Soft Computing Methods for Practical Environment Solutions:
Techniques and Studies

Marcos Gestal Pose
University of A Coruña, Spain

Daniel Rivero Cebrián
University of A Coruña, Spain

T0338667

Information Science REFERENCE

INFORMATION SCIENCE REFERENCE

Hershey · New York

Director of Editorial Content:	Kristin Klinger
Director of Book Publications:	Julia Mosemann
Acquisitions Editor:	Lindsay Johnston
Development Editor:	Joel Gamon
Publishing Assistant:	Keith Glazewski
Typesetter:	Keith Glazewski
Production Editor:	Jamie Snavely
Cover Design:	Lisa Tosheff
Printed at:	Yurchak Printing Inc.

Published in the United States of America by
Information Science Reference (an imprint of IGI Global)
701 E. Chocolate Avenue
Hershey PA 17033
Tel: 717-533-8845
Fax: 717-533-8661
E-mail: cust@igi-global.com
Web site: http://www.igi-global.com/reference

Library of Congress Cataloging-in-Publication Data

Soft computing methods for practical environment solutions : techniques and studies / Marcos Gestal Pose and Daniel Rivero Cebrián, editors.
    p. cm.
  Includes bibliographical references and index.
  Summary: "This publication presents a series of practical applications of different Soft Computing techniques to real-world problems, showing the enormous potential of these techniques in solving problems"--Provided by publisher.
  ISBN 978-1-61520-893-7 (hardcover) -- ISBN 978-1-61520-894-4 (ebook) 1. Soft computing. 2. Soft computing--Environmental aspects. 3. Soft computing--Industrial applications. I. Gestal Pose, Marcos, 1977- II. Rivero Cebrián, Daniel , 1978-
  QA76.9.S63S633457 2010
  006.3--dc22
                                        2009040713

British Cataloguing in Publication Data
A Cataloguing in Publication record for this book is available from the British Library.

All work contributed to this book is new, previously-unpublished material. The views expressed in this book are those of the authors, but not necessarily of the publisher.

Table of Contents

Section 1
Information Processing

Section 4
Natural Environment Applications

Detailed Table of Contents

Section 1
Information Processing

Chapter 1
Marcos Gestal, University of A Coruña, Spain
Daniel Rivero, University of A Coruña, Spain

This chapter is an introduction to two of the most significant techniques in the field of Soft Computing: artificial neural networks and evolutionary computation techniques, focusing on Genetic Algorithms and Genetic Programming. The basics of both techniques are outlined in a clear and simple way.

Chapter 2
Enrique Fernández, University of A Coruña, Spain
José Andrés Serantes, University of A Coruña, Spain
Nieves Pedreira, University of A Coruña, Spain
Julián Dorado, University of A Coruña, Spain

On the basis of biological adaptation generated in the internal functioning of cells, especially in terms of self-organization, a computational approach based on that behavior is raised. This approach is not merely theoretical, but a practical approach linked to an information processing system is shown.

Chapter 3

Oscar Déniz, Universidad de Castilla-La Mancha, Spain

Gloria Bueno, Universidad de Castilla-La Mancha, Spain

Modesto Castrillón, Instituto Universitario de Sistemas Inteligentes y Aplicaciones Numéricas en Ingeniería, Spain

Javier Lorenzo, Instituto Universitario de Sistemas Inteligentes y Aplicaciones Numéricas en Ingeniería, Spain

L. Antón, Instituto Universitario de Sistemas Inteligentes y Aplicaciones Numéricas en Ingeniería, Spain

M. Hernández, Instituto Universitario de Sistemas Inteligentes y Aplicaciones Numéricas en Ingeniería, Spain

This chapter describes the application of Soft computing techniques in order to solve two applications related to Human-Computer-Interaction. The first consists of the selection of video images of a structure (some glasses, in this case), whereas the second comprises a control application for an IM (instant messaging) tool based on face detection.

Chapter 4

Erik Cuevas, University of Guadalajara, México

Daniel Zaldivar, University of Guadalajara, México

Marco Perez-Cisneros, University of Guadalajara, México

Marco Block, Freie Universität Berlin, Germany

The segmentation of color images involves several difficulties, mainly due to the intensity changes produced by noise or shadows. This chapter presents an approach based on a special type of Artificial Neural Networks, LVQ (Learning Vector Quantization) networks, which seeks to provide a greater tolerance than traditional algorithms against these variations.

Chapter 5

G. N. Marichal, Universidad de La Laguna, Spain

A. Hernández, Universidad de La Laguna, Spain

E. J. González, Universidad de La Laguna, Spain

L. Acosta, Universidad de La Laguna, Spain

J. L. Saorin, Universidad de La Laguna, Spain

In this paper, the different interactions that occur between Artificial Intelligence and 3D- modeling are shown. Although there are certain applications focused on the engineering field (in particular robotics) detailed herein, the techniques shown in this chapter are general and can be applied in any other area.

The use of Soft Computing techniques is described in this chapter, with the aim of modelling the computer user's behavior. This kind of knowledge is of great importance for further improvement of the interaction between different programs and users.

Section 2
Industrial Applications

Several Soft Computing techniques have been used in the field of electromagnetics for some time: Simulated Annealing, Artificial Neural Networks and so on. This chapter shows the efficiency of using Genetic Algorithms for the electromagnetic optimization of single- and dual-band antennas.

The main focus of this chapter is a preference ranking analysis of a group of motor vehicles based on their chemical emissions. A multi-criteria decision making technique, named PROMETHEE, is used along with Trigonometric Differential Evolution. It shows the good behavior of Soft Computing techniques in this kind of problems.

The laser milling manufacture of high value steel components is an interesting and relatively new industrial technique used in the manufacture of steel components. This chapters presents how Soft Computing techniques can be used to optimize it, using a two-phase approach: first, an unsupervised neural projection determines if the data are good enough and secondly, a model is identified for the laser-milling process based on low-order models such as Black Box ones.

Juan L. Pérez, University of A Coruña, Spain
Juan R. Rabuñal, University of A Coruña, Spain
Fernando Martínez Abella, University of A Coruña, Spain

This chapter presents a practical example of applying Soft Computing techniques in the field of Civil Engineering. More specifically, there is a description of the implementation of the temporal behavior into Genetic Programming-based techniques in order to obtain a model that predicts the phenomenon of creep in structural concrete.

Laurenţiu Ionescu, University of Pitesti, Romania
Alin Mazare, University of Pitesti, Romania
Gabriel Iana, University of Pitesti, Romania
Gheorghe Şerban, University of Pitesti, Romania
Ionel Bostan, University of Pitesti, Romania

This chapter presents a general overview of an intrinsic evolvable hardware structure. An intrinsic evolvable hardware structure consists of two main modules: the hardware genetic algorithm and the dynamic reconfigurable circuit. The hardware genetic algorithm searches for the configuration that makes the reconfigurable circuit to respond correctly to the application requirements. The chapter proposes several design solutions and several applications that this kind of structures use.

Diego Ordóñez, University of A Coruña, Spain
Carlos Dafonte, University of A Coruña, Spain
Bernardino Arcay, University of A Coruña, Spain
Minia Manteiga, University of A Coruña, Spain

The volume of data offered by a satellite is enormous and their analysis is extremely complex and expensive. This paper describes the use of Artificial Neural Networks in order to determine automatically the characteristic parameters (temperature, gravity, metallicity, etc.) of a star from near infrared spectra in the wavelength region.

Section 3
Biomedical Approaches

Chapter 13

Carlos M. Travieso, University of Las Palmas de Gran Canaria, Spain

Jesús B. Alonso, University of Las Palmas de Gran Canaria, Spain

Miguel A. Ferrer, University of Las Palmas de Gran Canaria, Spain

Jorge Corsino, University of Las Palmas de Gran Canaria, Spain

This chapter presents an approach based on the use of Support Vector Machines (SVM) that provides an automatic detection of arrhythmias. This detection is carried out according to the Wavelet Transform of the Electrocardiogram (ECG). The control data employed come from the Arrhythmia Database, Massachusetts Institute of Technology (MIT), containing data from 8 different states, a normal one and the rest of them showing different pathologies.

Chapter 14

Vanessa Aguiar, University of A Coruña, Spain

Jose A. Seoane, University of A Coruña, Spain

Ana Freire, University of A Coruña, Spain

Ling Guo, University of A Coruña, Spain

Complex diseases comprise no clear relationship between the signs of a disease and its causes, since multiple genetic and environmental factors can be involved. This paper shows an algorithm based on Iterative Rule Learning that is meant to point out the association rules between a patient's genotype and phenotype, so that a better explanation for the cause of a disease can be provided.

Chapter 15

José Manuel Vázquez Naya, University of A Coruña, Spain

Marcos Martínez Romero, University of A Coruña, Spain

Javier Pereira Loureiro, University of A Coruña, Spain

Cristian R. Munteanu, University of A Coruña, Spain

Alejandro Pazos Sierra, University of A Coruña, Spain

Nowadays, ontologies are considered to be one of the most appropiate technologies for data sharing and reusing. However, like the rest of technologies, it has its challenges that have to be faced. One of these problems is how to map different ontologies to enable a common understanding. In order to solve this problem, different methods appeared, called ontology alignment techniques. This chapter proposes the use of a Genetic Algorithm in order to provide an optimal alignment between two techniques.

Section 4
Natural Environment Applications

Chapter 16

Antonio Geraldo Ferreira, University of Valencia, Spain & Fundação Cearense
de Meteorologia e Recursos Hídricos (FUNCEME), Brazil
Emilio Soria, University of Valencia, Spain
Antonio J. Serrano López, University of Valencia, Spain
Ernesto Lopez-Baeza, University of Valencia, Spain

This chapter gives an example of Artificial Neural Networks application in the prediction of qualitative and quantitative relationships between meteorological and soil parameters and net radiation. To this end, different types of networks, such as the Multilayer Perceptron and Self-Organizing Maps, have been employed.

Chapter 17

Juan Gómez-Sanchis, University of Valencia, Spain
Emilio Soria-Olivas, University of Valencia, Spain
Marcelino Martinez-Sober, University of Valencia, Spain
Jose Blasco, Centro de AgroIngeniería, IVIA, Spain
Juan Guerrero, University of Valencia, Spain
Secundino del Valle-Tascón, University of Valencia, Spain

The correct prediction of tropospheric ozone is important because excessive ozone concentrations may cause several problems related to public health. This paper describes a suggestion based on Machine Learning techniques, mainly including Artificial Neural Networks, and its validity is shown for this type of problems in accordance to the results obtained.

Chapter 18

Alejandro Peña, Escuela de Ingeniería de Antioquia, Colombia
Jesús A. Hernández, Universidad Nacional de Colombia, Colombia
María Victoria Toro, Universidad Pontificia Bolivariana, Colombia

One of the main concerns when it comes to reducing the concentration values for particulate matter PMx in a study area, is determining their spatial behavior over time. This chapter develops and analyzes a model based on the principles of Evolutionary Computation (EC) in order to determine this space-time behavior of the related concentration.

Chapter 19

Diana F. Adamatti, Universidade Federal do Rio Grande (FURG), Brazil

Marilton S. de Aguiar, Universidade Federal de Pelotas (UFPel), Brasil

There are three computational challenges in natural resources management: data management and communication; data analysis; and optimization and control. This chapter describes the use of the Cellular Automata and Multi-Agent-Based Simulation for the management of those aspects.

Chapter 20

M.P. Gómez-Carracedo, University of A Coruña, Spain

D. Ballabio, University of Milano-Bicocca, Italy

J.M. Andrade, University of A Coruña, Spain

R. Fernández-Varela, University of A Coruña, Spain

V. Consonni, University of Milano-Bicocca, Italy

This chapter shows two case studies, dealing with environmental studies of soil pollution caused by road traffic and sea pollution as a consequence of spilled hydrocarbons using, among other techniques, Self-Organizing Maps (SOM) and Counter-Propagation Artificial Neural Networks, a special SOM with a supervised layer.

Chapter 21

A. Moreno, Universidad de Valencia, Spain

E. Soria, Universidad de Valencia, Spain

J. García, Universidad de Valencia, Spain

J. D. Martín, Universidad de Valencia, Spain

R. Magdalena, Universidad de Valencia, Spain

This chapter is focused on obtaining an optimal forecast of one-month lagged rainfall. It is assessed by analyzing a period of 22 years of both satellite observations of vegetation activity and climatic data (precipitation, temperature). The approaches considered for rainfall forecasting include classical Auto-Regressive Moving-Average with Exogenous Inputs (ARMAX) models and Artificial Neural Networks (ANN).

Preface

Intelligence is one of the qualities that distinguish the human being from all the other animals. In spite of having inferior physical abilities to those of many other species, human intelligence has allowed him to overcome them and to become the dominant species. The ability to manipulate objects, and more fundamentally, his superior intellect, has allowed him to create tools and to develop complex reasoning and plans impossible for other species. This has allowed him, for example, to adapt to practically all conditions of planet Earth.

However, human inventiveness has been used not only to overcome the various problems in order to adapt and survive. Intellectual development entails different concerns, and perhaps one of the most interesting has been the determination to create a human being artificially, trying to simulate him both physically and intellectually. In general, this fact is applicable to the artificial development of a living organism.

From a physical point of view, the attempts to create a living organism artificially are well-known, and they have been carried out for a number of years. Sometimes, due to the fact they are made highly complex by means of clock mechanisms, these hominids and robots have reached such a point that they are able to reproduce everyday movements, usually succeeding to deeply impress those people who had the chance to see them. One early example is given in the Roman Empire, in which Heron of Alexandria built artificial actors that represented the Trojan War. Other significant examples are "The Pigeon" of Archytas of Tarentum, "The Mechanical Lion" of Leonardo da Vinci or "The Flute Player"-life-size figure of a shepherd that played the tabor and the pipe and had a repertoire of twelve songs, "The Tambourine Player" and "The Digesting Duck", with over 400 moving parts, able to flap its wings, drink water, digest grain and defecate, the latter three automatons belonging to Jacques Vaucanson. Other examples are the robots invented by Wolfgang von Kempelen, "The Turk", a chess-playing machine that played against the best opponents of its era, but later it was revealed to be a farce, and "The Mechanism of human speech", this time not an automaton but a talking machine.

From an intellectual point of view, there are also different approaches on creating machines that either exhibit a behavior that reproduces a certain level of intellect when it comes to solving a problem, or represent a support to humans in achieving intellectual tasks. The latter is the case, for example, of the abacus, designed to improve calculating abilities. Regarding the development of machines or systems that solve problems, they are a very old dream. The Arab mathematician al-Jwārizmī had already laid the foundations of algebra and especially of algorithmics around the 9th century. The algorithm is known as an established, ordered and finite step-by-step procedure for solving a problem. Given an initial state and an input, through well-established recursive steps, a final state is reached, which leads to the solution of the problem. Therefore, this set of steps could be programmed into a machine, so that it is able to solve a particular problem.

However, it was only with the emergence of the first computers and software when systems with features of living beings, such as memory or calculation, were developed and when complex algorithms that allowed the solution of problems began to be programmed. These algorithms, although they gave good results, lack some features, essential for the living beings, such as adaptation or learning abilities. Overall, the first algorithms that led unequivocally to the solution of a problem, had not the proper functioning when facing somehow uncertain data, noise or inaccuracy, as it usually occurs with real-world data. In an informal way, the techniques based on such algorithms are known as "hard computing" techniques.

In comparison to these techniques, a number of techniques aimed at solving real problems by imitating the way humans do it, have also arisen. They are known as "Soft Computing". This term was coined by Lotfi A. Zadeh in 1991, and ever since it has undergone a quick development both regarding the theoretical aspects, and above all, its applications. Soft Computing techniques approach problems of great diversity, both in their type (modeling, optimization, planning, monitoring, forecasting, data mining, ...) and in the field of their implementation (industrial production, telecommunications, energy, logistics, banking, food processing, ...)

Therefore, Soft Computing techniques could be considered as a branch of Artificial Intelligence (AI) focused on the design of intelligent systems able to operate properly with inaccurate, unclear and/or incomplete information. This property enables to approach real problems in order to find more reliable, manageable and less expensive solutions compared to those obtained by means of conventional techniques. The main techniques that make up Soft Computing are fuzzy logic, neural networks, evolutionary computation and probabilistic reasoning.

AI is a multi-disciplinary science field that deals with the study in depth of the possibility of creating artificial beings. Its starting point was Babbage's determination that his machine could "think, learn and create," so that the ability to perform these actions might be increased and applied to the problems that human beings face. AI, whose name is attributed to John McCarthy from the College Dormouth group in the summer of 1956, is divided into two main branches, known as symbolic and connectionist, depending on whether it is attempted to simulate or emulate the human brain in intelligent artificial beings, respectively. According to McCorduck and McCarthy, artificial beings are considered intelligent if they show a behavior that, when performed by a biological being, could be considered intelligent.

Nevertheless, and despite the high rate at which developments occur today, we are still far from reproducing artificially something that is inherent in all living beings, such as creativity, critical capacity (including self-critical capacity), consciousness or common sense, among others.

Although we are still far from reproducing the daily behavior of biological systems, all these studies and researches have achieved spectacular results. In recent decades, the attention of the scientific community has increased because of recent advances in computing, the latter due to the fact that the miniaturization of computers has evolved along with their increase in the information computing and storage capacities. Thus, more complex systems are being developed progressively in order to carry out more complex functions.

The efforts made so far approach two different situations. On the one hand, they are the basis for all the advances achieved so far in order to reproduce the defining features of the living beings. On the other hand, they also reflect the poor-but-spectacular advances regarding the creation of real intelligent beings. In spite of the fact that the connectionist systems are the most advanced in the field of emulation of intelligent biological systems, the latter show certain restrictions. These limitations are related mainly to the need to reduce training time and to optimize the architecture and also to the lack of explanation about their behavior. It is required to look back to Nature again, as it was done when great strides were taken to this end, to seek new information to inspire the search for these solutions. In general, Nature has provided guidance for the creation of a large number of techniques which are encompassed within the AI and Soft Computing.

Technology also provides solutions. In this respect, different technologies are meant to be integrated under a common label: MNBIC (Micro and Nanotechnologies, Biotechnology, Information Technologies, and Cognitive Technologies) Convergent Technologies. MNBIC is expected to be a revolution in scientific, technological and socio-economic fields since it helps making possible the construction of hybrid systems: biological and artificial.

Some possibilities consist of the use of micro- or nano-elements that could be introduced into biological systems with the aim of replacing damaged or non-functional parts, whereas biological particles could be embedded in artificial systems in order to perform certain actions. According to a recent report of the U.S. National Science Foundation, "The convergence of micro and nanoscience, biotechnology, information technology, and cognitive science (MNBIC) offers immense opportunities for the improvement of human abilities, social outcomes, the nation's productivity, and its quality of life. It also represents a major new frontier in research and development. MNBIC convergence is a broad, cross-cutting, emerging, and timely opportunity of interest to individuals, society, and humanity in the long term."

There is a significant scientific agreement on the fact that the most complex part to be integrated with the rest of converging technologies is the one representing cognitive science. The issues related to knowledge technologies have the highest level of integration by means of knowledge engineering models.

In general, considering the multidisciplinary nature of the AI and Soft Computing techniques, the scientific community benefits from their employment, since they can be applied in a wide variety of different fields. This publication presents a series of practical applications of different Soft Computing techniques to real-world problems. The aim is to show the enormous potential of these techniques in solving all kinds of problems. Thus, with the latest advances in these techniques, an extensive state-of-the-art and a vast theoretical study on them are provided.

Therefore, Soft Computing techniques are presented from a theoretical point of view, but above all from a practical point of view. This can be of great use to a student who wants to lean towards this branch of AI, as well as for a researcher that needs to become familiar with these techniques. Likewise, a professional or experienced researcher will also find this reading material very useful as it offers novel and recent applications, which gives a boost to expanding and exploring new research areas.

This publication is divided into four sections, which are meant to cover different areas of knowledge in which Soft Computing has been applied in order to solve various problems.

The first section is devoted to various tasks related to the employment of Soft Computing techniques in the field of information processing. This area is of great importance, since, due to its multidisciplinary nature, these techniques may be applied in several different fields.

- Chapter 1 provides an introduction to two of the most commonly used techniques in the Soft Computing: Artificial Neural Networks, Genetic Algorithms and Genetic Programming, the latter two categorized as being part of the Evolutionary Computation techniques.
- Chapter 2 presents a new technique within Evolutionary Computation, inspired by the adaptation of biological cells. This technique is used in this work to solve information processing problems.
- Chapter 3 uses Soft Computing techniques to carry out successfully two completely different applications in the field of human-computer interaction.
- Chapter 4 shows an application in the field of image processing: how it is possible to segment color images using a special type of Artificial Neural Networks: LVQ.

- Chapter 5 deals with 3D modelling. In this chapter, AI techniques are used in order to implement 3D environments, and, on the other hand, 3D models are employed in order to make the most of the AI techniques.
- Chapter 6 describes the use of Soft Computing techniques with the aim of developing computer user models. If this goal is achieved, a series of systems improving the interaction with the users could be created.

The second section, Industrial Applications, describes different ways of applying these techniques to solve various problems related to distinct industrial and, on the whole, engineering processes.

- Chapter 7 describes how a Genetic Algorithm can be used in order to optimize the design of single- and dual-band antennas.
- The basis of Chapter 8 is the effect exerted by the chemical emissions of motor vehicles on the environment. This chapter provides an analysis of these chemical emissions using various techniques.
- Chapter 9 shows a study in which a modelling of laser milling manufacture of steel components has been performed. As a result, this manufacturing process is optimized.
- Chapter 10 is related to an issue of Civil Engineering. This chapter describes how to use a technique of Evolutionary Computation, Genetic Programming, in order to predict the behavior of structural concrete.
- Chapter 11 presents the use of Evolutionary Computation techniques in the field of hardware development. More specifically, intrinsic evolvable hardware gives the possibility of being integrated into applications with high degree of autonomy and which require real-time response.
- Chapter 12 exposes a study in which Artificial Neural Networks were used in order to extract different atmospheric parameters (temperature, surface gravity, etc.) characterizing a particular star.

The third section contains a series of works related to the use of Soft Computing in the field of medicine and bioinformatics.

- Chapter 13 shows an application in which different techniques are used in order to give rise to a system capable of an automatic arrhythmia detection in ECG signals.
- Chapter 14 describes a new implementation of the Iterative Rule Learning algorithm for extracting the genotype-phenotype association rules in complex diseases.
- Chapter 15 describes an application in the field of Ontology. More specifically, it is shown how to perform the automatic combination of several measures into a single metrics using an Evolutionary Computation technique.

Finally, the fourth section, on Natural Environment Applications, is focused on the Soft Computing use to solve issues directly related to the environment, such as natural resource management or prediction or modelling of environmental effects.

- Chapter 16 shows the employment of an Artificial Neural Network to model net radiation starting from different meteorological parameters like temperature, precipitation, wind speed, etc.

- Chapter 17 describes a method to perform a prediction of tropospheric ozone in the atmosphere, of great importance to public health, using Machine Learning techniques.
- Chapter 18 presents a method to model PMx pollutant dispersion, with the aim of determining the spatio-temporal behavior of the concentration of these particles, using Evolutionary Computation techniques.
- Chapter 19 shows how Soft Computing techniques can be used to solve different challenges related to natural resources management: data analysis, optimization and control.
- Chapter 20 is related to the use of self-organizing maps employed for the study of soil pollution caused by road traffic, and sea pollution as a consequence of oil spillage.
- Chapter 21 focuses on the prediction of a weather phenomenon: rain. Starting from observations of vegetation activity and several climatic data, a model capable of predicting precipitation has been developed by means of different techniques.

As it can be seen, this publication aims at providing an outlook of the most recent works in the field of Soft Computing, including not only theoretical aspects but also describing implementations of these systems in fields with very different characteristics, thus proving the multi-disciplinary nature of these techniques.

That being said, we consider this book a proposal which, on the one hand, will contribute to solving a lot of problems but that, on the other hand, will also open new questions that will undoubtedly have a decisive role in the research progress within this field.

This book does not provide definitive solutions but it contributes to the creation of new and imaginative viewpoints instead.

Marcos Gestal Pose
University of A Coruna, Spain

Daniel Rivero Cebrián
University of A Coruna, Spain

Acknowledgment

First of all, editors are very grateful for the help received of all people involved in the different stages of this book. From the initial idea to the review process and the final submission, without this help this project could not be satisfactorily completed.

A special note of thanks must goes to all the staff of IGI Global. Their contributions all over the process have been invaluable. In particular, many thanks to Joel Gammon who continuously solved our doubts from the beginning of the project and encourage us to keep the project on schedule.

We wish to thank all the authors for their insights and excellent contributions to this book. Without them our efforts would be useless.

Most of authors also served as reviewers for the rest of articles on the book. Editorial Advisory Board members reviewed also some of the works. Our special thanks to all of them who provided comprehensive, objective, constructive and useful reviews which allow us to improve the final quality of this book.

We also want to thank the help of the staff of RNASA-Lab (Artificial Neural Networks and Adaptative Systems Laboratory) as well as the TIC Department (Department of Information and Communications Technologies) both of them belonging to the University of A Coruña.

Last but not least important, Marcos Gestal wants to thank his wife Noemí Carrillo for their love and patience; his daughter Iria for her smiles and his parents for their unconditional support. Daniel Rivero wants to thank his family and his girlfriend Beatriz for their support throughout this project and the huge love and patience they always have.

Marcos Gestal Pose
Daniel Rivero Cebrián
Editors

Section 1
Information Processing

Chapter 1

A Soft Computing Overview:
Artificial Neural Networks and Evolutionary Computation

Marcos Gestal
University of A Coruña, Spain

Daniel Rivero
University of A Coruña, Spain

ABSTRACT

Nature has proved to be the best testing system, where we can analyze the effectiveness of any method of solving problems. It provides one of the most complex problems to be resolved: the survival. Analyzing how the species behave to achieve that survival, soft computing methods try to mimic this behavior to provide meaningful solutions to diverse problems. This chapter offers an introduction the fundamentals that the different soft computing techniques translate from Nature. It includes an approach of the brain behavior (Artificial Neural Networks) or the evolution ideas taken from Darwin' laws (Evolutionary Computation algorithms).

INTRODUCTION

As time passes by, the complexity of the issues that different scientific fields tackle has been growing constantly. Along with this growth, there are the time and effort required to solve these issues by means of conventional techniques, either because at first the way to find a solution is not known, or because, even if it is known, the level of complexity of its implementation is also fairly high.

However, a solution to these issues can be found by observing our environment thoroughly. Perhaps the greatest challenge that any system may raise is the survival of organisms and species that inhabit it.;and Nature has provided a huge variety of valid solutions to this challenge ever since the beginning of time (Freeman, S & Herron, J, 2002).

And how does Nature provide these solutions? The answer to this question can be found in Darwin's theory of the evolution of species (Darwin, C., 1859): natural selection and survival of the fittest individuals.

Regarding the solutions provided by Nature to the challenge of survival, the human race itself plays a major role because of its predominant position.

DOI: 10.4018/978-1-61520-893-7.ch001

Due to what, exactly? Although the answer to this question can imply numerous nuances, perhaps one of the most widely accepted is the assumption that it is mostly because of human cognitive activity, that is, their highest intellectual capacity.

Both issues, the use of the intellectual capacity and the survival of the the fittest individuals, may be outlined so to conform the foundations of two methods, Artificial Neural Networks (ANNs) (Haykin, S., 1998), and Evolutionary Computation (EC), which, together or separately, provide excellent results in various types of problems.

The present chapter is aimed at giving an overview of each of these methods.

ARTIFICIAL NEURAL NETWORKS

As mentioned above, perhaps the supremacy of human over all the other living creatures is due to his high intellectual capacity and the basis of this capacity lies in the brain. However, reproducing the overall performance of the brain in order to achieve a problem solving system is not feasible at all.

The brain provides action responses to the whole range of stimuli received from the outside world: images, sounds, tastes, smells, temperatures, etc. To this end, it simply uses its collection of neurons (about 10^{11}) and its many synaptic connections between them (from about 1,000 to 10,000 synaptic connections can be found in one neuron). These scales are impossible to reach in a simulation system, but there is a possibility of building more simple models based on each of the major components of the above-mentioned performance: the neurons and interconnection architectures between them.

Both elements make up the basic structure of an ANN. Therefore, an ANN may be considered an attempt to produce learning systems inspired by nature (based on abstract models of how we think and how the brain works).

Biological Basis

Although the outline of the full performance of neurons is still to be discovered, we have quite a good understanding of the whole process.

Broadly speaking, a neuron receives through its extension branches, called dendrites, a series of impulses from its neighbouring neurons. Depending on the overall final intensity of the stimuli, there may be an excitatory or inhibitory effect on the neuron. In the first case, the neuron will cause an output signal which is transmitted through its axon to the dendrites of the neighbouring neurons. Information is stored by means of this exchange of impulses and in the capacity of neurons to be activated or inhibited by a certain set of inputs. Obviously this process occurs at the same time in millions of neurons, so the most fundamental characteristics of the brain: high redundancy, fault tolerance partial adaptability, and so on, are a consequence of this decentralized behaviour.

General Operation

Processing Element

Translation (and simplification) of the performance of a neuron to the field of ANN gives rise to the concept of processing element (PE) (see Figure 1).

Exactly like neurons, a PE is also associated to a number of inputs. The relative importance of each of these inputs is determined according to an adjustment factor called *weight*. Thus, a weight W_{ij} will indicate the relative importance of the input j of the PE i. The total input also called net or activation value – of the PE is determined by applying the adjustment factors to each input and by adding the different terms.

Moreover, each neuron is associated to a number called bias or threshold (θ_i), which can be taken into account as a number indicating from what postsynaptic potential value the neuron produces a significant output.

Figure 1. Processing element

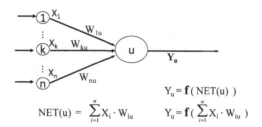

$$Y_u = \mathbf{f}(\, NET(u) \,)$$

$$NET(u) = \sum_{i=1}^{n} X_i \cdot W_{iu} \qquad Y_u = \mathbf{f}(\sum_{i=1}^{n} X_i \cdot W_{iu})$$

Like a biological neuron, the PE may exhibit an excitatory behaviour, giving a boost to its output, or an inhibitory one, the stimulation received at the input not causing any output. This will depend on the so-called transfer function (see Figure 2). This function will shape the output of the EP on the basis of its activation, for example, that the EP only acts as a repeater to the output value of the activation (linear transfer function), which provides a constant output once a certain value of activation is reached (threshold transfer function) or that varies in intensity within a specified range depending on the value of activation (sigmoid transfer function).

ANN Architecture

The same as neurons do not act independently in the brain, the PEs in the ANN do not either. The real power of an ANN does not lie in the PEs separately, but in their grouping. In this way, the output provided by a PE may act as an input in other PEs. In the same way as in the human brain,

this will allow the knowledge not to be centralized in a single place, but to be distributed, in this case, throughout the different connections of the ANN.

The PEs are divided into levels or layers. In a classical arquitecture, there are at least an input layer and an output layer. Between the two there may be several hidden layers or not.

Depending on the type of connection allowed between the different PEs of the ANN, two main types of topologies can be distinguished: feed-forward and feedback (see Figure 3). The former, referring to non-recurrent ANNs, is characterized by having unidirectional links where the PEs of the layer i are interconnected with those of the layer i +1. Generally, these are totally linked networks, that is, each PE of the layer i is interconnected with all the PEs of the layer i +1.

On the other hand, in recurrent architectures or feedback there is no such demand, there may be connections between elements of non-consecutive layers, between elements of the same layer, or between an element and itself.

Figure 2. Transfer function

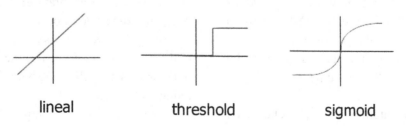

| lineal | threshold | sigmoid |

Figure 3. ANN architecture

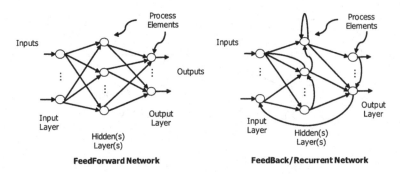

Learning

Learning or training of an ANN is the process of modifying the weights interconnecting the PEs in order to fit the output depending on the parameters entered as an input.

This change of weights is carried out through an iterative process that tries to minimize the error as the generations develop. Although there are many learning algorithms, the Backpropagation can be considered as the most widely used.

Depending on the training strategy, two different approaches can be distinguished: supervised and unsupervised learning.

In the supervised learning, the training algorithm starts from a set of patterns (where the input and the target output are provided by the user). The modifications are carried out considering the comparison between the outputs produced by the ANN and the desired outputs for the same set of input patterns. These modifications are supposed to ensure that the difference between the two outputs is as minimized as possible.

On the contrary, unsupervised learning does not have the knowledge provided by the set of desired outputs. In this case, the ANN organizes its weights by means of an autonomous process, seeking similarities or regularities between the entry patterns. Usually, this type of learning is used for classification tasks.

There are other intermediate approaches, such as hybrid learning or reinforcement learning. In the former, some ANN layers have a type of supervised learning and others have unsupervised learning, such as RBF networks. In the reinforcement learning, the ANN is not provided with a set of desired outputs, but it implies a certain degree of the error it may cause, even if it is a global error and not a standard one.

Advantages of Using ANN

Among the advantages shown by the use of ANN, it is worth pointing out, above all, its learning and generalization capacity. As mentioned above, the ANNs are able to extract knowledge from a set of examples. This knowledge can be successfully applied to input patterns not considered during the learning process, resulting in valid outputs. This is possible thanks to the generalization that could be defined as the capacity to summarize the useful information provided by the set of training, beyond particular cases. In this way, the ANN can respond to unknown cases.

Another interesting feature of the use of ANN is the error tolerance. Similar to what may happen in case of small brain errors, an ANN can keep providing fairly good results even if it gets partially damaged. This is due to the fact that, in both cases, brain and ANN, the information is not stored in a single place but it is properly and redundantly distributed.

Finally, it should be emphasised the ability of ANNs to work properly with changes on the

Figure 4. General outline of performance of an evolutionary algorithm

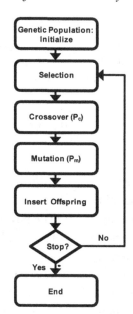

input information, such as modifications caused by noise, incomplete entries, etc. and the possibility to work in real time, since, once the training process finish, the responses are almost immediate.

EVOLUTIONARY COMPUTATION

The EC resumes the concepts of evolution and genetics to solve problems, mainly related to optimization tasks (Goldberg, D.E, 1989; Michalewiz, Z., 1998). However, it also must consider the important influence of the works carried out by Arthur Samuel and Alan Turing in the 50s: "Can machines think?", and "How can computers learn to solve problems without being explicitly programmed?"

Broadly speaking, the EC methods are search and optimization techniques consisting of the application of heuristic rules based on principles of natural evolution. In other words, algorithms that look for solutions based on genetics and evolution properties. Among these properties, the survival of the fittest individuals (which implies that the best solutions to a problem will be maintained

once they are found) and heterogeneity (basic heterogeneity so that algorithms have multiple types of information when generating solutions) are becoming particularly relevant.

General Outline of Performance

The performance of evolutionary algorithms is based on a relatively simple outline, as reflected in Figure 4. This iterative outline will perfect solutions generation by generation that will gradually approach the definitive solution to the problem.

But prior to the implementation of the evolutionary process specified by the algorithm, it is required to undertake two issues, perhaps the most important of the entire process: determining how to represent the solutions (encoding), and specifying a method to assess how accurate a solution may be (fitness function).

Regarding the encoding of the solutions, there are mainly two branches, as described in Figure 5: through value chains, usually named chromosomes (chains have a fixed or variable length, and the values are these integer, real, Boolean (bits), etc) or through trees (in which the leaves of the tree

Figure 5. Encoding of solutions: GA and GP

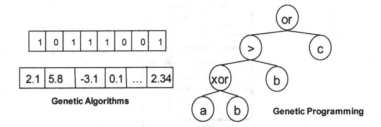

usually represent the values and the operating intermediate nodes. Depending on the encoding strategy selected, it will lead to some of the major techniques within the EC framework: Genetic Algorithm (GA) (Holland, J.H., 1975) or Genetic Programming (GP) (Koza, J.,1992) respectively. Whatever the encoding strategy is, the solutions that the algorithm involves are called genetic individuals. Each of its components (known as genes in the case of AG, or leaf nodes in the case of GP) will represent each variable or parameter involved in the solution of the problem.

Regardless of the encoding technique employed, the critical step when it comes to shaping an evolutionary algorithm is defining the fitness function. This function must evaluate each genetic individual, indicating a real value that would represent the goodness of the solution provided by the individual. This function is responsible for guiding the search process in one direction or another. Precisely because it is the function responsible for checking the goodness of each solution, this is a feature inherently linked to the problem to be solved.

The above-discussed evolution of solutions will occur thanks to genetic operators, crossover and mutation, that simulate the analogue processes of sexual and asexual reproduction that take place in natural enviroments.

Next, we will discuss in more detail each of the other steps to be performed in this kind of algorithms.

Initialization

The power of evolutionary algorithms lies in the large-scale parallel exploration of search space. This is feasible thanks to the existence of multiple solutions, each one represented by a genetic individual. Each individual will explore a region of the search space. The set of solutions, randomly initialized, is called population genetics.

The population size remains generally stable. The genetic individuals, as abovementioned, will be changing as the generations advance, led by the fitness function, so that the solutions involved meet constantly the global solution.

Selection

The selection algorithms are responsible for choosing the individuals which will have the opportunity to reproduce or not. Since this means to imitate nature's work, more opportunities should be given to the fittest individuals. Therefore, the selection of an individual will be related to its fitness value. However, the reproduction options of less fit individuals should not be completely counted out, since this would lead to a population uniformity in a few generations. There are several selection algorithms, but perhaps the best known ones are the roulette-wheel selection algorithm and the tournament selection algorithm, both deterministically and probabilistically.

In the roulette-wheel selection (Figure 6), each individual is given a share proportional to its fit-

Figure 6. Roulette-wheel selection

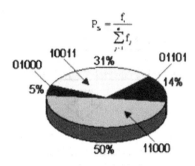

ness value of a roulette wheel, so that the sum of all percentages is a unit. The best individuals will be assigned a roulette-wheel proportion bigger than the one received by the weakest individuals. In order to select an individual, a random number is generated within the range [0..1] and the individual whose segment spans the random number is chosen.

On the other hand, the main idea of the tournament selection consists of carrying out the selection on the basis of direct comparisons between individuals. In the deterministic version, a number of individuals p (usually p = 2) is selected at random. Among the selected individuals, the fittest will be chosen as parent for the next generation. However, in the probabilistic version, a random number within the range [0..1] will be generated; if it is greater than a parameter p, the fittest individual is chosen and otherwise the least fit is selected.

Crossover

Once the individuals are selected, they are recombined to produce the offspring that are inserted into the next generation. Its importance for the transition between generations is high, since the usual crossover rates are around 90%.

The principle of the crossover is based on the fact that if two individuals, properly adapted to the environment, are selected and the offspring obtained share genetic information of both, there

is a possibility that the inherited information is precisely the cause of their parents' goodness. Since they share the good features of two individuals, the offspring, or at least part of them, should have better characters than each parent separately.

The crossover algorithms will depend on the type of encoding used. That is, specific crossovers will be available for GA and GP. If working with GA, there are many crossover algorithms, but perhaps the most widespread are the following: 1-point Crossover, 2-point Crossover and uniform Crossover (see Figure 7). When working with GP, the crossover par excellence is the exchange of subtrees (see Figure 8).

In the 1-point crossover, once two individuals are selected, their chromosomes are cut at a randomly selected point of the chromosome in order to generate two segments differentiated in each of them: the head and tail. The two individuals' tails are swapped to generate the new offspring. In this way, both descendants inherit genetic information from their parents.

The 2-point crossover is a generalization of the previous one. In this case, two cuts are performed in the chromosome (in the 1-point crossover the first cut is always the first gene in the chromosome). The offspring are generated by choosing the central segment of one of the parents and the lateral segments of the other parent.

The uniform crossover is a technique completely different from the previous ones. In this

Figure 7. Crossover operator in genetic algorithms

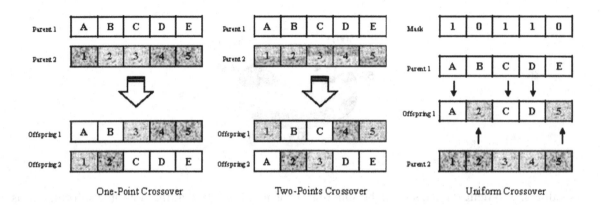

| | One-Point Crossover | Two-Points Crossover | Uniform Crossover |

case, each gene of the offspring has the same probability of belonging to one or the other parent. Although it can be implemented in many different ways, the technique involves the generation of a crossover mask with binary values. If there is a "1" in one of the mask positions, a gene located at that specific position in one of the offspring is copied from the first parent. If, on the contrary, there is a "0", the gene is copied from the second parent. To produce the second offspring, the parents' roles are exchanged or the interpretation of ones and zeros of the crossover mask is reversed.

In the case of GP, the genetic recombination is usually carried out by first selecting a non-terminal node in each parent and then swapping the subtrees hanging from these nodes.

Mutation

The mutation of an individual leads to a randomly variation in value of one of its genes or nodes, usually one only.

Although individuals can be selected directly from the current population and mutate before their insertion into the new population, the mutation is often used together with the crossover operator. First, two individuals from the population are selected for the crossover. If the crossover is successful then one of the offspring, or both of them, is/are mutated with some probability Pm. Thus, a behaviour that occurs in Nature is imitated, as when the offspring are generated there is always some kind of error, generally without any consequence

Figure 8. Crossover operator in genetic programming

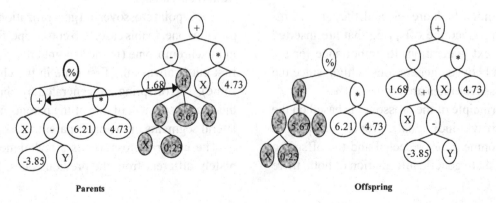

Parents **Offspring**

on the transmission of the genetic information from parents to offspring. Sometimes the mutation leads to a reduction in the fitness value of the individual (which may be rectified in subsequent generations). However, the new information provides a significant increase in the goodness of the solutions or may be taken into consideration for a better solution in future generations.

The probability of mutation is very low, usually less than 1%. This is due mainly to the fact that individuals tend to have a minor fitness after mutation. However, mutations are performed in order to ensure that no point of the search space has a zero probability of being explored

Again, the mutation algorithms depend on the type of encoding used. When working with GA, the most common mutations consist of the random variation of the value of one or more genes or they consist of the gene replacement (see Figure 9). In the case of GP, a choice can be made among simple mutations (functional or terminal) or subtree mutations (see Figure 10). In the first case, a tree node (intermediate or terminal) is selected at random and its value is replaced

randomly by another, obviously included within a set of allowed values. In the case of the subtree mutation, a subtree of an individual is selected, then it is entirely removed and a new randomly generated subtree is incorporated instead.

Replacement

In general, evolutionary algorithms (most often when working with GA) use a temporary population. This latter is gradually risen by copy operations of individuals and by the offspring resulting from crossover operations (and possibly mutation). When this population is complete – in this case it is said to have passed to a new generation– it becomes the population of the present generation, ruling out the old one and then restarting the process from a new empty temporary population. Such algorithms are usually called generational algorithms.

However, there is another approach called the steady-state algorithms. This option involves working with a single population, on which the selections and insertions are carried out, ruling

Figure 9. Mutation operator in genetic algorithms

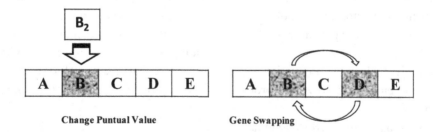

Figure 10. Mutation operator in genetic programming

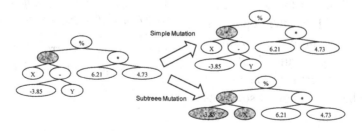

out the use of temporary population. That is, the offspring, instead of replacing their parents' generation, will be a part of it themselves. In this case, since the number of individuals in the population remains constant, it should be considered that, in order to insert a new individual, another one must be previously ruled out of the population.

The most common replacement methods are: the random replacement (in which the new individual is inserted anywhere into the population), the parent replacement (in which the space for the new offspring is obtained by emptying the one occupied by their parents), the replacement of similar individuals (once the offspring fitness is obtained, a group of individuals is selected from six to ten- from the population with a similar fitness, randomly replacing all the required individuals) or the replacement of the weakest individuals (the necessary number of individuals are selected randomly from the weakest group to make room for the offspring).

Stopping Criterion

As previously shown, the evolution process of solutions is a highly iterative mechanism. Therefore it will be necessary to specify a criterion in order to allow establishing when the execution is completed. Currently there are different options, but the most common ones are presented below:

- The fittest individuals in the population are solutions good enough to solve the problem raised.
- The population has converged. A gene has converged when 95% of the population has the same value (or very similar) for that particular gene. Once all the genes reach convergence it is said that the population has converged. When this occurs, the average goodness of the population is close to the goodness of the fittest individual.
- The difference between the best solutions among different generations is reduced.

This may indicate, in the best case, that population has already reached an overall solution or, on the contrary, has been at a standstill at a local minimum value.

- A predetermined maximum number of generations have been reached.

CONCLUSION

The possible advantage that stands out from these techniques is the simplicity of their implementation. No type of technique is required to solve the problem, only a way that can allow assessing a possible solution (so as to define the fitness function). Moreover, the simplicity of the ideas taken from Nature should also be highlighted, on which the development of solutions is based.

Furthermore, this type of techniques is easily adaptable to multimodal problems (those with several solutions) or multiobjective problems (those in which different criteria are tried to be optimized simultaneously).

When the computational cost is a criterion to be considered, due to its inherently parallel operation, we should take into account easily distributable techniques (at least the evaluation of the solutions, which often becomes a hurdle) with a marked improvement in the response times arising from such distribution.

Finally, we should note that this type of techniques, unlike others, always provides a solution to the problem raised and furthermore this solution will improve as the generations advances.

REFERENCES

Darwin, C. (1859). *On the Origin of the Species by Means of Natural Selection*.

Freeman, S., & Herron, J. (2002). Análisis Evolutivo. Madrid: Prentice Hall.

Goldberg, D. E. (1989). Genetic Algorithms in Search, Optimization and Machine Learning. Reading, MA: Addison-Wesley Pub.

Haykin, S. (1998). Neural Networks: A Comprehensive Foundation (2nd Ed.). Upper Saddle River, NJ: Prentice Hall.

Holland, J. H. (1975). Adaptation in Natural and Artificial Systems. Ann Arbor, MI: University of Michigan Press.

Koza, J. R. (1992). Genetic Programming: On the Programming of Computers by Means of Natural Selection. Cambridge, MA: The MIT Press.

Michalewicz, Z. (1998). Genetic Algorithms + Data Structures = Evolution Programs, 3rd revised & extended Ed. Berlin: Springer.

ADDITIONAL READING

Beasley, D., Bull, D. R., & Martin, R. R. (1993). An overview of genetic algorithms: Part 1, Fundamentals. *University Computing, 15*(2), 58–69.

Beasley, D., Bull, D. R., & Martin, R. R. (1993). An overview of genetic algorithms: Part 2, Research Topics. *University Computing, 15*(4), 170–181.

Bishop, C. M. (1995). Neural Networks for Pattern Recognition. New York: Oxford University Press.

DeJong, A. K., & Spears, W. M. (1993). On the State of Evolutionary Computation. In *Proceedings of the International Conference on Genetic Algorithms* (pp. 618-623).

Dreyfus, G. (2005). Neural Networks: Methodology and Applications. Berlin: Springer.

Fogel, D. B. (2006). Evolutionary Computation: Toward a New Philosophy of Machine Intelligence (3rd Ed.). Piscataway, NJ: IEEE Press.

Fogel, L. J., Owens, A. J., & Walsh, M. J. (1966). Artificial Intelligence Through Simulated Evolution. New York: Wiley Publishing.

Gestal, M., Cancela, A., Gómez-Carracedo, M. P., & Andrade, J. M. (2006). Several Approaches to Variable Selection by means of Genetic Algorithms. In Artificial Neural Networks in Real-Life Applications (pp. 141-164). Hershey, PA: Idea Group Publishing.

Goldberg, D. E. (2002). The Design of Innovation: Lessons from and for Competent Genetic Algorithms. Reading, MA: Addison-Wesley.

Koza, J. R. (1992). Genetic Programming: On the Programming of Computers by Means of Natural Selection. Cambridge, MA: The MIT Press.

Matlab: Genetic Algorithm and Direct Search Toolbox 2. (n.d.). Retrieved from www.mathworks.com/academia/student_version/r2007a_products/gads.pdf

Matlab: Neural Network Toolbox. (n.d.). Retrieved from http://www.mathworks.com/products/neuralnet/

Tomassini, M. (1995). A Survey of Genetic Algorithms. In []. New York: World Scientific.t]. *Annual Reviews of Computational Physics, 3*, 87–117.

Chapter 2
Artificial Cell Model Used for Information Processing

Enrique Fernández-Blanco
University of A Coruña, Spain

Jose A. Serantes
University of A Coruña, Spain

Nieves Pedreira
University of A Coruña, Spain

Julián Dorado
University of A Coruña, Spain

ABSTRACT

The main features of a new theoretical model inside the knowledge area called Artificial Embryogeny are described in this paper. Artificial Embryogeny is a term that identifies any model that uses embryological cells or embryological processes as inspiration. This chapter details the theoretical model and it also presents some its apllication to information processing problems. Specifically, this model was applied to solve classical problems such as pattern classification and pattern recognition problems. The Iris classification problem is the selected information processing problems presented in this paper. It must be remarked that a similar application was never been done with an artificial embryogeny model.

INTRODUCTION

Using biology as inspiration for the creation of computational models is not a new idea: Nature has already been the basis for artificial neuron models (McCulloch &Pitts, 1943), the genetic algorithms (Holland, 1975), etc. The cells of a biological organism are able to compose very complex structures from a unique cell, the zygote, with no need for centralized control (Watson & Crick, 1953). The cells can perform such process thanks to the existence of a general plan, encoded in the DNA for the development and functioning of the system. Another interesting characteristic of natural cells is that they form systems that are tolerant to partial failures: small errors do not induce a global collapse of the system. Finally, the tissues that are composed by biological cells present parallel information processing for the coordination of tissue functioning

DOI: 10.4018/978-1-61520-893-7.ch002

in each and every cell that composes this tissue. All these characteristics are very interesting from a computational viewpoint.

Another interesting point of view is to think that the biological structures process the input information of their environment and they use the DNA as a processor to operate with those inputs. to study the biological model as a design model. Actually, human designs use a top-down view, this methodology has served well. However the construction of software and hardware systems with a high number of elements, the design crisis is served. Verify formally the systems when interactions and possible states grows, becomes near impossible due the combinatorial explosion of configuration using a traditional way. Living systems suggest interesting solutions for these problems, such as that the information defining the organism is contained within each part. Consequently, if the designers want to increase the complexity of the systems, one way is to study the biological model trying to mimic its solutions.

This paper presents the development of a model that tries to emulate the biological cells and to take advantage of some of their characteristics by trying to adapt them to artificial cells. The model is based on a set of techniques known as *Artificial Embryogeny* (Stanley & Miikkulainen, 2003) or *Computational Embryology* (Kumar, 2004).

BACKGROUND

In 2003, Ken Stanley and Risto Miikulainen developed a methodology to classify the different models that appear in Evolutionary Computation (EC), which have defined the new Artificial Embryogeny (AE) area. This methodology is focused on the models which are inspired in abstractions of the embryological cells. This new research area has been called by different names, like Computational Embryology or AE, by different authors. The models try to keep features such as self-organizing, self-repairing, fault tolerance and parallel information processing, which are present in the biological model, in an abstraction to apply them to different problems.

Following this classification methodology, AE works can be classified in two main types which face the problem in two different ways. On one hand, works that are included under the grammatical approach can be found. These works are related with Lindermayer's studies and L-systems, which perform a top-down approach to the problem (1968). On the other hand, other works, with a chemical approach, are found. These last works are based in Turing's ideas and perform a bottom-up approach to the problem (1952).

Grammatical approach works have been mostly used to develop Artificial Neural Networks (ANNs). This process is called neuroevolution. The first neuroevolutive system was developed by Kitano (1990). This work shows how the connectivity matrix of an ANN can be evolved with a set of rewriting rules. Another remarkable work is the one developed by Hornby and Pollack (2002), where the authors develop both the structure of a body in a simulated 3D world and an ANN to control it. In this case, the authors use the L-systems to develop both parts. Finally, it is necessary to mention the work developed by Gruau (1994), where the authors use a grammatical tree to store the development of an ANN from a unique starting element.

On the chemical approach, the first work that has to be mentioned is the one done by Kauffmann (1969), where the theory about Gene Regulatory Networks is developed. From this one, different works that study how the expression of different genes causes the expression of other ones determining a complex behavior starts (Mjolness, Sharp, Reinitz, 1995).

One work that should be mentioned inside the chemical approach is the one developed by H. Kitano (1994). This work tries to develop a model close to the biological one, and its objective is to study the cell in deep. Other researchers have looked for this parallelism in the biological model through modeling the metabolism of the cell (Tomita, 2001, Kaneko,2006).

Other works focus their attention into applications to other problems far away from the cell study. These developments have been applied to different problems, such as approximating a simple shape in a 3D space (Kumar, 2004) or the design of evolutionary hardware (Tufte, Haddow, 2005).

Another significant work is the one proposed by Eggenberger (1996). The proposed model presents the concept of cellular differentiation and cellular movement. This is an important concept to develop self-organizing and cooperative models for complex task. The author presents different tests in 2D and 3D spaces and the objective is to develop the control of a robot. Unfortunately, the paper doesn't present any numeric result to provide a comparison.

Dellaert and Beer's work (1996) presents two models. The first one is more complex and closer to the biological system. The second one is more abstract but simpler. The more complex one adds the concept of operon for controlling the behavior of the model. This biological concept represents the relation among the different functionalities of a system. Only when some conditions are fulfilled, then a group of genes can be expressed. The main problem of this work is that the sets of rules are handmade, which limits the complexity of the developments.

Finally, one of the most important works into the last mentioned group is the one presented by Bentley and Kumar (2003). This work presents a model based on the evolution of a unique cell to develop an approximate shape in a 3D space. One of the most interesting parts is the use of the fractal proteins in the communication among the cells of the model (Bentley, 1999).

In 2003, J. Miller presented a different model. This one tries to grow from one single element and achieves different shapes, like the well known French flag test. The behavior of the cell is based on the inputs from its neighbors and the environ-

ment and a running program generated by Genetic Programming.

Other works do not fit their behavior so much to Biology. For example, in 2004 Federici presents a work that is a simulation of a tissue of artificial cells to develop a circuit for hardware. In this work, he does not mind if a division of a cell makes the solution tissue bigger than the admissible solution, only those cells that are out of the solution are not taken into account in the final solution.

Each one of these enumerated works can be characterized and classified following the methodology presented in Stanley and Miikulainnen's work (2003). The model presented in this paper is not an exception, and it can be included into the chemical approach. The classification methodology identifies five parameters to characterize a model, which are:

- Cell fate. This model can be defined as a self-organizing one instead of being based on a strict set of rules.
- Selection of objectives. This model presents a Cartesian system to message communication instead of a more physical like system based on angles and signal powers.
- Temporal variability. The proposed model implements the concepts of mitosis (cellular division) and apoptosis (cellular death).
- Canalization. This concept indicates how robust a model is. The presented here includes a certain component of randomness in the communication and buffering of the inputs of each cell. This model of communication gives the cells certain fuzzy computation capacities which imply fault tolerance.
- Complexity of solutions. It depends on the number of rules used by the system. This number of rules has been configured as variable to allow the system to explore the whole search space, independently of its complexity.

BIOLOGICAL INSPIRATION

A biological cellular system can be categorized as a complex system following the identification characteristics of a complex system stated by Nagl (Nagl, Parish, Paton & Warner, 1998). The cells of a biological system are mainly determined by the DNA strand, the genes, and the proteins contained by the cytoplasm. The DNA is the structure that holds the gene-encoded information that is needed for the development of the system. These genes are activated or transcribed by the protein shaped-information that exists in the cytoplasm. Genes have two main parts: the sequence, which identifies the protein that the gene will generate if the gene is transcribed, and the promoter, which identifies the proteins that are needed to activate the gene.

Another remarkable aspect of biological genes is the difference between constitutive genes and regulating genes. The latter are transcribed only when the proteins identified in the promoter part are present. The constitutive genes are always transcribed, unless inhibited by the presence of the proteins identified in the promoter part, acting then as gene oppressors.

The present work has tried to partially model this structure with the aim of fitting some of its abilities into a computational model; in this way, the system would have a structure similar that is similar to the above and will be detailed in following section.

PROPOSED MODEL

The present work uses for its tests an evolution of the model used in (Fernandez-Blanco, Dorado, Rabuñal, Gestal & Pedreira, 2007). In this section a description of this model can be found. This model represents the activity in a cell and how the cell cooperates with the neighborhood cells. The cells have as essential elements the DNA and the cytoplasm, which are related by using the proteins. Proteins are the responsible of the behavior expressed by the cells of the system. DNA is a set of rules which uses those proteins to express the behavior codified inside them. The DNA of a cell expresses a behavior depending on the proteins stored at the cytoplasm. When these proteins stored in the cytoplasm are in a certain concentration, they induce activations of genes of the DNA or communication of those proteins to a neighbor cell. These behavior and parts of the system are detailed in the following sections.

Protein

The protein is the basic piece of information of the system. In the biological model, proteins have a time to live, which determines how long the proteins can be in the system to be used, until they are degraded (deleted). In the artificial model, proteins are represented by a bit string that identifies each of the different proteins, and it also has a time to live (TTL). So, the system has a memory of previous non-used proteins, until they are used or degraded.

Cytoplasm

Cytoplasm is the part which has the responsibility of managing the information contained inside the artificial cell model. Therefore, this is the part which calculates the concentration of the different proteins which are inside the cell. This part is also the responsible of recovering the proteins needed for a transcription in the cell and checking the concentration level of the proteins inside and outside the cell to decide which proteins will be communicated. The cytoplasm of cells sets out a protein when its concentration is higher than a threshold.

Gene

Each gene of the system represents a rule, which has some conditions to perform a certain compu-

Figure 1. Gene schema

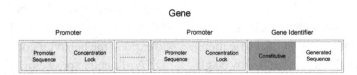

tation or process. The genes are bit strings which contains two main parts: Promoter and Gene Identifier (see Figure 1).

The description of the parts of the genes is the following:

- **Promoter region**. This part identifies the proteins needed to activate this gene. This section can appear several times, identifying more than one protein for a gene. Each Promoter region is composed by two subparts:
  - ○ **Promoter Sequence**. This section contains the identification sequences of the proteins required to activate the gene.
  - ○ **Concentration lock**. Each of the activation proteins needs a certain concentration level in the cytoplasm, identified in this field, to activate this gene.
- **Gene identifier**. This part identifies which is the protein generated by the gene and the type of the gene. It is composed by two subparts.

- ○ **Constitutive mark**, this bit indicates if the gene is a constitutive gene. This bit changes the normal behavior of a gene as it is explained below.
- ○ **Generated sequence**. When the gene is activated, the result of that activation is a protein which contains this sequence. This sequence can become in a simple protein or can allow some specific processes in the cell (death or division).

Genes need all their activation proteins for their activation (see Figure 2). These proteins have to be at least in a certain proportion inside the cell. However, it is not necessary to have a protein identical to the activation protein. In Nature, similar proteins in a high concentration can also activate the transcription of a gene. This last fact is modeled using this condition:

$$\text{Protein Concentration Percent} >= \text{(Distance} + 1) * \text{Concentration Lock} \tag{1}$$

Figure 2. Gene transcription example. This figure shows how a new protein is generated by a gen when all the promoters are present

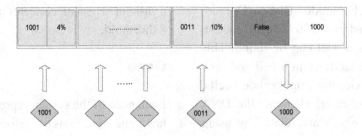

Figure 3. Operon schema. This figure shows a general schema of the parts that compose a operon in the model

In this condition, *Protein Concentration Percent* refers to the concentration of the tested protein into the cell, *Distance* is the hamming distance between the activation protein and the tested protein, and, finally, *Concentration Lock* is the required concentration for the activation protein. If the condition is fulfilled for all of the activation proteins or similar proteins, then the gene is activated and it generates a protein with the gene's generated sequence.

This is the normal behavior of a gene, but when it is marked as constitutive it changes drastically. Constitutive genes are transcript on every moment. This means that it is constantly generating proteins, until its activation proteins appear. In this case, those proteins are called inhibitor proteins. When these inhibitor proteins appear, the gene stops to transcript itself for a certain period. In the tests of this paper, the inhibition is set to one "cellular cycle", which is further explained in subsection Cell.

Operon

Operon is the name given to the group of genes that codify a task. In Nature, they codify the most complex parts of the development, but the genes have to act all or none. So, this model has tried to adapt this idea by creating a structure which applies some conditions to a group of genes. This structure has the same parts as a gene and acts in the same way but, instead of a generated sequence, it has a set of genes (Figure 3). The activation of the operon allows the activation of the genes from that moment for a period of time.

Figure 4. Gene encapsulates into DNA. The DNA is composed by genes and operons that have the parts showed in the Figure 1 and Figure 3

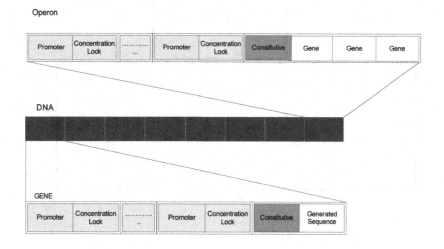

DNA

DNA is a structure composed by genes and operons, as shown in Figure 4. Its responsibility is to keep the instructions of the system and select the allowed genes to activate, when the cell asks for them in a certain moment of its development.

Cell

Cells are the basic elements of the system and contain all the parts previously described. They are the responsible to process information. Cells will be able to communicate with the environment or other cells, process the DNA, divide themselves or die. Cells define the cellular time or "cellular cycles" to coordinate the different actions. These cellular cycles contain all the events that can be considered to be done in a cell at the same time.

For example, a cell can communicate different proteins to the environment, but it can only divide itself once in a cellular cycle or a gene can be only transcript once in a cycle.

The behavior of a cell is determined by the tasks that can be executed in a single cycle. So, a scheme of the basic behavior can be seen in Figure 5. The steps in a cell functioning can be enumerated as following:

1. Update the proteins' TTL (Time to Live) and delete the degraded ones.
2. Process the DNA to transcript the genes with the information in the cytoplasm and generate the new proteins.
3. Execute the communications of the different proteins or execute the special actions (divide and death), if it's possible.

Figure 5. Workflow in a cellular cycle

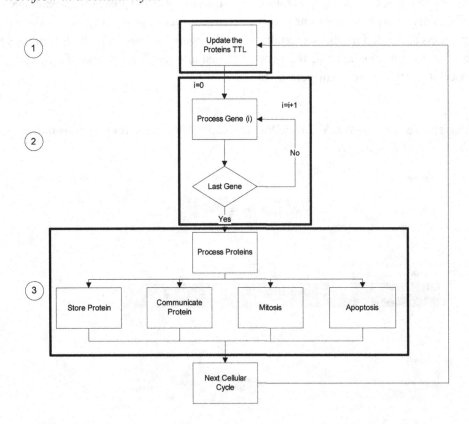

Figure 6. Communication probability function. Probability function around a certain position (left) and the decreasing value (right) of that probably when further positions are tested

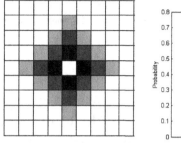
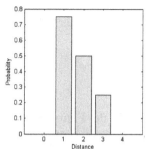

In short, after the update of the time to live of the proteins, when a cell activates a gene, four different actions can be performed: store the protein in the cytoplasm; communicate the protein to the neighborhood; division of the cell or death of the cell. These actions are performed by all of the cells in a tissue at the same time.

The division and death actions are regulated by a group of special proteins. There are four special proteins for growing that identify one of the four directions (Up, Down, Left, Right) in 2D. When a gene produces a protein with any of these sequences, then the action is performed, if the cell has not been already divided. The death operation is associated to another different protein. When this protein reaches a certain concentration threshold inside the cell at the end of a cellular cycle, this cell dies. The communication and the store of proteins are two linked actions for the rest of proteins. It is set a threshold when the concentration in the cytoplasm is higher than that threshold, then a protein of that type is communicated to the neighborhood in other case the protein is stored into the cytoplasm of the cell (the communication is further explained in the next section).

Environment

The environment is where the cells are, and, normally, it determines the type of communication among cells within a neighborhood. The main purpose of the environment is to manage the free proteins. The free proteins are the ones which have been set out by a cell and no cell has already required them. The environment determines how these proteins move themselves through it. This movement is performed until a cell requires those proteins or their TTL expire.

COMMUNICATION MODEL

Once the cells have been already defined, it is needed a system to coordinate the elements that compose the system. Therefore, a communication model is needed to define among the cells. In the communication, the cells check in each cellular cycle the concentration of the proteins inside them. When those concentrations are higher than a certain threshold, some proteins are put in the environment.

Once the proteins are put in the environment, they modify the value of a function. That function associates to each position of the environment a probability value to "find" each type of protein. The value of the function is determined by using the number of proteins put in a certain position and the distance between the positions of the cell and where the proteins are. This function has a space distribution as show Figure 6. The value

Figure 7. GA individual interpretation as DNA

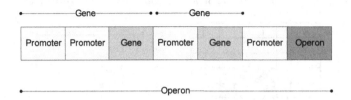

of the function is represented in the Figure 6 by the darkness of the positions, which fall from the maximum value to 0 as the position of the proteins is further from the cell's position. It must be mention that the position, where the proteins are, has a value of 0. That value is to erase the possibility that a cell gets its own proteins again and falls in an infinite loop. The cells check, each cycle, the protein values of near positions to determine the probability that those cells have to "find" a protein of a certain type. A higher amount of proteins of a certain type in a position and a closer distance to the origin position of those proteins implies a higher probability of finding a protein of that type by a neighbor cell. That probability is used to check if a protein of that type is found by the cell. When a protein is found by the cell, it reduces the number of proteins in the origin position and the value of the probability function. The proteins in the environment, as the ones inside a cell, update their TTL each cellular cycle. When that TTL reaches 0 the proteins are also deleted and the probability function modifies its value, too.

SEARCH METHOD

The DNA is the set of instructions that configures the behavior of the system, so the DNA will be the object to be searched to achieve the desired behavior. This is a difficult task because the number and the value of the different genes that compose the DNA is unknown.

In order to perform this search, a Genetic Algorithm (GA) (Fogel, 66, Holland, 1975, Goldberg,

1989) has been chosen. The reason for this selection is because GAs are one of the most robust and adaptable search methods. The codification of the individuals, the mutation operation and the crossover operation were modified in order to adapt the Genetic Algorithm to some peculiarities of the problem

The Figure 7 shows the different sections that can compose an individual of the GA and how they are associated to convert the GA individual into a DNA for the model. Each individual of the GA population represents one DNA, so the representation has to take into account some particularities of the DNA. First, the DNA is a set with an unknown number of rules, so the use of variable length individuals seems to be mandatory. Another particularity of the DNA is the shape of the genes, which have a variable number of conditions (activation proteins). Finally, the last particularity comes from the concept of operon. The operon has, like the gene, a variable part in the activation proteins, and it has another variable part in the group of genes that it allows to activate. So, the proposed solution with these particularities has the shape of the Figure 7.

In Figure 7, the sections that compose a GA individual can be seen. There are three different types:

- **Promoters sections**. They are functional sections that contain the identifier of an activation protein and the concentration lock associated to that protein.
- **Gene sections.** They identify a gene and contain the mark if the gene is constitutive

Figure 8. Crossover example

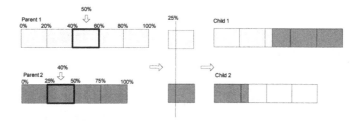

or not, and the sequence that will be generated. This section will be associated with the previous promoter sections that appear in the GA individual until another Gene identification section or operon section is found.

- **Operon section**. It is a mark of the creation of an operon for the cellular system and contains the number of genes that the operon has. This section associates itself with the promoters sections which appear before it until a Gene identification section or another operon identification section. An operon contains the genes which appear before it in the DNA, until the maximum number, which is identified at the section or is reached or it finds another operon identification section.

The different section types require different fields. The sections used by GA contain all those fields and the type of the section determines which ones are active. Using these sections and associating them like in Figure 7, the system is able to search all the possible combinations of rules. In order to allow the search with these sections, the next step is to adapt the GA crossover and mutation operators.

The Figure 8 shows how two sections of the GA parent individuals are selected and how that parents are crossed to generate two offspring. It begins by randomly selecting a crossover section which is chosen in function of a percent of its length. A random percent is generated and then the algorithm chooses, in each parent, the sections which are at those percent of the length. Length is understood as the number of functional sections of the individual. Once the sections are chosen, the algorithm selects one point inside each section to do the crossover. This point inside the sections is selected randomly but it is the sane in both sections to produce valid sections after the crossover. The sections are combined using that crossover point. The rest of the offspring's genetic material is the combination of the parents as shown in Figure 8

The mutation operator is not so simple, because variable length individuals are being using. In this way, the mutation operator can execute one of the three possible operations (Figure 9):

- Adding of a new section to an individual. This new section could be a new random one or the copy of an existing one.
- Delete a section.
- Change of a bit inside the section. This operation can change a value or change the type of the section.

The operation of copying a section is bioinspired, and allows biological systems to test alternatives maintaining a working copy as explained in other works (Force, Lynch, Pickett, Amores, Lin Yan, Poshlethwait, 1999).

The operation of change needs more explanation, because each block has two bits that identify its type. The first mark identifies if the section is a promoter section or not and the second mark determines if it is an operon or a gene, in case

Figure 9. Mutation operations: (A) Add a section, (B) delete a section and (C) modify a section

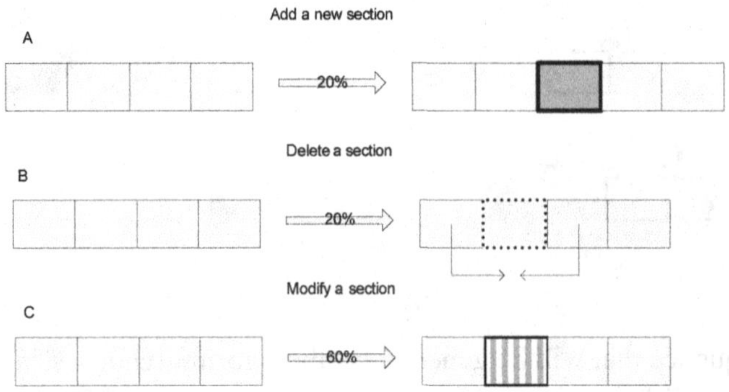

the section is not a promoter. A change in any of these bits makes the information of the block to be reinterpreted in its new role. This reinterpretation can produce a random generation of those fields that the section did not have before.

TESTS

This system was tested with different problems. The problems which the model was applied to do not have the ambition to become a very complex test. The motivation of this test is to understand how the system behavior is. This motivation of simplifying has leaded to use a 2D environment for the test. The reason of this selection is because the 2D environment simplifies the study of the results and the test, whereas a 3D environment does not add anything more than complexity to the analysis of the tests and their representation.

The kind of problems faced in this paper is those which try to solve information processing problems. This set of tests was done to know if the model can be trained to solve different kinds of problems. Particularly, pattern recognition and pattern non-linear classification were tested.

During the tests, a better behavior in the search was observed, if the mutation operation is divided in the three possibilities, the ones explained in the previous section, with a probability associated to

each type. The probabilities to execute each one of the actions in the mutation were empirically obtained: 20% of the times, that a mutation is performed, is to add a new block, 20% is to erase a block and 60% is to change a bit of the section changing its values or its type. These values have been used in the tests presented in this paper.

The model has source and sink points, which work like the inputs and the outputs, respectively. The objective of the tests is to search a DNA which minimizes the output error in the sink points when the inputs are present in the source points. Both, inputs and outputs, are codified as proteins to allow the system to work with the information. So, the DNA is put in the cells of the tissue and the input proteins are put in the source points. After a number of cellular cycles, the output values are tested in the sink points. The difference between the desired outputs and the obtained ones is the error of the system for that pattern. After each pattern is evaluated, the information in the buffer of the system is cleaned up not to mismatch the next input.

The number of cellular cycles, that the system is let to execute until the sink points are tested, is 5 for all the tests presented in this paper. This number was empirically obtained, and it was selected because it is time enough to let the cells to give a response and the tests do not last for too long.

Figure 10. Iris flower classification configuration

Iris Flower Classification Problem

The iris flower classification problem is a non-linear classification problem. The iris flower data were originally published by Fisher in 1936 as example of discriminate analysis and cluster analysis. Four parameters, sepal length, sepal width, petal length and petal width, were measured in millimeters on 50 iris specimens from each of three iris species, *Iris setosa*, *Iris versicolor* and *Iris virginica*. Given the four parameters, one should be able to determine which of the three classes a specimen belongs to. The data used in the experiment are 150 data points listed in the database, taken from UCI (Asuncion & Newman, 2007).

The model tries to search a DNA which classifies the different patterns of iris flowers. In order to adapt the cellular model to this new problem, the values of the variables were normalized between 0 and 1. One sink point and 4 source points, one for each variable, were used. Figure 10 shows how these elements were configured into the environment. The 4 source points where set in the same position of the environment in the shadowed position with an I, the cell was set at the position with a C and the sink point was set in the position with an O. The source points put into the environment 4 different proteins, one for each variable. The normalized value of a variable is the peek probability of receiving it around the source point. This probability decreases linearly from the source point into the around area, and it determines the presence probability of a protein in that point. The outputs of the system are the proteins received in the sink point. Three sequences are identified as the desired outputs and they determine the predicted class of the input data.

$$fitness = \sum_i \begin{cases} 100 & \text{no protein registered} \\ 1 & \text{no desired protein} \\ 0 & \text{desired protein in the first position of the list} \\ 0.5 & \text{desired protein in the second position of the list} \\ 0.75 & \text{desired protein in the third position of the list} \\ 0.85 & \text{desired protein in other position in the list} \end{cases}$$

(3)

The fitness function uses the list of the proteins received in the sink points which is ordered by the concentration of the proteins. The ordered list is needed to check the position of the desired sequence. The fitness function adds a different penalization depending on the position of the desired protein into the ordered list, as shown in Eq. 3. The value of that penalization was selected empirically. There are two special cases: when the desired protein is not present the penalization is set to 1 and when no protein is received the error is 100. The penalization of 100 is used to discard individuals. The i letter represents a pattern of the training set. The fitness is the sum of the penalizations for each pattern.

Finally, the GA used to search the DNA, which allows this classification, is the same as the previous test. The differences are that a better behavior was observed with a 70% crossover rate and a 30% mutation probability in populations between 50 and 100 individuals.

The Figure 11 shows on the top how many of the different iris types where classified. In the left it can be see the correct classification patterns and, on the right the wrong classified ones. The best individual has a fitness of 8.85 and it is composed by 583 sections which generate over 100 genes.

Figure 11. Iris flower classification: Correct (left) and errors (right)

TYPE	TOTAL NUMBER	CORRECT CLASSIFICATION
IRIS SETOSA: 1111(*)	50	50
IRIS VERSICOLOR: 1001(+)	50	46
IRIS VIRGINICA: 1010(□)	50	44

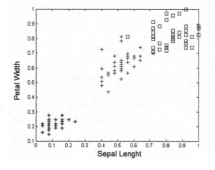 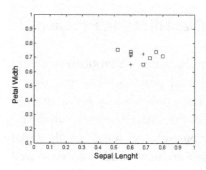

The results obtained by the best DNA string can be seen in Figure 11. This figure shows that the cellular system with that DNA string is able to classify 140 out of 150 data. So, the system is able to classify a 93.33% of the total data. In that figure, the three kinds of iris flowers can be seen represented by a star, a cross and a square. The correct classifications are represented by the marks on the left graph of Figure 11 and the wrong classifications are represented by marks on the right graph.

If the results are analyzed, it is clear that the wrong classified patterns are in the area between two classes of Iris. This result is the expected because the system does not have any problem to classify the clear ones. It may be remembered that this test only used one processing element (cell) and the system is expected to have a better behavior by increasing the complexity with more cells which cooperate to perform this classification (See Figure 12).

FUTURE TRENDS

The different lines opened by this work are very wide. Firstly, this paper has used the communication model based on probability of reception. This

Figure 12. Iris flower classification in training. Correct classified patterns are on the left graph and the wrong classified patterns are on the right graph

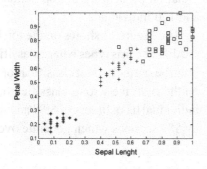 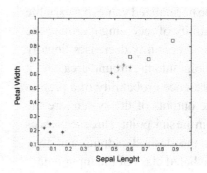

reduces and simplifies the model, but one open question is if the genes can be probabilistic, too.

The tests presented in this paper are a complementary work of the ones presented in (Fernandez-Blanco, Dorado, Rabuñal, Gestal, Pedreira, 2007), where it was presented how a similar model can evolve a shape. A possible future line is to combine the information processing with the shape development to generate self-organizing structure that can process information.

The simplification of the solutions obtained by the GA was already appointed in the text. The solutions normally have genes that are never activated. Deleting those genes can make the solutions quicker and more compact.

Another point of study in the model is the possibility of training the solution with the user interference, for example setting different Boolean functions executed by the environment when the correct proteins are present in certain position. If this idea is joined with the possibility of moving the cells or the division and self-organization of these ones, the system can have a high configuration level.

A specialization operator can open the cellular system to more complex developments. This operator could block the activation of a DNA section to the cell and its offspring, so it allows the creation of different roles among the cells. Therefore, this action will introduce different roles for each function having different types of cells to do it.

The information processing tests have to be improved and the model has to be applied to new problems in different areas far from the laboratory ones. Moreover, the information processing has to test its capacities to generate a tissue that solves the problems not only like the tests presented here (using a configuration that cannot grow).

Finally, the presented system has relation with the IBM's proposal under the name of Autonomic Computing (Kephart, Chess, 2003). To build a self-programming element, which contains all the characteristics mentioned into the IBM's text, is the objective of the work in long term.

CONCLUSION

This paper has presented a new application for models into Artificial Embryogeny. The proposed model is a different approach from its predecessors and its aim is, at least, to be able to be applied to any kind of different problem than the previous ones.

After setting the required objective, the system searches for a set of rules. This allows the achieving of an objective by the elements that compose the solution. This search and distributed organization is done without the participation of the user in the codification of the DNA, which is automatically generated by the system. Future developments with this system could be framed into the Autonomic Computing model proposed by IBM in 2003, because they present many of the features that these systems require, like self-organizing and self-configuration. The model could be the base for the communication between different elements. This is the objective of Autonomic Computing.

The information processing capacity of this model has been shown. The classification of iris flowers was performed. The aim of this problem was to study the performance of the cellular model in a complex problem. The result for this problem was that the system can classify a huge part of the patterns, however its results are not so good as ANNs have. This problem is expected to have a better result by increasing the number of processing elements because the tests presented here were done using only one cell.

FUTURE RESEARCH DIRECTIONS

On the last years the artificial embryogeny has had a very quickly development. As it was mentioned, models which are sorted as artificial embryogeny kind could be framed into the grammatical approach or into the chemical approach. On the last years, a lot of grammatical approach models have been adapted to generate artificial neural networks. This work is an interesting point of investigation, because it has application on evolvable artificial neural networks, such as archive an evolvable design of a network for a particular problem.

On the chemical approach models, as the one presented in this paper, could also include new characteristics such as the displacement of cells around their environment, or a specialisation operator that blocks pieces of DNA during the expression of its descendants, as happens in the natural model. These incorporations may induce new behaviours that make it applicable to new problems.

One of the questions is to develop models which could combine both approaches. The result will be a hybrid model which will has characteristics from both approaches.

Explore other possible applications of the artificial embryogeny models could be an interesting works in areas like the evolutionary robot controllers design, the evolutionary hardware, and design of generative encoding for the construction of artificial organisms in simulated physical environments, etc.

Another problem that could be easy detected is to find a strategy search to work with the model. Both approaches, chemical and grammatical, have to search into enormous search spaces. Many models have failed into their applicability because it was difficult to search the correct configuration for the rules of the system. Find a general way to develop that search may be an interesting work.

Finally, the model showed here has been used for information processing problems and the development of forms. The development of both aspects for the same problem, which may be an starting point to study self-organizing structures for information processing.

REFERENCES

Asuncion, A., & Newman, D. J. (2007). *UCI Machine Learning Repository*. Retrieved from http://www.ics.uci.edu/~mlearn/MLRepository.html

Bentley, P. J. (2002). Digital Biology. New York: Simon and Schuster.

Dellaert, F., & Beer, R. D. (1996). A Developmental Model for the Evolution of Complete Autonomous Agent. In *From animals to animats: Proceedings of the Forth International Conference on Simulation of Adaptive Behaviour*, Massachusetts, 9-13 September 1996 (pp. 394-401). Cambridge, MA: MIT Press.

Eggenberger, P. (1996). Cell Interactions as a Control Tool of Developmental Processes for Evolutionary Robotics. In *From animals to animats: Proceedings of the Forth International Conference on Simulation of Adaptive Behaviour*, Massachusetts, 9-13 September 1996 (pp. 440-448). Cambridge, MA: MIT Press.

Federici, D. (2004). Using embryonic stages to increase the evolvability of development. In *Proceedings of WORLDS Workshop on Regeneration and Learning in Developmental Systems hosted by GECCO 2004*. New York: ACM Press.

Fernandez-Blanco, E., Dorado, J., Rabuñal, J. R., Gestal, M., & Pedreira, N. (2007). A New Evolutionary Computation Technique for 2D Morphogenesis and Information Processing. In WSEAS Transactions on Information Science & Applications, April 2007 (Vol. 4, pp. 600-607).

Fogel, L. J., Owens, A. J., & Walsh, M. A. (1966). Artificial Intelligence through Simulated Evolution. New York: Wiley.

Force, A., Lynch, M., Pickett, F. B., Amores, A., Lin Yan, Y., & Poshlethwait, J. (1999). Preservation of duplicate genes by complementary, degenerative mutations. *Genetics, 151*, 1531–1545.

Goldberg, D. E. (1989). Genetics Algorithms in Search, Optimization and Machine Learning. Reading, MA: Addison-Wesley.

Gruau, F. (1994). *Neural networks synthesis using cellular encoding and the genetic algorithm.* Doctoral dissertation, Ecole Normale Superiere de Lyon, France.

Holland, J. H. (1975). Adaptation in natural and artificial systems. Ann Arbor, MI: University of Michigan Press.

Hornby, G. S., & Pollack, J. B. (2001). The advantages of generative grammatical encodings for physical design. In *Proceedings of the 2002 Congress on Evolutionary Computation*. Piscataway, NJ: IEEE Press.

Kaneko, K. (2006). Life: An Introduction to Complex Systems Biology. Berlin: Springer Press.

Kauffman, S. A. (1969). Metabolic stability and epigenesis in randomly constructed genetic nets. *Journal of Theoretical Biology, 22,* 437–467. doi:10.1016/0022-5193(69)90015-0

Kephart, J. O., & Chess, D. M. (2003). The vision of Autonomic Computing. IEEE Computer Magazine, (January), 41-50.

Kitano, H. (2005). Using process diagrams for the graphical representation of biological networks. *Nature Biotechnology, 23*(8), 961–966. doi:10.1038/nbt1111

Koza, J., et al. (1999). Genetic Programming III: Darwin Invention and Problem Solving. Cambridge, MA: MIT Press.

Kumar, S. (2004). *Investigating Computational Models of Development for the Construction of Shape and Form.* PhD Thesis, Department of Computer Science, University Collage London.

Kumar, S., & Bentley, P. J. (Eds.). (2003) On Growth, Form and Computers. London: Elsevier Academic Press.

Lindenmayer, A. (1968). Mathematical models for cellular interaction in development: Part I and II. *Journal of Theoretical Biology, 18,* 280–315. doi:10.1016/0022-5193(68)90079-9

McCulloch, W. S., & Pitts, W. (1990). A logical calculus of the ideas immanent in nervous activity. *The Bulletin of Mathematical Biophysics, 5,* 115–133. doi:10.1007/BF02478259

Mjolsness, E., Sharp, D. H., & Reinitz, J. (1995). A Connectionist Model of Development. *Journal of Theoretical Biology, 176,* 291–300. doi:10.1006/jtbi.1995.0199

Nagl, S. B., Parish, J. H., Paton, R. C., & Warner, G. J. (1998). Macromolecules, Genomes and Ourselves. In R. Paton, H. Bolouri, M. Holcombe, J. H. Parish & R. Tateson (Eds.), Computation in cells and tissues. Perspective and tools of thought. Berlin: Springer Press.

Rumelhart, D. E., Hilton, G. E., & Williams, R. J. (1986). Learning internal representations by error propagation. In Parallel distributed processing: Explorations in the microstructure of cognition (Vol. 1, pp. 318-362). Cambridge, MA: MIT Press.

Stanley, K., & Miikkulainen, R. (2003). A Taxonomy for Artificial Embryogeny. In *Proceedings* []. Cambridge, MA: MIT Press.]. *Artificial Life, 9,* 93–130. doi:10.1162/106454603322221487

Tomita, D. (2001). Whole-cell simulation: A grand challenge of the 21st century. *Trends in Biotechnology, 19*(6), 205–210. doi:10.1016/S0167-7799(01)01636-5

Tufte, G., & Haddow, P. C. (2005). Towards Development on a Silicon-based Cellular Computing Machine. *Natural Computing, 4*(4), 387–416. doi:10.1007/s11047-005-3665-8

Turing, A. (1952). The chemical basis of morphogenesis. *Philosofical Transactions of the Royal Society B, 237,* 37–72. doi:10.1098/rstb.1952.0012

Watson, J. D., & Crick, F. H. (1953). Molecular structure of Nucleic Acids. *Nature, 171*, 737–738. doi:10.1038/171737a0

ADDITIONAL READING

Bentley, P. J., & Kumar, S. (1999). The ways to grow designs: A comparison of embryogenies for an evolutionary design problem. In *Proceedings of the Genetic and Evolutionary Computation Conference (GECCO-1999)* (pp. 35-43) San Francisco, CA: Morgan Kaufmann

Bongard, J. C. (2002). Evolving modular genetic regulatory networks. In *Proceedings of the 2002 Congress on Evolutionary Computation.* Piscataway, NJ: IEEE Press.

Bongard, J. C., & Paul, C. (2000). Investigating morphological symmetry and locomotive efficiency using virtual embodied evolution. In *Proceedings of the Sixth International Conference on Simulation of Adaptative Behavior* (pp. 420-429). Cambridge, MA: MIT Press.

Bongard, J. C., & Pfeifer, R. (2001). Repeated structure and dissociation of genotypic abd phenotypic complexity in artificial ontogeny. In L. Spensor, E. D. Goodman, A. Wu, W. B. Langdon, H. M. Voight, M. Gen, S. Sen, M. Dorigo, S. Pezeshk, M. H. Garzon & E. Burke (Eds.), *Proceedings of the Genetic and Evolutionary Computation Conference* (pp. 829-836). San Francisco, CA: Morgan Kaufmann.

Clegg, K., Stepney, S., & Clarke, T. (2007). Using feedback to Regulate Gene expression in a developmental Control Architecture. In [New York: ACM Press.]. *Proceedings of GECCO, 2007*, 966–973. doi:10.1145/1276958.1277154

Dellaert, F. (1995). *Toward a biologically defensible model of development.* Master's thesis, Case Western Reserve University, Cleveland, OH.

Dellaert, F., & Beer, R. D. (1994). *Co-evolving body and brain in autonomous agents using a developmental model* (Tech. Rep. CES-94-16). Cleveland, OH: Dept. of Computer Engineering and Science, Case Western Reserve University.

Dellaert, F., & Beer, R. D. (1994). Toward an evolvable model of development for autonomous agent synthesis. In R. A. Brooks & P. Maes (Eds.), *Proceedings of the Fourth International Workshop on the Synthesis and Simulation of Living Systems (Artificial Life IV).* Cambridge, MA: MIT Press.

Devert, A., Bredeche, N., & Schoenauer, M. (2007). Robust Multi-Cellular Developmental Design. In [New York: ACM Press.]. *Proceedings of GECCO, 2007*, 982–989. doi:10.1145/1276958.1277156

Fleischer, K., & Barr, A. H. (1993). A simulation testbed for the study of multicellular development: The multiple mechanisms of morphogenesis. In C. G. Langton (Ed.), Artificial life III (pp. 389–416). Reading, MA: Addison-Wesley.

Gruau, F., Whitley, D., & Pyeatt, L. (1996). A *comparison between cellular encoding and direct encoding for genetic neural networks.* In J. R. Koza, D. E. Goldberg, D. B. Fogel, & R. L. Riolo (Eds.), *Genetic Programming 1996: Proceedings of the First Annual Conference* (pp. 81–89). Cambridge, MA: MIT Press.

Hart, W. E., Kammeyer, T. E., & Belew, R. K. (1994). *The role of development in geneticalgorithms* (Tech. Rep. CS94-394). San Diego, CA: University of California.

Hornby, G. S., & Pollack, J. B. (2002). Creating high-level components with a generative representation for body-brain evolution. *Artificial Life, 8*(3). doi:10.1162/106454602320991837

Jakobi, N. (1995). Harnessing morphogenesis. In Proceedings of Information Processing in Cells and Tissues (pp. 29-41). Liverpool, UK: University of Liverpool.

Kauffman, S. A. (1993). The origins of order. New York: Oxford University Press.

Kitano, H. (1990). Design neural networks using genetic algorithms with graph generation system. *Complex systems, 4,* 461-476.

Kumar, S. (2004). A Developmental Biology Inspired Approach to Robot Control. In *Artificial Life 9 (ALIFE), Proceedings of the Ninth Internacional Conference on the Simulation and Síntesis of Living Systems.* Cambridge, MA: MIT Press.

Kumar, S., & Bentley, P. J. (Eds.). (2003). On Growth, Form and Computers. London: Academic Press.

Kumar, S., & Bentley, P. J. (2003). Computational Embryology: Past, Present and Future. In A. Ghosh and S. Tsutsui (Eds.). Theory and Application of Evolutionary Computation: Recent Trends. London: Springer.

Lindermayer, A. (1974). *Adding continuous components to L-systems.*

Miller, J. (2003). Evolving Developmental Programs for Adaptation Morphogenesis, and Self-Repair. *7th European Conference on Artifial Life 2003.*

Otter, T. (2004). Toward a New Theoretical Framework. In *Proceedings of the Genetic and Evolutionary Computation Congress (GECCO-2004).* San Francisco, CA: Morgan Kaufmann.

Prusinkiewicz, P., & Lindenmayer, A. (1990). The algorithmic beauty of plants. Heidelberg, Germany: Springer-Verlag

Stanley, K., & Miikkulainen, R. (2002). Continual coevolution through complexification. In *Proceedings of the Genetic and Evolutionary Computation Congress* (GECCO-2002). San Francisco, CA: Morgan Kaufmann.

Stanley, K., & Miikkulainen, R. (2003). Evolving neural networkthrough augmenting topologies. *Evolutionary Computation, 10*(2), 99–127. doi:10.1162/106365602320169811

Steiner, T., Jin, Y., & Sendhoff, B. (2008). A Cellular Model for the Evolutionary Development of Lightweight Material with an Inner Structure. In [New York: ACM Press.]. *Proceedings of GECCO, 2008,* 851–858. doi:10.1145/1389095.1389260

Chapter 3
Soft Computing Techniques for Human–Computer Interaction

Oscar Déniz
Universidad de Castilla-La Mancha, Spain

Gloria Bueno
Universidad de Castilla-La Mancha, Spain

Modesto Castrillón
Instituto Universitario de Sistemas Inteligentes y Aplicaciones Numéricas en Ingeniería, Spain

Javier Lorenzo
Instituto Universitario de Sistemas Inteligentes y Aplicaciones Numéricas en Ingeniería, Spain

L. Antón
Instituto Universitario de Sistemas Inteligentes y Aplicaciones Numéricas en Ingeniería, Spain

M. Hernández
Instituto Universitario de Sistemas Inteligentes y Aplicaciones Numéricas en Ingeniería, Spain

ABSTRACT

Soft computing aims at using tricks or shortcuts that do not provide optimal solutions but useful approximations that can be computed at a reasonable cost. Such approximations often come in the form of heuristics and "rules of thumb." Computer vision relies heavily on heuristics, being a simple example the detection of faces by detecting skin color. Another approach that may also be considered as heuristics is the use of inductive learning, where the idea is to emulate humans in the sense that achieving certain skills require gradual learning. Thus, we would not make an effort to articulate solutions as equations, rules or algorithms. The solution would instead be sought automatically by feeding the system with training examples that would allow it to classify new samples. This chapter describes two successful applications of such soft computing approaches in the field of human-computer interaction, showing how the clever use of heuristics and domain restrictions can help to find solutions for the most difficult problems in this field.

DOI: 10.4018/978-1-61520-893-7.ch003

INTRODUCTION

For many problems in computing we can find solutions that are optimal in some sense. Brute force search or analytical solutions provide such optimality. However, the cost involved often makes this approach intractable, especially for some difficult problems. Within computer vision, for example, some problems like face detection and recognition are considered particularly challenging. The 'hard computing' approach of searching for optimal solutions is in such difficult tasks unfeasible not only because of the cost involved (images are typically treated as points in a high-dimensional space) but also because we do not know very much about how humans accomplish the tasks (Deniz et al, 2007). Think for example in face recognition, we recognize people's faces everyday without effort. Such good performance is probably associated to the automaticity of the ability, which can be carried out even unconsciously. Because of that we cannot articulate the features or procedures involved.

As opposed to hard computing, 'soft computing' aims at using tricks or shortcuts that do not provide optimal solutions but approximations that can be computed at a reasonable cost. Often, the term used is heuristics. Heuristics are "rules of thumb", educated guesses, intuitive judgments or simply common sense. They are used in many domains. Antivirus software, for example, use heuristic signatures to look for specific attributes and characteristics for detecting viruses and other forms of malware. Computer vision also relies heavily on heuristics, being a simple example the detection of faces by detecting skin color. Obviously, this approach does not detect all the faces that may be present in an image, although it detects most of them very quickly.

Another approach that may also be considered as heuristics is the use of inductive learning. The idea is to emulate humans in the sense that achieving certain skills require gradual learning. Thus, we would not make an effort to articulate

solutions as equations, rules or algorithms. The solution would instead be sought automatically by feeding the system with training examples that would allow it to classify new samples.

As in other "classical" soft computing techniques like genetic algorithms and fuzzy systems, inductive learning and heuristics aim at giving inexact but useful solutions to problems that are too complex to have a reasonable cost, analytic solution.

A central ability in human-computer interaction is human perception. As mentioned above, however, our perception abilities are mainly unconscious. This chapter describes two successful applications of soft computing in human-computer interaction, showing how the clever use of heuristics and domain restrictions can help to find solutions for difficult problems in this field.

EYEWEAR SELECTOR

The first application is a hardware-software system, intended for use at optical shops, which allows individuals to test different models of spectacles in a sort of real-time video mirror. The optical market is nowadays saturated with an increasingly complex array of lenses, frames, coatings, tints, photochromic and polarizing treatments, etc. The number of clients can grow only if the selection process is shortened or automated. A number of deployed systems have already demonstrated that eyeglass selectors can increase sales and customer satisfaction (Morgan, 2004).

From a research viewpoint, such systems represent an interesting application of Computer Vision, Multimedia and Human-Computer Interaction. The Augmented Reality, see a survey in (Azuma, 1997), of watching ourselves and try different "virtual" spectacles can be achieved by combining computer vision and graphics. The Magic Lens and Magic Mirror systems, for example, use the ARTag toolkit (Fiala, 2004), which mixes live video and computer-generated graphics. People can wear cardboard patterns that ARTag can detect. The graphics are placed in the visible positions of the patterns. The system can work in real-time on general-purpose hardware, although people have to wear the cardboard. Another approach is taken in (Lepetit et al 2003), where virtual glasses and moustaches are added to live video. Although the system works with an impressive frame rate of 25Hz the user must start the tracker by reaching a position that is close to a generic triangle-based face model shown on the screen. The ARMirror is a kiosk-based entertainment setup that shows live video overlaying virtual hats, skulls, etc., see (Lyn et al, 2005). Only the face as a whole is tracked, however.

Commercial systems for eyeglasses selection can be roughly classified according to a) use of live video or snapshots, and b) 3D or 2D-based rendering. With snapshots, two options are possible. Some systems use a photo of the user without glasses and then superimpose models on the image. Other systems simply take photos of the users wearing the different glasses, allowing them to select the frame they like by direct comparison of the captured images.

The use of snapshots is particularly convenient for web-based software. A number of sites are currently available that allow the user to upload his/her photo and see the glasses superimposed on it. Some systems can automatically extract facial features from the picture. In most of them, however, the user has to mark the pupils in the photo. In some cases the pupillary distance in millimeters has to be entered by the user.

3D systems model the user's head and have the advantage that a depiction can be rendered from different viewpoints (Activisu, 2009; Rodenstock, 2009; Visionix, 2009). 2D-based rendering does not work well for large out-of-plane rotations. 3D systems can also be of great help to opticians, as they can take measurements needed to manufacture the frames. However, 3D systems use special hardware and computing power, which can make them too expensive for most optical shops. The

system described in (Visionix, 2009), for example, uses six digital cameras. The system (Activisu, 2009) requires the user to wear a special plastic frame with markers.

Other possible features include: visual effect of tinted lenses on the whole displayed image, simulation of colored contact lenses, touch screens, compactness of the system, active sensing of the eyes (i.e. infrarred illumination for eye localization), etc.

Most commercial 2D systems use static pictures (ABS, 2009; Carl Zeiss Vision, 2009; CBC Co, 2009; CyberImaging, 2009; OfficeMate Software Systems 2009; Paperless Practice, 2009). Live video has an advantage over the use of static photos. Even if the user remains practically still, the experience is more realistic: other people near the user appear on the image, glasses can be placed on the face by the user, etc. Live video effectively creates the illusion of a mirror.

Using different heuristics and inductive learning techniques the system built by the authors is able to detect faces in real-time and superimpose a realistic render of real models of spectacles (the models were captured with real photos of the spectacles). Figure 1 shows the system's architecture:

The hardware has the following components: a Windows box and two Sony FCB cameras with motorized zoom, focus, white balance and shutter speed. The cameras are placed together on top of the screen (either a computer monitor or a projector can be used). Camera 1 has a resolution of 384x288 pixels and makes no use of the zoom, while Camera 2 (352x288 pixels) uses a (fixed) zoom such that only the user's face appears in the image. Camera 2 only captures gray scale frames and uses a larger zoom than Camera 1. The monitor displays the full-screen live video of Camera 1 with overlaid glasses and on-screen buttons.

The homeostatic module tries to keep image characteristics stable by using the motorized parameters of the cameras, see (Lorenzo et al, 2003) for details. It does this by modeling certain parameters like luminance or white balance as hormones

Figure 1.

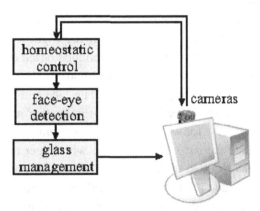

that must be in a set of acceptable performance states. When the hormone is far from the desired regime the homeostatic mechanism must recover it as soon as possible. The adaptive response of the homeostatic mechanism is governed by the hormone levels which are computed from the controlled variables by means of a sigmoid mapping. In this way, we can implement adaptive strategies more easily in the drives since the hormone levels that define the normal and urgent recovery zones are always the same independently of the values of the controlled variables. The methods used to compute these variables are described in (Lorenzo et al, 2004).

The luminance of the image is computed by dividing the image into five regions, similar to the method proposed in (Lee et al, 2001): an up-per strip (R0), a lower strip (R4) and the central strip is divided into three regions (R1, R2 and R3 from left to right), see Figure 2. These five regions allow us to define different auto exposure (AE) strategies according to the nature of the object of interest giving different weights to the average luminance in each region.

We have tested three different strategies for auto exposure that we have called uniform, centered and selective. The luminance for each of these strategies is computed as follows:

$$L_{uniform} = (L_0 + L_1 + L_2 + L_3 + L_4)/5$$

$$L_{centered} = 0.8\, L_2 + 0.2(L_0 + L_1 + L_3 + L_4)/4$$

$$L_{selective} = 0.8(L_2 + L_4)/2 + 0.2(L_0 + L_1 + L_3)/3$$

Figure 2.

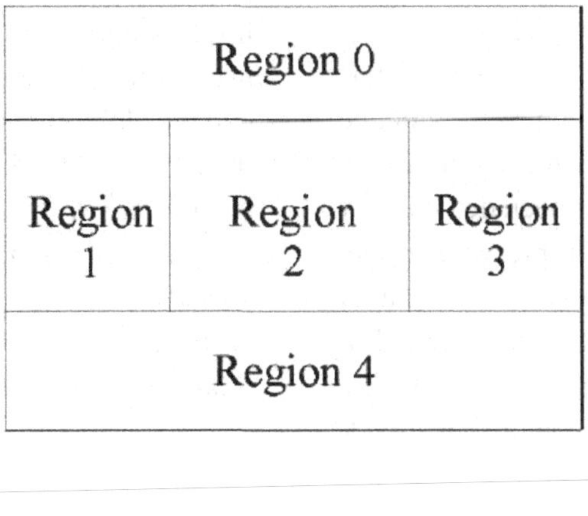

Region 0		
Region 1	Region 2	Region 3
Region 4		

where L refers to the total luminance of the image and L_i denotes the average luminance of region i. The $L_{centered}$ strategy is suitable for tracking tasks where the object of interest will be in the center of the image, whereas $L_{selective}$ is suitable for human-computer interaction because it considers the part of the image where normally a person appears when it is sat in front of a computer. As for white balance, we assumed a *grey world* scenario -see (Nanda and Cutler, 2001)- which tries to make the average amount of green, blue and red in the image constant by adjusting the red and blue gains.

The face and eye detection modules localize the position of the user's face and eyes. The face detection system developed for the selector (called ENCARA2, see (Castrillon et al, 2007) for details) integrates, among other cues, different classifiers based on the general object detection framework by Viola & Jones (2004), skin color, multilevel tracking, etc. In order to further minimize the influence of false alarms, we extended the facial feature detector capabilities, locating not only eyes but also the nose and the mouth. For that reason, several Viola-Jones' framework based detectors have been computed for the chosen inner facial elements.

Positive samples were obtained by annotating manually the eye, nose and the mouth location in 7000 facial images taken randomly from the Internet. The images were later normalized by means of eyes information to 59x65 pixels. Five different detectors were computed: 1-2) Left and right eye (18x12 pixels), 3) eye pair (22x5), 4) nose (22x15), and 5) mouth (22x15). These detectors are publicly available (Reimondo, 2009).

The facial elements detection procedure is only applied in those areas which bear evidence of containing a face. This is true for regions in the current frame, where a face has been detected, or in areas with detected faces in the previous frame. For video stream processing, given the estimated area for each feature, candidates are searched in those areas not only by means of Viola-Jones' based facial features detectors, but also by SSD-tracking previous facial elements. Once all the candidates have been obtained, the combination with the highest probability is selected and a likelihood based on the normalized positions for nose and mouth is computed for this combination.

The face and eye localization system works with images provided by Camera 1. The zoom camera (Camera 2) is used to capture the user's face with larger resolution than Camera 1. This can potentially provide a more precise and stable localization. Both eyes are searched for in the images taken by the zoom camera. A Viola-Jones detector is used along with tracking of eye patterns. ENCARA2 and complex eye localization methods were discarded in order to keep an acceptable frame rate of the whole system. As the glasses will have to be superimposed in the images taken from Camera 1, the localizations found in each Camera-2 frame have to be mapped onto the Camera-1 frame.

Whenever an eye pair localization is obtained, the eye patterns in those localizations are scaled down. The scale factor is the ratio of intereye distances found in frames of the two cameras. The scaled eye patterns are then searched for in the images captured by Camera 11. This search is carried out in the vicinity of the last eye pair localization obtained for Camera 1.

Once eye positions are obtained, the glass management module is in charge of overlaying lasses and controlling glass fitting (and on-screen next/previous spectacle model buttons). Superimposition is done via alpha blending. This process is basically a mixing of two images, with the mixing weights given by a third image. The models are made up of two images: the glasses and the alpha channel. The alpha channel defines the zones of the glasses that are translucent (i.e. the mixing weights). The glasses models were obtained by taking frontal photographs of real glasses of a local optical shop. The pictures were cropped and the alpha channels extracted using image editing software.

Figure 3.

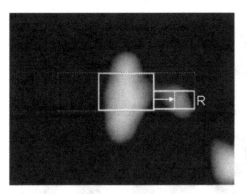 

Glasses models are scaled according to the intereye distance, rotated, and finally placed on screen according to the eye midpoint. Blending is performed only in the affected image region. Note that eye localization has an inherent error, which is also present in the midpoint. The eye midpoint has to be obtained robustly. The glasses should move with the face, otherwise the rendition will appear unrealistic. Thus, a Lucas-Kanade pyramidal tracker (Bouguet, 1999) tracks strong corners within the face region. The average displacement vector of the tracking points is used in each frame to correct the displacement of the eye midpoint.

The current glasses model can be changed with on-screen Previous-Next buttons. Button pressing detection is achieved by detecting skin color blobs within the button zones. Each button pressing is followed by a feedback sound. With on-screen buttons there is no need to use keyboard or mouse to control the system (note that the system activates as soon as a face is detected by the system, no other user interaction is necessary). Additional buttons may be added to change tints, coatings, frame thickness, etc.

Glass models are stored as images. The center of the glass image is placed on the eye midpoint. This may lead to undesired results if the glass image is not well centered. Horizontal centering is not difficult to achieve, though the vertical center is subjective. Besides, each user's facial characteristics may require different placements over

his/her nose. In order to tackle this, glass placement gesture detection was added to the system. The user is given the possibility of adjusting the spectacles (vertically) with the real gesture (i.e. by moving the hand towards the head as if fitting real spectacles. To this end, the information obtained from the zone with the face detected is used to estimate a histogram-based (Sanchez-Nielsen et al, 2005) skin color model for the individual (see a similar technique in (Swain & Ballard, 1991)). The skin color model is employed to locate other skin-like blobs in the image, and in consequence to find the hands for a given face using coherent skin blobs and considering anthropomorphic dimensions. The glass placement gesture is detected by looking for a skin-colored blob (different from the face itself) that touches the face blob at a height similar to that of the eyes.

The whole process is illustrated in more detail in Figure 3. Along the vertical sides of the face rectangle a series of small lateral rectangles are considered. Their size is proportional to the size of the detected face, considering anthropomorphic relations. The skin-color image is softened using a Gaussian filter with an aperture that equals the detected face width. Thus, isolated pixels and small blobs are removed, while the face and hand blobs create consistent high-valued regions. The hand vertical position is given by the position of the rectangle R containing the highest sum of skin-color pixels. However, the hand must be

Figure 4.

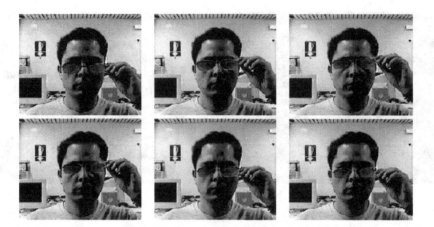

in contact with the head. In order to check the "touching the head" condition, pixel values are analyzed in R. Skin-color continuity is checked from the face side through half the width of R. Every column should contain at least one pixel with a high enough skin-color value (32 on normalized conditions). Otherwise, the hand may be still approaching the face or leaving it. Once the hand is detected as "touching the head", its relative displacement is used to move the glasses upward and downward. When the hand no longer touches the head the final relative displacement is stored with the current glass model so that the glasses can be always displayed in the right position.

Figure 4 shows a sequence in which the user is fitting the glasses.

The different parts of the system were put to test in experiments. First, and in order to test the effect of homeostatic regulation in the face detection task, a performance measure was defined as the ratio between the number of detected faces in a second and the number of images per second. As the ENCARA2 face detector depends heavily on skin color and pattern matching to detect faces, the influence on performance of luminance and white balance was studied. Figure 5 shows the values of the luminance and white balance hormones along with the face detection rate for an individual moving in front of the camera. The

dashed lines represent the changes in the environmental condition (lighting).

When the system starts the detection rate is high and it decreases slightly when more lights are switched on (30-57 secs.). When the lights are switched on, both the luminance and white balance hormones go out of their desired states but the homeostatic mechanism recovers them after a delay, larger for the white balance hormone than for the luminance one.

The homeostatic mechanism is deactivated after 70 seconds, so when the conditions change again the state of the hormones is not recovered and the performance of the system decreases with a low rate of detections.

In order to measure the localization capabilities of the system, seven video sequences were recorded in which a subject moves his head, from almost no motion to extreme movements. The eyes of the subject were manually located so as to have ground truth data. Figure 6 shows the number of frames, average intereye distance and amount of motion of each video sequence. In sequences 6 and 7 the head movements were exaggerated for testing purposes and they do not represent a typical situation (most of the time the individual is not even looking at the screen).

The effect of the zoom camera (Camera 2) is shown in the Figure 7. The first thing to note is

Figure 5.

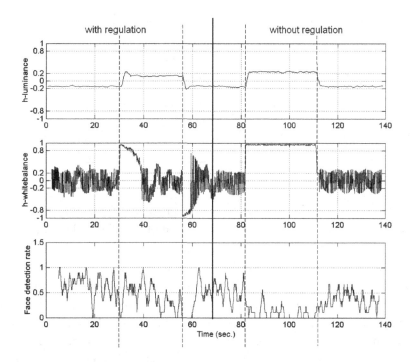

that localization errors using information from the zoom camera (Camera 2) are larger than those of Camera 1. Despite the higher resolution available in the zoom camera, this finding is explained by two reasons:

- The eye localizer of the second camera is much simpler than the ENCARA2 face detector (though 80% faster).
- Head motion often makes the eyes go out of the zoomed image.

As Camera 1 data are better for localization, they have priority in the combination. That is, whenever localization data are available from ENCARA2 they are used to place the glasses on screen. Data obtained with Camera 2 are only used when ENCARA2 cannot provide an eye pair localization.

The combined use of information of the two cameras does not improve either one of them alone, except in the cases marked with bold in the

figure. However, the use of the second camera is advantageous in terms of number of frames with available eye localization. This allows the glasses to remain longer on screen, even if the individual is moving.

Currently, the whole system runs at 9.1 frames per second, with peaks of 16.1 fps, on a CPU at 1.86Ghz.

INSTANT MESSAGING CONTROL

Instant Messaging is a form of real-time communication based on typed text. Since IM appeared in the 1970s to facilitate communication with other users logged in to Unix machines, it has expanded enormously. Currently, IM is actively used as a fast communication tool, specially among young people (Boneva et al, 2006) and in the workplace (Isaacs et al, 2002). The benefits of IM include the ability to know when personal contacts are available, nearly instantaneous communication,

Figure 6.

Video sequence	Number of frames	Average intereye distance (std.dev.)	Variance of eye position
1	126	42.7 (1.6)	8.2
2	175	42.9 (2.2)	11.1
3	176	44.1 (1.8)	11.3
4	148	40.0 (2.8)	27.1
5	119	42.9 (2.8)	37.7
6	129	42.9 (4.4)	120.8
7	208	41.6 (3.1)	164.4

and the ability to carry on several informal conversations at once.

Some computer-vision-based enhancements have been proposed to enhance IM communication. One of the problems with current one-to-one videoconferencing is that the speakers do not appear to be looking at each other. The incorrect eye-gaze problem is due to the fact that the webcam looks at each person at an angle. The i2i technology from Microsoft Corp. can correct the eye gaze of the speakers by generating new (virtual) images as if they were acquired by a camera placed along the direction of the gaze. Other abilities include background subtraction or smart focus, some of which require two cameras. Logitech has also introduced Video Effects in its cameras. Facial detection and tracking is used to insert 3D avatars that move with the user's facial features, leading to funny effects.

Despite advances in clients and network speeds, however, current IM software is still based on typed text. The well-known emoticons are used as an attempt to convey user's facial expression or emotion. The lack of verbal and visual cues can otherwise cause what were intended to be humorous, sarcastic, ironic, or otherwise non-100%-serious comments to be misinterpreted, resulting in arguments. Nevertheless, the user has to specifically type the keystroke sequence of the emoticon to show. User status (i.e. online, away, etc.) also has to be specifically controlled by the user. User status is not a trivial aspect of IM communication. A typical misunderstanding occurs when someone is writing to you but you forgot to change your status to 'Away'. The other user may interpret that you were simply ignoring him/her. In this section we describe a face and smile detector intended for controlling an instant messaging application (Microsoft Messenger).

There is a significant number of papers that have tackled facial expression recognition, see the surveys (Fasel & Luettin, 2003; Pantic & Rothkrantz, 2000). Few systems, however, have been specifically designed for smile detection.

Figure 7.

Video sequence	Camera 1		Camera 2		Combination	
	REE	LEE	REE	LEE	REE	LEE
1	1.68(1.01)	1.53(0.87)	3.08(2.41)	2.85(1.78)	**1.61(1.01)**	1.53(0.87)
2	2.78(2.91)	2.81(1.21)	5.44(5.17)	4.27(3.25)	**2.71(2.92)**	**2.73(1.25)**
3	2.39(1.00)	2.03(0.80)	1.38(0.93)	2.37(1.23)	2.36(0.98)	**2.03(0.78)**
4	1.86(1.21)	2.69(1.41)	2.96(2.94)	2.22(1.43)	1.99(1.19)	2.40(1.27)
5	2.63(1.39)	2.37(1.16)	2.48(1.57)	2.69(1.78)	2.54(1.34)	**2.33(1.51)**
6	3.03(2.75)	2.64(1.76)	6.82(7.86)	9.81(10.03)	6.14(7.22)	7.79(9.27)
7	2.29(1.24)	2.22(1.55)	5.36(4.82)	7.91(11.48)	2.82(2.13)	4.81(9.93)

Figure 8.

The smile detector of (Ito et al, 2005) used a vector of lip measures (extracted from an edge image) and a perceptron classifier. Edge features, however, may not be robust enough for practical use. More elaborated is the method of (Shinohara & Otsu, 2004), which used HLAC (Higher-order Local Autocorrelation) along with Fisher weight maps, achieving recognition rates of 97.9%. The BROAFERENCE system was developed to assess TV or multimedia content through smile measurement (Kowalik et al, 2005). In this case, 8 mouth points are tracked, feeding a neural network classifier with the 16 feature vector. Unfortunately the authors do not give precise figures for its performance, although they claim that it achieves a 90% detection rate (Kowalik et al, 2006). On a commercial level, sensing component company Omron has recently developed a "smile measurement software", which measures the amount of happiness that human subject of a photo are exhibiting (Omron Corp., 2008).

In our system, after detecting the face a smile detector is applied inside the face area. This detector is based on a Viola-Jones cascade classifier (feature-based detection proved very unrobust). Training was carried out using 2436 positive (smiling) images and 3376 negative images. The images were first extracted from Internet, then detected and normalized by the face detection system described above, see Figure 8.

The search for a smile starts whenever a face is detected and is carried out only inside the face region (inside the normalized face image). Note that this approach is actually taking advantage of the face detector as, obviously, a smile/non-smile can only be present inside a face. When the cascade detector is searching over the image, it may produce multiple positives around the positive region (the smile). Those detected rectangles largely overlap. Usually, isolated detections are false and they should be discarded.

Note that the number of neighbor detections can also be considered as a confidence measure. The more neighbors detected around an image region, the more confidence that the region contains a smile. If the negative images of the training set contain mostly neutral faces then the number of neighbors can be considered as a measure of smile intensity, which can be used to detect big smiles and small smiles.

The application uses a standard webcam to measure both presence (user status) and smile. In particular, it can control two features of the IM client: Away/online status and Smile emoticons. The application developed is able to detect when the user is in front of the laptop or away. The smile detector automatically inserts smile emoticons in the conversation window when the user is smiling. High intensity smiles can also be detected, using the number of neighbors as a measure. The IM

Figure 9.

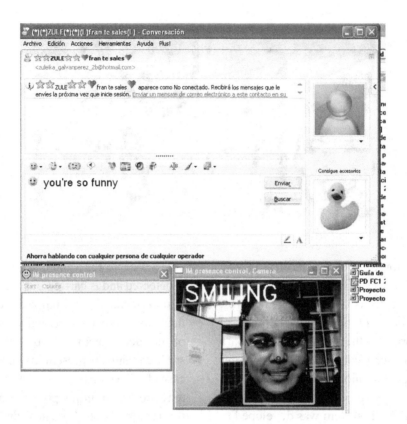

client application is controlled through keystrokes sent to its window (as specified by its title). Keystrokes sent will not interfere with user's typing.

Keystroke strings, both of status change and of the emoticons to insert, can be adjusted by the user. An example keystroke string is ":-) ", the typical smiley. Special keys can be inserted too, between "<" and ">." For example, the string "<HOME><HOME>)<HOME>-<HOME>:<END>" would insert a smiley (plus a blank space) at the beginning of the current text line in the conversation window (the <HOME> key must be sent before each character because in IM clients the conversation window is continually placing the cursor at the end of the line). Status change can be typically achieved with strings such as "<ALT>ade" that navigate through the options of the main menu. The options of the application include: IM application window title string, IM conversation window title

string, Smile keystroke string, Big smile keystroke string (typically ":-D"), Time between sending of smile keystroke strings (in seconds, 0 to wait for a no-smile before sending a new smiley), Away keystroke string, Online keystroke string, Time without face before sending an Away keystroke string (in seconds), Smile detections before a smile or big smile keystroke string is sent, Sensitivity (the smaller the more smile detections), Smile/ Big smile threshold and Show/hide live video window (the video window is hidden by de-fault). The application can be executed with the argument '-s', which makes it start automatically and remain minimized in the tray. This way it will run unobtrusively. In Figure 9 the live video window is shown, working with Windows Live Messenger (Copyright of Microsoft Corp.).

In order to test smile detection, experiments were carried out using a set of 4928 images of

Figure 10.

Smile	Number of neighbors	
intensity	Mean	Std. dev.
Low	7.63	5.31
Medium	11.31	8.01
High	18.40	10.09

108 individuals. The images were previously processed by the face detector. This particular set and the individuals were different from those used for training. Detection rates are above 96% with less than 3% false acceptance rate. This would compare well with Omron's system, of which we only know that is more than 90% accurate. On the other hand, the smile detector spends on average 0.36ms per (normalized) face image (running on a CoreTM2 Duo CPU at 2.4Ghz, using a 16 stage classifier). This means that the total (face detection+smile detection) processing time per image is roughly 46ms.

The ability to estimate smile intensity was also put to test. In this case, a different dataset was used. In the DaFEx database (Battocchi and Pianesi, 2004) 8 professional actors show 7 expressions (6 basic facial expressions + 1 neutral) on 3 intensity levels (low, medium, high). The 'happy' pictures were extracted of the database video sequences, and the intensity level was compared with the number of neighbors given by the smile detection system. Figure 10 shows the results. It can be seen from the table that smile intensity (as given by the database labels) and the number of neighbors are correlated.

Still, as the intensity discretization is sparse in the DaFEx database (i.e. only low, medium and high labels), a second database was tested. The Japanese Female Facial Expression (JAFFE) (Lyons et al, 1998) database contains 213 images of 7 facial expressions (6 basic facial expressions + 1 neutral) posed by 10 Japanese female models. Each image had been rated on 6 emotion adjectives

by 60 Japanese subjects. This database allowed us to have numerical intensity values for the happy emotion (the averages of the scores given by the 60 subjects). The correlation ratio between these values and the number of neighbors given by the smile detection system was 0.64 (95% confidence interval: [0.55,..,0.71]). Again, this supports the fact that the number of neighbors is a good indicator of smile intensity.

The application itself was tested by fourteen IM users. Before using it, they answered these questions:

- How often do you use the IM? (1=seldom, 2=at least once a week or once a fortnight, 3=every day)
- Would it be useful a program that inserts smileys automatically in the messenger window by observing your face with the webcam?
- Would it be useful a program that automatically changes your Away/Online status by observing your face with the webcam?

After using the application, they had to answer these two:

- What do you think of the smiley insertion feature of the program?
- What do you think of the Away/Online status control feature of the program?

85.7% of the participants used IM every day. The second and third questions acted as a kind of hypothesis test, and they produced interesting answers. As an example, for the second question some participants considered what would be the case with multiple conversation windows (the application only inserts smileys in the active conversation window). In general, all the participants considered such a program useful. The Away/Online status change was rated as comparatively more useful (one participant illustrated this with the following comment: public toilets are more intelligent than modern computers, as they know when there is a user present and hence when to flush).

After using the program, the acceptance was very good in general. The smiley insertion was considered useful especially because it shows the real facial gesture of user at the other end. One participant stated that typing the emoticon keystrokes was still more convenient for him. As for the Away/Online feature the participants noted that it could avoid the frequent misunderstandings mentioned above. Three participants noted a slight delay between the smile and the icon appearing in the conversation window (note that this is affected by the option "Smile detections before a smile" of the program) or in the status change control (there is also an option that allows to control this delay). Four participants expressed their desire for a similar program recognizing more facial expressions. Also, one participant suggested that the Away/Online change be used to control the power saving mode of the computer. Overall, the results were encouraging and seem to justify further effort to develop more features.

CONCLUSION

This chapter describes some of the heuristics involved in the development of two human-computer interaction applications. Heuristics and machine learning are two aspects of soft computing that are widely used in the computer vision community. Those "tricks" that combine domain restrictions with simple but clever solutions are important to produce useful systems. The best two examples given here have been the fitting gesture detection for the eyewear selector and the use of machine learning for smile detection.

Future research will aim at improving the two applications described. First, the eyewear selector will be made portable, as a modern laptop has all the necessary resources to run the application. Second, out-of-plane rotations will be considered to improve the experience for the user. As for smile detection, future work shall include the use of the smile detector in other applications that could take advantage of joy assessments: film previews, email clients, intelligent desktops, human-robot interaction, video games, wearable computing, etc. The natural extension would be to use the same methods described here to build a general facial expression recognizer which can give intensity values. Another aspect for future work is the effect of other parts of the face other than the mouth. Smiles can involve subtle cheek raising around the eyes (the so-called Duchenne smile). However, this may not be a reliable cue, not least because it does not appear in every smile.

REFERENCES

ABS. (2009). *Smart Look*. Retrieved June 30, 2009, from http://www.smart-mirror.com

Activisu. (2009). *Activisu Expert*. Retrieved June 29, 2009, from http://www.activisu.com

Azuma, R. T. (1997). A survey of augmented reality. *Presence (Cambridge, Mass.)*, *6*, 355–385.

Battocchi, A., & Pianesi, F. (2004). Dafex: Un database di espressioni facciali dinamiche. In SLI-GSCP Workshop Comunicazione Parlata e Manifestazione delle Emozioni.

Boneva, B., Quinn, A., Kraut, R., Kiesler, S., Cummings, J., & Shklovski, I. (2006). Instant messaging in teen life. In R. Kraut, M. Brynin & S. Kiesler (Eds.), Computers, Phones, and the Internet: The Social Impact of Information Technology. Oxford, UK: Oxford University Press.

Bouguet, J. (1999). *Pyramidal implementation of the Lucas Kanade feature tracker*. Technical report, Intel Corporation, Microprocessor Research Labs, OpenCV documents.

Carl Zeiss Vision. (2009). *Lens Frame Assistant*. Retrieved June 30, 2009, from http://www.zeiss.com

Castrillón, M., Déniz, O., Hernández, M., & Guerra, C. (2007). ENCARA2: Real-time detection of multiple faces at different resolutions in video streams. *Journal of Visual Communication and Image Representation*, *18*(2), 130–140. doi:10.1016/j.jvcir.2006.11.004

Co, C. B. C. (2009). *Camirror*. Retrieved June 30, 2009, from http://www.camirror.com

CyberImaging. (2009). *CyberEyes*. Retrieved from http://www.cyber-imaging.com

Déniz, O., Hernández, M., Lorenzo, J., & Castrillón, M. (2007). An Engineering Approach to Sociable Robots. *Journal of Experimental & Theoretical Artificial Intelligence*, *19*(4), 285–306. doi:10.1080/09528130701208174

Fasel, B., & Luettin, J. (2003). Automatic facial expression analysis: a survey. *Pattern Recognition*, *36*, 259–275. doi:10.1016/S0031-3203(02)00052-3

Fiala, M. (2004). Artag, an improved marker system based on artoolkit. *Technical Report ERB-1111*, NRC Canada.

Isaacs, E., Walendowski, A., Whittaker, S., Schiano, D., & Kamm, C. (2002). The character, functions, and styles of instant messaging in the workplace. In *Proceedings of the 2002 ACM conference on Computer supported cooperative work* (pp. 11-20).

Ito, A., Wang, X., Suzuki, M., & Makino, S. (2005). Smile and laughter recognition using speech processing and face recognition from conversation video. In *Procs. of the 2005 IEEE Int. Conf. on Cyberworlds (CW'05)*.

Kowalik, U., Aoki, T., & Yasuda, H. (2005). Broaference - a next generation multimedia terminal providing direct feedback on audience's satisfaction level. In INTERACT (pp. 974-977).

Kowalik, U., Aoki, T., & Yasuda, H. (2006). Using automatic facial expression classification for contents indexing based on the emotional component. In EUC (pp. 519-528).

Lee, J.-S., Jung, Y.-Y., Kim, B.-S., & Sung-Jea, K. (2001). An advanced video camera system with robust AF, AE and AWB control. *IEEE Transactions on Consumer Electronics*, *47*(3), 694–699. doi:10.1109/30.964165

Lepetit, V., Vacchetti, L., Thalmann, D., & Fua, P. (2003). Fully automated and stable registration for augmented reality applications. In *Proceedings of International Symposium on Mixed and Augmented Reality*, Tokyo, Japan.

Lorenzo, J., Castrillón, M., Hernández, M., & Déniz, O. (2004). Introduction of Homeostatic Regulation in Face Detection. In A. Fred (Ed.), *Proceedings of the 4th International Workshop on Pattern Recognition in Information Systems, PRIS 2004*, Porto (Portugal), April 13-14, 2004 (pp. 5-14).

Lorenzo, J., Déniz, O., Guerra, C., & Hernández, D. (2003). A Proposal of a Homeostatic Regulation Mechanism for a Vision System. In X Conferencia de la Asociación Española para la Inteligencia Artificial, CAEPIA, San Sebastián.

Lyons, M., Akamatsu, S., Kamachi, M., & Gyoba, J. (1998). Coding facial expressions with gabor wavelets. In *Procs. of the Third IEEE International Conference on Automatic Face and Gesture Recognition*.

Lyu, M. R., King, I., Wong, T. T., Yau, E., & Chan, P. W. (2005). Arcade: Augmented reality computing arena for digital entertainment. In *Proceedings 2005 IEEE Aerospace Conference, Big Sky* (pp. 5-12).

Morgan, E. (2004). Dispensing's new wave. *Eyecare Business*. Retrieved from http://www.eyecarebiz.com

Nanda, H., & Cutler, R. (2001). Practical calibrations for a real-time digital onmidirectional camera. In *Proceedings of the Computer Vision and Pattern Recognition Conference (CVPR 2001)*.

OfficeMate Software Systems. (2009). *iPoint-VTO*. Retrieved June 30, 2009, from http://www.opticalinnovations.com

Omron Corp. (2008). *Omron OKAO vision system*. Retrieved from http://www.omron.com/r_d/technavi /vision/okao/authentication.html

Pantic, M. S., & Rothkrantz, L. J. M. (2000). Automatic analysis of facial expressions: The state of the art. *IEEE Transactions on Pattern Analysis and Machine Intelligence, 22*, 1424–1445. doi:10.1109/34.895976

Paperless Practice. (2009). *FrameCam*. Retrieved June 30, 2009, from http://www.paperlesspractice.com

Reimondo, A. (2007). *OpenCV Swiki*. Retrieved from http://alereimondo.no-ip.org/OpenCV/

Rodenstock. (2009). *ImpressionIST*. Retrieved June 30, 2009, from http://www.rodenstock.com

Sánchez-Nielsen, E., Antón-Canalís, L., & Guerra-Artal, C. (2005). An autonomous and user-independent hand posture recognition system for vision-based interface tasks. In *Procs. of the 11th Conference of the Spanish Association for Artificial Intelligence (CAEPIA 2005)* (pp. 113-122).

Shinohara, Y., & Otsu, N. (2004). Facial expression recognition using Fisher weight maps. In Procs. of the IEEE Int. Conf. on AFGR.

Swain, M. J., & Ballard, D. H. (1991). Color indexing. *International Journal of Computer Vision, 7*(1), 11–32. doi:10.1007/BF00130487

Viola, P., & Jones, M. J. (2004). Robust real-time face detection. *International Journal of Computer Vision, 57*(2), 151–173. doi:10.1023/B:VISI.0000013087.49260.fb

Visionix. (2009). *3DiView 3D virtual try-on*. Retrieved June 30, 2009, from http://www.visionix.com

Chapter 4
LVQ Neural Networks in Color Segmentation

Erik Cuevas
Universidad de Guadalajara, México

Daniel Zaldivar
Universidad de Guadalajara, México

Marco Perez-Cisneros
Universidad de Guadalajara, México

Marco Block
Freie Universität Berlin, Germany

ABSTRACT

Segmentation in color images is a complex and challenging task in particular to overcome changes in light intensity caused by noise and shadowing. Most of the segmentation algorithms do not tolerate variations in color hue corresponding to the same object. By means of the Learning Vector Quantization (LVQ) networks, neighboring neurons are able to learn how to recognize close sections of the input space. Neighboring neurons would thus correspond to color regions illuminated in different ways. This chapter presents an image segmentator approach based on LVQ networks which considers the segmentation process as a color-based pixel classification. The segmentator operates directly upon the image pixels using the classification properties of the LVQ networks. The algorithm is effectively applied to process sampled images showing its capacity to satisfactorily segment color despite remarkable illumination differences.

INTRODUCTION

The color discrimination plays an important role in humans for individual object identification. Humans usually do not search in a bookcase for a previously known book solely by its title. We try to remember the color on the cover (e.g., blue) and then search among all of the books with a blue cover for the one with the correct title. The same applies to recognizing an automobile in a parking site. In general, humans do not search for model **A** of company **B,** but rather we look for a red car. It is only when a red vehicle is spotted, when it is

DOI: 10.4018/978-1-61520-893-7.ch004

decided according to its geometry, whether that vehicle is the one of the required kind.

Image segmentation is the first step in image analysis and pattern recognition. It is a critical and essential component but also it is one of the most difficult tasks in image processing. The actual operation of the algorithm determines the quality of the overall image analysis.

Color image segmentation is a process of extracting from the image domain one or more connected regions satisfying the uniformity (homogeneity) criterion (Ridder & Handels, 2002) which is derived from spectral components (Cheng et al., 2001; Gonzalez & Woods, 2000). These components are defined within a given color space model such as the RGB model -the most common model, which considers that a color point is defined by the color component levels of the corresponding pixel, i.e. red (R), green (G), and blue (B). Other color spaces can also be employed considering that the performance of an image segmentation procedure is known to depend on the choice of the color space. Many authors have sought to determine the best color space for their specific color image segmentation problems. Unfortunately, there is not an ideal color space to provide satisfying results for the segmentation of all kinds of images.

Image segmentation has been the subject of considerable research activity over the last two decades. Many algorithms have been elaborated for gray scale images. However, the problem of segmentation for color images that implies a lot of information about objects in scenes has received much less attention of the scientific community. Although color information allows a more complete representation of images and more reliable segmentations, processing color images requires computational times considerably larger than those needed for gray-level images as it is very sensitive to illumination changes.

This chapter considers the color image segmentation as a pixel classification problem. By means of the LVQ neural networks and their clas-

sification schemes, classes of pixels are detected by analyzing the similarities between the colors of the pixels.

In particular, color image segmentation techniques described in the literature can be categorized into four main approaches: Histogram thresholding and color space clustering; region based approaches, edge detection, probabilistic methods and soft-computing techniques. The following section discusses on each techniques, summarizing their main features.

Histogram Thresholding and Color Space Clustering

Histogram thresholding is one of the widely used techniques for monochrome image segmentation. It assumes that images are composed of regions with different gray levels. The histogram of an image can be separated into a number of peaks (modes), each corresponding to one region, and there exists a threshold value corresponding to valley between the two adjacent peaks. As for color images, the situation is different from monochrome images because of multi-features. Multiple histogram-based thresholding divides the color space by thresholding each component histogram.

The classes for color segmentation are built by means of a cluster identification scheme which is performed either by an analysis of the color histogram (Park et al., 2001) or by a cluster analysis procedure (Chen & Lu, 2002). When the classes are constructed, the pixels are assigned to one of them by means of a decision rule and then mapped back to the original image plane to produce the segmentation. The regions of the segmented image are composed of connected pixels which are assigned to the same classes. When the distribution of color points is analyzed in the color space, the procedures generally lead to a noisy segmentation with small regions scattered through the image. Usually, a spatial-based post-processing is performed to reconstruct the actual regions in the image (Nikolaev & Nikolaev, 2004).

Region Based Approaches

Region based approaches, including region growing, region splitting (Ohlander et al., 1980), region merging (Cheng et al., 2002) and their combination (Tremeau & Borel, 1997), attempt to group pixels into homogeneous regions. In the region growing approach, a seed region is first selected. Thus it is expanded to include all homogeneous neighbors, repeating the process until all pixels in the image are classified. One problem with region growing is its inherent dependence on the selection of seed region and the order in which pixels and regions are examined. In the region splitting approach, the initial seed region is simply the whole image. If the seed region is not homogeneous, it is usually divided into four squared sub-regions, which become new seed regions. This process is repeated until all sub-regions are homogeneous. The major drawback of region splitting is that the resulting image tends to mimic the data structure used to represent the image and comes out too square. The region merging approach is often combined with region growing or region splitting to merge similar regions for making a homogeneous section as large as possible.

Edge Detection

Edge detection is extensively employed in gray level image segmentation, which is based on the detection of gray levels discontinuity among points with abrupt changes. However, in color images, the information about an edge is much richer than that in monochrome case. For example, edges between two objects with the same brightness but different hue can be detected in color images (Macaire et al., 1996). Accordingly, in a color images, an edge should be defined by a discontinuity within a three-dimensional color space. Thus the basic approach falls into computing gradients for each

dimension (RGB), while adding them to produce the total color gradient (Zenso, 1986). The image a thresholding value is used for segmentation.

Probabilistic Methods

Probabilistic color segmentation estimates the probability $P_i(x, y) \in [0,1]$ for a given pixel $I(x,y)$ of belonging to a region i in the image I. Although the probability density $P_i(x, y)$ is usually determined, its parameters are often unknown. Jepson, McKenna & Raja (1998, 1999) have already discussed color segmentation when the joint distribution of color is modeled by a mixture of Gaussians within a 3-dimensional space. Since no spatial coordinates are incorporated, once the model has been inferred, it needs a spatial grouping step which applies a maximum-vote filter and uses the connected component algorithm.

Isard & MacCormick (2001) have employed color information to implement particle filtering. Lately, Perez et al. (2001) introduced an approach that also uses color histograms and particle filtering for multiple object tracking. Both methods differ in the initialization procedure for the tracker, the model updating, the region shape and the observation of the tracking performance. Bradski (1998) modified the mean-shift algorithm (Camshift) which operates on probability distributions to track colored objects in video frame sequences.

Soft-Computing Techniques

A trendy issue is the use of soft-computing approaches for image processing systems. Artificial neural network models have been proposed to segment images directly from pixel similarity or discontinuity. More than 200 neural networks used in image processing are presented by de-Ridder & Handels (2002) by means of an 2D taxonomy. Cheng et al. (2001) also discusses on many color image segmentation techniques, including the histogram thresholding, characteristic feature clustering, edge detection, region-based methods, fuzzy methods, and neural networks.

Color segmentation is successfully computed by Self-organizing Maps (SOMs) and competitive networks in (Dong & Xie, 2005; Ong et al., 2002; Yeo et al., 2005). In (Ong et al., 2002) a two-stage strategy includes a fixed-size two dimensional feature map (SOM) to capture the dominant colors of an image by unsupervised training. In a second stage, the algorithm combines a variable-sized one-dimensional feature map and color merging to control the number of color clusters that are used for segmentation. The model in (Dong & Xie, 2005) is based on a two-step neural network. In the first step, a SOM performs color reduction and then a simulated annealing step searches for the optimal clusters from SOM prototypes. The task involves a procedure of hierarchical prototype learning (HPL) to generate different sizes of color prototypes from the sampled object colors.

Proposed Scheme

Learning Vector Quantization (LVQ) networks learn to recognize groups of similar input vectors in such a way neurons that locate nearby to others in the neuron layer respond to similar input vectors. The learning is supervised and the inputs vectors into target classes are chosen by the user.

The LVQ algorithm presented in this chapter works only with image pixels, with no dynamic model or probability distribution, which in turn, improves the processing speed and facilitates the implementation process. The approach naturally avoids the complex structures commonly resulting from other neural methods such as those in (Dong & Xie, 2005; Ong et al., 2002; Yeo et al., 2005). It incorporates a decision function which eases the segmentation of the objective color. The method has been applied on several color segmentation problems (face localization and color tracking), showing enough capacity to comprehensively segment color even under illumination differences.

The chapter is organized as follows: Section 2 revisits some background concepts while Section 3 presents an introductory study of competitive neural networks and their main features. Section 4 explains relevant details of LVQ networks and Section 5 shows the architecture and characteristics of the proposed color-segmentation system, including some practical discussions. Section 6 offers a simple explanation on the algorithm's implementation. Finally, Section 7 reports on the results and their conclusions. The chapter also contains an appendix with some guidelines to train and simulate the segmentation algorithms by using Matlab©.

BACKGROUND ISSUES

RGB Space Color

Color is perceived by humans as a combination of triple stimuli R (red), G (green), and B (blue) which are usually named as primary colors. From R,G,B representation, it is possible to derive other kinds of color representations (spaces) by using either linear or nonlinear transformations. The *RGB* color space can be geometrically represented within a 3-dimensional cube as shown in Figure 1. The coordinates of each point inside the cube represent the values of red, green and blue components, respectively.

The laws of color theory are: (1) any color can be created by these three colors and the combination of the three colors is unique; (2) if two colors are equivalent, they will be again equivalent after multiplying or dividing the three components by the same number; (3) the luminance of a mixture of colors is equal to the sum of the luminance of each color. The triple stimuli values that served as the color basis are: 425.8 nm for blue, 546.1 nm for green and 700.0 nm for red. Any color can be expressed by these three color bases.

RGB is the most widely accepted model for television systems and pictures acquired by digital

Figure 1. RGB space color

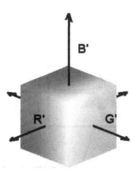

cameras. Video monitors commonly display color images by modulating the intensity of the three primary colors (red, green, and blue) at each pixel of the image (Comaniciu & Meer, 1997). *RGB* is suitable for color display as it is complicated for color segmentation's purposes, considering the high correlation among the *R*, *G*, and *B* components (Pietikainen, 2008). High correlation refers to the intensity changes which assume that all the three components will change accordingly. The measurement of a color in *RGB* space does not represent color differences in a uniform scale and hence it is impossible to evaluate the similarity of two colors from their distance in *RGB* space.

Neural Networks

Artificial Neural Networks are composed from simple elements that commonly mimic biological systems following parallel arrangements. By nature, a network function is determined by the connections between such neural elements. It is possible to train a neural network to "learn" a given function by adjusting the values of the connections (**W** weights) between elements.

A common training algorithm seeks to match a given neural input to a specific target output as shown in Figure 2. The network is adjusted by comparing the network's output and the target value, until the network output matches, as close

as possible, the target. Typically, a great number of input/target pairs are used following the *supervised learning* scheme to train the network.

Batch training of a network proceeds by making weight and bias changes based on an entire set (batch) of input vectors. Incremental training changes are applied to the weights and biases of a network after the presentation of each individual input vector. Incremental training is sometimes referred as on-line or adaptive training.

Neural networks may be employed to solve several sorts of problems, ranging from pattern recognition, identification, classification, speech, control systems and computational vision. The supervised training methods are widely known in the school. Other kind of networks can be obtained from *unsupervised training* techniques or from direct design methods. Unsupervised networks can be applied, for instance, to identify groups of data.

COMPETITIVE NETWORKS

Competitive Networks (Kohonen, 1997) learn to classify input vectors according to how they are grouped in the input space. They differ from other networks in that neighboring neurons learn to recognize neighboring sections of the input space. Thus, competitive layers learn both the distribu-

Figure 2. Supervised learning in neural networks

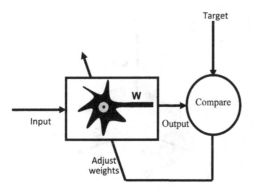

tions and topology of the input vectors in which they are trained on. The neurons in the layer of a competitive network are arranged originally in physical positions according to a topology pattern such as grid, hexagonal, or random topology.

The architecture of a competitive network is shown in Figure 3. The |*Ndist*| box in the figure receive the input vector **p** and the input weight matrix **IW** and produces a vector or a matrix **S** according to the topological configuration. The elements are the negative distances between the input vector **p** and the matrix **IW**. The net value *v* of the competitive layer is computed by finding the negative distance between input vector **p** and the weight matrix **IW** and then adding the biases **b**. If, all biases are zero, the maximum net input that a neuron can have is 0. This occurs when the input vector **p** equals the neuron's weight vector contained in the matrix **IW**.

The competitive transfer function *C* receive a net value *v* and returns outputs of 0 for all neurons except for the *winner*, the neuron associated with the most positive element of input *v*. Thus, the winner's output is 1. The weights of the winning neuron are adjusted by the Kohonen learning rule. Supposing that the ith neuron wins, the elements of the ith row of the input weight matrix and all neurons within a certain neighborhood radius *Ni(d)* of the winning neuron are adjusted as shown in Eq. (1). In other words, *Ni(d)* is the neighbor's number around of the winner neuron to be affected.

$$_i\mathbf{IW}^{1,1}(q) = {}_i\mathbf{IW}^{1,1}(q-1) + \alpha(\mathbf{p}(q) - {}_i\mathbf{IW}^{1,1}(q-1))$$
(1)

Here α is the learning rate and *Ni(d)* contains the index for all of the neurons that lie within a radius *d* of the ith winning neuron. Thus, when a

Figure 3. Architecture of a competitive network

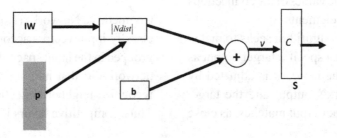

Figure 4. Left, two dimensional neighborhood with radius d = 1. Right, neighborhood with radius d = 2

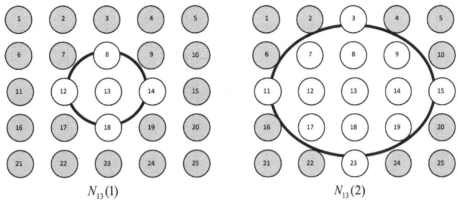

$$N_{13}(1) \qquad\qquad N_{13}(2)$$

vector **p** is presented, the weights of the winning neuron and its closest neighbors move toward **p**. Consequently, after many presentations, neighboring neurons will have learned vectors similar to each others. The winning neuron's weights are altered accordingly by the learning rate. The weights of neurons in its neighborhood are altered proportional to half of the learning rate. In this work, the learning rate and the neighborhood distance (used to determine which neurons are in the winning neuron's neighborhood) are not altered during training.

To illustrate the concept of neighborhoods, consider the Figure 4. Left, it is shown a two dimensional neighborhood of radius $d = 1$ around neuron 13. Aside it is shown a neighborhood of radius $d = 2$.

These neighborhoods could be written as:

$$N_{13}(1) = (8,12,13,14,18), N_{13}(2) = (3,7,8,9,11,12,13,14,15,17,18,19,23)$$

LEARNING VECTOR QUANTIZATION NETWORKS

An LVQ network (Kohonen, 1987) has first, a competitive layer and second, a linear layer. The competitive layer learns to classify input vectors like the networks of the last section. The linear layer transforms the competitive layer's classes into target classifications defined by the user. We refer to the classes learned by the competitive layer as *subclasses* and the classes of the linear layer as *target classes*. Both the competitive and linear layers have one neuron per class. However the neurons in the competitive layer can be arranged according to a topology pattern.

Thus, the competitive layer can learn **S1** classes, according to how they are grouped in the topological space. These, in turn, are combined by the linear layer to form **S2** target classes. This process can be considered as a lineal transformation carried out on the learned classes **S1** (in unsupervised manner) by the competitive layer to a mapping on **S2** defined by **LW**. This transformation allows distributing similar patterns around the target neuron in the linear layer. The LVQ network architecture is shown in Figure 5.

ARCHITECTURE OF THE COLOR SEGMENTATION SYSTEM

The core of the proposed algorithm is a LVQ network whose inputs are connected directly to each RGB pixel component of the image **I**. The output

Figure 5. Schematic representations of the LVQ net

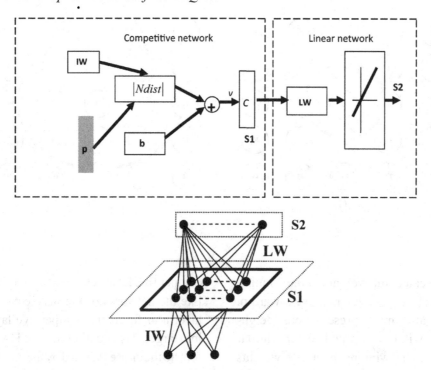

of the LVQ network is a vector **S2** connected to the decision function **f**$_d$. If the RGB components of the original pixel represents the color to be segmented, then the **f**$_d$ function output is 1, if not is 0. The result is a new image **I'**. The segmentator takes advantage of the LVQ property to learn to recognize neighboring sections of the input space. Figure 6 shows the segmentator's architecture.

Considering that the LVQ net is configured with a grid of 6 x 5 neurons in the competitive layer and 30 one-dimensional output neurons (linear layer), then would be possible to train the competitive network to learn the color-pixel space and its topology (described as the vector **p** with elements **p**$_R$, **p**$_G$ and **p**$_B$ coming from the image). The 6 x 5 grid in the competitive layer was chosen after considering a tradeoff between the neuron distribution and the computational cost (Ong et al., 2002). The size of the linear layer (30) is considered only as being coherent to the neurons contained on the grid (6x5).

The net training is achieved in two phases: Ordering phase and tuning phase. In the ordering phase the neurons of competitive layer learn to recognize groups of similar color vectors in an *unsupervised* manner. Using *supervised* learning, they learn the tuning phase for the linear layer. It was for supported, we suppose that the image **I** contains an object *O* with the color to be segmented, being **p**$_O$ a RGB pixel corresponding to the object, we train the linear network in such a way, that the class of this pixel is assigned in the middle of the linear layer (15). Using the neuron 15th as objective helps to have symmetry in the class distribution. This defines a pattern similarity, depending on the presented neighborhood with regard to this class.

The idea is that the winning neuron activated in the competitive layer (as consequence of have been excited by the RGB color combination to be segmented) will be located halfway of the linear layer as consequence of the **LW** mapping. This intrinsic LVQ property allows to locate similar

Figure 6. Architecture of the color segmentation system

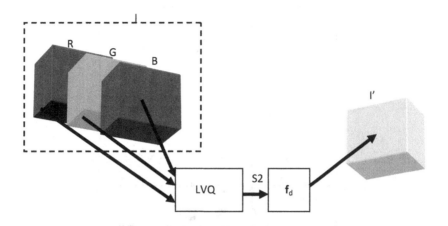

colors in the neighboring neurons. Thus, if exists a color vector $\mathbf{p}_1$ that correspond, in fact, to the same object, however due to the illumination conditions and noise, it is a little different to the target pattern, this color could not be classified by the neuron 15 but for some close to it.

The classification performed by the LVQ network finds a vector of elements categorized by $\mathbf{S}^2$ of 30 elements corresponding to 30 classes. Each element of $\mathbf{S}^2$ vector could have two possible values, 1 or 0 and only an element from each vector could be 1, while the other elements will be 0. Then for the color to be segmented, the activation of the neurons is concentrated in the middle of the vector, Thus, neurons nearest to the 15 will have a bigger possibility to be activated, for similar color patterns.

Considering the problematic above described, is necessary to describe a function $\mathbf{f}_d$ who defines the neuron's density which will be taken to consider if a pixel corresponds or not to the color to be segmented, this function will be called in this work "decision function". Is possible to formulate many functions which could solve the decision problem satisfactorily. In this work the Gaussian function has been chosen to resolve the decision problem, although it is possible to use other, including non-symmetrical distributions functions. Figure 7 shows graphically the Gaussian function

and its relationship with the output layer. Eq. (2) shows mathematically this function where $\mathbf{g}$ is the index $(1,\ldots,30)$ of the activated neuron, N is the neuron number of the linear layer (for this paper, N=30) and σ is the standard deviation. Therefore, $\mathbf{f}_d$ has only a calibration parameter represented by σ which determines the generalization capacity of the complete system. Thus, for example, if the value of σ is chosen small enough, the segmentation capacity will be more selective than in the case of a bigger σ.

$$\mathbf{f}_d(\mathbf{g}) = \frac{1}{\sqrt{2\pi\sigma}} \exp\left(-\frac{(\mathbf{g} - (N/2)^2}{2\sigma^2}\right) \qquad (2)$$

IMPLEMENTATION

The implementation is divided in two parts, the net training and the segmentator application.

First, the training process requires an image frame containing the object whose color will be segmented. Then, a pixels block is selected to train the LVQ net according to the color to be segmented but specifying that this pixel must be located at the 15th neuron that means, at the middle of the 30

Figure 7. Decision function model

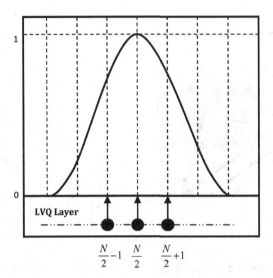

neurons array. Using this selection, the patterns are similarly distributed around the 15th neuron.

The weight matrix **IW** and **LW** are randomly initialized for the training. During the unsupervised training the learning rate α=0.1 was used as well as a distance radius $Ni(d)$ =3. This conditions assure that winner neurons weights will be affected in a reason of 0.1. While its three neighboring neurons weights (in both ways) be affected in a

reason of 0.05. During the training of the lineal layer the values of **LW** are calculated. These values transform the classes lineally allowing distributing them around the neuron 15. Initially due to the aleatory configuration, the learned classes by the competitive layer cannot be correctly mapped to the output vector, however after some iteration; these values are classified correctly as consequence of the adaptation of **LW**. The Figure

Figure 8. Classification performed by a LVQ network with 10 neurons in the competitive layer

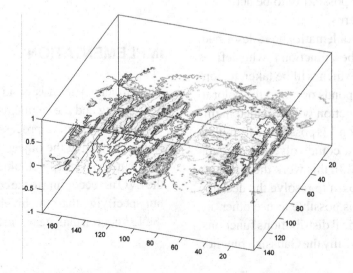

Figure 9. Result Images. (a) original image, (b) image of the pixels corresponding to the class represented by the 15th neuron, (c) image of the pixels corresponding to the class represented by the 14th neuron and (d) output of the decision function

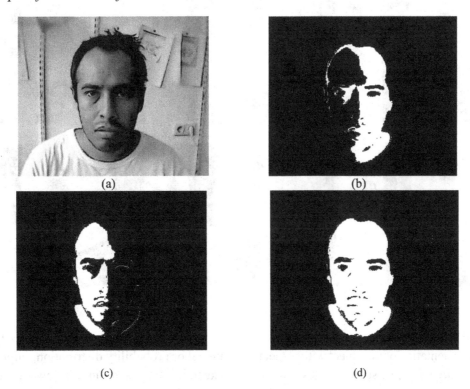

8 shows the classification results of the neurons in the competitive layer arranged in a 5 x 2 grid on an image obtained of Webcam. More information about the training algorithm is available in Appendix A.

For the segmentator use, a decision function **fd** with parameters $\mu = 15$ and $\sigma = 3$ was integrated to the previously trained network. The complete system was programmed using Visual C ++ and tested on a PCx86 at 900 MHz with 128 MBytes RAM. The Figure 9 shows an image with irregular illumination and different images obtained during the segmentation process of the flesh color. The resulting images correspond to the classes represented by the 15th neuron (9(b)) and the 14th neighbor neuron (9(c)), as well as the output of the decision function (9(d)).

RESULTS AND DISCUSSION

In order to test the robustness of the segmentation algorithm, the approach is applied to video-streamed images. The patch of color to be segmented may exhibit illumination changes within the video sequence; however the algorithm's operation prevails despite such changes.

The overall performance is tested considering two different experiments. First, the system performance is tested over an indoor footage as shown by Figure 10. In order to train the LVQ Network, one video-frame is considered to choose some pixels that belong to the skin of a couple of human individuals who are participating in a handshaking gesture. Once the system is fully trained, a full-long video sequence is tested. It is important to consider all changes in the skin color that are related to variable illumination. The effect

Figure 10. Sequence performed by the LVQ segmentator in indoor environment

is generated as a result of changes in the relative position and orientation of the object with respect to the light source. Despite such changes and the closeness of other similar colors in the scene, the algorithms have been able to acceptably segment the skin color as shown by Figure 10.

The second experiment tests the algorithm's sensitivity in response to abrupt changes on illumination. An external setting is used to generate the video sequence which naturally includes changes in sun lighting and therefore shading too. Figure 11 shows the resulting sequence once the algorithm is segmenting a red spot representing one backpack. Although the shape of the object of interest exhibits several irregular holes generated from lighting variations, the algorithm is still capable to segment the patch yet if it is located under the shade, or passing by a transition zone or under full illumination from the sun.

The overall performance of the algorithm can be successfully compared to other algorithms such as those in (Jang & Kweon, 2001; Nummiaro et al., 2001). However, the LVQ algorithm works directly on the image pixels with no dynamical model or probability distribution, improving the execution time and simplifying the implementation. However, contrary to other approaches (Chiunhsiun, 2007) the average execution time required by the algorithm to classify one pixel is always constant depending solely on the color complexity.

It is remarkable the influence of the σ parameter over the decision function itself. Best results were achieved with σ falling between 3 and 5. It is easy to envision that improving the robustness of the system may evolve considering an adaptable σ parameter. As an example, Figures 12(a)-(b) show several cases when using different values for σ.

The proposed algorithm also exhibits better generalization properties compared to other classical lookup table algorithms. In particular, if it considers images with changing illumination. As shown by Figure 9, the LVQ algorithm is capable of segmenting one face completely while one lookup-table-based algorithm, in the best case, merely reaches similar images to those generated

Figure 11. Image sequence as processed by the LVQ segmentator while segmenting for the backpack within an outdoor environment

by neighboring output neurons (Figures 9(b) or 9(c) of the LVQ net).

The robustness of the LVQ algorithm facing variable lighting can be compared to the popular CamShift algorithm. Aiming for a fair comparison, three indexes are considered just as it is proposed in (Salmond, 1990). The first performance index is related to "tracking failure". Both algorithms run until a failure in the tracking process is registered. According to this measurement, a track is assumed to be lost either when the center of the segmented object is sufficiently far from the true center, i.e. when the object position determined by the algorithm does not match to the real position or when the computed center falls outside the image location in five consecutive steps. Finally, the "track-lifetime" is defined according to the number of time steps until the tracking was lost. This index is commonly averaged across all trials. Figure 13 shows the results from these experiments. Both algorithms were tested considering 100 lux as an initial point –a standard office's illumination–. At

Figure 12. Results obtained using (a) σ = 4 and (b) σ = 1

Figure 13. Comparison of LVQ and Camshift algorithms

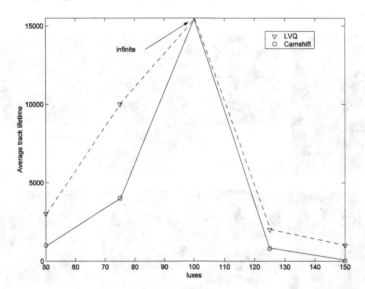

this point, the averaged track-lifetime is infinite for both algorithms. Measurements are taken in both directions, showing that the LVQ algorithm has a higher robustness, particularly in case of low intensity lighting.

CONCLUSION

This chapter presents an image segmentator approach based on LVQ networks which considers the segmentation process as a pixel classification which is fully based on color. The segmentator operates directly upon the image pixels using the classification properties of the LVQ networks. The algorithm is effectively applied to the segmentation of sampled images showing its capacity to satisfactorily segment color despite remarkable illumination differences, considering indoor and outdoor scenes. The results demonstrate the operation of the LVQ algorithm which in turn is capable of organizing topologically the input space, accomplishing the segmentation process, despite a small number of neurons.

The proposed system has two important features. First, since the LVQ algorithm works directly on the image pixels with no dynamic model or probability distribution, the execution time is faster than other approaches. Second, the algorithm exhibits interesting generalization properties, in particular considering images with changing illumination.

Further increases in the segmentator performance might be reached, if the parameter σ is also adapted using some kind of optimization technique.

ACKNOWLEDGMENT

This document was prepared with economical support of the European Community, the European Union and CONACYT under grant FONCICYT 93829.

REFERENCES

Bradski, G. R. (1998). Computer vision face tracking as a component of a perceptual user interface. In *Workshop on Applications of Computer Vision* (pp. 214-219).

Chen, T. Q., & Lu, Y. (2002). Color image segmentation: an innovative approach. *Pattern Recognition, 35*(2), 395–405. doi:10.1016/S0031-3203(01)00050-4

Cheng, H., Jiang, X., & Wang, J. (2002). Color image segmentation based on histogram thresholding and region merging. *Pattern Recognition, 35*(2), 373–393. doi:10.1016/S0031-3203(01)00054-1

Cheng, H. D., Jiang, X. H., Sun, Y., & Wang, J. L. (2001). Color image segmentation: advances and prospects. *Pattern Recognition, 34*(12), 2259–2281. doi:10.1016/S0031-3203(00)00149-7

Chiunhsiun, L. (2007). Face detection in complicated backgrounds and different illumination conditions by using YCbCr color space and neural network. *Pattern Recognition Letters, 28*, 2190–2200. doi:10.1016/j.patrec.2007.07.003

Comaniciu, D., & Meer, P. (1997). Robust analysis of feature spaces: color image segmentation. In *IEEE Conference on Computer Vision and Pattern Recognition* (pp. 750-55).

deRidder, D., & Handels, H. (2002). Image processing with neural networks – a review. *Pattern Recognition, 35*, 2279–2301. doi:10.1016/S0031-3203(01)00178-9

Dong, G., & Xie, M. (2005). Color clustering and learning for image segmentation based on neural networks. *IEEE Transactions on Neural Networks, 16*(4). doi:10.1109/TNN.2005.849822

Gonzalez, R. C., & Woods, R. E. (2000). Digital Image Processing. São Paulo, Brasil: Edgard Blücher.

Isard, M., & MacCormick, J. (2001). BraMBLe: A Bayesian Multiple-Blob tracker. In *International Conference on Computer Vision, 34-31.*

Jang, G. J., & Kweon, I. O. (2001). Robust Real-time Face Tracking Using Adaptive Color Model. In *International Conference on Robotics and Automation* (pp. 138-149).

Jepson, A., Fleet, D., & El-Maraghi, T. (2001). Robust Online Appearance Models for Visual Tracking. *Computer Vision and Pattern Recognition, 25*(10), 415–422.

Kohonen, T. (1987). Self-Organization and Associative Memory (2nd Ed.). Berlin: Springer-Verlag.

Kohonen, T. (1997). Self-Organizing Maps (2nd Ed.). Berlin: Springer-Verlag.

Macaire, L., Ultre, V., & Postaire, J.-G. (1996). Determination of compatibility coefficients for color edge detection by relaxation. In *International Conference on Image Processing* (pp. 1045-1048).

Martinez, A. M., & Benavente, R. (1998). The AR Face Database. *CVC Technical Report #24.*

McKenna, S., Raja, Y., & Gong, S. (1999). Tracking Colour Objects using Adaptive Mixture Models. *Image and Vision Computing, 17*(3-4), 225–231. doi:10.1016/S0262-8856(98)00104-8

Nikolaev, D., & Nikolayev, P. (2004). Linear color segmentation and its implementation. *Computer Vision and Image Understanding, 94*(3), 115–139. doi:10.1016/j.cviu.2003.10.012

Nummiaro, K., Koller-Meier, E., & Van-Gool, L. (2002). A color-based Particle Filter. In *Proceedings of the 1st International Workshop on Generative-Model-Based Vision* (pp. 353-358).

Ohlander, R., Price, K., & Reddy, D. R. (1980). Picture segmentation using a recursive region splitting method. *Computer Graphics Image Processing, 8*, 313–333. doi:10.1016/0146-664X(78)90060-6

Ong, S. H., Yeo, N. C., Lee, K. H., Venkatesh, Y. V., & Cao, D. M. (2002). Segmentation of color images using a two-stage self-organizing network. *Image and Vision Computing, 20*, 279–289. doi:10.1016/S0262-8856(02)00021-5

Park, S. H., Yun, I. D., & Lee, S. U. (2001). Color image segmentation based on 3D clustering: morphological approach. *Pattern Recognition, 31*(8), 1061–1076. doi:10.1016/S0031-3203(97)00116-7

Perez, P., Hue, C., Vermaak, J., & Gangnet, M. (2002). Color-Based Probabilistic Tracking. In *European Conference on Computer Vision* (pp. 661-675).

Pietikainen, M. (2008). Accurate color discrimination with classification based on feature distributions. In *International Conference on Pattern Recognition* (pp. pp. 833-838).

Raja, Y., McKenna, S., & Gong, S. (1998). Tracking and Segmenting People in Varying Lighting Condition using Color. In *International Conference on Face and Gesture Recognition* (pp. 228-233).

Salmond, D. (1990). Mixture Reduction Algorithms for Target Tracking in Clutter. *SPIE Signal and Data Processing of Small Targets, 1305*, 434–445.

Tremeau, A., & Borel, N. (1997). A region growing and merging algorithm to color segmentation. *Pattern Recognition, 30*(7), 1191–1203. doi:10.1016/S0031-3203(96)00147-1

Yeo, N. C., Lee, K. H., Venkatesh, Y. V., & Ong, S. H. (2005). Colour image segmentation using the self-organizing map and adaptive resonance theory. *Image and Vision Computing, 23*, 1060–1079. doi:10.1016/j.imavis.2005.07.008

Zenso, S. (1986). A note on the gradient pf multi-image. *Computer Vision Graphics and Image Processing, 33*(1), 116–125. doi:10.1016/0734-189X(86)90223-9

A. APPENDIX

A.1 Creating a Competitive Neural Network in Matlab®

Competitive layers and self organizing maps can be simulated by the Matlab© Neural Networks Toolbox. In particular, commands *newc* and *newsom*, may be used to initialize both architectures respectively. It is also possible to specify different topologies for initial neuron locations by using other built-in functions such as: *gridtop*, *hextop* or *randtop*.

There exist four different ways to calculate distances from a particular neuron to its neighbors. In this chapter, the function *dist* calculates the Euclidian distance from the home neuron to any other neuron.

Suppose that it is required to create a network considering 2 input vectors whose values fall into the range of 0 to 2 and 0 to 1 respectively. Further suppose that only 10 neurons are considered following a linear structure and one 1-by-10 network. The code to define such network may be written as follows:

```
net=newsom([0 2; 0 1],[1,10]);
```

A.2 Training a Competitive Neural Network in Matlab©

Learning within a self-organizing map may occur for one vector at the time, independently from whether the network is trained directly (with the Matlab© function *trainr*) or it is trained adaptively by the Matlab© function *trans*. In either case, *learnsom* is the weight learning function for self-organizing maps.

By revisiting the algorithm, several assumptions must be reviewed as follows: the neuron identifies the winning neuron, the weights of the winning neuron and also the neighboring neurons that are moved closer to the input vector at each learning step by using the self-organizing learning map (Matlab function *learnsom*). Such parameters are hosted by the following values:

```
LP.order_lr
LP.order_steps
LP.tune_nd
```

In turn, they represent the learning rate, the number of steps and the neighborhood distance, respectively. Thus, it is possible to train the network for 100 epochs, a learning rate of 0.1 and a neighborhood distance of 1. The code thus is as follows:

```
net.trainParam.epochs=100;
net.trainParam.order_lr=0.1;
net.trainParam.tune_nd=1;
net=train(net,P);
```

A.3 Creating and training an LVQ Neural Network

Linear layers can be created by using the *newlin* command. For instance, in order to create a network with two elements in the range of -1 to 1 and one output, the following command sentence may be employed:

```
net=newlin([-1 1; -1 1], 1);
```

Linear networks can be trained to perform linear classification together to Matlab© function *train*. This function applies to each vector a set of input vectors and calculates the network weights and bias increments as a result of such inputs and according to the *learnp* function.

A.4 Auxiliary Functions

For the image capture, the *VFM* utility was used. This is a Matlab© tool that captures images in *RGB* format. The image is embedded into a $m \times n \times 3$ matrix (being $m \times n$ the image dimension and 3 base colors known as *Red*, *Green* and *Blue*). This data matrix is represented by an integer format and it should be converted into a float point matrix (double). An example code for an image capture is shown below.

```
Im=vfm ('grab',1);
```

The image is stored in **Im**, which in turn should be transformed into the training data vector of $m \times n$ dimensions, i.e. the R, G and B color channels. The code below shows the overall operation:

```
R=Im(:,:,1);
V=Im(:,:,2);
A=Im(:,:,3);
[m,n]=size(R);
index=0;
for a1=1:m
for an=1:n
data=R(a1,an);
data1=V(a1,an);
data2=A(a1,an);
index=index+1;
VR(index)=data;
VV(index)=data1;
VA(index)=data2;
end
end
VP=[VR;VV;VA];
VP=double(VP);
```

Thus, from the training vector **VP,** it is possible to perform training. The following sequence of functions support the training environment.

```
net=newsom([0 255;0 255;0 255],30);
net.trainParam.epochs=500;
net.trainParam.order_lr=0.1;
net.trainParam.tune_nd=3;
net=train(net,VP);
```

Once the competitive neuronal network has been acceptably trained, it is trivial to find a point and its correct identification within the data vector, enabling the supervised training of the lineal network by using Matlab© function *learnp*. During the training, any parameters combination may eventually offer acceptable results.

By now, it is feasible to consider the data from the neuronal network as an image. In order to prevent such situation, a new function was created. It allows modifying the vector format to an *mxn* image by following the code below:

```
index=0;
for a1=1:m
for an=1:n
index=index+1;
data=Image(index);
MR(a1,an)=data;
end
end
```

with Image being the data vector obtained by the neural network.

Chapter 5
3D Modelling and Artificial Intelligence:
A Descriptive Overview

G. N. Marichal
Universidad de La Laguna, Spain

A. Hernández
Universidad de La Laguna, Spain

E. J. González
Universidad de La Laguna, Spain

L. Acosta
Universidad de La Laguna, Spain

J. L. Saorin
Universidad de La Laguna, Spain

ABSTRACT

This paper explains the different interactions between the Artificial Intelligence (AI) techniques and 3D modelling, not only the wide-used application of AI in order to the implementation of 3D environments, but the less explored use of 3D models in order to take advantage from AI techniques. The authors will be especially interested in real Engineering applications, but the techniques presented in this paper are general and can be used in other research fields. Moreover, a particular robotic application is shown.

INTRODUCTION

The amazing growth and development of technology features in 20th and 21st centuries have implied the coining of new terms. One of the most known is that of Artificial Intelligence, born in the 50s, that includes a wide range of topics and tools, such as Logic, Neural networks, classifiers, statistical learning methods, etc.

AI domains clearly interact with other research activities, since it is an extremely wide field. This paper focuses on the exploration of these interactions related to 3D modelling.

DOI: 10.4018/978-1-61520-893-7.ch005

3D modelling can be defined as

the process of developing a mathematical, wire-frame representation of any three-dimensional object (either inanimate or living) via specialized software. The product is called a 3D model (Wikipedia, 2009).

Keeping in mind this definition, it is clear that 3D modelling and Artificial Intelligence (AI) are not disjoint researching fields but several interactions between these fields occur. These interactions usually require the joint work of specialists in different disciplines. A field where these are interactions have been shown as useful is that of Engineering, and in particular Robotics: simulation of real devices, artificial vision, virtual environments, etc. However the authors consider that this field has not taken completely advantage from the potential that this interaction offers.

The objectives of this paper can be summarized as follows:

1. 3D modelling and Artificial intelligent are usually applied in different engineering problems in an independent way. However, this chapter will be show the interest of fusing both approaches.
2. Different hybrid approaches will be presented, where 3D modelling and Artificial Intelligence are combined.
3. A new perspective will be shown, where the 3D Modelling is used as a resource for collecting the data. These data could be used as a source data, necessary to apply an intelligent strategy to a particular engineering problem.

BACKGROUND

Humans are used to interpret bidimensional images as part of a three dimensional world. However computers have not this spatial reference. So,

artificial vision, means, mainly, to create a 3D virtual model based on a bidimensional image captured by an artificial eye (such as a camera or similar). In this context, researchers can simulate the human stereovision and capture several images at the same time (human vision use two images to create a 3D model), but in a lot of problems only a single image is available. In both cases, the computer recognizes and understands the 3D space, usually making use of mathematical methods to solve the problem but also a certain amount of intelligence.

These mathematical methods are based on nonlinear partial differential equations, stochastic and statistical methods, and signal processing techniques, as Wavelet and other transform types. These techniques achieve image smoothing and denoising, image enhancement, morphology, image compression, and segmentation (determining boundaries of objects, including problems of camera distortion and partial occlusion). The development of the theory is fundamental since it enables achieve the high level vision. Some examples of this are stochastic processes, that they have been used in a Bayesian framework to incorporate prior constraints on smoothness and the regularities of discontinuities into algorithms for image restoration and reconstruction. This has a considerable number of applications such as handwriting recognizers, printed-circuit board inspection systems and quality control devices, motion detection, robotic control by visual feedback, reconstruction of objects from stereoscopic view and/or motion, autonomous road vehicles, and many others.

Other field where AI has been included is in the design of intelligent behaviour of 3D elements, mainly focused in Entertainment and Education fields, such as intelligent agents virtual environments, computer games, online social worlds and educational platforms. Recent advances in Multimedia and Internet technology are giving rise to interactive virtual worlds, which are is essential for certain types of applications, both in education and entertainment. Most of these applications are referred to the design of 3D virtual worlds as a society of agents or intelligent animated 3D agents that provide assistance to students and researchers in order to carry some tasks (Rickel and Johnson, 1999). Although there are many definitions of the concept, an agent can be defined as a system that has goals and beliefs (Russell and Norvig 1995), and executes actions based on those ones, seeking to achieve its goals by interacting with its environment. Extending the definition, a virtual agent can be defined as an autonomous entity in a virtual environment (Soto and Allongue, 2002) that also it behaves as a living organism, and be able to interact with it and its inhabitants (real users in the form of avatars, or other virtual agents).

In this kind of systems, the same digital media and 3D model used in visualizing, simulating and documenting architectural designs for the physical world, are often used for the design and the creation the virtual word. The designs need to go beyond the geometric representation and to include the virtual presence of the people in the world and object behaviours, so these 3D virtual worlds are not very useful as tools for designing since the design involves change. There are two levels at which modifications occur: the users directly, through their direct actions, and the world can modify itself as a consequence of the user's actions. For example, an agent model of 3D virtual worlds that assumes a persistent object oriented representation of the world was developed by Maher et al. (Maher et al, 2002), including a cognitively-based agent model (Gero and Fujii 2000), which use Sensor and Effectors as the interface with the virtual worlds, identifying the main computational processes as sensation, perception, conception, hypothesizer, and action activation. As example, a wall consists of a combination of a 3D model that provides a visual boundary to a room and agent software that allows the wall to react to the use of the place.

In this type of 3D simulations, a key problem (especially in real-time specifications) is that of collision detection. The related algorithms are often divided into four categories: space-time volume intersection, swept volume interference, multiple interference detection and trajectory parameterization (Jimenez, Thomas and Torras, 2001) and usually involves a bottleneck in the 3D modelling. Thus, proper optimized AI algorithms are welcomed such that based on neural networks for multi-armrobotic systems (Rana, 1997).

The authors note that the use of Virtual Environments as a user interface should not be limited to just browsing a beautiful 3D scene, These worlds are even more attractive for the user when they are neither static nor pre-scripted, but have dynamic characteristics and are populated by autonomous entities, that is, the virtual agents. The authors will cite a tool for the construction of virtual worlds with autonomous entities, targeted for a specific group of applications, such as simple simulation systems, virtual environments, educational applications or multimedia presentations, developed by Vosinakis and Panayiotopoulos (Vosinakis and Panayiotopoulos, 2005). This tool, called *SimHuman*, consists of a programming library and two utilities and, as it is not based on fixed scenes and models, it is highly dynamic and configurable. Moreover, it incorporates some important features for designing and building virtual environments and turns out to be an effective tool for interactive 3D applications with virtual agents, because of *SimHuman* has embedded characteristics such as Inverse Kinematics, Physically Based Modeling, Collision Detection and Response, and Vision.

Amiguet, Szarowicz and Forte (2001) propose the application of AI techniques for automatic generation of crowd scenes in all those aspects regarding to the processes of space sensing and perceiving, goal planning, collision avoidance, taking appropriate actions and other cognitive tasks. Generation and animation of human figures especially in crowd scenes have many applications, such as the special effects industry or computer games, but it is both a labour-intensive and time-consuming task. Currently, animators have developed techniques can decrease both factors, but the process is still tedious and expensive. Those problems especially affect to the special effects industry because they need generate scenes involving many interacting human figures and most of the work in such scenes must be done manually by skilled professionals because characters still lack autonomy and self-awareness. The designed prototype, namely FreeWill, issues these problems by proposing and implementing an extendable cognitive architecture designed to accommodate goals, actions and knowledge, and supported by a well engineered design, thus endowing animated characters with some degree of autonomous intelligent behaviour. The design allows for easy co-operation of different software packages, namely a geometry engine, AI engine, sensing/actuating models, simulation managing unit and a visualization environment. Therefore, FreeWill utilises the features of animation packages (inverse kinematics, object modelling, virtual worlds industrial standards) and an extensible behavioural engine which allows for autonomous behaviour of the avatars and easy control of the parameters of the animated sequences. Each such a sequence consists of characters (avatars) interacting within a graphically defined setting. The key objective was to create an avatar based on the idea of agent presented by Russel and Norvig. Each avatar comprises two main components, its body and an AI engine (so called mind). The body is the 3D representation of the avatar (with all its properties and position), whereas the "mind" supplies all functionality necessary for world representation, goal planning, sensing and acting, and emotions. Apart from the mentioned AI engine (responsible for managing the processes of space sensing and perceiving, goal planning…), the project includes a Geometry engine, Sensing/actuating modules, World objects (models of all physical entities within the virtual world) and a Visualization module.

It can be distinguished many efforts in the development of tools for easy development of intelligent virtual environments populated with synthetic characters (Prada and Paiva, 2005), since believability (in both visual and behaviour sense – including severe real time requirements) is a key feature for this kind of applications if a good interaction experience to the user is needed. Moreover, from other point of view, a proper connection between intelligent and visual aspects integration is other problem to be solved as both aspects present several dependences. They are difficult to manage at most cases. As example of this approach, OpenSG Agents are developing libraries and an *Application Programming Interface* (API) to allow intelligent synthetic characters to be easily incorporated into virtual worlds using the OpenSG system (Voss et al, 2002). These libraries make use of Multi-agent technology in order to define an abstract layer that promotes the interdependency of the intelligent and visual components of a virtual environment. OpenSG is an Open Source real-time rendering system based on a scenegraph metaphor on top of OpenGL, which is a very thin layer above the graphics hardware and is designed as a state machine, which means it does not know anything about the whole scene.

It is clear that these 3D environments can be enriched with sophisticated AI techniques in order to obtain some results for other fields. Simo et al. (Simo, Kitamura, Nishida, 2005) integrate virtual humans in a 3D environment in the field of behavior simulation related to children accidents. The system integrates accident database and physiology with a realistic visual simulation in a 3D environment representing different settings and scenarios. The virtual child is attached to an action plan of succeeding, in other words, unintentional children's accidents can been seen as a mixture of "intentional" accidents ande there is an unpredictability factor related to the corresponding accident's type.

Other approach consists of using 3D modelling for simulation of environments difficult to reproduce or in which the proofs are expensive to be carried out. Researchers can obtain feedback from these 3D models in order to improve their design of an AI system. Carnevale et al. (2007) propose the use of neural networks and Neuro-Fuzzy for the source-receptor identification in air quality plans (in particular it has been applied to ozone and PM10 concentrations in Nothern Italy) using a 3D modelling system. Their work presents a 3D eulerian multiphase model simulating tropospheric secondary pollution at mesoscale called Transport and Chemical Aerosol Model (TCAM). This model has been validated since it has reproduced ozone, nitrogen oxides and aerosol observed patterns for both winter and summer pollution regimes.

Martínez-Lastra et al (2005) propose the use of a 3D software suite for the three-dimensional creation, simulation and visualization of agent societies. This suite is compatible with the FIPA (Foundation for Intelligent Physical Agents) set of standards as a facilitator for the interoperation of heterogeneous agents and it is applied to the 3-dimensional creation, simulation and visualization of these societies in industrial applications (in particular industry assembly operations).

Liu. Wu and Cheng (2007) propose a 3D visual intelligent simulation for a railway container yard. This simulation includes the four parts in which railway container yards consists of: railway loading and unloading line, truck operations corridor, container yard and handling machinery. These authors apply 3D modelling based on computer GUI and texture technology in order to get a visual intelligent simulation for real-time control of the target.. This approach influences the real-time of system since it requires many computational resources. This is the reason why special disposal and previous treatment of the scene model is carried out. The fact of real-time interaction is one of the key aspects that need to be improved in the interaction AI-3D modelling. Liu, Wu and Cheng improve the real-time response creating the scene graphics profile by establishing the 3D

model of each object one by one. Apart from this, the scene simulation is accomplished by fusion of the pre-installed texture and map. For complex objects, the authors apply the LOD (level of detail) technique. This technique involves decreasing the complexity of a 3D model in special occasions such as when it moves away from the viewer. This visual quality change is often unnoticed by the user. Other improvement in the computational cost is that a moving object is decomposed into basic movement units according to transitive relation of the kinematics chain.

An analogue application is described by Bruno et al (Bruno, Francesco and Pisacane, 2008) for the support in the assessment of the optimal loading configuration for several carriers (containers, trucks…), that is the known as Bin-Packaging Problem, visualized by a 3D graphics representation. In this case, the Tabu Search algorithm is the used AI approach. In detail, the algorithm starts an initial solution, obtained considering a total number of bins equal to the number of items and assigning each item to a specific bin. Then, it tries to improve the current solution by applying some feasible moves on the base of the specific problem instance.

A novel point of view consists of the use of 3D models in AI systems. A significant part of Artificial Intelligence techniques are strongly based on the existence of a set of patterns. These patterns are often used in order to train a system (as example, a neural network) with a training set, allowing the system to "learn" about the problem to resolve (identification, determination of parameters, etc) and to take decisions based on this knowledge. In fields like Computer Vision, Robotic, Automation etc. it is not always possible to get an appropriate training set through data obtained in real environments making use of sensors like ultrasound devices or cameras. In this case, researchers make use of the application of mathematical calculations for the definition of the training set of patterns.

In this context, the design of an adequate 3D environment where the research could take these types of data, could considerably simplify this process. In fact, 3D models designed making use of Computer Aided Design (CAD) software are the graphical expression of a set of geometrical restrictions. Thus, 3D modelling is a quick way to the generation of patterns for AI applications, especially when these patterns represent the interaction of several elements in a scene. In this way, a trained real robot could be able to recognize 3D elements in its path (identity, position, orientation, etc.) and/or design an alternative trajectory in order to avoid them. One approach is the creation of 3D graphical databases in order to allow AI applications to be properly trained.

SOME LINKS BETWEEN 3D MODELLING AND AI TECHNIQUES IN ENGINEERING

In Engineering, a key feature provided by both 3D modelling and AI is the step of obtaining tridimensional models from bidimensional images (in particular in the case of single images), usually obtained by a camera. This is especially interesting when there is interaction with elements placed in an uncertained environment, for example, in the case of a robotic vehicle. There are two different types of single image. On the one hand, it can be geometrical, such as engineering pieces, or in the other hand, a general image, such as a landscape or the interior of a room. An intelligent program should be able to recognize a piece or a space in which a vehicle should move. Geometrical Reconstruction, is in charge of geometrical recognition for pieces, while there is a specific word for a generic recognition. The Geometric Reconstruction is a process that transforms a bidimensional geometric image (usually an axonometric image, denominated "single-view reconstruction") into a 3D model. This problem implies the determination of geometrical and topological relations

of one object. There are different approaches for this task and some of them are mainly geometrical or mathematical (labelling approaches, gradient space approaches, linear programming approaches, optimization approaches, etc.). There are a few basic references of the state of the art in geometric reconstruction: Sugihara (1986), Nagenda and Guijar (1988), Wang and Grinstein (1993), Company (1997), Hartley and Zisserman (2000) and Kahl and Henrion (2005).

Nevertheless reconstruction is not only a numerical process based on geometric rules but the geometric information contained in the figures is usually incomplete. This is why the 2D figures must "be perceived" by the computer (in the psychological sense of the term "perception"). So there is a perceptual approach to Geometrical Reconstruction that can be considered as a small part of the Artificial Intelligence (Artificial Vision, or Computer Vision field). In the perceptual approach, the general idea is to generate an interpretation of the geometry using different heuristic rules. This approach does not use numerical methods, but has also some limitations, because the rules tend to be too rigid, for a human point of view. Because of that, most reconstruction methods use a mathematical or numerical part, mixed with a set of rules that "perceive" the figure (Seitz, 2006).

In the case of a 3D-scene, such as a landscape, humans understand the depth of the scene, and recognize that one part is nearer that the other. This is not obvious for a computer, so it is needed a special algorithm to simulate this recognition. This is important for Engineering applications such as mobile monocular robots moving in unknown environments.

Make-3D, developed for Stanford University is a good example for this purpose (Saxena, Sun and Ng, 2007). In a mathematical point of view it is impossible to recover a 3D model from a single image. However, human can do it easily and researchers try to copy this capability using artificial intelligence in their algorithms. Make-3D includes algorithms that infer depth from single images by combining assumptions about what must be ground or sky. For that, it makes use of some simple cues such as vertical lines in the image that represent walls or trees. This system is based on Machine Learning. The training consists on teaching the algorithm about parameters (depth, orientation, position) in 2D images using known 3D data of the same scenes gathered with laser scanners. The proposed algorithm matches the data and it is able to extract some patterns. For example, it concludes that "things that are far away can be just a little hazier and more bluish than things that are close". In detail, the algorithm breaks the image up into tiny planes called "superpixels". These superpixels are zones in the image that have very uniform brightness, colour and other attributes. Analyzing the variations among neighbour superpixels (variations in texture and so on), the algorithm makes a judgment about how far the related object is from the viewer and what its orientation in space is. Feedback is obtained for users in the Make3d website, refining the algorithm. As result, Ng concludes that the algorithm works better with landscapes and scenery than close-ups of individual objects.

Simbad (Hugues and Bredeche, 2006) is an example of free Java 3D robot simulator recommended as a simple basis for studying AI algorithms, in the context of Autonomous Robotics and Autonomous Agents. It enables to write a robot controller, modify the environment and using the available sensors. Simbad provides 3D visualization and sensing, single or multi-robot simulation, vision sensors – color monoscopic camera-, range sensors – sonars and infrared -, contact sensors – bumpers and two AI extensions for Evolutionary Robotics (a methodology that uses evolutionary computation to develop controllers for autonomous robots): PicoNode (a Neural network library) and PicoEvo (an Evolutionary Algorithms library). As example of its use, the following code excerpt from the tutorial is reproduced:

```
static public class Robot extends Agent {
    RangeSensorBelt sonars;
    CameraSensor camera;
    public Robot(Vector3d position, String name) {
        super(position, name);
        // Add camera
        camera = RobotFactory.addCameraSensor(this);
        // Add sonars
        sonars = RobotFactory.addSonarBeltSensor(this);
    }
    /** This method is called by the simulator engine on reset. */
    public void initBehavior() {
        // nothing particular in this case
    }
    /** This method is call cyclically (20 times per second) by the simulator engine. */
    public void performBehavior() {
        // progress at 0.5 m/s
        setTranslationalVelocity(0.5);
        sonars.getMeasurement(0);
    }

}
```

Another application is to use the 3D Modelling as a data source. Sometimes it is not easy to take the data directly from the real scenario. There are many situations where it is not possible, for example, in dangerous environments, when so

Figure 1. Visualization of the interaction between the sonar cone and the simulated scenario

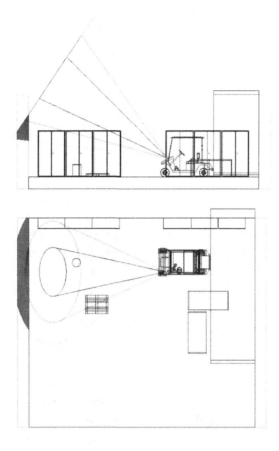

many measurements are necessary or when the measurement process is tedious. One example is the use of a simulator of a sonar system inside a virtual scenario (SIBTRA, 2009). In Figure 1, the 3D modelling is shown.

In this case, a 3D modelling of a warehouse has been built by a computer aided design software (CAD). The 3D modelling has focused on building a graphical representation of a car, a set of sonar sensors on the bodywork and the different objects included in the warehouse. In addition to, a sonar model has been incorporated as it is shown in Figure 2.

The sonar model has to include all possible real effects, such as, the temporal requirements of the ultrasonic signals and sensor electronics, or the accuracy of the obtained distances between the sensors and the objects. In this work, the data provided by the 3D modelling has been used for determining by a Neuro-Fuzzy approach the objects around the vehicle. In fact, a spatio-temporal approach has been considered. That is, distance data to the environment objects from the vehicle in movement has been considered. A big amount of data are necessary for the training phase of the Neuro-Fuzzy system in this way. It is necessary to obtain the object distances from each position of the vehicle and it is necessary to identify the target objects for the sonar system at each position along with its approximate accuracy. Because of that, a 3D model is very useful, overall considering the three-dimensional structure of the problem. In a spite of using the data obtained by the 3D model, real data has been acquired in order to determine

Figure 2. A sonar sensor on the bodywork

the deviations between the 3D model and the real scenario. These real data confirm the performance of the method. However, it is important to remark that this is the weak point of the methods, that is, it is necessary to elaborate a 3D model without so many deviations from the real scenario.

FUTURE TRENDS

As technology provides faster and more efficient computers, the interactions of AI techniques and 3D modelling are supposed to become increasingly popular, since computational cost in these cases is usually heavy, like in the presented case of the railway container yard. That improvement in the computer capacity and some emerging techniques will imply that other AI methods and 3D technologies - impossible to be currently applied in some fields - will be introduced in an efficient way in a near future. This is especially interesting in some fields such as System Engineering, where real time features are required.

As stated above, the authors consider that this field has not taken completely advantage from the potential that this interaction offers. As example of this fact, researchers have almost ignored the advantages of the use of 3D modelling as source data for the training process in AI systems, when it is clear that this application offers many advantages such as avoiding a lot of experimental and tedious measurements. The authors hope that the mentioned improvement in computer technology will repair this fault.

CONCLUSION

The combined application of 3D modelling with traditional Artificial Intelligence tools has been shown as a powerful tool in order to obtain better results and/or simplify the design/learning process of an AI system. This chapter shows in a summarized manner a state-of-the-art of the interaction between both branches, covering aspects such as artificial vision, intelligent behaviour of 3D elements, intelligent virtual environments populated with synthetic characters, simulation of environments difficult to reproduce, etc. Concerning System Engineering, despite the described applications, the use of the interaction AI-3D modelling is far from being widespread. There could be many reasons for that fact, but the main reason seems to lie on the high computational cost of 3D modelling and the real-time requirements in most of the System Engineering applications, not fulfilled by the present-day technology. With these restrictions, a not-completely explored field of application is that of the use of 3D-modelling as data source.

ACKNOWLEDGMENT

This work has been supported by the Spanish Government under the Project DPI2007-64137.

REFERENCES

Amiguet-Vercher, J., Szarowicz, A., & Forte, P. (2001). Synchronized Multi-agent Simulations for Automated Crowd Scene Simulation. In *AGENT-1 Workshop Proceedings, IJCAI 2001*, August 2001.

Bruno, F., Caruso, F., & Pisacane, O. (2008). A web3D application for the bin-packaging problem. In *20th European Modeling and Simulation Symposium (Simulation in Industry), EMSS08*, Calabria, Italy.

Carnevale, C., Finzi, G., Pisoni, E., Singh, V., & Volta, M. (2007). Neuro-fuzzy and neural network systems for air quality control. In Urban Air Quality 2007, UAQ 2007, March 27-29, Cyprus.

Company, P. (1997). Integrating Creative Steps in CAD Process. In *International Seminar on Principles and Methods of Engineering Design. Proceedings, 1*, 295–322.

Hartley, R. I., & Zisserman, A. (2000). Multiple View Geometry in Computer Vision. Cambridge, UK: Cambridge Univ. Press.

Hugues, L., & Bredeche, N. (2006). Simbad: an Autonomous Robot Simulation Package for Education and Research. In *Proceedings of The International Conference on the Simulation of Adaptive Behavior 2006*.

Jimenez, P., Thomas, F., & Torras, C. (2001). A neural networks based collision detection engine for multi-arm robotic systems. *Computers & Graphics, 25*(2), 269–285. doi:10.1016/S0097-8493(00)00130-8

Kahl, F., & Henrion, D. (2005) Globally Optimal Estimates for Geometric Reconstruction Problems. In *10th IEEE International Conference on Computer Vision (ICCV 2005)* (pp. 978-985).

Liu, F., Wu, X., & Cheng, W. (2007). Visual Intelligent Simulation For Railway Container Yard Based on Agent. *International Conference on Intelligent Systems and Knowledge Engineering (ISKE2007)*.

Maher, M. L., & Gero, J. S. (2003). Agent models of 3D virtual worlds. In *Proceedings of ACADIA 2002*, Panoma, California.

Martinez Lastra, J. L., López-Torres, E., & Colombo, A. W. (2005). A 3D Visualization and Simulation Framework for Intelligent Physical Agents. *HoloMAS, 2005*, 23–38.

Nagendra, I. V., & Gujar, U. (1988). 3-d objects from 2-D Orthographic Views – A survey. *Computer Graphics, 12*(1), 111–114. doi:10.1016/0097-8493(88)90015-5

Prada, R., & Paiva, A. (2005). Intelligent virtual agents in collaborative scenarios. In *Proceedings of the 5th International Working Conference on Intelligent Virtual Agents (IVA2005)*, Kos, Greece.

Rana, A. S., & Zalzala, A. M. (1997). *Fifth International Conference on Artificial Neural Networks* (Conf. Publ. No. 440).

Rickel, J., & Johnson, W. L. (1999). Animated Agents for Procedural Training in Virtual Reality: Perception, Cognition, and Motor Control. *Applied Artificial Intelligence, 13*(4-5), 343–382. doi:10.1080/088395199117315

Russel, S., & Norvig, P. (1995). Artificial Intelligence, A modern approach. Upper Saddle River, NJ: Prentice-Hall, Inc.

Saxena, A., Sun, M., & Ng, A. (2007). Make3D: Learning 3-D Scene Structure from a Single Still Image. *ICCV workshop on 3D Representation for Recognition* (3dRR-07).

Seitz, S. M., Curless, B., Diebel, J., Scharstein, D., & Szeliski, R. (2006). A comparison and evaluation of multiple stereo reconstruction algorithms. *CVPR*, 519–528.

SIBTRA. (2009). *Sistema Inteligente de Bajo Coste Para el Transporte y la Vigilancia en Entornos Ecológicos No Estructurados*. Ministerio de Educación y Ciencia. Plan Nacional de I+D (DPI2007-64137).

Simo, A., Kitamura, K., & Nishida, Y. (2005). Behavior based Children Accidents' Simulation and Visualization: Planning the Emergent Situations. *Computational Intelligence*, 164–169.

Soto, M., & Allongue, S. (2002). Modeling Methods for Reusable and Interoperable Virtual Entities in Multimedia Virtual Worlds. *Multimedia Tools and Applications*, *16*(1/2), 161–177. doi:10.1023/A:1013249920338

Sugihara, K. (1986). Machine interpretation of line Drawings. Cambridge, MA: The MIT Press.

Vosinakis, S., & Panayiotopoulos, T. (2005, February). A tool for constructing 3D Environments with Virtual Agents. *Multimedia Tools and Applications*, *25*(2), 253–279. doi:10.1007/s11042-005-5607-y

Voss, G., Behr, J., Reiners, D., & Roth, M. (2002). A Multi-Thread Safe Foundation for Scenegraphs and its Extension to Clusters. *Eurographics Workshop on Parallel Graphics and Visualisation*.

Wang, W., & Grinstein, G. (1993). A Survey of 3D Solid Reconstruction from 2D Projection Line Drawings. *Computer Graphics Forum*, *12*(2), 137–158. doi:10.1111/1467-8659.1220137

Wikipedia. (2009). *Article on 3D modelling*. Retrieved from http://en.wikipedia.org/wiki/3D_modelling

Chapter 6
User Modeling in Soft Computing Framework

Jose Antonio Iglesias
Carlos III University, Spain

Agapito Ledezma
Carlos III University, Spain

Araceli Sanchis
Carlos III University, Spain

ABSTRACT

Nowadays, the systems that interact with the user, including computers, are improving very quickly. In this improvement, a great goal for the near future is to create systems able to adapt its behavior according to the needs of a particular user. The key element for this purpose is the user model. In this context, a goal of user modeling is to increase the effective use of computers and many other systems that require more sophistication in its interaction with the user. To achieve this goal, it is necessary to know how the users behave. Then, the anticipation of certain aspects of human behavior, such as goals, actions or preferences is possible. In this chapter, the development of user models using soft computing is presented. The main approaches to different user modeling are reviewed, and the main techniques used to develop user models are discussed. Also, a particular example is explained in detail.

INTRODUCTION

Recognizing the behavior of others is a significant aspect of many different human tasks in different environments. There are new theories which claim that a high percentage of the human brain is used for predicting the future, including the behavior of other humans (Mulcahy & Call, 2006). If we consider a social context, there are many situations in which humans recognize (or try to recognize) the plan underlying the behavior of others in order to make predictions based on that recognition.

In addition, humans usually think about the past and plan for the future. To illustrate this idea, the Estonian neuroscientist Endel Tulving (2004) uses the following tale: A girl attended a party but she was not able to eat her favorite dessert because there were no spoons available. Facing the possibility of attending the party again, she took a spoon to bed. This girl took the spoon not because she

DOI: 10.4018/978-1-61520-893-7.ch006

currently needed it, but because she would need it in the future.

To predict the behavior of others is important, for instance, in assisting them (Kuniyoshi et al., 1994), imitating them (Bakker & Kuniyoshi, 1996) or detecting changes in their behavior (which can serve as indicator of malicious or damaging misuse in many services). When this process is carried out by a software agent or a robot based on set of observations, it is known as *plan recognition* or *agent recognition*. Most existing techniques for *plan recognition* assume the availability of carefully hand-crafted *plan libraries,* which encode the a-priori known behavioral repertoire of the observed agents; during run-time, plan recognition algorithms match the observed behavior of the agents against the plan-libraries, and matches are reported as hypotheses. Unfortunately, techniques for automatically acquiring plan-libraries from observations, e.g., by learning or data-mining, are only beginning to emerge.

In this chapter we will focus on User Modeling (UM) and we mainly consider systems developed using soft computing techniques. These systems acquire information about a user (or group of users) so as to be able to adapt their behavior to that user or group. Therefore, if a system is able to create a user model, the system can be tailored to the needs of a particular use. For example, a TV system could be able to create the model of the user who use it and suggest different choices based on past preferences. In this case, if the user always record his/her favorite TV series, the system should recognize this task and shows a message when the TV system was not activated for recording it, or recommend similar TV series or movies about the same topic, etc. For this purpose, the information arising from the human-computer system interface should be treated and analyzed to create the TV user profile.

Finally, we need to consider that nowadays large quantities of information are produced at a fast rate by users of the Internet, consumer markets, etc. Therefore, there exists the need to cope with huge amounts of data and it is very interesting to use it for analyzing the user who created that information.

WHAT IS USER MODELING (UM)?

UM is the process of profiling users by observing them in action. It is very important to consider that the model is created by observation. It is different from asking users about how they behave when they are using a certain system. It is different from talking with expert users who may know how users are suppose to behave. In fact, users themselves usually do not know how to describe what they do, especially if they are familiar with the tasks they perform. It happens because users usually behave leaving out activities that they do not even notice they are doing. They emphasize activities that they find difficult or boring and they do not realize that there are other ordinary activities that they perform, too. It means that the *true* could not exactly be what they believe to be true (Hackos & Redish, 1998).

Research on UM can be traced back to the early 1970s, but it was in the mid-1980 when interesting research works on this area appear. Since the early 1990s, we are witnessing and information revolution; currently, the World Wide Web and other new platforms have populated the lives of an increasing number of people with many different computing systems and large quantities of information are produced at a fast rate. These aspects tend to increase the need for user modeling and personalization.

Cohen et al (1982) propose two kinds of plan recognition depending on the role the observed agent plays in the recognition task: *keyhole* and *intended* recognition. This classification can be also considered in the area of UM. In *keyhole* recognition, the observed agent does not attempt to impact the recognition process, as if it is recognized through a *keyhole*. In *intended* recognition, the observed agent knows that it is being observed and deliberately performs actions to help the recognition. This last kind of recognition can be used in cooperative environments in which the agents cannot communicate to each other but they can observe the environment and how the other agents behave. Geib and Goldman (2001) consider a third kind of recognition, *adversarial* plan recognition. In this case, the observed agent attempts to thwart the recognition, typically in competitive environments. In the UM field, the *agent* is considered as the *user* to be modeled in a certain context. In this case, the kind of recognition most common and useful is the *keyhole*. Thus, only by observing users we can understand deeply how they behave, it means how they perform their tasks in a certain environment.

A user model could be constructed using personal information about the user, such as age, occupation, marital status, etc. This information can be used to anticipate some of the behavior of the user before observing the actions. However, this information can be uncompleted or not available (for example, when we create the behavior of a computer user, a visitor to a web site, etc). In this chapter, it is considered that this kind of personal information is not available and the user is modeled only by observing their actions in a certain environment.

Once a user model has been created, one of the main goals of UM is to make information systems user-friendly, by adapting the system to the needs of the user. This aspect is very important in the information systems and there are many areas in which UM have already been applied: adaptive user interface, computer-supported learning environments, information retrieval, systems which require "intelligent help" for performing complex tasks, etc.

Finally, we need to bear in mind that the construction of effective user profiles is a difficult problem because of different aspects:

- Human behavior is usually erratic.

- Sometimes humans behave differently because of a change in their goals.

SOFT COMPUTING IN USER MODELING

To model, recognize, or classify the behavior of others is very useful in different fields. The literature of UM is very vast, therefore we focus on the most notable work in which soft computing techniques are used. Different methods have been used to find out relevant information under a user behavior in many different areas:

- *Student modeling:*

The students are modeled to personalize their learning process in order to create environments which can be adapted to the needs and knowledge of individual students. Such models can assist an intelligent tutoring system, an intelligent learning environment, or an intelligent collaborative learner in adapting to specific aspects of student behavior. Historically, the first users to be modeled were students; therefore, student modeling proceeds UM and it can be considered as one of the causes for the development of UM technology.

In this area, several soft computing techniques have been used:

Chiu and Webb (1999) propose and evaluate two issues used in any student modeling system that constructs models for multiple observations over time: First, how to improve prediction rate without degrading prediction accuracy. And second, how to improve prediction accuracy without affecting prediction rate.

Sison and Shimura (1998) examine how machine learning techniques have been used to create student models automatically as well as the background knowledge necessary for student modeling. They also describe how results in student modeling research are useful in machine learning research, mainly because student modeling requires dealing with nearly all the problems of machine learning, and more.

Bull et al. (2009) present *OLMlets* and *UK-SpecIAL*: independent open learner models to promote learner reflection and learner independence within courses, and a greater understanding of how courses fit together to build the "bigger picture" of their degree and how this relates to their future professions. This approach is proposed to be used in comparable university departments to promote metacognitive skills and independent learning by students outside lecture.

• *Discovery of user navigation patterns:*

Discovering and extracting interest navigation patterns is one of the top demanding tasks in the personalization services. For this purpose, several implicit schemes have been proposed: based on intelligent agents, frequent user traversal paths discovery, site organization learning and re-classification.

Wu et al. (2007) present a Portal-independent mechanism of interest elicitation with privacy protection. Moreover, they present a hidden Markov model extension with personalization interest description of Portal to form interest navigation patterns for different users.

Spiliopoulou and Faulstich (1998) present the *Web Utilization Miner WUM*, a mining system for discovering interesting navigation patterns in web sites. *WUM* prepares the web log data for mining and the language *MINT* mining the aggregated data according to the directives of the human expert. This work is complementary to "*Footprints*" tool, which focuses on the visualization of frequently accessed patterns and on the identification of pattern types that may be of importance (Wexelblat, 1996).

Buechner et al. (1999) introduces an algorithm (called *MiDAS*) to discover marketing related navigation patterns. *MiDAS* extends traditional sequence discovery with a wide range of web-specific features.

Recently, Farzan and Brusilovsky (2009) present an interesting multifaceted study of social navigation support (*SNS*) in a controlled experiment designed for factual information seeking tasks. The result of this study confirms that users follow social navigation cues for finding information. However, time constraint did not increase the applicability of SNS and traditional navigational support such as search rank proved to be more reliable for users.

• *Web page filtering:*

Two issues need to be addressed when developing a web search engine: how to locate relevant documents on the web and how to filter out irrelevant documents from a set of documents collected from the web. In this case, the second issue is taken into account.

Gody and Amandi (1998) present a technique to generate readable user profiles that accurately capture interests by observing their behavior on the Web. The proposed technique is built on the *Web Document Conceptual Clustering* algorithm, with which profiles without an a priori knowledge of user interest categories can be acquired.

In a similar field, another example is to determine which news articles to read from a web page (Pazzani, & Billsus, 1997). In this situation, different learning methods are proposed in which the training data are decisions made by the users. These decisions can be used to create a model which can be used to emulate the decisions of the user in future problems.

An approach to track user interaction data and preserving semantic knowledge on complex and interactive Web sites is proposed by Plumbaum et al. (2009).

• *Recommender systems:*

Recommender systems can be considered as a specific type of information filtering technique that attempts to present information items that are likely of interest to the user. The recommender technology (Goldberg et al., 1992) was invented more than a decade ago. The current systems based on this technology are in the mainstream practice of e-commerce and social websites.

Macedo et al. (2003) propose a system (*Web-Memex*) that (a) provides recommended information based on the captured history of navigation from a list of well-known users, (b) allows users to have access from any networked machine, (c) demands user authentication to access the repository of recommendations and, (d) allows users to specify when the capture of their history should be performed. *WebMemex* captures information such as IP addresses, user Ids and URL accessed for future analysis.

Zhu et al. (2003) present a novel method for predicting the current information need of a web user from the content of the pages the user has visited and the actions the user has applied to these pages. This inference is based on a parameterized model of how the sequence of actions chosen by the user indicates the degree to which page content satisfies the user´s information need. These authors are also the developers of *WebIC*, a client-side Web recommender system that predicts the user's information need based on his browsing patterns, then points him to web pages from essentially anywhere on the Web, that contain information useful to that user.

Brun et al. (2009) focus on context dependent recommender systems and present the *AKSMM* model, a low-order Markov model that has a high coverage and a low space complexity. Experiments show in this case that the accuracy of the model increases according to the size of the history used to perform recommendations.

- *Computer security:*

Knowledge about computer users is very beneficial for detecting masqueraders.

Pepyne et al. (2004) describe a method using queuing theory and logistic regression modeling methods for profiling computer users based on simple temporal aspects of their behavior. In this case, the goal is to create profiles for very specialized groups of users, who would be expected to use their computers in a very similar way.

In a related area (computer intrusion detection problem), Coull et al. (2003) propose an algorithm that uses pair-wise sequence alignment to characterize similarity between sequences of commands. The algorithm produces an effective metric for distinguishing a legitimate user from a masquerader. Schonlau et al. (2001) investigate a number of statistical approaches for detecting masqueraders.

Angelov and Zhou (2008) propose to use evolving fuzzy classifiers for computer intrusion detection. A new approach to the online classification of streaming data is introduced and successfully tested on a number of benchmark problems as well as on data from an intrusion detection data stream where it demonstrated its advantages. An important demonstration in this research is that flexible classifiers can be generated online from streaming data, achieving high classification rates.

A method very used and powerful for UM is the artificial neural networks (ANN). ANNs have been mainly used for classification and clustering users with a similar profile. In 2003, Bidel et al. (2003) use ANN for the classification of hypermedia users. For this task, the data generated from an on-line encyclopedia are used as training data. Hsieh et al. (2004) propose a behavioral scoring model for analyzing bank users. In that research, the training data are the bank databases provided by a major Taiwanese credit card issuer. This classification is very interesting for customer marketing purposes.

As we can see, a lot of research on user modeling uses the *World Wide Web* environment, which provides a well-known interaction environment and a huge set of information to filter. However, it is not clear that they can be transferred to other environment.

USER MODELING AS SEQUENCE LEARNING

As we already mentioned, the actions performed by a user are usually influenced by his/her past experiences. A current situation or the action that an agent performs usually depends on what has happened before and sometimes on what happened long time ago. This aspect motivates the idea of automated sequence learning for UM; if we do not know the features that influence the behavior of a user, we can consider a sequence of past actions to incorporate some of the historical context of the user. Indeed, sequence learning is arguable the most common form of human and animal learning. Sequences are absolutely relevant in human skill learning (Sun et al., 2001) and in high-level problem solving and reasoning (Anderson, 1995). This aspect is usually taken into account in the related researches; however, there are some models which have problems dealing with such dependencies. For example, recurrent neural network models (Godoy & Amandi, 2005) or reinforcement learning cannot manage efficiently the long-range dependences.

Taking this aspect into account, the problem of behavior recognition can be examined as a problem of learning to characterize the behavior of a user in terms of sequences of atomic behaviors. Therefore, the behavior recognition problem is transformed into a sequence classification problem where a sequence represents a specific behavior. This transformation can be done because it is clear that any behavior has a sequential aspect, as actions are performed in a sequence.

According to this aspect, Horman and Kaminka (2007) present a learner with unlabelled sequential data that discover meaningful patterns of sequential behavior from example streams. Popular approaches to such learning include statistical analysis and frequency based methods. In addition, it is carried out an in-depth empirical comparison and analysis of popular sequence learning methods in terms of the quality of infor-

mation produced. The conclusions of this work are really interesting and are detailed as follows: both frequency-based and statistics-based approaches suffer from common statistical biases based on the length of the sequences considered; and are unable to correctly generalize the patterns discovered, thus flooding the results with multiple instances of the same pattern. Lane and Brodley (1999) present an approach based on the basis of instance-based learning (IBL) techniques, and several techniques for reducing data storage requirements of the user profile.

There are many other areas in which sequential data need to be analyzed in order to solve a problem. In general, the sequence learning problem can be categorized in four basic categories: sequence prediction, sequence generation, sequence classification and sequential decision making. Considering the sequence classification, the main reason to need to handle sequential data is because of the observed data from some environments are inherently sequential. An example of these data is the DNA sequence. Ma et al. (2001) present new techniques for bio-sequence classification. Given an unlabeled DNA sequence S, the goal in that research is to determine whether or not S is a specific promoter (a gene sequence that activates transcription). Also, a tool for DNA sequence classification is developed by Chirn et al. (1997).

In a different area, Iglesias et al (2007) present a technique to discover a pattern from a given sequence and a general method to classify the sequence. The method considers mainly the dependencies among the neighboring elements of a sequence. In a very different area (simulated soccer player modeling), the same idea is evaluated by Iglesias et al (2009). In that research a method used by the team CAOS (*CAOS Coach 2006Simulation Team)* which models successfully the behavior of a multi-agent system. The main idea of the research is to compare two different simulated soccer team behaviors and a *trie* data structure is proposed in a novel way. It was demonstrated that this structure can be very useful to detect predictable and exploitable behaviors. Also, there are many other domains related to multi-agent systems where this method could be applied: Kaminka et al. (2002) recognize basic actions based on descriptive predicates, and learn relevant sequences of actions using a statistical approach. This structure is also used in (2003) to create frequent patterns in dynamic scenes.

APPLICATIONS: PROFILING UNIX USERS USING SOFT COMPUTING TECHNIQUES

The aim of this section is to propose a complete example in which a user model is obtained from the UNIX commands (s)he types in a command-line interface. We present and evaluate different methods which can represent and classify the behavior of different users in different domains. Also, we will considerer that sequences are very relevant in human skill learning and in high-level problem solving and reasoning and that the actions performed by an agent could be influenced by his past experiences. For example, in a human-computer interaction by commands, the sequentiality of these commands is essential for the result of the interaction and we will study if this aspect is important for recognizing a computer user.

The goal of UNIX user classification is the recognition of a UNIX user profile from the commands (s)he types and the classification of this user into a predefined profile. Therefore, as most of the agent modeling techniques, in the implemented methods in this research, we classify the UNIX commands into the profiles stored in a library. The result of this classification can be very useful, for example, in computer intrusion detection.

In this example, the profile of a UNIX user is defined by the commands typed during a period of time. The actions executed by a user being inherently sequential, there are many different behaviors that can be represented by a sequence of events. Therefore, the methods proposed in this research can be used in many other environments (such as GUI events, network packet traffic and so on). As a behavior is represented by a sequence of elements, the behavior classification can be defined as follows: Let us define a sequence of n elements as $E = \{e_1, e_2,.. e_n\}$. Given a set of m classes $C = \{c_1, c_2,...,c_m\}$ we wish to determine which class $c_i \in C$ the sequence E belongs to.

In this section we propose four different classifiers; two of them are proposed because they are very used in this kind of environment (*TFIDF* and *HMMs*), the other two are soft computing techniques (**Bayesian Networks** and **Artificial Neural Networks**). These techniques are evaluated with real-data analyzing 50 different UNIX users and respective results can be compared. The data[1] used for these experiments were used by Schonlau et al. (2001) in masquerade-detection studies. These user commands were captured from the UNIX *acctt* auditing mechanism. However, this analysis is only based on two fields: *Command name* and *User*. Thus, a user is identified by a set of commands concatenated by date order; for example the first 10 commands of the *User1* are: *cpp, sh, xrdb, cpp, sh, xrdb, mkpts, env, csh, csh.*

In the command extracting process done by Schonlau et al., the first 15,000 commands for each of about 70 users were recorded over a time period of several months. Some users generate 15,000 commands in a few days, others in a few months. Some commands recorded by the system are not explicitly typed by the user. For example, a *shell file* contains multiple commands, and running it will cause all of its commands to be recorded. Scholen et al. (2001) use the data of 50 users randomly selected in which data from the remaining 20 users are interspersed as masqueraders data. However, in this chapter we describe a research in which we obtain the data of the 50 users without data interspersed. For evaluating the different classifiers, we use the sequences of commands typed by 50 different users. In our case, each subsequence contains 12,500 commands.

In order to measure the performance of the proposed classifiers using the above data, the well-established technique of cross-validation is used. For this research, 10-fold cross-validation is chosen. Thus, the 12,500 commands typed by a user (training set) are divided into 10 disjoint subsets with equal size (1,250 commands). Each of the 10 subsets is left out in turn for evaluation.

First User Model: Term Weighting - TFIDF

This kind of classifier is based on the relevance feedback algorithm proposed by Rocchio (1971). TFIDF (Term Frequency–Inverse Document Frequency) is a common method often used in Information Retrieval (IR) problems. This method is based on a statistical measure (*weight*) used to evaluate how *important* a word is to a document in a collection: First, it evaluates the word frequency in the document (the more a word appears in the document, the more it is considered to be significant in the document). In addition, IDF measures how frequent a word is in the collection.

There are different variants of *TFIDF*; in this case, we consider the following weight, as explained in (Salton, 1999):

$$\text{weight}_{wd}\text{TFIDF} = \text{tf}_{wd} * \log (N_d / n_w)$$

where tf_{wd} is the frequency of a the word w in the document d, N is the number of documents in the collection and n_w is the number of documents in which the word w appears.

In order to classify a UNIX user, her/his profile must be created in advance. To apply the proposed classifier, a profile based on *TFIDF* is created for each UNIX user. The *importance* of each command will be used to identify the user. Therefore, we calculate the *TFIDF* weight for each command of the sequence of a user.

In this case, the TFIDF weight is calculated as follows:

$$\text{TFIDFweight}_{cs} (\text{User u}) = \text{tf}_{cs} * \log (N_u / n_c)$$

where tf_{cs} is the frequency of the command c in the sequence s which belongs to the user u, N_u is the number of users and n_c is the number of users who have typed the command c at least once.

Once the *importance* (TFIDF weight) of each command is calculated, the model of a UNIX user is represented by the distribution of these values. Finally, each user profile is stored in a library (similar to the plan-libraries used in the plan recognition) where it is labeled with a *name* that identifies them.

After creating all the user profiles, a given sequence of commands is obtained and it needs to be classified. Therefore, given a set of profiles stored in a library and a sequence of commands, the goal is to determine into which profile the given sequence fits. Firstly, the distribution of *TFIDF* weights is calculated from the sequence to classify. Then, it is matched with all the behavior models stored in the library.

As both models are represented by a distribution of elements, the proposed classifier applies a statistical test for matching these distributions. A non-parametric test (or distribution free) is used because this kind of test does not assume a particular population distribution. The proposed test applied is a modification of *Chi-Square* Test for two samples. The profile to classify is considered as an observed sample and all the profiles stored in the library are considered as expected samples. This test compares the observed distribution with all the expected distributions objectively and evaluates if a deviation appears.

The proposed test is the comparison of two sets of *TFIDF weights* in which *Chi-Square* is the sum of the terms $(\text{Exp} - \text{Obs})^2/\text{Obs}$. This comparison obtains a value (*comparing value*) that indicates the difference (deviation) between the two distributions. The lower this value, the closer the similarity between the two profiles. This comparison test is applied once for each

Figure 1. Framework - the proposed TFIDF classifier

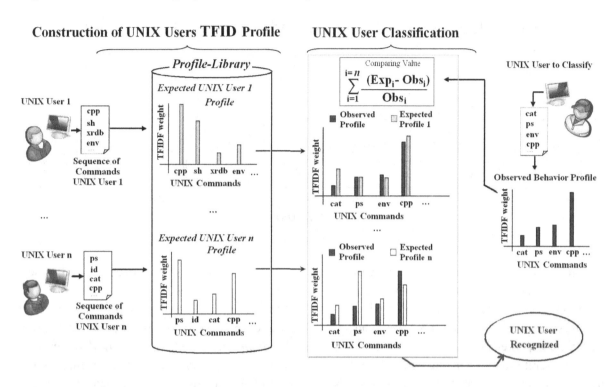

library profile. The profile which obtains the lowest deviation is considered as the most similar one. An advantage of the proposed test is its rapidity because only the observed subsequences are evaluated. However, there is no penalty for the expected relevant subsequences which do not appear in the observed distribution.

Figure 1 graphically represents the proposed classifier. Finally, it is remarkable that with this method, we have not considered that the commands typed by a user are sequential. This aspect will be taken into account in the next three proposed classifiers.

In this case, a full program to profile and classify UNIX users using the TFIDF classifier has been implemented. For evaluating the results, each user classification returns a ranking list with the most similar users (*training profile*) to the sequence to classify (*testing profile*). There are users whose behavior is quite similar and the results of the comparison could be similar. How-

ever, in these results, a comparison is considered correct only if the user who typed the sequence of commands to classify holds the first position of the ranking list.

Figure 2 shows the result of the classification of 50 UNIX users using 10-fold cross-validation. Each UNIX user evaluated is represented in the X-axis. The Y-axis represents the percentage of folds that has been correctly classified. Observing this graph, we can see that all the users are correctly classified at least once of the 10 times executed and the **average correct classification** percentage value is: *57,1%*.

Second User Model: Hidden Markov Models (HMM)

Recent researches have demonstrated the effectiveness of Hidden Markov Models (*HMMs*) for information extraction and they are very used in speech recognition. Also, related with this

Figure 2. Classification results - TFIDF classifier}

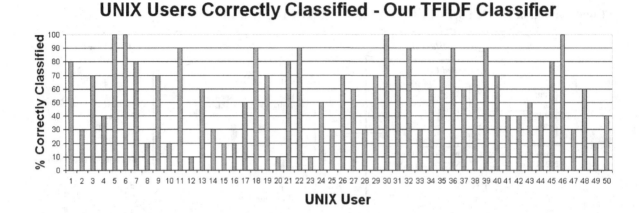

research, *HMMs* have been used for recognizing automated robot behavior (Han & Veloso, 2000).

A *HMM* is a finite state automaton with stochastic state transitions and symbol emissions. At each time step, the *HMM* system (represented by a set of discrete states) is in one state s_i. The state transitions occur according to a certain probability distribution: $Pr\ (S_{t+1} = s_j \mid S_t = s_i)$ for the state transition $s_i \rightarrow s_j$. However, the system state at time t is not directly observable (*Hidden*). Instead, a set of state dependent observation variables, o_i, are available. For each state s_i, an observation probability $b_i(o)$ is defined over *o*.

In the proposed HMM classifier, the set of Markov states is not previously defined; however, it could correspond to a model of the different *mental states* of the UNIX user. For applying this classifier to identify UNIX users, we need previously to create each UNIX user profile. In this case, each user is represented by a HMM with a number of states chosen by the designer (for the experiments conducted in this research, we have used different number of states). Therefore, a *HMM* is created and trained for each user (class). This step requires that the training data (sequence of command) be *labeled* (with the user typed the commands). All the user profiles based on *HMMs* are stored in a library.

Once the profiles have been created, a sequence of commands is given for classifying it. Then, the probability of the sequence is evaluated under each *HMM*. For this process, the *Viterby algorithm* can be used. The *Viterby algorithm* is a dynamic programming algorithm for finding the most likely sequence of hidden states that result in a sequence of observed elements. Finally, the given sequence is classified by the *HMM* (user profile) which gave it the highest likelihood.

For creating a system to classify UNIX users using the *HMM* classifier proposed, we have used *UMDHMM: Hidden Markov Model Tool* (Kanungo, 1999). In this case, as the result can vary depending of the number of states used for creating the *HMM profile*, we obtain the results using 3, 5 and 10 states. As the TFIDF classifier, this classifier returns a ranking list with the most similar users to the sequence to classify and only if the correct user holds first position, it is considered a correct classification.

Figure 3 shows the results of the *HMM* classification in this example. In this case, the results depend of the number of states used for creating the *HMM* profile. The average correct classification percentage value is: **71,8%** (3 States), **73,6%** (5 States) and **76,4%** (10 States). As we can see, this percentage is higher if the *HMM* profile consists

Figure 3. Classification results – HMM classifier

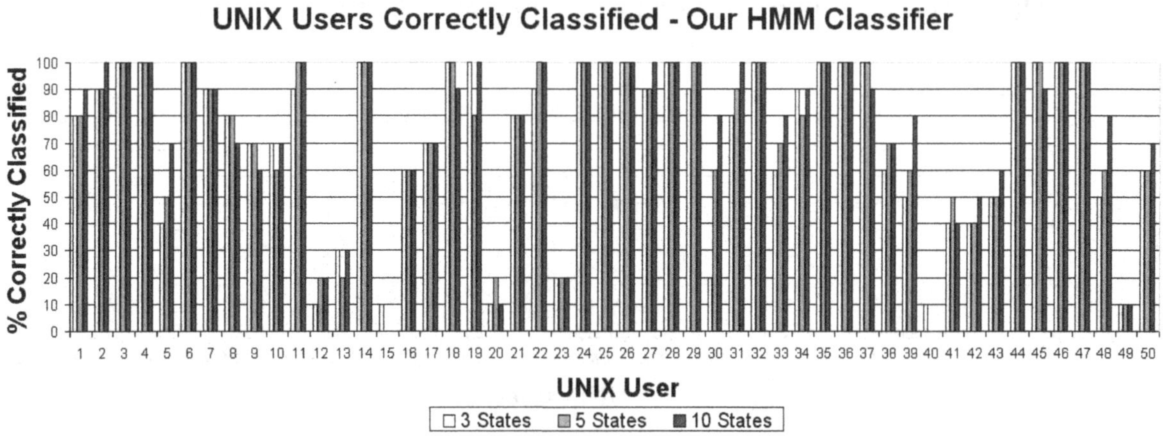

UNIX Users Correctly Classified - Our HMM Classifier

of more states; however, using more states, the *HMM* created is more complex and the process for classifying a user is more time-consumed.

Third User Model: Graphical Model - Bayesian Networks

A Bayesian network is a graphical model that encodes probabilistic relationships among variables of interest. Over the last decade, the Bayesian network has become a popular representation for encoding uncertain expert knowledge in expert systems (Heckerman et al., 1995).

Let $U=\{x_1, x_2,...,x_n\}$, $n\geq 1$ be a set of variables. A *Bayesian network B* over a set of variables U is a *network structure* B_s, which is a directed acyclic graph (*DAG*) over U and a set of probability tables $B_p=\{p(u|pa(u))|u \in U\}$ where *pa* (u) is the set of parents of u in B_s. A bayesian network represents a probability distribution $P(U) = \Pi_{u \in U} p(u|pa(u))$.

Using this technique, the classification task consists of classifying a variable $y = x_0$ (called *class variable*) given a set of variables $x = x_1$, $x_2,..., x_n$ (called *attribute variables*). In this case, a classifier h: $x \rightarrow y$ is a function that maps an instance of x to value of y. The classifier is learned from a dataset D consisting of samples over (x,y).

The learning task consists of finding an appropriate *Bayesian network* given a data set D over U. Therefore, as is shown in (Bouckaert, 2004), to use a *Bayesian network* as a classifier, the *argmax*$_y$ P(y|x) is calculated using the distribution P(U) represented by the *Bayesian network*. Also, as all variables in x are known, complicated inference algorithms are not needed, but just calculate *P(y|x)* $\Pi_{u \in U} p(u|pa(u))$ for all class values.

In this example, in order to create the corresponding classifier for UNIX users, the data set consists of sequences of commands that the user have typed consecutively. For obtaining these instances (data set), the sequence of commands is segmented in subsequence of equal length from the first to the last element. Thus, the sequence $A=A_1, A_2,..., A_n$ (where *n* is the number of commands of the sequence) will be segmented in the subsequences described by $A_i,...,A_{i+length}$ $\forall i$, i=[1, n-*length*+1], where *length* is the size of the subsequences created and this value determines how many commands are considered as dependent.

For example, let us consider the sequence typed by User1 is: *{cpp, sh, xrdb, mkpts, env, ps, hostname, id, cat}* and each instance consists of 5 attribute variables (subsequences of 5 commands); therefore, the following instances are

Figure 4. Classification results - Bayesian Network classifier

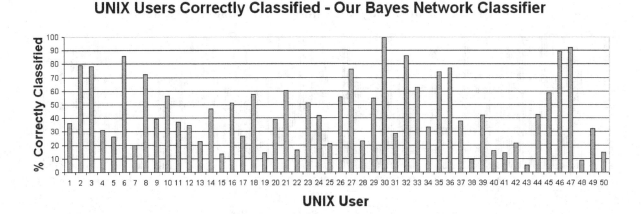

obtained: *{cpp, sh, xrdb, mkpts, env, user1}, {sh, xrdb, mkpts, env, ps, user1}, {xrdb, mkpts, env, ps, hostname, user1}, {mkpts, env, ps, hostname, id, user1},{env, ps, hostname, id, cat, user1}* where the 5 first words represent the *attribute variables* and the last word represents the *class variable*.

Once the instances are created, the classification can be performed using *WEKA* (Waikato Environment for Knowledge Analysis). *WEKA* is a Java software package (Garner, 1995) with an open source issued under the GNU General Public License. The package provides a collection of machine learning algorithms for data mining tasks.

In this study, the Bayesian Network classifier has been implemented using WEKA. Also, these results have been conducted using 5 attribute variables. The results have been obtained using WEKA's default settings. In this case, we calculate the percentage of the instances correctly classified using the confusion matrix obtained.

As in the previous result, Figure 4 shows the result of the Bayesian Network classification of 50 UNIX users using 10-fold cross-validation. In this case, although we consider that the order of the commands is relevant for classifying a user, the average correct classification percentage value is: *44.2%.*

Fourth User Model: Artificial Neural Networks

An Artificial Neural Network (ANN) is a computational (or mathematical) model that is able to capture and represent complex input/output relationships. The purpose of an ANN is to learn to recognize patterns in the input data. The ANN needs to be trained on samples data, and then, it can make predictions by detecting similar patterns in future data. The main advantage of an ANN lies in their ability to represent both linear and non-linear relationships and in their ability to learn these relationships from the input data.

The most common ANN model is the multilayer perceptron (MLP) which requires a desired output to learn (supervised network). This type of network creates a model which maps the input to the output using historical data so that the model can then be used to produce the output when it is unknown.

In this case, the data set of the ANN classifier is the same than the used in the Bayesian network classifier (subsequences of commands that the user have typed consecutively). The Artificial Neural Network classifier has been implemented using WEKA and the results have been conducted using

Figure 5. Classification results – Artificial Neural Network classifier

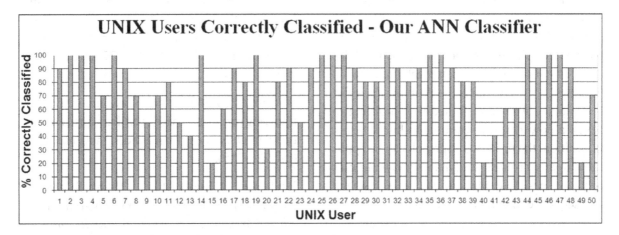

5 attribute variables. The parameters of the ANN created are as follows:

- number of hidden layers: 1
- number of neurons in the hidden layer: (attributes + classes)/2 = 28
- Learning rate (amount the weights are updated): 0,3
- Momentum applied to the weights during updating: 0,2
- Number of epochs to train through: 300
- Percentage size of the validation set: No validation set will be used and instead the network will train for the specified number of epochs
- Validation testing (how many times in a row the validation set error can get worse before training is terminated): 20

Figure 5 shows the result of the ANN classification of 50 UNIX users. In this case, the average correct classification percentage value is: *77,8%* and we can see that a large number of users are always recognized. After obtaining these results and comparing them with the other techniques use, we can conclude that this soft computing technique is adequate for this kind of environment.

Comparing the Proposed Techniques in this Section

After obtaining the results with the different techniques, we can conclude that ANN is an appropriate technique for our purpose. However, the time consuming for training the ANN is a longer than the classifier based on Bayesian Networks and *TFIDF*, but similar to the HMM classifier.

Using soft computing techniques can be very useful in the different tasks of UM, there are a lot of research which use this techniques obtaining very good results. But it could be very interesting to do a previous research according to the characteristics of the environment to know if this kind of techniques is the most adequate.

FUTURE RESEARCH DIRECTIONS

It is difficult or in general impossible, to create a user model that will have a full description of all possible behaviors of the user because the user behavior evolves with time, they are not static and new patterns may emerge as well as an old habit may be forgotten or stopped to be used. Therefore, because of a user profile is not necessarily fixed but rather it evolves/changes, new proposals use evolving methods to date the created profiles. For example, Iglesias et al. (2009) propose an evolving method to keep up to date the created profiles using an evolving system approach (Angelov et al., 2007). In this research, the evolving classifier is combined with a *trie*-based user profiling to obtain a powerful self-learning on-line scheme. In addition, the proposed approach can be applicable to any problem of dynamic/evolving user behavior modeling where it can be represented as a sequence of actions and events.

CONCLUSION

The aim of UM is to make information systems user-friendly, by adapting the system to the needs of the user. For this purpose, many research projects have used soft computing techniques obtaining promising results. However, several problems can arise: The collection of training data is essential in a user modeling process but this information sometimes is hard to obtain or it is not available.

In addition, the time to train is an important aspect that needs to be taken into account in the user modeling process. The different evaluated techniques show us that soft computing techniques (mainly ANN) can be efficiently used for this task.

Finally, changes in the behavior of a user are inevitable, a user evolves and it is shown in his/her behavior. Therefore, the user profiles created with soft computing techniques need to be keeping up to date constantly.

REFERENCES

Anderson, J. (1995). Learning and Memory: An Integrated Approach. New York: John Wiley and Sons.

Angelov, P., & Zhou, X. (2008). Evolving Fuzzy-Rule-Based Classifiers From Data Streams, Fuzzy Systems. *IEEE transactions on Fuzzy Systems*, *16*(6), 1462–1475. doi:10.1109/TFUZZ.2008.925904

Angelov, P., Zhou, X., & Klawonn, F. (2007). Evolving fuzzy rule-based classifiers. In Computational Intelligence in Image and Signal Processing (pp. 220-225).

Bakker, P., & Kuniyoshi, Y. (1996). Robot see, Robot do: an overview of robot imitation. In the *AISB Workshop on Learning in Robots and Animals*, Brighton, UK.

Bidel, S., Lemoine, L., & Piat, F. (2003). Statistical machine learning for tracking hypermedia user behavior. In *Proceedings of the 2nd workshop on machine learning, information retrieval and user modeling* (pp. 56-65).

Bouckaert, R. R. (2004). *Bayesian networks in Weka.* Computer Science Department. University of Waikato, 14.

Brun, A., Bonnin, G., & Boyer, A. (2009). History dependent Recommender Systems based on Partial Matching. In G-J. Houben, G. McCalla, F. Pianesi & M. Zancanari (Eds.), User Modeling, Adaptation and Personalization 2009 (pp. 343-348). Berlin: Springer-Verlag.

Buechner, A. G., Baumgarten, M., Anand, S. S., Mulvenna, M. D., & Hughes, J. G. (1999). Navigation Pattern Discovery from Internet Data. *Workshop on Web Usage Analysis and User Profiling* (pp.92-111), Springer.

Bull, S., Gardner, P., Ahmad, N., Ting, J., & Clarke, B. (2009). Use and Trust of Simple Independent Open Learner Models to Support Learning Within and Across Courses, in G-J. Houben, G, McCalla, F. Pianesi and M. Zancanari (eds), User Modeling, Adaptation and Personalization 2009 (pp. 42-53). Springer-Verlag, Berlin Heidelberg.

Chirn, G., Wang, G. T., & Wang, Z. (1997). Scientific Data Classification: A Case Study. In Tools with Artificial Intelligence (pp. 216-222).

Chiu, B. C., & Webb, G. I. (1999). Dual-model: An Architecture for Utilizing Temporal Information in Student Modeling, International conference on Computers in Education, Amsterdam, vol. 1., (pp. 111-118). IOS Press.

Cohen, P. R., Perrault, C. R., & Allen, J. F. (1982). Beyond Question Answering, In W. G. Lehnert and M. H. Ringle(Ed.), Strategies for Natural Language Processing, 245-274. Hillsdale, NJ.

Coull, S. E., Branch, J. W., Szymanski, B. K., & Breimer, E. (2003). Intrusion Detection: A Bioinformatics Approach. In *Computer Security Applications Conference* (pp.24-33).

Farzan, R., & Brusilovsky, P. (2009). Social Navigation Support for Information Seeking: If You Build It, Will The Come? In G-J. Houben, G, McCalla, F. Pianesi and M. Zancanari (Ed.), User Modeling, Adaptation and Personalization 2009 (pp. 66-77). Springer-Verlag, Berlin Heidelberg.

Garner, S. (1995). WEKA: The waikato environment for knowledge analysis. In *Proc. of New Zealand Computer Science Research Students Conference* (pp. 57-64).

Geib, C. W., & Goldman, R. P. (2001). Plan Recognition in Intrusion Detection Systems, In DARPA Information Survivability Conference and Exposition (DISCEX).

Giles, C. L., & Gori, M. (1998). Adaptive Processing of Sequences and Data Structures. Summer School on Neural Networks, 1387, Springer.

Godoy, D., & Amandi, A. (2005). User Profiling for Web Page Filtering. *IEEE Internet Computing*, *9*(4). doi:10.1109/MIC.2005.90

Goldberg, D., Nichols, D., Oki, B. M., & Terry, D. (1992). Using collaborative filtering to weave an information tapestry. *Communications of the ACM*, *35*, 61–70. doi:10.1145/138859.138867

Hackos, J. T., & Redish, J. C. (1998). User and Task Analysis for Interface Design. Hoboken, NJ: Wiley.

Han, K., & Veloso, M. (2000). Automated Robot Behavior Recognition Applied to Robotic Soccer. In *Robotics Research: the Ninth International Symposium,* (pp. 199-204). London: Springer-Verlag.

Heckerman, D., Geiger, D., & Chickering, D. M. (1995). Learning Bayesian Networks: The Combination of Knowledge and Statistical Data. *Machine Learning*, *20*(3), 197–243.

Horman, Y., & Kaminka, G. (2007). Removing biases in unsupervised learning of sequential patterns. *Intelligent Data Analysis*, *11*(5), 457–480.

Hsieh, N. (2004). An integrated data mining and behavioural scoring model for analyzing bank customers. *Expert Systems with Applications*, *27*, 623–633. doi:10.1016/j.eswa.2004.06.007

Huang, Z., Yang, Y., & Chen, X. (2003). An approach to plan recognition and retrieval for multi-agent systems. In *Workshop on Adaptability in Multi-Agent Systems (AORC 2003)*.

Iglesias, J. A., Ledezma, A., & Sanchis, A. (2007). Sequence classification using statistical pattern recognition. *Intelligent Data Analysis*, *2007*, 207–218. doi:10.1007/978-3-540-74825-0_19

Iglesias, J. A., Ledezma, A., & Sanchis, A. (2009). CAOS Coach 2006 Simulation Team: An opponent modelling approach. *Computing and Informatics Journal*, *28*(1), 57–80.

Iglesias, J. A., Ledezma, A., & Sanchis, A. (2009). Modelling Evolving User Behaviours. In *ESDIS 2009 IEEE Workshop on Evolving and Self-Developing and Self-Developing Intelligent Systems* (pp. 16-23).

Kaminka, G., Fidanboylu, M., Chang, A., & Veloso, M. (2002). Learning the sequential coordinated behavior of teams from observations. In RoboCup 2002 (pp. 111-125). Berlin: Springer.

Kanungo, T. (1999). UMDHMM: Hidden Markov Model Toolkit. Extended Finite State Models of Language, Cambridge University Press.

Kuniyoshi, Y., Rougeaux, S., Ishii, M., Kita, N., Sakane, S., & Kakikura, M. (1994). Cooperation by observation - the framework and the basic task patterns. In *IEEE International Conference on Robotics and Automation* (pp. 767–773).

Lane, T., & Brodley, C. E. (1999). Temporal sequence learning and data reduction for anomaly detection. *International Journal ACM Transactions on Information and System Security, 2*(3), 150–158.

Ma, Q., Wang, J. T., Shasha, D., & Wu, C. H. (2001). DNA sequence classification via an expectation maximization algorithm and neural networks: a case study. *International Journal IEEE Transactions on Systems, Man, and Cybernetics. Part C, 31*(4), 468–475.

Macedo, A. A., Truong, K. N., Camacho-Guerrero, J. A., & Pimentel, M. G. (2003). Automatically sharing web experiences through a hyperdocument recommender system. In ACM conference on Hypertext and hypermedia (pp. 48-56). New York: ACM.

Mulcahy, N. J., & Call, J. (2006). Apes save tools for future use. *Science, 312*(5776), 1038–1040. doi:10.1126/science.1125456

Pazzani, M., & Billsus, D. (1997). Learning and revising user profiles: The identification of interesting web sites. *Machine Learning, 27*, 313–331. doi:10.1023/A:1007369909943

Pepyne, D. L., Hu, J., & Gong, W. (2004). User Profiling for Computer Security. In *Proceedings of the American Control Conference* (pp. 982-987).

Plumbaum, T., Stelter, T., & Korth, A. (2009). Semantic Web Usage Mining: Using Semantics to Understand User Intentions. In G-J. Houben, G. McCalla, F. Pianesi & M. Zancanari (Eds.), User Modeling, Adaptation and Personalization 2009 (pp. 391-396). Berlin: Springer-Verlag.

Rocchio, J. (1971). Relevance feedback in information retrieval. In The SMART retrieval system: Experiments in Automatic Document Processing (pp. 313-323).

Salton, G. (1989). Automatic Text Processing: The Transformation, Analysis, and Retrieval of Information by Computer. Reading, MA: Addison-Wesley Longman Publishing Co., Inc.

Schonlau, M., Dumouchel, W., Ju, W. H., Karr, A. F., Theus, M., & Vardi, Y. (2001). Computer Intrusion: Detecting Masquerades. *Statistical Science, 16*(1), 58–74. doi:10.1214/ss/998929476

Sison, R., & Shimura, M. (1998). Student Modeling and Machine Learning. *International Journal of Artificial Intelligence in Education, 9*, 128–158.

Spiliopoulou, M., & Faulstich, L. C. (1998). WUM: A Web Utilization Miner. In EDBT Workshop WebDB98 (pp. 109-115). Berlin: Springer Verlag.

Sun, R., Merrill, E., & Peterson, T. (2001). From implicit skills to explicit knowledge: a bottom-up model of skill learning. *Cognitive Science, 25*(2), 203–244.

Tulving, E. (2004). The Missing Link in Cognition: Evolution of Self-Knowing Consciousness. (H. Terrace & J. Metcalfe, Eds.). New York: Oxford Univ. Press.

Wexelblat, A. (1996). An environment for aiding information-browsing tasks. *AAAI Spring Symposium on Acquisition, Learning and Demonstration: Automating Tasks for Users*. Birmingham, UK, AAAI Press.

Wu, J. Z., Xiong, P., & Sheng, H. (2007). Mining Personalization Interest and Navigation Patterns on Portal. In PAKDD (pp. 948-955). Berlin: Springer.

Zhu, T., Greiner, R., & Häubl, G. (2003). Predicting Web Information Content, Intelligent Techniques for Web Personalization. In B. Mobasher & S. S. Anand (Eds.), ITWP 2003 (pp. 1-36). Berlin: Springer-Verlag.

ENDNOTE

[1] These data are available from the Schonlau web page: http://www.schonlau.net/

Section 2
Industrial Applications

Chapter 7
Electromagnetic Optimization Using Genetic Algorithms

P. Mukherjee
Institute of Engineering & Management, India

E. L. Hines
University of Warwick, UK

ABSTRACT

This chapter focuses on the application of Genetic Algorithms (GAs) techniques in overcoming the limitations of microstrip antennas in terms of several key parameters such as bandwidth, power-handling capacity etc. In this chapter the effectiveness of GAs is discussed in relation to Electromagnetic optimization. A matching network has been designed for single band and dual band matching of microstrip antenna using GA.

INTRODUCTION

Microstrip geometries were originally contemplated in the 1950s (Grieg &Englemann, 1952). The microstrip antenna integrated with microstrip transmission line developed by Deschamps [1953] was the earliest known realization of this kind of structure. Figure 1 shows the structure of a simple microstrip patch antenna. The antenna is fabricated on one side of a substrate and on the other side the copper metallization is retained. A microstrip antenna can be modeled as a resonator with considerable radiation loss. The top and bottom metallization forms two electric walls and the

four side slots form the magnetic walls. Radiation from the structure can be explained in terms of the leakage of field lines through the side slots. The length of the patch is chosen to be approximately half wavelength, so that out of the four side slots, only two radiates efficiently. Due to its resonant structure a microstrip antenna has a very narrow impedance bandwidth that limits the applicability of the antenna. The motivation behind the present work is to overcome this limitation with some simple structures of the antenna, so that it can be used as a wideband antenna that has a large range of application in the field of satellite or mobile communication. Artificial Neural Networks (ANNs), Genetic Algorithms (GAs), Swarm Intelligence (SI), etc. are well known in the field of Soft Computing for their

DOI: 10.4018/978-1-61520-893-7.ch007

Copyright © 2010, IGI Global. Copying or distributing in print or electronic forms without written permission of IGI Global is prohibited.

Figure 1. Geometry of a microstrip Antenna (h=substrate thickness, W=patch width, L= patch length)

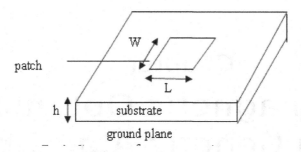

ability to solve real world problems in areas such as design, optimization and so on. GAs provide a mechanism by which the solution space for a particular problem is searched for "good solutions". GAs are inspired by Darwin's theory about evolution and models his principles of 'Natural Selection' and 'Survival of the Fittest'. Goldberg (1989) presented the first GA optimizer. GAs have been successfully applied in designing printed antennas (Michael Johnson. & Rahmat Samii, 1997; Rahmat Samii & Michielson, 1999; Sun, Hines, Mias, Green, & Udrea, 2005; Namkung, Hines, Green, &Leeson, 2007). Popovic (1982) has shown that a monopole which is inclined at a particular angle can be perfectly matched and can also exhibit a directive pattern in the horizontal plane. A good match and a given pattern can be achieved simultaneously by properly choosing the angles of inclination of the different segments. In a particular example the length of each of the five segments have been chosen to be $l = \lambda_0/6$ (f = 0.964 GHz) and θ (angle of inclination) can vary from 0° up to 180°. The optimized values of the angles of the different segments can be obtained with the aid of GAs. Dual-frequency operation can be obtained with two slots printed on the patch. The number of slots, the positions of the slots, and the slot lengths on the patch are important parameters in the design. The effects of all the parameters of the antenna can be described successfully by the theory. Both the resonant frequency and input impedance of the slotted antenna depend on the loading slot length and position.

The main difficulty of these kinds of designs is how to choose the loading slot that will satisfy the desired frequency and the input resistance at resonance simultaneously. In this case, the objective function can be chosen to be the summation of reflection coefficients at the two frequencies. The GA has been successfully applied by a number of researchers to improve the impedance bandwidth with an optimized patch shape (Delabie, Villegas, & Picon, 1997). In a particular method the patch has been considered to be made of a number of metallic cells and GAs have been used to remove some of the cells to obtain the desired impedance bandwidth. Artificial Neural Networks (ANN) also has been successfully applied for impedance matching of microstrip antenna (Pattnaik , Panda & Devi, 2002); for the optimization of the input impedance of rectangular microstrip patch antenna (Sharma & Gupta, 2007);in the analysis and synthesis of these antennas, to predict both patch dimensions and resonant frequency (Sagiroglu, Güney & Erler, 1999).

In many applications, it is desired to operate the same antenna in two or more discrete frequency bands with an arbitrary separation of bands. There are many techniques that ensure wideband and multiband operation of microstrip antennas. For example the frequencies of operation for an annular ring can be adjusted by choosing the inner and outer radii. However, the ratio of the two frequencies is somewhat limited (Wang & Lo, 1994). By modifying the geometry of the basic antenna it is possible to obtain a shift in the operating frequency

Figure 2. A basic genetic algorithm

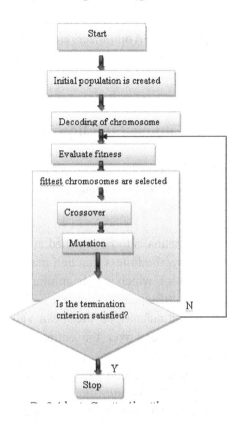

(Kerr, 1977). But this technique requires permanent physical changes to the antenna and cannot be used to electronically modify or control the antenna's performance. A microstrip antenna is generally designed for dominant mode of operation. In the next higher mode, the radiation efficiency and impedance pattern deteriorate. Since a patch is a high Q resonant structure, dual band operation requires stacking of radiating elements, such that the structure no longer remains planar (Pozar, 1995). The bottom patch may be fed by coaxial probe or microstrip feed line, or by aperture coupling. The impedance bandwidth of the probe coupled rectangular microstrip antennas can be effectively enhanced by optimal positioning of feed and choice of aspect ratio, the bandwidth achieved may still be inadequate for many applications. The aim of the present work is to present and demonstrate a method for design of a matching network for microstrip antenna, using GAs. By utilizing a GA, a dual band antenna is designed. As we will show this improves the performance of the antenna in both the bands.

BACKGROUND TECHNIQUES

Before describing the specific details of the optimization of microstrip antenna, some relevant Soft Computing concepts are reviewed below.

Genetic Agorithms (GAs)

Genetic Algorithm (GA) optimizers are robust, stochastic search methods modeled on the principles and concepts of natural selection and evolution (Haupt & Haupt, 1998). A block diagram of a simple GA optimizer is presented in Figure 2. In GAs a set of populations of potential solutions is caused to evolve towards a global optimal solution. A gene is the basic element of GA and a chromosome is an array of genes, see Table 1. Each parameter is encoded as a gene. The number of genes in a chromosome depends on the number of parameters to be optimized in the process.

In any typical GA optimizer an initial population is created with a predetermined number of randomly created parameter strings, also called chromosomes. Each of these chromosomes represents an individual. The set of individuals forms the current generation. A fitness value is associated with each chromosome. Choice of the fitness function totally depends on the nature of the problem. The performance requirements of the GA lead to the existence of three phases in

Table 1. Binary encoding of chromosomes

Chromosome A	10111010
Chromosome B	11100101

a typical GA optimization. Three phases in GA optimization process are (1) generation of initial population (2) reproduction and (3) generation replacement. Each individual in the generation is assigned a fitness value by evaluating the fitness function for them. In the reproduction phase, a new generation is formed from the current generation. In this process, pairs of individuals are selected from the population to act as parents. The selection may be based on the fitness function. Crossover and mutation are performed on the parent chromosomes, and a population of children is produced. In the crossover process a node is selected randomly in each pair of parent chromosomes (shown in Figure 3). Then two parts of the chromosomes are exchanged to form two new chromosomes. In the mutation process a bit is randomly selected in a chromosome and the value is changed (in binary GA a '0' will become '1' and vice versa). Then a new generation is formed with these children. The selection, crossover and mutation operations are repeated until enough children have been generated to fill the new generation. In some GA implementations this scheme is modified slightly. Selection is used to fill the new generation and then crossover and mutation are applied to the individuals in the new generation through random pairings.

Genetic algorithms work slower than most direct search methods, but examine much more of the solution space. GA optimizers are particularly effective when the goal is to find an approximate global maximum in a near-optimal manner for a function.

Choice of Fitness Function in GA

The fitness function can be chosen in different forms for different applications. Some of them are discussed here:

- If the antenna is to be matched at a single frequency, the fitness function may be the return loss Γ which is to be minimized.
- For multifrequency antenna, the fitness function may be the mean value of the return loss over the entire range of frequencies.
- The desired radiation pattern can be introduced in the optimization procedure. In such a case the fitness function is the difference value $|\Delta_t|$ between a specified pattern and the calculated value for a given angle.
- Both the return loss and the pattern can be optimized together and an objective function F can be defined as:

Figure 3. Single point crossover

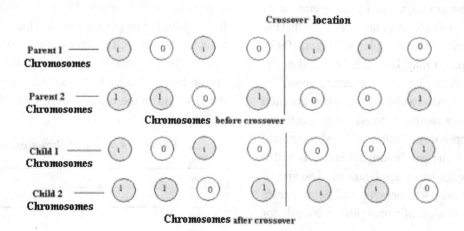

96

$$F = a_1 |\Gamma_t| + a_2 |\Delta_t| \tag{1}$$

where a_1 and a_2 are the weights.

CASE STUDY APPLICATION

Design of a Matching Network for Microstrip Antenna

Compared to other antennas such as dipoles, slots, and waveguide horns, the traditional microstrip patch element has a 2:1 Voltage Standing Wave Ratio(VSWR) bandwidth of only a fraction of a percent to 1-2%. It is required that the bandwidth increase be obtained without sacrificing the radiation characteristics and losing as little of the 'real estate' as possible. For these applications, impedance bandwidth of the microstrip antenna can be improved with a separate matching network without altering the antenna element itself. This can be done conveniently in microstrip form using a coplanar matching network or with an offboard network. However, we preferred the off-board approach for the obvious advantage of savings in real estate. Here GAs are applied to design the matching network for a microstrip antenna. The GA is used to find optimized values of characteristic impedance for those transformers that will give the best possible matching. The total design of the system includes the following steps:

- **Step 1:** Design and fabrication of the antenna.
- **Step 2:** Measurement of the input impedance of the antenna for a range of frequency around the design frequency.
- **Step 3:** Design and fabrication of the matching network.
- **Step 4:** The matching network and the antenna is integrated as a single module.

Step 1: Design and fabrication of the antenna

A suitable patch length is the first step in the design of the antenna. The patch length L for the TM_{10} mode is given by

$$L = c/(2f_r \sqrt{\varepsilon_r}) \tag{2}$$

where f_r is the resonant frequency of the patch and ε_r is the permittivity of the dielectric. In practice, the fields are not strictly confined to the region underneath the patch metallization only. A fraction of the fields lie outside the dimensions L X W of the patch. This fraction of field lines is called the fringing field, for which the field lines are shared between the substrate and air. The effect of the fringing field along the edges y=0 and y=W can be included through consideration of an effective dielectric constant ε_e and an additional line length Δl on either ends of the patch length. Considering all these effects the element length is obtained as

$$L = (c/2f_r \sqrt{\varepsilon_e}) - 2\Delta l \tag{3}$$

where ε_e is the effective permittivity given by

$$\varepsilon_e = (\varepsilon_r + 1)/2 + [(\varepsilon_r - 1)/2] (1 + 12h/W)^{-1/2} \tag{4}$$

and additional line length Δl is given by

$$\Delta l/h = 0.412[(\varepsilon_e + 0.3)(W/h + 0.264)]/ [(\varepsilon_e - 0.258)(W/h + 0.8)] \tag{5}$$

For a substrate of thickness h and relative permittivity ε_r, a practical width for a patch is

$$W = (c/2f_r)[(\varepsilon_r + 1)/2]^{-1/2} \tag{6}$$

Step 2: Measurement of the input impedance of the antenna for a range of frequency around the design frequency.

Figure 4. A two section quarter-wave transformer (l=λ/4 at the design frequency)

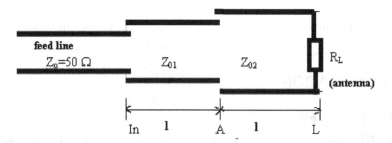

The input impedance of the patch antenna is measured with a vector network analyzer over a range of frequency around the design frequency of the antenna.

Step 3: Design and fabrication of the matching network

The Quarter-Wave Transformer

For a quarter-wavelength transmission line of characteristic impedance Z_0 and terminated with load impedance Z_L, the input impedance is given by

$$Z_{in} = Z_0^2 / Z_L \qquad (7)$$

where a quarter wave line acts as an impedance inverter. For a single section quarter wave transformer of fixed length l, the input reflection coefficient $|\Gamma_{in}|$ varies with frequency since $\beta l = \omega l / c$. At the design frequency ($\beta l = \pi/2$), $|\Gamma_{in}|=0$ indicating a perfect match. It is the frequency sensitivity of l/λ that degrades the standing wave ratio (SWR) at the band edges. Very low values of SWR over a wide frequency range can be achieved with a properly designed multisection quarter wave transformer. For a single section of quarter wave transformer, the wave gets reflected at both load and input planes. At the design frequency, due to quarter wave spacing the load reflection arrives at the input plane 180^0 out of phase with the input reflection and these two reflected waves cancels each other forcing

the input SWR to unity. At other frequencies, the round trip phase delay is not 180^0 and only partial cancellation takes place, which results in an input SWR greater than unity. Figure 4 shows two quarter wave line sections with characteristic impedance Z_{01} and Z_{02}. The Z_{02} line causes the impedance at plane A to be Z_{02}^2/R_L and the Z_{01} line transforms this impedance to Z_{01}^2/Z_A.

By properly choosing Z_{01} and Z_{02}, Z_A can be adjusted to be equal to the characteristic impedance of the feed line, resulting in perfect matching and an input SWR of unity (Collin, 1966). At other than the design frequency, the center line spacing differs slightly from the $\lambda/4$ value, which results in partial cancellation of two identical reflections. As a result, its input SWR at the band edges differs from unity.

The matching network is designed using microstrip lines with different characteristic impedances. Accordingly GA has been applied to determine the dimensions of the matching network that provides best or almost best impedance matching.

Parameters for Optimization

The matching network consists of a multisection quarter wave transformer with different characteristic impedance values. The characteristic impedance of each section is considered as a gene (a parameter for the optimization) and all the genes together form a chromosome, shown in Figure 5. Each gene is binary encoded with 9 bits.

Figure 5. Chromosome structure for the multisection quarter wave transformer

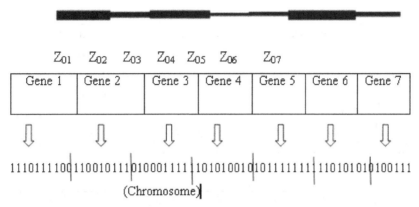

Z_{On} : Characteristic impedance of the nth section

There are total 7 genes (parameters) in a chromosome since it is a 7-section quarter-wave transformer. Thus the total length of one chromosome is 63 bits. A number of binary encoded chromosomes are randomly generated to form an initial population. Two chromosomes are randomly selected and crossover is performed on them depending on the probability of crossover (which is also randomly generated). This procedure is repeated a number of times and mutation is performed on them on the basis of a randomly chosen probability of mutation. From this population, a number of the best chromosomes are chosen depending on their fitness function. The probability of crossover is often in the range of 0.65-0.80. Here it is chosen as 0.7. Mutation consists of changing an element's value at random, often with a constant probability. The probability of mutation ideally varies between 0.001 and 0.01. Here it is chosen as 0.002.

Fitness Function

The fitness function is given by

$$\sum_f T = \sum_f (Z_{in}^{(f)} - Z_0)/(Z_{in}^{(f)} + Z_0)$$

Here $\sum T$ is the sum of reflection coefficients over the entire frequency band evaluated at closely spaced intervals. $Z_{in}^{(f)}$ is the input impedance of the multisection transformer at frequency f and Z_0 is the characteristic impedance of the line. The higher the fitness, the more likely it is the chromosome will be selected for the new generation.

The widths of the microstrip lines having characteristics impedances obtained from step 3 are then found using standard software and the network is etched on a separate substrate.

The characteristic impedances of different sections, as obtained from the simulation program and the corresponding widths are given in Table 2.

Step 4: The matching network and the antenna patch is integrated as a single module.

The matching network consisting of seven quarter wave transformers in microstrip form is etched on a substrate placed immediately below a common ground plane with connection to the antenna being made through a via as shown in Figure 6.

The GA based optimization was applied to the impedance data of a rectangular patch antenna (f_R=9.75 GHz) and a fractional bandwidth as high as 11.8% was obtained for maximum tolerable VSWR 2:1 with the matching network (Raychowdhury, Gupta & Bhattacharjee, 2000). Figure 7 shows the refection coefficient plot for the single

Table 2. Width and Characteristic Impedance of different sections of the multisection quarter wave transformer

	Width of different sections (mm) of the matching network	Characteristic Impedance Z_0 (Ω)
Section1	1 mm	81
Section2	1.5 mm	66
Section3	5 mm	29.52
Section4	2.5 mm	48.53
Section5	1.5 mm	66
Section6	2 mm	55.9
Section7	1 mm	81

(Length of each section–5 mm)

Figure 6. Structure of the antenna and the matching network (a) Front view (b) Back view

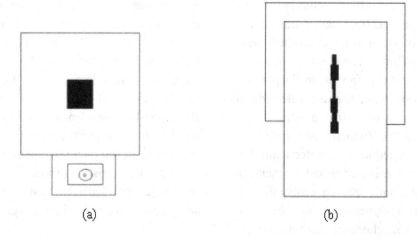

(a)   (b)

band patch antenna. This amount of bandwidth is obtained with this simple structure. Table 3 show the antenna and feed network parameters.

The results for the reflection coefficient are presented in Figure 7.

The same concept can be applied for dual band matching of the antenna. The fundamental design philosophy is to operate the same patch at a higher order mode, corresponding to a different resonant frequency efficiently. Normally this is not possible since the antenna radiates efficiently only for the dominant mode and for the higher order modes there is considerable loss due to impedance mismatch with the feed. This problem

is overcome with the aid of a dual band matching network, designed by using GA. Sufficient number of matching sections are designed to have a length equal to one quarter of a wavelength at the higher resonant frequency and the patch is designed at lower operating frequency. Again the characteristic impedance of each section is obtained by treating its binary encoded version as a gene and all such genes being combined to form a chromosome and finally the best chromosome being selected through genetic operations and 'Survival of Fittest' strategy. The fitness function employed is the average reflection coefficient at the antenna input summed over both frequency

Table 3. Antenna and Feed network parameters

Antenna substrate dielectric constant	2.4
Antenna substrate thickness	0.305cm
Matching network substrate dielectric constant	2.4
Matching network substrate thickness	0.254 cm
Matching network design frequency	9.75 GHz

Figure 7. Reflection Coefficient versus frequency plot for a rectangular-patch antenna

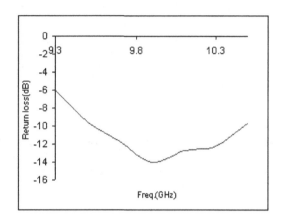

bands. This method may be useful in many cases like a mobile telephone antenna operating at two different allotted frequency bands or in satellite transceivers.

RESULTS AND DISCUSSIONS

Figures 8(a) & (b) show the measured reflection coefficient plot for the antenna at the two different frequency bands. Figures 9(a) & (b) show the measured radiation pattern for the antenna at the two frequency bands. These plots indicate that a good amount of matching has been obtained in both the bands without deteriorating the radiation patterns. The VSWR 1.8 at 7.08 GHz and 1.199 at 10.16 GHz.

The significance of this work is that it is superior to other dual band techniques such as when stacking of antenna elements is used.

Stacking of antenna elements reduces radiation efficiency due to aperture blockage or increases aerodynamic drag. The present design ensures impedance matching without any degradation of radiation pattern; as can be seen from Figure 8. Cross polarized radiation is also very low in both the frequency bands, the cross polar discrimination is -11 dB in the C band and too small to be measured in X band. Also since the matching network will be inside the aerodynamic body, it does not produce aerodynamic drag.

FUTURE RESEARCH DIRECTIONS

Genetic algorithm can be applied to other feed techniques of microstrip antenna for improving bandwidth. Aperture coupled microstrip antennas are broadband in nature. The feed line is electro-magnetically coupled to the antenna elements, so

Figure 8. (a) VSWR plot in C band (VSWR 1.8 at 7.08 GHz) (b) VSWR plot in X band (VSWR 1.199 at 10.16 GHz)

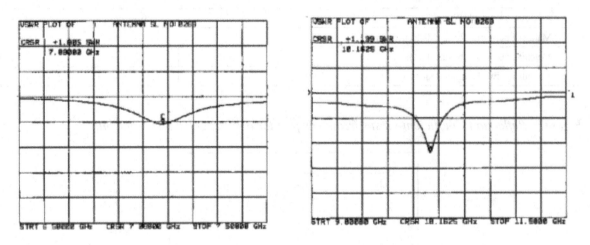

Figure 9(a) Radiation pattern in X band (measured at 10.18 GHz) (b) Radiation pattern in C band (measured at 7 GHz)

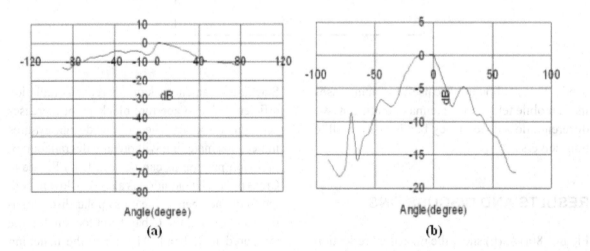

(a)   (b)

problems such as large probe reactance or wide microstrip line, which are critical at microwave frequencies, are avoided. Concepts of genetic algorithm can be applied to study the effect of aperture dimensions and stub length on the VSWR bandwidth of a simple microstrip patch antenna. The dual band antenna may be found extensive areas of possible application in communication systems and radars, where there is a need for dual frequency operation with polarization diversity.

The structure of the antenna can be modified to realize different polarization characteristics at the two frequency bands. In the work reported here only the impedance bandwidths of the antenna have been optimized. However the same technique can be applied for axial ratio bandwidth optimization. A Genetic algorithm can be developed to optimize both the impedance pattern and axial ratio. A rigorous study can be carried out on the effects of probability of crossover and probability of mutation. In addition there are a range of other techniques which may be applied in order to improve the performance. For example modified versions of the genetic algorithm approach could be applied to improve the bandwidth in each individual band.

CONCLUSION

In this chapter we presented Genetic Algorithm approach to the design of single as well as dual band antennas. Some of the main points can be summarized as follows:

- A matching network for microstrip antenna is designed using microstrip lines.
- The matching network consists of a multisection quarter wave transformer, having different characteristic impedance values.
- Genetic algorithms have been applied to determine the dimensions of the matching network that provides best or almost best impedance matching.
- The same technique is used for single and dual band impedance matching.

REFERENCES

Collin, R. E. (1966). Foundations for Microwave Engineering. New York: McGraw-Hill Book Co.

Delabie, C., Villegas, M., & Picon, O. (1997). Creation of new shapes for resonant microstrip structures by means of a genetic algorithm. *Electronics Letters*, *33*, 1509–1510. doi:10.1049/el:19971017

Deschamps, G. A. (1953). Microstrip Microwave Antennas. In *The Third Symposium on The USAF Antenna Research and Development Program* (pp. 18-22), University of Illinois, Monticello, Illinois.

Goldberg, D. E. (1989). Genetic Algorithms in Search, Optimization and Machine Learning. Boston, MA: Addison-Wesley Longman Publishing Co. Inc.

Grieg, D. D., & Englemann, H. F. (1952). Microstrip –A New Transmission Technique for the Kilomegacycle Range. *Proceedings of The IRE*, *40*(12), 1644–1650. doi:10.1109/JRPROC.1952.274144

Haupt, R. L., & Haupt, S. E. (1998). Practical genetic Algorithm. New York: John Wiley & Sons.

Johnson, J. M., & Samii, Y. R. (1997). Genetic Algorithms In Engineering Electromagnetics. *IEEE Magazine on Antennas and Propagation*, *39*, 7–25. doi:10.1109/74.632992

Karaboga, D., Güney, K., Sagiroglu, S., & Erler, M. (1999). Neural Computation Of Resonant Frequency Of Electrically Thin And Thick Rectangular Microstrip Antennas. *Microwaves, Antennas and Propagation. IEEE Proceedings*, *146*(2), 155–159.

Kerr, J. L. (1977). Other Microstrip Antenna Applications. In *Proc. 1977 Antenna Applications Symp.*, Univ. Illinois.

Namkung, J., Hines, E. L., Green, R. J., & Leeson, M. S. (2007). Probe-fed microstrip antenna feed point optimisation using genetic algorithms and the method of moments. *Microwave and Optical Technology Letters, 49*(2), 325-329. Pattnaik, S. S., Panda, D. C., & Devi, S. (2002). Input Impedance Of Rectangular Microstrip Patch Antenna Using Artificial Neural Networks. *Microwave and Optical Technology Letters, 32*(5), 381–383.

Popovic, B. D., Dragovic, M. B., & Djordjevic, A. R. (1982). Analysis and synthesis of wire antennas. New York: Research studies Press.

Pozar, D. M., & Schaubert, D. H. (Eds.). (1995). Microstrip Antennas. New York: IEEE Press.

Raychowdhury, A., Gupta, B., & Bhattacharjee, R. (2000). Bandwidth improvement of microstrip antennas through a genetic-algorithm based design of feed network. *Microwave and Optical Technology Letters, 27*, 273–275. doi:10.1002/1098-2760(20001120)27:4<273::AID-MOP17>3.0.CO;2-8

Samii, R., & Michielson, E. (1999). Electromagnetic Optimization by Genetic algorithm. Hoboken, NJ: John Wiley & Sons Inc.

Sharma, V., & Gupta, G. K. (2007). Using Artificial Neural Network to Model Microstrip Inset Fed Rectangular Patch Antenna. In *Microwave and Millimeter Wave Technology, ICMMT International Conference* (pp. 1 - 2).

Sun, L., Hines, E. L., Mias, C., Green, R., & Udrea, D. (2005). Quarter-wave phase-compensating multidielectric lens design using genetic algorithms. *Microwave and Optical Technology Letters, 44*(2), 165–169. doi:10.1002/mop.20577

Wang, B. F., & Lo, Y. T. (1984). Microstrip Antennas For Dual Frequency Operation. *IEEE Transactions on Antennas and Propagation, 32*, 938–943. doi:10.1109/TAP.1984.1143459

ADDITIONAL READING

Altshuler, E. E. (1993). A Monopole Antenna Loaded With A Modified Folded Dipole. *IEEE Transactions on Antennas and Propagation, 41*, 871–876. doi:10.1109/8.237616

Balanis, C. (1982). Antenna Theory-Analysis and Design. New York: John Wiley & Sons Inc.

Carver, K. R., & Mink, J. W. (1981). Microwave Antenna Technology. *IEEE Transactions on Antennas and Propagation, 29*(1), 2–24. doi:10.1109/TAP.1981.1142523

Choo, H., Iiutani, A., Trintinalia, L. C., & Ling, H. (2000). Shape Optimization Of Broadband Microstrip Antennas Using Genetic Algorithm. *Electronics Letters, 36*, 2057–2058. doi:10.1049/el:20001452

Das, S., & Gupta, B. (1992). Tapering Of Microstrip Antenna Patches For Bandwidth Enhancement. In *Proc APSYM-CUSAT* (pp. 205-208).

Davis, L. (Ed.). (1991). Handbook of Genetic Algorithms. New York: Van Nosttand Reinhold.

Dawoud, M. M., & Nuruzzaman, M. (2000). Null Steering In Rectangular Planar Arrays By Amplitude Control Using Genetic Algorithms. *International Journal of Electronics, 87*(12), 1473–1484. doi:10.1080/002072100050192498

Garg, R., Bhartia, P., Bahl, I., & Ittipiboon (Eds.). (2000). *Microstrip Antenna Design Handbook.* Boston: ArtechHouse. Hall, P. S. Wood, C., & Garret, C. (1979). Wide Bandwidth Microstrip Antennas For Circuit Integration. *Electron Letters, 15*, 458-460.

Haupt, R. L. (1994). Thinned Arrays Using Genetic Algorithm. *IEEE Transactions on Antennas and Propagation, 42*, 993–999. doi:10.1109/8.299602

Iierscovici, N., Osorio, M. F., & Peixciro, C. (2001). Minimization of a Rectangular Patch Using Genetic Algorithms. In IEEE antennas & propagation international symposium, Boston, MA, USA.

James, J. R., Hall, P. S., & Wood, C. (1981). Microstrip antennas: Theory & Design. London: Peter Perengrinus Ltd.

Linden, D. S., & Altshuler, E. E. (1996). Automating Wire Antenna Design Using Genetic Algorithm. *Microwave Journal, 39*, 74–86.

Marcano, D., & Duran, F. (2000). Synthesis Of Antenna Arrays Using Genetic Algorithms. *IEEE Antenna and Propagation Magazine, 42*(3), 12–20. doi:10.1109/74.848944

Mukherjee, P., & Gupta, B. (2002). Genetic Algorithm Based Optimization For Impedance Bandwidth Of Microstrip Patch Antenna. *Indian Journal Of Physics, 76B*(6), 727–730.

Mukherjee, P., Gupta, B., & Bhattacharjee, R. (2003). Dual Band Coplanar Microstrip Antenna With Polarization Diversity. *Journal of Electromagnetic Waves and Applications, 17*(9), 1323–1330. doi:10.1163/156939303322520098

Muscat, A. F., & Parini, C. G. (2000). Design Of Novel Microstrip Antenna Structures Using Knowledge Intensive CAD. In *Millenium Conference on Antennas & Propagation*, Davos, Switzerland.

Poddar, D. R., Chatterjee, J. S., & Chowdhury, S. K. (1983). On Some Broadband Microstrip Resonators. *IEEE Transactions on Antennas and Propagation, 31*, 193–194. doi:10.1109/TAP.1983.1142999

Pues, H. F., & Van de Capelle, A. R. (1989). An Impedance Matching Technique For Increasing The Bandwidth Of Microstrip Antennas. *IEEE Transactions on Antennas and Propagation, 37*, 1345–1354. doi:10.1109/8.43553

Rawlins, G. H. E. (Ed.). (1991). Foundations of Genetic Algorithm. San Mateo, CA: Morgan Kaufmann.

Rodriguez, J. A., Ares, F., Moreno, E., & Franceschetti, G. (2000). Genetic Algorithm Procedure For Linear Array Failure Correction. *Electronics Letters, 36*(3), 196–197. doi:10.1049/el:20000236

Shimizu, M. (1994). Determining The Excitation Coefficients Of An Array Using Genetic Algorithm. In IEEE Antenna and Propagat. So. Int. Symp. (pp. 530-533).

Tennant, A., Dawoud, M. M., & Anderson, A. P. (1994). Array Pattern Nulling By Element Position Perturbations Using A Genetic Algorithm. *Electronics Letters, 30*(3), 174–176. doi:10.1049/el:19940139

Vicente-Lozano, M., & Ares-Pena, F. (1999). Antenna Array Pattern Synthesis In The Presence Of Near-Zone Scatterers. Three-dimensional Case. In *29ᵗʰ European Microwave Conference 99. Incorporating MIOP'99* (pp. 138-141).

Yeo, B. K., & Lu, Y. (1999). Mutual Coupling Compensation For Circular Arrays Using Genetic Algorithm. *Annual Review of Progress in Applied Computational Electromagnetics, 1*, 365–370.

Chapter 8

Motor Vehicle Improvement Preference Ranking:
A PROMETHEE and Trigonometric Differential Evolution Analysis of their Chemical Emissions

Malcolm J. Beynon
Cardiff University, UK

Peter Wells
Cardiff University, UK

ABSTRACT

The central theme of this chapter is a preference ranking analysis of a group of motor vehicles based on their chemical emissions. Beyond the initial ranking of the motor vehicles, operationalised using the multi-criteria decision making technique PROMETHEE, further analysis is given on how the manufacturers of a motor vehicle could improve its preference rank position, based on reducing it current levels of chemical emissions. The rank improvement analysis, is defined a constrained optimisation problem, solved here using Trigonometric Differential Evolution. Further, an identification of a prescribed order to these chemical emissions reductions is then identified, offering practical findings to motor vehicle manufacturers when considering their position in a competitive market. The employment of Trigonometric Differential Evolution along with PROMETHEE in this chapter demonstrates a clear example of soft-computing in a practical problem.

INTRODUCTION

The motor vehicle has provided mobility and individual freedom for millions of people; however, it also embodies the dilemma of contemporary industrialisation in the environmental costs of automobility (Zachariadis *et al.*, 2001), with the environmental impact of vehicle emissions (Karlsson, 2004). Vehicle manufacturers have invested considerable research and development resources to create new combustion control technologies (to reconcile toxic and climate change emissions criteria including, carbon monoxide and hydrocarbons).

DOI: 10.4018/978-1-61520-893-7.ch008

Historically, consumers purchasing ranking preferences have not included the environmental performance of a vehicle (Prothero, 1994), but more recently environmental issues have become more prominent in consumer choice (Noblet *et al.,* 2006). Ranking systems are well established with respect to other associated consumer choice criteria, which often use toxic emissions per vehicle in their criteria (Walton *et al.,* 2004). Manufacturers are aware consumer interest has grown over recent years, importantly, the ranking systems intermediate between consumers and the vehicle manufacturers. Typical of the interests of government in terms of vehicle environmental performance and consumer choice are the views expressed in ABC Online (2004),

For those of us with an interest in all aspects of a vehicle's performance you can now check up closely on its environmental performance, and establish and weigh appropriately in your own mind about how you ought to go about combining your practical needs with your commitment to the environment.

The details presented in this chapter are in the spirit of these views, and we consider a number of issues arising from an initial preference ranking analysis of a small number of motor vehicles, based on certain criteria, namely exhaust chemical emissions levels. These issues include the motor vehicles' subsequent perceived preference rank improvement opportunities - identifying chemical emission levels to achieve this (defined as a constrained optimisation problem) and targeted rank improvement - the order in which a motor vehicle's chemical emissions levels should be changed to the previously identified levels to achieve improvement (defined through the iterative employment of ranking analyses).

The ranking findings are found using the multi-criteria decision making technique PROMETHEE (Preference Ranking Organization Method for Enrichment Evaluation, Brans *et al.,* 1986). The

PROMETHEE technique is employed since it is characterised by simplicity and clarity to a decision-maker (Brans *et al.,* 1986). PROMETHEE is also considered to have a transparent computational procedure (Georgopoulou *et al.,* 1998). Put simply, the ranking achieved using PROMETHEE produces a series of final 'net' values which are used to rank objects (vehicles), found from the aggregation of constituent 'criterion' values, which express the levels of preference of the objects over different individual criteria.

These characteristics of PROMETHEE have made it a versatile methodology in many areas of study, including in particular energy management (Pohekar and Ramachandran, 2004; Simon *et al.,* 2004). It is noted, there exist other ranking techniques, such as ELECTRE (Beccali *et al.,* 1998; Wang, and Triantaphyllou, 2008) and TOPSIS (Lai *et al.,* 1994; Abo-Sinna and Amer, 2005), offer alternative approaches to the ranking problem considered here, and could potentially be employed instead of PROMETHEE in the analysis in this chapter.

Beyond the initial preference ranking findings using PROMETHEE, the preference rank improvement opportunities consider the changes to a motor vehicle's chemical emissions levels to improve its preference rank position, and require the solution to a constrained optimisation problem, solved using the evolutionary computation algorithm, Trigonometric Differential Evolution - TDE (Fan and Lampinen, 2003). The evolutionary computation work (using TDE), originally termed the PROMETHEE based uncertainty analysis in Hyde *et al.* (2003) and Hyde and Maier (2006), here utilises the minimisation of the Euclidean distance measure (and concomitant constraints). Moreover, it identifies the minimum changes necessary to the chemical emissions levels of a considered low preference ranked motor vehicle that improves its preference rank position to that of a comparatively higher preference ranked motor vehicle. Evolutionary computing, in the form of genetic algorithms, has been used previously in the form of rank aggregation on the world wide web (Beg and Ahmad, 2003).

The targeted rank improvement analysis performs multiple PROMETHEE iterations, using results from the TDE based preference rank improvement opportunity findings, to order the changes to the considered chemical emissions levels of a motor vehicle. This ordering, using certain 'small changes' values to the different chemical emissions, is of practical use to motor vehicle manufactures in that, for instance, it identifies where to start first in terms of making changes to the chemical emissions levels of a motor vehicle in order to improve its preference 'marginally', but the most in this marginal sense, relative to a considered comparative motor vehicle.

The intention of this chapter is to demonstrate one of the main constituents of soft computing, namely evolutionary computing (Bodenhofer *et al.*, 2007; Nikravesh, 2008). Regularly associated with the identification of optimisation strategies, evolutionary computing can be incorporated with more traditional techniques, such as the ranking technique PROMETHEE, to achieve practical results beyond those normally found with the technique. Indeed, the inclusion of soft computing (TDE) and numerical processing (PROMETHEE) closely aligns the details of the chapter with the area of computational intelligence (Dote and Ovaska, 2001).

BACKGROUND

The background presented in this chapter, covers the two main techniques employed in the described motor vehicle preference rank based analysis, namely PROMETHEE and Trigonometric Differential Evolution.

PROMETHEE

PROMETHEE (**P**reference **R**anking **O**rganization **METH**od for **E**nrichment **E**valuation) was introduced in Brans *et al.* (1984, 1986) to preference rank a set of decision alternatives, based on their values over a number of different criteria. Put simply, a ranking of alternatives is established based on the accumulative preference comparisons of pairs of alternatives' values over the different criteria (using generalized preference functions).

More formally, to express the preference structure of alternatives and to withdraw the scaling effects of the different K criteria considered (c_1, ..., c_K), with PROMETHEE, generalized criterion preference functions are defined, $P_k(\cdot, \cdot)$ ($k = 1, ..., K$). Each is a function of the difference between criterion values of pairs of alternatives (from $a_1, ..., a_N$), where $P_k(a_i, a_j) \in [0, 1]$ confers the directed intensity of the preference of alternative a_i over a_j, with respect to a single criterion c_k. The often exposed limiting qualitative interpretations to the $P_k(a_i, a_j)$ values are (from Brans *et al.*, 1986);

$P_k(a_i, a_j) = 0 \Leftrightarrow a_i$ is not better than a_j with respect to criterion c_k,

$P_k(a_i, a_j) = 1 \Leftrightarrow a_i$ is 'strictly' better than a_j with respect to criterion c_k.

This qualitative interpretation given previously highlights that at least one of the values, $P_k(a_i, a_j)$ and $P_k(a_j, a_i)$ will be zero, depending on whether a_i or a_j is the more preferred between them. Expressing the $P_k(a_i, a_j)$ by;

$$P_k(a_i, a_j) = \begin{cases} \mathrm{H}(d) & a_i - a_j > 0, \\ 0 & a_i - a_j \leq 0, \end{cases}$$

where $a_i - a_j > 0$ and $a_i - a_j \leq 0$ refer to whether a_i or a_j is the more preferred on that criterion (taking into account the direction of preferment of the criterion values), and $d = v(a_i) - v(a_j)$ is the specific difference between the criterion values of a_i and a_j. The extant research studies have worked on the utilization of six types of generalized preference functions for H(d). Their names,

Figure 1. (Brans et al., 1986)

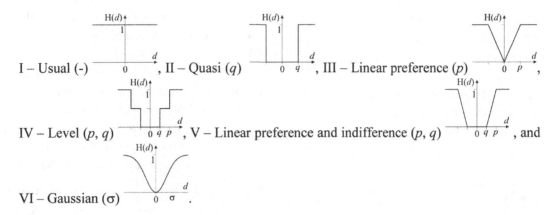

labels (also required parameters) and graphical representations are given as shown in Figure 1.

The graphical representations shown for the generalized preference functions highlight an important point, namely that some of them are continuous (III, V and VI) and the others not continuous (I, II and IV), with respect to the $P_k(a_i, a_j)$ value over the $v(a_i) - v(a_j)$ domain. The non-continuous feature means that small changes to criteria values may mean a dramatic change in the associated preference function values (see later).

The augmentation of the numerical preference values throughout the operation of PROMETHEE is described through the notion of flows. A *criterion flow* $\varphi_k(a_i)$ value for an alternative a_i from a criterion c_k can be defined by;

$$\varphi_k(a_i) = \sum_{a_j \in A} \{P_k(a_i, a_j) - P_k(a_j, a_i)\},$$

where A is the set of N alternatives, $a_1, \ldots, a_N$, considered, it follows $-(N-1) \le \varphi_k(a_i) \le N-1$ and $\sum_{a_i \in A} \varphi_k(a_i) = 0$ (the bounds are due to not normalizing by $(N-1)$ in each case). In words, a criterion flow represents the preference of an alternative over the other $(N-1)$ alternatives, with respect to a single criterion. A subsequent *net flow* $\varphi(a_i)$ value is defined by;

$$\varphi(a_i) = \sum_{k=1}^{K} w_k \varphi_k(a_i),$$

where w_k, $k = 1, \ldots, K$ denote the relative importance of the criterion c_k (the criteria importance weights). The conditions, $-(N-1) \le \varphi(a_i) \le N-1$ and $\sum_{a_i \in A} \varphi(a_i) = 0$, similarly hold for the net flow values (when w_k are normalized so they sum to one). The magnitudes of the net flow values subsequently exposit the relevant rank order of the N alternatives considered. The larger an alternative's net flow value, the higher its rank position.

Uncertainty Analysis – Trigonometric Differential Evolution

An associated issue recently considered is the uncertainty in the ranking results found using PROMETHEE (Hyde *et al.*, 2003), re-defined here as the consideration of the rank improvement of those alternatives ranked below the top rank alternative. Hyde and Maier (2006) investigated the possibility of changes to the criteria values of an alternative and the concomitant criteria importance weights, which reversed the ranks of two alternatives. Considering only changes to criteria values and concentrating on the rank improvement of an alternative a_{r_i}, it is necessary for a change of the r_1^{th} ranked alternative's criteria values so its net flow value is larger than or equal to that of the r_2^{th} ranked, $\varphi(a_{r_1}) \geq \varphi(a_{r_2})$.

The minimum changes necessary to achieve this are evaluated by minimizing some distance function (d_{r_1,r_2}) between the original and proposed criteria values of the considered alternative. Here the Euclidean distance measure d_{r_1,r_2} is employed, given by (from Hyde and Maier, 2006);

$$d_{r_1,r_2} = \sqrt{\sum_{k=1}^{K}\left(v_{r_1,k}^i - v_{r_1,k}^o\right)^2},$$

where $v_{r_1,k}^i$ and $v_{r_1,k}^o$ are the initial and optimized criteria values. The changes to the criteria values of the r_1^{th} ranked alternative are kept within known domains, given by $LL_{v,k} \leq v_{r_1,k}^o \leq UL_{v,k}$, where $[LL_{v,k}, UL_{v,k}]$ is the allowed interval domain of the kth criterion value. With the presence of non-continuous preference functions, the requirement for $\varphi(a_{r_1}) \geq \varphi(a_{r_2})$ may not be strong enough. That is, small changes in the proposed criteria values may cause disproportionate changes in the resultant net flow value (as in Hyde and Maier, 2006), so other alternatives may take the desired rank position (since $\sum_{a_i \in A} \varphi(a_i) = 0$). A stronger condition is simply that the new $\varphi(a_{r_1})$ value affords the desired rank position for the considered alternative.

The constrained optimisation problem formulated within the rank improvement analysis using PROMETHEE is solved here using Trigonometric Differential Evolution (TDE) (Storn and Price, 1997; Fan and Lampinen, 2003). The domain of TDE is the continuous space made up of the K criteria domains. For an alternative, its series of criteria values are represented as a point in this continuous space (parameter/target vector). In TDE, a population of NP parameter vectors, $\overrightarrow{y_i^G}$,

$i = 1, \ldots, NP$, is considered at each generation G of the progression to an optimum solution, measured through a defined objective function (OB - d_{r_1,r_2} in this chapter).

Starting with an initial population, TDE generates new parameter vectors by adding to a third member the difference between two other members (this change subject to a crossover operator). If the resulting vector yields a lower OB value then a predetermined population member it takes its place. More formally, a parameter vector $\overrightarrow{y_i^G}$ is *made up* of the values $y_{i,j}^G$, $j = 1, \ldots, K$ in the Gth generation. In the next generation the possible change in a value $y_{i,j}^G$ to a *mutant vector* value $z_{i,j}$ is given by;

$$z_{i,j} = y_{r_1,j}^G + F(y_{r_2,j}^G - y_{r_3,j}^G), \qquad (1)$$

where $r_1, r_2, r_3 \in [1, NP]$, are integer and mutually different, with $F > 0$ and controls the amplification of the differential variation. This construction of a trial vector $\overrightarrow{z_i}$ is elucidated in Figure 2, where an example two dimensional (X_1, X_2) case is presented.

In Figure 2, the effect of the 'vector' difference between $\overrightarrow{y_{r_2}^G}$ and $\overrightarrow{y_{r_3}^G}$ on the constructed mutant vector $\overrightarrow{z_i}$ from $\overrightarrow{y_{r_1}^G}$ is elucidated. A further operation takes into account the OB values associated with the three vectors $\overrightarrow{y_{r_1}^G}$, $\overrightarrow{y_{r_2}^G}$ and $\overrightarrow{y_{r_3}^G}$ chosen, used to perturb the trial vector according to the following formulation;

$$z_{i,j} = (y_{r_1,j}^G + y_{r_2,j}^G + y_{r_3,j}^G)/3 + (p_2 - p_1)(y_{r_1,j}^G - y_{r_2,j}^G)$$
$$+ (p_3 - p_2)(y_{r_2,j}^G - y_{r_3,j}^G) + (p_1 - p_3)(y_{r_3,j}^G - y_{r_1,j}^G),$$

where $p_1 = OB(\overrightarrow{y_{r_1}^G})/p_T$, $p_2 = OB(\overrightarrow{y_{r_2}^G})/p_T$ and $p_3 = OB(\overrightarrow{y_{r_3}^G})/p_T$ with $p_T = OB(\overrightarrow{y_{r_1}^G}) + OB(\overrightarrow{y_{r_2}^G}) + $

Figure 2. Example of an OB with contour lines and process for generation of the new vector $\vec{z}_i$

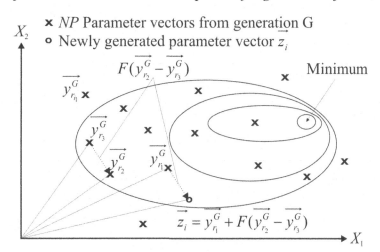

OB($\vec{y}_{r_3}^{G}$). This trigonometric operation, which is the development in TDE (Fan and Lampinen, 2003) from the original differential evolution (Storn and Price, 1997), on occasions, takes the place of the original mutation (see (1)) using a 'trigonometric mutation probability' parameter M_t, where a random value less than M_t implies the use of the trigonometric mutation. A crossover operator then combines the mutant vector $\vec{z}_i = [z_{i,1}, z_{i,2}, ..., z_{i,4n_C}]$ with the target (old) vector $\vec{y}_i^{G}$ $= [y_{1,j}^{G}, y_{2,j}^{G}, ..., y_{i,4n_C}^{G}]$ into a trial vector $\vec{y}_i^{T} = [y_{1,j}^{T}, y_{2,j}^{T}, ..., y_{i,4n_C}^{T}]$ according to;

$$y_{i,j}^{T} = \begin{cases} z_{i,j} & \text{If rand}(j) \leq CR, \\ y_{i,j}^{G} & \text{If rand}(j) > CR, \end{cases}$$

where rand$(j) \in [0, 1]$ is a random value and CR is the defined crossover constant. It follows, if OB($\vec{y}_i^{T}$)<OB($\vec{y}_i^{G}$) then replacement takes place and the progression continues. The progression of the construction of new generations continues until a satisfactory OB value is achieved. This may mean a required level has been attained or a zero decrease in the OB value is identified (over a number of generations).

MOTOR VEHICLE IMPROVEMENT PREFERENCE RANKING

The main thrust of this chapter is an investigation of the possibility of improving the preference of a motor vehicle amongst other motor vehicles based on pertinently changing the levels of certain chemical emissions associated with that motor vehicle.

This section is partitioned into four subsections, which succinctly describe; The considered data set of motor vehicles and their chemical emissions; Preference ranking, using PROMETHEE of the motor vehicles based on their chemical emissions; Preference rank improvement 'uncertainty' analysis of motor vehicles within the established rank orderings, using TDE; and Progressive targeted change of chemical emission levels for preference rank improvement of a motor vehicle or "what chemical emission to lessen to most greatly improve the preference of a motor vehicle".

Table 1. Emissions of selected chemical emissions (criteria) from the sample vehicles (g/km)

Manufacturer and model of car	CO2	CO	HCO	NOx
CC4 - Citroen C4	193	0.814	0.068	0.017
FCS - Ford Focus 2004½ Model Year Onwards	222	0.698	0.056	0.058
FMN - Ford Mondeo Pre-2004½ Model Year	218	0.120	0.070	0.050
RMG - Renault New Megane Scenic	205	0.424	0.079	0.034
AVN - Toyota Avensis	221	0.350	0.050	0.020
RV4 - Toyota RAV4	224	0.310	0.050	0.010
BTL - Volkswagen Beetle	228	0.390	0.036	0.024
SHN - Volkswagen Sharan	264	0.775	0.088	0.066
Mean	221.9	0.485	0.062	0.035
Standard deviation	19.21	0.233	0.016	0.019

Motor Vehicle Chemical Emissions Data Set

The motor vehicles considered in this analysis represent a range of choices available to a typical family buyer, where the vehicle chosen should have a petrol engine, of a nominal 2.0 litre capacity, and an automatic gearbox. Furthermore, there is an assumption that the basic engineering choices for vehicle size and configuration have been made (including vehicle weight). The analysis excludes cars with diesel engines, on the grounds that the use of such cars is prevalent only in Europe rather than the US or Japan. There are further health-effects issues associated with diesel engines, notably with particulate matter emissions (Reed *et al.*, 2004; Sydbom *et al.*, 2001), and these could be incorporated into the methodology demonstrated here. Equally, the use of automatic transmissions is relatively rare in Europe compared with the US and Japan, but this configuration was chosen because it would have a broader relevance to other markets. The chemical emissions (criteria) considered in this chapter were CO_2, CO, HCO and NOx.

The emissions figures used are those obtained under the official EU Type Approval test cycle and are published on the UK Vehicle Certification Agency website (VCA, 2004). Motivation for their utilisation comes from (Hummel *et al.*, 2000), which includes these chemical emission criteria for reduction due to concern about the effects of the traffic pollution to the citizens' health, associated with the ERLIVE (European Reference Laboratory on Incineration and Vehicle Emissions)-Project. Further research studies that have utilised these emission criteria include (Martin *et al.*, 1999; Mierlo *et al.*, 2003; 2004). Within these criteria there are identified engineering compensatory effects including that higher fuel efficiency (lower CO_2) tends to be associated with higher combustion temperatures, which in turn results in higher NOx emissions. The eight cars and their chemical emissions levels are presented in Table 1 (including vehicle abbreviations defined), and reflect a typical range of choice available, given our criteria, acknowledging the ongoing fragmentation in the market.

The vehicles chosen here all comply with the so-called Euro IV limit values for toxic emissions (SMMT, 2004), though actual CO_2 emissions are not regulated as such in the European Union currently they will be by 2012, and will be in most other leading markets (ICCT, 2007).

Table 2. Criterion and net flow values for preference of the eight motor vehicles

Vehicle	$\varphi_{CO_2}(\cdot)$	$\varphi_{CO}(\cdot)$	$\varphi_{HCO}(\cdot)$	$\varphi_{NOx}(\cdot)$	$\varphi(\cdot)$	Rank
CC4	4.620	−4.453	−1.282	2.947	0.458	4
FCS	−0.066	−3.294	1.389	−4.019	−1.497	7
FMN	0.375	4.660	−1.684	−2.854	0.124	6
RMG	2.535	1.188	−3.430	0.359	0.163	5
AVN	0.364	2.011	2.500	2.605	1.788	3
RV4	−0.273	2.422	2.500	3.770	2.105	1
BTL	−0.754	1.589	4.894	2.092	1.955	2
SHN	−6.473	−4.123	−4.886	−4.900	−5.096	8

Under European law (as in the US) the official CO_2 emission figure for a new vehicle has to be displayed alongside the price information, with the intention it becomes a key decision factor for any consumer. More importantly, the various consumer information websites noted above, such as that provided by the US EPA, allow consumers to rank vehicles by environmental performance according to those within the same segment, or indeed to obtain individual rankings to create personal choice lists. In other words, all else being of indifference to the consumer, relative environmental performance can be the decisive factor. Also included in Table 1 are the mean and standard deviation values of the four chemical emissions (utilised later).

PROMETHEE Analyses of Motor Vehicle Chemical Emissions Data Set

The intention of the PROMETHEE method, described previously, is to identify a rank ordering of alternatives (of motor vehicles as in Table 1) based on their values over a number of associated criteria (chemical emissions CO_2, CO, HCO, NOx). This subsection reports a series of standard PROMETHEE analyses on the motor vehicle chemical emissions data set.

In this exposition of the application of PRO-METHEE in the motor vehicle preference problem the four criteria, chemical emissions CO_2, CO, HCO, NOx, are initially considered of equal importance ($w_k = 1/4$, $k = 1, ..., 4$) (see later for different levels of importance). The PROMETHEE method was then employed, with the criterion flow values ($\varphi_k(\cdot)$) found for the eight motor vehicles on each criterion, and then the subsequent net flow values ($\varphi(\cdot)$) evaluated (see the description of the PROMETHEE given previously), see Table 2.

The results in Table 2 identify a preference rank ordering of the eight motor vehicles, with the Toyota RAV4 (RV4 - $\varphi(RV4)$ = 2.105) and Volkswagen Sharan (SHN - $\varphi(SHN)$ = −5.096), top and bottom ranked, respectively. The criterion flow values ($\varphi_k(\cdot)$) elucidate the contribution of each criterion (chemical emissions) to the net flow value of a motor vehicle and their subsequent preference ranking. In the case of the top ranked RV4 vehicle, the evidence from the chemical emissions in decreasing order of contribution is, NOx ($\varphi_{NOx}(RV4)$ = 3.770), HCO (2.500), CO (2.422) and CO_2 (−0.273).

It is the net flow value based rank ordering (or ones like it) that the manufacturers are aware consumers could be viewing, or it is a ranking model of how they (consumers) have taken on board the chemical emissions details associated with the motor vehicles. Further, vehicle manufacturers are mindful of how they may improve their identified rank position.

Following on from this PROMETHEE analysis, with equal weight of importance of the different chemical emissions, the effects of different rank orderings of importance of these emissions is next considered. This sensitivity issue comes from differing perceptions of the relative importance of environmental pollutants and their effects (as well as issues such as fuel economy). Here, three rank orderings are considered, described with the chemical emissions presented in decreasing order of importance as;

i) CO2, HCO, NOx, CO *ii*) CO2, HCO = NOx, CO *iii*) CO2, NOx, HCO, CO

In each of the chemical emissions importance rankings given, the CO2 and CO chemical emissions are consistently considered most and least important. The CO is usually the product of inefficient combustion, in modern engines CO emissions are low and can be assigned the least importance. CO2 emissions are not themselves toxic, but are the focus of much policy concern for government, both from fuel consumption and global warming perspectives (OMB, 2004; Europa, 2007; Bandivadekar *et al.,* 2008). The difference is with respect to HCO and NOx, which are interchanged in their importance in the presented orderings, between being second and third, as well as being equal in importance. Broadly, HCO emissions are associated with carcinogens, whereas NOx emissions are associated with respiratory problems.

This knowledge on chemical emissions importance rankings needs to be quantified into a series of weight values, used in the subsequent PROMETHEE analysis. Weight elicitation is a well studied problem (Barron and Barrett, 1996), here we consider the rank order centroid (ROC) approach, given by $w_i = \left(1/n\right)\sum_{k=i}^{n}\left(1/k\right)$, n - number of criteria (Barron and Barrett, 1996; Edwards and Barron, 1994; Solymosi and Dombi,

1986). However, it must be remembered that these contrived weights are only surrogates to those the decision maker might identify (Barron and Barrett, 1996). Motivation for the utilisation of the ROC weights includes its employment in SMARTER (Edwards and Barron, 1994).

In the motor vehicle chemical emissions data set, with four chemical emissions criteria, the four ROC weight values are found to be; 0.521, 0.271, 0.149 and 0.603. Depending on the rank order of the chemical emissions, these four weights will be assigned to the chemical emissions appropriately (and aggregated in the case of having equal importance of chemical emissions criteria). For each identified chemical emissions importance rank order, a concomitant PROMETHEE analysis is undertaken, with the subsequent criterion and net flow values can be found, see Table 3.

The results in Table 3 report the net flow values and subsequent ranking of the eight motor vehicles when different levels of chemical emissions importance are known. The rankings in Table 3 show a level of difference with those in Table 2 where equal importance ranking of all chemical emissions presumed. Most noticeable is the identified constant top ranking of CC4 (Citroen C4) in Table 3, compared to RV4 top ranked in Table 2, now either second or third ranked. One reason for the improved ranking of the CC4 is its low CO2 emissions which are now very potent in its preference evidence since it is top ranked in importance (the most importance weight assigned to it).

Within the results reported in Tables 2 and 3, when different rank orders of importance of the chemical emissions are known, a level of rank reversal amongst the motor vehicles is noticed. The changes in rank order of the motor vehicles are amongst (between) the second to fifth placed vehicles. For example, with the Volkswagen Beetle (BTL), its rank position changes from second to fifth, depending on whether the CO2, HCO, NOx, CO or CO2, NOx, HCO, CO rank orders of chemical emissions importance are considered. Further

Table 3. Net flow values for performance of motor vehicles (different importance of chemical emissions)

Motor Vehicle	CO2, HCO, NOx, CO		CO2, HCO=NOx, CO		CO2, NOx, HCO, CO	
	$\varphi(\cdot)$	Rank	$\varphi(\cdot)$	Rank	$\varphi(\cdot)$	Rank
CC4	2.211	1	2.475	1	2.739	1
FCS	−0.450	7	−0.788	7	−1.126	7
FMN	−0.386	6	−0.459	6	−0.532	6
RMG	0.518	5	0.755	5	0.991	4
AVN	1.201	4	1.208	3	1.215	3
RV4	1.236	3	1.315	2	1.395	2
BTL	1.337	2	1.162	4	0.987	5
SHN	−5.667	8	−5.668	8	−5.669	8

rank reversals are shown on the Toyota Avensis (AVN) and RV4 vehicles across these different ranks of chemical emissions importance. These findings still leave an open mind to the sensitivity of PROMETHEE analyses when there are changes to the importance of chemical emissions. In this case there were considerable changes, but only in the rank importance of the two chemical emissions, HCO and NOx.

Preference Rank Improvement 'Uncertainty' Based Analysis of Motor Vehicles Using TDE

This subsection presents an 'uncertainty' based analysis of established preference rank orderings of the motor vehicles (based on their chemical emissions). Moreover, the pertinence here, with respect to the motor vehicle preference problem, is the ability to identify the minimum changes necessary to the chemical emissions of a motor vehicle that would infer an improvement to its previously established preference rank order. Within this problem it is expected that changes to the chemical emissions are downwards when attempting to improve a motor vehicles preference rank order.

Throughout this subsection the Volkswagen Sharan (SHN) is considered in terms of potential changes to its chemical emissions and potential preference rank improvement. With its identified bottom preference rank order position in each PROMETHEE analysis, there is the possibility to improve (attain) its rank position to any of the seven higher rank positions. Here, the minimum changes necessary to its chemical emissions, to achieve only the sixth, fourth and second rank positions are considered (i.e. moving up the different quartiles), subject to minimising the d_{r_1,r_2} measure using TDE described previously (distance between original SHN chemical emissions and its proposed emissions), see Table 4, considering when there is equal importance between the chemical emissions.

The results in Table 4 identify the proposed new chemical emissions of the Volkswagen Sharan, which collectively offer the minimum d_{r_1,r_2} from its original chemical emission values, subject to equating its net flow value with that of the motor vehicle it is being compared with (sixth, fourth and second placed motor vehicles - shown in each column). The bracketed values are the respective $\Delta v_{r_1,k}$, indicating their relative change from the original chemical emission values. The net flow values associated with the Volkswagen Sharan ($\varphi(SHN)$) and the comparison motor vehicles are given to nine decimal spaces to show their almost

Table 4. Changes in chemical emissions of Volkswagen Sharan (SHN) to improve its preference rank position from eighth to sixth, fourth and second positions

Criteria	Changes to Volkswagen Sharan (SHN)		
	6th (FMN)	4th (CC4)	2nd (BTL)
CO_2 (264.0 g/km)	232.6 (−11.9%)	231.6 (−12.3%)	228.7 (−13.4%)
CO (0.775 g/km)	0.436 (−43.7%)	0.424 (−45.3%)	0.180 (−76.7%)
HCO (0.088 g/km)	0.060 (−32.2%)	0.057 (−35.4%)	0.048 (−45.5%)
NOx (0.066 g/km)	0.031 (−53.1%)	0.028 (−57.2%)	0.025 (−62.0%)
φ(SHN)	−0.473891002	−0.149623395	1.064894336
$\varphi(\cdot)$	−0.473891002	−0.149623397	1.064894336
d_{r_1, r_2}	3.341 (3.951)	3.560 (4.650)	4.536 (4.628)

equal values in each case, while the φ(SHN) values are slightly larger, as desired to achieve the necessary improved preference rank position.

The bottom row of this table gives two distance values for each analysis, the first is the distance of the proposed new chemical emission values to the original set associated with the Volkswagen Sharan, the second (in brackets) is the distance of the original set of chemical emission values of the Volkswagen Sharan to those of the comparison vehicle. In all of the analyses, the first distance value is less than the second value, and this indicates in each case that the changes described are less than what would have been necessary to exactly match the chemical emission values of the compared to vehicle. This highlights the subtlety of this analysis, where using PROMETHEE (with equal criteria importance), these are the chemical emission values the manufacturer of the Volkswagen Sharan should strive towards on order to improve their rank position (through engineering modifications etc.).

Considering the actual results for the equating of the SHN with sixth placed Ford Mondeo Pre-2004½ Model Year (FMN), the CO_2 emissions would need to be reduced from its original 264g/

km down to 232.6g/km, a −11.9% change in its level. Similar changes of −43.7%, −32.2% and −53.1% are necessary to the CO, HCO and NOx emissions, so the preference ranking of SHN is equal to that of FMN. To improve to the fourth rank position, a further small reduction in their emission levels is required. The largest of these is a −57.2% change in NOx. Considerably more reduction in the SHN's chemical emissions is necessary to achieve the second rank position, the largest in this case a −76.7% change in CO.

To further exposit the relationship between the considered Volkswagen Sharan and the other vehicles, two graphical presentations are next reported, for all four PROMETHEE analyses undertaken (with the different importance rankings of the chemical; emissions - see Tables 2 and 3). The first considers the changes in the net flow values associated with all the motor vehicles, subject to the changes of the criteria values of the bottom ranked SHN (since the sum of the net flow values associated with all the motor vehicles must equal zero), see Figure 3.

In Figure 3, each graph shows the effects of improving the rank position of the bottom ranked SHN vehicle to the respective sixth, fourth and

Figure 3. Changes in net flow values of motor vehicles when changing preference rank position of SHN from eighth to sixth, fourth and second positions (with different orderings of chemical emissions importance)

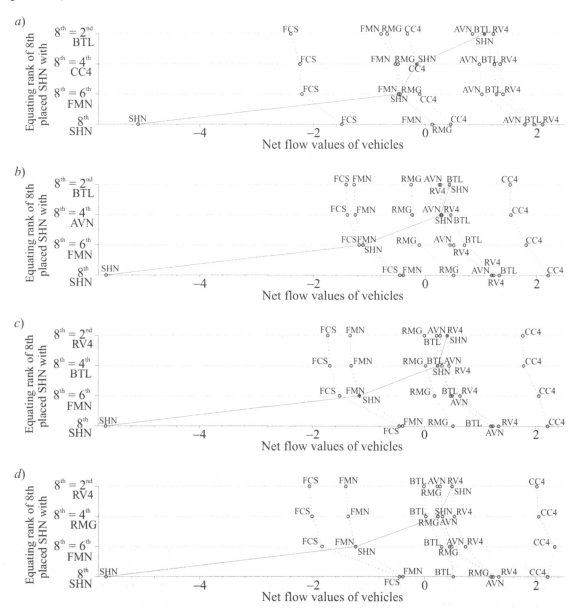

second rank positions. The four graphs relate separately to when equal importance of chemical emissions (Figure 3a), decreasing importance; CO2, HCO, NOx, CO (Figure 3b), CO2, HCO = NOx, CO (Figure 3c) and CO2, NOx, HCO, CO (Figure 3d), are utilised. Describing the graphs, along the y-axis is the rank position of the vehicle

the bottom placed SHN vehicle was compared to (to equate net flow values), with the x-axis showing the scale of the net flow values (each circle represents a net flow value). At the base of the graph is the original net flow values associated with each vehicle (see Table 2). Successive horizontal lines of circles report the changes in the net flow

Figure 4. Progressive changes of the chemical emissions of the SHN vehicle to improve its preference rank position from eighth to sixth, fourth and second positions (with different orderings of chemical emissions importance)

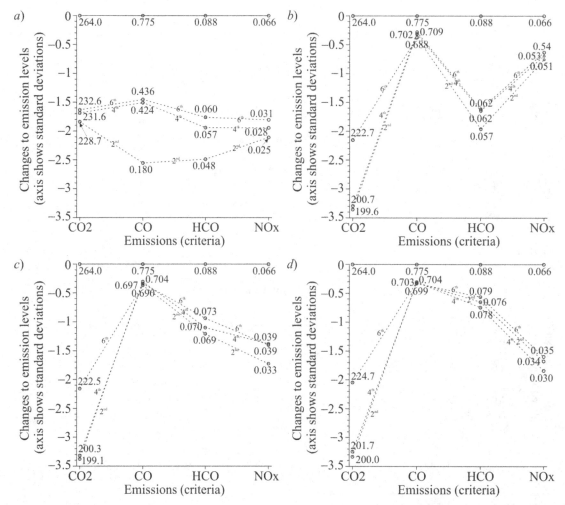

values of the eight vehicles when comparing SHN with the other higher ranked vehicles.

In each graph there is a dramatic change in the net flow value associated with the SHN vehicle to equal that of the higher sixth placed FMN vehicle, with lesser changes apparent to move up to the fourth (CC4) and second (BTL) rank positions. There is a near uniform decrease in the net flow values associated with the other vehicles to accommodate the improved preference of SHN. This is interpreted as showing that the improvement of SHN is at the expense of all the

other vehicles and not just one or two (including the vehicle it is particularly compared with) and is directly related to the constraint that the sum of the net flow values is zero.

The next consideration is on the progressive changes required in the chemical emissions levels of the SHN vehicle to achieve each improved preference rank position, see Figure 4.

In the graphs reported in Figure 4, the *x*-axis lists the four chemical emissions used to discern the preference ranking of the eight motor vehicles (using PROMETHEE). The *y*-axis identifies the level of change in a particular chemical emission, from its original value (using a general standard deviation scale). Moreover, the tops of the graphs identify the original chemical emissions levels of the SHN motor vehicle (see Table 1). The series of points connected by dashed lines are the changes of the respective chemical emissions levels (given in Tables 2 and 3), to improve to a higher rank position (sixth, fourth and second). Each vertical set of circles described the progressive change of a particular level of chemical emission.

A discussion of these graphs starts with Figure 4a, where there existed equal weight importance of the four criteria. For the improvement of the SHN vehicle from eighth place to sixth and fourth there is little difference in the levels of change to the CO_2, CO, HCO and NOx emissions (in terms of the number of standard deviations away from their original values, between -1.5 and -1.9 standard deviations). To achieve the second place position (from eighth) there is a noticeable change (further reduction) necessary to the CO and HCO emission levels (compared to that for CO_2 and NOx). When a rank order of importance of the chemical emissions is made (Figures 4b, c and d), there are relatively similar looking sets of graphs, each noticeably different to that in Figure 4a (equal importance of chemical emissions).

In Figures 4b, c and d, the most and least chemical emissions changes are necessary to the CO_2 and CO emissions, respectively, which are consistently the most and least importance ranked (see previously). When the importance of the two middle ranked chemical emissions, HCO and NOx, are altered some noticeable change is identified. This is most noticeable for the HCO emission between when it is ranked above NOx (Figures 4b), compared to when they are equal ranked (Figures 4c) or NOx is ranked above it (Figures 4d). That is, only on this occasion do its chemical emissions levels need to be reduced by between 1.6 and 1.9 standard deviations when ranked above NOx, whereas by not more than 1.3 standard deviations on the other two occasions.

Progressive Targeted Change of Chemical Emissions Levels for Preference Rank Improvement of a Motor Vehicle

A 'next stage' understanding of the notion of preference rank improvement is the consideration of the practical problem of the order of the progressive proposed changes to the different chemical emissions (criteria) to achieve the necessary preference rank improvement results.

At the technical level, the ability to identify where to start the preference improvement, in terms of decreasing certain chemical emissions levels is next described. The first requirement is the level of incremental change intended for each chemical emission that will be considered. Beyond this, the iterative procedure requires the repetitive employment of PROMETHEE to identify which of a chemical emission's change (decrease) would most greatly improve the net flow value of the considered motor vehicle relative to the comparison motor vehicle (to greatly improve and at each incremental stage). The quantity of change possible with a chemical emission is constrained by the level of improvement identified by the associated 'uncertainty' analysis (see the previous sub-section). This is because, the 'uncertainty' analysis identified the minimum 'collective' levels of changes to the chemical emissions, which would be required to achieve the desired preference rank improvement of a particular motor vehicle.

This progressive targeted preference rank improvement approach is demonstrated on the SHN (Volkswagen Sharan) motor vehicle, from the overall preference ranking results in Tables 2 and 3. Only the intent for the SHN to achieve the second place preference rank position is considered, from its original eighth place identified. Using the established minimum changes necessary to the chemical emissions to achieve second place (see Table 4 and Figure 4), change to all chemical emissions is required. Throughout this investigation, potential incremental decreases of

Figure 5. Order of prescribed 1% changes to chemical emissions of SHN to achieve the second place preference rank order position (with different orderings of chemical emissions importance)

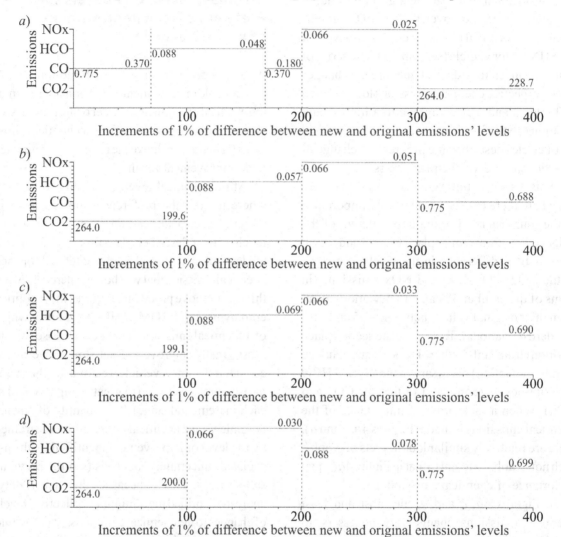

1% of the difference between on any of the original chemical emissions of the SHN and identified optimum levels are considered (a generalisation that understandably would be criterion specific). So, for example, in the case of when equal importance of the criteria was considered, the incremental changes would be; for CO2 - (264 – 228.7)/100 = 0.353g/km, CO - 0.00595g/km, HCO - 0.0004g/km and NOx - 0.00041g/km. The progressive targeted preference rank improvement results for the SHN, in terms of the order in which changes

to its chemical emissions should be undertook are shown in Figure 5.

In each of the graphs in Figure 5, the points shown from left to right across the graph each represent proposed 1% (or final remainder) changes to the respective chemical emission identified on the left axis. The four graphs relate separately to when equal importance of chemical emissions (Figure 5a), decreasing importance; CO2, HCO, NOx, CO (Figure 5b), CO2, HCO = NOx, CO

(Figure 5c) and CO2, NOx, HCO, CO (Figure 5d), are utilised.

When equal importance of the chemical emissions is considered (Figure 5a), inspection shows the first target should be to the decrease the CO level down from 0.775g/km to 0.370g/km. This is followed by the full decrease of HCO from 0.088g/km down to 0.048g/km, followed by the remaining decrease of the CO down to 0.180g/km. Finally the NOx and CO2 emissions should be reduced down to their identified levels in turn. The interesting feature of these results is the two stage decrease of the CO emissions, indicating this approach could identify a piecemeal approach to how to attain the identified reduced levels of chemical emissions to achieve second place preference rank position. With respect to the results in the other graphs (Figure 5b to 5d), the order of changes to the chemical emissions follows consistently the order of importance defined on them (in the case of Figure 5c with equal importance of HCO and NOx, HCO is undertaken before NOx).

The defined reason for these prescribed orders being identified was to make as much gain in the relative improvement of the SHN motor vehicle (at each iteration), in terms of its net flow value, to ultimately achieve second place in the preference rankings of the eight motor vehicles. That is, each identified decrease of 1% (or remainder) on a chemical emissions level is dependent on the fact that it optimally decreases the difference in the net flow values of the SHN motor vehicle and the second placed motor vehicle. The progressive decreases in this difference based on the changes of the chemical emissions (exposited in Figure 4), are shown in Figure 6.

In Figure 6, the net flow values of the eight motor vehicles are shown as the proposed changes to the chemical emissions levels of the SHN motor vehicle are imposed. The order of the emissions changes, as described in Figure 5, was based on the greatest movement of the net flow value for the SHN motor vehicle (φ(SHN)) to that of the second ranked. The movement of the φ(SHN)

increases, in contrast to the other net flow values which decrease (to maintain their sum equals zero, see description of PROMETHEE). The level of increase is more pronounced at the start before levelling off, exposing the chemical emissions on with which most effect will take place (progressively).

FUTURE TRENDS

The future trends associated with this chapter are in both application and technical terms. For the motor vehicle industry the findings here can be replicated (by a manufacturer) to rank any series of motor vehicles in which they are interested, either their own or competitors, using a range of chemical emissions (and other criteria). This could be taken further through comparison with the costings associated with the engineering required to reduce the individual chemical emissions, then these could be the main constituent of the distance measure based uncertainty analysis (using TDE).

At the technical level, the PROMETHEE technique, like many other techniques, has been developed, in a soft computing environment, namely using fuzzy set theory (Zadeh, 1965), with the introduction of fuzzy PROMETHEE (Fernández-Castro and Jiménez, 2005; Goumas and Lygerou, 2000). The fuzzy PROMETHEE technique enables the ranking of alternatives which are described by criteria values for which a level of imprecision surrounds them. How the rank improvement and targeted rank improvement analyses can be worked when using fuzzy PROMETHEE would be of interest for future research.

CONCLUSION

Motivation for this chapter originates from the continuous debate on the effect of motor vehicle chemical emissions on the environment - a concern identified by governments, manufacturers and

Figure 6. Progressive changes of the net flow values of the SHN and other motor vehicles, during the progressive changes of the SHN's chemical emissions levels (with different orderings of chemical emissions importance)

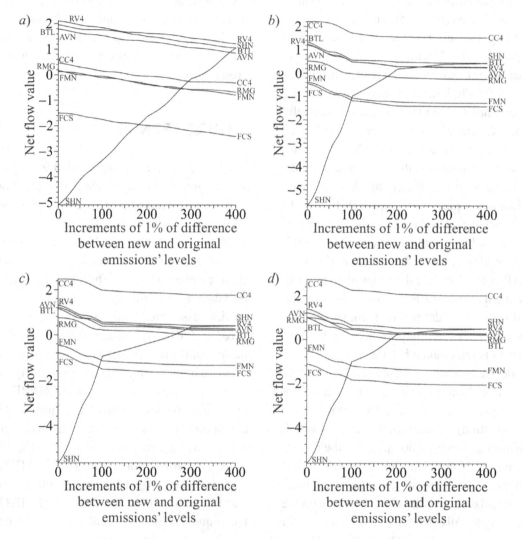

consumers alike. Through the employment of a traditional ranking technique like PROMETHEE and the evolutionary computing approach Trigonometric Differential Evolution to constrained optimisation, a number of findings are attempted.

The utilisation of the PROMETHEE method of multi-criteria decision making (MCDM) here attempts to model a preference rank preference of eight 'similar' motor vehicles based on their levels of chemical emissions of carbon dioxide (CO_2), carbon monoxide (CO), hydrocarbons

(HCO) and nitrous oxide (NOx), considered as criteria. The rank orders identified are of interest to manufacturers since it offers evidence on the preference of a motor vehicle they produce, and how it is perceived when compared with other vehicles. Four analyses are undertaken, different in terms of the importance placed on the different chemical emissions. The variation in results over the four different rank orderings of the chemical emissions suggests further understanding is necessary.

Further investigation in this chapter takes the form of an uncertainty based analysis of the different PROMETHEE results. Within this motor vehicle preference problem the investigation takes the important role of identifying the lean (minimum) changes necessary to the emission levels of a motor vehicle to improve its identified rank position. The practicalities of the results are with respect to a manufacturer and the constraints (changes in emission levels) on the engineering performance modifications required to be made. The operation to identify the lean (minimum) changes needed is defined a constrained optimisation problem, solved here using Trigonometric Differential Evolution.

The graphical results presented in the chapter offer two types of findings. Firstly, those which are practical (Figures 4 and 5), and contain information that could be acted upon to improve the rank position of a particular motor vehicle (Figure 4) and where to start first in making changes to criteria values to achieve rank improvement (Figure 5). Secondly, those which are technical, and simply confirm the impact of the more practical graphs (Figures 3 and 6), showing changes in net flow values of motor vehicles.

In a more applied problem context, the graphs showing the progressive changes in the criteria values that necessitate the rank improvement of the bottom ranked motor vehicle clearly elucidate the collected changes required across the different chemical emissions. Their information content is crucial to a manufacturer to guide the necessary engineering modifications required in the process of engine calibration because it allows insight into the optimum combination of improvements in the various variables. An important development necessary is the acknowledgement that the presented changes cannot be considered on the criteria chemical emissions. The effects of the relationships between changing emissions levels needs to be taken into account, either as part of the optimisation process or in the re-calibration stage post optimisation.

REFERENCES

Abo-Sinna, M. A., & Amer, A. H. (2005). Extensions of TOPSIS for multiobjective large-scale nonlinear programming problems. *Applied Mathematics and Computation, 162*, 243–256. doi:10.1016/j.amc.2003.12.087

Bandivadekar, A., Cheah, L., Evans, C., Groode, T., Heywood, J., & Kasseris, E. (2008). Reducing the fuel use and greenhouse gas emissions of the US vehicle fleet. *Energy Policy, 36*(7), 2754–2760. doi:10.1016/j.enpol.2008.03.029

Barron, F. H., & Barrett, B. E. (1996). Decision Quality Using Ranked Attribute Weights. *Management Science, 42*(11), 1515–1523. doi:10.1287/mnsc.42.11.1515

Beccali, M., Cellura, M., & Ardente, D. (1998). Decision Making in Energy Planning: The ELECTRE Multicriteria Analysis Approach Compare to a Fuzzy-Sets methodology. *Energy Conversion and Management, 39*(16-18), 1869–1881. doi:10.1016/S0196-8904(98)00053-3

Beg, M. M. S., & Ahmad, N. (2003). Soft Computing Techniques for Rank Aggregation on the World Wide Web. *World Wide Web: Internet and Web Information Systems, 6*, 5–22.

Bodenhofer, U., Hüllermeier, E., Klawonn, F., & Kruse, R. (2007). Special issue on soft computing for information mining. *Soft Computing, 11*, 397–399. doi:10.1007/s00500-006-0105-3

Brans, J. P., Mareschal, B., & Vincke, P. H. (1984). PROMETHEE: A New Family of Outranking Methods in MCDM. In *International Federation of Operational Research Studies (IFORS 84)*, North Holland (pp. 470-490).

Brans, J. P., Vincke, P. H., & Mareschal, B. (1986). How to select and how to rank projects: the PROMETHEE method. *European Journal of Operational Research, 24*, 228–238. doi:10.1016/0377-2217(86)90044-5

Dote, Y., & Ovaska, S. J. (2001). Industrial Applications of Soft Computing: A Review. *Proceedings of the IEEE, 89*(9), 1243–1265. doi:10.1109/5.949483

Edwards, W., & Barron, F. H. (1994). SMARTS and SMARTER: Improved simple methods for multiattribute utility measurement. *Organizational Behavior and Human Decision Processes, 60*, 306–325. doi:10.1006/obhd.1994.1087

Europa. (2007). *Commission proposal to limit the CO2 emissions from cars to help fight climate change, reduce fuel costs, and increase European competitiveness.* Retrieved June 19, 2008, from http://europa.eu/rapid/pressReleasesAction.do?reference=IP/07/1965

Fan, H.-Y., & Lampinen, J. (2003). A Trigonometric Mutation Operation to Differential Evolution. *Journal of Global Optimization, 27*, 105–129. doi:10.1023/A:1024653025686

Fernández-Castro, A. S., & Jiménez, M. (2005). PROMETHEE: an extension through fuzzy mathematical programming. *The Journal of the Operational Research Society, 56*, 119–122. doi:10.1057/palgrave.jors.2601828

Georgopoulou, E., Sarafidis, Y., & Diakoulaki, D. (1998). Design and implementation of a group DSS for sustaining renewable energies exploitation. *European Journal of Operational Research, 109*, 483–500. doi:10.1016/S0377-2217(98)00072-1

Goumas, M., & Lygerou, V. (2000). An extension of the PROMETHEE method for decision making in fuzzy environment: Ranking of alternative energy exploitation projects. *European Journal of Operational Research, 123*, 606–613. doi:10.1016/S0377-2217(99)00093-4

Hummel, R., Krasenbrink, A., & De Santi, G. (2000). Characterisation of Vehicle Emissions. *Journal of Aerosol Science, 31*(Supplement 1), S246–S247. doi:10.1016/S0021-8502(00)90255-6

Hyde, K. M., & Maier, H. R. (2006). Distance-based and stochastic uncertainty analysis for multicriteria decision analysis in Excel using Visual Basic for Applications. *Environmental Modelling & Software, 21*(12), 1695–1710. doi:10.1016/j.envsoft.2005.08.004

Hyde, K. M., Maier, H. R., & Colby, C. B. (2003). Incorporating Uncertainty in the PROMETHEE MCDA Method. *Journal of Multi-Criteria Decisions Analysis, 12*, 245–259. doi:10.1002/mcda.361

ICCT. (2007). Passenger vehicle greenhouse gas and fuel economy standards: a global update. Sacramento, CA: International Council on Clean Transportation.

Karlsson, H. L. (2004). Ammonia, nitrous oxide and hydrogen cyanide emissions from five passenger vehicles. *The Science of the Total Environment, 335*, 125–132. doi:10.1016/j.scitotenv.2004.04.061

Lai, Y. J., Liu, T. Y., & Hwang, C. L. (1994). TOPSIS for MODM. *European Journal of Operational Research, 76*, 486–500. doi:10.1016/0377-2217(94)90282-8

Martin, N. J., St. Onge, B., & Waaub, P.-W. (1999). An integrated decision aid system for the development of Saint Charles river alluvial plain, Quebec, Canada. *International Journal of Environment and Pollution, 12*(2/3), 264–279.

Mierlo, J. V., Timmermans, J.-M., Maggetto, G., Bossche, P. V., Meyer, S., & Hecq, W. (2004). Environmental rating of vehicles with different alternative fuels and drive trains: a comparison of two approaches. *Transportation Research Part D, Transport and Environment, 9*, 387–399. doi:10.1016/j.trd.2004.08.005

Mierlo, J. V., Vereeken, L., Maggetto, G., Favrel, V., Meyer, S., & Hecq, W. (2003). How to define clean vehicles? Environmental impact rating of vehicles. *International Journal of Automotive Technology, 4*(2), 77–86.

Nikravesh, M. (2008). Soft Computing for Intelligent Reservoir Characterization and Decision Analysis. In M. Nikravesh et al. (Eds.), Forging the New Frontiers: Fuzzy Pioneers II. Berlin: Springer-Verlag.

Noblet, C. L., Tiesl, M. F., & Rubin, J. (2006). Factors affecting consumer assessment of eco-labelled vehicles. *Transportation Research Part D, Transport and Environment, 11*, 422–431. doi:10.1016/j.trd.2006.08.002

OMB. (2004). *Analytical statement in support of 2004 budget: transportation.* Retrieved December 30, 2004, from http://www.whitehouse.gov/omb/budget/fy2004/text/energy.html.

Online, A. B. C. (2004). *Website rates environmental performance of cars.* Retrieved July 12, 2004, from http://www.abc.net.au/newsitems/200408/s1169582.htm

Pohekar, S. D., & Ramachandran, M. (2004). Application of multi-criteria decision making to sustainable energy planning – A review. *Renewable & Sustainable Energy Reviews, 8*, 365–381. doi:10.1016/j.rser.2003.12.007

Prothero, A. (1994). Green marketing in the car industry. In P. Nieuwenhuis & P. Wells (Eds.), Motor Vehicles in the Environment: Principles and Practice. Chichester, UK: John Wiley.

Reed, M., Gigliotti, A., McDonald, J., Seagrave, J., Seilkop, J., & Manderly, J. (2004). Health effects of subchronic exposure to environmental levels of diesel exhaust. *Inhalation Toxicology, 16*(4), 177–193. doi:10.1080/08958370490277146

Simon, U., Brüggemann, R., & Pudenz, S. (2004). Aspects of Decision Support in Water Management - Example Berlin and Potsdam (Germany) I - Spatially Differentiated Evaluation. *Water Research, 38*, 1809–1816. doi:10.1016/j.watres.2003.12.037

SMMT. (2004). The 4th Annual Sustainability Report. London: Society of Motor Manufacturers and Traders.

Solymosi, T., & Dombi, J. (1986). A method for determining weights of criteria: The centralized weights. *European Journal of Operational Research, 26*, 35–41. doi:10.1016/0377-2217(86)90157-8

Storn, R., & Price, K. (1997). Differential Evolution - A Simple and Efficient Heuristic for Global Optimisation over Continuous Spaces. *Journal of Global Optimization, 11*, 341–359. doi:10.1023/A:1008202821328

Sydbom, A., Blomberg, A., Parnia, S., Stenfors, N., Sandstrom, T., & Dahlen, S.-E. (2001). Health effects of diesel exhaust emissions. *The European Respiratory Journal, 17*(4), 733–746. doi:10.1183/09031936.01.17407330

VCA. (2004). *Vehicle Certification Agency Car Fuel / CO2 data.* Retrieved from http://www.vca.gov.uk/carfueldata/index.shtm

Walton, D., Thomas, J. A., & Dravitzki, V. (2004). Commuters' concern for the environment and knowledge of the effects of vehicle emissions. *Transportation Research Part D, Transport and Environment, 9*, 335–340. doi:10.1016/j.trd.2004.04.001

Wang, X., & Triantaphyllou, E. (2008). Ranking irregularities when evaluating alternatives by using some ELECTRE methods. *Omega, 36*, 45–63. doi:10.1016/j.omega.2005.12.003

Zachariadis, T., Ntziachristos, L., & Samaras, Z. (2001). The effect of age and technological change on motor vehicle emissions. *Transportation Research Part D, Transport and Environment, 6*, 221–227. doi:10.1016/S1361-9209(00)00025-0

Zadeh, L. A. (1965). Fuzzy Sets. *Information and Control, 8*(3), 338–353. doi:10.1016/S0019-9958(65)90241-X

KEY TERMS AND DEFINITIONS

Alternative: Abstract or real objects, or actions, which can be chosen. Here, one of a number of objects/options considered for preference ranking, each described by values over a series of criteria.

Criterion: A feature or standard that alternatives are preferenced on, which has a known direction of improving preference.

Evolutionary Algorithm: An algorithm that incorporates mechanism inspired by biological evolution, including; reproduction, mutation, recombination, natural selection and survival of the fittest.

Flow Values: Within PROMETHEE, totals of preference function values on alternatives, including; criterion, outgoing, incoming and net.

Objective Function: A positive function of the difference between predictions and data estimates that are chosen so as to optimize the function or criterion.

Preference Function: A function to standardize (remove scale effects) the difference between two alternative's values over a single criterion.

PROMETHEE: The multi-criteria decision making technique **P**reference **R**anking **O**rganization **METH**od for **E**nrichment **E**valuation.

Ranking: An ordering of alternatives with respect to some preface.

Trigonometric Differential Evolution: The evolutionary algorithm **T**rigonometric **D**ifferential **E**volution (TDE), belongs to the class of evolution strategy optimizers. The central idea behind TDE-type algorithms is to add the weighted difference between two population vectors to a third vector within the optimisation process.

Chapter 9
A Soft Computing System for Modelling the Manufacture of Steel Components

Javier Sedano
University of Burgos, Spain

José Ramón Villar
University of Oviedo, Spain

Leticia Curiel
University of Burgos, Spain

Emilio Corchado
University of Burgos, Spain

Andrés Bustillo
University of Burgos, Spain

ABSTRACT

This chapter presents a soft computing system developed to optimize the laser milling manufacture of high value steel components, a relatively new and interesting industrial technique. This applied research presents a multidisciplinary study based on the application of unsupervised neural projection models in conjunction with identification systems, in order to find the optimal operating conditions in this industrial issue. Sensors on a laser milling centre capture the data used in this industrial case of study defined under the frame of a machine-tool that manufactures steel components for high value molds and dies. Then a detailed study of the laser milling manufacture of high value steel components is presented based mainly on the analysis of four features: angle error, depth error, surface roughness and material removal rate. The presented model is based on a two-phases application. The first phase uses an unsupervised neural projection model capable of determine if the data collected is informative enough. The second phase is focus on identifying a model for the laser-milling process based on low-order models such as Black Box ones. The whole system is capable of approximating the optimal form of the model. Finally, it is shown that the Box-Jenkins and Output Error algorithms, which calculate the function of a linear system based on its input and output variables, are the most appropriate models to control such indus-

DOI: 10.4018/978-1-61520-893-7.ch009

trial task for the case of the analysed steel tools. The model can be applied to laser milling optimization of other materials of industrial interest and also to other industrial multivariable processes like High Speed Milling or Laser Cladding.

INTRODUCTION

Soft computing represents a collection or set of computational techniques and intelligent systems principles in machine learning, computer science and some engineering disciplines, which investigate, simulate, and analyze very complex issues and phenomena in order to solve real-world problems. Laser Milling is nowadays a very interesting industrial task, which, in general, consists on the controlled evaporation of waste material due to its interaction with high-energy pulsed laser beams.

The operator of a conventional milling machine is aware at all times of the amount of waste material removed, but the same can not be said of a laser milling machine. In this case, the amount of vaporized material depends not only on laser pulse characteristics, but also on the composition of the material to be removed. Indeed, in industrial conditions, the input process variables that could be measured show a too complex relation between then to obtain a proper modelisation using analytical or empirical models. Then a soft computing model that could predict the exact amount of material that each laser pulse is able to remove would contribute to the industrial use and development of this new technology. In this case we are focus on laser milling of steel components. It is an especially interesting industrial process, due to the broad use of steel as base material for different kind of manufacture tools, like molds and dies. One of the applications of this technology to these industrial tools is the deep indelible engraving of serial numbers or barcodes for quality control and security reasons for automotive industry (Wendland et al., 2005). The soft computing model proposed in this paper is able to optimize the manufacturing process and to control laser milling to the level of accuracy

that is required for the manufacture of these deep indelible engravings. It has been developed using a combination of Soft computing models and it is applied here to a data set taken from micro-manufacturing laser milling of steel components.

Unsupervised connectionist models can be used as an initial phase or step before a model is established. They are used to analyze the internal structure of the data sets in order to establish that they are sufficiently informative. In the worst case, experiments have to be carried out again.

System identification is a field that refers to the set of techniques used to provide a mathematical model M for estimating the behaviour of a signal of a process for a certain period of time prediction interval (Ljung, 1999). In this study is applied after the use of connectionist models in order to identify the exact amount of material that each laser pulse is able to remove.

The rest of the chapter is organized as follows. Following the introduction, a two-phase process is described to identify the optimal conditions for the industrial laser milling of steel components. The case study that outlines the practical application of the model is then presented. Finally, some different modelling systems are applied and compared, in order to select the optimal model, before ending with some conclusions and future work.

AN INDUSTRIAL PROCESS FOR STEEL COMPONENTS MODELLING

Analyse of the Internal Structure of the Data Set

Cooperative Maximum-Likelihood Hebbian Learning (CMLHL) (Corchado & Fyfe, 2003; Corchado et al., 2003) is used in this research in order to analyze the internal structure of a data set describing an industrial task: a laser milling manufacture of steel components, to identify whether it is "sufficiently informative" by means of the identification of clusters or groups. In the worse case, the experiments have to be performed again in order to collect a proper and informative data set.

CMLHL is a Exploratory Projection Pursuit (EPP) method (Diaconis & Freedman, 1984; Freedman & Tukey, 1974; Corchado et al., 2004). In general, EPP provides a linear projection of a data set, but it projects the data onto a set of basic vectors which help reveal the most interesting data structures; interestingness is usually defined in terms of how far removed the distribution is from the Gaussian distribution (Seung et al., 1998).

One connectionist implementation is Max-imum-Likelihood Hebbian Learning (MLHL) (Corchado et al., 2004; Fyfe & Corchado, 2002). It identifies interestingness by maximising the probability of the residuals under specific prob-ability density functions that are non-Gaussian. An extended version is the CMLHL (Corchado et al., 2003) model, which is based on MLHL (Corchado et al., 2004; Fyfe & Corchado, 2002) but adds lateral connections (Corchado & Fyfe, 2003; Corchado et al., 2003) that have been derived from the Rectified Gaussian Distribution (Corchado et al., 2004). Considering an N-dimensional input vector (x), and an M-dimensional output vector (y), with w_{ij} being the weight (linking input j to output i), then CMLHL can be expressed (Corchado & Fyfe, 2003; Corchado et al., 2003) as:

1. Feed-forward step:

$$y_i = \sum_{j=1}^{N} W_{ij} x_j, \forall i \tag{1}$$

2. Lateral activation passing:

$$y_i(t+1) = \left[y_i(t) + \tau(b - Ay) \right]^+ \tag{2}$$

3. Feedback step:

$$e_j = x_j - \sum_{i=1}^{M} W_{ij} y_i, \forall j \tag{3}$$

4. Weight change:

$$\Delta W_{ij} = \eta . y_i . sign(e_j) \mid e_j \mid^{p-1} \tag{4}$$

Where: η is the learning rate, τ is the "strength" of the lateral connections, b the bias parameter, p a parameter related to the energy function (Corchado & Fyfe, 2003; Corchado et al., 2004; Fyfe & Corchado, 2002), and A a symmetric matrix used to modify the response to the data (Corchado et al., 2004). The effect of this matrix is based on the relation between the distances separating the output neurons.

System Identification and the Knowlegde Based Systems

System identification is a well known knowledge area that refers to the set of techniques used in obtaining a mathematical model M for estimating the behaviour of a signal of a process for a certain period of time prediction interval (Ljung, 1999) For such modeling task, a dataset of representative of the process input, perturbations, and output -or controlled-signals are given. The model M estab-lishes not only the structure or formulae but also is responsible for fitting its parameters $\theta = \hat{\theta}$. Given the characteristics of the real process, behaviour or signal to be modeled, the identification procedures establish the optimization and testing the model.

In the identification literature there has been a great deal of successful applications of system identification in different areas: control, robotics, forecasting, power systems, predictions, signal processing. Some examples are mentioned below to catch a glimpse of the wide influence of system identification. In (Jurado, 2004), SOFC energy plants and the distribution system modelling were afforded using ARX and BJ structures. In (Pacheco & Steffen, 2004), the modelling of a nonlinear mechanical system using nonlinear models and Volterra series is studied. A duffy ostrictive actuator and an electrostrictive actuator have been identified by means of the high order frequency response functions of the associated linear equations (Vazquez et al., 2004). The development of a fault detection model in Civil Engineering is detailed in (Liu et al., 2001). The identification of a delignification process (Chen & Billings, 1989), the modeling and prediction of machining errors (Fung et al., 2003), and the identification of a gas turbine power plant (Basso et al., 2002) are some examples of using nonlinear models with NARMAX structures.

The prediction of the heat transfer coefficient is analysed in (Mihir & Kishor, 2009), where a zero-order fuzzy model is compared with the prediction obtained with ANFIS. Also, several works using neural networks in practical identification applications can be found in the literature: the prediction of a machine operation conditions faults using ANFIS and pre-processing the data using nearest neighbours with the mutual information measure (Tran et al., 2009), the modelling of the termosyphon close loop cooling process (Fichera & Pagano, 2002), the prediction of the relationship between the fuel flow and the shaft speed dynamics of a gas turbine engine (Neophytos et al., 2002), the vitrations modelling in a magnetorheological damper (Xia, 2003) and the detection of the structural damage in PVC sandwich plates in the aeronautical and locomotion industry (Yam et al., 2003). In (Esen & Inalli, 2009) a vertical ground coupled heat pump system is modelled using artificial neural networks and back-propagation training method. Support vector machines have been satisfactorily applied in modelling the efficiency of a solar-air heating system (Esen et al., 2009). In (Venkatesh, 2004) some requisites for a robustness identification are analysed. Especifically, the prediction of a pulsed-

laser process conditions is solved by means of neural networks hybridised with Particle Swarm Optimization in (Ciurana et al., 2009).

Nowadays there are some computer tools helping in the development of models, but they require the users´ expertise in order to obtain good results. Some computer tools are standardised in the system identification community. Mat-lab suite from The Mathworks (MathWorks) is the best known computer tool, and the greater part of the published works makes use of it. The R project (The R_project) is an equivalent, lesser used computer tool. Also, LabView is a well known commercial software tool in system identification (Labview, 2004).

The Identification Criterion

The identification criterion evaluates which of the group of candidate models is best adapted to and which best describes the data sets collected in the experiment; i.e., given a model $M(\theta_*)$ its prediction error may be defined by equation (5); and a good model (Ljung, 1999) will be that which makes the best predictions, and which produces the smallest errors when compared against the observed data. In other words, for any given data group Z^t, the ideal model will calculate the prediction error $\varepsilon(t,\theta)$, equation (5), in such a way that for any one t=N, a particular $\hat{\theta}_N$ (estimated parametrical vector) is selected so that the prediction error $\varepsilon(t,\hat{\theta}_N)$ in t=1,2,3…N, is made as small as possible.

$$\varepsilon(t,\theta_*) = y(t) - \hat{y}(t \mid \theta_*) \tag{5}$$

The estimated parametrical vector $\hat{\theta}$ that minimizes the error, equation (8), is obtained from the minimization of the error function (6). This is obtained by applying the least-squares criterion for the linear regression, i.e., by applying the quadratic norm $\ell(\varepsilon) = \frac{1}{2}\varepsilon^2$, equation (7).

Table 1. Black-box model structures

Polynomials in (10)	Polynomials used in (10)	Name of model structure
$A(q^{-1}) = 1 + a_1(q^{-1}) + a_2(q^{-2}) + \cdots + a_{n_a}(q^{-n_a})$ $B(q^{-1}) = b_1(q^{-1}) + b_2(q^{-2}) + \cdots + b_{n_b}(q^{-n_b})$ $C(q^{-1}) = 1 + c_1(q^{-1}) + c_2(q^{-2}) + \cdots + c_{n_c}(q^{-n_c})$ $D(q^{-1}) = 1 + d_1(q^{-1}) + d_2(q^{-2}) + \cdots + d_{n_d}(q^{-n_d})$ $F(q^{-1}) = 1 + f_1(q^{-1}) + f_2(q^{-2}) + \cdots + f_{n_f}(q^{-n_f})$	B AB ABC AC BF BFCD	FIR ARX ARMAX ARMA OE BJ

$$V_N(\theta, Z^N) = \frac{1}{N} \sum_{t=1}^{N} \ell(\varepsilon_F(t, \theta)) \qquad (6)$$

$$V_N(\theta, Z^N) = \frac{1}{N} \sum_{t=1}^{N} \frac{1}{2} (y(t) - \hat{y}(t \mid \theta))^2 \qquad (7)$$

$$\hat{\theta} = \hat{\theta}_N(Z^N) = \arg \min_{\theta \in D_M} V_N(\theta, Z^N) \qquad (8)$$

The methodology of black-box structures has the advantage of only requiring very few explicit assumptions regarding the pattern to be identified, but that in turn makes it difficult to quantify the model that is obtained. The discrete linear models may be represented through the union between a deterministic and a stochastic part, equation (9); the term *e(t)* (white noise signal) includes the modelling errors and is associated with a series of random variables, of mean null value and variance λ.

$$y(t) = G(q^{-1})u(t) + H(q^{-1})e(t) \qquad (9)$$

The structure of a black-box model depends on the way in which the noise is modelled $H(q^{-1})$; thus, if this value is 1, then the OE (Output Error) model is applicable; whereas, if it is different from zero a great range of models may be applicable; one of the most common being the BJ (Box Jenkins) algorithm. This structure may be represented

in the form of a general model, where $B(q^{-1})$ is a polynomial of grade n_b, which can incorporate pure delay n_k in the inputs, and $A(q^{-1})$, $C(q^{-1})$, $D(q^{-1})$ and $F(q^{-1})$ are autoregressive polynomials ordered as n_a, n_c, n_d, n_f respectively, equation (10). Likewise, it is possible to use a predictor expression, for the on-step prediction ahead of the output $\hat{y}(t \mid \theta)$, equation (11),. In Table 1, the generalized polynomial expressions are presented, as well as those that represent the polynomials used in the case of each particular model.

$$A(q^{-1})y(t) = q^{-n_k} \frac{B(q^{-1})}{F(q^{-1})} u(t) + \frac{C(q^{-1})}{D(q^{-1})} e(t) \qquad (10)$$

$$\hat{y}(t \mid \theta) = \frac{D(q^{-1})B(q^{-1})}{C(q^{-1})F(q^{-1})} u(t) + \left[1 - \frac{D(q^{-1})A(q^{-1})}{C(q^{-1})} \right] y(t) \qquad (11)$$

Procedure for Modelling the Laser Milling Process. The identification procedure used to arrive at a parameterized model M, which will eventually be selected as the best from among those that modelled the laser milling characteristics on the basis of the variable measurements, is carried out in accordance with two fundamental patterns: a first pre-analytical and then an analytical stage that assists with the determination of the parameters in the identification process and the model estimation. The pre-analysis test is run to establish the identification techniques (Ljung, 1999; Nögaard et al., 2000; Söderström & Stoica, 1989; Nelles, 2001; Haber & Keviczky, 1999b; Haber & Keviczky, 1999a), the selection of the model structure and its order estimation (Stoica & Söderström, 1982; He & Asada, 1993) the identification criterion and search methods that minimize it and the specific parametrical selection for each type of model structure.

A second validation stage ensures that the selected model meets the necessary conditions for estimation and prediction. Three tests were performed to validate the model: residual analysis $\varepsilon(t, \hat{\theta}(t))$, by means of a correlation test between inputs, residuals and their combinations; final prediction error (FPE) estimate, as explained by Akaike (Akaike, 1969); and the graphical comparison between desired outputs and the outcome of the models through simulation one (or k) steps before.

MODELLING STEEL COMPONENTS: AN INDUSTRIAL TASK

This research is interested on the study and identification of the optimal conditions for laser milling of deep indelible engraving of serial numbers or barcodes on steel components using a commercial Nd:YAG laser with a pulse length of 10μs. Three parameters of the laser process can be controlled: laser power (u_1), laser milling speed (u_2) and laser pulse frequency (u_3). The laser is integrated in a laser milling centre (DMG Lasertec 40).

To simplify this industrial problem a test piece was designed and used in all of the laser milling experiments. It consisted on an inverted, truncated, pyramid profile that had to be laser milled on a flat metallic piece of steel. The truncated pyramid had angles of 135°, and a depth of 1 mm, but as the optimized parameters for the laser milling of steel were not known at that point in time, both

parameters showed errors, which are referred as angle error (y_1) and depth error (y_2). A third parameter to be considered was the surface roughness of the milled piece (y_3), measured on the flat surface of the truncated pyramid. A last parameter is the removal rate, that is the number of cubic millimeters of steel removed by the laser per minute (y_4). These four variables have to be optimized, because the industrial process required a precise geometrical shape, a good surface roughness of the piece and the shorter manufacturing time. We applied different modelling systems to achieve the optimal conditions of these four parameters.

The experimental design was performed on a Taguchi L25 with 3 input parameters and 5 levels, so as to include the entire range of laser milling settings that are controllable by the operator. Table 2 summarizes the input and output variables of the experiment which define the case of study. The experiment was performed on the test piece described above. After the laser milling, actual inverted pyramid depth, walls angle and surface roughness (y_3) of the bottom surface were measured using optical devices. Considering the whole time required for the manufacture of each sample and the actual volume of removed material the material removal rate (y_4) was also calculated. The measured walls angle and the pyramid depth were compared with the nominal values in the CAD model, thereby obtaining the two errors (y_1 and y_2). The test piece and the prototype were described in detail beforehand (Arias et al., 2007).

Application of the Two Phases of the Modelling System

The study has organized into two phases or steps.

- **Step 1:** Analysis of the internal structure of the data set based on the application of several unsupervised connectionist models.
- **Step 2:** Application of several identification models in order to find the one

Table 2. Variables, units and values used during the experiments. All values are common to this laser milling process. Output y(t), Input u(t)

Variable (Units)	Range
o Angle error of the test piece, $y_1(t)$	-1 to 1
o Depth error of the test piece, $y_2(t)$	-1 to 1
o Surface roughness of the test piece (µm), $y_3(t)$	0.8 to 15
o Material removal rate (mm³/min), $y_4(t)$	$0.32 - 4.38$
o Laser power in percent of the maximum power performed by the laser (%), $u_1(t)$.	20 to 100
o Laser milling speed (mm/s), $u_2(t)$.	200 to 800
o Laser pulse frequency (kHz), $u_3(t)$.	20 to 100

that best defines the dynamic of the laser milling process.

Step 1. Figure 1 shows the results obtained by means of CMLHL projections. This model is able to identify three different clusters or groups order mainly by power. Also each group is formed by three subgroups organized by frequency and speed. After studying each cluster it can be noted a second classification based on the speed and frequency as it is shown in Figure 1. The existence of such organized internal structure indicates that the data analysed is sufficiently informative.

Step 2. Modelling the laser milling process. Figure 2, shows the results of output $y_1(t)$, angle error and $y_4(t)$, material removal rate, respectively. Figure 3, shows the results of output $y_2(t)$, depth error and $y_3(t)$, surface roughness, respectively.

They show the graphic representations of the best results, for OE y BJ models, in relation to the polynomial order and the delay in the inputs; various delays for all inputs and various polynomial orders $[n_{b1}\ n_{b2}\ n_{b3}\ n_c\ n_d\ n_f\ n_{k1}\ n_{k2}\ n_{k3}]$ were considered to arrive at the highest degree of precision, in accordance with the structure of the models that have been used; see Table 1. In Figure 2, Figure

Figure 1. The first of two projections obtained by CMLHL

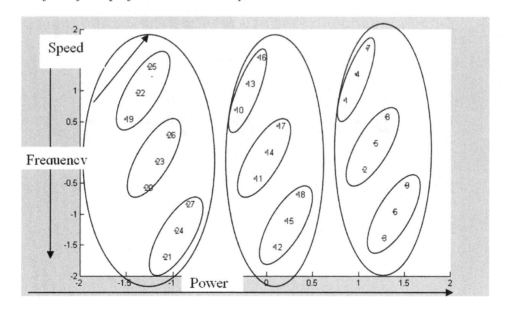

Figure 2. Representation of measured output, simulated output and one-step-ahead prediction for two–box models. The model generated by the OE and the BJ models for angle error, output $y_1(t)$, are shown in rows 1, 2, respectively. On the left, measured output vs. simulated output, on the right, measured output vs. one-step-ahead prediction. The OE and the BJ models for output $y_4(t)$, Material removal rate are shown in rows 3, 4, respectively. The validation data set was not used for the estimation of the model. The order of the structure of the model is [1 1 1 2 2 2 1 1 1] for $y_1(t)$ and [2 1 1 2 1 1 2 1 1] for $y_4(t)$. The solid line represents true measurements and the dotted line represents estimated output

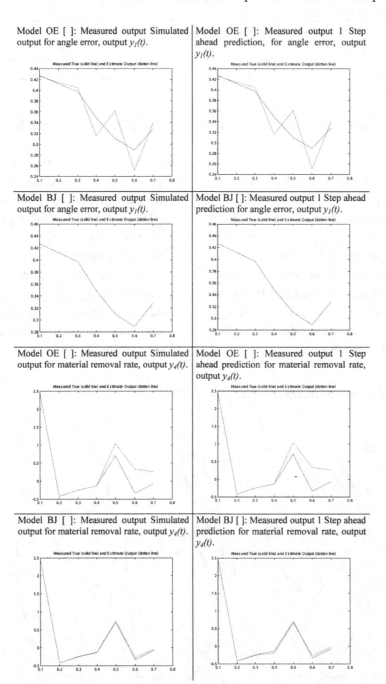

Figure 3. Representation of measured output, simulated output and one-step-ahead prediction for two–box models. The model generated by the OE model for Depth error, output $y_2(t)$, is shown in row 1. On the left, measured output vs. simulated output, on the right, measured output vs. one-step-ahead prediction. The OE and the BJ models for output $y_3(t)$, surface roughness are shown in rows 2, 3, respectively. The validation data set was not used for the estimation of the model. The order of the structure of the model is [1 2 1 2 1 2 1] for $y_2(t)$ and [3 1 1 2 1 1 2 1 1] for $y_3(t)$. The solid line represents true measurements and the dotted line represents estimated output

Model OE [ ]: Measured output Simulated output for depth error of the test piece, output $y_2(t)$.

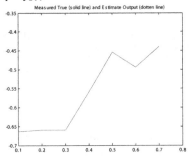

Model OE [ ]: Measured output 1 Step ahead prediction, depth error of the test piece, output $y_2(t)$.

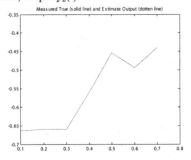

Model OE [ ]: Measured output Simulated output for surface roughness, output $y_3(t)$.

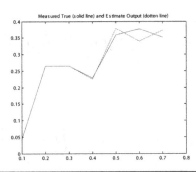

Model OE [ ]: Measured output 1 Step ahead prediction for surface roughness, output $y_3(t)$.

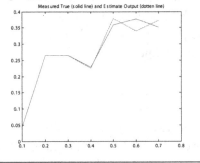

Model BJ [ ]: Measured output Simulated output for surface roughness, output $y_3(t)$.

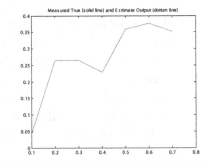

Model BJ [ ]: Measured output 1 Step ahead prediction for surface roughness, output $y_3(t)$.

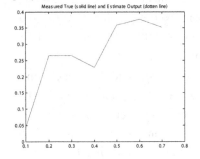

Table 3. Indicator values for several proposed models of the angle error

Model	Indexes
Black-box OE model with $n_{b1}=2$, $n_{b2}=1$, $n_{b3}=1$, $n_f=2$, $n_{k1}=1$, $n_{k2}=1$, $n_{k3}=1$. The model is estimated using the prediction error method, the degree of the model selection is carried out from the best AIC criterion (the structure that minimizes AIC).	FIT:44.04%, FIT1:44.04% FIT10:44.04%, V: 0.02 FPE:0.23, NSSE:7.71e-4
Black-box OE model $n_{b1}=1$, $n_{b2}=1$, $n_{b3}=1$, $n_f=2$, $n_{k1}=1$, $n_{k2}=1$, $n_{k3}=1$. The model is estimated using the prediction error method, the degree of the model selection is carried out with the best AIC criterion (the structure that minimizes AIC).	FIT:21.2%, FIT1: 21.2% FIT10: 21.2%, V: 0.023 FPE:0.162, NSSE:0.0015
Black-box BJ model with $n_{b1}=1$, $n_{b2}=1$, $n_{b3}=1$, $n_c=2$, $n_d=2$, $n_f=2$, $n_{k1}=1$, $n_{k2}=1$, $n_{k3}=1$. The model is estimated using the prediction error method, the degree of the model selection is carried out with the best AIC criterion (the structure that minimizes AIC).	FIT:100%, FIT1:100% FIT10:100%, V: 0.12 FPE:0.27 NSSE:2.73e-31
Black-box BJ model with $n_{b1}=2$, $n_{b2}=1$, $n_{b3}=1$, $n_c=2$, $n_d=2$, $n_f=2$, $n_{k1}=1$, $n_{k2}=1$, $n_{k3}=1$. The model is estimated using the prediction error method, the degree of the model selection is carried out with the best AIC criterion (the structure that minimizes AIC).	FIT:100%, FIT1:100% FIT10:100%, V: 0.97 FPE:1,75 NSSE:4.17e-30

3, the X-axis shows the number of samples used in the validation of the model, while the Y-axis represents the range of output variables.

Table 3, Table 4, Table 5 and Table 6 show a comparison of the qualities of estimation and prediction of the best models obtained, as a function of the model, the estimation method, and the indexes, which are defined as follows:

- The percentage representation of the estimated model (expressed as so many percent "%") in relation to the true system: the numeric value of the normalized mean error that is computed with one-step prediction (FIT1), with ten-step prediction (FIT10), or by means of simulation (FIT). Also shown are the graphical representations of true system output and both the one-step prediction $\hat{y}_1(t \mid m)$, the ten-step prediction $\hat{y}_{10}(t \mid m)$, and the model simulation $\hat{y}_\infty(t \mid m)$. The equations (12), (13) and (14) show as is calculated the percentage representation of the estimation of model from the one-step ahead prediction (FIT1), in the same form are calculated the others indexes FIT10 and FIT.

$$\hat{y}_1(t \mid m) = \hat{H}^{-1}(q)\hat{G}(q)u(t) + (1 - \hat{H}^{-1}(q))y(t)$$

(12)

$$J_1(m) = \frac{1}{N}\sum_{t=1}^{N} \mid y(t) - \hat{y}_1(t \mid m) \mid^2$$

(13)

$$FIT1\ (\%) = \left[1 - \frac{\sqrt{J_1(m)}}{\sqrt{\frac{1}{N}\sum_{t=1}^{N} \mid y(t) \mid^2}}\right]100$$

(14)

- The loss or the error function (V): the numeric value of the mean square error that is calculated from the estimation data set, equation (13).
- The generalization error value (NSSE): the numeric value of the mean square error that is calculated from the validation data set, equation (13).
- The average generalization error value (FPE): This is the numeric value of the FPE

Table 4. Indicator values for several proposed models of the depth error

Model	Indexes
Black-box OE model with n_{b1}=1, n_{b2}=2, n_{b3}=1, n_f=2, n_{k1}=1, n_{k2}=2, n_{k3}=1.. The model is estimated using the prediction error method, the degree of the model selection is carried out from the best AIC criterion (the structure that minimizes AIC).	FIT:100%, FIT1:100% FIT10:100%, V: 0.051 FPE:0.636 NSSE:1.08e-27
Black-box BJ model with n_{b1}=1, n_{b2}=3, n_{b3}=1, n_c=2, n_d=1, n_f=1, n_{k1}=1, n_{k2}=2, n_{k3}=1. The model is estimated using the prediction error method, the degree of the model selection is carried out with the best AIC criterion (the structure that minimizes AIC).	FIT:100%, FIT1:100% FIT10:100%, V: 0.07 FPE:1.331 NSSE:1.24e-28
Black-box BJ model with n_{b1}=2, n_{b2}=2, n_{b3}=2, n_c=2, n_d=1, n_f=1, n_{k1}=2, n_{k2}=2, n_{k3}=1. The model is estimated using the prediction error method, the degree of the model selection is carried out with the best AIC criterion (the structure that minimizes AIC).	FIT:65.16%, FIT1:59.98% FIT10:63.32%, V: -0.12 FPE:0.471 NSSE:0.0014

Table 5. Indicator values for several proposed models of the surface roughness

Model	Indexes
Black-box OE model with n_{b1}=2, n_{b2}=1, n_{b3}=1, n_f=1, n_{k1}=1, n_{k2}=1, n_{k3}=1. The model is estimated using the prediction error method, the degree of the model selection is carried out from the best AIC criterion (the structure that minimizes AIC).	FIT:59.31%, FIT1: 59.31% FIT10: 59.31%, V: 0.005 FPE:0.0172, NSSE:0.0019
Black-box OE model with n_{b1}=3, n_{b2}=1, n_{b3}=1, n_f=1, n_{k1}=2, n_{k2}=1, n_{k3}=1. The model is estimated using the prediction error method, the degree of the model selection is carried out with the best AIC criterion (the structure that minimizes AIC).	FIT:83.15%, FIT1: 83.15% FIT10: 83.15%, V: 0.055 FPE:0.031 NSSE:3.20e-4
Black-box BJ model with n_{b1}=2, n_{b2}=1, n_{b3}=1, n_c=2, n_d=1, n_f=1, n_{k1}=1, n_{k2}=1, n_{k3}=1. The model is estimated using the prediction error method, the degree of the model selection is carried out with the best AIC criterion (the structure that minimizes AIC).	FIT:61.68%, FIT1:60.85% FIT10:59.15%, V: 0.0024 FPE:0.045, NSSE:0.0019
Black-box BJ model with n_{b1}=3, n_{b2}=1, n_{b3}=1, n_c=2, n_d=1, n_f=1, n_{k1}=2, n_{k2}=1, n_{k3}=1. The model is estimated using the prediction error method, the degree of the model selection is carried out with the best AIC criterion (the structure that minimizes AIC).	FIT:100%, FIT1:100% FIT10:100%, V: 0.0015 FPE:0.0281 NSSE:5.3e-23

Table 6. Indicator values for several proposed models of the material removal rate

Model	Indexes
Black-box OE model with n_{b1}=2, n_{b2}=1, n_{b3}=1, n_f=1, n_{k1}=1, n_{k2}=1, n_{k3}=1. The model is estimated using the prediction error method, the degree of the model selection is carried out from the best AIC criterion (the structure that minimizes AIC).	FIT:48.26%, FIT1: 48.26% FIT10: 48.26%, V: 0.88 FPE:3.05, NSSE:0.244
Black-box OE model with n_{b1}=2, n_{b2}=1, n_{b3}=1, n_f=1, n_{k1}=2, n_{k2}=1, n_{k3}=1. The model is estimated using the prediction error method, the degree of the model selection is carried out with the best AIC criterion (the structure that minimizes AIC).	FIT:67.82%, FIT1: 67.82% FIT10: 67.82%, V: 0.34 FPE:1.29, NSSE:0.094
Black-box BJ model with n_{b1}=2, n_{b2}=1, n_{b3}=1, n_c=2, n_d=1, n_f=1, n_{k1}=1, n_{k2}=1, n_{k3}=1. The model is estimated using the prediction error method, the degree of the model selection is carried out with the best AIC criterion (the structure that minimizes AIC).	FIT:90.34%, FIT1:89.34% FIT10:89.5%, V: 0.3 FPE:2.11, NSSE:0.02
Black-box BJ model with n_{b1}=2, n_{b2}=1, n_{b3}=1, n_c=2, n_d=1, n_f=1, n_{k1}=2, n_{k2}=1, n_{k3}=1. The model is estimated using the prediction error method, the degree of the model selection is carried out with the best AIC criterion (the structure that minimizes AIC).	FIT:96.73%, FIT1:95.58% FIT10:95.5%, V: 0.15 FPE:1.42, NSSE:0.0018

Table 7. Function and parameters that represent the behaviour of the laser milled piece for the angle error. The degree of the BJ model polynomials are $n_{b1}=1$, $n_{b2}=1$, $n_{b3}=1$, $n_c=2$, $n_d=2$, $n_f=2$, $n_{k1}=1$, $n_{k2}=1$, $n_{k3}=1$. [1 1 1 2 2 2 1 1 1]

Parameters and polynomials.	
B1(q) = 0.01269 q^{-1}	D(q) = 1 + 1.208 q^{-1} + 0.3098 q^{-2}
B2(q) = 0.0004895 q^{-1}	F1(q) = 1 + 0.4094 q^{-1} - 0.16 q^{-2}
B3(q) = 0.01366 q^{-1}	F2(q) = 1 - 1.678 q^{-1} + 0.7838 q^{-2}
C(q) = 1 + 1.541 q^{-1} + 1.02 q^{-2}	F3(q) = 1 - 1.1 q^{-1} + 0.7671 q^{-2} e(t) is white noise signal whit variance 0.08

criterion that is calculated from the estimation data set. The equation (15) shows as is calculated the value FPE, where: d_M is the dimension of θ -estimated parametrical vector- and Z^N are the estimation data set.

$$FPE = \bar{J}_p(m) \approx J_1(m) + \frac{J_1(m)}{1-(d_M/N)}\frac{2d_M}{N}$$

(15)

From the graphical representation (Figure 2, Figure 3) it can be concluded that the BJ model is capable of simulating and predicting the behaviour of the laser milled piece (for angle error, for surface roughness and for material removal rate) as it meet the indicators and is capable of modelling more than 95% of the true measurements. The OE model is capable of simulating and predicting the behaviour of the other output (depth error) and it's capable of modelling 100% of the true measurements. The tests were performed using Matlab and the System Identification Toolbox.

Tables 7, 9, 10 and Table 8 show the finals BJ and OE models, respectively.

The obtained models can be used not only to predict the angle error, the depth error, the surface roughness and the material removal rate, but also to determine the optimal conditions to minimize the errors. Considering that the model is a polynomial model, if all except one input variable are fixed, then the remaining variable could be calculated and fixed in order to minimize the angle error and the depth error of the flat metallic test piece of Steel.

FUTURE RESEARCH DIRECTIONS

Future work will be focus on the study and application of this model to other kinds of materials of industrial interest, such as cast single-crystal nickel superalloys for high-pressure turbine blades and also the application of this model to the optimization of other but similar industrial problems, like laser cladding, laser super-polishing and laser drilling. Also the upgrading of this model

Table 8. Function and parameters that represent the behaviour of the laser milled piece for the depth error. The degree of the OE model polynomials are $n_{b1}=1$, $n_{b2}=2$, $n_{b3}=1$, $n_f=2$, $n_{k1}=1$, $n_{k2}=2$, $n_{k3}=1$. [1 2 1 2 1 2 1]

Parameters and polynomials.	
B1(q) = 0.003554 q^{-1}	F1(q) = 1 - 0.4365 q^{-1} - 0.1936 q^{-2}
B2(q) = -0.00224 q^{-2} - 0.003145 q^{-3}	F2(q) = 1 - 0.5375 q^{-1} - 0.4496 q^{-2}
B3(q) = -0.02758 q^{-1}	F3(q) = 1 - 1.677 q^{-1} + 0.9613 q^{-2} e(t) is white noise signal whit variance 0.34

Table 9. Function and parameters that represent the behaviour of the laser milled piece for the surface roughness. The degree of the BJ model polynomials are $n_{b1}=3$, $n_{b2}=1$, $n_{b3}=1$, $n_c=2$, $n_d=1$, $n_f=1$, $n_{k1}=2$, $n_{k2}=1$, $n_{k3}=1$. [3 1 1 2 1 1 2 1 1]

Parameters and polynomials.	
$B1(q) = -0.0110 \ q^{-2} + 0.014 \ q^{-3} - 0.07 \ q^{-5}$	$D(q) = 1 + 0.7715 \ q^{-1}$
$B2(q) = -0.0005157 \ q^{-1}$	$F1(q) = 1 - 1.006 \ q^{-1}$
$B3(q) = 0.003764 \ q^{-1}$	$F2(q) = 1 - 0.001624 \ q^{-1}$
$C(q) = 1 - 0.4865 \ q^{-1} - 0.528 \ q^{-2}$	$F3(q) = 1 - 0.3292 \ q^{-1}$ e(t) is white noise signal whit variance 0.01

will be analysed to be improved, establishing an intermediate step allowing a feature selection process, in order to speed up the last step. Then several feature selection models will be applied and compared to identify the best one in each case/material.

CONCLUSION

We have done an investigation to study and identify the most appropriate modelling system for laser milling of steel components. Several methods were investigated to achieve the best practical solution to this interesting problem. The study shows that the BJ model is best adapted to the case of angle error, the surface roughness and the material removal rate, whereas OE model is best adapted, with lower variance of the error e(t), to the case of the depth error, in terms of identifying the best conditions and predicting future circumstances.

It is important to emphasize that a relevant aspect of this research lies in the use of a two-step model when modelling the laser milling process for steel components: a first step, which applies projection methods to establish whether the data describing the case study is "sufficiently informative". As a consequence, the first phase eliminates one of the problems associated with these identification systems, which is that of having no prior knowledge of whether the experiment that generated the data group may be considered acceptable and will present sufficient information in order to identify the overall nature of the problem. It is important to emphasize that this soft-computing based model can be applied to some other material as explained before but also to several many industrial problems related to process simulation and prediction.

Table 10. Function and parameters that represent the behaviour of the laser milled piece for the material removal rate.. The degree of the BJ model polynomials are $n_{b1}=2$, $n_{b2}=1$, $n_{b3}=1$, $n_c=2$, $n_d=1$, $n_f=1$, $n_{k1}=2$, $n_{k2}=1$, $n_{k3}=1$ [2 1 1 2 1 1 2 1 1]

Parameters and polynomials.	
$B1(q) = 0.093 \ q^{-2} - 0.06508 \ q^{-3}$	$D(q) = 1 + 0.647 \ q^{-1}$
$B2(q) = -0.006598 \ q^{-1}$	$F1(q) = 1 + 0.3556 \ q^{-1}$
$B3(q) = 0.0004217 \ q^{-1}$	$F2(q) = 1 + 0.9642 \ q^{-1}$
$C(q) = 1 - 0.3523 \ q^{-1} - 0.6638 \ q^{-2}$	$F3(q) = 1 + 0.04872 \ q^{-1}$ e(t) is white noise signal whit variance 0.78

ACKNOWLEDGMENT

This research has been partially supported through project BU006A08 of JCyL and CIT-020000-2008-2 of Spanish Ministry of Education Innovation. The authors would also like to thank the manufacturer of components for vehicle interiors, Grupo Antolin Ingeniería, S.A. in the framework of the project MAGNO 2008 - 1028.- CENIT Project funded by the Spanish Ministry of Science and Innovation.

This work has been made possible thanks to the support received from ASCAMM Technological Centre (www.ascamm.com), which provided the laser milling data and performed all the laser tests. The authors would especially like to thank Mr. Pol Palouzie and Mr. Javier Diaz for their kind-spirited and useful advice.

REFERENCES

Akaike, H. (1969). Fitting autoregressive models for prediction. *Annals of the Institute of Statistical Mathematics*, *20*, 425–439. doi:10.1007/BF02911655

Arias, G., Ciurana, J., Planta, X., & Crehuet, A. (2007). Analyzing Process Parameters that influence laser machining of hardened steel using Taguchi method. In *Proceedings of 52nd International Technical Conference SAMPE 2007,* Baltimore.

Basso, M., Bencivenni, F., & Giarre, L. Groppi, S., & Zappa., G. (2002, December). Experience with NARX Model Identification of an Industrial Power Plant Gas Turbine. In *41ˢᵗ IEEE Conference on Decision and Control*, Las Vegas, Nevada, USA (pp. 3710–3711).

Chen, S., & Billings, S.A. (1989). Representations of Non-linear Systems: The Narmax model. *International Journal of Control*, *49*(3), 1013–1032.

Ciurana, J., Arias, G., & Ozel, T. (2009). Neural network modeling and particle swarm optimization of process parameters in pulsed laser micromachining of hardened AISI H13 steel. *Materials and Manufacturing Processes*, *24*, 358–368. doi:10.1080/10426910802679568

Corchado, E., & Fyfe, C. (2003). Connectionist Techniques for the Identification and Suppression of Interfering Underlying Factors. *International Journal of Pattern Recognition and Artificial Intelligence*, *17*(8), 1447–1466. doi:10.1142/S0218001403002915

Corchado, E., Han, Y., & Fyfe, C. (2003). Structuring Global Responses of Local Filters Using Lateral Connections. *Journal of Experimental & Theoretical Artificial Intelligence*, *15*(4), 473–487. doi:10.1080/0952813031000161 1603

Corchado, E., MacDonald, D., & Fyfe, C. (2004). Maximum and Minimum Likelihood Hebbian Learning for Exploratory Projection Pursuit. *Data Mining and Knowledge Discovery*, *8*(3), 203–225. doi:10.1023/B:DAMI.0000023673.23078.a3

Diaconis, P., & Freedman, D. (1984). Asymptotics of Graphical Projections. *Annals of Statistics*, *12*(3), 793–815. doi:10.1214/aos/1176346703

Esen, H., & Inalli, M. (2009). Modelling of a vertical ground heat pump system by using Artificial Neural Networks. *Expert Systems with Applications*, *36*(7), 10229–10238. doi:10.1016/j.eswa.2009.01.055

Esen, H., Ozgen, F., Esen, M., & Sengur, A. (2009). Modelling of a new solar air heater through least-squares support vector machines. *Expert Systems with Applications*, *36*(7), 10673–10682. doi:10.1016/j.eswa.2009.02.045

Fichera, A., & Pagano, A. (2002). Neural Network based Prediction of the oscillating behaviour of a closed loop Thermosyphon. *International Journal of Heat and Mass Transfer*, *45*, 3875–3884. doi:10.1016/S0017-9310(02)00095-9

Friedman, J. H., & Tukey, J. W. (1974). Projection Pursuit Algorithm for Exploratory Data-Analysis. *IEEE Transactions on Computers, 23*(9), 881–890. doi:10.1109/T-C.1974.224051

Fung, E., Wong, Y., Ho, H. F., & Mignolet, P. (2003). Modelling and Prediction of Machining Errors using ARMAX and NARMAX Structures. *Applied Mathematical Modelling, 27*, 611–627. doi:10.1016/S0307-904X(03)00071-4

Fyfe, C., & Corchado, E. (2002). Maximum Likelihood Hebbian Rules. In *Proc. of the 10th European Symposium on Artificial Neural Networks (ESANN 2002)* (pp. 143-148).

Haber, R., & Keviczky, L. (1999). Nonlinear System Identification, Input-Output Modeling Approach, Part 1: Nonlinear System Parameter Estimation. London: Kluwer Academic Publishers.

Haber, R., & Keviczky, L. (1999). Nonlinear System Identification, Input-Output Modeling Approach, Part. 2: Nonlinear System structure Identification. London: Kluwer Academic Publishers.

He, X., & Asada, H. (1993). A new method for identifying orders of input-output models for non-linear dynamic systems. In Proc. Of the American Control Conf., California (pp. 2520–2523).

Jurado, F. (2004). Modelling SOFC plants on the distribution system using identification algorithms. *Journal of Power Sources.*

Liu, J. J., Cheng, S., Kung, I., Chang, H., & Billings, S. A. (2001). Non-linear System Identification and fault diagnosis using a new gui interpretation tool. *Mathematics and Computers in Simulation, 54*, 425–499. doi:10.1016/S0378-4754(00)00274-3

Ljung, L. (1999). System Identification, Theory for the User. Upper Saddle River, NJ: Prentice-Hall.

Mihir, K., & Kishor, N. (2009). Adaptive Fuzzy Model Identification to Predict the Heat Transfer coefficient in pool boiling of distilled water. *Expert Systems with Applications, 36*(2-1), 1142 – 1154.

National Instruments Corporation. (2004). LABVIEW System Identification Toolkit User Manual.

Nelles, O. (2001). Nonlinear System Identification, From Classical Approaches to Neural Networks and Fuzzy Models. Berlin: Springer.

Neophytos, C., Evans, C., & Rees, D. (2002, June). Nonlinear Gas Turbine Modelling using Feedforward Neural Networks. In *Proceedings of ASME TURBO EXPO 2002*, GT-2002-30035, Amsterdam, The Netherlands. Nögaard, M., Ravn, O., Poulsen, N. K., & Hansen, L. K. (2000). *Neural Networks for Modelling and Control of Dynamic Systems*. London, U.K: Springer-Verlag.

Pacheco, R., & Steffen, V. (2004). On the identification of non-linear mechanical systems using orthogonal functions. *International Journal of Non-linear Mechanics, 39*, 1147–1159. doi:10.1016/S0020-7462(03)00112-4

Seung, H. S., Socci, N. D., & Lee, D. (1998). The Rectified Gaussian Distribution. *Advances in Neural Information Processing Systems, 10*, 350–356.

Söderström, T., & Stoica, P. (1989). System identification. Englewood Cliffs, NJ: Prentice Hall.

Stoica, P., & Söderström, T. (1982). A useful parametrization for optimal experimental design. In *IEEE Trans. Automatic. Control*, AC-27. The Math Works, Inc. (n.d.). *The Matlab and Simulink products*. Retrieved from http://www.mathworks.com/

The r project. (n.d.). *The R Project for Statistical Computing*. Retrieved from http://www.r-project.org/

Tran, V. T., Yang, B. S., & Chiow Tan, A. C. (2009). Multi-step Ahead Direct Prediction for a Machine Conditions Prognosis using regression trees and Neuro-fuzzy Systems. *Expert Systems with Applications, 36*(5), 9378–9387. doi:10.1016/j.eswa.2009.01.007

Vazquez Feijoo, J. A., Worden, K., & Stanway, R. (2004). System identification using associated linear equations. *Mechanical Systems and Signal Processing, 18,* 431–455. doi:10.1016/S0888-3270(03)00078-5

Venkatesh, S. (2004). Necessary and sufficient conditions for robust identification of uncertain LTI systems. *Systems & Control Letters, 53,* 117–125. doi:10.1016/j.sysconle.2003.10.007

Wendland, J., Harrison, P. M., Henry, M., & Brownell, M. (2005). Deep Engraving of Metals for the Automotive Sector Using High Average Power Diode Pumped Solid State Lasers. In *Proceedings of the 23nd International Conference on Applications of Lasers and Electro-Optics (ICALEO 2005)* Laser Institute of America, Miami, USA.

Xia, P. (2003). An inverse model of MR damper using optimal neural network and system identification. *Journal of Sound and Vibration, 266,* 1009–1023. doi:10.1016/S0022-460X(02)01408-6

Yam, L. H., Yan, Y. J., & Jiang, J. S. (2003). Vibration-based damage detection for composite Structures using wavelet transform and Neural Network identification. *Composite Structures, 60,* 403–412. doi:10.1016/S0263-8223(03)00023-0

Chapter 10
Soft Computing Techniques in Civil Engineering:
Time Series Prediction

Juan L. Pérez
University of A Coruña, Spain

Juan R. Rabuñal
University of A Coruña, Spain

Fernando Martínez Abella
University of A Coruña, Spain

ABSTRACT

Soft computing techniques are applied to a huge quantity of problems spread in several areas of science. In this case, Evolutionary Computation (EC) techniques are applied, in concrete Genetic Programming (GP), to a temporary problem associated to the field of Civil Engineering. The case of study of this technique has been centered in the prediction, over time, of the behavior of the structural concrete in controlled conditions. Given the temporary nature of the case of study, it has been necessary to make several changes to the classical algorithm of GP, among whom it can be emphasized the incorporation of a new operator that gives the GP the ability to be able to solve problems with temporary behavior. The obtained results shown that the proposed method has succeeded in improving the adjustment to the current regulations about creep in the structural concrete.

INTRODUCTION

The existence of numerous database in the field of Civil Engineering, and in particular in the field of structural concrete, has opened new research lines through the introduction of techniques of analysis based on the Artificial Intelligence. Two methods of working are mainly applied in this new field:

the ones based on the Artificial Neural Networks (ANN) and the ones developed from the Evolutionary Computation (Arciszewski & De Jong, 2001). In the case of ANN (Wasserman, 1989) it has been mainly used the recurrent ANN to be able to obtain temporary behavior of the case of study. The result is a black box that, with enough training (a wide database), is capable of predicting the result of new cases.

DOI: 10.4018/978-1-61520-893-7.ch010

Genetic Programming (Koza, 1990), a sub-group in the techniques of EC, lead to similar results regarding the capability of prediction, but with the difference that the process of learning leads to the establishment of mathematical expressions that join the variables taking part in the problem. The achievement of expressions starts generating at random a group of initial formulas (individuals), which will be selected, crossing and mutating among them, evolving only those that are better adjusted to the expected results (Koza, 1992).

This chapter shows the use of GP techniques to specific field of Engineering as the one of structural concrete. For this reason and due to the nature of the concrete problem to solve (modelling the creep of the concrete in controlled laboratory conditions), it has been necessary to make several changes and adjustments to the GP algorithm. Once the changes have been made, it has been applied to data coming from the Réunion Internationale des Laboratoires et Experts des Matériaux, systèmes de constructionet ouvrages - RILEM (International union of laboratories and experts in construction materials, systems and structures) (RILEM, 2009), as a whole (existing database referred to tests in Civil Engineering) with whom it has been obtained several expressions that shape the creep and they are compared to the currrent models.

DEVELOPMENT SYSTEM

Within Soft computing there are several strategies when it comes to deal with the solution of a certain problem. Soft computing is a group of techniques and methodologies that can work together to obtain in any case a flexible ability and adapted to situations of the real world (Zadeh, 1994). Its main advantage is the ability to make the most of the lack of precision, the uncertainty and the approximate reasoning to achieve strength and solutions without and excessive knowledge of the problem. The principle in which it is based is the one of designing the methods of calculus that lead to an acceptable solution through the search of an approximate solution to a given problem (Pal & Mitra, 1999).

A field where Soft Computing techniques can be applied is to the tasks of prediction, according to the type of prediction (generally classification or regression), several techniques exist to solve these tasks.

The fundamental objective that is pursued is the carrying out of prediction of the value that a certain data coming from the experimentation, that is, making symbolic regression about data. Regression uses the existing values to predict what other values are going to happen.

When it comes to deal technically with this situation, it is suggested the use of several possibilities. The techniques based on the use of the ANN have shown their solvency making tasks of regression. We can quote an example as Cladera and Mari who use ANNs to study the shear strength response of concrete beams without web reinforcement (Cladera & Marí, 2004). In this case, once the training has been made, the training ANN has been used as a virtual laboratory, predicting the values of tests that have not been made physically. The main problem of the use of ANN, within the field of Civil Engineering, is its own functioning. The ANN is able, once they have been well trained, to make good predictions, but without explaining how, that is, they work as black boxes. That is why, together with the difficulty in the decision of the ideal setup of the architecture, experts in Civil Engineering do not use them with regularity. Another technique is the use of Genetic Programming. Among other qualities, it can be emphasized the fact of being able to connect the input data (coming from experimental tests) with the result (output data) producing mathematical expressions. An example of the use of this ability of the GP is the work of Ashour et al. (Ashour, Alvarez & Toropov, 2003) where they deal with the achievement of several expressions, of variable complexity, that get several degrees of accuracy in the prediction of the strength of concrete beams.

In any case, in most of the cases studied in Civil Engineering, GP cannot get to create a model capable of predicting the results of a test using the "classical" or common operators (addition, subtraction, multiplication, etc.). The case of study of this chapter is an example where GP does not get to produce a successful result with the classical operators. Following this, it is shown the physical model where GP techniques have been applied.

Creep Phenomenon of Structural Concrete

The structural concrete is the material resulting from mixing mainly three elements, in determined proportions, which are: cement, water and arid materials. These arid materials are small pieces of rocks of different genesis; if the size does not overcome the mm. it is named sand; but if it is bigger, they are named gravels or crushed stones.

Additives or additions are usually added to be able to modify some of the characteristics or behavior of the structural concrete. Additives are components of organic (resins) or inorganic nature, whose inclusion has as its object to modify the properties of the conglomerate materials in fresh state. They are usually presented in powder-shaped or liquid-shaped as emulsions. The proportion is inferior from the rest of the components. In Spain, it cannot overcome the 5% of the weight of the cement used. Examples of additives are the accelerators, retardant materials of hardening, fluidifying materials, etc. On the other hand, the additions are materials of inorganic nature that highlight by their pozzolanic or hydraulic characteristics. Examples of additions are the flying ashes or silica smoke. The proportion against the weight of the cement overcomes the five per cent from the total.

The adjective structural is due to the fact that its habitual use is in Architecture or Engineering works, such as buildings, bridges, dykes, ports,

channels, tunnels, etc. Even in those buildings whose main structure is made of steel, its use is essential to shape the foundation.

It can be considered that the concrete is made up by three stages: the solid one, the liquid one and the gaseous one. The presence of tiny interstices, partially or totally full of water, means the existence of forces resulting from surface phenomena, due to whom the water contained in the pores acquires a solid viscose consistence and it does not behave as free water.

The model to study is the concrete creep phenomenon under a constant load in controlled laboratory conditions. It is observed examining the evolution of the deformations that a piece of concrete (test-tube) experiences subjected to a constant compressive stress over time (see Figure 1). In this type of tests, an initial elastic deformation is produced firstly (Figure 1, variable ε_i in the moment t_1), and next a growing deformation that tends to an asymptotic value (in a moment t_x, the total deformation is the addition of ε_i and the deformation produced by the creep ε_t).

The creep in the concrete begins to be considered at the beginning of the twentieth century. The first study known about creep belongs to Woolson (Woolson, 1905). In the middle of the twentieth century, Troxel et all, (Troxell, Raphael, & Davis, 1958), were the first to bring out the important influence of the humidity of the curing medium on creep. The most recent studies belong to Bazant (Bazant & Baweja, 1995) and to Gardner and Lockman (Lockman, 2000).

Predictive Models of Creep

Different approximations exist to predict the deformation of the creep, generally embodied through codes or norms. The most spread out is the Normative ACI-209 (ACI Committee 209, 1982) developed by the Committee 209 from the American Concrete Institute (ACI), as well as the one proposed by the European Committee of Bèton (CEB), summarized in the model CEB-

Figure 1. Creep phenomenon

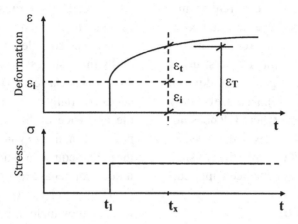

MC90 (Müller & Hilsdorf, 1990) in the year 1990. This model has been adopted as the proposal for the Eurocode 2 (EC2) (Eurocode 2, 2002). As an example, and to have an idea of the complexity of the norms, in the equations 1 to 10 the Normative ACI-209 is shown, being presented in Table 2 the description of each of the variables used. The function J represents the unitary deformation of the concrete, and it is formed by the elastic component ($1/E_{cmt0}$) and the deferred component or component of creep, represented by the coefficient φ of creep, dependent on the time.

$$J(t,t_0) = \frac{1+\varphi}{E_{cmto}} \qquad (1)$$

$$\varphi = 2.35\gamma_1\gamma_2\gamma_3\gamma_4\gamma_5\gamma_6 \frac{\left(t-t_0\right)^{0.6}}{\left(t-t_0\right)^{0.6}+10} \qquad (2)$$

Where γ_1, is a correction term for the effect of age of loading. For moist cured concrete the value of γ_1 is obtained by the Equation 3 where t_0 is greater than or equal to 7 days. And for stream cured concrete the value of γ_1 is obtained by the Equation 4 where t_0 is greater than or equal to 3 days.

$$\gamma_1 = 1.25t_0^{-0.118} \qquad (3)$$

value of γ1 for moist cured concrete when $t_0 \geq$ 7.

Table 2. Variables used in the ACI 209 method 1978

Variable	Description
t	Age of concrete at loading (days)
a	Air content expressed as a decimal
-	Curing method
Ψ	Fine aggregate to total aggregate ratio, by weight
E_{cmto}	Modulus of elasticity of concrete when loading commenced (MPa)
h	Relative humidity (expressed as a decimal)
s	Slump of fresh concrete (mm)
V/S	Volume to surface ratio (mm)

Table 1. γ_3 as a function of V/S (when V/S ≤ 37.5 mm), ACI 209 method

V/S	γ_3
12.5	1.30
18.8	1.17
25.0	1.11
31.2	1.04
37.5	1.00

$$\gamma_1 = 1.25 t_0^{-0.094} \qquad (4)$$

value of γ1 for stream cured concrete when $t_0 \geq 3$.

The γ_2 is a correction term for the effect of humidity and it is applied (see Equation 5) if the humidity value is greater than 40%

$$\gamma_2 = 1.27 - 0.67h \qquad (5)$$

value of γ2 for h > 40%.

The γ_3 is a correction term for the effect of size. When *V/S* less than or equal 37.5 mm, the modification factors given in Table 1 can be used. However if *V/S* is between 37.5 mm and 95 mm then applies the Equation 6 if the difference between the age of concrete at loading and concrete age when applying load is less than or equal to 365 otherwise applies the Equation 7. Finally, if *V/S* is greater than or equal to 95 mm applies the Equation 8.

$$\gamma_3 = 1.14 - 0.00368 \left(V / S \right) \qquad (6)$$

value of γ_3 when $(t - t_0) \leq 365$ days and V/S in [37.5-95.0]mm

$$\gamma_3 = 1.10 - 0.00268 \left(V / S \right) \qquad (7)$$

value of γ_3 when $(t - t_0) > 365$ days and V/S in [37.5-95.0]mm

$$\gamma_3 = \frac{2}{3} \left[1 + 1.13 \exp \left(1 - 0.0213 \left(V / S \right) \right) \right] \qquad (8)$$

value of γ_3 when V/S > 95.0 mm

The last three correction terms (γ_4, γ_5, γ_6) are related to the composition of concrete. See the Equations 9,10 and 11.

$$\gamma_4 = 0.82 + 0.00264s \qquad (9)$$

value of γ_4, related to the slump of fresh concrete

$$\gamma_5 = 0.82 + 0.24\Psi \qquad (10)$$

value of γ_5, related to the fine to total aggregate ratio

$$\gamma_6 = 0.46 + 9a \geq 1.0 \qquad (11)$$

value of γ_6, related to the air content

Another of the existent models nowadays has been, for example, the one developed by Bazan and named B3 (Bazant & Baweja 1995); and finally, the model developed by Gardner and Lockman called GL2000 (Lockman, 2000).

These models are developed from the experimental results, sustained to some extent (especially the B3) by theoretical approaches. It has been verified through contrasted essays, specific essays, or essays grouped in uniform bases. Probably the experimental base is the tuning by the RILEM (2009). From the work of the Committee TC 107, it includes comparable test between different concretes and in which the same variables related to the creep intervene.

Proposed Method

As it can be observed in Figure 1, for every test, a time series is obtained with the values of deformations at a specific time. The objective is to be able to predict completely the time series only from the characteristics of the concrete, that is, from the static data, to predict a dynamic behavior.

To achieve the objective described previously it has been opted for the use of Evolutionary Computation. With this term it has been included a group of techniques that are based on the realization of models that emulate certain characteristics of nature, mainly the one related to the capacity that human beings have to adapt to their environments, what had been taken as base by Darwin to make his theory of the evolution according to the principle of natural selection of the species (Darwin 1859).

This theory supports that those individuals of an area that possess the most advantageous characters will leave proportionally more offspring in the following generation; and if such characters are due to genetic differences that can be transmitted to the descendants, it will tend to change the genetic composition of the population, raising the number of individuals with such characteristics. In this way, the whole of human beings are adapted to the variable circumstances of its environment. The final result is than human beings tend to improve themselves in relation to the surrounded circumstances.

John Holland was conscious of the importance of the natural selection: for this reason, he developed a technique that let him to incorporate it in a computer program. His objective was to achieve that the machines learnt by Holland has originally called "reproductive plans", but it was made popular under the name of Genetic Algorithm (GA) after the publication of his book "Adaptation in Natural and Artificial Systems", in 1975 (Holland 1975).

A GA is an algorithm of search based on the observation of the fact that sexual reproduction and the principle of the most suitable survivor let biological species to adapt themselves to his environment and compete for the resources. The GA establish an analogy between the whole of solutions of a problem and the whole of individuals of a natural population, codifying the information of each solution in a string of values (bits or numbers called genes), so-called chromosome. Chromosomes evolve through the iterations, called generations. In each generation, chromosomes are evaluated using some measure of fitness (evaluating the values that act as variables and assigning a value that determine the capacity of those individuals to solve the problem). The following generations (new chromosomes), called offspring, are formed using two operations, the one of crossover and the one of mutation.

In the elaboration of a new generation, it is named reproduction to the creation of new individuals from the preexisting in the population that constitute the previous generation. A very important fact in the running of this algorithm is the selection of individuals for the reproduction. In order that the algorithm functions, the best individuals (those whose adjustments or level of fitness is better) will have to breed more times than the rest. With this idea, it has been developed multiple algorithm of selection.

All the existent algorithms or selection are based on the same: choosing individuals (in a probabilistic or deterministic way) giving more possibilities to the best but giving the possibility that the worst also are selected. If it is not just like that, if only the best are chosen, the algorithm would converge prematurely making that all the population would be equal, what it is translated into it would be left without exploring a great part or the space of states to explore in an intensive way only a small area.

Afterwards the creation of new individuals, and with low probability (commonly it is usually used values between 1% to 5%), each new individual is submitted to a process of mutation: the string of bits is varied making a change at random.

Finally, the new individuals are inserted in the new generation creating in this way, a new population that shapes the following generation.

This process is repeated until some criterion of stop established is satisfied. The most habitual criteria are usually of 3 types. The first one, an individual has achieved a determined adjustment (it is good enough to give the solution as valid). The second type of stop is that it has been made the maximum prefixed number of generations. Lastly, the population has converged. That is, it is considered that a population has converged when the 95% of the population has the same value (in the case of working with binary codifications, or values within a specific rank, in the case of making with another type of codification). When this happens, the average of goodness of the population approaches to the goodness of the best individual.

Given that each individual represents a possible solution to the problem, the existence of a great number of individuals in the population implies that the algorithm makes a search in a lot of areas different from the space of states at the same time.

An additional advantage of Genetic Algorithms is that the problem solving strategy uses a measure of adjustment to direct the search, and it does not require any specific knowledge about space of search, being efficient in spaces that have jumps, noise, valleys, etc. As each individual within the population directs the search, the GA makes a parallel search in numerous points of the space of states whit numerous directions of search (Fuchs 1990).

The technique in which the proposed method is based is the GP. This appears as an evolution of the traditional GA, keeping the same principle of natural selection. What now is pretended is to provide solutions to the problems through the induction of programs and algorithm that solve them. In the case of a GA, the result that provides the algorithm is the adjustment of a series of codified numerical values shaped like a chromosome that solve the problem. In the case of the GP, the result that provides, according to the technique

used, can be a program, another algorithm, or even a mathematical expression that solves the problem. The basic difference between the GA and the GP is the way of encoding the solutions, while the GA it is made through a sequence of values, in the GA it is represented through a structure named "tree", in which a mathematical formula is encoded. This structure so-called "tree" represents in the nodes the operators (arithmetic operations, trigonometric functions, etc.) and in the "leaves" of terminals the constants and the variables.

In the book: *"Genetic Programming. on the Programming of Computers by means of Natural Selection"*, is where Koza lays the foundations of what from that moment is known as Genetic Programming (Koza, 1992) and that originally it had been implemented in LISP language. His technique is almost independent on the domain and it has been used in numerous applications as the image compression, the design of electronic circuits, the recognition of models, the movements of robots, etc.

Afterwards (Koza, 1995) Koza extended his technique through the incorporation of what has been named as Automatically Defined Functions (ADF), which can be reused as the subroutines and they serve to increase in a demonstrable way the power of the GP to generate programs automatically.

As it has been previously said, the solutions are encoded through the representation of a tree. Two types of nodes exist in the tree. The first type would be the **non-terminal** nodes where the operators of the algorithm to be developed (for example addition, subtraction, etc.) They are characterized because they have one or more children. The second type is the **terminal** nodes, or leaves of the tree, where the constant values and the defined variables are previously situated. These nodes do not have children. For example Figure 2 represents a possible solution to a problem where input variables (a,b) are wanted to relate with output variables f(a,b), through the expression $f(a,b) = a*((b/2)+5)$. In this example

Figure 2. Tree for the expression a*((b/2)+5))

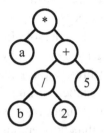

the non-terminal nodes would correspond to the product, the addition and the division, whereas the non-terminal nodes would be the values 2 and 5, together with the variables *a* and *b*.

An essential part in the functioning of the GP is the specification of the whole of terminal and non-terminal elements before the beginning of the evolutionary process. With the nodes that are specified to it, the algorithm will build the trees. So, it is necessary a minimum process of the analysis of the problems to form the algorithm, since it is necessary to tell it what operators or functions (sine, cosine, exponential, etc.) can use. As a general rule, it is desirable to adjust the number of operators to only those necessary, since the addition of items not needed will not cause that is not the solution but the algorithm that take longer to find it.

When it comes to specify the set of terminal and non-terminal elements, it is necessary that these sets possess two requirements, which are *adequacy and completeness* (Montana, 1993). The adequacy requirement says that the solution to a problem must be able to be specified with the whole of operators specified. The requirement of completeness says that it must be possible to build correct trees with the specified operators.

Given that the process of construction of trees is a process based on chance, most of the built trees will not be correct. It is by following the rules of grammar but is by the application of operators (non-terminal nodes) to elements that are not under its dominion. For this reason these operators are not directly applied, but a modification of them in which their dominion of application is enlarged. The most obvious example is the division operator, whose dominion is the set of real numbers except the zero value. Enlarging its dominion, it is defined a new operator (%).

Table 3. Variables, ranks and standardization used in the development

Variable	Name of the variable in the expressions	Ends of standardization (min – max)	Ends of real variations (min – max)
V/S (mm)	VS	0 – 220	17.5 – 200
HR (%)	H	0 – 110	20 – 100
t_c (days)	t_c	0 – 440	0.4 – 400
t_0 (days)	t_0	0 – 3600	0.5 – 3300
t (days)	t	0 – 10000	0.5 – 8525
Ctype	Ctype	1 – 2 – 3	1 – 2 – 3
c (kg/m³)	C	250 – 600	275 – 564
a (kg/m³)	A	1500 – 2300	1661 – 2110
w/c	W/C	0.2 – 0.8	0.25532 – 0.70957
E_{cmt0} (MPa)	$Ecmt_0$	10000 – 50000	10554 – 47620
f_{cm28} (MPa)	fcm_{28}	0 – 130	17.2 – 119
J(t, t_0) - J(t_0) x10⁻⁶ (1/MPa)	out	0 – 300	0 – 262

Figure 3. Operator "ln(t-t$_0$+1)" introduced in the process

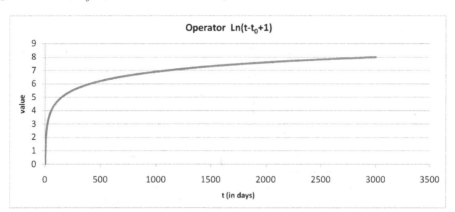

$$\%(a,b) = \begin{cases} 1, & b = 0 \\ \dfrac{a}{b}, & b \neq 0 \end{cases} \quad (12)$$

This new operation is named *operation of protected division*, and in general when a new operation that enlarges the dominion of another is extended, it is named *protected operation*.

As for the process of training and test, a database that contains experimental series of 185 tests has been used. The database belongs to the RILEM. This database contains values that characterize each test (data not dependent on the time) and values dependent on the moment in which the measuring is taken. Within the first group it is found: the volume/surface rate (*V/S* in mm), the relative humidity of the environment (*HR* in %), the age drying commenced, end of moist curing (t_c, in days), the age of the concrete in which the load is introduced (t_0, in days), the type of cement (*C type*), the cement content (*c*, in kg/m³), the aggregate content (*a*, in kg/m³), and the connection water/cement (*w/c*), the modulus of elasticity of concrete at the age of the initial load (E_{cmt0}, in MPa) and the concrete mean compressive strength at 28 days (f_{cm28}, in MPa). Regarding the time dependent data it is had: the day in which the measuring is made (*t*, in days) and the deformation produced from the beginning of the test (computed at unit

of load and subtracted the initial deformation through (*J(t, t$_0$)* - *J(t$_0$)x10^{-6}*), in MPa^{-1}). There are 2323 readings in all. In Table 3 the variables are shown, their ranks and the standardization values used in the developed system.

After studying carefully the behavior of the set of cases the operator "*ln(t-t$_0$+1)*" is incorporated given the temporary nature of the series and the asymptotic tendency to the deformation of the creep (compare Figure 1 with Figure 3).

Schema of the Algorithm

The developed system is based on the use of GP techniques adding the new operator "*ln(t-t$_0$+1)*" defined in the previous section. In this way, the GP algorithm will be able to choose the classical operators (addition, subtraction…) together with the operator "*ln(t-t$_0$+1)*" for the creation/mutation of new individuals. As a consequence of GP's own nature, it will be used the new operator as long as the resultant individuals obtain a good adjustment. Besides, it has been established as a condition for the evolutionary process that this operator will be applied only once.

In Figure 4 it is shown the developed system in a schematic way: in the central part, it is found the typical algorithms in any system based on Genetic Programming. On the lower left side, the

Figure 4. Scheme of the developed system

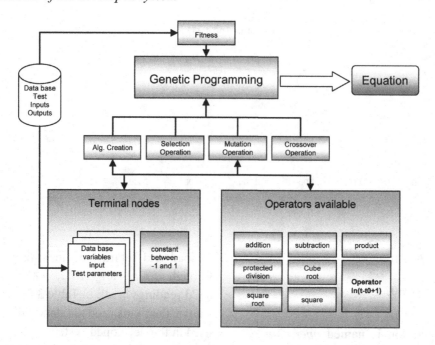

terminal nodes are depicted, and in this case, both the algorithms of creation and the mutation will be able to be select the input variables from the database and constants between -1 and 1. On the lower right side, the operators that can be chosen in the system appear. Finally, in the upper side of the scheme, it is shown the fitness function used to evaluate the individual, in this case the mean square error between the obtained value and the output value from the database.

To avoid redundancy in the expressions that the GP produces and an excessive growth of them, in the developed algorithm is included a parsimony factor in the fitness function than modifies the calculation of the adjustment (Soule & Foster, 1997; Soule 1998). This technique can be used to reduce the complexity of the tree that is being evaluated, and it functions through the punishment in the adjustment of the individual *"i"*. See Equation 13, fitness function with parsimony.

$$f(i) = P(i) + \alpha \cdot s_i \qquad (13)$$

Where *P(i)* is a measure of the goodness of the individual (in this case, worst if the value is bigger), α is the level of parsimony and S_i is the size (number of nodes) of the individual. With this coefficient the number of nodes of a tree is being punished, and its maximum value is usually 0.1. With this value, it will be needed that the tree has 10 nodes to increase in one unit the value of adjustment. However, such a high value is very harmful in the evolution, lower values are usually taken (0.05, 0.01, etc.), depending on the rank of values in which the adjustments of individuals are expected to be.

With this parameter, as the GP algorithm is evolving, those equations that before a value of similar adjustment are simpler are going to be selected, which is a key factor in the final result that the system will produce, since selecting a suitable value it will be possible to obtain results that are understood by the expert. As well, the user will be able to decide whatever he prefers to obtain a value of maximum adjustment, not using this parameter (parsimony=0) and being able to obtain a mathematical expression very complex; or using a value of parsimony that lets the algorithm to evolve and to obtain simple expressions, although with a worse value of adjustment. It is important to indicate that in the algorithm developed during the extraction of expressions is possible to modify the value of parsimony. As a general rule it is usual to initiate with a low value and next, when acceptable results are obtained, to raise the value of the parsimony to favor the reduction of the expressions.

Another factor that influences broadly the complexity of the expressions is the maximum height that is allowed in the creation of individuals. This restriction prevents the creation of too high trees and it forces a search in solutions whose size is enclosed beforehand. With this restriction it is avoided that trees possess a lot of redundant code and the excessive growth of the trees (Soule & Foster, 1997; Soule 1998). The excessive growth of the trees is a phenomenon known as the name of *"bloat"*. This phenomenon is produced in a spontaneous way because of the advance of the evolutionary process, since trees evolve generating parts that do not influence in their behavior. This is produced to alleviate the noxious effects of the crossover and the mutation operators, since the more useless parts a tree has, the less probabilities there will be that this is modified when a crossover or mutation operator is applied. In this manner, individuals protect themselves. An example of a useless part of tree would be, in an individual that represents a mathematical expression, a subtree which will be multiplied by zero.

In a lot of cases, when a mathematical expression that represents the functioning of a physical process is being searched, it must be allowed to control the mechanism of search towards certain indispensable characteristics of operation. An example is the fact that the calculation of a structure is made through mathematical equation, but there is a security coefficient that determines that the calculation value will be oversizing a certain

value, for example, the calculation of resistance in a concrete beam. In these cases, when it is searched a formulae that explains the functioning of a process, it is not only important that a good adjustment to the experimental data is produced, but they are also secure, that is, if the wish is to calculate the resistance that a beam will have, it is important that the prediction is not higher than the real value; then, on the contrary, the beam will be able to break and that supposes a catastrophe from the point of view of Engineering.

To increase the security of the generated formula, it is incorporated a process of punishment to the individuals that predict insecure values, in this case lower values than the real ones. In this way, individuals with a good predictive capacity that give back insecure values, will have less adjustment than more conservative individuals but with less fidelity with regard to the real values.

Equally with the parsimony factor, it has been modified the classical fitness function with a parameter of punishment incorporating, in this way, the security factor.

The process operates in a dynamic way; at the same time that it is evaluated the obtained expressions, it is calculated the security coefficient and it is punished if the result produces insecure values; for that reason, it is established criteria that indicate for each case of the training card index whether it is secure or not. Finally, all the insecure values are added and it is punished proportionally to the quantity of "insecurity" of the equations.

The fitness function with security coefficient used can be seen in the Equation 14. Notice that it appears combined with the parsimony value. Where x_i represents the value predicted by the genetic formulae, d_i is the real value; p is the security punishment, α the coefficient of parsimony and c_i represents the complexity of the individual, measured in number of nodes.

Table 4. Parameters used in GP configuration

Parameters of configuration	Value
Selection algorithm	Tournament
Mutation rate	20
Crossover rate	95
Population size	400
Maximum tree height	9

$$\frac{\sum |x_i - d_i| + s_i}{n} + \alpha \cdot c_i$$

$$s_i = p \cdot \sum |x_i - d_i| \quad \text{if} \quad x_i > d_i$$

$$s_i = 0 \quad \text{if} \quad x_i \leq d_i \tag{14}$$

In this way, the obtained insecure values will make the represented expressions not to be good and, within the evolutionary process, it will tend to disappear in future generations. That is why it is favored the fact of obtaining expressions that have a high behavior of security.

Results

As it can be seen in Table 1, the expressions are developed for the standardized variables, and they only affect the deformation produced after the initial elastic deformation (Figure 1, ε_i). To obtain the results, it has been necessary to make several tests with different parameters of configuration. In Table 4 it is shown the one which has been obtained the better result.

Once the ideal configuration of the GP algorithm has been obtained for the case of study, two significant formulas have been obtained: the Equation 15 (*f1*) with few complexity but with adjustments similar to the current codes and regulations, and the Equation 16 (*f2*) more complex than the previous one, not very different from the current codes and regulations but with much better adjustments than these ones. In both

formulas it is observed that the introduced operator "$ln(t-t_0+1)$" only appears once.

$$f1 = 0.069 \cdot \frac{W}{C} \cdot \ln\left(t - t_0 + 1\right) \tag{15}$$

$$f2 = -0.19 \cdot \left(\gamma_1 \cdot h + \gamma_2\right) \cdot \ln\left(t - t_0 + 1\right) \cdot \gamma_3$$

$$\gamma_1 = 1.27 \cdot \left(\frac{W}{C}\right)^2 \left(VS - 0.37\right) + 0.5$$

$$\gamma_2 = \frac{0.42 \cdot t_0}{t_0 + VS} - 0.15 \cdot t_c - 0.64$$

$$\gamma_3 = -0.77 \cdot Ecmt_0 - 0.09 \, t_o + 0.93 \tag{16}$$

In Table 5 it can be observed (sorted by error from small to large in the line of Mean Absolute Error) the errors and the coefficient of correlation that are obtained applying the current models and the obtained formulation. In all the calculations it has been proceeded previously to undo the standardization.

The correlation that can be obtained after applying the current models (GL, Gardner y Lockman (Lockman, 2000); CEB, European Committee of concrete (Müller & Hilsdorf, 1990); ACI, American Concrete Institute (ACI Committee 209, 1982); and B3, Bazant (Bazant & Baweja, 1995)) to the data as a whole, it doesn't overcome the value of 0.795, being GL the best model from the ones that have been considered.

With the GP it has been obtained the improvement of the correlation reaching, with the equation 2, a correlation of 0.842.

Future Research Directions

One of the uses of the systems based on GP is the search of mathematical relations over a set of data

Table 5. Results from the different models (real values)

	F2	GL	CEB	ACI	F1	B3
Mean Absolute Error	10.5	12.0	13.7	14.7	17.4	17.6
Mean Square Error	276.3	362.7	410.4	549.0	679.5	622.8
Coefficient R^2	0.84	0.79	0.78	0.76	0.61	0.72

providing, applying for it the symbolic regression technique. These systems are used in several fields as the one in which has been applied this work or another ones such as in Physics, Biology, etc.

Although in a lot of cases it is successful, as it has been shown in this work, they present some limitations regarding the solution of these problems in an easy way. That is, it is necessary to enlarge and/or modify the algorithms to apply them to each specific case. For that reason, it would be interesting the possibility to incorporate the expert knowledge in a way that it permits to modify the behaviour of the system, making it effective and efficient. That is, it is pretended that, when some mechanism or rule of functioning of the mathematical expressions previously mentioned is known, such knowledge can be incorporated to the system letting this to be able to use it, facilitating and directing the search process. The mechanism to make the incorporation of the formula will have to be dynamic, with the aim that every researcher can use the system without the necessity to codify any method. Besides the inclusion of rules with the form of mathematical expressions, it would be interesting to define another type of rules of a high level, that is, to build a system based on knowledge that directs the evolution of the population. The possibility of giving some probabilities of emergence of the operators, to be able to determine the number of times that an operator appears (both terminal and non-terminal operator) in a tree, or simplification rules of trees that have branches "without sense", unproductive or branches that can be simplified (for example, it would be formula as "X-X, 1/1, (1+1-1)), are examples of characteristics that can be added to the process of search.

Another future research direction would be the use of co-evolutionary strategies, that is, to run the algorithm with several populations of different nature that interact between them and go evolving as a whole. With this strategy the progress in a population causes a reaction on the rest, and the evolution is produced in a collective way. Making what has been proposed here, it would be necessary to redesign the Genetic Programming algorithm, incorporating different techniques of clustering, achieving the distribution of individuals in different populations. Given the computational cost of the genetic process of the populations, it would be essential to distribute and parallelize the execution of the Genetic Programming requests, developing different strategies of distribution, with whom it will be achieved to reduce the execution time and the computational cost that entails the evaluation of the individuals in the population, and it will improve the efficiency of the techniques based on Genetic Programming.

CONCLUSION

After making this study, it can be drawn the following conclusions:

Soft Computing techniques, and specifically Genetic Programming, are a powerful tool of analysis and data processor even capable of suggesting expressions that combine the variables. The results usually improve the current techniques of adjustment.

One of the usual procedures in any technique of regression is the process of standardization of information. Although it is not strictly necessary to make the standardization of the data in the appliance of the Genetic Programming, better results have been obtained after standardizing the variables as a whole.

It has been obtained an expression, named F2, which predicts the concrete creep deformation. With this formula it is obtained the best result over the database developed by the RILEM. For this achievement it has been crucial the incorporation of the specific operator "ln(t t0+1)" and the restriction that each individual only appears once. From the point of view of Civil Engineering, this expression could be incorporated (according to experts in the field) as a model of creep of the concrete in the regulations of the structural concrete, provided that it improves the results that any of the current expressions provide, both theoretical and regulatory as: CEB, ACI, B3 and GL.

There are many areas within the field of structural concrete capable of being treated with these techniques. All of them are characterized by counting on wide experimental database and by being nowadays formulated through empirical rules, outside theoretical approaches in most of the cases and absent from dimensional coherence.

ACKNOWLEDGMENT

This work was partially supported by the Spanish Ministry of Development (Ministerio de Fomento) (Ref. CLEAM-CENIT, AIE), grants (Ref. 202/ PC08/3-03.2) funded by the Spanish Environmental Ministry (Ministerio de Medio Ambiente) and grants from the General Directorate of Research, Development and Innovation (Dirección Xeral de Investigación, Desenvolvemento e Innovación) of the Xunta de Galicia (Ref. 07TMT011CT, Ref. 08TIC014CT and Ref. 08TMT005CT). The work of Juan L. Pérez is supported by an FPI grant (Ref. BES-2006-13535) from the Spanish Ministry of Science and Innovation (Ministerio de Ciencia e Innovación).

REFERENCES

ACI Committee. 209. (1982). Prediction of Creep, Shrinkage and Temperature Effects in Concrete Structures. ACI 209-82. American Concrete Institute, Detroit.

Arciszewski, T., & De Jong, K. A. (2001). Evolutionary computation in civil engineering: research frontiers. In B. H. V. Topping (Ed.), *Proceedings of the Eight International Conference on Civil and Structural Engineering Computing*, Eisenstadt, Vienna, Austria.

Ashour, A. F., Alvarez, L. F., & Toropov, V. V. (2003). Empirical modelling of shear strength of RC deep beams by genetic programming. *Computers & Structures*, *81*, 331–338. doi:10.1016/S0045-7949(02)00437-6

Bazant, Z. P., & Baweja, S. (1995). Creep and Shrinkage Prediction Model for Analysis and Design of Concrete Structures - Model B3. *Materials and Structures*, *28*, 357–365. doi:10.1007/BF02473152

Cladera, A., & Marí, A. R. (2004). Shear design procedure for reinforced normal and high-strength concrete beams using artificial neural networks. Part I: beams without stirrups. *Engineering Structures*, *26*, 917–926. doi:10.1016/j.engstruct.2004.02.010

Darwin, C. (1859). On the origin of species by means of natural selection or the preservation of favoured races in the struggle for life. Cambridge, UK: Cambridge University Press.

Eurocode 2. (2004). *Design of Concrete Structures* (EN 1992-1-1:2004). European Committee for Standardization.

Fuchs, M. (1998). Crossover Versus Mutation: An Empirical and Theoretical Case Study. In J. R. Koza, W. Banzhaf, K. Chellapilla et al. (Eds.), *3rd Annual Conference on Genetic Programming* (pp. 78-85) Madison, WI: Morgan-Kauffman.

Goldberg, D. E. (1989). Genetic Algorithms in Search, Optimization & Machine Learning. Reading, MA: Addison-Wesley.

Holland, J. H. (1975). Adaptation in Natural and Artificial Systems. Ann Arbor, MI: The University of Michigan Press.

Koza, J. (1990). Genetic Programming: A paradigm for genetically breeding populations of computer programs to solve problems (Tech. Rep.). Stanford, CA: Stanford University, Computer Science Department.

Koza, J. (1992). Genetic Programming. On the Programming of Computers by means of Natural Selection. Cambridge, MA: The MIT Press.

Koza, J. R., Bennett, F. H., III, Andre, D., & Keane, M. A. (1999). Genetic Programming III: Darwinian Invention and Problem Solving. San Francisco, CA: Morgan Kaufmann Publishers.

Lockman, M. J. (2000). *Compliance, relaxation and creep recovery of normal strength concrete* (Thesis). Ottawa, Canada: University of Ottawa, Department of Civil Engineering.

Montana, D. J. (1993). Strongly Typed Genetic Programming. *Evolutionary Computation*, *3*, 199–230. doi:10.1162/evco.1995.3.2.199

Müller, H. S., & Hilsdorf, H. K. (1990). Evaluation of the Time Dependent Behavior of Concrete. (Bulletin d'Information No. 199). France: CEB Comite Euro-International du Beton.

Pal, S. K., & Mitra, S. (1999). Neuro-Fuzzy Pattern Recognition: Methods in Soft Computing. New York: Wiley.

RILEM. (2009). *Réunion Internationale des Laboratoires et Experts des Matériaux, systèmes de constructionet ouvrages*. Retrieved from http://www.rilem.net

Soule, T. (1998). *Code Growth in Genetic Programming* (Thesis). Moscow, ID: University of Idaho.

Soule, T., & Foster, J. A. (1997). Code Size and Depth Flows in Genetic Programming. Genetic Programming. In *Proceedings of the Second Annual Conference*. San Francisco, CA (pp. 313-320).

Troxell, G. E., Raphael, J. M., & Davis, H. E. (1958). Long term creep and shrinkage test of plain and reinforced concrete. In *Proceedings of the American Society for Testing and Materials (ASTM)*, Philadelphia, PA (Vol. 58, pp. 1101-1120).

Wasserman, P. (1989). Neural Computing. New York: Van Nostrand Reinhold.

Woolson, I. H. (1905). Some remarkable tests indicating flow of concrete under pressure. *Engineering News*, *54*, 454.

Zadeh, L. A. (1994). Fuzzy logic, neural networks, and soft computing. *Communications of the ACM*, *37*, 77–84. doi:10.1145/175247.175255

ADDITIONAL READING

Baker, J. E. (1987). Reducing Bias and Inefficiency in the Selection Algorithm. Genetic Algorithms and their Applications. In *Proceedings of the Second International Conference on Genetic Algorithms* (pp. 14-22) Hillsdale, NJ: Lawrence Erlbaum Associates.

Booker, L. B. (1982). *Intelligent Behavior as an Adaptation to the Task of Environment* (Thesis). University of Michigan.

Brindle, A. (1981). *Genetic Algorithms for Function Optimization* (Thesis). University of Alberta.

Cagnoni, S., Rivero, D., & Vanneschi, L. (2005). A purely evolutionary memetic algorithm as a first step towards symbiotic coevolution. In *Proceedings of the IEEE Congress on Evolutionary Computation, CEC 2005* (Vol. 2, pp. 1156-1163). Edinburgh, UK: IEEE.

Cantú-Paz, E., & Kamath, C. (2005). An Empirical Comparison of Combinatios of Evolutionary Algorithms and Neural Networks for Classification Problems. In IEEE Transactions on systems, Man and Cybernetics – Part B: Cybernetics (pp. 915-927).

Chul-Hyun, L., Young-Soo, Y., & Joong-Hoon, K. (2004). Genetic algorithm in mix proportioning of high-performance concrete. *Cement and Concrete Research, 34*, 409–420. doi:10.1016/j.cemconres.2003.08.018

Cladera, A. (2003). *Shear design of reinforced high-strength concrete beams* (Thesis). Universitat Politècnica de Catalunya, Departament d'Enginyeria de la Construcció, Spain.

Dorado, J., Fernandez, E., Ibañez, O., & Rabuñal, J. R. (Eds.). (2007). Tecnologías de la Información y las Comunicaciones en la Ingeniería Civil. Santiago de Compostela, A Coruña, Spain: Fundación Alfredo Brañas.

Friedberg, R. M., Dunham, B., & North, J. H. (1959). A Learning Machine: Part II. *IBM Journal of Research and Development, 3*, 282–287. doi:10.1147/rd.33.0282

Fujiki, C. (1986). *An Evaluation of Holland's Genetic Operators Applied to a Program Generator* (Thesis). Moscow, ID: University of Idaho.

Kicinger, R., Arciszewski, T., & De Jong, K. (2005). Evolutionary computation and structural design: A survey of the state-of-the-art. *Computers & Structures, 83*, 1943–1978. doi:10.1016/j.compstruc.2005.03.002

Kohonen, T. (1988). Self-Organization and Associative Memory (2nd Ed.). New York: Springer-Verlag.

Luke, S., & Spector, L. (1998). A Revised Comparison of Crossover and Mutation in Genetic Programming. In *3rd Annual Conference on Genetic Programming*. New York: Morgan-Kauffman.

Rabuñal, J. R. (2008) *Uso de Técnicas de Inteligencia Artificial en Ingeniería Civil* (Thesis). A Coruña, Spain: Universidade da Coruña, Departamento de Métodos Matemáticos y de Representación.

Rabuñal, J. R., & Dorado, J. (Eds.). (2005). Artificial Neural Networks in Real-Life Applications. Hershey, PA: Idea Group Inc.

Rabuñal, J. R., Varela, M., Dorado, J., González, B., & Martínez, I. (2005). Aplicación de la Programación Genética para determiner la adherencia en hormigón armado. In *Proceedings of IV Congreso Español sobre Metaheurísticas, Algoritmos Evolutivos y Bioinspirados MAEB'2005* (pp. 76-84). Madrid: Thompson.

Rivero, D., Rabuñal, J. R., Dorado, J., & Pazos, A. (2005). Time Series Forecast with Anticipation using Genetic Programming. In A. P. Cabestany & D. F. Sandoval (Eds.), IWANN 2005 (LNCS 3512, pp. 968-975).

Rodriguez-Vazquez, K. (2001). Genetic Programming in Time Series Modelling: an Application to Meteorological Data. In [Washington, DC: IEEE Press.]. *Proceedings of Congress on Evolutionary Computation, CEC2001*, 261–266.

Shah, S. P. (1993). Recent trends in the science and technology of concrete, concrete technology, new trends, industrial applications. In *Proceedings of the international RILEM workshop* (pp. 1–18). London: E & FN Spon.

Shaw, D., Miles, J. C., & Gray, A. (2003). Genetic programming within civil engineering: a review. In O. Ciftcioglu & E. Dado (Eds.), *Proceedings of the 10th International Workshop of the European Group for Intelligent Computing in Engineering (EG-ICE)*, Delft, The Netherlands (pp. 29-39).

Yang, Y., & Kiong, C. (2002). Automated optimum design of structures using genetic programming. *Computers & Structures, 80*, 1537–1546. doi:10.1016/S0045-7949(02)00108-6

KEY TERMS AND DEFINITIONS

Compression: Stress generated by pressing or squeezing.

Compressive Strength: The measured maximum resistance of a concrete or mortar specimen to axial compressive loading; expressed as force per unit cross-sectional area; or the specified resistance used in design calculations.

Concrete: A building material made of cement, sand, stone and water that hardens to a stone like mass

Creep: A slow flow or deformation of material when under high temperature or great pressure.

Crossover: The interchange of sections between pairing homologous chromosomes during the prophase of meiosis. In Genetic Programming the crossover operation selects two branches of the parents trees and are exchanged to create offspring.

Fitness: The state or condition of being fit; suitability or appropriateness.

Mutation: The process by which such a change occurs in a chromosome. In Genetic Programming the mutation operation selects a node in the parse tree and replaces the branch at that node by a randomly generated branch.

Parsimony: The preference for the least complex explanation for an observation.

Stress: The force per unit area applied to an object. Objects subject to stress tend to become distorted or deformed.

Structural Safety: Structural response stronger than the internal forces produced by external loading.

Chapter 11
Intrinsic Evolvable
Hardware Structures

Laurenţiu Ionescu
University of Pitesti, Romania

Alin Mazare
University of Pitesti, Romania

Gabriel Iana
University of Pitesti, Romania

Gheorghe Şerban
University of Pitesti, Romania

Ionel Bostan
University of Pitesti, Romania

ABSTRACT

The main target of this chapter is to present the intrinsic evolvable hardware structures: concept, design and applications. The intrinsic evolvable hardware structures concept join more research areas like: bio–inspired searching methods (evolutionary algorithms), optimization of algorithms by parallel processing and reconfigurable circuits. First, a general overview about intrinsic evolvable hardware structure is presented. The intrinsic evolvable hardware structure consists of two main modules: hardware genetic algorithm and dynamic reconfigurable circuit. The hardware genetic algorithm searches the configuration that makes the reconfigurable circuit to correctly respond to application requirements. The background section present the genetic algorithm concept as a bio-inspired search solution, the hardware reconfiguration concept with sub areas classifications and the research directions in the evolvable hardware structures areas with application examples. The main section presents the design solutions for hardware implementation of genetic algorithm and for the reconfigurable circuit. Finally, several applications are presented that illustrate the usefulness of the intrinsic evolvable hardware structure.

DOI: 10.4018/978-1-61520-893-7.ch011

Figure 1. Intrinsic evolvable hardware structure

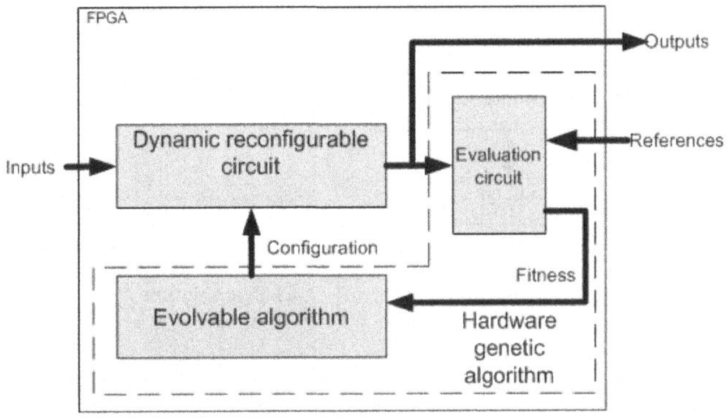

INTRODUCTION

The reconfigurable hardware area, with one of its branches, evolvable hardware, is very dynamic and has experienced great developments in recent years. With 10 years ago from the time of writing the paper (2009) implementation of a logic circuit with a high degree of complexity on a programmable logic involves a series of problems caused by the limitation of existing technology. The market was dominated by complex programmable logic circuits and logic gates for areas of low resolution. Main problem was the number of available logic cells on the chip and response time. Extremely rapid evolution of technology has made at present on an area of programmable gate can be implemented a core processor for high speed, comparable in performance with versions of dedicated integrated circuits. Meanwhile the price of production has decreased very much what makes a modern configurable logic circuit to be available on the market. Therefore, it is necessary to have an evolution in design techniques, synthesis and implementation of logic circuits, techniques, still rely on classical logic programmable array. In those circumstances arise and develop areas of dynamic reconfigurable hardware with its new branch evolvable hardware. This tries to answer the question: in the context of current development of configurable logic circuits, it is

not possible to print a new direction in design, synthesis and implementation of logic circuits, so that performance is improved compared to classical methods? As in any new field, lines of research are multiple. One of the objectives of this work is to try to synthesis the assumptions made in a single theory concerning the evolutionary synthesis of logical circuits.

The starting point for this chapter is the intrinsic evolvable hardware structure (configurable through its own resources) illustrated in Figure 1.

It is composed of several modules, each allocate the sections in this chapter. A **reconfigurable circuit** is a circuit which can change their behavior according to a map of configurations that is generated.

The process of generating the map of connections, from a structural or functional description of the new behavior is called logic synthesis of the circuit. There are several classical methods for synthesis of logic circuits, but in principle the synthesis is a laborious process, requiring a high volume of operations (performed with the DeMorgan rules, minimization).

The evolutionary algorithms are search algorithms in an expanded space of multiple objective solutions. They are used in several areas in which other search methods are not effective. The use of evolutionary algorithms (EA) to solve multi objective problem has be motivated mainly

Figure 2. Flowchart of an optimization process

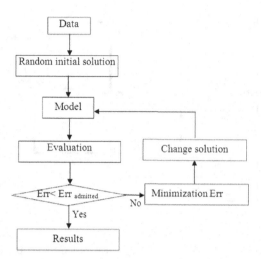

because of the nature of the solution based on population which allow generation of several optimal set in a single run (Coello 2002). In the evolvable hardware structures, EA are used to found a map of configurations in a search space that exceed limits imposed by classical methods of synthesis of logic circuits. The complexity of the electronic design search space has encouraged the use of Evolutionary Electronic Design (Ali 2004). This would mean that the solution to be found more quickly and possibly be better than with classical methods of synthesis.

On the other hand, evolutionary algorithms are meant to run on computers (software implementations). This means a limitation on the running speed due to the sequential characteristic of the computers.

A first objective we propose it in the following, is to increase the speed of convergence of evolutionary algorithm by parallel implementation in hardware structures. Hardware implementation of genetic algorithms has another major advantage. They can be integrated in the circuits of which can then be run for the search of solutions. Thus, the intrinsic evolvable hardware structure, shown in Figure 1, can have all the components in the same chip!

Another objective is to present solutions for the implementation of reconfigurable circuits that can be configured internally by the evolutionary algorithms. The solutions presented here begin with the classical namely programmable logic array with multilevel logic gates and reach to configurable generic functions array. Finally, we present three different types of applications that illustrate how you can utilize intrinsic evolutionary hardware structures: applications auto adaptive, fault tolerant and real time.

BACKGROUND

Evolutionary Algorithms

Evolutionary algorithms are search methods inspired by natural evolution principles, which are simulated on the computer (Chaitin 1997). They are used, primarily, in solving optimization problems, especially problems that do not require obtaining an optimal solution but a solution that falls within a reasonable margin of error (See Figure 2).

Genetic algorithms (GA) represent the most known field of evolutionary algorithms. Metaphor of cryptographic genetic refers to natural evolution since is based on natural genetic selection mechanisms. GA operates on a population (artificial) of characters rows. Reproduction operators, crossover and mutation apply generation's successive rows in view to the creation of new populations of rows. Often, they say genetic algorithms are an underclass of population reproduction algorithms. At each generation creates a new set of artificial creatures (defined by rows of characters) using the best elements of the preceding generation (Holland 1975).

An evolutionary algorithm has more components. They can be grouped into three basic modules:

- population module includes a method for initializations of chromosomes population. This module contains the technique of chromosomes representation and techniques for creating and handling new generations of the population. In this manner, it is specific the procedure through which passes from one population to another. The transition is made by replacing all or parts of old population chromosomes with the new generation of chromosomes. The module indicate method for selecting the chromosomes, population size and the total number of generations;
- the evaluation module contains fitness functions used for determining chromosomes performance in relation to the purpose;
- recombination and mutation module contains methods used to generate new solutions - new chromosomes - starting from the parent's genetic dot – chromosomes selected for reproduction. There are specified parameters for each genetic operator used, such as the probability of crossover, the of mutation, etc.

For implementation of an evolutionary algorithm will have to take account of how are implemented its components and their interconnection. For software implementing will be designed distinguish functional modules which then will be called on the main program. In a hardware implementation, after having been made components, they will be connected in a circuit according to the solution tackled. For example, to increase significantly the speed of convergence, the components may work each on a given set of individuals. (Gordon 1994)

Parameter Problem Coding

The implementation of an evolved algorithm implies, before all, to find a mechanism for scrambling/both to make correspondence between solutions field and representation their field for evolved algorithms. In other words, correspondence between phenotype – solution space – and genotype – representation space evolved algorithm or individuals spaces.

Each individual of a population - chromosome or genome (if presents several chromosomes) - means, in an encoded manner, a potential solution to the problem to be solved by evolved algorithm. In turn a chromosome consists of a genes sequence.

Genes representation are made using a particularly alphabet. Such an alphabet, can be composed of binary numbers ("0" and "1"), the integer numbers, the real numbers, symbols (letters "a", "b", "c", "d", etc. - this representation being used and for biology and the amino acids sequences of genetic code), arrays, etc. Usually, a gene encodes a parameter what occurs in the process to be optimized. A private value of a gene from one moment to bears the name of allele. (Davis 1991).

In the standard case of evolved algorithms proposed by Holland, the chromosome consists of a string of binary fixed length. Method "Messy coding scheme" proposed by Goldberg (Goldberg 1989), consists in the association of gene place in a row (locus) and its value (allele).

In some case, evolutionary algorithms may be used more efficiently if they use and other methods of representation. For example, instead binary alphabet can use alphabets formed with integer numbers or real numbers.

Fitness Functions

At beginning of each generation, by using a fitness function, determine to what extent performance achieved by each individual in relation to the issue to be solved. Usually, the measure performance of an individual cannot be transferred directly into reproductive facilities, which is need another function, called the fitness function, which realize this thing.

Many times the notions of evaluation or fitness are used in the same way. However it is useful to make a distinction between the evaluation and fitness functions. For example, evaluating a chromosome is independently of others evaluation and fitness calculation is made in relation to other members of current population. Typically, the fitness's a chromosome is computed after the relationship (Shaefer1987):

$$F_i = \frac{eval(i)}{\overline{eval}} = \frac{eval(i)}{\sum_{j=1}^{\dim\_pop} eval(j)}$$

where through the eval (i) have noted fitness function.

Selection Functions

The mechanism of selection use fitness value to decide which individuals of current population will be retained for future generations to become parents.

Introduction of the genetic operators into intermediate population lead at creation of a new individuals that will stay at the base of the creation of next generation. Because individuals of the intermediate population transmit genes in the next generation, usually they will be with best fitness.

So far, selecting methods known are divided into two major classes: methods for probabilistically selection and methods for deterministic selection.

Probabilistic methods use as a criterion for selection relatively fitness of individual in rapport with fitness of other individuals of the population. The best known methods in this class are: roulette method, stochastic selection of the rest and universal stochastic section.

In the roulette method selection probability associated to each member of population is:

$$P_i = \frac{F(i)}{\sum_{j=1}^{\dim\_pop} F(j)} \qquad \text{[Holland, 1975]}$$

where F(i) represent the fitness value for the i individual.

In this method, each individual is allocated a sector of roulette in proportionally mode with self fitness normalized. In moving of roulette deciding who will be individuals who will pass the intermediate generation.

In stochastic universal selection method around the roulette it puts N markers equally, and the roulette playing once.

At deterministic methods the choice depending on the rank held by individuals in the population. Basically, the rank sorting implies sorting of individuals by the absolute value of their fitness map. In this way, the selection is based only on the relative order of the population and does not take account of the fitness distribution over the population. The best known selection methods of this type are: the selection by competition (tournament selection), selection $\mu - \lambda$, truncated selection, linear rank selection (Syswerda1989).

The work of these selection methods based on individuals ranking is follows: first is running a sort of solutions depending on your fitness levels after the selection is made according to rank. Rank individuals represent its position in the population ordered by fitness.

Table 1. Genetic operators

Operator type	Description	Example
Copy	Copy the same parent in one or more children	a b c d $\rightarrow$ a b c d a b c d
Crossover	Combine the two parents who get one or many sons	$a_1 b_1 c_1 d_1$ $a_2 b_2 c_2 d_2 \rightarrow a_1 b_1\ c_2 d_2$ $a_2 b_2\ c_1 d_1$
Mutation	Change a random bit from the string "parent" as the son resulting	a b c d $\rightarrow$ a b m c

The tournament selection method consists of random selection (using a uniform probability distribution) of a number of k individual, then one that has the fitness biggest winner is declared, and consequently, will be training for the intermediate population. The number k represents the order size or tournament. This process is repeated several times (N) until the completion of the intermediate population (Goldberg 1991).

Operators Used in Evolutionary Algorithms

Fundamental mechanisms of evolutionary search algorithms specific are provided by the genetic operators. The role of genetic operators is to create new solutions using the genetic material of individuals leaving the intermediate population. Due to their property to produce new individuals (within the meaning and distribution of genes in the chromosome) these operators are appointed and reproduction operators.

Reproduction (reproduction) - is a process in which each string is copied according to the objective function value (adaptation to environment). The reproduction operator may be in different forms:

• crossover is a reproduction process by which two parent chromosomes produce two chromosome copies.
• mutation is a technique of reproduction, which amended one or more genes in a chromosome, so one or more bits in a string, with a time
• copying, duplication or cloning is unaltered genetic information transfer (chromosomes) of one or more survivors (See Table 1).

Terms Used in Genetic Algorithms

• Chromosome – refers to the code (usually binary) obtained from the encoding parameters
• Gene – is the smallest sequence of chromosome. For example in a string of bits, gene is a bit.
• Genotype – represent all the chromosomes that determine the potential solutions vector.
• Phenotype – is the solutions space that can be encoded in chromosome.
• Generation – it is all chromosomes derived from a time after the cross-mutation processes.
• Fitness - refers to the concordance of solutions obtained from a chromosome with the best solutions which is desired to be obtained. For example, if the fitness of potential solutions is better the solution is closer than optimal.
• Locus - the position of a gene in chromosome, position of the bit in a string of bits.

Figure 3. Reconfigurable circuit structure

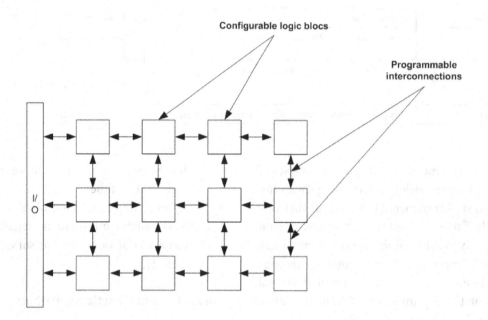

Reconfigurable Circuits

A reconfigurable structure allows more functions description on the same hardware device. A static reconfigurable structure allows external reconfiguration. This is done in the presence of a specialized programming device in the presence of a human developer. Instead, a dynamic reconfigurable structure can be self configurable. (Lomb 1998)

An alternative to Application-Specific Integrated Circuits (ASIC) structures would be using static reconfigurable circuits like Field Programmable Gates Array (FPGA). Standard structure of these devices consists in programmable logic cells and programmable interconnections.

Each programmable logic block (each cell) contains a Boolean function generator, a group of basics logic gates and one or more storage circuits. The Boolean function generator can be reprogrammed more times because it is SRAM based.

Manufacturers of integrated circuits FPGA (Xilinx, Cypress, Altera, Lucent, etc.) provide different circuit and development environments for them. Here, the algorithm is transposed in a Hardware Description Language (HDL) by enter the circuit in the form of instruction or describing it as a finite state machine or a schematics. In addition, development environments (Electronic Design Automation – EDA – tools) allow simulation of the design which makes them extremely useful in debug operations. Unlike ASIC, FPGA structures can be reconfigurable (See Figure 3).

Xilinx provide ISE EDA environment (now 10.1 version) which work with Xilinx FPGA (Xilinx 2009). It integrates VHDL/Verilog editor, schematic editor, finite state machine editor, tools for synthesis and implementation and others tools (constraints placing, simulation, core generator, etc.). For its own FPGA's and other reconfigurable circuits family Altera provide Quartus II environment (now 9.1 version) (Altera 2009). This contains editor (HDL/Schematic/FSM), Synthesis & Implementation Tools, simulation and optimization tools (TimeQuest timing analyze, PowerPlay power optimization).

There are environments which work with more FPGA/CPLD/PLD families. They can integrate tools provide by the circuits manufactures and can be used to design project with more circuits families under the same environment. In this category would be Active HDL (8.1 version) (Aldec 2009) and Mentor Graphics (DO-254) (Mentor 2009). Both have support to design circuit using a high level language like SystemC and C/C++.

All these environments use classic synthesis tools. At the end of the backgrounds section we place a very short description of classic synthesis stages and make a comparison with evolved synthesis used in intrinsic evolved hardware.

All systems using static reconfigurable hardware are no more than pseudo-dynamic. This means that allow modifying in the design stage. Once designed, the system behavior will not be changed until the next reconfiguration stage.

But there are some applications where system must respond to various external factors, difficult to predict at the initial stage of the design. There is a large class of applications: recognition of shapes, automatic control systems, guidance systems, systems of "routing" (including GSM network), image processing based on predictions, etc. where to use classical algorithms (like the list of events to be treated - treatment) would not lead to satisfactory results. For these cases, are needed to automatically control algorithms: genetic algorithms (GA), evolutionary strategies, neural networks. Here is needed capacity for self reconfiguration that can be performed by dynamically reconfigurable circuits.

Evolvable Hardware

The idea of "evolutionary machine", which has its roots in the cybernetics movement in the years 1940 and 1950, was based in theory and put in practice in two new areas of design of electronic circuits: the hardware reconfigurable structures and the search bio-inspired algorithms. Inaugural

seminar "Towards evolutionary hardware" was held in Laussane - Switzerland in October 1995 and was followed by "First International Conference on System Evolution: From biology to hardware" (ICES96) in Japan in October 1996. (eletters1997)

After the enthusiastic echoes they have raised these two events was the "Second International Conference on System Evolution: From biology to hardware" (ICES98) Laussane in Switzerland, in 1998, where participants from academic research and industrial are presented their latest discovers in the area of hardware systems that implement the concepts inspired by biology. They reached a wide range of topics including: the evolution of digital systems, analog systems development, embryonic electronics, bio-inspired systems, artificial neural networks, adaptive robotics, hardware platform with Adaptive and molecular calculation.

Field of evolvable hardware is relatively new one, it proposes that the main to expansion area of designing electronic circuits beyond the limits imposed by conventional design methods.

First demonstration that a structure with the FPGA can be used to implement evolvable hardware structure for design space expansion was Thompson (Thompson 1996). His work was interested for several reasons: first by the fact that using a FPGA circuit which allow dynamic reconfiguration (Xilinx XC6200) and thus illustrated the need for dynamic reconfigurable circuit inside evolvable hardware structure. Secondly, he illustrates the possibilities that may provide evolutionary circuits synthesis by extending the design space. In his paper, he has ordered circuit design to address both the functional requirements (to fulfill a certain function logic: signal generator with a certain frequency) and requirements that are not related to functionality (requirements related to variations in temperature and the tolerance to errors).

He used a genetic algorithm to run on a host computer and configuration was discharged into the dynamic reconfigurable circuit (Thompson

1999). He made three assumptions in the evolvable hardware area which then has proven by the implementation in FPGA Xilinx XC6200:

- Conventional methods of designing digital circuits can be applied in areas of limited space design. So much of the design space remain unexploited;

- Evolutionary algorithms can exploit areas of the design which can be accessed by conventional design methods. From this point of view it is expected that some solutions offered by evolutionary algorithms are better than solutions offered by classical methods of design.

- Evolutionary algorithms can in practice generate design solutions that cannot be obtained through traditional methods but are best.

The three hypotheses have been demonstrated by implementing a circuit using an algorithm from evolutionary algorithms class (genetic algorithm).

In Fogarty work (Fogarty 1998) described how the circuits can be synthesized directly into a structure without the need for routing operations and generating configurations, operations very demanding of resources and a long lasting time. Usually these operations are performed on an external computer. Tufte (Tufte 1999) has completed implementation of a system evolving hardware based on pipeline architecture which allows parallelization in hardware synthesis. The system is based on the solutions offered by an evolutionary algorithm (genetic algorithm) running on a computer.

Levi (Levi 1999) described a method that allows generation of FPGA configurations in avoiding the generation of illegal configuration which provides stability to FPGA (use genetic algorithm).

Hardware Implementations of Evolutionary Algorithms

From performances point of view has being more research about hardware implementation of genetic algorithm. A partial implementation of a genetic programming algorithm, only evaluation, crossover and mutation was performed by Heywood (Heywood 2000). Graham (Graham 1995) has implemented an entire genetic algorithm which runs to 4 FPGA circuits. Each FPGA has a different function: selection, crossover, mutation and evaluation. The performance of this system has been compared with those of a software implementation on a RISC architecture (PA-RISC) working at 125MHz frequency and has observed an improvement of 4 times the speed of processing. Perkins has implemented a GA on a Xilinx Virtex chip (Perkins 2000). Performances were compared with those of a software implementation on a system with Pentium processor working at 366MHz frequency and have been observed to improve the speed of hardware solution 320 times. Koza has used an FPGA structure to increase the speed of evaluation through a sort network for genetic programming (Koza 1997). Initial population was created by a computer and then the individuals download in a pre-programmed FPGA to evaluate the individual's fitness.

A solution of synthesis of the above, assembled in a customized form, probably first block diagram of parallel genetic algorithm, is given in Scott's work in that it presented a genetic algorithm architecture implemented hardware (Scott 1995) (Scott 1997). He realized the functions of selection, crossing and mutation in a number of Xilinx XC4005 circuits. Resulting scheme allows implementation of parallel modules and through a pipe-line mechanism, allows for increased processing speed for a generation (See Figure 4).

On the basis of organization proposed by Scott remain researching performed in the

Figure 4. Hardware genetic algorithm - Scott version

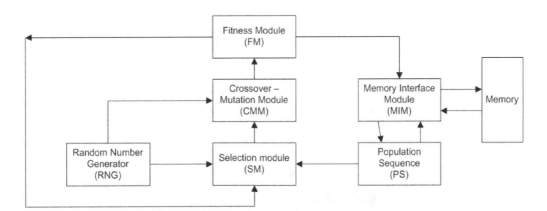

implementation of software algorithms field, i.e. serial execution of instructions, parallel hardware structures to improve performance related to speed of processing (Cantu 1995). As shown in the related concept of evolutionary hardware section, a direction of development in improving evolutionary algorithms to increase the speed of convergence of them is a parallelization through their implementation in hardware structures. The problem here is how to design modules for the complex functions of evolutionary algorithms in hardware structures. In the first phase was tried to describe the form of a combinatorial array of separate modules, which are considered time consuming such as sorting or selection (Chan 1995). Using these modules, and designing adequate command interfaces was demonstrated the optimization of the speed shown by the calculation in their applications that solve problems typical for evolutionary algorithms (Graham 1995) or in applications of hardware design for real-time systems (Turon 1995). Another direction was the implementation of parallel computing machine dedicated to run of evolutionary algorithms type (Stikoff 1995) (Shackleford 1997).

A fundamental problem in the hardware architectures of hybrid structure – the computer represents hardware - software interface that is "bottleneck" on these structures (Page 1996). This is one of the reasons for the continued research in the field of hardware intrinsically evolutionary. Using combinatorial arrays as a means of implementation of logical functions is investigated before the hardware changing. The basic idea is the decomposition of complex functions in simple function represented recursively simpler. Along with this research are noted by Mengson for use the combinatorial circuits in describing the various functions (Megson 1992). In the first phase it was the combination use of combinatorial array as a method of logic circuits synthesis (Megson 1994). He, along with Bland, presented as a possibility for implementing these types of circuits and to describe complex functions of the genetic algorithm (Megson 1997).

The solution can be completed with a pseudo-random sequences generator that is implemented with combinatorial array too (Bland 1996) and a pipe-line mechanism between modules (Bland 1997) (See Figure 5).

Synthesis of Logic Circuits Using Evolutionary Algorithms

If the field of research to implement evolutionary algorithms in hardware equipment have been

Figure 5. Hardware genetic algorithm as combinational array blocs: FPGA integrated combinational blocs and storing / evaluation to a remote computer

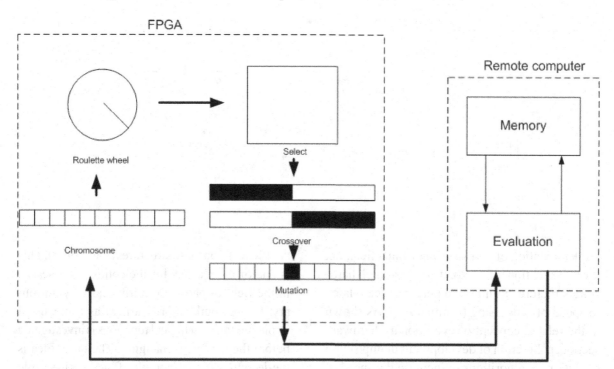

started in 90 years the research undertaken towards a synthesis of logical circuits using evolutionary algorithms, as practical applications that can be used, have been started since with 2000.

First, Miller presented in the paper "The principle of evolutionary design" (Miller 2000) a solution by which an algorithm from evolutionary algorithms class - evolutionary computing - achieving synthesis of logic circuits. Interest here is it the reconfigure hardware structure composed from cells that can implement each 16 basic logic functions.

A similar structure is used in this chapter below with the following changes: the number of elementary functions is lower and the command module is changed to a best allocation of resources in the FPGA. Also note that the algorithm used for the synthesis of logical circuits is a genetic algorithm unlike evolutionary computing aborted

in the paper cited because provides a better convergence (Langdon 2001).

Hardware implementation of a genetic algorithm with its application in the synthesis of logic circuits has been developed by Shackleford (Shackleford 2001). The paper itself does not produce an evolutionary structure within the meaning of hardware reconfiguration was classified. He used a pipeline configuration to implement a genetic algorithm such as those presented in the previous section to minimize logic circuits. He made a comparative study with an algorithm to run the same problems on a workstation with the processor at 100MHz and at 366MHz and obtained performance of 2200 or, respectively 320 times faster in hardware version.

Yasunaga's paper (Yasunaga 2001) illustrates an ingenious method of encoding solutions using an evolutionary algorithm (genetic algorithm) for a concrete application: speech recognition.

Figure 6. Basic sorting module – symbolic representation

The problem that occurred was during the "convergence" which was about 2 hours more than the other solutions. That is because this algorithm was run entirely on computer.

Classic Synthesis versus Evolvable Synthesis

There is a lot of synthesis traditional algorithms which can decompose a complex function in elementary function like F(a,b,c)=y. An example of traditional synthesis is described below:

1. The target function which must be implemented is:

$F(x_1, x_2, \ldots x_n)$

2. By using DeMorgan's rules obtain description of the function using more simple function:

$F'(x_1, x_2, \ldots x_{n1}) \ldots F'_y(x_1, x_2, \ldots x_{ny})$

3. Next the function is described using elementary functions (like F(a,b,c)):

$f_1(x_1, x_2, \ldots x_{k1}) \circ f_2(x_1, x_2, \ldots x_{k2}) \ldots \circ f_i(x_1, x_2, \ldots x_{ki})$

4. Associate elementary function with basics cell (like multiplexer) which are included inside FPGA:

$e_1(x_1, x_2, \ldots x_{n1}), e_2(x_1, x_2, \ldots x_{n2}), \ldots e_j(x_1, x_2, \ldots x_{nj}),$

5. The computation of the routing function which give the implementation:

$$\Re_{j=1}^{c} e_j(x_1, x_2, \ldots x_{nj})$$

The classic synthesis begins from the target function and, by using more Boolean rules and computation, goes to its description using elementary functions. These suppose operations like minimization which are performed with strong computation hardware.

On the other side, evolvable synthesis uses a genetic algorithm and begins from basic functions to obtain the description of complex target function, like below:

1. Elementary Boolean cells:

$e_1(x_1, x_2, \ldots x_{n1}), e_2(x_1, x_2, \ldots x_{n2}), \ldots e_j(x_1, x_2, \ldots x_{nj})$

2. Individual makes association between basics functions and gives a route:

$$\Re_{j=1}^{c} e_j(x_1, x_2, \ldots x_{nj})$$

3. Result a function which can be a potential solution:

$F'(x_1, x_2, \ldots x_n)$

4. Give fitness by comparing potential solution with the target function:

$F'(x_1, x_2, \ldots x_n) \diamond= F'(x_1, x_2, \ldots x_n)$

5. The steps are repeated until the potential solution is same with target. In this case this is the description of the target function.

The operations involved here are simplest but a genetic algorithm implementation is required.

INTRINSIC EVOLVABLE HARDWARE SYSTEM

Hardware Genetic Algorithm

Combinational Networks Used for Hardware Implementation of Basic Functions

There are two types of fundamental combinational networks in building modules of genetic algorithm: sorting networks and permutation networks. In this section are presented sorting networks and how they can be used to build selection module in GA. The others modules are designed in the same way using combinatorial sorting networks and permutation networks.

Sorting Networks

Sorting function is as an input string consisting of numbers leaving in the same range but ordered ascending or descending. A sorting network can be structured using sorted elementary module which has two inputs and two outputs characterized relations:

$$y_1 = min(x_1, x_2)$$

$$y_2 = max(x_1, x_2)$$

to sorting in ascending sense of

$$y_1 = max(x_1, x_2)$$

$$y_2 = min(x_1, x_2)$$

to sorting in descending sense.

In (Stefan 2000) the symbol of sorting elementary module is shown in Figure 6.

For example, a 4-operands sorting module is composed as in Figure 7.

Relations on output will be:

$$y_1 = min(min(x_1, x_2), min(x_3, x_4)),$$

$$y_2 = min(min(max(x_1, x_2), max(x_3, x_4)), max(min(x_1, x_2), min(x_3, x_4))),$$

$$y_3 = max(min(max(x_1, x_2), max(x_3, x_4)), max(min(x_1, x_2), min(x_3, x_4))),$$

$$y_4 = max(min(x_1, x_2), min(x_3, x_4)).$$

Selection Module Implementation Using Sorting Networks

The basic sorting module can be implemented using a subtracted circuit and selection circuit like in Figure 8. The module can be connected with others similar modules in a 2D sorting array like in Figure 9.

Individuals, with fitness computed, enter in the left side of the array. Each cell collates fitness values from two inputs x_{in} and y_{in}. The output x_{out} get the individual with the smallest fitness value

Figure 7. 4-operands sorting module

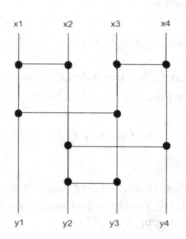

Figure 8. Basic sorting module implementation

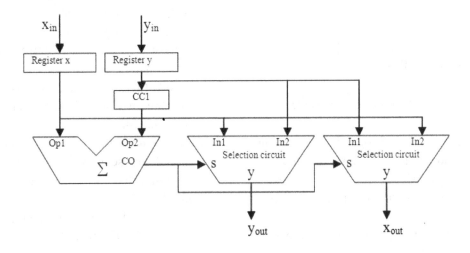

Figure 9. Selection module as a combinatorial sorting network

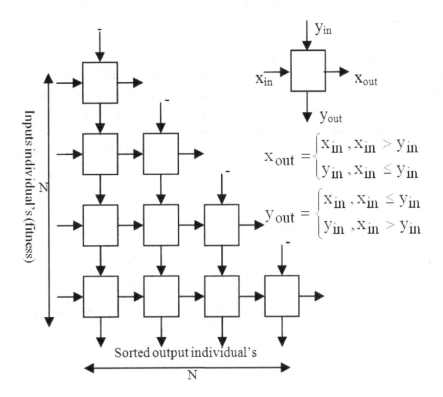

$$x_{out} = \begin{cases} x_{in}, x_{in} > y_{in} \\ y_{in}, x_{in} \le y_{in} \end{cases}$$

$$y_{out} = \begin{cases} x_{in}, x_{in} \le y_{in} \\ y_{in}, x_{in} > y_{in} \end{cases}$$

from the inputs and the output y_{out} individual with the biggest one. So, the individuals with bad fitness will cross array on horizontal, from the left to right and individuals with good fitness will cross array from top to bottom on vertical.

Finally, we have in the left side outputs with the best fitness. In bottom side of each columns is applied the smallest number possible represented here by sign minus ('-'). This number can be zero or any number which can't be great than the small fitness value.

Hardware Implementation of the Genetic Algorithm

Figure 10 is a block diagram for a possible HGA solution

HGA Each module is designed to concurrent work with the others. Thus, processing speed will increase significantly.

Basic functionality for HGA is as follows:

- the first step will be the initial storing of the individuals values in memory;
- the population generator will start a sequence that will requirements to access memory for reading the initial population. This will send address and will receive in response content from memory from those addresses which will be sent to the module selection;
- the task of selection module is to receive the individuals to the inputs and to returns classified by the fitness value. Thus, following modules will take some individuals to apply genetic operators ;

- When crossing module receives a pair of members of the unit of selection will decide whether he will apply the operator to be bits (gene). The decision will be based on random values from the random numbers generator;
- Mutation module will act on some bits of a randomly selected individual. And it will be connected to the generator of random numbers;
- The steps above will continue until the algorithm decides to end.

Certain aspects of how it will work modules will be specified separately in the detailed description of each module in the next sections. Some modules were presented in (Ionescu 2008). The modules will be designed so as to provide a high level of generality and to allow easy implementation of a large range of algorithms. Thus all modules, except for one to calculate the fitness, were designed to consist of some basic structure that can then be multiplied easily.

Figure 10. Bloc diagram for HGA module

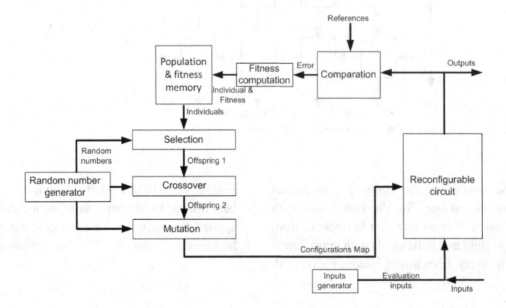

Figure 11. Individual (bits string) sequence

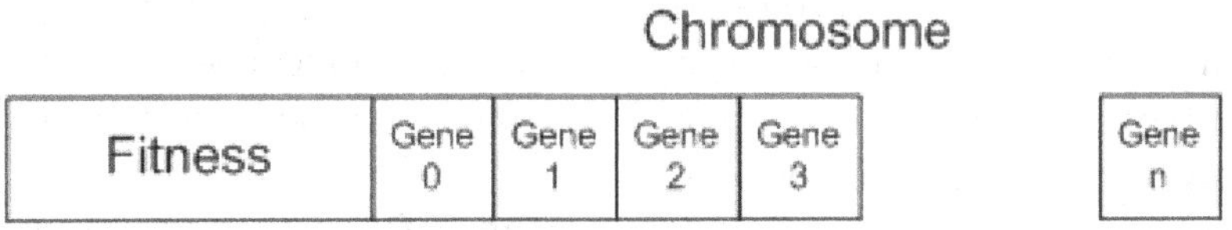

Chromosome

Fitness	Gene 0	Gene 1	Gene 2	Gene 3		Gene n

For the calculation of fitness will have designed a structure dedicated to the application.

Coding Schema

An optimization problem depends, usually, of n inputs parameters, which take real values:

$$\overline{x}(x_1, x_2, ..., x_n) \text{ with } x_i \in \Re.$$

We have solution space:

$$\overline{x} \in \underbrace{\Re \times \Re \times \Re \times ... \times \Re \in \Re^n}_{n \, solutions}$$

If we use the binary coding schema on 16 bits for each parameter: $x_i \rightarrow B^{16}$ when $B = \{0,1\}$ then we have the translation from real space in binary:

$$\Omega \rightarrow \Lambda : \Re \times \Re \times \Re \times \Re ... \times \Re \rightarrow B^{16} \times B^{16} \times B^{16} \times B^{16} ... \times B^{16}$$

By concatenating the binary string for each parameter we obtain the chromosome:

$$I = B^{16} \times B^{16} \times B^{16} \times B^{16} ... \times B^{16}$$

The binary coding schema is usually used in implementation of algorithm on digital hardware structures because is very easy to make transition from issues in digital circuits to binary strings and work with binary string in digital circuits.

We choose a binary coding schema because it can be applied to a large class of solution, it can be implemented in digital circuits (storing cell can be a latch or flip-flop circuit), and genetic operators can be easily implemented for a bits string.

We have already test system for individuals (bits strings) with one single chromosome (string) but we can extend to more, function of applications requirement. Each individual must be follow by its fitness. So, we use the sequence as shown in Figure 11 which describes an individual.

C is the size in bits for individuals (numbers of bits) and application decides how many numbers are required. F is compute from numbers of individuals per generation (N):

$$F = \begin{cases} [\log_2 N] \, if \, \{\log_2 N\} = 0 \\ [\log_2 N] + 1 \, if \, \{\log_2 N\} \neq 0 \end{cases}.$$

For example, if we have an 8 individual's population then F is 3 and if we have a 9 individual's population then F is 4.

Dynamic Reconfigurable Circuit

In this section we present architecture solution for more dynamic reconfigurable circuits. We design three reconfigurable circuit types:

a.   min terms reconfigurable circuit;
b.   INV-AND-OR multi-layer reconfigurable circuit;
c.   Basic functions multi-layer reconfigurable circuit.
  a.   Min-terms circuit is the most close of the traditional design methods. It is based on min terms synthesis but use the bits string provide by the genetic algorithm to select desired min terms in synthesis.

b. INV-AND-OR multi-layer reconfigurable circuit consists in more configurable layer. We design this circuit in three layers: an input layer INV, am AND layer and OR output layer. Each layer has its own configuration circuit which connects inputs for this layer with outputs for preceding layer.

c. Elementary functions multi-layer reconfigurable circuit has three layers of elementary Boolean functions. On this circuit can be configured connections between layers also each elementary function. Each elementary circuit has three inputs and one output. There are 16 functions: two INV, four AND, four OR, two XORS and four MUX.

This is the fully reconfigurable circuit. It allows configurations of the elementary functions and routing algorithm. The solutions provide here has different deep and different circuit number.

The circuit is based to a Boolean F(a,b,c) functions network implemented by the basic multiplexers. The selection of Boolean function and of the inputs parameters is made by a genetic algorithm (See Figure 12).

An 8:1 multiplexor (Figure 13) can be watch as a Boolean function $F(x_0,x_1,x_2) = y$, with 3 inputs and one output.

Like is illustrated in Figure 13, to each main input of the multiplexer (Iijk) can be connected to an output from one of the three the neighbors from former layer or to 0 or 1 values. The selection of these connection possibilities is coded as one gene in the chromosome. Also, the multiplexer selection inputs (Sijk) are connected to one of the eight inputs of the target complex function (here noted with a,b,c…h) or to 0 or 1. Here the selection is coded as a gene in the chromosome.

The last layer, the right one, will generate the eight outputs of the complex target function.

By having a complex function:

$$F(x_0,x_1,x_2,x_3,x_4,x_5,x_6,x_7) = (y_0,y_1,y_2,y_3,y_4,y_5,y_6,y_7)$$

the main problem is to represent this function as composition of elementary $F(x_0,x_1,x_2)$ functions.

Reconfigurable Hardware and HGA System. Example of Applications

Application 1: Boolean Function Evolvable Synthesis

In Figure 14 a bloc diagram for application 1 is presented.

The objective is the synthesis of logical function which is give as truth table: target Boolean function. The algorithm run until an individual is found which configure reconfigurable circuit to respond that the target function. After the target function is reached, the evolution stop until a new target function is required.

In Figure 15.a is presented the target function which is required. In Figure 15 b) presents the results taken with the oscilloscope on the evolution of genetic algorithm.

Application 2: Fault Tolerance Evolvable Circuit

Target is the same that in 1 application but here we simulate the change of some interconnections or circuits inside reconfigurable circuit (Figure 16).

The result displayed to oscilloscope, to channel 1 (Figure 17), illustrate the output stabilized of the reconfigurable circuit that has been applied some interconnections variation. These variations acts as perturbation and the application illustrate the capacity of fault tolerance of evolvable structure. The signal shape from Figure 17 must be read from right to left to compare with the required signal.

Figure 12. Reconfigurable circuits; a. INV-AND-OR reconfigurable circuit; b. Elementary functions multi-layer reconfigurable circuit

a.

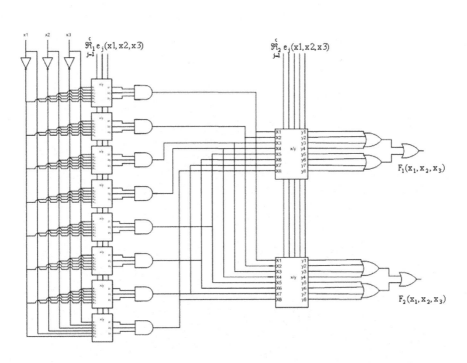

b.

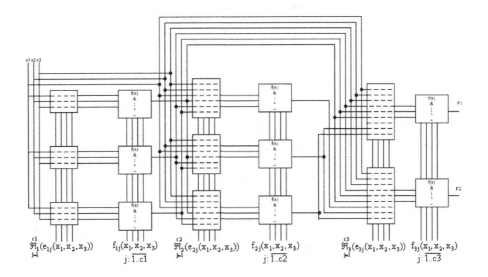

Figure 13. Boolean functions array; a. 8:1 multiplexer as 3 inputs Boolean function; b. Connections inside multiplexer (Boolean functions) array

a.

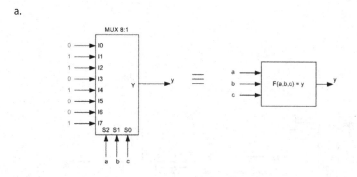

b.

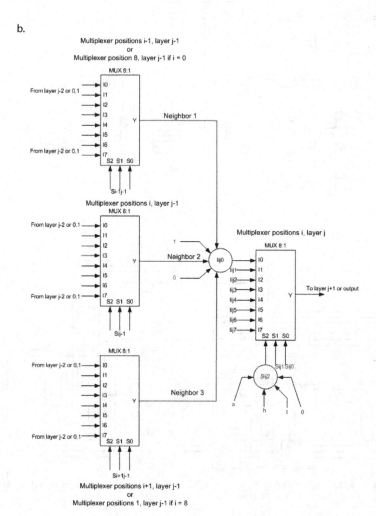

Figure 14. Application 1: Synthesis of Boolean functions

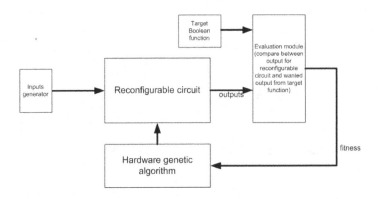

Figure 15. Dynamic reconfigurable circuit output; a. Target function output (simulation); b. Output results (oscilloscope capture)

a.

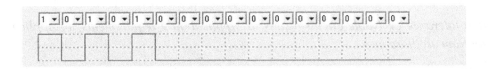

b.

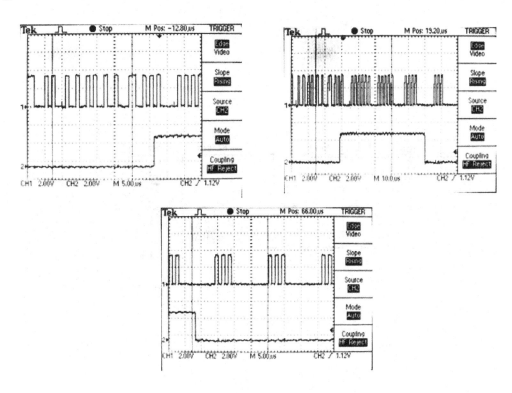

Figure 16. Fault tolerance evolvable circuit application

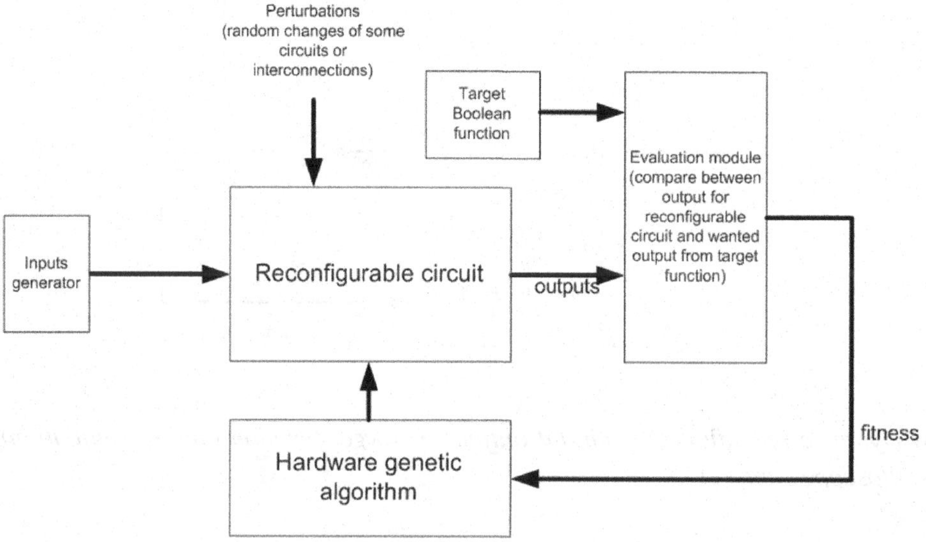

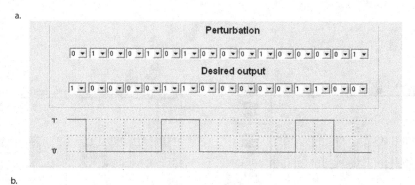

Figure 17. Fault tolerance evolvable circuit results; a. Application 2 requirements; b. Application 2 results (capture from oscilloscope)

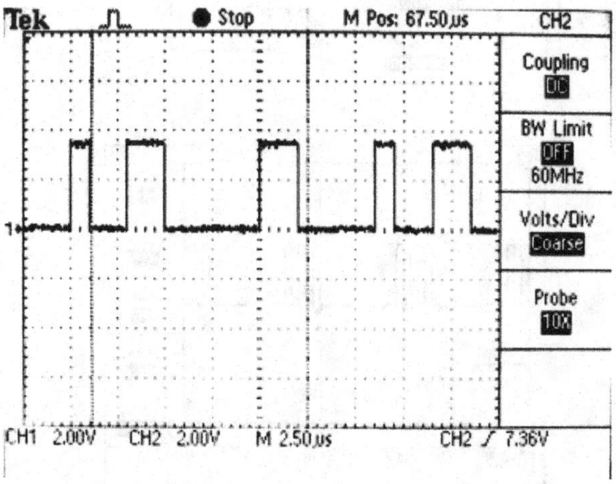

Application 3: Real Time Command for a Power Supply Regulator

In Figure 18, a block diagram of evolvable power regulator is presented.

Each individual, from evolutionary algorithm module, is a bit string which represent the configuration map for dynamic reconfigurable circuit. This module give a response as digital output data which are then PWM (pulse width modulation) encoded. A single-wire PWM signal commands power converter. Here, voltage input is translated as regulated voltage by taking in account PWM command.

Output voltage is compared with a reference voltage in evaluation circuit and fitness associated with individual will result. Fitness illustrates how close output voltage value from reference is.

Evolution loop give more individuals and increase the quality of solution until an output voltage with a value very close to reference voltage appear.

In Table 3 are present more results for application 3. The input value represents the voltage value (after AD converter) and the reference is the desired value of the output (See Table 3)

The convergence time of the algorithm prove that application can be used to work in real time. Initialization field indicates whether to go with a generation of individuals initialized or continued with the generation who converged in the last experiment.

FUTURE RESEARCH DIRECTIONS

It outlined several possible directions for development:

a. Description of reconfigurable circuit using primitive

Older series of field programmable gates array like XC300 from Xilinx allow dynamic reconfiguration. Here, the configuration table can be accessed during operation. The connection table entity was regarded as primitive (a logical drive that cannot be divided). Accessing table primitive means that a rewrite of the circuit configuration.

Figure 18. Real time command for power regulator

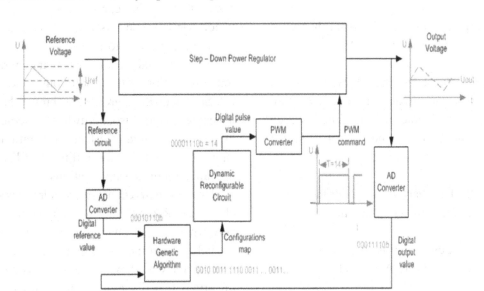

Table 3. Experimental results

Experiment	Input	Reference	Convergence time (ns)	Initialization?
1	00h	00h	16153920	Yes
2	01h	01h	13461600	No
3	00h	01h	74038800	Yes
4	00h	02h	1,88E+08	No
5	04h	09h	3,16E+08	Yes
6	04h	06h	2,88E+08	Yes
7	04h	08h	7,31E+08	No
8	05h	09h	3,89E+08	Yes
9	05h	0ah	3,38E+08	Yes
10	0ah	05h	3,55E+08	Yes

To further family a particular priority has been an increase number of cell logical component and has not been developed the dynamic reconfiguration. To family like Spartan or Virtex 2 the access to configuration resource is allowed, but without the possibility to change the configuration while operation. With Virtex 5 family have appeared reconfigurable circuits where the access to the primitive table connections is allowed. Under these conditions foresee the future direction of development to use configurations table from the FPGA as dynamic reconfigurable circuit. Resource allocation is more efficient using cells of FPGA.

b.   Storing partial configurations using hardware implemented neural networks

In the previous chapter has shown that hardware structures require memory circuit to store the individuals and fitness. A possible research direction would be to use neural networks for learning certain configurations.

c.   Using the hardware structure for the evolvable synthesis of analog circuits

An area where evolvable hardware is often used is analog circuit synthesis. A research direction is to replace dynamic reconfigurable circuit with a Field Programmable Transistors Array (FPTA).

CONCLUSION

Evolvable hardware structures and especially intrinsic evolvable hardware can be used in a large range of applications, generally where the functional requirements cannot be established in design stage. Intrinsic evolvable hardware can integrate in applications with high degree of autonomy and which require real-time response. Solution space that can be accessed is extended in comparison with classical solutions due of bio inspired, evolved algorithms.

There are many challenges that they raise the implementation of these solutions. One of them is speeding up the search algorithms by hardware implementation. Also, hardware implementation brings the advantages of the integration inside single chip and the possibility of utilization in into an autonomous applications.

The design of reconfigurable circuit is another challenge. Reconfiguration is dynamic: a fixed core where evolutionary algorithm runs, change the behavior of the reconfigurable circuit.

Chapter ended with the submission of applications that illustrate methods of using these types of structures. Evolvable synthesis of logic circuits, presented here as application can be used itself in more applications including: autonomous guidance systems, pattern recognition, decisional systems, and robots. For these reason, application 2 illustrate how the system can be used in error detection and correction. Application 3 has presented the real time operation possibilities and its possible use in control systems for power supply management.

REFERENCES

Aldec Active, H. D. *L.* (2009). Retrieved from http://www.aldec.com/ActiveHDL/

Ali, B., Almaini, A., & Kalganova, T. (2004). Evolutionary Algorithms and Their Use in the Design of Sequential Logic Circuits. []. Amsterdam: Kluwer Academic Publisher.]. *Genetic Programming and Evolvable Machines*, *5*, 11–29. doi:10.1023/B:GENP.0000017009.11392.e2

Altera. (2009). Retrieved from http://www.altera.com/products/software/quartus-ii/subscription-edition/qts-se-index.html

Bland, I. M., & Megson, G. M. (1996). Systolic random number generation for genetic algorithms. Electronic Letters.Bland, I. M., & Megson, G. M. (1997, June). Efficient operator pipelining in a bit serial genetic algorithm engine. Electronic Letters.

Cantu-Paz, E. (1995). A summary of research on parallel genetic algorithms. University of Illinois.

Chaitin, G. J. (1997). Algorithmic information theory. Cambridge, UK: Cambridge University Press.

Chan, H., & Mazumder, P. (1995). A systolic architecture for high speed hypergraph partitioning using genetic algorithms. Berlin: Springer-Verlag.

Coello Coello, C. A., Van Veldhuizen, D. A., & Lamont, G. B. (2002). Evolutionary Algorithms for Solving Multi-Objective Problems. New York: Kluwer Academic Publishers.

Cohoon, J. P., Martin, W. N., & Richards, D. S. (1991). Genetic algorithms and punctuated equilibria in VLSI. In *Proceedings of 1st Workshop*, October 1991. Berlin: Springer-Verlag

Davis, L. (1991). Handbook of Genetic Algorithms. New York: Van Nostrand Reinhold.

Fogarty, T., Miller, J., & Thompson, P. (1998). Evolving digital logic circuits on Xilinx 6000 family FPGAs. In P. Chawdhry, R. Roy, & R. Pant (Eds.), Soft Computing in Engineering Design and Manufacturing (pp. 299–305). Springer: Berlin.

Goldberg, D. E. (1989). Genetic Algorithms in Search, Optimisation and Machine Learning. Reading, MA: Addison-Wesley Publishing Company.

Goldberg, D. E., & Deb, K. (1991). A comparative analysis of selection schemes used in genetic algorithms. San Francisco: Morgan Kaufmann.

Gordon, V. S., & Whitley, D. (1994, June). A machine-independent analysis of parallel genetic algorithms. *Complex Systems,* Complex Systems Publication.

Graham, P., & Nelson, B. (1995). A hardware genetic algorithm for the travelling salesman problem on SPLASH, Lecture Notes in Computer Science, Springer – Verlag.

Heywood, M. I., & Zincir-Heywood, A. N. (2000). Register based genetic programming on FPGA computing platforms. In R. Poli, W. Banzhaf, W. B. Langdon, J. F. Miller, P. Nordin, & T. C. Fogarty (Eds.), Genetic Programming, Proc. EuroGP'2000, Edinburgh, 15–16 April 2000 (LNCS 1802, pp. 44–59). Berlin: Springer.

Holland, J. (1975). Adaptation in Natural and Artificial Systems. Ann Arbor, MI: University of Michigan Press.

Ionescu, L., Mazare, A., Serban, G., & Sofron, E. (2008). Evolved synthesis of digital circuits. In J. R. Rabunal Dopico, J. Dorado de la Calle, & A. Pazos Sierra (Eds.), Encyclopedia of Artificial Intelligence (pp. 609-617). Hershey, PA: IGI Global.

Koza, J. R., Bennett, F. H., III, Hutchings, J. L., Bade, S. L., Keane, M. A., & Andre, D. (1997). Evolving sotring networks using genetic programming and the rapidly reconfigurable xilinx 6216 Field Programmable Gate Array. In *Proc. 31st Asilomar Conf. Signals, Systems, and Comp.* New York: IEEE Press.

Langdon, W. (2001). Long random linear programs do not generalize. []. Amsterdam: Kluwer Academic Publishers.]. *Genetic Programming and Evolvable Machines, 2,* 95–100. doi:10.1023/A:1011590227934

Levi, D., & Guccione, S. (1999, July). Genetic FPGA: evolving stable circuits on mainstream FPGA devices. In A. Stoica, D. Keymeulen, & J. Lohn (Eds.), *Proc. First NASA/DoD Workshop on Evolvable Hardware* (pp. 12–17). Silver Spring, MD: IEEE Computer Society.

Megson, G. M. (1992). An Introduction to Systolic Algorithm Design. Oxford, UK: Clarendon Press.

Megson, G. M. (1994). Transformational approaches to systolic design, Chapman-Hall Parallel and Distributed Computing, Megson, G. M., & Bland, I. M. (1997, March). Generic systolic array for genetic algorithms. IEEE Proc. Computers and Digital Techniques.

Mentor Graphics. (2009). Retrieved from http://www.mentor.com/products/fpga/do-254/

Miller, J., Job, D., & Vassiliev, V. (2000). Principles in the evolutionary design of digital circuits – Part 1. []. Amsterdam: Kluwer Academic Publishers.]. *Genetic Programming and Evolvable Machines, 1,* 7–35. doi:10.1023/A:1010016313373

Miller, J., Job, D., & Vassiliev, V. (2000). Principles in the evolutionary design of digital circuits – Part 2. []. Amsterdam: Kluwer Academic Publishers.]. *Genetic Programming and Evolvable Machines, 1,* 259–288. doi:10.1023/A:1010066330916

Page, I. (1996). Closing the gap between hardware and software: Hardware-software cosynthesis at Oxford. IEEE Colloquium Digest.

Perkins, S., Porter, R., & Harvey, N. (2000). Everything on the chip: A hardware-based self-contained spatially-structured genetic algorithm for signal processing. In J. Miller, A. Thompson, P. Thompson, and T. Fogarty (Eds.), *Proc. 3rd Int. Conf. Evolvable Systems: From Biology to Hardware (ICES 2000),* Edinburg, UK (LNCS 1801, pp. 165–174). Springer: Berlin.

Scott, D., Seth, S., & Samal, A. (1997, July 4). *A hardware engine for genetic algorithms.* Technical Report UNL-CSE-97-001, Dept. Computer Science and Engineering, University of Nebraska-Lincoln.

Scott, S. D., Samal, A., & Seth, S. (1995). HGA: A hardware-based Genetic Algorithm. In *Proc of the ACM-SIGDA Third Int. Symposium on Field-Programmable Gate Arrays* (pp. 53-59).

Shackleford, B., Okushi, E., Yasuda, M., Koizumi, H., Seo, K., & Iwamoto, T. (1997, July). Hardware framework for accelerating the execution speed of a genetic algorithm. *IEICE Transactions on Electronics.*

Shackleford, B., Snider, G., Carter, R., Okushi, E., Yasuda, M., Seo, K., & Yasuura, H. (2001). A high performance, pipelined, FPGA-based genetic algorithm machine. *Genetic Programming and Evolvable Machines, 2*(1), 33–60. doi:10.1023/A:1010018632078

Shaefer, C. G. (1987, July). The ARGOT strategy: adaptive representation genetic optimizer technique. In *Proceedings of the 2nd International, Conference on Genetic Algorithmsi and their Applications.* New York: Lawrence Erlbaum Associates.

Stefan, G. (2000). Circuits and digital systems (Circuite si sisteme digitale). Bucharest: Tehnical Publishing House.

Stikoff, N., Wazlowski, M., Smith, A., & Silverman, H. (1995). Implementing a genetic algorithm on a parallel custom computing machine. *IEEE Workshop on FPGAs for Custom Computing Machines.*

Syswerda, G. (1989). Uniform crossover in genetic algorithms. In *Proceedings of the Third International Conference on Genetic Algorithms and their Applications.* San Francisco: Morgan Kaufmann.

Thompson, A. (1996). Silicon evolution. In J. R. Koza, D. E. Goldberg, D. B. Fogel, & R. L. Riolo (Eds.), *Genetic Programming 1996: Proc. First Ann. Conf.,* Stanford University, CA, 28–31 July 1996 (pp. 444–452). Cambridge, MA: MIT Press.

Thompson, A., & Layzell, P. (1999). Analysis of unconventional evolved electronics. *Communications of the ACM, 42*(4), 71–79. doi:10.1145/299157.299174

Tufte, G., & Haddow, P. (1999). Prototyping a GA pipeline for complete hardware evolution. In A. Stoica, D. Keymeulen, & J. Lohn (Eds.), *Proc. First NASA/DoD Workshop on Evolvable Hardware* (pp. 18–25). New York: IEEE Computer Society.

Turon, B. C. H., & Arslan, T. (1995). A parallel genetic VLSI architecture for combinatorial real-time application. *IEEE Int. Conf. Genetic Algorithms in Engineering Systems: Innovations and Applications.*

Xilinx. (2009). Retrieved from http://www.xilinx.com/ise/logic_design_prod/foundation.htm

Yasunaga, M., Kim, J., & Yoshihara, I. (2001). Evolvable reasoning hardware: its prototyping and performance evaluation. []. Amsterdam: Kluwer Academic Publishers.]. *Genetic Programming and Evolvable Machines, 2,* 211–230. doi:10.1023/A:1011939025340

ADDITIONAL READING

Ali, B., Almaini, A., & Kalganova, T. (2004). Evolutionary Algorithms and Their Use in the Design of Sequential Logic Circuits. []. Amsterdam: Kluwer Academic Publisher.]. *Genetic Programming and Evolvable Machines, 5,* 11–29. doi:10.1023/B:GENP.0000017009.11392.e2

Coello Coello, C. A., Van Veldhuizen, D. A., & Lamont, G. B. (2002). Evolutionary Algorithms for Solving Multi-Objective Problems. New York: Kluwer Academic Publishers.

Heywood, M. I., & Zincir-Heywood, A. N. (2000). Register based genetic programming on FPGA computing platforms. In R. Poli, W. Banzhaf, W. B. Langdon, J. F. Miller, P. Nordin, & T. C. Fogarty (Eds.), Genetic Programming, Proc. EuroGP'2000, Edinburgh, 15–16 April, 2000, (LNCS 1802, pp. 44–59). Berlin: Springer.

Megson, G. M., & Bland, I. M. (1997, March). Generic systolic array for genetic algorithms. *IEEE Proc. Computers and Digital Techniques.*

Miller, J., Job, D., & Vassiliev, V. (2000). Principles in the evolutionary design of digital circuits – Part 1. []. Amsterdam: Kluwer Academic Publishers.]. *Genetic Programming and Evolvable Machines, 1,* 7–35. doi:10.1023/A:1010016313373

Miller, J., Job, D., & Vassiliev, V. (2000). Principles in the evolutionary design of digital circuits – Part 2. []. Amsterdam: Kluwer Academic Publishers.]. *Genetic Programming and Evolvable Machines, 1,* 259–288. doi:10.1023/A:1010066330916

Perkins, S., Porter, R., & Harvey, N. (2000). Everything on the chip: A hardware-based self-contained spatially-structured genetic algorithm for signal processing. In J. Miller, A. Thompson, P. Thompson, and T. Fogarty (Eds.), *Proc. 3rd Int. Conf. Evolvable Systems: From Biology to Hardware (ICES 2000),* Edinburg, UK (LNCS 1801, pp. 165–174). Springer: Berlin.

Rabunal Dopico, J. R., Dorado de la Calle, J., & Pazos Sierra, A. (Eds.). (2009). Encyclopedia of Artificial Intelligence. Hershey, PA: IGI.

Scott, D., Seth, S., & Samal, A. (1997, July 4). *A hardware engine for genetic algorithms*. Technical Report UNL-CSE-97-001, Dept. Computer Science and Engineering, University of Nebraska-Lincoln.

Shackleford, B., Okushi, E., Yasuda, M., Koizumi, H., Seo, K., & Iwamoto, T. (1997, July). Hardware framework for accelerating the execution speed of a genetic algorithm. *IEICE Transactions on Electronics*.

Stefan, G. (2000). *Circuits and digital systems*. Retrieved from http://arh.pub.ro/gstefan/digital_circuits.html

Thompson, A. (1996). Silicon evolution. In J. R. Koza, D. E. Goldberg, D. B. Fogel, & R. L. Riolo (Eds.), *Genetic Programming 1996: Proc. First Ann. Conf.*, Stanford University, CA, 28–31 July 1996 (pp. 444–452). Cambridge, MA: MIT Press

Wikipedia. (n.d.). *Evolutionary algorithm*. Retrieved from http://en.wikipedia.org/wiki/Evolutionary_algorithm

Yasunaga, M., Kim, J., & Yoshihara, I. (2001). Evolvable reasoning hardware: its prototyping and performance evaluation. []. Amsterdam: Kluwer Academic Publishers.]. *Genetic Programming and Evolvable Machines*, *2*, 211–230. doi:10.1023/A:1011939025340

Zhao, S., & Jiao, L. (2006). Multi-objective evolutionary design and knowledge discovery of logic circuits based on an adaptive genetic algorithm. []. Amsterdam: Kluwer Academic Publisher.]. *Genetic Programming and Evolvable Machines*, *7*, 195–210. doi:10.1007/s10710-006-9005-7

Chapter 12

Connectionist Systems and Signal Processing Techniques Applied to the Parameterization of Stellar Spectra

Diego Ordóñez
University of A Coruña, Spain

Carlos Dafonte
University of A Coruña, Spain

Bernardino Arcay
University of A Coruña, Spain

Minia Manteiga
University of A Coruña, Spain

ABSTRACT

A stellar spectrum is the finger-print identification of a particular star, the result of the radiation transport through its atmosphere. The physical conditions in the stellar atmosphere, its effective temperature, surface gravity, and the presence and abundance of chemical elements explain the observed features in the stellar spectra, such as the shape of the overall continuum and the presence and strength of particular lines and bands. The derivation of the atmospheric stellar parameters from a representative sample of stellar spectra collected by ground-based and spatial telescopes is essential when a realistic view of the Galaxy and its components is to be obtained. In the last decade, extensive astronomical surveys recording information of large portions of the sky have become a reality since the development of robotic or semi-automated telescopes. The Gaia satellite is one of the key missions of the European Space Agency (ESA) and its launch is planned for 2011. Gaia will carry out the so-called Galaxy Census by extracting precise information on the nature of its main constituents, including the spectra of objects (Wilkinson, 2005). Traditional methods for the extraction of the fundamental atmospheric stellar parameters (effective temperature (Teff), gravity (log G), metallicity ([Fe/H]), and abundance of alpha elements [α/Fe], elements integer multiples of the mass of the helium nucleus) are time-consuming and unapproachable

DOI: 10.4018/978-1-61520-893-7.ch012

for a massive survey involving 1 billion objects (about 1% of the Galaxy constituents) such as Gaia. This work presents the results of the authors' study and shows the feasibility of an automated extraction of the previously mentioned stellar atmospheric parameters from near infrared spectra in the wavelength region of the Gaia Radial Velocity Spectrograph (RVS). The authors' approach is based on a technique that has already been applied to problems of the non-linear parameterization of signals: artificial neural networks. It breaks ground in the consideration of transformed domains (Fourier and Wavelet Transforms) during the preprocessing stage of the spectral signals in order to select the frequency resolution that is best suited for each atmospheric parameter. The authors have also progressed in estimating the noise (SNR) that blurs the signal on the basis of its power spectrum and the application of noise-dependant algorithms of parameterization. This study has provided additional information that allows them to progress in the development of hybrid systems devoted to the automated classification of stellar spectra.

INTRODUCTION

Spectral parameterization is a well-known problem in Astrophysics, and many previous studies have worked with a wide range of data sources (Bailer-Jones, 2008; Christlieb, 2002; Recio-Blanco, 2002; Von Hippel 2002). The purpose of these works was the study of the electromagnetic radiation spectra radiated from stars and other astronomical objects. Spectroscopy can be used to infer most stellar properties and also many attributes of distant galaxies.

Historically, the techniques that have most often been applied to automated spectra parameterization have been artificial neural networks and the minimal distance methods. Various studies have tried to determine the physical parameters of stellar spectra using artificial neural networks (ANN) and synthetic data sets (Kaempf, 2005; Bailer-Jones, 2000; Harrinder, 1998; Allende, 2000; Fiorentin., 2007). The main objective is to ascertain the fundamental stellar atmospheric parameters, particularly effective temperatures, superficial gravities, metallicities, possible overabundances of alpha elements, and individual abundances of certain chemical elements.

Stellar physico-chemical parameterization represents a fundamental step for the understanding and modelling of the Galaxy and its components. The classification of stars present in a sample or a wide collection of objects is opening new horizons in galactic astrophysics, and is helping to untangle the sequence of phenomena that have led to the present structure of the Via Lactea. The study of the metal content and chemical abundances of wide samples of stars is providing evidence on the history of stellar formation and information on the chemical enrichment from previous populations, with a detail that was inimaginable before. The Gaia ESA space mission was designed as a primarily astrometric mission that will extend the Hipparcos mission legacy with several orders of magnitude, both with respect to astrometric precision and the number of observed sources. But Gaia is a complex project, conceived to provide much more information about the Galaxy and its vicinity. It will take back two spectrophotometers that will measure the spectral energy distributions of the observed sources (between 330 and 1050 nm) and will allow us to determine their physical nature. It will also be equipped with a radial velocity spectrograph (RVS), designed to determine radial velocities and stellar parameters up to magnitude 17 (approximately) with a resolution of R=11500, and an operative wavelength range around the near IR CaII triplet (847 to 874 nm). Our study focuses on the preparation of automated analysis tools for the RVS survey.

The Gaia satellite, which is foreseen to be launched near the end of 2011, is one of the present key scientific missions of the European Space Agency (ESA). The Gaia mission will carry out the most accurate study of the Galaxy components by compiling exact information on their nature and motion. Over the course of its five operative years, it will perform precise astrometry. The RVS domain is the Ca II infrared region, 847-874 nm, a region which is rich in diagnostic lines for the determination of stellar atmospheric parameters, i.c. effective temperatures, surface gravities, overall metallicities and non canonical alpha-elements abundances. This wavelength range was selected to coincide with the energy-distribution peaks of G and K-type stars, which are the most abundant RVS targets. For these late-type stars, the wavelength interval displays three strong ionized Calcium lines and numerous weak lines, mainly due to Fe, Si, and Mg. In early- type stars, RVS spectra will be dominated by Hydrogen Paschen lines and may contain weak lines due to carriers such as CaII, HeI, HeII, and NI. The instrument operates in time-delayed integration mode, observing each source about 40 times during the 5 years of the mission. Over the 5 years mission, RVS will observe around 5 billion transit spectra of the brightest 100-150 million stars on the sky. The on-ground analysis of these spectroscopic data set will be a complex and challenging task, not only because of the volume but because of the interdependence of different instruments and observation modes.

Our aim is therefore to develop automated algorithms for the parameterization of the fundamental properties of stars that enable us to analyse, in an efficient and robust manner, the extensive volume of stellar spectra that the Gaia RVS instrument is expected to provide. For these reasons Artificial Intelligence techniques, and ANN in particular, are being tested for the case of the Gaia-RVS dataset.

In the course of the last four years, our group has been involved in the Gaia scientific team as members of the Data Processing and Analysis Consortium (Gaia DPAC): as Coordination Unit 8 "Astrophysical Parameters", we have been responsible for the classification tasks. We have tested different algorithms, based on Artificial

Intelligence techniques, for the extraction of physical parameters of stars, and worked with synthetic stellar spectra in the spectral region of RVS that were specifically calculated for the Gaia instrument (Gaia; 2009). Preliminary results have shown that artificial neural networks in different data domains represent a very competitive and robust method for such a derivation. This article presents and discusses both the methodology and the parameters accuracies obtained for several typical stellar populations of the Galaxy. The chapter is divided into 9 sections. Following this Introduction, Section 2 describes the synthetic spectra datasets and how the input domain changes when both the Fourier and the Wavelet transforms were applied to the spectra. Multilevel wavelet decomposition (Mallat, 1989) in 5 different approach and detail levels was considered. Section 6 explains the algorithm for the estimation of the signal-to-noise ratio of the spectra, as well as the tests that identify the optimal data domain for the ANN, yielding the best estimation of each of the four basic astrophysical parameters (Teff, logg, [Fe/H], [αFe]) depending on the noise level. Section 8 presents the best results obtained for each of the astrophysical parameters depending on the SNR; and, finally, Section 9 presents our conclusions and introduces our future prospects.

SPECTRALIB: A LIBRARY OF SYNTHETIC SPECTRA FOR GAIA RVS

Our initial approach consisted in performing simulations on stellar parameter extraction by means of synthetic spectra. For these first tests we used the Gaia RVS Spectralib, a library of 9285 stellar spectra compiled by A. Recio-Blanco and P. De Laverny from the Nice Observatory, and B. Plez from the University of Montpellier. The spectra are based on the new generation of MARCS models from the Uppsala Observatory in the RVS region. A technical note, describing the models used for

Table 1. Parameter Ranges

Parameter	Values
Teff	4500 7750 4500 4750 5000 5250 5500 5750 6000 6250 6500 6750 7000 7250 7500 7750
Log G	-0.5 5 -0.5 0 0.5 1 1.5 2 2.5 3 3.5 4 4.5 5
[Fe / H]	-5 1 -5 -4 -3 -2 -1.5 -1 -0.75 -0.5 -0.25 0 0.25 0.5 0.75 1
[α/Fe]	-0.2 0.4 -0.2, 0, 0.2, 0.4

the atmospheres from which the synthetic spectra were calculated and the parameters that were used, is available (Recio-Blanco A., 2005). This set of spectra will be named RVS1. The range of values of the different atmospheric parameters is presented in Table 1. The grid closely covers HR diagram positions for A5, F, G, and K stars.

RVS will be operated in windowed mode, as will be the other Gaia instruments. The windows are 1104 pixels long by 10 pixels wide. The length of the windows includes pixels out of the filter bandwidth to measure the background. The effective number of pixels is 971, and the dispersion per pixel 0.26 A. The spectra will be sampled with three different modes:

- The brightest stars, $4.75 \leq G_{RVS} \leq 7$, will be recorded with samples of 1 per 1 pixel. The corresponding spectra will therefore be made of 971 x 10 samples.
- The spectra of the stars in the magnitude range $7 \leq G_{RVS} \leq 10$ will be recorded with samples of 1 per 10 pixels. The corresponding spectra will be made of 971 x 1 samples.
- The spectra of the stars fainter than G_{RVS} =10 will be recorded with samples of 3 per 10 pixels. Larger samples are used for the faint stars in order to reduce the total read-out noise as well as the telemetry flux. The corresponding spectra will be made of 324 x 1 samples, and the dispersion 0.86 Å per pixel. These low resolution RVS spectra will not be considered in the present work.

This work focuses on the parameterization of single star spectra, which, for the effects of these tests, are supposed to be previously selected from the bulge of all the RVS Gaia observations. The ensemble of RVS simulated data, made to be used for testing and the performance assessment of the data parameterization algorithms provided by the CU8 team, was calculated by means of MARCS models of stellar atmospheres. The set of values of the atmospheric parameters that was considered in the models computation is presented in Table 1.

Next, a simple model of additive white noise at different signal to noise levels was considered (SNR: 5, 10, 25, 50, 75, 100, 150, 200 1000 and ∞). The consideration of a preprocessing stage, prior to the proper process of parameterization of the stellar spectra, was decided upon in order to improve the algorithms performance for the case of low SNR. Additionally, the fact that the spectral features sensitive to the different parameters (Teff, log G, metallic lines, α-elements lines) could be broad or narrow, together with the consideration that they are located at specific wavelengths along the spectrum, suggested that a Fourier transform and/or a multilevel wavelet decomposition could provide good results for a selective filtering of the information.

Our work has two purposes: determine the optimal domain for work with data, and develop an adequate noise detection and filtering algorithm. The concept of "domain" refers to the data format that results from the transformations that were applied to the stellar spectra in order for the parameterization algorithm to behave in the best possible way. We considered the three follow-

Figure 1. Example of RVS synthetic spectra at several signal-to-noise ratios

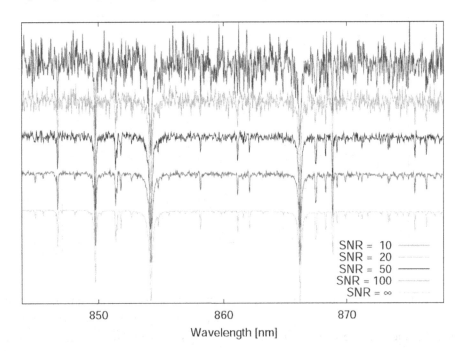

ing domains: the original domain, i.e. a flow of light received according to the wavelength; the transformed domain, i.e. the result of applying the Fourier Transform (Cooley, 1965) to the spectra in wavelength; and the Wavelet Transform, which allows us to use the multilevel analysis of signal approaches and details (Mallat, 1989) as inputs of the neural network.

The choice of the data domain, the selection of an adequate neural network for the classification, and the detection of SNR are related tasks that allow us to work towards hybrid systems for information processing in which specific techniques can be applied to each case.

INPUT DOMAINS

The dataset represents the total amount of examples that will be used to carry out the first stage of the experiment (comparison of results according to input domains). This set was arbitrarily divided

into two subsets, in a proportion of 70%-30%; the first subset will be used to train the algorithms, the second for testing (the results are shown in the comparison).

As was explained in the Introduction, the input domains on which we focus are the following:

- The spectrum in **wavelength:** in this case, the processing consists only in normalizing the spectrum and scaling its values in the [0,1] interval, so that they can be used as input signals for the ANN.

- The result of transforming the spectra into wavelength by applying the **FFT** (Cooley & Tukey, 1965). The process of transformation into the selected domain is described in Figure 2. The input of the algorithm is the original signal in units of intensity flux per wavelength interval. From that point onwards, we apply the classical steps in signal processing by Fourier transform, as can be seen in Figure 1. The entire process

Figure 2. Fourier analysis

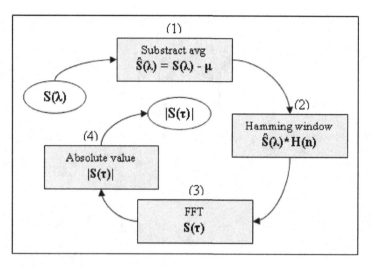

consists of four stages (Bendat & Piersol, 1971):

○ Substract the average value from the signal

○ Apply a window function of the Hamming type

○ Apply the FFT

○ Calculate the absolute value of the resulting signal.

• Application of the **wavelet transform** (Meyer, 1989) to the synthetic spectra. An efficient way of implementing this scheme by means of filters was developed in 1988 by Mallat (1989), whose practical filtering algorithm produced a rapid wavelet transform. We shall refer to this analysis as the multilevel analysis.

For many signals, the low frequency content is the most important part, because it provides them with an identity, whereas the high frequency content merely conveys nuances. In wavelet analysis, we frequently speak of approaches and details: the former are signal components with high scales and low frequencies, the latter are components with low scales and high frequencies. In our case, the

signal is a stellar spectrum, generally composed by high frequency absorption lines with variable intensity, some wider lines, and molecular bands of various types, which leads us to think that a wavelet analysis may be very adequate for our problem. The concept of multilevel analysis refers to the repeated application of filtering to each of the successive signal approaches, obtaining a new level after each filtering stage. Figure 3 shows how the filters are used to obtain the approaches and details.

We consider up to five levels of approaches and details, which yield a total of 5x2 = 10 different signals for each spectrum. We carry out the tests for each signal in order to determine where the relevant information for each parameter is to be found.

All these approaches and details constitute what we consider to be our third study domain. With regard to the wavelet analysis, an important parameter remains to be determined: the election of the mother wavelet. In this case, we decided to carry out the analysis with the help of the Daubeschies wavelets (Daubechies, 1988), because they are orthogonal and easily implementable by means of digital filtering techniques (Meng et al., 2000).

Figure 3. Discrete wavelet analysis

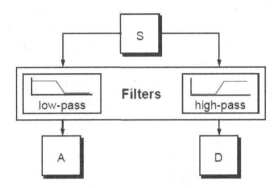

EXPERIMENT DESIGN

The previous section described the three formats or input data domains that are to be considered in the extraction of stellar parameters and the comparison of various experiments. The dimension of the input data can be observed in Table 2. For the spectrum in wavelength, the dimensionality results from using all the information provided by the signal of the normalized spectrum, i.e. a total of 971 points. However, for the result of the algorithms that were used to analyse the transformed domains, the dimensions change. In the case of the Fourier analysis, we know that the resulting signal is symmetric and band-limited. It is for this reason that we have 335 points, of which we discard half (for symmetry), as well as the highest frequencies (because they cancel the signal).

Table 2. Dimensions of the data formats

Format	Signal points
FFT	335
Wavelength	971
A1/D1	490
A2/D2	249
A3/D3	129
A4/D4	69
A5/D5	39

In the case of the multiresolution analysis with wavelets, as we descend the filtering sublevels, the number of signal points decrease with a factor of approximately 1/2, which results in signals with the amount of points indicated in Table 2. The algorithm used to evaluate the adjustment to each of the input domains is an ANN. We generate one network for each parameter to be predicted (Teff, logg, [Fe/H], [α/Fe]). The network design is based on experiments that were described in related articles and have proven their usefulness in parameterization (Bailer-Jones et al., 2005; Bailer-Jones, 2000). All these experiments point towards feed-forward networks with three layers (input, hidden, and output) and trained with the error backpropagation algorithm (Rumelhart et al., 1986). After deciding the network architecture, we must determine the dimension of the neural network. For each experiment, the number of neurons in the input layer coincides with the number of points of the format that was selected for the signal. The output layer consists of one single processing element, determined by the parameter to be predicted.

The activation function for the output neuron of the network is a sigmoid function that finds its values in the closed [0,1] interval; this requires a subsequent interpretation of the network result by adapting it to the value range of the parameter to be predicted. Even though there is no formula with which to calculate the amount of hidden process elements that are adequate for the network training, we were able to determine the correct approach by following a heuristic strategy with several adjustments. The number of input layers added to the number of output layers divided by 2 will be the number of process elements in the hidden layer, provided that this number is not higher than 200. The reason for limiting the number of process elements is that we want to make good use of the available computer resources: a network of, for instance, 1000 inputs and 500 process elements in the hidden layer with 10.000 training patterns would be too expensive in terms of resources, requiring an additional week of work, with the equipment described in Section 5, just to complete each network training. In any case, experimentation has shown that an increase in the number of process elements does not result in any significant improvement.

Since parameterization of spectra is not a linear problem, the network architecture requires more than one layer. The derivation of a given parameter on the basis of a spectrum can be seen as a function whose input is the spectrum that is presented in the corresponding format (wavelength, FFT, or wavelet analysis) and whose value is the parameter that must be predicted. It has been shown that multilayer neural networks, with hidden process elements whose activation function is no-polynomial, can approach any function (Leshno, 1993). The configuration with three network layers (input, hidden layer, and output) is very frequently used for many purposes, not only to solve parameterization problems, and has provided excellent results in the present work.

EQUIPMENT AND TOOLS

Our experiment required a rack of four servers equipped with two Intel Xeon Quad Core processors and 16 GB RAM each. This hardware architecture allowed us to launch a total of 32

parallel trainings (eight per computer) without any significant impact on the equipments productivity. The time needed to finish training was highly variable and depended on three main factors:

- Number of process elements of the hidden layer
- Dimension of the input domain
- Number of training stages with which the algorithm is configured

The neural networks and the processing algorithms were implemented in JAVA (requirement of the GAIA project). The neural networks were defined and trained with a tool that was developed by our research group: XOANE (Ordoñez et al., 2007), eXtensible Object Oriented Artificial Neural Networks Engine, is a tool that allows us to arbitrarily shape network architectures, training algorithms, and tests. We use this framework instead of other, more popular ones (e.g. Matlab), because its execution times are shorter and it enables us to obtain intermediate results that finally lead to the network's point of generalization for each experiment.

The search for the network generalization point is a recurring question when we tackle a classification problem with neural networks. The best network is not the one with the smallest mean error in the training set, but the one with the best results in the test set. In a normal training iteration, with correct network parameterization conditions, training network, and weights initialization, it is usual for both sets to decrease their error during the training stages until they reach a point at which the error decreases for the training set but negatively affects the results of the test; this point is called the network generalization point. XOANE allows us to save the state of the network by stage intervals that are selected by the user. For instance, if we configure a training with 1000 stages, stored at intervals of 100 stages, at the end of the algorithm we are saving 10 networks that correspond to the state of the network in stages

100, 200,... up to 1000. The networks are saved in an XML format according to a format that was specified in an XML schema. These XML documents can afterwards be recuperated so as to reproduce the tests or transformed to be used in another environment that is external to the tool.

Experience tells us that by saving the network every 100 stages, we are not likely to find the exact generalization point, but we will be nearby, with an error of maximum 50 training stages (half of the defined interval). If we want more precision, we reduce the interval, but a smaller interval also means that more networks will be saved, and this is a costly operation that considerably increases the execution time of the trainings in the case of very large networks. In the case of the present experiment, the networks were saved at intervals of 25 stages.

It has been already mentioned that the neural networks and the processing algorithms were implemented in JAVA, as required by the Gaia project. XOANE provides an ideal framework to develop neural networks, because it produces a direct conversion between the developed networks and the technology used in the implementation platform, independently from the final software platform of exploitation. XOANE is a very flexible tool for the development of neural networks, including not only feed-forward multilayer architectures and the error backpropagation algorithm for the training, but a wide variety of network architectures, such as RBF, SOM, SVM, Cascade Correlation, CPN, etc. It also integrates training algorithms that allow its use for a wide range of problems.

Furthermore, XOANE allows the translation of the networks represented in its internal format to several programming languages, being possible the extraction of a specific network in XML to a file containing the source code of the network in ANSI C. This property offers the developer the following advantages:

- **Transparency** with respect to the implementation platform. The developer carries out the tests independently of the final platform of implementation.
- **Reusability** of components. A particular network used to solve a problem can be reused to solve the same problem in new contexts. This avoids the duplication or re-iteration of the training and test phases for the same problem.

NATURE OF THE SPECTRAL SIGNAL AND PREDICTION OF THE NOISE LEVEL

The reliability of the parameterization algorithm largely depends on the wavelength coverage, the spectral resolution, and the noise intensity. From the point of view of the design, we must know the quality of the parameterization for a given set of observations. Since the wavelength interval and the resolution are determined in advance, the treatment of the noise problem and the configuration of the information extraction algorithm that will be applied determine the extraction quality of the parameters (Bailer-Jones, 2000).

Our experiment assumes an additive noise of the Gaussian type, the noise that the GAIA development team is initially considering in each cycle. We know that noise of this nature has a spectral density that is continuous in all the frequencies. Unlike noise, the Fourier Transform of any clean spectrum is band-limited and even cancelled at high frequencies. Therefore, if the noise is additive and has constant spectral density, and if the signals' only spectral density components other than zero appear in low frequencies, in a noisy spectrum the highest values of the transformed variable correspond only with spectral components of the noise. We will further develop this aspect in order to try to taxonomize the noise and predict its intensity. Figure 4 describes this behaviour

Figure 4. Comparison of the spectral strength of a clean signal and a signal with SNR 10

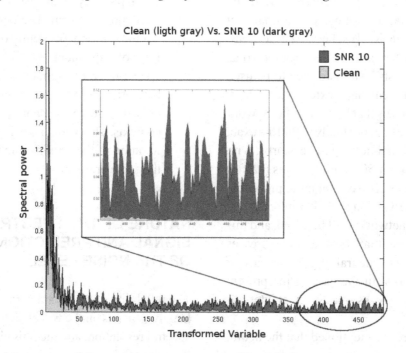

for the highest frequencies. Another important aspect is that more noise intensity in the studied signal (spectrum) implies more intense values in the higher frequencies. Therefore, in Figure 4 the signal of the lower values corresponds to spectra of SNR 100, then SNR 25, 10, and 5 (values with the highest intensity).

After determining the nature of the signal and the noise, we now only need to introduce a method to predict the adequate level of noise. Our point of departure are the data of which we already dispose, i.e. the sets at various SNRs mentioned in Section 2, which amount to a total of 9 sets, including the clean sets of the same examples with different noise intensities. For each resulting signal, we calculate the value of the integral for the last signal points, because more noise means more intensity in the last points and therefore a larger integral value. For each signal-to-noise set, we calculate the average values while taking into account the value of the integral for all the data of the set. This results in a numeric value for each

set. With the reference of the values that were calculated during the previous step, we proceed to calculate the intervals that will allow us to serve as a basis to determine the noise category of a new example. Given the integral values I_{SNR5}, I_{SNR10}, I_{SNR25}, I_{SNR50}, I_{SNR75}, I_{SNR100}, I_{SNR150}, I_{SNR200}, and $I_{SNR10000}$, we calculate the average values (I_{SNRX} - I_{SNRX}+1/2) to conclude that a spectrum has noise with intensity S_{NR50} if the value of the integral in the last points lies in the interval [(I_{SNR25} - I_{SNR50})/2, (I_{SNR50} - I_{SNR75})/2].

This strategy has a low error rate (90% hits for the available data), but by experimenting with the spectra we were able to observe that if we train with the examples of a specific signal-to-noise level and try with examples of the previous or next level, the results do not deteriorate substantially. On the basis of that fact, we decided to establish noise level groups, considering the same algorithm for SNR 5, 10, and 25; for SNR 50, 75, and 100, and for SNR 150 and 200. This strategy allows us to minimize the error probabilities (all the examples in the test set are placed in the correct category).

This calculation allows us to use the couple input domain plus SNR specific algorithm to optimize the behaviour for any level of intensity in the signal. If we know the intensity of noise in a signal, we can elaborate a specific treatment for that signal. The idea behind this is to use the knowledge that was gathered in the course of numerous experiments by applying a wide range of signal processing algorithms and carrying out specific trainings for each particular input domain, parameter, and noise level. As a result of all these tests, we know with a high level of certainty which is the most adequate way of parameterizing according to the noise and parameter type. This knowledge will be used to generate the final classifier.

The final classifier is the result of combining the acquired knowledge. Noise is a determinant factor in the quality of the adjustment, but thanks to the algorithm described in this section, we can apply the adequate transformation to the spectrum for the parameter to predict and for that specific noise level or range of noise levels, and we can select the network that is most adequate to process that input. In other words, the final classifier was designed to give the best response possible for each particular case.

PARAMETERIZATION ALGORITHM

The parameterization algorithm is based on a system of *feed-forward* neural networks trained with the error *backpropagation* algorithm (Rumelhart et al., 1986). The *network design* is as follows:

- **Input layer**, the number of process elements in this layer is determined by the preprocessing of the spectra and varies from **385** (fourier processing, removing highest frecuencies) to **971** (wavelenght

domain) process elements, and activation function of the linear type.
- **Hidden layer**, variable range (between **100** and **200** process elements), and activation function of the tangent hyperbolic type.
- **Output layer**, only **one** process element, the output value provides us with one parameter value. The output activation function is of the sigmoid type, which provides values between 0 and 1.

In this sense, it is obvious that we will need to train an ANN for each parameter that is to be predicted: Effective Temperature (Teff), gravity (log G), metallicity ([Fe/H]), and abundance of alpha elements ([α/Fe]). We will need to select four networks in order to obtain the complete set of parameters for a given spectrum.

The network will provide us with the parameterization, but the quality of the adjustment depends to a large extent on the selection of the network training set and the specific preprocessing for each SNR case. The noise level detection algorithm allows us to select the training set. We start by detecting the noise level, applying the specific preprocessing, and obtaining parameters with the neural network. The network is specialized in two senses: on the one hand, each network is able to extract a single parameter; on the other hand, the quality of the results is directly related to the noise level of the data used for the ANN training (we dispose of different ANN for different noise levels).

With clean or almost clean spectra, the combination of the above processing algorithm and a neural network for each parameter to be predicted yields good results. However, the results are less satisfactory for signals with a high SNR ratio in transformed domains, because the noise distorts the spectrum too much and is not band-located (if it were, we could solve the problem with a band-pass filter); we are using this information to perform the SNR detection, because in highest frequencies we have *only* noise and we can characterize it.

We must also consider the fact that when we use the described processing technique, as a step prior to parameterization with the neural network, we are not taking into account the last points of the spectrum, since, as mentioned above, these correspond to spectral components of the noise.

RESULTS

The results of the experiments are exposed in Figures 5 to 8. The values of the data must be seen in their context: for instance, a temperature error of 100 K should be compared within the parameter interval of possible values, which in this case lies between 4500 and 7750 K. For this reason, and in order to gain a better sense of our results, the errors presented in the figures are provided in a relative way, normalized by the interval of values possible for each of the parameters (for instance, log G should belong to the (-1,5) dex interval, therefore every log G error value is divided by 6).

As can be seen in the figures, the three signal domains (FFT, Wavelengths, and Wavelet) and each of the SNR levels were considered in this study.

We notice that the algorithm that provides the best results for clean spectra (FFT) does not function as well in the presence of noise. This is mainly due to the characteristics of the spectrum (the noise is additive and affects all the frequencies). The most consistent results are found in the wavelength domain, with slight variants in which certain approaches and details provide slight improvements (e.g.: A3 with SNR 10 and predicting temperature).

If we knew in advance what the noise level in the signal were to be, we could select the input domain and the network that provide the best result under the given circumstances for a given parameter. But a real situation does not provide this prior knowledge, so we are, in theory, obliged to choose an intermediate alternative that gives good results in the presence of noise and acceptable results with clean spectra. In such a scenario, and considering the mean error results, the wavelength domain would be the best solution. However, thanks to the proposed algorithm, we can apply the processing algorithm that is most suitable for each case.

The use of the wavelet transform fits for purpose when the SNR of the spectra is small, i.e. for the noisier spectra. This can be explained by the fact that the application of the wavelet transform preserves the high frequency components in the details and the low frequency components in the approximations. Although, in the case of study, the noise is additive at all frequencies, we know that the signal has almost no energy from some (high) value of frequency onwards (see Section 6), becoming mostly noise. Filtering those high frequencies improves the SNR and lowers the errors of the derived parameters. The loss of information (particularly in the case of high metallicity spectra) could be assumed providing that lower mean errors and error dispersions are found, as is the case in Figure 8.

CONCLUSION

Signal processing techniques allow us to select the information that is relevant for the derivation of a specific stellar atmosphere parameter, while taking into account the presence of noise that is unavoidable for real data. For the first time, a parameterization algorithm (artificial neural networks) has been applied to stellar spectra after the calculation of the Fourier and wavelet transforms of the signals. These new input domains for the neural networks have been applied systematically to a representative set of synthetic stellar spectra, compiled by the scientific team of the Gaia ESA missio, in order to determine the best numerical algorithms to derive atmospheric stellar param-

Figure 5. Clean spectra results (no noise)

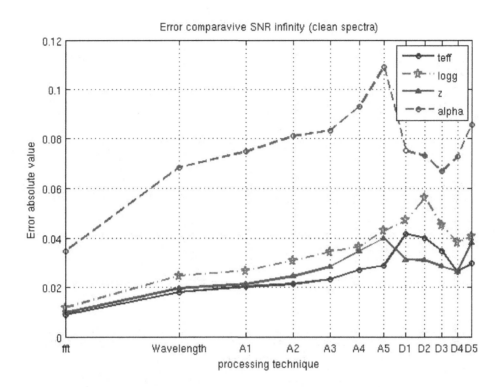

Figure 6. Spectra SNR=200 (low noise)

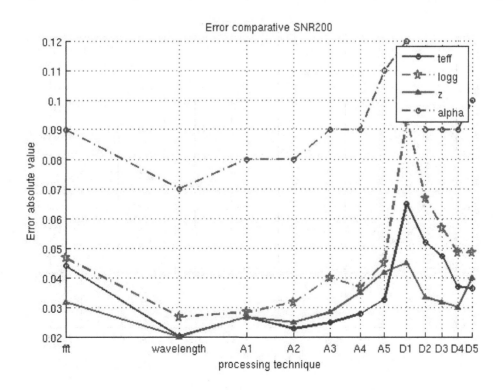

Figure 7. Spectra SNR=75 (moderate noise)

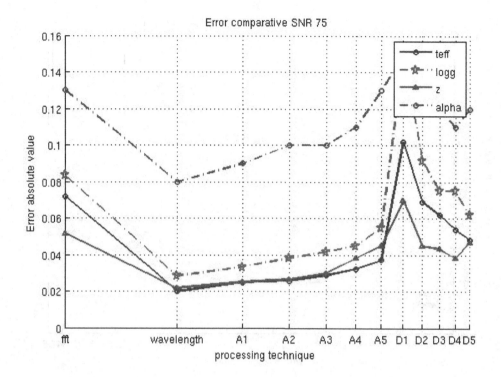

Figure 8. Spectra SNR=10 (huge noise)

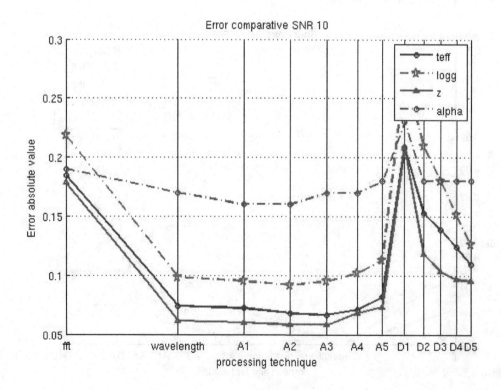

eters from the spectra that will be obtained by the astronomical space mission in a near future.

The study of the distribution of the errors obtained in the derivation of the parameters prove that the SNR definitively influences the learning process, and that characterizing the noise and training with noisy spectra is essential to improve the functioning of the networks. The noise detection algorithm plays a fundamental role in blind tests, i.e. tests for which we do not know the noise level in advance, as happens with real problems. The good results in parameterizing clean spectra by training neural networks in transformed domains (FFT) open the door to future explorations with noisy spectra. The results show that a completely automatic system, based on ANN, can successfully determine the main physical parameters of stars on the basis of their spectroscopic data.

ACKNOWLEDGMENT

This work is supported by the Spanish Ministry for Science and Education, project MEC ESP 2006-13855-C02-02.

REFERENCES

Allende, C., Rebolo, R., Garcia, R., & Serra-Ricart, M. (2000). The INT Search for Metall-Poor Stars. Spectroscopic Observations and Classification via Artificial Neural Networks. *The Astronomical Journal, 120,* 1516–1531. doi:10.1086/301533

Bailer-Jones, C. A. L. (2000). Stellar parameters from very low resolution spectra and medium band filters. *Astronomy & Astrophysics, 357,* 197–205.

Bailer-Jones, C. A. L. (2008). A method for exploiting domain information in astrophysical parameter estimation. In *Astronomical Data Analysis Software and Systems XVII. ASP Conference Series* (Vol. 30).

Christlieb, N., Wisotzki, L., & Graßhoff, G. (2002). Statistical Methods of automatic spectral classification and their application to the Hamburg/ESO sourvey. *Astronomy & Astrophysics, 391,* 397–406. doi:10.1051/0004-6361:20020830

Cooley, J. W., & Tukey, J. W. (1965). An algorithm for the machine calculation of complex Fourier series. *Mathematics of Computation, 19,* 297–301. doi:10.2307/2003354

Daubechies, I. (1988). Orthonormal bases of compactly supported wavelets. *Communications on Pure and Applied Mathematics, 41,* 909–996. doi:10.1002/cpa.3160410705

Fiorentin, P. R., Bailer-Jones, C. A. L., Lee, Y. S., Beers, T. C., Sivarani, T., & Wilhelm, R. (2007). Estimation of stellar atmospheric parameters from SDSS/SEGUE spectra. *Astronomy & Astrophysics, 467,* 1373–1387. doi:10.1051/0004-6361:20077334

Gaia. (2009). *The galactic census problem.* Retrieved from http://www.rssd.esa.int/gaia/

Harinder, P., Gulati, R. K., & Gupta, R. (1998). Stellar Spectral Classification using Principal Component Analysis and Artificial Neural Networks. *Monthly Notices of the Royal Astronomical Society, 295,* 312–318. doi:10.1046/j.1365-8711.1998.01255.x

Kaempf, T. A., Willemsen, P. G., Bailer-Jones, C. A. L., & de Boer, K. S. (2005). Parameterisation of RVS spectra with Artificial Neural Networks First Steps. In 10th RVS workshop, Cambridge.

Leshno, M., & Schocken, S. (1993). *Multilayer Feedforward Networks with non-Polynomial Activation Functions can Approximate any Function.* Center for Digital Economy Research, Stern School of business. Working Paper IS-91-26.

Mallat, S. (1989). A theory for Multiresolution Signal Decomposition: The Wavelet representation. *Proc. IEEE Trans on Pattern Anal., & Math. Intel., 7*(11).

Meng, H., Wang, Z., & Llu, G. (2000). Performance of the Daubeschies wavelet filters compared with other orthogonal transforms in random signal processing. In *Proceedings ICSP*.

Ordóñez, D., Dafonte, C., Arcay, B., & Manteiga, M. (2007). A canonical integrator environment for the development of connectionist systems. *Dynamics of continuous. Discrete and Impulsive Systems*, *14*, 580–585.

Recio-Blanco, A., Bijaoui, A., & de Laverny, P. (2002). Automated derivation of stellar atmospheric parameters and chemical abundances: the MATISSE algorithm. R. Astron. Soc.

Recio-Blanco, A., de Laverny, P., & Plez, B. (2005). *RVS-ARB-001*. European Space Agency technical note.

Rumelhart, D. E., Hinton, G. E., & Williams, R. J. (1986). Learning representations by back-propagating errors. *Nature*, *323*, 533–536. doi:10.1038/323533a0

Von Hippel, T., Allende, C., & Sneden, C. (2002). Automated Stellar Spectral Classification and Parameterization for the Masses. *The Garrison Festschrift conference proceedings*.

Wilkinson, M. I., Vallenary, A., & Turon, C. (2005). Spectroscopic survey of the Galaxy with Gaia- II. The expected science yield from the Radial Velocity Spectrometer. *Monthly Notices of the Royal Astronomical Society*, *359*, 1306. doi:10.1111/j.1365-2966.2005.09012.x

Section 3
Biomedical Approaches

Chapter 13
Automatic Arrhythmia Detection

Carlos M. Travieso
University of Las Palmas de Gran Canaria, Spain

Jesús B. Alonso
University of Las Palmas de Gran Canaria, Spain

Miguel A. Ferrer
University of Las Palmas de Gran Canaria, Spain

Jorge Corsino
University of Las Palmas de Gran Canaria, Spain

ABSTRACT

In the present chapter, the authors have developed a tool for the automatic arrhythmias detection, based on time-frequency features and using a Support Vector Machines (SVM) as classifier. Arrhythmia Database Massachusetts Institute of Technology (MIT) has been used in the work in order to detect eight different states, seven are pathologies and one is normal. The unions of different blocks and its optimization have found success rates of 99.82% for RR' interval detection from electrocardiogram (PQRST waves), and 99.23% for pathologic detection. In particular, the authors have used wavelet transform in order to characterize the wave of electrocardiogram (ECG), based on Biorthogonal family, achieving the most discriminative coefficients. A discussion on arrhythmia ECG classification methods is also presented in this paper.

INTRODUCTION

Nowadays, cardiovascular diseases are one of most important causes of death, with a great repercussion on the health assistance budget. For instance, to obtain an early exact cardiovascular diagnosis is one of the most important missions for the physicians.

Blood cannot pump effectively when the heart does not beat properly. Therefore the lungs, brain and all other organs cannot work properly and may shut down or be damaged.

Cardiology departments have become one of the most important areas within Health Services all over the world, due to the number of deaths caused by cardiology related problems. In particular, in Spain, according to the National Statistics Institute (INE), approximately a third of the total number of fatalities had its origin in a cardiac disease. As the single largest cause of death it cannot be ignored.

DOI: 10.4018/978-1-61520-893-7.ch013

Nevertheless, research carried out in this area to date is considered to be insignificant, bearing in mind the high rate of deaths caused by cardiac diseases. European Union countries invest on average a minimal value of 3%, considerably less than countries such as the USA (6.8%) or South Korea (5.4%).

The ECG is the graphic description of the heart's electric activity registered from the body surface in exquisite detail. This is a basic element in the diagnosis of different heart diseases. This diagnosis depends on the medical experience. Normally a big knowledge is needed to obtain great results.

Some of the reasons of identification error are: signal with no good quality; details under noise or miniature details such as human subjectivity.

Therefore, the objective of this present work is to design and implement computer aided software for detecting arrhythmias based on the time-frequency features and using an automatic classification system. The term arrhythmia refers to any change from the normal sequence of electrical impulses. The electrical impulses may happen too fast, too slowly, or erratically causing the heart to beat too fast, too slowly, or erratically. This idea is based on the feature extraction from Electrocardiogram (ECG) signal, using physicians as supervised knowledge for labeling ECG signals. The function of these tools is to help on medical tasks against the prevention of cardiovascular diseases.

BACKGROUND

In the 60's the ECG analysis had a wide number of studies about its process in different ways and for different applications, for example, some of them apply mathematical or statistical concepts.

Most cardiovascular diseases can be diagnosed by the analysis of the significant time intervals in the ECG signal. The ECG features extracted can determine whether a patient presents any kind of cardiac pathology or not. However, in order to extract these values a previous signal processing is required to delete noise and to make the analysis lighter. The common noise sources are: baseline wander, power line interference and muscle noise. Baseline wander, or stranger low-frequency high-bandwidth components, can be caused by: perspiration (effects electrode impedance), respiration and body movements. These noises can cause problems to analysis, especially when examining the low-frequency ST-T segment.

On the frequency domain, the main information is placed under 35 Hz. Power line normally affect over 50 and 60 Hz and the muscle noisy can be approximated as white noise because his frequency spectrum is practically plane.

The inherent morphology of the electrocardiographic (ECG) signal is a key factor to determine if the reliable feature detection can be made. As a non-stationary signal, ECG has to be pre-processed using frequency adaptive tools. Several techniques have been used to perform the detection of these features over the last decades, such as the Short Time Fourier Transform (STFT) or the Wavelet transform.

In the arrhythmias detection there are two main kinds for the feature extraction. On the one hand, features extracted directly from the ECG signal, time, sizes, areas, delays, etc. And on the other hand, features extracted from domain transforms. Both methods will be discussed in this present work (Mallat, 1998; Kunzmann et al. 2002; Alonso et al., 1999; Moraes et al., 2002; Bahoura et al., 1997; Hosseini & Reynolds, 2001; Zimmerman & Povinelli, 2004).

The block diagram of both approaches is very similar; the difference is the feature extraction module. In the Figure 1, we can see a block diagram of the whole classification system.

As shown, after extracting the features from the entire database, a first training stage is obtained. Through this model system a new block of features is applied to see the answer of the model. If it this solution is optimal, the final Classifier

Figure 1. Block Diagram of automatic Arrhythmia detection

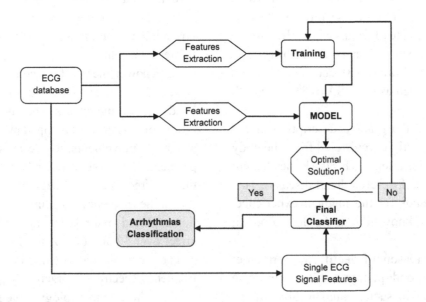

is completed, on the other way, the training stage has to be redo with new characteristics.

In a brief literature review or state-of-the-art, the previous two research lines it can be seen. Senhadji et al. (1995) firstly proposed a Wavelet-based feature extraction system for ECG signals, showing its performance on R peak detection varying between three Wavelets families. This study shows a capability of discrimination between normal, premature ventricular contraction, and ischemic beats by means of linear discriminant analysis. The good results obtained motivated Sahambi et al. (1997) to develop a system able to detect not only the R peak, but also the QRS complex and the P and T waves using the Discrete Wavelet Transform (DWT), overcoming the limitations of other methods of complexes QRS detection. In fact, Sahambi et al. (1997) show that the rapid and objective measurement of timing intervals of the electrocardiogram (ECG) by automated systems is superior to the subjective assessment of ECG morphology. Since then several feature detection systems using DWT have been developed, improving its performances. Sivannaryana & Reddy (1999) added amplitude features to a time feature

based detector, obtaining better results. Recently published works, such as, Shyu's et al. (2004) or Martinez's et al. (2004) based on an improvement of Li's et al. (1995) detection algorithm, achieved about 99% success rates using wavelet transform and fuzzy neural network (FNN) with the MIT Arrhythmia Database (MIT-BIH Arrhythmia Database, 2009).

Size and power requirements, characteristic of mobile devices such as mobile heart monitors, restricted these authors to use the DWT on feature extraction pre-processing. DWT presents a good response on time calculation and pre-processing, demonstratins that it can eliminate the influence of high and low frequency noise. However, discrete Wavelet techniques have disadvantages such as low time-frequency resolution. Continuous Wavelet Transform (CWT) solves the resolution problem, but more load time is required for the process. Nowadays, processor execution times have been reduced, which allows for the implementation of CWT detectors on mobile devices. In 2005, Romero Legarreta et al. (2005) proposed a CWT detector based on maximum modulus curves, which obtained 99.7% on sensitivity and a 99.6% success rate. Continuous wavelets transform modulus maxima reduces the computational requirements by representing only the relevant information contained within the scale obtained from continuous wavelet analysis. This new domain has an easy interpretation and offers a useful tool for the automatic characterization of the different components observed in the ECG in health and disease.

Heart activity monitoring has become an essential tool in cardiac diagnosis. Mostly, a single cardiologist has to analyze a full sequence of heart beeps which in Holter records last for up to 48 hours. To facilitate the diagnosis process, various automatic ECG classification systems have been presented in the last years which have obtained good results, although reliability is still less than 100%, and the supervision of the specialist after the automatic classifying is compulsory. The aim of these systems is to minimize the greatest possible degree the number of signals that have to be revised by the specialist, thus saving time on analysis.

In recent years several classification systems have been implemented using classifying techniques, such as Neural Networks, and recently SVM. The widely used Neural Networks techniques on biomedical signals motivated us to choose it as the initial classification technique. Lagerholm et al. (1998) developed a neural network based classifier using Self Organized Maps (SOM), achieving success rates of over 98%. Silippo et al. (1999) used static neural networks and improved the performance of the Lagerholm classifier. They developed a good fuzzy classifier for a three-class arrhythmia using fourteen ECG measures to characterize each beat. However, as the number of different signals increased in the classification process, the performance decreased notably.

Support Vector Classification (SVC) was introduced by Vapnik (1995), but it was not commonly used until the late 1990's. It was presented for use in any field of action; in Biomedical Engineer-

ing works such as Liu's et al. (2001) proposing a cancer diagnosis system, or Huang (2001) face recognition system, for example. In Jankolowski et al. (2003) firstly applied SVM to ECG classification achieving a 98.3% success rate on arrhythmia classifying. More recently, Song et al. (2005) developed a 6 classes ECG classifier with a 99.3% success rate over 10 signals of the MIT Arrhythmia DB. This last algorithm was based on the generalized discriminant analysis (GDA) feature reduction scheme and the support vector machine (SVM) classifier. Initially 15 different features are extracted from the input heart rate variability (HRV) signal by means of linear and nonlinear methods. These features are then reduced to only five features by the GDA technique.

Our proposal focuses on the use of DWT in order to detect and classify the arrhythmias, and distinguishing different 7 classes of pathologies. But the adequate Wavelet family and the classification system must be applied in order to obtain the most discriminative information and a good success, respectively.

ARRHYTHMIA DETECTION SYSTEM

This work presents a Wavelet feature extraction using the Multiresolution Analysis (MRA) which provides Wavelet techniques (Mallat, 1998). This system is developed from a database labeled (MITD). Although there are many databases, the most extended arrhythmia databases are MITDB (MIT-BIH Arrhythmia Database, 2009) and UCI database (Blake & Merz, 2009). Firstly, the detection of EGC waves is carried out by Wavelet transform, and in the next step, the classification is carried out with the ECG wave parameters. This system has been implemented as supervised classification, and therefore, training and test modes have been made (Vapnik, 1995; Huang et al., 2001; Jankolowski et al., 2003). Both modes, using the medical labels of each signal and beat.

ECG Data

The electrocardiogram (ECG) is a time-varying signal that reflects the electric current that stimulates cardiac muscle to contract and relax. The ECG signal is acquired using at least two electric sensors applied at specific points of the patient's body, recording the electric potential between these two points. Basically, heart activity can be described as a continuous two step movement, depolarization/repolarisation, contraction and relaxation of the muscle.

Contraction is the result of the electrical activity of the myocardial cells. This electrical signal begins in the sinoatrial (SA) node, located at the top of the right atrium. The SA node is sometimes called the heart's natural pacemaker. When an electrical impulse is released from this natural pacemaker, it causes the atria to contract. The signal then passes through the atrioventricular (AV) node. The AV node checks the signal and sends it through the muscle fibers of the ventricles, causing them to contract.

The SA node sends electrical impulses at a certain rate, but heart rate may still change depending on physical demands, stress, or hormonal factors.

A single normal cycle of the ECG represents the atrial depolarization/repolarisation and the ventricular depolarization/repolarization present in every beat.

As blood collects in the upper chambers (the right and left atria), the SA node sends out an electrical signal that causes the atria to contract. This contraction pushes blood through the tricuspid and mitral valves into the resting lower chambers (the right and left ventricles). This part of the cardiac cycle (the longer of the two) is called diastole.

The second part of the cardiac cycle begins when the ventricles are full of blood. The electrical signals from the SA node travel along a pathway of cells to the ventricles, causing them to contract. This is called systole. As the tricuspid and mitral valves shut tight to prevent a back flow of blood, the pulmonary and aortic valves are pushed open.

While blood is pushed from the right ventricle into the lungs to pick up oxygen, oxygen-rich blood flows from the left ventricle to the heart and other parts of the body.

After blood moves into the pulmonary artery and the aorta, the ventricles relax, and the pulmonary and aortic valves close. The lower pressure in the ventricles causes the tricuspid and mitral valves to open, and the cycle begins again.

Each of the above mentioned movements are reflected in the ECG waveform and labeled as P, Q, R, S, and T waves: Atrial contractions (both right and left) show up as the P wave; Ventricular contractions (both right and left) show as a series of 3 waves, Q-R-S, known as the QRS complex; the T wave reflects the electrical activity produced when the ventricles are recharging for the next contraction (repolarizing).

The electrical activity results in P, QRS, and T waves that have a myriad of sizes and shapes. When viewed from multiple anatomic-electric perspectives, these waves can show a wide range of abnormalities of both the electrical conduction system and the muscle tissue of the heart's four pumping chambers.

The normal delay between the contraction of the atria and of the ventricles is 0.12 to 0.20 seconds. This delay is perfectly timed to account for the physical passage of the blood from the atrium to the ventricle. Intervals shorter or longer than this range indicate possible problems.

A simple relation between these waves and anomalies is:

- The relationship between P waves and QRS complexes helps distinguish various cardiac arrhythmias.
- The shape and duration of the P waves may indicate atrial enlargement.
- Absence of the P wave may indicate atrial fibrillation.
- A sawtooth pattern instead of a P wave may indicate atrial flutter.

- The duration, amplitude, and morphology of the QRS complex is useful in diagnosing cardiac arrhythmias, conduction abnormalities, ventricular hypertrophy, myocardial infarction, electrolyte derangements, and other disease states.
- Q waves can be normal (physiological) or pathological. Pathological Q waves refer to Q waves that have a height of 25% or more than that of the partner R wave and/or have a width of greater than 0.04 seconds. Normal Q waves, when present, represent depolarization of the interventricular septum.
- A PR interval of over 200 ms may indicate a first-degree heart block.
- A short PR interval may indicate a pre-excitation syndrome via an accessory pathway that leads to early activation of the ventricles, such as seen in Wolff-Parkinson-White syndrome.
- A variable PR interval may indicate other types of heart block.
- PR segment depression may indicate atrial injury or pericarditis.
- Flat, downsloping, or depressed ST segments may indicate coronary ischemia.
- And others.

One of the most common values, which are obtained from the extraction, is the RR' interval, or its inverse, the beep rate. Heart Rate Variability (HRV) can show the presence of abnormal heart activity. Several other time intervals, such as the QT interval or the ST segment, can also determine pathologic beats. Not only are time related values extracted from the ECG signal, but also amplitude related values like the QRS complex area or even frequency related values, such as LF/HF ratio, defined as the power difference between 0.015 Hz and 0.15 Hz, are obtained. Using all these values previously extracted as an input to a classifying system can provide the cardiology specialist with an extremely useful tool capable of automatically detecting the presence of abnormal beats in a patient's ECG.

The most common cardiovascular diseases can normally be detected with an in-depth analysis of the electrocardiogram, as heart malfunction is reflected in the ECG signal by variations of the characteristic waves. Cardio pathologies can be classified into three groups according to their origin: sinus, atrial and ventricular. A noticeable decrease of heart rate is known as bradycardia and its inverse effect is called tachycardia. An irregular increase of tachycardia rhythms derives into fibrillation. Within the cardiac diseases, atrial fibrillation is the most commonly diagnosed and consequently treated.

In this paper, we establish the use of approximated wavelet coefficients taken out from the ECG signal in order to classify eight types of beat: normal pulse (N), extra-systole (L), premature ventricular contraction (V), premature auricular contraction (A), blockade left branch (L), blockade right branch paced beat (R), fusion of normal and paced beat (f) and fusion of normal and premature ventricular contraction (F).

Types of Arrhythmia to Detect

Atrial Premature Beat describes a beat arising from the atrium and occurring before the expected sinus beat. Premature beats can occur randomly or in a pattern. P-wave morphology differs from sinus beats and varies, depending on the origin of the impulse in the atria.

Premature ventricular contraction: is premature heartbeat originating from the ventricles of the heart that occurs before the regular heartbeat.

Left bundle branch block is a cardiac conduction abnormality seen on the electrocardiogram (ECG). In this condition, activation of the left ventricle is delayed, which results in the left ventricle contracting later than the right ventricle.

Right bundle branch block: During a right bundle branch block, the right ventricle is not directly activated by impulses travelling through the right bundle branch. The left ventricle however, is still normally activated by the left bundle branch and these impulses travel through the left ventricle's myocardium to the right ventricle and activate the right ventricle.

Fusion of ventricular and normal beat, in electrocardiography, the complex resulting when an ectopic ventricular beat coincides with normal conduction to the ventricle.

Fusion of paced and normal beat: is usually narrower than a paced impulse and has various morphologies that reflect the relative contributions of the impulse to the ventricular depolarization.

The MIT Arrhythmia Database will be used for the classification system testing process. This database is composed by 48 half hour length records, sampled 360 samples per second with 11 bits resolution for level of 10 mili Volts. These 48 records are divided into two groups: 23 with common arrhythmias, and the remainder, a further 25, presenting abnormal cases. All these records have been labeled to facilitate their reading and for testing purposes. The MITDB is the most commonly used, and is generally regarded as the standard in ECG classification. For training process, different files of the MIT/BIH arrhythmia database were selected as representatives of mentioned classes.

Feature Extraction

Although the decomposition in well defined blocks in time and frequency, wavelet transform can characterise the local sign regularities. This skill allows distinguishing electrocardiogram waves (ECG) from noise and other artefacts.

The ECG features are extracted through a pre-processing stage in which the Wavelet transform is applied to original ECG signal. R peaks and QRS complex detection is carried out using the continuous wavelet transform (CWT) of the whole ECG signal.

The CWT is defined as follows:

$$W_{\psi(a,b)} = \int_{-\infty}^{\infty} f(t)\psi_{a,b}(t)dt \qquad (1)$$

where ψ is the transform function or "mother wavelet":

$$\psi_{a,b}(t) = \frac{1}{\sqrt{|a|}} \psi\left(\frac{t-b}{a}\right) \qquad (2)$$

An example of relation between scales and time can be observed in Figure 2. The CWT is thresholded using a signal independent threshold fixed at:

$$T = 1.5 * std(WT) \qquad (3)$$

All the values over the threshold are selected in order to find the maximums corresponding to the peak. A detection window is used avoiding interferences from P and T waves, i.e. if a peak is detected it cannot be any other peak in the next n samples. The parameter will be initially fixed to 100 samples (equivalent to 200 beeps per minute) and sequentially modified according to the signal beep rate calculated with previously detected peak values.

Once the R peaks are extracted, the next step is to obtain the location of the QRS complex by finding the adjacent minimums of the peak previously detected. This process is used in QRS complex detection, removing the P and T Waves. This process is applied to every single beat previously detected. The QRS complexes detected are evaluated as an input to the P and T detection process. However, on the P and T waves extraction a DWT method is presented in Figure 3. This system has achieved a success rate of 99.82% for the feature extraction.

Finally, as we are processing digital signal, it is inevitable to transfer the process to digital domain, where the DWT is defined as;

Figure 2. Relation between wavelet coefficients and time

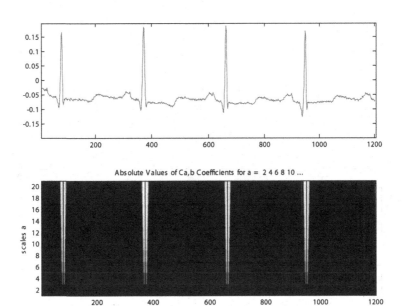

$$C[j,k] = \sum_{n \in \mathbb{Z}} f[n]\psi_{j,k}[n] \qquad (4)$$

where $\psi_{j,k}$ is the transform function:

$$\psi_{j,k}[n] = 2^{\frac{-j}{2}} \cdot \psi[2^{-j}n - k] \qquad (5)$$

The DWT follows a dyadic scale, as shown, the scale factor i and the transfer factor j are modified by a factor of 2 every time that DWT is calculated.

Thanks to DWT, a new concept appears Multi Resolution Analysis (MRA), whose main characteristic is that every frequency component is analysed with a different resolution. The most important advantage is that high frequencies are analysed with high time resolution and low frequency resolution, and for low frequencies, the time resolution is high and the frequency is low.

The QRS Complexes previously extracted are removed from the P and T wave analysis range. Then a level 4 DWT with Biorthogonal family

is obtained from the ECG signal range defined. The P and T waves are detected by means of a signal-independent thresholding process.

Classification System

A supervised classification system based on discrete wavelet coefficients is proposed in this chapter, being physicians who supervised the process. We have checked with two different classifiers, Artificial Neural Network and Support Vector Machines. The first approach is more robust versus noise, and the second approach is minus robust the previous classifier, but it has a good method to determinate the decision frontier.

Support Vector Machine (SVM)

The Support Vector Machine (SVM) resolves by maximizing the margin separation the classification of geometric parameters of the separate hyperplane from the training data (Cristianini et al. 2000; Burges 1998; Schöfkopf et al. 1999).

Figure 3. Process for P and T waves extraction

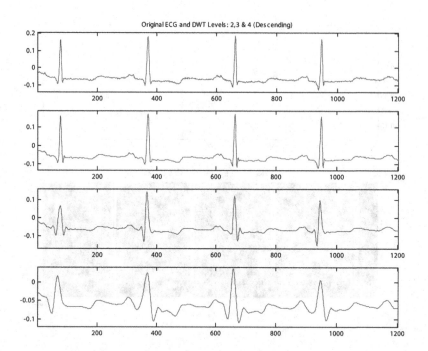

Besides, this solution introduces methods, which will enable to work with no separable and lineally separable cases of the data. The decision boundary is determined with the calculation of a separate hyperplane that discriminates between the positive and the negative samples; therefore a SVM treats the classification as two different classes. This decision boundary or separate hyperplane can be designed with different kernels: linear, polynomial, gaussian, etc.

Supposing that all the data of training satisfy the following conditions:

$$x_i \cdot w + b \geq +1 \quad for \quad y_i = +1 \qquad (6)$$

$$x_i \cdot w + b \leq -1 \quad for \quad y_i = -1 \qquad (7)$$

being x_i the vector of characteristics and y_i the class of a determinate observation i.

These two conditions can be transformed in a set of inequations:

$$y_i(x_i \cdot w + b) - 1 \geq 0 \qquad \forall i \qquad (8)$$

The points which comply with the equality of the equation 6, are found in the hyperplane H1: $x_i \cdot w + b = 1$ with normal w and distance perpendicular since the origin $\dfrac{|1-b|}{\|w\|}$.

Similarly, the contained points in the equality of the equation 7 are found in the hyperplane H2: $x_i \cdot w + b = -1$ with normal w and distance perpendicular since the origin $\dfrac{|-1-b|}{\|w\|}$. The distances between H1 and H2 will be equal to $\dfrac{1}{\|w\|}$, for which the margin will be $\dfrac{2}{\|w\|}$.

The above H1 and H2 are parallel (have the same normal) and no point of the training is located between them. It will possible to find the pair of hyperplanes which give the most maximum margin minimizing, subject to the conditions of the equation 8.

Firstly, a neural network classification system using time intervals obtained from the previous extraction process is implemented. The input was defined as a 10 features group for every beat, including commonly used features such as beep rate, QRS width, PR interval, QT interval, P wave area, etc. These types of features were chosen because time interval, delays and amplitude characteristics are the traditional aspects used in cardiac diagnosis.

These features, were so variable for the different arrhythmias and even between the same class, that after conducting several tests with different characteristics such as hidden neurons, number of epochs or weights, and viewing the results obtained with the analysis features block reserved for testing process completely foreign to the classifier another classification, system was proposed using the DWT coefficients associated to a PQRST segment. Every single beat of the MIT DB that is labeled is processed, being previously normalized to 256 samples to have the same numbers of DWT coefficients. Once the beats are normalized, the level 4 DWT is calculated using the Biorthogonal mother wavelet. This family was chosen analyzing other studies and comparing results. The result is a 30 coefficients group for every beat of the MIT DB. Finally a combination of these 2 input groups was tested, but better results were obtained using only 30 DWT coefficients. The Neural Network classifier is implemented by Perceptions Multi-layer (MLP), using Back-propagation algorithm for training process. In this case, the NN system has used one hidden layer, where the dimension of the vector of features gives the number of input units and the number of output units is given by the number of pathologies to identify.

The implementation of the Support Vector Machines classifier is based on SVM_Light. These machines attempt to fix maximum margins to divide the space into classes by means of vector operations with the input vectors, in this case two classes. For this case multiclass, "one-versus-all" strategy was implemented. Once the SVM has been trained, the test mode is carried out. Exactly the same group of test features has been used in NN and SVM classification in order to test systems in identical conditions.

Our experiments were repeated in 10 times, using cross validation strategy. The success rates for NN were very low, 73%, but for SVM, this system has achieved 99.23%. Besides, we show the load time for test mode for one sample (RR' interval). The feature extraction has a computational time of 10.62 milliseconds and the SVM test process 1.62 milliseconds. This system have been developed in MATLAB language, and a Dual Core II Processor with 2 GB RAM Memory (standard Computer), therefore, this process ca be considered as a real time application.

FUTURE RESEARCHS DIRECTIONS

For future works, there are some important aspects for commenting. The first aspect is about the database. The typical database for experiment is MITDB, this database has to be labeled again, because the knowledge during these years has been improved, and it must reflect in this database. The learning algorithms can train with bad labels and can damage its improvement. Besides, the number of pathologies can be increased, and the number of samples per pathology can be balanced. Nowadays, that number of samples is very significant for some pathology, and much reduced for others.

Secondly, the main aspect in future trends is the feature extraction. During the last year, researchers have been working for improving this block and the main line has looked for different methods of time-frequency features, as this present work. In order to avoid the noise from feature extraction, some authors is included feature selection methods. It allows improve a bit the success rates. Nowadays, it is a main task. Moreover, the last year have begun new works with other modalities, in particular, the echocardiography have advanced many studies in order to detect the working of heart. The techniques based on snakes from images are reaching good results.

Another aspect is the classification system. In this area, references are not increasing their approaches. The most representative classifier is Support Vector Machines, but the building of our kernels and mapping to high dimensionality can be a solution in order to improve these systems.

One more way to detect arrhythmia is to detect arrhythmic rhythms, which are a group of several abnormal beats, such as atrial bigemini, atrial flutter, ventricular bigeminy or ventricular trigeminy.

Finally, we have detected a problem concerning making comparisons with other authors' works, because there is not a protocol of competition, and for this reason, it must establish a protocol for training and test ECG signals, as other kind of pathologies for MIT Databases, like for example, Apnea identification on ECG signals.

CONCLUSION

The ECG automatic analysis is a key process, saving time on medical diagnosis. In the last two decades, several techniques for automatic arrhythmia detection have been proposed. Techniques such as Wavelet Analysis or Measures of ECG waves have been applied to the detection of ECG beat features and its classification, obtaining good performances.

For this present work, we have developed a very good, simple and robust automatic arrhythmia detection system, in two steps, ECG feature extraction and pathologic detector. We have used wavelet coefficients for calculating parameters and SVM by classifier. For this purpose, we have used 20 different ECG signals from MIT Arrhythmia Database. For RR' interval extraction, the success rate found is 99.82%. And for pathologic detection is 99.23%. The computational time is considered as real time.

With respect to load time, we have achieved good and low results, bearing in mind that we have used MATLAB language, and in successive works we will be able to optimise it in order to reduce this time, for example by using C or Java Language.

Our study used wavelet transforms to describe and recognize isolated cardiac beats. The choice of the selection of the analyzing function has been discussed. The ECG signal used is from MIT arrhythmias database, and it has been parameterized with DWT coefficients.

The choice of Wavelet family and the classification system have been discussed even the criterion followed.

The goal if this work is to help the public and healthcare professionals learn more about arrhythmias detection or classification, and ultimately reduce disability and death from heart disease and stroke.

REFERENCES

Afonso, V. X., Tompkins, W. J., Nguyen, T. Q., & Luo, S. (1999). ECG beat detection using filter banks. *IEEE Transactions on Bio-Medical Engineering, 46*, 192–201. doi:10.1109/10.740882

Arrhythmia Database, M. I. T.-B. I. H. (n.d.). Retrieved April 14, 2009, from http://www.physionet.org/physiobank/mitdb

Bahoura, M., Hassani, M., & Hubin, M. (1997). DSP implementation of wavelet transform for real time ECG wave forms detection and heart rate analysis. *Computer Methods and Programs in Biomedicine, 52*, 35–44. doi:10.1016/S0169-2607(97)01780-X

Blake, C., & Merz, C. (1998). *UCI repository of ML databases*. Retrieved April 14, 2009, from http://archive.ics.uci.edu/ml/

Burges, C. (1998). A Tutorial on Support Vector Machines for Pattern Recognition. *Data Mining and Knowledge Discovery, 2*(2), 121–167. doi:10.1023/A:1009715923555

Cristianini, N., & Shawe-Taylor, J. (2000). An introduction to support vector machines. Cambridge, UK: Cambridge University Press.

Hosseini, H., & Reynolds, K. J. (2001). A Multistage Neural Network Classifier for ECG Events. In *Proceedings of the 23rd International Conference of the IEEE Engineering in Medicine and Biology Society* (Vol. 2, pp. 1672-1675).

Huang, J., Blanz, V., Heisele, B., Lee, S. W., & Verri, A. (2002). Face Recognition Using Component-Based SVM Classification and Morphable Models. *Lecture Notes in Computer Science, 2388,* 334–341. doi:10.1007/3-540-45665-1_26

Jankowski, S., & Oreziak, A. (2003). Learning System for Computer-Aided ECG Analysis Based on Support Vector Machines. *International Journal of Bioelectromagnetism, 5*(1), 175–176.

Kunzmann, U., Von Wagner, G., Schöchlin, J., & Bolz, A. (2002). Parameter extraction of the ECG-signal in real-time. *Biomedizinische Technik, 47,* 875–878. doi:10.1515/bmte.2002.47.s1b.875

Lagerholm, M. (1998). Mean Field Neural Network Techniques. (Tech. Rep.). Lund, Sweden: Lund University, Department of Theoretical Physics.

Li, C., Zheng, C., & Tai, C. (1995). Detection of ECG characteristic points using wavelet transforms. *IEEE Transactions on Bio-Medical Engineering, 42,* 21–28. doi:10.1109/10.362922

Liu, W., Shen, P., Yingge, Q., & Xia, D. (2001). Fast Algorithm of Support Vector Machines in Lung Cancer Diagnosis. In *International Workshop on Medical Imaging and Augmented Reality* (pp. 188).

Mallat, S. (1998). Wavelet Tour of signal Processing. Boston: American Press.

Martinez, J. P. (2004). A Wavelet-Based ECG Delineator. Evaluation on Standard Databases. *IEEE Transactions on Bio-Medical Engineering, 51*(4), 570–581. doi:10.1109/TBME.2003.821031

Moraes, J., Freitas, M., Vilani, F., & Costa, E. (2002). A QRS complex detection algorithm using electrocardiogram leads. *Computers in Cardiology, 29,* 205–208.

Romero-Legarreta, I., Addison, P. S., Reed, M. J., Grubb, N. R., Clegg, G. R., Robertson, C. E., & Watson, J. N. (2005). Continuous wavelet transform modulus maxima analysis of the electrocardiogram: Beat-to-beat characterization and beat-to-beat measurement. *International Journal of Wavelets, Multresolution, and Information Processing, 3,* 19–42. doi:10.1142/S0219691305000774

Sahambi, J., Tandon, S., & Bhatt, R. (1997). Using wavelet transforms for ECG characterization an on-line digital signal processing system. *IEEE Engineering in Medicine and Biology Magazine, 16,* 77–83. doi:10.1109/51.566158

Schöfkopf, B., Burges, C., & Smola, A. (1999) Pairwise Classification and Support Vector Machines. Cambridge, MA: The MIT Press.

Senhadji, L., Carrault, G., Bellanger, J. J., & Passariello, G. (1995). Comparing wavelet transforms for recognizing cardiac patterns. *IEEE Engineering in Medicine and Biology Magazine, 14,* 167–173. doi:10.1109/51.376755

Shyu, L.Y., & al. (2004). Using Wavelet Transform and Fuzzy Neural Network for VPC Detection From the Holter ECG. *IEEE Transactions on Bio-Medical Engineering, 51*(7), 1269–1273. doi:10.1109/TBME.2004.824131

Silippo, R., Zong, W., & Berthold, M. (1999). ECG Feature Relevance in a Fuzzy Arrhythmia Classifier. *Computers in Cardiology,* 679–682.

Sivannarayana, N., & Reddy, D. C. (1999). Biorthogonal wavelet transforms for ECG. *Medical Engineering & Physics, 21,* 167–174. doi:10.1016/S1350-4533(99)00040-5

Song, M. H., Lee, J., Cho, S. P., Lee, K. J., & Yoo, S. K. (2005). Support Vector Machine Based Arrhythmia Classification Using Reduced Features. *International Journal of Control, Automation, and Systems, 3*(4), 571–579.

Vapnik, V. (1995). The Nature of Statistical Learning Theory. Berlin: Springer.

Zimmerman, M. W., & Povinelli, R. J. (2004). On Improving the Classification of Myocardial Ischemia Using Holter ECG Data. *Computers in Cardiology,* 377–380. doi:10.1109/CIC.2004.1442951

ADDITIONAL READING

Abedin, Z., Conner, R. P., & Conner, R. (2007). Essential Cardiac Electrophysiology: Self Assessment. New York: Blackwell Pub.

Al-ahmad, A., Natale, A., Hsia, H. H., & Callans, D. J. (2008). Electroanatomical Mapping: An Atlas for Clinicians. Hoboken, NJ: John Wiley & Sons Inc.

Al-Fahoum, A., & Qasaimeh, A. (2006). ECG arrhythmia classification using simple reconstructed phase space approach. *Computers in Cardiology,* 757–760.

Amien, M. B. M., Bo, C., & Jiarui, L. (2007). Robust techniques for designing remote real-time arrhythmias classification system. In Life Science Systems and Applications Workshop (pp. 200–204)

Azemi, A., Sabzevari, V. R., Khademi, M., Gholizade, H., Kiani, A., & Dastgheib, Z. S. (2006). Intelligent Arrhythmia Detection and Classification Using ICA. In *28th Annual International Conference of the IEEE Engineering in Medicine and Biology Society* (pp. 2163–2166).

Bayes-De-Luna, A., Furlanello, F., Zipes, D. P., & Maron, B. J. (2000). Arrhythmias and Sudden Death in Athletes. Berlin: Springer Verlag.

Bennett, D. H. (2006). Cardiac Arrythmias: Practical Notes on Interpretation and Treatment. Oxford, UK: Oxford Univ. Pr.

Bishop, C. M. (1995). Neural Networks for Pattern Recognition. Oxford, UK: Oxford University Press.

Cnockaert, L., Migeotte, P.-F., Daubigny, L., Prisk, G. K., Grenez, F., & Sa, R. C. (2008). A Method for the Analysis of Respiratory Sinus Arrhythmia Using Continuous Wavelet Transforms. *IEEE Transactions on Bio-Medical Engineering, 55*(5), 1640–1642. doi:10.1109/TBME.2008.918576

de Bianchi, M. F., Guido, R. C., Nogueira, A. L., & Padovan, P. (2006). A wavelet-PCA approach for content-based image retrieval. In *Proceedings of the Thirty-Eighth Southeastern Symposium on System Theory* (pp. 439–442).

De Buck, S., Maes, F., Ector, J., Bogaert, J., Dymarkowski, S., Heidbuchel, H., & Suetens, P. (2005). An augmented reality system for patient-specific guidance of cardiac catheter ablation procedures. *IEEE Transactions on Medical Imaging, 24*(11), 1512–1524. doi:10.1109/TMI.2005.857661

Dobbs, K. D. (1999). Arrhythmias. Amsterdam: Elsevier Science Health Science.

Gharaviri, A., Teshnehlab, M., & Moghaddam, H. A. (2007). PVC Arrhythmia Detection Using Neural Networks. In *5th International Symposium on Image and Signal Processing and Analysis* (pp. 234–237).

Goldberger, A. L. (2006). Clinical Electrocardiography: A Simplified Approach. Amsterdam: Elsevier Science Health Science.

Gussak, I., Antzelevitch, C., & Wilde, A. A. (2008). Electrical Diseases of the Heart: Genetics, Mechanisms, Treatment, Prevention. Berlin: Springer.

Inagaki, M., Kawada, T., Lie, M., Zheng, C., Sunagawa, K., & Sugimachi, M. (2006). Intravascular parasympathetic cardiac nerve stimulation prevents ventricular arrhythmias during acute myocardial. In *27th Annual International Conference of the Engineering in Medicine and Biology Society* (pp. 7076 – 7079).

Jalife, J., Delmar, M., Davidenko, J. M., & Anumonwo, J. (1998). Basic Cardiac Electrophysiology for the Clinician. Oxford, UK: Blackwell Pub.

Juang, B. H., & Rabiner, L. R. (1992). Spectral representations for speech recognition by neural networks: a tutorial. In *Proceedings of the Workshop Neural Networks for Signal Processing* (pp. 214 – 222).

Kafieh, R., Mehri, A., & Amirfattahi, R. (2007). Detection of ventricular Arrhythmias using roots location in AR-modelling. In *6th International Conference Information, Communications & Signal Processing* (pp. 1 – 4).

Kanai, D., Fukuoka, Y., Oyama, O., & Armoundas, A. A. (2004). A saline tank study of a catheter guiding method for ablative therapy of cardiac arrhythmias by application of an inverse solution to body surface electrocardiographic signals. *Computers in Cardiology*, 781–784. doi:10.1109/CIC.2004.1443056

Karimifard, S., & Ahmadian, A. (2007). Morphological Heart Arrhythmia Classification Using Hermitian Model of Higher-Order Statistics. In *29th Annual International Conference of the IEEE Engineering in Medicine and Biology Society* (pp. 3132 – 3135).

Kass, R., & Clancy, C. E. (2005). Treatment of Cardiac Arrhythmias. Berlin: Springer Verlag.

Khadra, L., Al-Fahoum, A. S., & Binajjaj, S. (2005). A quantitative analysis approach for cardiac arrhythmia classification using higher order spectral techniques. *IEEE Transactions on Bio-Medical Engineering*, *52*(11), 1840–1845. doi:10.1109/TBME.2005.856281

Klein, G. J., & Prystowsky, E. N. (1997). Clinical Electrophysiology Review. New York: McGraw-Hill.

Lee, J., Park, K. L., Song, M. H., & Lee, K. J. (2006). Arrhythmia Classification with Reduced Features by Linear Discriminant Analysis. In *27th Annual International Conference of the Engineering in Medicine and Biology Society* (pp. 1142 – 1144).

Lin, C. C., & Hu, W. C. (2007). Analysis of unpredictable intra-QRS potentials based on multistep linear prediction modeling for evaluating the risk of ventricular arrhythmias. *Computers in Cardiology*, 793–796. doi:10.1109/CIC.2007.4745605

Mandel, W. J. (1995). Cardiac Arrhythmias: Their Mechanisms, Diagnosis, and Management. Philadelphia, PA: Lippincott Williams & Wilkins.

Munson, C., Mayer, B. H., Haworth, K., & Labus, D. (2004). ECG Interpretation Made Incredibly Easy! Philadelphia, PA: Springhouse.

Oreziak, A., Piatkowska-Janko, E., Lewandowski, Z., & Opolski, G. (2006). Prediction of the supraventricular arrhythmias in hypertensive patients with different forms of the left ventricular geometry. Computers in Cardiology.

Podrid, P. J., & Kowey, P. R. (1996). Handbook of Cardiac Arrhythmia. Philadelphia, PA: Lippincott Williams & Wilkins.

Shenasa, M., Borggrefe, M., Breithardt, G., & Hindricks, G. (2009). Cardiac Mapping. Hoboken, NJ: John Wiley & Sons Inc.

Smeets, J. L., Smeets, J., Doevendans, P. A., Kirchhof, Ch., Doevendans, P., Josephson, M., & Vos, M. (2000). Professor Hein J. J. Wellens: 33 Years of Cardiology and Arrhythmology. Berlin: Springer Verlag.

Spooner, P. M., & Rosen, M. R. (2000). Foundations of Cardiac Arrhythmias: Basic Concepts and Clinical Approaches. Philadelphia, PA: Taylor & Francis.

Stevenson, W. G., Stevenson, W. G., Epstein, L. M., Maisel, W. H., Sweeney, M. O., & Stevenson, L. W. (2002). Arrhythmias in Heart Failure. Oxford, UK: Blackwell Pub.

Takeuchi, A., Ikeda, N., Mamorita, N., Miyahara, H., & Sato, T. (2005). Simulation system of arrhythmia and HRV analyzer. *Computers in Cardiology*, 897–900. doi:10.1109/CIC.2005.1588251

Valenza, G., Lanata, A., Ferro, M., & Scilingo, E. P. (2008). Real-time discrimination of multiple cardiac arrhythmias for wearable systems based on neural networks. *Computers in Cardiology*, 1053–1056.

Vespry, L. A. (2008). Cardiac Arrhythmia Research Advances. New York: Nova Science Publishers.

Walraven, G. (2005). Basic Arrhythmias. Upper Saddle River, NJ: Prentice Hall.

Zipes, D. P., & Jalife, J. (2004). Cardiac Electrophysiology: From Cell to Bedside. Amsterdam: Elsevier Science Health Science.

Zuo, W. M., Lu, W. G., Wang, K. Q., & Zhang, H. (2008). Diagnosis of cardiac arrhythmia using kernel difference weighted KNN classifier. *Computers in Cardiology*, 253–256.

Chapter 14

GA-Based Data Mining Applied to Genetic Data for the Diagnosis of Complex Diseases

Vanessa Aguiar
University of A Coruña, Spain

Jose A. Seoane
University of A Coruña, Spain

Ana Freire
University of A Coruña, Spain

Ling Guo
University of A Coruña, Spain

ABSTRACT

A new algorithm is presented for finding genotype-phenotype association rules from data related to complex diseases. The algorithm was based on genetic algorithms, a technique of evolutionary computation. The algorithm was compared to several traditional data mining techniques and it was proved that it obtained better classification scores and found more rules from the data generated artificially. It also obtained similar results when using some UCI Machine Learning datasets. In this chapter it is assumed that several groups of Single Nucleotide Polymorphisms (SNPs) have an impact on the predisposition to develop a complex disease like schizophrenia. It is expected to validate this in a short period of time on real data.

INTRODUCTION

Complex diseases are those that result from the interaction of multiple factors, usually including both genetic and environmental factors (Risch, 2000). Due to their nature, it is hard to establish a relationship between a gene and the disease. In general, this type of disease is caused by combination of effects of several sets of Single Nucleotide Polymorphisms (SNPs) which, separately, have a low effect. There is a high prevalence and impact of complex diseases like cancer, mental disorders and cardiovascular diseases. This situation has a

DOI: 10.4018/978-1-61520-893-7.ch014

high repercussion on the costs of hospitals and, therefore, on the costs of the national health system.

A SNP (Den Dunnen & Antonarakis, 2000) is a single nucleotide site where two (of four) different nucleotides occur in a high percentage of the population, that is, at least in 1% of the population. Since there exist 14 million of SNPs in human beings then a huge amount of data obtained from DNA genotyping needs to be dealt with, thus many variables have to be taken into account.

This data can be analysed carrying out association studies. In a genetic association study, the frequency of a SNP variant in people affected by the same disease is compared to the frequency of a SNP variant in healthy people (control population). There has to be no familiar relationship between these subjects, they have to belong to the same ethnic group and have the same geographic origin.

Carrying out such studies is expensive, mostly due to the cost of genotyping. Genotyping is the process of determining the genotype of an individual using a biological test. In Spain, for example, the cost of genotyping 74 SNPs for 720 samples reaches nearly 8.000€. The accuracy rate of the technologies used for this purpose ranges between 85-98%, depending on which one has been chosen. The technology used is chosen depending on the approach and purpose of the study and the number of SNPs to be genotyped. Not having an accuracy rate of 100% will make the analysis of genetic data more difficult as there will be missing data.

An important challenge that molecular association study faces in the post genomic era is to understand the inter-connections between networks of genes and their products. These networks are initiated and regulated by a variety of environmental changes. The variety of genotype definitions leads to an increase of the number of tests that need to be run and also involves a large amount of comparisons. Non-reproducibility of many results obtained in several studies has led to criticism of association studies.

SNP data and haplotypes used in association studies of complex diseases have three main characteristics which represent important challenges in data analysis. These characteristics are: complexity, heterogeneity and a constantly evolving nature. In addition to this, this type of data is large, redundant, diverse and distributed.

It is heterogeneous in the sense that it involves a large amount of data types, including categorical and continuous data, sequences, as well as temporal data, incomplete and missing data. There is a lot of redundancy in SNP and haplotype databases. This type of data is very dynamic and evolves continuously. Not only the data but also the schema evolves, which means that it requires special knowledge when designing modelling techniques. Finally, SNP and haplotype data is complex and has intrinsic features and subtle patterns, in the sense that it is very rich in associated complex phenotype traits or common multifactor diseases.

In complex diseases, in general, the combination of certain genes predisposes to develop a disease and the environmental factors are those which increase the impact of these genes in the disease development. This is known as epistasis or epistatic effect. In addition, environmental factors, which at the population level seem to have only a moderate impact, might have higher risks in subpopulations with certain genetic predispositions. There are major methodological challenges in the study of gene-gene and gene-environment interactions. Another important challenge is to study large datasets in order to identify combinations of SNPs which interact increasing the predisposition to develop a certain complex disease. Thus, there is a need to develop methods capable of performing a massive analysis of SNP data related to complex diseases beyond that of traditional statistical approaches.

Hence, the objective of this chapter is to develop an algorithm that will analyse data obtained from genotyping as part of an association study.

This will help reduce the costs of this type of study. The chapter has the following structure:

- In the *Introduction* the problem to be solved is described and some basic concepts are explained.
- The *Background* section contains a summary of the state of the art of different types of methods used to perform association studies, such as statistical and soft computing methods.
- *Methods* describes in detail the algorithm developed and shows the problems other techniques have in this field.
- In the *Results* section, results obtained after applying the algorithm developed on different databases are shown.
- *Future research directions* describes the possible research lines that could be followed to continue improving the work presented in this chapter.
- Finally, in the *Conclusions* section, conclusions obtained after developing this work are explained.

BACKGROUND

During recently years, the amount of data generated by association studies has increased remarkably and, due to this, a large number of methods have been developed. Not only statistical methods, but also computational methods have been designed to perform SNP-based genotype-phenotype association study analysis. These methods, as Kelemen et al. proposed in (2009), can be divided in three major groups: statistical methods, supervised and unsupervised data mining methods and soft computing methods.

Statistical Methods

There are statistical methods based on measures and on statistical tests (Thomas 2004; Balding,

2006). These studies can be divided in preliminary analysis and genotype-phenotype association. The objective of the first group is to check the quality of the data, that is, to check the deviation of the Handy-Weinberg Equilibrium (HWE) (Wittke-Thompson, Pluzhinikov & Cox, 2005). This may help to choose an adequate set of SNPs or to infer haplotypes from genotypes. The Pearson goodness-of-fit is mainly used to analyse the HWE deviation.

Tests for detecting missing (genotype) data are also part of this group (Little & Rubin, 2002). Even though missing data is not a problem when analysing a single SNP, when analysing multiple SNPs this situation can lead to some problems because many subjects could have one or more lost genotypes. The most common solution to this problem is to replace the missing genotypes with values predicted using the neighbours' genotypes. "Maximum likelihood estimate" or random selection based on a probability distribution are mostly used. The second approach has an advantage over the first one: random selection allows softening the effects caused by the existence of missing data in results.

There are three possibilities to perform association analyses. The first one corresponds to a single SNP association test. This type of test is based on proving the following null hypothesis: there is no association between the values of each SNP and the case or control value. The Pearson test and the exact Fisher test are mostly used and especially the last one, even though it is computationally more costly. In complex diseases, there are very few cases in which there exists a clear genotype-phenotype relationship, so the Pearson and the Fisher test may not be powerful enough. In this case, the Cochran-Armitage test (Armitage, 1955), which is more conservative than the previous ones and does not depend on the HWE, can be applied.

The second type of analysis refers to continuous result analysis. Linear regression and analysis of variance (ANOVA) are classical methods used in studies that involve variables with a continuous outcome. ANOVA is equivalent to the Pearson test and it compares the non-association null hypothesis with the general alternative. Linear regression reduces the degrees of freedom assuming that a linear relationship exists between the outcome value considered in the study and the genotype. In both cases the tests need the genotypes to follow a normal distribution. If case-control studies are taken into account, linear regression is not very powerful due to the non-linear distribution followed by the case and control outcome values. Logistic regression is a more elaborate approach for this type of task, though it is mostly used to apply a score to a prediction instead of being used as a predictive method. Despite this, logistic regression is a flexible tool which can be easily adapted for multiple SNPs and it will allow including environmental interactions and covariates such as age or sex. When tests are applied to multiple SNPs, the aim of the test, given a set of SNPs in case and control subjects, is to find the set of SNPs related to a disease and/or, when an association is given, find the nearest SNPs to the current polymorphism.

As mentioned previously, multiple SNP logistic regression is one of the most widely used methods. This method is a logical extension of single SNP analysis.

When the number of SNPs is too large, being capable of selecting the most relevant SNPs and deleting those with correlations increases the power of the analysis at the expense of losing some information.

Another solution to the problem of having too many correlated SNPs is to use techniques such as "stepwise selection procedure" (Cordell & Claiton, 2002) or "bayesian shrinkage methods" (Wang et al., 2005).

One of the major problems of multiple SNP analysis is related to the existence of too many predictors, some of them strongly related. One possible strategy, inspired in the block structure followed by the human genome, is to use haplo-types to delete the correlation in low recombination regions. This approach allows obtaining analyses with a lower number of degrees of freedom and also highlights the importance of combined effects of these accidental variables.

Data Mining Methods

Data mining methods have a number of characteristics which make them very attractive to perform association study analysis. These methods are usually computationally efficient and scalable when high dimensionality data is used, as happens in GWAs (Genome-Wide Association studies). However, the models obtained tend to be considered simple with regard to those obtained by statistical methods. In addition, these methods usually tend to explore and discover. That is, unlike statistical methods, which are hypothesis-driven, data mining methods are hypothesis generators. Results obtained by analyses which use these techniques are often considered as a complement to traditional statistical analyses. Finally, data mining methods usually handle discrete data and use symbolic structures, providing more useful and understandable results and explanations than those provided by statistical methods, which are usually complex. Sometimes data mining is poorly defined as "non-trivial extraction of implicit, previously unknown and potentially useful information from data". Data mining techniques used in association study analysis can be divided in two groups: classification methods, which try to find markers and other relevant characteristics in order to be able to predict a disease, and clustering techniques, which try to find subsets of subjects based on their genotypic and phenotypic similarity.

Classification Methods

As mentioned previously, the aim of classification methods is to find rules or patterns which would help predict the value of a variable according to independent variables. Applied to association studies, this involves finding a group of patterns of SNPs or haplotypes that, together, form a good phenotype predictor and which may predict the susceptibility of a subject to a disease. Regression/ Classification/Decision trees is one of the most popular techniques. This type of technique is based on data recursive partitioning and it obtains a model with a tree structure. Some examples of the application of these techniques to association study analysis can be found in (Young & Ge, 2005; Cook, Zee & Ridker, 2004).

Symbolic discriminant analysis (SDA) is used in large dataset analysis as it performs automatically and simultaneously a variable reduction and the development of the method. Some examples of the application of these techniques to genomics can be found in (Reif, White & Moore, 2004).

An example of association analysis using association rules can be found in (Rova, Haataja, Marttila et al., 2004). This method is based on generating rules that describe co-occurrences of sets of characteristics. This classification method will be described in detail later.

Other methods such as DICE (an automated method for the Detection of Informative Combined Effects) (Tahri-Daizadeh, Tregouet, Nicaud et al., 2003), multifactor dimensionality reduction (Ritchie, Hahn, Roodi et al., 2001; Moore, 2004) or support vector machine (SVM) (Waddell, Page, Zhan et al., 2005) have also been widely used for association study analysis.

Clustering Methods

Clustering methods try to find relatively homogenous subsets in a dataset. Applied to association studies, these techniques try to find subsets of subjects which may share genetic characteristics. This type of clustering can be applied to genotypes and phenotypes. Once clustering has been applied, finding genetic factors in each cluster should be easier. An application of these techniques can be found in (Tzeng, Devlin, Wasserman et al., 2003; Toivonen, Onkamo, Hintsanen et al, 2005; Molitor,

Marjoram & Thomas, 2003; Wilcox, Wyszynski, Panhuysen et al., 2003).

Soft Computing

Soft computing includes methods such as neural networks, evolutionary computation and fuzzy logic. In this area, there exist two main tasks in association study analysis.

The first task is SNP pattern discovery in complex diseases and it includes subtle SNP selection from thousands of SNPs related to a disease. There are two possible approaches. One approach is the use of tagSNPs. TagSNPs are based on unsupervised methods. Methods which follow this approach try to identify the blocks of SNPs related to a disease. The other approach, SNP-disease association, is based on supervised methods which relate sets of SNPs to diseases without taking into account any preestablished blocks.

The second task is gene-gene and gene-environment interaction modelling in complex diseases. Due to the complexity of the problem, there are few research projects that deal with it.

Jourdan et al. (2002) developed a genetic algorithm capable of extracting association rules from data obtained from diabetic patients. Later, the algorithm was adapted for use in distributed environments (Vermeulen-Jourdan, Dhaenens & Talbi, 2005).

Clark et al. (2005) developed a genetic algorithm which builds logic trees. These trees consist of boolean expressions which group SNPs. This genetic algorithm was applied to studies about genetic variation of candidate genes. In each generation of the genetic algorithm a population of modified logic trees is generated using mutation, crossover and selection operators. The best trees are generated based on the fitness value, which is the outcome of the bayesian regression of the tree.

Recent studies show that genetic programming improves the performance of many traditional statistical methods, as well as data mining and machine learning methods, such as linear regression and SVM. Ritchie et al. (2003) used an optimized neural network. Genetic programming is used to optimize the architecture of the neural network. This is done to improve the identification of combination of genes related to the risk of developing a disease.

Motsinger et al. (2006) also used genetic programming for neural network optimization in order to detect gene-gene relationships in SNP data.

Hubley et al. (2003) present an evolutionary algorithm for multiobjective SNP selection, which is able to approximate a set of optimal solutions. This design works well in large studies. They implemented a modified version of the Strength-Pareto evolutionary algorithm. This algorithm is especially adequate for solving optimization problems with several objectives or complex search spaces where more exhaustive heuristics cannot be used.

Banzhaf et al. (2006) used genetic algorithms, as well as other evolutionary computation techniques, to model gene-gene relationships. They also used evolved trees for haplotype analysis.

Moore and White (2006) developed a hybrid method which combines genetic programming with multifactor dimensionality reduction (MDR) to choose SNPs. They found that this method worked better than random search when using simulated data.

Several approaches to perform association study analysis have been explained so far. A review of the state of the art of association rule techniques is shown below.

Association rules are a very popular structure for expressing patterns in a dataset. These patterns can be useful to understand the general behaviour of the problem generated by the dataset. This way, more information will be available to help solving problems such as decision-making, diagnosis, etcetera. The dataset can be expressed as a table. The rows of the table can be interpreted as samples, whereas the columns can be interpreted as types of characteristics presented by each sample. An

association rule can be defined as a probabilistic proposition about the occurrence of certain states in the data. A typical association rule could be "IF C1=2 AND C2=4 THEN CONSEQUENT". An association rule can be formally seen as "IF A THEN B", where A and B are disjoint item sets. Given an association rule, two measures are usually used to calculate the quality of the rule: coverage and confidence. The coverage of a rule can be defined as the number of instances that the rule is able to predict correctly. The confidence measures the percentage of times the rule is satisfied when it can be applied. The different search algorithms used to find association rules are based on searching rules that meet certain coverage and confidence minimum requirements. Several implementations of association rules can be found in (Lucrédio, Almeida & Prado, 2004; Srikant & Agrawal, 1995; Hipp, Guntzer & Nakaeizadeh, 2000).

Usage of Genetic Algorithms for Rule Extraction

Evolutionary algorithms have a global search feature which makes them especially adequate for solving problems found along the different stages of a knowledge discovery process. In rule extraction processes, evolutionary algorithms treat interactions between attributes adequately because they evaluate a rule as a whole using a fitness function instead of evaluating the impact due to adding or deleting a condition of a rule. This last part is what local search processes do, including the majority of induction rule algorithms and decision trees. Genetic algorithms and genetic programming are the most used evolutionary algorithms for rule discovery. These two techniques differ mostly in how individuals are represented. In the case of genetic algorithms, individuals are represented as a linear string of conditions. When considering rules, each condition is usually a pair attribute-value. In the case of genetic programming, an individual is usually represented as a tree where the leaf nodes are the values of the attributes and the intern nodes represent functions. Genetic algorithms can follow two approaches depending on how rules are codified in a population of individuals (De Jong, 1988). The first possibility is to follow the "chromosome = rule" approach, in which each individual represents one rule. The second possibility is to follow the "chromosome = rule base" approach, also known as Pittsburg (Smith, 1980), in which each individual represents a set of rules. If the first approach is followed, there are two possibilities. In the first one, known as "Michigan approach" (Holland & Reitman, 1978), each individual modifies only one rule but the final solution is the final population or a subset of it. In this case, the behaviour of the whole set of rules needs to be evaluated, as well as the contribution of each single rule. The second possibility is to follow the IRL (Iterative Rule Learning) approach (González & Herrera, 1997), in which each chromosome represents a rule but the solution of the genetic algorithm is the best individual, whereas the global solution consists of the best individuals obtained from several consecutive runs.

Choosing one approach or another depends on the task the rule search algorithm has to do. If the objective is to obtain a set of classification rules, then the behaviour of the whole set of rules must be evaluated and not only the quality of a single rule. In this case, the most adequate is to follow the "chromosome = rule base" approach, which considers the interactions among rules. Some examples in which genetic algorithms are used for classification and in which the previous approach has been followed can be found in (De Jong, Spears & Gordon, 1993; Janikow, 1993). However, this approach has some problems due to the usage of longer individuals (sometimes the length is even variable), increasing the algorithm's computational cost, and due to the modification of genetic operators. Because of this, genetic algorithms following the "chromosome = rule" approach have also been designed (Greene & Smith, 1995; Giordana & Neri, 1995). In these

examples reduced individuals have been used, simplifying the design of genetic operators. This approach has two drawbacks. On one hand, calculating the fitness function is difficult as each rule is evaluated individually and, due to this, it is hard to determine the quality of the whole set of rules. On the other hand, the algorithm should not converge only to one individual as the objective is to obtain a set of rules. To prevent this from happening, a niche technique (Beasley, Bull & Martin, 1993) is needed to promote the existence of different individuals in the population.

For association rule discovery, the best approach is "chromosome = rule" as the objective is usually to find a set of rules in which the quality of each rule is evaluated independently.

METHODS

Issues, Controversies, Problems

In the *Background* section, different approaches to the same type of problem have been described. In each case, the drawbacks of each existing method were explained. Thus, to overcome the problems the different methods have, an algorithm based in evolutionary computation (EC) has been developed. Given that this type of technique has been designed to solve optimization problems, an application of genetic algorithms is proposed with the aim of making rule extraction possible. The chromosome of the genetic algorithm (GA) will represent one rule.

Solutions and Recommendations

A genetic algorithm was initially developed in order to solve the problem of analysing a large amount of data with the objective of finding association rules. The structure of this algorithm is described as follows.

Figure 1. A possible rule

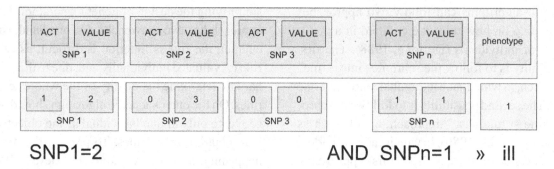

Definitions

Terms Used

When referring to the genetic algorithm, the terms individual, rule and population will be used. Individual represents a GA individual (or chromosome), which is a possible solution for the problem. In this case, the solutions will be rules. The structure of the association rules is explained below. The population of the GA is the set of individuals that will evolve through the iterations.

The terms subject, example or sample will be used when we want to refer to the data extracted from a patient (in this case, SNP data) or the data generated simulating real data.

Structure of the Association Rules

It is assumed that the influence of SNPs in genetic predisposition to develop a complex disease can be represented as several rules extracted from the data. These rules have the following structure:

If the following conditions are met

SNP1=X AND SNP2=Y AND … AND SNPn=Z

the individual is genetically predisposed, or not, to develop the complex disease studied.

Each rule represents an individual of the GA population.

Genetic Algorithm

GA Individual

As mentioned above, each individual of the population represents a candidate rule. In a genetic algorithm, each individual is considered to be a chromosome. Below, the structure of this chromosome is described.

The chromosome of the GA, shown in Figure 1, represents a candidate rule containing n SNPs plus a position for the phenotype. In this case, each SNP consists of two genes. One gene represents if the SNP is part, or not, of the rule (ACT) and the other one represents its real value (VALUE). The value taken by this gene will depend on the problem studied.

All the positions of the chromosome, except the last one, represent the genotype. The last position of the chromosome, which represents the phenotype, can take 1 if the subject is a case or 0 if it is a control. Hence, the structure of an individual of the GA consists of 2n+1 genes that represent a chromosome.

Each rule represents an individual of the GA population.

For example, if the complex disease considered is schizophrenia, we could have the following rule extracted from the data: If SNP1=2 and SNPn=1 then the individual is genetically predisposed (Figure 1). Thus, a subject which has those values in those SNPs, would be considered to be predisposed to develop schizophrenia.

Table 1. Implementation of the GA operators

Operator	Implementation
Selection	Deterministic tournament selection has been used.
Crossover	One point and two point crossover algorithms have been implemented. For each algorithm there are two possible versions: one in which the crossover point (or points) belongs to one of the ancestors, and another one in which that point (or those points) is obtained combining the values the other ancestors had in that point. In this case, the algorithms will be known as one real point crossover and two real point crossover.
Mutation	Random replacement has been used.

If another problem is considered, such as the Breast Cancer problem described in the *Results* section, we could have the following rule extracted from the data: If the age belongs to the range 60-69 and the tumour size is between 50 and 54, then the subject is likely to develop breast cancer again. In this case, the data presents different attributes and not SNPs. As these attributes have been classified in several categories or ranges, the algorithm proposed in this chapter can be applied to this dataset.

Fitness Function

The fitness function will depend on the number of examples which is correctly and incorrectly classified. In this way, a GA individual will be penalised if it classifies incorrectly a high number of examples and will be rewarded if it classifies correctly a high number of examples. There is also a penalisation so that the rules obtained do not consist of one attribute (or one SNP) and to avoid obtaining rules with all the attributes (or SNPs) considered.

The fitness function used, which has to be minimized, has the following structure:

```
IF the rule doesn't classify
correctly any example THEN
fitness = Number of examples of
the training set + 0.1 x (Number
of SNPs part of the rule / Num-
ber of SNPs in the examples)
ELSE
fitness = Number of examples of
```

```
the training set - Number of
correctly classified examples +
Number of incorrectly classified
examples
```

In the first part (the IF part) individuals are penalised adding the number of SNPs part of the rule divided by the total number of SNPs and multiplied by a coefficient to the number of examples. This addend is added in order to avoid the tendency of obtaining rules with all the SNPs. It is multiplied by 0.1 so that it will not have too much impact on the fitness value and to avoid obtaining rules with only one SNP. The value used as coefficient has been determined after a large number of experiments.

In the second part (the ELSE part) individuals are penalised adding the number of incorrectly classified examples and are rewarded subtracting the number of correctly classified examples (See Table 1).

Operators

Parameters

The parameters in Table 2 can be configured to obtain different results.

The GA is executed until the fitness value changes less than a certain threshold (*minimum change*) or until a *maximum number of generations* is reached. Deterministic tournament selection has been used, as well as random replacement for mutation. Configuring the GA using a two-real-point crossover algorithm with a crossover rate of

Table 2. Description of the parameters that can be configured

Parameter	Description
Maximum number of generations	Represents the number of generations or iterations the GA will be executed.
Minimum change	If the GA population changes less than this threshold, then the GA will stop.
Number of GA individuals	Represents the number of individuals the GA will have in each generation. This parameter is directly proportional to the genotype length.
Genotype length	Represents the length of the GA chromosome, the number of attributes or variables considered for a given problem.
Crossover rate	Represents the percentage of individuals affected by the crossover operator in one iteration of the GA.
Mutation rate	Represents the percentage of individuals affected by the mutation operator in one iteration of the GA.
Crossover algorithm	Represents the type of crossover algorithm chosen. The possible choices are: one point crossover, two point crossover, one real point crossover and two real point crossover.

90% and a mutation rate of 10% have proved to obtain the best results. For the problems in which there are, for example, 50 attributes (including the class), an adequate value for the *number of GA Individuals* would be between 750 and 1000.

Iterative Algorithm

Using only a genetic algorithm has some problems. Firstly, the genetic algorithm can fall in local minimums and can have difficulties in finding a solution when the search space is uniform. What is more, the individuals of the GA population can also become very similar after several generations. In addition to this, the genetic algorithm offers only one solution and, in this type of problem, there could be more than one solution. Moreover, it would be more interesting to obtain several solutions, which could be separated in the search space, as a result.

In order to allow obtaining different solutions which meet the previous conditions, the *Iterative Rule Learning* (Venturini, 1993) approach (explained in the previous section) has been followed. Thus, the final method is capable of extracting several rules and has the advantage of being able to explore different parts of the search

space in one execution. The structure of this algorithm, which will be called iterative algorithm, is described below.

This algorithm (Figure 2) consists of a loop that executes, in each iteration, a GA.

Every time the GA is executed, a list of candidate rules is obtained. These rules, which correspond to the final population of the GA, are filtered in order to choose the best rule between those which classify a case or a control subject and cover at least a certain percentage of the samples from the training set. This percentage is a parameter set by the user (See Table 3).

From the iterations of the iterative algorithm a set of rules covering the search space is obtained. That set will be called rule pool. Once there are enough rules, the rules from the Final Rule Pool are validated using a test set composed of control and case (disease) subjects. This happens when all the search space is covered or when a maximum number of iterations is reached.

The algorithm developed is capable of finding logical expressions. These expressions classify a subject based on the values that the alleles of certain SNPs have.

The method proposed in this chapter was initially developed with the idea of applying

Figure 2. Iterative algorithm structure

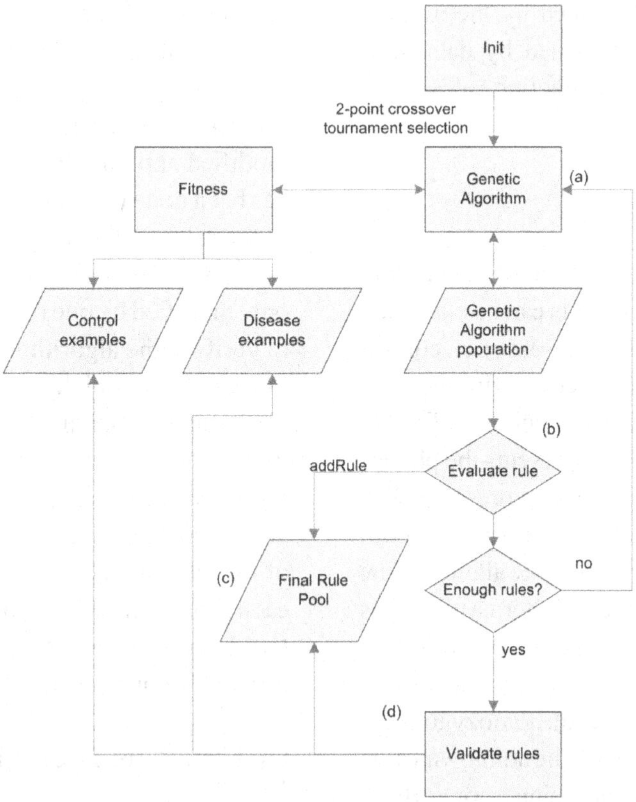

it to problems related to a complex disease, such as schizophrenia. In these problems, each sample of the data consisted of a set of SNPs, which represents the genotype, and a value for the phenotype. This is the reason why the GA individuals were designed simulating this situation. Despite this, this method can be applied to other problems where SNPs would correspond to different categorical attributes and the phenotype would represent the class.

RESULTS

Test Bed

Two different groups of datasets have been used. The first one, generated artificially, was used with the objective of observing if the algorithm was able to find the patterns existing in the data. This dataset was also used to compare the results obtained by the method described in this chapter with those obtained by other traditional data min-

Table 3.

Parameter	Description
Minimum percentage of correctly classified subjects	Represents the percentage of subjects from the training set that have to be correctly classified by the rule in order to add it to the rule pool.

ing techniques. The second one was used in order to compare the results obtained by the method presented to the results obtained by data mining techniques capable of extracting rules using published datasets.

Real Clinical Data

This data was obtained as a result of genotyping DNA of patients. These patients can be classified as case (they developed the disease) or control (healthy). This data is presented in a file and each patient is represented as a list of numbers. Except for the first position, which represents the phenotype (case or control), the numbers represent SNPs. SNPs can take different values: homozygous (both copies of a given gene have the same allele) for the first allele (one of a number of alternative forms of the same gene occupying a given position on a chromosome), heterozygous (the patient has two different alleles of a given gene), homozygous for the second allele or unknown. The unknown value appears when there is a genotyping error as these techniques are not 100% accurate (mentioned in the *Introduction* section).

Due to the nature of the data and that it is still under study, artificial data had to be generated. Artificial data, described below, will simulate real clinical data and, in this case, patterns introduced will be known.

Generation of Artificial Input Data

In order to observe how the algorithm presented works, datasets have been generated. This is done so that a pattern simulating real clinical data exists in the data created.

First of all, 360 random datasets were generated. Each dataset was divided in two groups: case subjects and control subjects. Each group represents 50% of the dataset. After that, rules with two, three or four SNPs have been randomly generated.

Some examples representing case subjects have been modified in different percentages (between 20% and 80%). The datasets can be firstly divided into three groups: sets modified applying one rule, those modified applying two rules and those modified applying three rules. The modification has been done introducing the values of the SNPs of the rules generated previously in the subjects' corresponding positions. Each subject should be only modified by one rule. This way, it is possible to verify if the algorithm is able to find the rules introduced artificially.

Another division can be done according to the percentage of case subjects modified. Thus, four groups of sets will be available for testing the algorithm. In each group 20%, 40%, 60% or 80% of the case subjects has been modified. Also, in each group, one third of the sets have been modified by rules of two SNPs, one third by rules of three SNPs and one third by rules of four SNPs.

UCI Machine Learning Repository

Three datasets from the UCI Machine Learning Repository (Asuncion & Newman, 2007) were used. Results obtained from applying the algorithm developed were compared to those obtained by several classification methods that generated rules. The characteristics of each database are detailed below.

The first dataset used was the Breast Cancer Dataset. This is one of three domains provided by the Oncology Institute that has repeatedly appeared in the machine learning literature. This breast cancer domain was obtained from the University Medical Centre, Institute of Oncology, Ljubljana, Slovenia.

This dataset includes 201 instances of one class and 85 instances of another class, that is, 286 instances in all. The instances are described by 9 attributes, some of which are linear and some are nominal, all of them categorical. This database has

9 missing values, distributed uniformly between case and control subjects.

The second dataset which was used was the Breast Cancer Wisconsin (Original) dataset (Wolberg & Mangasarian, 1990; Bennet & Mangasarian, 1992). This breast cancer database was obtained from the University of Wisconsin Hospitals, Madison from Dr. William H. Wolberg.

It includes 699 instances. There are 10 attributes represented as integers. There are also missing values. In this case, the 16 missing values appear mostly in control subjects. In fact, only two appear in case subjects, the rest appear in control subjects.

The third dataset used is the Chess (King-Rook vs. King-Pawn) Dataset (Holte, Acker & Porter, 1989). This dataset includes 3196 instances. Each instance has 36 categorical attributes. In this case, there is not missing information.

Results

To validate the algorithm 10-fold cross validation has been used. Therefore, the original data was divided into 10 subsets. Only one subset was used as test data, while the other 9 subsets were used for training. The cross validation is repeated ten times, using each time, only, each subset. The ten results obtained after doing the 10-fold cross validation have been combined in order to obtain global classification measures.

The algorithm proposed has been compared, firstly, to 29 traditional data mining techniques using the artificial data generated. These techniques can be classified in the following categories: decision rule learning, classification trees, bayesian nets and other techniques such as neural networks, metaclassifiers, regression-based techniques… The data mining suite Weka (Witten & Frank, 2005) was used and the 29 techniques were applied to the 360 sets created artificially. After that, the techniques that obtained rules were applied to

the three datasets from the UCI Machine Learning Repository described above.

Data Mining Techniques

The four main categories in which the techniques used for the comparison have been divided are described in the following paragraphs.

The objective of decision rule learning techniques is to generate a set of decision rules in order to obtain hypothesis which could explain a concrete system. In a classification problem, the set of rules obtained will follow an IF-THEN-ELSE structure. Some examples of this type of method are the following: conjunctive rule, decision table, JRip, NNge, Ridor, DTNB…

Classification trees build trees in which each leaf represents a class. To classify a pattern, this type of method starts in the root node and, depending on the values the variable (attribute) observed has, the instances are distributed along the child nodes. This process is repeated until a leaf node is reached. Some examples of classification trees are the following: J48, REPTree…

Bayesian nets are a graphical representation of the dependencies used in probabilistic reasoning in which the nodes stand for random variables and the branches stand for direct dependence relationships among the variables. A bayesian classifier can be considered a special case of a Bayesian net in which there is a special variable, the class, and there are other variables, the attributes. The structure of the net will depend on the type of classifier. Some examples of techniques that use bayesian learning are the following: AODE, Bayes Net, HNB, Naive Bayes…

As mentioned previously, some other techniques have been used, such as: Attribute Selected Classifier, LBR, Multilayer Perceptron, VFI, RBF Network, Adaboost M1, Bagging, Classification Via Regression…

Figure 3. Comparison of classification percentages

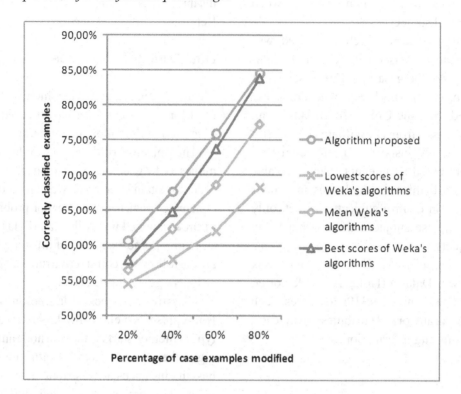

Results

Firstly, results of the comparison using the artificial input data are shown. In Figure 3, the evolution of the percentages of correctly classified samples obtained for the different groups can be observed. The algorithm proposed obtains better results than all of the traditional methods used.

These results are significantly better when less percentage of the case subjects is modified. Classification scores are shown in Table 4.

Ridor (Gaines & Compton, 1995) is the traditional algorithm that gets the best classification scores most of the times using these datasets. However, when 20% or 40% of the case subjects is modified, the number of rules found by Ridor is clearly less than the number of rules found by the algorithm presented in this chapter.

For example, in the left part of Figure 4, it can be observed that while this algorithm extracts nearly 70% of the rules introduced artificially, Ridor is only able to find 30% of them when one rule is introduced in 20% of case subjects. If the

Table 4. Classification scores

	20%	40%	60%	80%
Lowest scores of Weka's algorithms	54.51%	58.00%	62.14%	68.41%
Mean Weka's algorithm	56.47%	62.30%	68.66%	77.37%
Best scores of Weka's algorithms	57.84%	64.83%	73.72%	83.81%
Algorithm proposed	60.68%	67.72%	75.86%	84.62%

Figure 4. Comparison of found rules

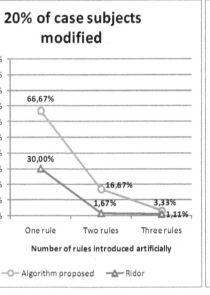 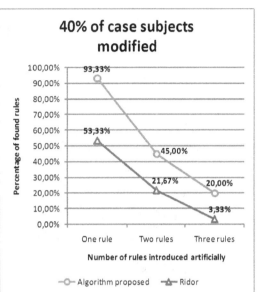

right part of Figure 4 is observed, when one rule is introduced in 40% of case subjects, again, the algorithm presented obtains better results, finding more than 90% of the rules while Ridor is only able to find half of them.

Moreover, in most of the situations where the algorithm presented does not find the exact rule, it finds a part of it (for example, for a rule made

of four SNPs it could find a rule with three SNPs), while Ridor, in many situations, is unable to find any of the rules introduced artificially.

Below, results of the comparison using the UCI Machine Learning Repository are shown. In this case, only the methods that obtained rules were considered.

Table 5. Classification scores using UCI datasets

	Breast Cancer	**Wisconsin Breast Cancer**	**King Rook vs King Pawn**
Conjunctive rule	69.30%	91.97%	66.05%
Decision table	73.73%	95.49%	97.32%
DTNB	69.94%	96.85%	96.31%
JRip	71.45%	95.61%	99.21%
NNge	67.80%	96.18%	98.44%
OneR	66.91%	92.01%	66.91%
PART	69.41%	94.69%	99.17%
Ridor	72.50%	95.35%	88.06%
ZeroR	70.30%	65.52%	52.22%
Mean	*70.15%*	*91.52%*	*84.85%*
Method presented	76.07%	93.19%	94.39%

Figure 5. Mean of the classification scores obtained using UCI datasets

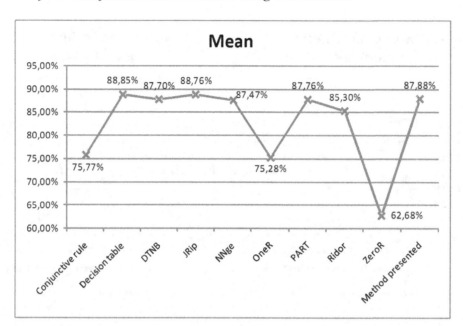

As can be observed in Table 5, the method presented obtains better results than any other method capable of extracting rules when there is missing data and there is approximately the same number of case and control subjects with missing values. This is the case of the Breast Cancer Dataset, in which there are 2 attributes with missing values. For the other two datasets, the results obtained by the method presented are still adequate.

Figure 5 shows the mean of the classification scores of the different methods. The method presented obtains a higher rate than seven of the nine methods used in this comparison.

FUTURE RESEARCH DIRECTIONS

Future work will focus, firstly, on continuing to refine the algorithm. With that purpose, more tests will be run and the fitness function will be modified in order to try to obtain better classification scores. The possibility of using trees instead of rules as the structure which represents the pattern existing in the data will be considered.

Another research direction will be to consider the possibility of modifying the algorithm in order to allow using not only categorical data, but also real data. In addition to this, the option of allowing another type of classification will also be considered. That is, modifying the algorithm in order to add the capacity of classifying in more than two classes.

This method has been designed in such a way that it allows changing or adding new modules. Taking this into account, the use of genetic programming instead of using genetic algorithms will be studied. Genetic programming allows obtaining sets of rules structured as trees and opens a broad range of new possibilities.

The results of both designs will be compared, and also with the current one, in order to see which one is capable of finding more rules and which one is able to classify with higher accuracy scores. We hope to determine, with this, which approach is better: a tree-based approach or an IF-THEN rule approach; and which technique, genetic programming or genetic algorithms, seems to be better for the current problem.

CONCLUSION

In complex diseases, the factors that increase the risk of developing a certain disease do not correspond to the values of one or more genes. There is then a likelihood of several combinations of values of different sets of SNPs affecting the increase of the risk factor. The method described in this chapter is capable of finding several sets of SNPs related to control or case subjects. It is also able to find patterns structured as rules which represent a dataset with categorical attributes and classify new instances presented to the method.

When comparing to 29 existing techniques using artificially generated data, it classifies better than all of them and it was able to find a higher percentage of the rules introduced artificially. The more noise the data has, the better classifies the method presented.

When using datasets from the UCI Repository, this method achieves better results when there is missing data and it is distributed uniformly between case and control subjects. In addition to this, it obtains better classification scores than 7 of the 9 methods capable of extracting rules used.

ACKNOWLEDGMENT

This work was partially supported by the Spanish Ministry of Science and Innovation (Ref TIN2006-13274) and the European Regional Development Funds (ERDF), grant (Ref. PIO52048 and RD07/0067/0005) funded by the Carlos III Health Institute, grant (Ref. PGDIT 07TMT011CT) and (Ref. PGDIT08SIN010105PR) from the General Directorate of Research, Development and Innovation of the Xunta de Galicia and grant (2007/127 and 2007/144) from the General Directorate of Scientific and Technologic Promotion of the Galician University System of the Xunta de Galicia. The work of Vanessa Aguiar is supported by a grant from the General Directorate of Quality and Management of Galicia's University System of the Xunta. The work of José A. Seoane is supported by an Isabel Barreto grant from the General Directorate of Research, Development and Innovation of the Xunta. Thanks go to M. Zwitter and M. Soklic for providing the data of the Breast Cancer Dataset, and to Dr. William H. Wolberg from the University of Wisconsin Hospitals for providing the Breast Cancer Wisconsin dataset.

REFERENCES

Armitage, P. (1995). Test for linear trends in proportions and frequencies. *Biometrics*, *11*, 375–386. doi:10.2307/3001775

Asuncion, A., & Newman, D. J. (2007). *UCI Machine Learning Repository*. Irvine, CA: University of California, School of Information and Computer Science. Retrieved from http://www.ics.uci.edu/~mlearn/MLRepository.html

Balding, D. (2006). A tutorial on statistical methods for population association Studies. *Nature Reviews. Genetics*, *7*, 781–791. doi:10.1038/nrg1916

Banzhaf, W., Beslon, G., Christensen, S., Foster, J. A., Kepes, F., & Lefort, V. (2006). Guidelines: from artificial evolution to computacional evolution: a research agenda. *Nature Reviews. Genetics*, *7*(9), 729–735. doi:10.1038/nrg1921

Beasley, D., Bull, D. R., & Martin, R. R. (1993). A sequential niche technique for multimodal function optimization. *Evolutionary Computation*, *1*(2), 101–125. doi:10.1162/evco.1993.1.2.101

Bennett, K. P., & Mangasarian, O. L. (1992). Robust linear programming discrimination of two linearly inseparable sets. *Optimization Methods and Software*, *1*, 23–34. doi:10.1080/10556789208805504

Clark, T. G., De Iorio, M., Griffiths, R. C., & Farrall, M. (2005). Finding associations in dense genetic maps: a genetic algorithm approach. *Human Heredity*, *60*, 97–108. doi:10.1159/000088845

Cook, N. R., Zee, R. Y. L., & Ridker, P. M. (2004). Tree and spline based association analysis of gene-gene interaction models for ischemic stroke. *Statistics in Medicine, 23,* 1439–1453. doi:10.1002/sim.1749

Cordell, H. J., & Clayton, D. G. (2002). A unified stepwise regression approach for evaluating the relative effects of polymorphisms within a gene using case/control or family data: application to HLA in type 1 diabetes. *American Journal of Human Genetics, 70,* 124–141. doi:10.1086/338007

De Jong, K. A. (1988). Learning with genetic algorithms: an overview. *Machine Learning, 3*(2/3), 121–138. doi:10.1023/A:1022606120092

De Jong, K. A., Spears, W. M., & Gordon, D. F. (1993). Using genetic algorithms for concept learning. *Machine Learning, 13*(2/3), 161–188. doi:10.1023/A:1022617912649

Den Dunnen, J. T., & Antonarakis, S. E. (2000). Mutation Nomenclature Extensions and Suggestions to Describe Complex Mutations: A Discussion. *Human Mutation, 15,* 7–12. doi:10.1002/(SICI)1098-1004(200001)15:1<7::AID-HUMU4>3.0.CO;2-N

Gaines, B. R., & Compton, P. (1995). Induction of Ripple-Down Rules Applied to Modeling Large Databases. *Journal of Intelligent Information Systems, 5*(3), 211–228. doi:10.1007/BF00962234

Giordana, A., & Neri, F. (1995). Search intensive concept induction. *Evolutionary Computation, 3*(4), 375–416. doi:10.1162/evco.1995.3.4.375

González, A., & Herrera, F. (1997). Multi-stage genetic fuzzy systems based on the iterative rule learning approach. *Mathware & Soft Computing, 4*(3), 233–249.

Greene, D. P., & Smith, S. F. (1993). Competition based induction of decision models from examples. *Machine Learning, 13*(2), 229–257. doi:10.1023/A:1022622013558

Hipp, J., Guntzer, U., & Nakaeizadeh, G. (2000) Algorithms for Association Rule Mining - a General Survey and Comparison. In U. Fayyad (Ed.), *Sixth ACM SIGKDD International Conference on Knowledge Discovery and Data Mining* (Vol. 2, pp. 58 - 64). Boston: ACM.

Holland, J. H., & Reitman, J. S. (1978). Cognitive Systems Based on Adaptive Algorithms. In D. A. Waterman & F. Hayes-Roth (Eds.), Pattern-Directed Inference Systems (pp. 313-329). New York: Academic Press.

Holte, R. C., Acker, L., & Porter, B. W. (1989). *Concept Learning and the Problem of Small Disjuncts* (Tech. Rep. AI89-106). Austin, TX: University of Texas at Austin, Computer Sciences Department.

Hubley, R. M., Zitzler, E., & Roach, J. C. (2003). Evolutionary algorithms for the selection of single nucleotide polymorphisms. *BMC Bioinformatics, 4*(30), 30–39. doi:10.1186/1471-2105-4-30

Janikow, C. Z. (1993). A knowledge-intensive genetic algorithm for supervised learning. *Machine Learning, 13*(2/3), 189–228. doi:10.1023/A:1022669929488

Jourdan, L., Dhaenens, C., Talbi, E.-G., & Gallina, S. (2002). A Data Mining Approach to Discover Genetic and Environmental Factors involved in Multifactorial Diseases. *Knowledge-Based Systems, 15*(4), 235–242. doi:10.1016/S0950-7051(01)00145-9

Kelemen, A., Vasilakos, A. V., & Liang, Y. (2009). Computational Intelligence for genetic association study in complex diseases: review of theory and applications. *International Journal of Computational Intelligence in Bioinformatics and System Biology, 1*(1), 15–31. doi:10.1504/IJCIBSB.2009.024041

Little, R. J. A., & Rubin, D. B. (2002). Statistical Analysis with Missing Data. New York: John Wiley.

Lucrédio, D., Almeida, E. S., & Prado, A. F. (2004). A Survey on Software Components Search and Retrieval. In R. Steinmetz & A. Mauthe (Eds.), *30th IEEE EUROMICRO Conference. Component-Based Software Engineering Track* (pp. 152-159). Rennes, France: IEEE Press.

Molitor, J., Marjoram, P., & Thomas, D. (2003). Fine-scale mapping of disease genes with multiple mutations via spatial clustering techniques. *American Journal of Human Genetics*, *73*, 1368–1384. doi:10.1086/380415

Moore, J. H. (2004). Computational analysis of gene – gene interactions using multifactor dimensionality reduction. *Expert Review of Molecular Diagnostics*, *4*, 795–803. doi:10.1586/14737159.4.6.795

Moore, J. H., & White, B. C. (2006). Exploiting expert knowledge for genome-wide genetic analysis using genetic programming. In T. P. Runarsson, H-G. Beyer, E. Burke, J. J. Merelo-Guervos, L. D. Whitley & X. Yao (Eds.), Parallel Problem Solving from Nature – PPSN IX (Vol. 4193, pp.969-977). Reykjavik, Iceland: Springer.

Motsinger, A. A., Lee, S. L., Mellick, G., & Ritchie, M. D. (2006). GPNN: power studies and applications of a neural network method for detecting gene-gene interactions in studies of human disease. *BMC Bioinformatics*, *7*(39).

Reif, D. M., White, B. C., & Moore, J. H. (2004). Integrated analysis of genetic, genomic and proteomic data. *Expert Review of Proteomics*, *1*, 67–75. doi:10.1586/14789450.1.1.67

Risch, N. (2000). Searching for genetic determinants in the new millennium. *Nature*, *405*, 847–856. doi:10.1038/35015718

Ritchie, M. D., Hahn, L. W., & Roodi, N. (2001). Multifactor dimensionality reduction reveals high-order interactions among estrogen metabolism genes in sporadic breast cancer. *American Journal of Human Genetics*, *69*, 138–147. doi:10.1086/321276

Ritchie, M. D., White, B. C., Parker, J. S., Hahn, L. W., & Moore, J. H. (2003). Optimization of neural network architecture using genetic programming improves detection and modelling of gene-gene interactions in studies of human diseases. *BMC Bioinformatics*, *4*(28).

Rova, M., Haataja, R., & Marttila, R. (2004). Data mining and multiparameter analysis of lung surfactant protein genes in bronchopulmonary dysplasia. *Human Molecular Genetics*, *13*, 1095–1104. doi:10.1093/hmg/ddh132

Smith, S. F. (1980). *A learning system based on genetic adaptive Algorithms*. Doctoral dissertation, University of Pittsburgh.

Srikant, R., & Agrawal, R. (1995). Mining generalized association rules. In U. Dayal, P. Gray & S. Nishio (Eds.), *21st International Conference on Very Large Data Bases* (pp. 407-419). Zurich, Germany: Morgan Kaufmann.

Tahri-Daizadeh, N., Tregouet, D. A., & Nicaud, V. (2003). Automated detection of informative combined effects in genetics association Studies of complex traits. *Genome Research*, *13*, 1952–1960.

Thomas, D. C. (2004). Statistical Methods in Genetic Epidemiology. Oxford, UK: Oxford University Press.

Toivonen, H., Onkamo, P., Hintsanen, P., et al. (2005). Data mining for gene mapping. In M. M. Kantardzic & J. Zurada (Eds.), New Generation of Data Mining Applications (pp. 263-293). Hoboken, NJ: IEEE Press.

Tzeng, J. Y., Devlin, B., & Wasserman, L. (2003). On the identification of disease mutations by the analysis of haplotype similarity and goodness of fit. *American Journal of Human Genetics*, *72*, 891–902. doi:10.1086/373881

Venturini, G. (1993). SIA: A supervised inductive algorithm with genetic search for learning attributes based concepts. In P. Brazdil (Ed.), *Machine Learning: ECML-93: Vol. 667. European Conference on Machine Learning* (pp. 280-296). Vienna: Springer.

Vermeulen-Jourdan, L., Dhaenens, C., & Talbi, E.-G. (2005). Linkage disequilibrium study with a parallel adaptive GA. *International Journal of Foundations of Computer Science, 16*(2), 241–260. doi:10.1142/S0129054105002978

Waddell, M., Page, D., Zhan, F., et al. (2005). Predicting cancer susceptibility from single-nucleotide polymorphism data: A case study in multiple myeloma. In S. Parthasarathy, W. Wang & M.J. Zaki (Eds.), *Fifth ACM SIGKDD Workshop on Data Mining in Bioinformatics (BIOKDD)* (pp. 21-28). Chicago: ACM.

Wang, H. (2005). Bayesian shrinkage estimation of quantitative trait loci parameters. *Genetics, 170*, 465–480. doi:10.1534/genetics.104.039354

Wilcox, M. A., Wyszynski, D. F., & Panhuysen, C. I. (2003). Empirically derived phenotypic subgroups - qualitative and quantitative trait analyses. *BMC Genetics, 4*(1), S15. doi:10.1186/1471-2156-4-S1-S15

Witten, I. H., & Frank, E. (2005). Data Mining: Practical machine learning tools and techniques (2nd Ed.). San Francisco, CA: Morgan Kaufmann.

Wittke-Thompson, J. K., Pluzhinikov, A., & Cox, N. J. (2005). Rational Inferences about departures from Hardy-Weinberg equilibrium. *American Journal of Human Genetics, 76*, 967–986. doi:10.1086/430507

Wolberg, W. H., & Mangasarian, O. L. (1990). Multisurface method of pattern separation for medical diagnosis applied to breast cytology. *Proceedings of the National Academy of Sciences of the United States of America, 87*(23), 9193–9196. doi:10.1073/pnas.87.23.9193

Young, S. S., & Ge, N. (2005). Recursive partitioning analysis of complex disease pharmacogenetic studies I. Motivation and overview. *Pharmacogenetics, 6*, 65–75.

ADDITIONAL READING

Banzhaf, W., Beslon, G., Christensen, S., Foster, J. A., Képès, F., & Lefort, V. (2006). Guidelines: From artificial evolution to computational evolution: a research agenda. *Nature Reviews. Genetics, 7*, 729–735. doi:10.1038/nrg1921

Bishop, C. M. (2006). Pattern Recognition and Machine Learning. Second Edition. New York: Springer.

Cardon, L. R., & Bell, J. I. (2001). Association study designs for complex diseases. *Nature Reviews. Genetics, 2*, 91–99. doi:10.1038/35052543

Coello Coello, C. A., Lamont, G. B., & Van Veldhuizen, D. A. (2007). Evolutionary algorithms for solving multi-objective problems (2nd Ed.). New York: Springer.

Craig, J. (2008). Complex diseases: Research and applications. *Nature Education, 1*(1).

Dunham, H. (2003). Data mining: introductory and advanced topics. Upper Saddle River, NJ: Prentice Hall.

Engelbrecht, A. P. (2007). Computational intelligence: an introduction (2nd Ed.). New York: Wiley.

Foster, J. A. (2001). Computational genetics: Evolutionary computation. *Nature Reviews. Genetics, 2*, 428–436. doi:10.1038/35076523

Halldórsson, B. V., Istrail, S., & De La Vega, F. M. (2004)... *Human Heredity, 58*, 190–202. doi:10.1159/000083546

Han, J., & Kamber, M. (2006). Data mining: concepts and techniques (2nd Ed.). San Francisco, CA: Morgan Kaufmann.

Hastie, T., Tibshirani, R., & Friedman, J. (2009). The elements of statistical learning: data mining, inference and prediction (2nd Ed.). New York: Springer.

Haupt, R. L. (2004). Practical genetic algorithms (2nd Ed.). Hoboken, NJ: Wiley-Interscience.

Hernández Orallo, J., Ramírez Quintana, M. J., & Ferri Ramírez, C. (2008). Introducción a la Minería de Datos. Madrid: Pearson Prentice Hall.

Kantardzic, M. (2003). Data mining: concepts, models, methods, and algorithms. Totowa, NJ: Wiley-IEEE.

Kiberstis, P., & Roberts, L. (2002). It's not just the genes. *Science*, *296*(5568), 685. doi:10.1126/science.296.5568.685

Lewis, C. M. (2002). Genetic association studies: Design, analysis and interpretation. *Briefings in Bioinformatics*, *3*(2), 146–153. doi:10.1093/bib/3.2.146

Man, K. F., Tang, K. S., & Kwong, S. (1999). Genetic algorithms: concepts and designs. (Advanced textbooks in control and signal processing). London: Springer.

Molitor, J., Marjoram, P., Conti, D., & Thomas, D. (2004). A survey of current Bayesian gene mapping methods. *Human Genomics*, *1*(5), 371–374.

Ott, J. (2001). Neural networks and disease association studies. [Neuropsychiatric Genetics]. *American Journal of Medical Genetics*, *105*, 60–61. doi:10.1002/1096-8628(20010108)105:1<60::AID-AJMG1062>3.0.CO;2-L

Reeves, C. R., & Rowe, J. E. (2003). Genetic algorithms: principles and perspectives: A Guide to GA theory. Boston, MA: Kluwer.

Rothlauf, F. (2006). Representations for genetic and evolutionary algorithms (2nd Ed.). Berlin: Springer.

Sierra, B. (2006). Aprendizaje Automático: Conceptos básicos y avanzados. Aspectos prácticos utilizando el software Weka. Madrid: Pearson Prentice Hall.

Tan, P.-N., Steinbach, M., & Kumar, V. (2006). Introduction to Data Mining. Boston, MA: Pearson Addition Wesley.

Thomas, D. C., Stram, D. O., Conti, D., Molitor, J., & Marjoram, P. (2003). Bayesian spatial modeling of haplotype associations. *Human Heredity*, *56*, 32–40. doi:10.1159/000073730

Todd, J. A. (2001). Human genetics: Tackling common disease. *Nature*, *411*, 537–539. doi:10.1038/35079223

Willard, H. F., Angrist, M., & Ginsburg, G. S. (2005). Genomic medicine: genetic variation and its impact on the future of health care. *Philosophical Transactions of the Royal Society B*, *360*, 1543–1550. doi:10.1098/rstb.2005.1683

Chapter 15
Improving Ontology Alignment through Genetic Algorithms

José Manuel Vázquez Naya
University of A Coruña, Spain

Marcos Martínez Romero
University of A Coruña, Spain

Javier Pereira Loureiro
University of A Coruña, Spain

Cristian R. Munteanu
University of A Coruña, Spain

Alejandro Pazos Sierra
University of A Coruña, Spain

ABSTRACT

Ontology alignment is recognized as a fundamental process to achieve an adequate interoperability between people or systems that use different, overlapping ontologies to represent common knowledge. This process consists of finding the semantic relations between different ontologies. There are different techniques conceived to measure the semantic similarity of elements from separate ontologies, which must be adequately combined in order to obtain precise and complete results. Nevertheless, combining multiple measures into a single similarity metric is a complex problem, which has been traditionally solved using weights determined manually by an expert, or calculated through general methods that does not provide optimal results. In this chapter, a genetic algorithm based approach to find out how to aggregate different similarity metrics into a single measure is presented. Starting from an initial population of individuals, each one representing a specific combination of measures, the algorithm finds the combination that provides the best alignment quality.

DOI: 10.4018/978-1-61520-893-7.ch015

INTRODUCTION

At present, the role of ontologies for allowing a more effective data and knowledge sharing and reusing is widely recognized (Neches et al., 1991; Guarino, 1998) and a variety of public ontologies exist for different application domains. This innovative technology is considered to be an appropriate solution to the problem of heterogeneity in data, since ontological methods make it possible to reach a common understanding of concepts in a particular domain, supporting the exchange of information between people (or between systems) that utilize different representations for the same or similar knowledge (Ashburner et al., 2000; Gómez-Pérez et al., 2004; Gruber, 1995).

Nevertheless, given that different tasks or different points of view usually require different conceptualizations, utilizing a single ontology is neither always possible nor advisable. This can lead to the usage of different ontologies, although in some cases the different ontologies collectively might contain information that could be overlapping. This, in turn, represents another type of heterogeneity that can result in inefficient processing or misinterpretation of data, information, and knowledge. Having into account that ontologies can interoperate only if correspondences between their elements have been identified and established (Kalfoglou and Schorlemmer, 2003), addressing this problem while at the same time insure an appropriate level of interoperability between heterogeneous systems, requires to find correspondences or mappings that exist between the elements of the different ontologies being used. This process is commonly known as *ontology alignment*, *ontology matching* or *ontology mapping*. The resulting set of inter-ontology relations can be used to adequately exchange information between people, systems and organizations.

As such, ontology engineers face the problem of how to map various ontologies to enable a common understanding (Ding et al., 2002), and

several methods for identifying the relationships or correspondences between elements associated with different ontologies have been conceived during the last years. Collectively these methods are called *ontology alignment techniques*. Each one of these techniques provides a numerical value of similarity between elements from separate ontologies that can be used to decide (frequently, according to a predefined threshold) if those elements are semantically similar or not.

Ontology alignment is considered to be a complex, tedious, and time-consuming task, especially when working with ontologies of considerable size (containing, for instance, thousands of elements). In addition, the true potential of ontology alignment is realized when different information-exchange processes are achieved automatically and on real time, thereby providing the framework for reaching a suitable level of efficient interoperability between heterogeneous systems. The importance of automatically aligning ontologies has therefore been a topic of major interest in recent years, and there has been a surge in a variety of software tools dedicated to aligning ontologies in either a fully or partially automated fashion. These tools are commonly referred to as *ontology alignment systems*.

Due to the complex nature of the ontology alignment problem, the application of a single ontology alignment technique normally is not enough to provide satisfactory alignment results. Because of this reason, most ontology alignment systems combine a set of different alignment techniques, which can be based on different approaches (e.g. lexical, structural, etc.), into a single value of aggregated similarity between ontological elements, and subsequently select the semantic mappings on the basis of the aggregated similarity function. Finding the optimal combination of similarity measures is a complex and hard process, which should be achieved automatically in order to get optimal results. Nevertheless, current similarity aggregation approaches generally use weights determined manually by an expert, or calculated through general methods (e.g. average or sigmoid function) that do not always provide acceptable results. This situation demands an automatic manner of obtaining an acceptable set of weights in a reasonable amount of time.

Given a set of existing ontology alignments (reference alignments), this work proposes the utilization of Genetic Algorithms (GAs) to ascertain how to combine multiple similarity measures into a single aggregated metric, in order to provide the optimal alignment result. Genetic Algorithms (GAs) are considered to be a flexible and robust technique, which can deal successfully with a wide range of difficult optimization problems and they are generally good at finding acceptably good solutions to problems acceptably quickly. These characteristics make them apparently suitable to be applied to a complex process such as aggregating different similarity values. The obtained aggregated similarity measure can be useful to automatically tune an ontology alignment system addressed to work in environments such as the one of the reference alignments, improving the results provided by the system.

The paper proceeds as follows: a brief background of ontology alignment and genetic algorithms, as well as related work, are first presented in the background section; this is followed by the main thrust of the chapter, where a specific description of the methods planned to improve the ontology alignment task is presented. We discuss some future research directions and, finally, we present the conclusions of the work.

BACKGROUND

Towards the end of the 20th and beginning of the 21st centuries, the term "ontology" (or ontologies) gained usage in computer science to refer to a research area in the subfield of artificial intelligence primarily concerned with the semantics of concepts and with expressive (or interpretive)

processes in computer-based communications. In this context, there are many definitions of ontology, and these definitions have evolved over the years. Gruber offered one of the first definitions of ontology in 1993, as follows (Gruber, 1993):

An ontology is an explicit specification of a conceptualization.

Gruber's definition became the most frequently referenced one in the literature, and it was soon considered as the base or working definition for those researching in this area.

At present, ontologies are viewed as a practical way to conceptualize information that is expressed in electronic format, and are being used in many applications belonging to different areas. For example, there are multiple applications of ontologies in health, medicine and biomedicine (e.g., Smith and Brochhausen, 2008; Gustafsson and Falkman, 2005; Spasic et al., 2005), car industry (e.g., Syldatke et al., 2007), learning (e.g., Snae and Brueckner, 2007), administration and government (e.g., Gómez-Pérez and Villazon-Terrazas, 2006), energy (e.g., Van Dam and Lukszo, 2006), finances (e.g., Bas, 2007) or tourism (e.g., Campos et al., 2008). The basic idea behind these applications is to use ontologies to reach a common level of understanding or comprehension within a particular domain.

However, certain systems that encompass a large number of components associated with different domains would generally require the use of different ontologies. In such cases, using ontologies would not reduce heterogeneity but rather would recast the heterogeneity problem into a different (and higher) framework wherein the problem becomes one of ontology alignment, thereby allowing a more efficient exchange of information and knowledge derived from different (heterogeneous) data bases, knowledge bases, and the knowledge contained in the ontologies themselves.

Figure 1. A simple example illustrating the alignment between two ontologies, A and B

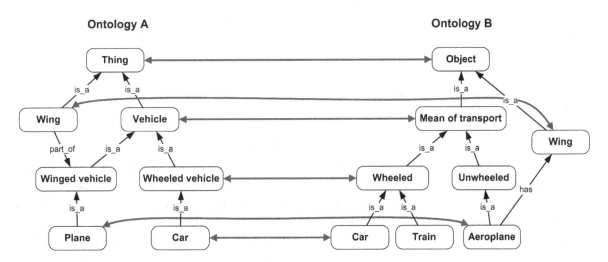

Ontology Alignment

Euzenat et al. defined the problem of ontology alignment as follows (Euzenat et al., 2004):

Given two ontologies which describe each a set of discrete entities (which can be classes, properties, rules, predicates, etc.), find the relationships (e.g. equivalence or subsumption) holding between these entities.

The key issue in ontology alignment is finding which entity in one ontology corresponds (in terms of meaning) to another entity in one (or many) ontology (or ontologies). Essentially, one might say that ontology alignment can be reduced to defining a similarity measure between entities in different ontologies and selecting a set of correspondences between entities of different ontologies with the highest similarity measures.

In the Figure 1, a basic example of ontology alignment between two simple ontologies is showed.

The pair of ontologies shown in Figure 1 contain *classes* (e.g., *Wing, Car, Object*, etc.), each one represents a set of elements in the real world that share certain characteristics; and *relations* between classes (e.g. *is_a*, *part_of* and *has*). Both ontology A and ontology B have their own set of entities organized according to a specific taxonomy. The two representations arise due to the fact that they correspond to two different perspectives or points of view of similar domains. However, some pairs of entities can be identified in these ontologies that share the same or similar semantics. Thus, it's probable that the *Plane* class in ontology A and *Aeroplane* in ontology B refer to the same concept in general (in the real world), given that the terms that describe them are synonymous terms.

There are different methods to calculate the similarity measures between entities, and collectively these methods are known as *ontology alignment techniques*. Many of these techniques are derived from other fields (for instance, discrete mathematics, automatic learning, data base design, pattern recognition, among others). Consequently, some of these techniques attempt to compare text strings that describe the entities in the ontologies (terminology-based ontology alignment) while others calculate the similarity measures between entities taking into account the structure of their corresponding ontologies (structural ontology alignment). Due to that each ontology alignment technique is based on comparing a specific feature, reliability of results depends on the adequate selection of the most suitable technique for each problem. Thus, an ontology alignment technique could provide good results at aligning a specific pair of ontologies, but it could be bad at aligning another different pair of ontologies, with different characteristics. Up to the moment, several studies have been published dedicated to the classification of these techniques. The most referenced ones have been written by Euzenat et al., (2004), Euzenat & Valtchev (2004), Rahm & Bernstein (2001) and Shvaiko & Euzenat (2005).

Due to its cognitive complexity, ontology alignment has been traditionally performed by human experts. However, manual ontology alignment in dynamic environments that require real-time processing (e.g. the Semantic Web, Berners-Lee et al., 2001) is inefficient and at times close to impossible. This has resulted over the past few years in the emergence of multiple software tools that have been developed by diverse research groups and well-established international organizations, primarily associated with the academic community. The tools, designed to automatically identify the correspondences that may exist between entities of different ontologies, are called *ontology alignment systems* or *matchers*.

Since ontology alignment started to be considered as an important research area, a considerable number of ontology alignment systems have become available. Each one of these systems offers a unique set of advantages, disadvantages, and performance characteristics. A complete classification of ontology alignment systems can be found in (Euzenat and Shvaiko, 2007). An ontology alignment system accepts one (or more) ontologies as input, and provides, as output, a set of correspondences between their elements. This set of correspondences is referred to as *alignment*. The quality of a particular alignment depends on the correctness and completeness of the cor-

respondences it has found, and it is normally assessed on the basis of two measures from the information retrieval field, commonly known as *precision* and *recall*.

Precision (or correctness, or accuracy) measures the fraction of found alignments that are actually correct. A precision of 1 means that all found alignments are correct, but it does not imply that all alignments have been found. Typically, precision is balanced against recall (or completeness), which measures the fraction of correct alignments found in comparison to the total number of correct existing alignments. A high recall means that many of the alignments have actually been found, but no information about the number of additionally falsely identified alignments is given. Therefore, often precision and recall are balanced against each other with the so-called *f-measure* (Van Rijsbergen, 1975), which is the uniformly weighted harmonic mean of precision and recall. F-measure will be used as the reference quality metric in the rest of this paper, in such a way that we will consider that the best alignment is the alignment with highest f-measure.

Given a reference alignment R and some alignment A, precision and recall are given by the following expressions:

$$precision = \frac{|R \cap A|}{|A|} \; ; \; recall = \frac{|R \cap A|}{|R|}$$

while f-measure for a given precision and recall is calculated as follows:

$$f - measure = 2 \cdot \frac{precision \cdot recall}{precision + recall}$$

As it was explained before, aligning ontologies requires comparing the semantic similarity of pairs of entities from different ontologies, and there are different methods or measures to calculate this similarity. However, aligning two ontologies is not simply the application of a similarity measure in an isolated manner: rather, the goal is mainly to find the appropriate combination of techniques to be applied, such that the strengths of one technique can compensate another technique's weaknesses and limitations, with the overarching objective of uncovering an optimal set of correspondences between the ontologies of interest. Actually, it is recognized that a combination of several similarity techniques or measures leads to better alignment results than using only one at a time (Ehrig, 2007).

Because of these facts, an alignment system typically calculates the similarity between a pair of entities from two different ontologies by means of a set of multiple similarity techniques and obtained similarity values are combined in a unique similarity measure. This process of aggregating different similarity assessments for one pair of entities into a single measure is commonly known as *similarity aggregation*. In a simplified manner, similarity aggregation can be calculated according to the expression:

$$sim_{agg}(e_i, e_j) = \sum_{k=1}^{n} w_k \cdot sim_k(e_i, e_j), \quad subject\ to \quad \sum_{k=1}^{n} w_k = 1$$

with (e_i, e_j) being a candidate alignment between the entities e_i and e_j, from two different ontologies, and w_k being the weight for each separate similarity measure sim_k.

As an example, if we have two similarity measures, sim_1 and sim_2, with $sim_1(e_1, e_2)=0.78$ and $sim_2(e_1, e_2)=0.56$, and we wish to give a weight of 0.3 to sim_1 an of 0.7 to sim_2, then the aggregated similarity would be calculated as follows:

$$sim_{agg}(e_1, e_2) = 0.3 \cdot 0,78 + 0.7 \cdot 0.56 = 0.626$$

Optimal aggregation of different similarity measures consist of finding out the combination of weights w_k that provide the best alignment result between the elements from two ontologies. However, finding the adequate values for these weights is not an easy task. It is a complex process that normally is achieved manually by an expert or by means of general approaches (e.g. averaging, linear summation, sigmoid function, etc.), which are not appropriate to provide optimal results for all alignment problems. Providing solutions to this problem is a research area that is still in an early-stage, but that is considered to be essential to obtain high quality alignments in an automatic manner and, therefore, to reach an adequate semantic interoperability between systems in domains that require real-time processing and response.

This work proposes a GA-based approach to automatically find the best manner of aggregating different similarity measures into a single similarity metric. Starting from one (or several) existing alignments (reference alignments) between ontologies with specific characteristics (e.g. with high structural similarity, from the medical domain, etc.), we propose a GA which is able to find the combination of weights that provides the best value according to a well known measure for quality of ontology alignment. This set of optimal weights can be used to compute the optimal alignment between ontologies with characteristics similar to the ontologies whose alignment was used as reference.

Genetic Algorithms

At the end of the 60's, the American scientist John Holland and a group of students and colleagues from the University of Michigan[1] were researching about the learning capacities of machines. They discovered that learning could happen not just through the adaptation of just one organism, but also trough the evolving adaptation of multiple generations of a specie. His work was inspired by the Darwinian notion of evolution, which states that only the most valid organism survives. Holland proposed that the construction of a machine that were able to learn should be achieved through the descendants of several strategies in a population of candidates, in spite of proposing it as the construction and refinement of just one strategy. Holland and his collaborators called their technique *reproductive plans*, but the term *genetic algorithms* (GAs) became popular after the publication of his book (Holland, 1975), in which the basic principles of GAs were first rigorously laid down.

GAs are adaptative methods, generally used in search and parameter optimization problems, based on sexual reproduction and survival of the fittest individual in a population. In order to achieve the solution to a problem, the GA starts from an initial set of individuals, called population, which is randomly generated. Each one of these individuals represents a possible solution to the problem. These individuals will evolve on the basis of the schemes about natural selection proposed by Darwin (Darwin, 1859), and they will adapt themselves to the required solution while they pass from one to another generation.

At the beginning of 80's, GAs seemed to be very promising, and the leaders in the area started to give periodical conferences each year. In 1989, David Goldberg, from the University of Alabama[2] published a book (Goldberg, 1989) containing and explaining multiple successful real applications of GA, which provided a solid scientific base in the field. In this work, Goldberg defined GAs as follows:

Genetic algorithms are search algorithms based on the mechanics of natural selection and natural genetics. They combine the principle of survival of the fittest among string structures with a structured yet randomized information exchange to form a search algorithm with some of the innovative flair of human search.

Three years after the publication of Goldberg's book, in 1992, Lawrence Davis published his "Handbook of Genetic Algorithms" (Davis, 1991), which soon became a reference work in the field. Since then, the area turned into an incredible

mine of gold to develop applications in fields like optimization, searching and machine learning.

One year later, J.R. Koza (1992) gave another good definition of genetic algorithm as follows:

The genetic algorithm is a highly parallel technique that transforms a population of individual objects, each with an associated fitness value, into a new generation of the population using the Darwinian principle of reproduction and survival of the fittest and naturally occurring genetic operations such as crossover (recombination) and mutation. Each individual in the population represents a possible solution to a given problem.

Nevertheless, in spite of all the previously mentioned definitions and as explained in (Mitchell, 1996), there is no rigorous definition of GA accepted by all in the evolutionary computation community that differentiates GAs from other evolutionary computation methods. However, it can be said that most methods called GAs have at least the following elements in common: population of chromosomes, selection according to fitness (performance), crossover to produce new offspring, and random mutation of new offspring.

Due to the already mentioned characteristics, the problem of finding a good aggregation of similarity measures can be potentially solved by using GAs. In this work, a GA-based approach to find an optimal combination of multiple similarity measures is proposed, with the final aim of discovering the best set of semantic correspondences between two ontologies. We hope that this work can be useful to researchers and developers who need a manner of automatically tuning their ontology alignment systems in order to find the best alignment results.

Related Work

After ontology alignment became an important research field, several authors tried to apply techniques from other research areas to this process in order to get the best results. Qazvinian et al. (2008) are among the small number of authors who have tried, up to the moment, to apply GA to the ontology alignment task. They consider the problem of finding an ideal mapping from a set of existing correspondences between two ontologies as an optimization problem in which the objective is maximizing the overall similarity value between the input ontologies, and they use a GA to find the optimal mapping. In a similar way, another interesting example to solve the ontology alignment problem by using GAs is GAOM (Wang et al., 2006). In this work, features of ontology are defined from two aspects: intensional and extensional, and ontology alignment problem is modeled as a global optimization of a mapping between two ontologies. Then GA is used to achieve an approximate optimal solution.

Besides the approaches in which GAs have been proposed to improve the ontology alignment process, there are also other set of works which show that combining ontologies and GAs is a promising research field which can provide good solutions in a wide range of problems. An example is the research made by Nammuni et al. (2002), who investigated the use of a GA in producing optimal allocations of tasks to resources, using an ontology to support partial matching; it helps to determine which tutors' skills (i.e. resources) are ontologically close to the optimal skill. These are then matched against the skill requirements of the task. Another example is the approach by Rocha et al. (2004), which discusses the use of concept maps (CMs) in learning assessment. They showed how to use ontologies and machine learning, through GAs, to assess CMs in learning assessment. The ontologies they use store knowledge, in the form of concepts and propositions, and functions to measure the semantic distance between CMs. The GA, using the ontology, generates the search space (collections of CMs) used to show learners the alternatives to their possible faults when learning concepts and propositions.

A GENETIC ALGORITHM BASED APPROACH TO OPTIMIZE THE AGGREGATION OF MULTIPLE SEMANTIC SIMILARITY MEASURES

As previously explained, ontology alignment is the process of determining a semantic correspondence or mapping between two (or several) ontologies. That is, for every entity in an ontology finding out its corresponding or related entity in another ontology with the same or the closest intended meaning. When the process finishes, the set of correspondences can be used to exchange information between people or systems in situations where using a unique ontology is not possible, correct or enough. During the last years, multiple ontology alignment techniques have been conceived to identify these correspondences. These methods are based on computing a similarity (or distance) value between elements of different ontologies. When computing the ontology alignment between two ontologies, it is frequently to use several ontology alignment techniques, based on different similarity approaches (e.g. lexical similarity, structural similarity, etc.) and then aggregating them into a unique similarity value. However, calculating the optimal similarity aggregation is a computationally expensive task that requires new, more efficient methods to get precise and complete alignments.

In the following, a GA to find the optimal aggregation of multiple similarity measures is presented. This GA starts from a randomly generated aggregation (set of weights) of similarity measures, and tries to find the weight value for each measure that optimizes the global quality of the alignment.

Description of the Problem

In order to reliably describe the existing problem, it is necessary to define the following elements (see Figure 2):

Figure 2. Graphical representation of the problem. The figure shows the hierarchical tree of two different ontologies: ontology A and ontology B, and a possible set of semantic correspondences (s_{ij}) between them ($i \in [1,n], j \in [1,m]$)

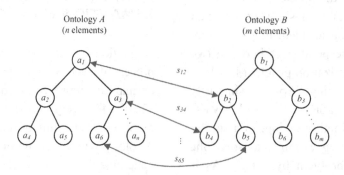

- A and B are two ontologies with n and m elements (entities) respectively. A is composed by the entities $a_1,...,a_n$ while B has the entities $b_1,...,b_m$.

- S is an existing set of semantic mappings or correspondences s_{ij} between A and B, being s_{ij} a semantic mapping between the entity a_i from A and the entity b_j from B, with $0<i<n$ y $0<j<m$.

- $F = \left\{ F_1(a_i, b_j),...,F_p(a_i, b_j) \right\} = \left\{ F_1(s_{ij}),...,F_p(s_{ij}) \right\}$

  is a set composed by p functions, or ontology alignment techniques, to compute a value of semantic similarity (in the [0, 1] interval) between pairs of entities from separate ontologies. Examples of these functions can be found in Shvaiko & Euzenat (2005).

- t is a similarity threshold belonging to the interval [0, 1], which indicates the minimum value of similarity required to consider that exists semantic correspondence between two different entities.

- $Q(S) \rightarrow [0,1]$ is a function that measures the quality of a set of semantic correspondences between two ontologies. As previously mentioned, in this work we will consider that the quality measure is the f-measure metric.

- $F_{agg}(a_i, b_j) = \sum_{k=1}^{p} w_k \cdot F_k(a_i, b_j)$, with

  $\sum_{k=1}^{p} w_k = 1$, is a function to compute an aggregated similarity measure between two entities. This function combines the similarity values provided by p different similarity functions into a single value belonging to the interval [0, 1]. The aggregation is based on the values of a set of p weights w_k, which quantify the contribution of each separate similarity measure to the aggregated value.

Having this into account, the main aim of this work is to find the values of the weights w_k that maximize the quality of the alignment between the input ontologies A and B, that is, the function $Q(S)$. The obtained set of weights could be subsequently used to compute the alignment of ontologies with similar characteristics, or from the same domain than the ontologies whose alignment was selected as a reference.

At this point, it is also important to mention that although the problem has been described on the basis of a unique reference alignment between two ontologies, it can be generalized to use more than one reference alignment. This can be useful when it is necessary to obtain a more general ag-

Figure 3. Graphical representation of a chromosome and the set of weights obtained after decoding it. Each position of the chromosome contains a value belonging to the interval [0, 1] that represents a cut, or separation point between weights. $C' = \{c_1, ..., c_{p-1}\}$ is an unordered set of cuts, while $C = \{c_1, ..., c_{p-1}\}$ is the result obtained after ordering C' from lower to higher. $W = \{w_1, ..., w_p\}$ is the set of weights that constitute the solution to the problem

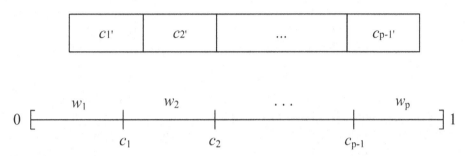

gregated measure of similarity, able to provide good results in a wider range of ontological domains (e.g., medicine, industry, commerce, etc.) or characteristics (e.g. high structural similarity, low lexical similarity, etc.).

The proposed implementation of GAs in application to the ontology alignment problem incorporates five basic steps so that the algorithm is formulated for the specific application: (i) the presentation of an individual, i.e. the encoding mechanism of the problem, (ii) the description of the reproduction methods used to get a new generation of individuals from a specific generation, (iii) the formulation of the fitness function, which gives to each individual a measure of performance, and (iv) the selection of the criterion that will be followed to stop the execution of the algorithm. Finally, a simple example of the GA execution is provided. In the following, each one of the mentioned steps is described.

Encoding Mechanism and Initialization

Having into account that each individual of the population represents a potential solution to the problem, it is clear that each individual must provide the values for the set of weights w_k which, as explained before, indicate the contribution of each similarity function to the aggregated similarity function.

We propose an encoding mechanism which is based on that each position in the chromosome contains a value belonging to the interval [0, 1] which represents a *cut*, or *separation point* that limits the value of a weight (remember that summation of all weights is equal to 1). Considering that p is the number of required weights, the set of cuts can be formally represented as $C' = \{c_1, ..., c_{p-1}\}$. The chromosome decoding is carried out by ordering C' from lower to higher, which constitutes the ordered set of values $C = \{c_1, ..., c_{p-1}\}$, and calculating the weights according the following expression:

$$w_k = \begin{cases} c_1, & k = 1 \\ c_i - c_{i-1}, & 1 < k < p \\ 1 - c_{p-1}, & k = p \end{cases}$$

A graphical representation of the chromosome and the decoded values are showed in Figure 3, while Figure 4 presents an example that can be useful to understand the encoding and decoding mechanisms.

After deciding the encoding mechanism, the initial population would be constituted by a ran-

Figure 4. Example showing a specific individual from the population and the weight values after decoding it. Each gene in the chromosome contains a numerical value belonging to the [0, 1] interval, which represents a point that restricts the value of a weight. In this example, 6 different weights are considered, which would measure the contribution of 6 different similarity functions to an aggregated metric. As can be observed, the chromosome values are ordered before calculating the set of weights

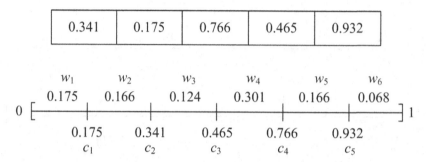

domly generated group of chromosomes, each one coding a possible solution to the problem.

Reproduction Methods

To go from one generation to the next, we propose to apply the following genetic operators:

- **Selection.** Like in nature, in GAs the most suitable individuals must have more opportunities of reproducing themselves. The best individuals in a population are the individuals that have the best fitness value and the genetic information of these individuals can potentially provide the best solutions to the problem. Anyway, reproduction opportunities of the less suitable individuals should not be completely removed, because it is important to keep diversity in the population. Having this into account, we propose to use a roulette wheel selection method, which consists in that individuals are given a probability of being selected that is directly proportionate to their fitness, so the best individuals will have more opportunities of reproduction. Two individuals are then chosen randomly

based on these probabilities and produce offspring.

- **Crossover.** When the set of individuals have been selected, they must be recombined to produce the descendants that will be inserted in the following generation. The crossover will use a non-destructive strategy, in such a way that the descendants will pass to the following generation only if they exceed the fitness of their parents. A single-point crossover will be used, which consists in randomly selecting a crossover point on both parent chromosomes and then interchanging the two parent chromosomes at this point to produce two new offspring.

- **Copy.** The best individual from one generation will be also copied to the following generation (elitist strategy). This decision has been taken to keep the best set of weights (best solution) that has been obtained up to the moment.

- **Mutation.** When the crossover has been achieved, genes will be mutated with a low probability. This mutation will consist of replacing the selected gene by a randomly generated one.

Figure 5. Graphical representation of ontologies A and B, and the reference alignment S

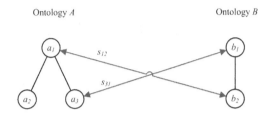

Fitness or Objective Function

For the smooth running of a GA, it is necessary to have a method that allows to show if the individuals of the population are or are not good solutions to the problem. That is the aim of the fitness function, which establishes a numerical measure for the goodness of a solution. In the application of GAs to the ontology alignment problem, we propose to use the f-measure, previously explained in this paper, as the fitness function:

$$fitness = f - measure = 2 \cdot \frac{precision \cdot recall}{precision + recall}$$

The previous expression represents the adequate fitness function when starting the GA from a unique reference alignment from two ontologies. If it is necessary to work on the basis of several reference alignments (between several pairs on ontologies), the fitness function must be modified to have into account the quality of all the reference alignments. This could be done by means of the average of all the f-measures for each reference alignment, as follows:

$$fitness = \frac{f - measure_1, f - measure_2, ..., f - measure_k}{k}$$

Stop Criterion

We propose to use a hybrid criterion to stop the execution of the algorithm. Thus, the GA would stop when one of the following conditions is true:

- A fixed number of iterations have been reached.
- The value for the fitness function is higher than a particular threshold.

Example

In the following, we provide a simple example with two small ontologies, which can be useful to understand how the proposed GA works.

In this example, we will suppose that:

- A and B are two ontologies from a specific domain. Ontology A has 3 entities ($n = 3$), while ontology B is composed by just 2 entities ($m = 2$).
- S is the reference alignment between A and B. In this example $S = \{s_{12}, s_{31}\}$, that is, it will be supposed that there is a semantic mapping between the pairs of entities (a_1, b_2) and (a_3, b_1), as shown in Figure 5. We also will suppose that between the entities (a_1, b_1) exists some similarity, but not enough to be considered a semantic mapping.
- $F = \{F_1(s_{ij}), F_2(s_{ij}), F_3(s_{ij}), F_4(s_{ij}), F_5(s_{ij})\}$ is a set composed by five different similarity functions. We need to aggregate the similarity values provided by these functions into a single measure. We will also suppose that the functions $F_4(s_{ij})$ and $F_5(s_{ij})$, due to the particular characteristics of A and B, are not adequate to align those ontologies, so they will not provide reliable similarity values.
- Finally, it will be supposed that the similarity threshold $t = 0.7$.

Having into account these data, the aggregated similarity function would be:

Table 1. Results of initial similarity computation.

	s_{11}	s_{12}	s_{21}	s_{22}	s_{31}	s_{32}
$F_1(s_{1j})$	0.75	0.81	0.59	0.43	0.86	0.32
$F_2(s_{2j})$	0.64	0.75	0.20	0.03	0.91	0.19
$F_3(s_{3j})$	0.68	0.85	0.44	0.50	0.79	0.37
$F_4(s_{4j})$	0.65	0.74	0.60	0.83	0.34	0.25
$F_5(s_{5j})$	0.71	0.20	0.45	0.63	0.66	0.10

$$F_{agg}(a_i, b_j) = w_1 F_1(s_{ij}) + w_2 F_2(s_{ij}) + w_3 F_3(s_{ij}) + w_4 F_4(s_{ij}) + w_5 F_5(s_{ij}),$$

with $w_1 + w_2 + w_3 + w_4 + w_5 = 1$.

The proposed GA will be used to find the values of weights w_1, w_2, w_3, w_4 and w_5 that provide the optimal alignment between the ontologies.

Firstly, it is necessary to compute the values of similarity for the $n \times m$ possible correspondences between A and B, according to the five different similarity functions. We will suppose that the results of this computation are the ones in Table 1.

The following step is to generate the initial population (first generation). In this case, it is composed by 10 randomly generated individuals, and it is shown in Table 2.

After that, it is necessary to calculate the fitness value for each individual. To do that, it is required to decode each chromosome in order to obtain the

values of the 5 weights. Then, these weights are used to compute the aggregated similarity value for each possible correspondence. Correspondences with a value of similarity higher than the threshold $t = 0.7$ would be considered valid semantic mappings. Using these mappings, the fitness value (f-measure) can be calculated according to the reference alignment. All of these parameters for the initial population are shown in Table 3.

The following task is selecting the individuals that will reproduce themselves to create the following generation. We will suppose that the roulette selection method chooses the individuals 2 and 10 to reproduce themselves. The results of a single-point crossover (in the middle point) between these elements are shown in Table 4. Table 5 shows the results obtained to calculate the fitness function for each chromosome.

As Table 5 shows, the crossover between individuals 2 and 10 produces two new individuals, 11 and 12. The individual 12 has a fitness value of 1, which is the maximum value for the fitness function. Having reached this value, the GA is stopped (according to the stop criterion). The solution provided by the GA would be the set of weights obtained after decoding the individual 12:

$w_1 = 0.11$; $w_2 = 0.40$; $w_3 = 0.36$; $w_4 = 0.07$; $w_5 = 0.06$

Given those weights, the aggregated similarity function for this example would be calculated through the following expression:

Table 2. Initial population

Individual	Chromosome			
1	0.47	0.52	0.31	0.59
2	0.51	0.11	0.92	0.57
3	0.37	0.76	0.64	0.81
4	0.80	0.75	0.61	0.71
5	0.20	0.64	0.21	0.72
6	0.79	0.57	0.12	0.21
7	0.46	0.01	0.22	0.70
8	0.17	0.59	0.58	0.39
9	0.05	0.06	0.46	0.77
10	0.45	0.52	0.87	0.94

Table 3. Weights, valid mappings and fitness value for the initial population

Solution	w_1	w_2	w_3	w_4	w_5	Mappings	Fitness
1	0.31	0.16	0.05	0.07	0.41	s_{11}, s_{31}	0.50
2	0.11	0.40	0.06	0.35	0.08	s_{12}	0.67
3	0.37	0.27	0.12	0.05	0.19	s_{31}	0.67
4	0.61	0.10	0.04	0.05	0.20	s_{11}, s_{31}	0.50
5	0.20	0.01	0.43	0.08	0.28	s_{31}	0.67
6	0.12	0.09	0.36	0.22	0.21	-	-
7	0.01	0.21	0.24	0.24	0.30	-	-
8	0.17	0.22	0.19	0.01	0.41	s_{31}	0.67
9	0.05	0.01	0.40	0.31	0.23	-	-
10	0.45	0.07	0.35	0.07	0.06	s_{11}, s_{12}, s_{31}	0.80

$$F_{agg}(c_{ij}) = 0.11\, F_1(c_{ij}) + 0.40\, F_2(c_{ij}) + 0.36\, F_3(c_{ij}) + 0.07\, F_4(c_{ij}) + 0.06\, F_5(c_{ij})$$

As it can be observed, this function practically does not consider the values of the functions $F_4(s_{ij})$ and $F_5(s_{ij})$. We had supposed that these two functions were not reliable, so the GA has provided a sensible result. Using this function, we could align any pair of ontologies with similar characteristics than A and B, expecting to obtain good results.

FUTURE RESEARCH DIRECTIONS

In this work, we have proposed a possible manner of using GAs to optimize the aggregation of different similarity measures into a single similarity metric, with the final aim of improving the ontology alignment quality. The most immediate future work is to exhaustively test the GA using as reference alignments the public set of tests provided by the Ontology Alignment Evaluation Initiative

(OAEI[3]), which is an international campaign commencing in 2004 that aims at establishing a consensus on the evaluation and comparison of matching systems, whose proposed alignment tasks cover a large portion of real world domains.

After that, we will also embed our GA into a real existing ontology alignment system that achieves similarity aggregation in a traditional manner (i.e., either through manual, user-based aggregation or by means of general methods), in order to measure the improvement of alignment quality.

Another important subarea that we hope to explore in a near future is the automatic configuration or tuning of ontology alignment systems through GAs. In dynamic environments, such as the Web, it is natural that applications are constantly changing their characteristics. Therefore, approaches addressed to tune and adapt automatically alignment solutions to the settings in which an application operates are of high importance. We think that the application of GAs to the au-

Table 4. Results of the crossover between the individuals 2 and 10

Individual	Chromosome			
11	0.45	0.52	0.57	0.92
12	0.11	0.51	0.87	0.94

Table 5. Weights, valid mappings and fitness value for the individuals 11 and 12

Solution	w1	w2	w3	w4	w5	Mappings	Fitness
11	0.45	0.07	0.05	0.35	0.08	s_{11}, s_{12}	0.50
12	0.11	0.40	0.36	0.07	0.06	s_{12}, s_{31}	1

tomatically adaptation of an ontology alignment solution to the settings in which an application operates, involving the run time reconfiguration of an alignment system by finding its most suitable parameters (e.g., thresholds, weights, and coefficients) could provide great results. As explained by Gal and Shvaiko (2009), the challenge is to be able to perform aligner self-tuning at run time, and therefore, efficiency of the aligner configuration search strategies becomes crucial. In this case, the configuration space can be arbitrary large, thus, searching it exhaustively may be infeasible.

CONCLUSION

Ontology alignment is recognized as an important step in ontology engineering that needs more extensive research to fit the requirements of modern applications. Although a lot has been done towards tackling this problem, the research community still reports open issues that impose new challenges for researchers and underline new directions for the future. One of these issues, which represents an emerging research area, is the aggregation of different similarity measures into a single similarity metric. This problem can be viewed as an optimization problem, which can be faced by using techniques from other research areas, like GAs.

In this work, we have proposed a GA-based approach to combine different measures into a single metric, optimizing the quality of the alignment results. The presented GA can be useful to automatically configure the similarity aggregation process in ontology alignment systems that are ad-dressed to provide precise and complete results in domains that require rapid processing. Through a simple example, we have showed how the GA can find the similarity combination that provides an optimal alignment result between two ontologies.

In continuation of our research, work is now being done on implementing the proposed GA and embedding it into a real ontology alignment system. We are also interested in extending our theory and mechanisms for providing an ontology alignment system with full self-configuration capabilities, in order to obtain good results in dynamic environments that require immediate response, without requiring user interaction.

ACKNOWLEDGMENT

This work was partially supported by the following: Spanish Ministry of Education and Culture (Ref TIN2006-13274); European Regional Development Funds (ERDF); grant (Ref. PIO52048) funded by the Carlos III Health Institute; grant (Ref. PGIDIT 05 SIN 10501PR) from the General Directorate of Research of the Xunta de Galicia; and grant (File 2009/58: "Colorectal Cancer Research Network in Galicia") from the General Directorate of Scientific and Technologic Promotion of the Galician University System of the Xunta de Galicia. The work of José M. Vázquez is supported by an FPU grant (Ref. AP2005-1415) from the Spanish Ministry of Education and Science. The work of Marcos Martínez is supported by a predoctoral grant from the University of A Coruña.

REFERENCES

Ashburner, M., Ball, C. A., Blake, J. A., Botstein, D., Butler, H., & Cherry, J. M. (2000). Gene Ontology: tool for the unification of biology. *Nature Genetics, 25*(1), 25–29. doi:10.1038/75556

Bas, J. L. (2007). Real Time Suggestion of Related Ideas in the Financial Industry. *W3C Semantic Web use cases and case Studies*. Retrieved May 5, 2009, from http://www.w3.org/2001/sw/sweo/public/UseCases/Bankinter/

Berners-Lee, T., Hendler, J., & Lassila, O. (2001). The semantic web. *Scientific American, 284*(5), 34–43. doi:10.1038/scientificamerican0501-34

Campos, A., Fernández, M. J., Berrueta, D., Polo, L., & Mínguez, I. (2008). CRUZAR: An application of semantic matchmaking for eTourism in the city of Zaragoza. *W3C Semantic Web case studies and use cases*. Retrieved April 16, 2009, from http://www.w3.org/2001/sw/sweo/public/UseCases/Zaragoza-2/

Darwin, C. (1859). On the origin of species by means of natural selection. London: John Murray.

Davis, L. (1991). Handbook of Genetic Algorithms. New York: Van Nostrand Reinhold.

Ding, Y., & Foo, S. (2002). Ontology research and development. Part 2-a review of ontology mapping and evolving. *Journal of Information Science, 28*(5), 375.

Ehrig, M. (2007). Ontology alignment: bridging the semantic gap. New York: Springer-Verlag Inc.

Euzenat, J., Le Bach, T., Barrasa, J., Bouquet, P., De Bo, J., Dieng, R., et al. (2004). *State of the art on ontology alignment*. Deliverable D2.2.3 v1.2. Knowledge Web. Retrieved December 21, 2008, from http://knowledgeweb.semanticweb.org/

Euzenat, J., & Shvaiko, P. (2007). Ontology matching. Berlin: Springer-Verlag.

Euzenat, J., & Valtchev, P. (2004). Similarity-based ontology alignment in OWL-Lite. In *Proceedings of 16ᵗʰ European Conference on Artificial Intelligence (ECAI)*, Amsterdam (pp. 333-337).

Gal, A., & Shvaiko, P. (2009). Advances in Ontology Matching. In Advances in Web Semantics, I: Ontologies, Web Services and Applied Semantic Web (pp. 176).

Goldberg, D. E. (1989). Genetic algorithms in search and optimization. Reading, MA: Addison-Wesley.

Gómez-Pérez, A., Fernández-López, M., & Corcho, O. (2004). Ontological Engineering: with examples from the areas of Knowledge Management, e-Commerce and the Semantic Web. Berlin: Springer.

Gómez-Pérez, A., & Villazon-Terrazas, B. (2006). Legal Ontologies for the Spanish e-Government. In *Lecture Notes in Computer Science, 11th Conference of the Spanish Association for Artificial Intelligence*.

Gruber, T. R. (1995). Toward principles for the design of ontologies used for knowledge sharing. *International Journal of Human-Computer Studies, 43*(5-6), 907–928. doi:10.1006/ijhc.1995.1081

Guarino, N. (1998). Formal ontology in information systems. Amsterdam: IOS press.

Gustafsson, M., & Falkman, G. (2005). Representing clinical knowledge in oral medicine using ontologies. *Studies in Health Technology and Informatics, 116*, 743.

Holland, J. H. (1975). Adaptation in natural and artificial systems. Ann Arbor, MI: University of Michigan Press.

Kalfoglou, Y., & Schorlemmer, M. (2003). Ontology mapping: the state of the art. *The Knowledge Engineering Review, 18*(1), 1–31. doi:10.1017/S0269888903000651

Koza, J. R. (1992). Genetic Programming: on the programming of computers by means of natural selection. Cambridge, MA: MIT press.

Lambrix, P., & Tan, H. (2007). Ontology alignment and merging. *Anatomy Ontologies for Bioinformatics: Principles and Practice, 133.*

Mitchell, M. (1996). An introduction to Genetic Algorithms. Cambridge, MA: Bradford Books.

Nammuni, K., Levine, J., & Kingston, J. (2002). Skill-based Resource Allocation using Genetic Algorithms and an Ontology. In *Proceedings of the International Workshop on Intelligent Knowledge Management Techniques (I-KOMAT 2002).*

Neches, R., Fikes, R., Finin, T. W., Gruber, T. R., Patil, R., & Senator, T. E. (1991). Enabling technology for knowledge sharing. *AI Magazine, 12*(3), 36–56.

Qazvinian, V., Abolhassani, H., Haeri, S. H., & Hariri, B. B. (2008). Evolutionary coincidence-based ontology mapping extraction. *Expert Systems: International Journal of Knowledge Engineering and Neural Networks, 25*(3), 221–236. doi:10.1111/j.1468-0394.2008.00462.x

Rahm, E., & Bernstein, P. A. (2001). A survey of approaches to automatic schema matching. *The International Journal on Very Large Data Bases, 10*(4), 334–350. doi:10.1007/s007780100057

Rocha, F. E. L., Costa, J. V., & Favero, E. L. (2004). A new approach to meaningful learning assessment using concept maps: Ontologies and genetic algorithms. In *Proceedings of the First International Conference on Concept Mapping.*

Shvaiko, P., & Euzenat, J. (2005). A Survey of Schema-based Matching Approaches. [JoDS]. *Journal on Data Semantics, 4*, 146–171.

Smith, B., & Brochhausen, M. (2008). Establishing and Harmonizing Ontologies in an Interdisciplinary Health Care and Clinical Research Environment. *Studies in Health Technology and Informatics, 134*, 219.

Snae, C., & Brueckner, M. (2007). Ontology-driven e-learning system based on roles and activities for Thai learning environment. *Interdisciplinary Journal of Knowledge and Learning Objects, 3*, 1–17.

Spasic, I., Ananiadou, S., McNaught, J., & Kumar, A. (2005). Text mining and ontologies in biomedicine: making sense of raw text. *Briefings in Bioinformatics, 6*(3), 239–251. doi:10.1093/bib/6.3.239

Syldatke, T., Chen, W., Angele, J., Nierlich, A., & Ullrich, M. (2007). How Ontologies and Rules Help to Advance Automobile Development. *Lecture Notes in Computer Science, 4824*, 1. doi:10.1007/978-3-540-75975-1_1

Van Dam, K. H., & Lukszo, Z. (2006). Modelling Energy and Transport Infrastructures as a Multi-Agent System using a Generic Ontology. In *Systems, Man and Cybernetics IEEE International Conference 2006 (SMC06).*

Van Rijsbergen, C. J. (1975). Information Retrieval. London: Butterworth.

Wang, J., Ding, Z., & Jiang, C. (2006). GAOM: Genetic Algorithm Based Ontology Matching. In *Proceedings of IEEE Asia-Pacific Conference on Services Computing 2006 (APSCC2006).*

ADDITIONAL READING

Alasoud, A., Haarslev, V., & Shiri, N. (2008). An empirical comparison of ontology matching techniques. *Journal of Information Science.*

Albertoni, R., & De Martino, M. (2008). Asymmetric and context-dependent semantic similarity among ontology instances. Journal on Data Semantics.

An, Y., Borgida, A., & Mylopoulos, J. (2005). Constructing Complex Semantic Mappings between XML Data and Ontologies. In *Proceedings of International Semantic Web Conference 2005 (ISWC'05)*.

Aumueller, D., Do, H. H., Massmann, S., & Rahm, E. (2005). Schema and ontology matching with COMA++. In *Proceedings of the 2005 ACM SIGMOD international conference on Management of data*.

Bodenreider, O. (2004). The Unified Medical Language System (UMLS), integrating biomedical terminology. *Nucleic Acids Research, 32*(Database Issue), 267D. doi:10.1093/nar/gkh061

Choi, N., Song, I. Y., & Han, H. (2006). A survey on ontology mapping. *SIGMOD Record, 35*(3), 34–41. doi:10.1145/1168092.1168097

Doan, A., Madhavan, J., Domingos, P., & Halevy, A. (2004). Ontology Matching: A Machine Learning Approach. In S. Staab & R. Studer, (Eds.), Handbook on Ontologies in Information Systems (pp. 397-416). Berlin: Springer-Verlag.

Ehrig, M., Staab, S., & Sure, Y. (2005). Bootstrapping Ontology Alignment Methods with APFEL. In *Proceedings of the 4th International Semantic Web Conference, ISWC 2005* (LNCS 3729, pp. 186-200). Berlin: Springer.

Euzenat, J., Loup, D., Touzani, M., & Valtchev, P. (2004). Ontology alignment with OLA. In *Proceedings of 3rd ISWC 2004 workshop on Evaluation of Ontology-based tools (EON)* (pp. 59-68).

Evermann, J. (2009). Theories of meaning in schema matching: An exploratory study. *Information Systems, 34*(1), 28–44. doi:10.1016/j.is.2008.04.001

Garey, M., & Johnson, D. (1979). Computers and intractability: a guide to the theory of NP-completeness. New York: W. H. Freeman & Co.

Giunchiglia, F., Yatskevich, M., Avesani, P., & Shvaiko, P. (2009). A Large Scale Dataset for the Evaluation of Ontology Matching Systems. Knowledge Engineering Review Journal.

Gruber, T. R. (1993). A translation approach to portable ontology specification. *Knowledge Acquisition, 5*(2), 199–200. doi:10.1006/knac.1993.1008

Haeri, S. H., Abolhassani, H., Qazvinian, V., & Hariri, B. B. (2007). Coincidence-Based Scoring of Mappings in Ontology Alignment. *Journal of Advanced Computational Intelligence, 11*(7).

Hu, W., & Qu, Y. (2008). Falcon-AO: A practical ontology matching system. *Web Semantics: Science. Services and Agents on the World Wide Web, 6*(3), 237–239. doi:10.1016/j.websem.2008.02.006

Hu, W., Qu, Y., & Cheng, G. (2008). Matching large ontologies: A divide-and-conquer approach. *Data & Knowledge Engineering, 67*(1), 140–160. doi:10.1016/j.datak.2008.06.003

Isaac, A., Wang, S., Zinn, C., Matthezing, H., van der Meij, L., & Schlobach, S. (2009). Evaluating Thesaurus Alignments for Semantic Interoperability in the Library Domain. *IEEE Intelligent Systems, 24*(2), 76–86. doi:10.1109/MIS.2009.26

Jaroszewicz, S., Ivantysynova, L., & Scheffer, T. (2008). Schema matching on streams with accuracy guarantees. *Intelligent Data Analysis, 12*(3), 253–270.

Jeong, B., Lee, D., Cho, H., & Lee, J. (2008). A novel method for measuring semantic similarity for XML schema matching. *Expert Systems with Applications, 34*(3), 1651–1658. doi:10.1016/j.eswa.2007.01.025

Jung, J. J. (2007). Taxonomy alignment for interoperability between heterogeneous virtual organizations. Expert Systems with Applications.

Kotis, K., Vouros, G., & Stergiou, K. (2005). Towards Automatic Merging of Domain Ontologies: The HCONE-merge approach. [JWS]. *Elsevier's Journal of Web Semantics, 4*(1), 60–79. doi:10.1016/j.websem.2005.09.004

Lambrix, P., & Tan, H. (2006). SAMBO - A System for Aligning and Merging Biomedical Ontologies. *Journal of Web Semantics, Special issue on Semantic Web for the Life Sciences, 4*(3), 196-206.

Meilicke, C., Stuckenschmidt, H., & Tamilin, A. (2008). Reasoning support for mapping revision. *Journal of Logic and Computation.*

Noy, F. N., & Musen, A. M. (2003). The PROMPT Suite: Interactive Tools for Ontology Merging and Mapping. *International Journal of Human-Computer Studies, 59*(6), 983–1024. doi:10.1016/j.ijhcs.2003.08.002

Shvaiko, P., & Euzenat, J. (2008). Ten challenges for ontology matching. In *Proceedings of OD-BASE-2008.*

Vaccari, L., Shvaiko, P., & Marchese, M. (2009). A geo-service semantic integration in Spatial Data Infrastructures. *International Journal of Spatial Data Infrastructures Research, 4*, 24–51.

Wang, P., & Xu, B. (2008). Debugging Ontology Mappings: A Static Approach. *Computing and Informatics, 27*(1), 21.

ENDNOTES

[1]   http://www.umich.edu/
[2]   http://www.ua.edu/
[3]   http://oaei.ontologymatching.org/

Section 4
Natural Environment Applications

Chapter 16
Characterization and Modelization of Surface Net Radiation through Neural Networks

Antonio Geraldo Ferreira
University of Valencia, Spain & Fundação Cearense de Meteorologia e Recursos Hídricos (FUNCEME), Brazil

Emilio Soria
University of Valencia, Spain

Antonio J. Serrano López
University of Valencia, Spain

Ernesto Lopez-Baeza
University of Valencia, Spain

ABSTRACT

Artificial neural networks have shown to be a powerful tool for system modeling in a wide range of applications. In this chapter, the focus is on neural network applications to obtain qualitative/quantitative relationships between meteorological and soil parameters and net radiation, the latter being a significant term of the surface energy balance equation. By using a Multilayer Perceptron model an artificial neural network based on the above mentioned parameters, net radiation was estimated over a vineyard crop. A comparison has been made between the estimates provided by the Multilayer Perceptron and a linear regression model that only uses solar incoming shortwave radiation as input parameter. Self-Organizing Maps, another type of neural model, made it possible to get knowledge in an easy way on how the input variables are related to each other in the data set. The results achieved show the potential of artificial neural networks as a tool for net radiation estimation using more commonly measured meteorological parameters.

DOI: 10.4018/978-1-61520-893-7.ch016

INTRODUCTION

Artificial Neural Networks (ANN) applications on atmospheric science have experienced considerable growth in the last years if we consider the increasing number of publications in the topic. The most significant applications refer to solar radiation (Elizondo, Hoogenboom, & McClendon, 1994; Reddy & Ranjan, 2003), evapotranspiration (Landeras, Ortiz-Barredo, & López, 2008), ozone concentrations in urban areas (Yi & Prybutok, 1996; Prybutok, Yi, & Mitchell, 2000) or thunderstorms prediction (MacCann, 1992; Manzato, 2007), processing of Earth observation satellite data (Krasnopolsky & Schiller, 2003; Diego & Loyola, 2006), etc. But to the authors' knowledge, surface net radiation (Q^*) estimation has not been attempted yet using ANNs. In effect, surface net radiation estimation is a complex problem because according to Venäläinen *et al.* (1998), there are complicated feedback mechanisms between the surface energy balance quantities and the surface characteristics. The usual approach to this problem has been through conventional statistical modeling techniques. In spite of finding successful applications by using regressions models to estimate Q^* (Glover, 1972; Iziomon *et al.*, 2000; Sentelhas & Gillespie, 2008), the input parameters used sometimes are difficult to obtain or measure. Thus, the objective of this chapter is to develop a *Multilayer Perceptron* ANN model, based on *in situ* measured micrometeorological and soil parameters, to estimate Q^* and compare and evaluate this model against the performance of a more commonly used Q^* linear regression model (LM) that only uses incoming solar radiation as input parameter. A *Self-Organizing Map* (SOM) was applied to extract knowledge of the possible relationships between the measured micrometeorological and soil parameters. The SOM, which is another neural model, preserves the topological relationships among the data while mapping this data into a two-dimensional map.

BACKGROUND

The energy exchanges between the land surface and the atmosphere can be described by the surface energy balance equation given by the algebraic sum of fluxes over the surface

$$Q^* + Q_H + Q_{\lambda E} + Q_G = 0 \qquad (1)$$

where Q^* is net radiation at surface, Q_H is the sensible heat flux, $Q_{\lambda E}$ is the latent heat flux, a product of the evaporative rate E and the latent heat per unit quantity of water evaporated, λ, and Q_G is the soil heat flux, the rate at which heat is transferred from the surface downward into the soil profile, all in units of W m^{-2}. In Eq. (1), the fluxes are considered as positive if directed toward the surface and negative in the opposite case (Hillel, 2004) (See Figure 1).

In Eq. (1), Q^* is also the algebraic sum of net components of shortwave (K^*) and longwave (L^*) radiation, which can be written as

$$Q^* = K^* + L^* \qquad (2)$$

where the symbol * represents net flux. The K^* and L^* in Eq. (2) can be written as

$$K^* = K\downarrow - K\uparrow \qquad (3)$$

and

$$L^* = L\downarrow - L\uparrow \qquad (4)$$

finally resulting

$$Q^* = K\downarrow - K\uparrow + L\downarrow - L\uparrow \qquad (5)$$

where the downward arrows ($\downarrow$) and upward arrows ($\uparrow$) indicate incoming and outgoing radiation components respectively, and the energy moving toward the surface is also considered positive and the energy moving away from the surface is considered negative.

Figure 1. Typical variation of terms of the surface energy balance for: (a) daytime over land and (b) night-time over land. The arrow size indicates the relative magnitude

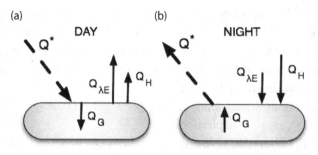

The outgoing shortwave radiation $K{\uparrow}$ is the fraction of the shortwave incoming radiation $K{\downarrow}$ that is reflected by the surface under consideration, i.e.,

$$K{\uparrow} = \alpha\, K{\downarrow} \qquad (6)$$

where α is the surface albedo. Thus equation (5) can be rewritten as

$$Q^* = K{\downarrow}\,(1 - \alpha) + (L{\downarrow} - L{\uparrow}) \qquad (7)$$

Eq. (7) clearly shows that Q^* constitutes the fundamental parameter which governs the climate of the lower atmosphere and is a measure of the total amount of energy available at the ground (Iziomon *et al.*, 2000; Oke, 1987). It is therefore the driving force in many physical and biological processes such as evapotranspiration, air and soil heating, as well as other small energy-consuming processes such as photosynthesis. When available, the Q^* measurements are used in agricultural, biological and engineering sciences for estimation of evapotranspiration, which in turn is used to optimize crop yield and quality, crop modeling, water resource planning, climate predictions, etc (Bennie *et al.*, 2008; Ji *et al.*, 2009; Li *et al.*, 2009; Trezza, 2006).

Although the surface meteorological stations (conventional/automatic) around the world normally record air temperature, wind velocity and direction, pressure, relative humidity, and incoming solar radiation, however, Q^* is rarely measured, and therefore, not generally available. According to this, many studies have put major efforts into the accurate determination of Q^* from conventional meteorological data, and various models have been proposed and evaluated for that purpose (Federer, 1968; de Jong *et al.*, 1980; Irmak *et al.*, 2003; Kjaersgaard *et al.*, 2007). One of the most commonly used equations to estimate Q^* is

$$Q^* = a_1\, K{\downarrow} + b_1 \qquad (8)$$

where a_1 and b_1 are regression coefficients and $K{\downarrow}$ is the incoming solar radiation, that is more commonly measured than Q^*. The investigations have shown that the regression coefficients in those models are, among other things, dependent on the type and conditions of the surface (Kessler, 1985; Kjaersgaard et *al.*, 2007). Concerning the ANN, the literature shows many studies that were developed/evaluated in order to estimate $K{\downarrow}$ (Äženkal & Kuleli, 2009; Elizondo *et al.*, 1994; Mohandes *et al.*, 1998a; Reddy & Ranjan, 2003; Jiang, Y., 2008). Rehman & Mohandes (2008), for example, by applying feedforward ANNs, estimated global solar radiation, for Abba city in Saudi Arabia. An ANN was trained with 3 inputs (day of the year, daily mean relative humidity and daily mean temperature), 24 hidden neurons in one layer and one output ($K{\downarrow}$). The mean squared data error found by the mentioned authors, on testing data, was about 3×10^{-5} and the absolute mean

Figure 2. Scheme of a typical neuron; x_i are the inputs and w_j are the neuron weights

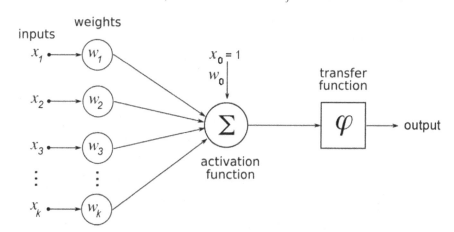

percentage error was about 4.5%. Concerning Q^* estimation using ANN models, references have not been found by the authors in the literature.

As a consequence of what has been mentioned above and taking into account that several meteorological factors, together with land cover and land use, do affect the quantity of Q^* that is registered at any particular place, an automatic micrometeorological station was installed inside a vineyard field (latitude 39° 31 '23 "N and longitude 1° 17' 22" W), at the Valencia Anchor Station area located on the natural region of the Utiel-Requena Plateau, Spain, in order to understand the behavior of Q^* during the vine growing season. The field campaign denominated *FESEBAV-2007* (*Field Experiment on Surface Energy Balance Aspects over the Valencia Anchor Station area*) was carried out between June 18 - September 19, 2007.

Based on the collected data, a new model utilizing ANNs, which consists in a layered arrangement of individual computation units known as artificial neurons (Bishop, 2007; Haykin, 2008), was proposed.

The Multilayer Perceptron

A *Multilayer Perceptron* (MLP) is an ANN that is composed of elementary processing units, the so-called neurons. A typical neuron model is shown in Figure 2 (Haykin, 1999).

The main components of the model are:

- *Sum function*. It carries out a linear combination of the neuron inputs through the use of a set of coefficients, known as synaptic weights. Being $\mathbf{w}=[w_0, w_1,....., w_k]$ the vector of coefficients, and $\mathbf{x}=[1, x_1,....., x_k]$ the input vector, the sum function is given by the scalar product of both vectors. When using a neural model, the goal is to find the optimal synaptic weights to solve the problem, the process of searching the optimal weights is known as network learning.

- *Activation function*. It is a non-linear function which gives the network its non-linear nature. The most used activation functions are the sigmoid function (its values ranging between 0 and 1) and the hyperbolic tangent, which ranges between −1 and +1 (Figure 3).

Neurons are arranged in layers to form an MLP. The first layer is known as input layer, and the last one is called output layer. All the other layers are called hidden layers (Haykin, 1999). This kind of arrangement enables the neuron outputs to be used as inputs to neurons of following layers

Figure 3. Sigmoid function and hyperbolic tangent

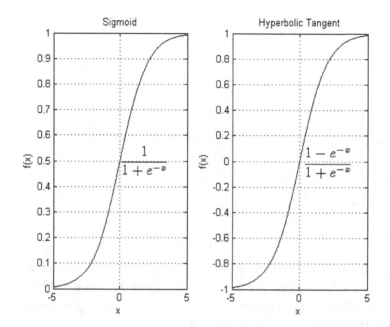

(non-recurrent network) and/or previous layers (recurrent networks). Figure 4 shows a typical MLP structure.

Several remarks should be made regarding the learning process (Haykin, 1999; Bishop 1996):

1. The learning rate must be chosen appropriately. The learning algorithm is based on finding the closest minimum, being this learning rate a parameter which measures the speed of approaching the minimum.
2. The network architecture must also be chosen appropriately. While the number of neurons in the input layer and the output layer is given by the problem, the number of hidden layers, and the quantity of neurons in each hidden layer must be chosen depending on the particular problem.
3. Due to the iterative nature of the learning process, it is necessary to choose the initial values of the synaptic weights. Different initial values are usually tested in order to achieve an optimal model and avoid a local minimum.
4. Due to the high adaptability of the model, which is capable of determining any

Figure 4. Scheme of a Multilayer Perceptron (MLP)

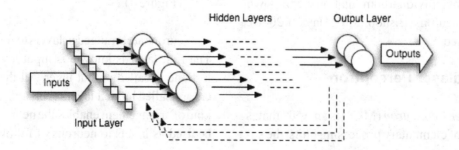

relationship between two data sets, the usual procedure is based on dividing the whole data set into two groups, known as the training set and the validation set, respectively. The first set is used to determine the synaptic weights, and the second one is used to test the behaviour of the neural model with data that the network has not yet seen.

5. Two different approaches can be carried out to train the network. The first one is based on updating the synaptic weights for each pattern of the data set (*on-line* approach) whereas the other approach is based on updating the synaptic weights once for all the training data set (*batch* approach).

The data utilized to build the ANN model proceed from the *FESEBAV-2007* experiment. Wind velocity (m s^{-1}), wind direction (degrees), air and surface temperature (°C), soil temperature at 5 cm depth (°C), relative humidity (%), soil moisture at 5 cm depth (m^3 m^{-3}), and net radiation (W m^{-2}), was the data used as input during training and validation sets, standing out that Q^* is the output variable.

Self-Organizing Map

The *Self-Organizing Map* is a neural network proposed by Teuvo Kohonen in 1984 (Haykin, 1999; Kohonen, 2001). Neurons are arranged in two layers: an input layer, formed by n neurons (one neuron for each input variable) and an output layer in which information is processed; this second layer is usually arranged in a two-dimensional structure (see Figure 5).

Neurons of the output layer are characterised by a weight vector with the same dimension as the input vector. For instance, neuron i,j (i-th row, j-th column) is characterised by the weight vector $\mathbf{w}_{ij} = \left[w_{ij}^1 \ w_{ij}^2 .... w_{ij}^n \right]$. Similar input patterns are mapped close to each other in the output layer (Kohonen, 2001). The algorithm procedure can be summarized, as follows (Haykin, 1999):

1. Weight initialisation.
2. Choice of an input pattern $x = [x_1 \ x_2 .... x_n]$.
3. Measurement of the similarity between weights and inputs. If the Euclidean distance is taken into account, then the similarity measure is given by $d(\mathbf{w}_{ij}, \mathbf{x}) = \sum_{k=1}^{M} (w_{ij}^k - x_k)^2$. The most similar neuron to the input pattern is called *Best Matching Unit* (BMU).
4. Synaptic weights are updated as $\mathbf{w}_{st} = \mathbf{w}_{st} + \alpha \cdot h(BMU, \mathbf{w}_{st}) \cdot (\mathbf{x} - \mathbf{w}_{st})$, where here α represents the learning rate and h is known as neighbourhood function. The value of this function depends on the distance between the BMU and the neuron to be updated, the closer the two neurons the higher the value of this function.
5. The previous steps are performed a predetermined number of iterations. When this number is reached, the learning algorithm is stopped. While the number of iterations is lower than the predetermined value, go to step 2.

Once the map training is finished, the visualisation of the two-dimensional map provides qualitative information about how the input variables are related to each other for the data set used to train the map. SOM is a visualisation tool rather than a clustering tool, although it is possible to obtain clusters of similar patterns from the two-dimensional map.

ANALYSIS OF NET RADIATION WITH ARTIFICIAL NEURAL NETWORKS

1. Issues, Controversies, Problems

When analyzing data we are looking not only for relationships between variables by fitting an equation to the observed data set, but also for relationships to define and establish models. In

Figure 5. Kohonen SOM topology showing the input vectors x_i and the output space (SOM) in 2D space

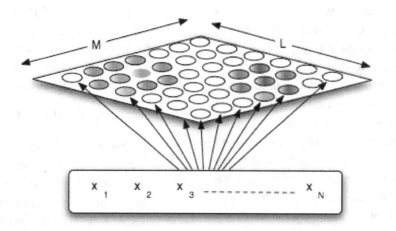

the case of environmental modeling, a variety of approaches and combinations can be made. Choosing the most suitable approach depends on the complexity of the problem being addressed and on the degree to which the problem is understood (Gardner & Dorling, 1998). Normally, the models used to estimate Q^* require geophysical non-operational parameters such as surface albedo, surface temperature, air vapor pressure, fraction of cloud cover, emissivity of the surface and of the atmosphere, etc. as input to the model (Amarakoon & Chen, 1999; de Jong *et al.*, 1980; Iziomon *et al.*, 2000; Jegede, 1997; Ortega-Farias *et al.*, 2000; Sentelhas & Gillepie, 2008). These parameters are not routinely measured at meteorological stations so that it is too difficult to apply these models in an operational way. Another point is that some parameters used in these models are estimated and not measured, so that estimations made for them can lead to increasing errors in Q^* estimations. Gladly, Q^* can be estimated by using a linear regression model (Gentle, Härdle, & Mori, 2004) between both measured incoming solar radiation ($K\downarrow$) and Q^*. The problem is that during the night the earth surface does not receive solar radiation and the regression equation to predict Q^* during the night cannot be used, limiting its application only for daytime. But observations show that Q^*

is not zero during the night. For this reason, efforts should be made to estimate Q^* from others geophysical parameters.

2. Solutions and Recommendations

In order to accurately determine Q^* in an operational way, an alternative approach has been presented by using ANNs. The proposed ANN model uses as input a limited number of meteorological parameters measured in conventional/automatic meteorological stations, being this one of its practical advantages.

The first step is starting the data analysis by plotting different SOM graphs for the *in situ* measured micrometeorological and soil parameters such as those listed in Table 1 which will allow a visualization of the possible relationships among them. This is because the SOM preserves the topology of the input vectors in a bidimensional visualization (Kalteh *et al.*, 2008; Kohonen, 2001). In the SOM's learning process; firstly the two possible types of learning (on-line and batch) have been considered and, secondly, the most common neighbourhood functions (Gaussian and Mexican hat) have been varied as well as the learning constants and the neurons coefficients initialization (50 different initializations for each possibility).

Table 1. Meteorological and soil parameters measured during FESEBAV-2007

Graphs SOM Title (Figure 7)	Parameter	Unit
G12.5 and G7.5	Soil heat flux at depths of 12.5 and 7.5 cm, respectively	W m⁻²
Rad_inc, Rad_ref, and Rad_net	Incident, reflected and net radiation at 2 m height	W m⁻²
Wind_vel	Wind speed at 2.10 m height	m s⁻¹
Wind_dir	Wind direction at 2.10 m height	degrees
T_soil25, T_soil15, T_soil10, T_soil5	Soil temperature at depths of 25, 15, 10 and 5 cm, respectively.	°C
T_sup	Surface temperature	°C
T_air	Air temperature at 2.0 m height	°C
Rel_hum	Relative humidity at 2.0 m height	%
Soil_moisture	Soil moisture at 5 cm depth in the ground	m³ m⁻³
Prec	Precipitation	dmm

The self-organized maps were analyzed in order to determine the quantization error (adjustment of the neurons' vectors to the input data) and the topographic error (a measure of how well the neighbourhood relationship is maintained between the original and the final bidimensional space), finally choosing the map that presented a lower product of the quantization error times the topographic one.

As far as the architecture is concerned, the algorithm used was the one implemented in Matlab's SOM library (www.cis.hut.fi/projects/somtoolbox), which takes into account the scattering of the data and the number of variables (Kohonen, 2001). The final map had a size of 22x11 neurons.

Figure 6a shows the number of patterns assigned to each neuron, where the more filled up is the hexagon (the hexagon represents a neuron). In addition, the SOM contents can show the different behaviour presented by the data (Figure 6b).

Figure 6. (a) Patterns number assigned to the neuron (winners), and (b) number of different types of behaviour in the data set (cluster): Dark color indicates weak similarity between categories and clear color indicates strong similarity between categories

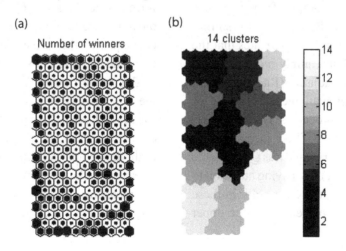

Figure 7. Self-Organizing Maps (SOM) of meteorological and soil parameters. Each SOM graph contains 22 rows and 11 columns of neurons

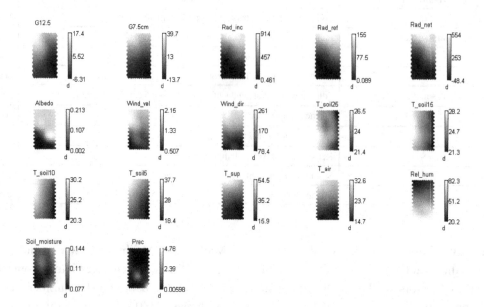

The neuron assigned will be the unit whose incoming connection weights are the closest to the input topology in terms of Euclidean distance. Figure 7 shows the SOM visualization graphs of the meteorological variables listed in Table 1, where we can directly, with just a glance to the maps, see the relationships between the variables used. In this sense, the SOM provides, literally, a visual map of our data thus allowing a fast understanding on how everything fits together.

It can be seen, for example, from Figure 7, that Rad_inc, Rad_ref, Rad_net, show similar patterns, where the clear color indicates that the higher values of Rad_inc, imply more reflected (Rad_ref) and more net radiation (Rad_net). More $Q*$ implies more energy available at the surface for physical and biological processes. The opposite is also true, i. e., lower values of Rad_inc, imply less reflected radiation (Rad_ref) and less $Q*$ available at the surface (dark color). By paying attention to G_75, T_sup and T_air, the clear color in these SOM maps suffer a displacement in the upper

left corner direction in relation to Rad_inc. This means that the incoming shortwave radiation that reaches the surface begins, after a lag in time, to heat it up. Then, part of this energy is transferred to the soil, heating it up, from where a part is used to heat up the air near the surface. During the day, the surface receives more quantity of Rad_inc from the sun (clear color), consequently, the surface heats up, and more quantity of heat is transferred from the surface to the soil in the Q_G form and to the air in Q_H and $Q_{\lambda E}$ form. During the night, the Rad_inc is cut off (dark color), and consequently the surface does not receive energy from the sun and the surface cools up, and heat begins to be transferred from deeper layers of the soil towards the surface. Now comparing, for example, Rel_hum and T_air, they present an opposite pattern, i.e., when the Rel_hum is low/high (dark color/clear color) the T_air is high/low (clear color/dark color). Relative humidity (RH) is a measure of the amount of moisture in the air. Expressed as a percentage, it describes the amount

Figure 8. SOM of the meteorological and soil parameters used as input layer in the ANN modeling

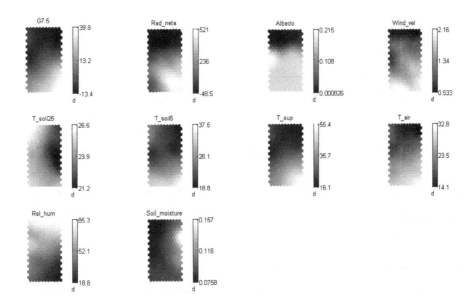

of water vapor in the air compared to the amount needed for the air to be saturated (i.e. 100% RH). Humidity varies with temperature – as temperature increases humidity decreases and when temperature decreases humidity increases. This indicates that the SOM pattern makes physical sense.

After analysing the SOM maps presented in Figure 7, the variables chosen to develop de ANN models are presented in Figure 8. Since the *Multilayer Perceptron* requires no prior knowledge between variables and their relationships, the criteria to choose the variables that will be used in the ANN model input layer were: (i) meteorological variables not linked directly with our target variable, i. e., (Q^*), and (ii) variables that are usually measured routinely at meteorological stations. For these reason, Rad_inc, Rad_ref, G12.5; T_soil25, T_soil15 and T_s10, were not used in the model development.

The next step was, considering that Q^* can be positive, negative, or even zero, to divide the data set in three parts: The first part considering all the Q^* measured data, the second one considering only the negative net radiation ($Q^* < 0$) values, and the third one considering only the positive

net radiation ($Q^* > 0$) values, hereafter referred as $Q^*_{\pm}$, Q^*_{-} and Q^*_{+}, respectively. This procedure allows to find a model for $Q^*_{\pm}$ overall values, and more specific models for Q^*_{-} and Q^*_{+}, Then, each of these data sets were divided into two subsets, the first one with 2/3 of the data for developing LMs / training ANN and the remaining 1/3 for testing the models.

In the same way that was made in the SOM's case, in order to train the *Multilayer Perceptron*, all its parameters were varied, namely the number of hidden layers (1 and 2) and the number of neurons per layer (from 2 to 10). According to Cybenko's Theorem, no more layers were necessary (Haykin, 2008) and in order to avoid overfitting problems no more neurons were considered (Alpaydin, 2004). The learning algorithm chosen was that of Levenberg-Marquardt's with a variable learning constant because of its performance characteristics with respect to speed and accuracy (Haykin, 2008). Due to the local minima problem, the networks of each structure were initialized 50 times using a normal distribution of mean zero and unity variance to avoid the neurons saturation

Table 2. Statistical results for Q* using linear regression models (developing / testing phase) and networks (training / validation sets)

Linear Model	R^2	RMSE	MAE	ME	N
$Q_+^* = 0.657\,K{\downarrow} - 4.273$	0.96 / 0.96	39.48 / 35.38	34.19 / 30.87	0.006 / 7.10	4397 / 2198
Neural Models					
Q_-^*	0.92 / 0.92	6.23 / 6.54	4.59 / 4.76	0 / 0.089	4435 / 2218
Q_+^*	0.97 / 0.96	42.9 / 48.75	26.81 / 29.29	-0.33 / 0.26	4397 / 2198
$Q_\pm^*$	0.98 / 0.98	38.09 / 39.26	21.67 / 22.60	0.0209 / 1.41	8832 / 4416

RMSE and MAE are in units of W m^{-2}, and N is the number of data utilized

problem: if the initial weights are very high, the network does not learn because the neurons act in the flat zone of the activation function (Haykin, 2008). The best architecture for each case, using the RMSE of the generalization set as index were: $Q_\pm^*$: 1 hidden layer and 10 neurons; Q_-^*: 1 hidden layer and 10 neurons; and Q_+^*: 2 hidden layers and 9 and 10 neurons.

The accuracy of the (different) Q^* estimated values using both the LM and the ANN models was assessed through the correlation coefficient (R^2), the Root Mean Square Error (RMSE), the Mean Absolute Error (MAE) and the Mean Error (ME). These statistical values (those corresponding to the best networks and using RMSE as the performance index) are presented in Table 2.

According to the results shown in Table 2, the proposed ANN provides similar results to the LMs when considering Q_+^*. But when considering Q_-^* and Q_+^*, the performance of the ANN was markedly high. The value of $R^2 = 0.92$ and 0.98 were obtained respectively for both training and validation sets. Taking into account that during the night there is no solar radiation, in order to develop a Q_-^* linear model, which depends only on solar radiation, it makes no sense. But Q^* is neither zero nor constant during the night period as it is observed in the field data collected, and this

is because net radiation depends not only on $K{\downarrow}$ but also on other radiation fluxes and atmospheric parameters (Table 1). The good results provided by the ANNs Q_-^*, Q_+^*, and $Q_\pm^*$, is because the ANNs learn from the data. On the one hand, $K{\downarrow}$, is not used as an input parameter in the ANN model because the model sought should not be influenced directly for any parameter in particular, and solar radiation has a direct influence on the amount of Q* available at the surface. However, the ANN model accounts very well for the rest of the surface and atmospheric parameters. On the other hand, because the Q^* LM depends only on $K{\downarrow}$ and not on the other parameters, it can only perform correctly during the day but not during the night. Therefore, the ANN provides good results for Q_-^*. The ANN's ability to learn from a given set of collected data makes them attractive and exciting because no prior knowledge about the relationship between variables inside the data set is needed. It's one of the advantages that ANN's present over conventional regression analyses.

Figure 9 shows the time series of Q^* (measured, predicted by the LMs and ANN), for two different periods, August 01 - 08, 2007 and September 01 – 08, 2007. From these time series, four different days were chosen for analysis, where two of them are cloudy days: August 01, 2007 (Figure

Figure 9. Time series of Q* observed, estimated by using ANN and LM for the periods between: (a) August 01 – 08, 2007 and (b) September 01 – 08, 2007

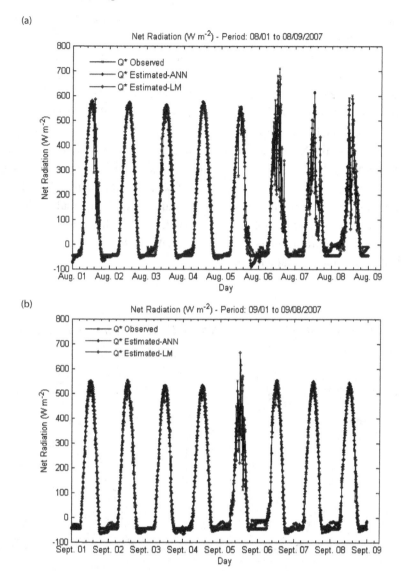

(a)

(b)

10a), and September 05, 2007 (Figure 10d). The other two cloudless days: August 02, 2007 and September 04, 2007, are shown in Figures 10b and 10c respectively.

An accurate prediction is achieved in a global point of view. Nevertheless, it seems that in general, over cloudless conditions, the LMs have a tendency to slightly underestimate Q^* during morning hours, approximately between 9:00 h and 11:00 h, and overestimate Q^* in the afternoon hours, approximately between 13:00 h and 18:00 h. Over overcast conditions, it seems that the LMs present better performance. Perhaps this is because only $K\downarrow$, a meteorological parameter linked directly to Q^*, is used as input parameters in LMs. As mentioned earlier, the ANN uses other meteorological parameters as input layer.

FUTURE RESEARCH DIRECTIONS

One possible extension of this work is to apply the ANN models to other sites around the study area, i. e., the Valencia Anchor Station area, considering different soil types, land cover, and meteorological parameters collected by the existing meteorological stations in the area. After building ANN models for each considered site, the next step would be to look for a general ANN model. It would be obtained by averaging the ANN models generated for each site.

Along this chapter, the application of two neural models has been discussed. These models can be considered as classical neural models by the number of practical developments made from them, but there are other models that could be applied to compare their performance with the procedures described here, so we would have:

Alternative models to the MLP. Here feedback or Multi-Layers models as Elman and Jordan network, Finite Impulse Response (FIR) or Infinite Impulse Response (IIR) networks (depending on the type of digital filter applied as synapses), as well as, models that utilize other types of temporal memory in the ANN, for example, Laguerre models (Haykin, 2008). If multilayer ANN models are not used, other elements of the learning machine that can work as universal modellers are the Support Vector Machines (SVM) and the regression trees (Alpaydin, 2004).

*Figure 10. **Q*** observed and estimated by using ANN and LM for: cloudy days (a) and (d); and for cloudless days (b) and (c)*

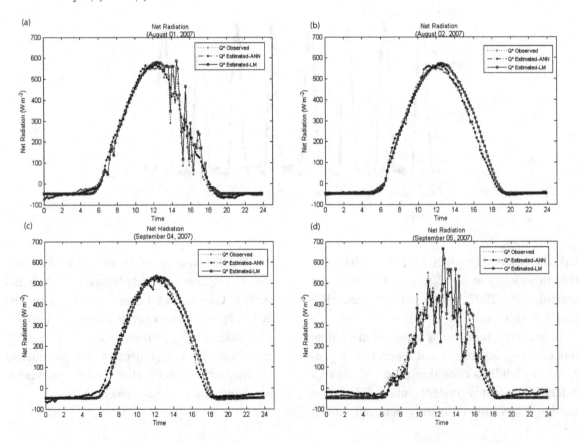

Alternative models to the SOM. In this case, the solution could be given by the model known as Generative Topographic Mapping (GTM). In this case, the approach is of Bayesian type which complicates the algorithm utilized to obtain the parameters if compared to a *Self-Organizing Map* (Bishop, 2007).

The estimation of geophysical parameters such as net and solar radiation, surface temperature, wind (velocity and direction) over land and ocean, phytoplankton concentration in the ocean, aerosol concentration in the atmosphere, soil moisture etc, is required with high quality and adequate spatial and temporal scales, depending on the applications under consideration, but this is not generally available. Presently, only satellites can retrieve many of these parameters with good quality and accuracy. But, the quality of geophysical parameters derived from satellite measurements varies significantly depending, not only on the strength and uniqueness of the signal from the mentioned geophysical parameters but also on the mathematical methods applied to extract these parameters, i. e., to solve forward inverse remote sensing problems. In this way, the ANN technique is a very promising mathematical tool to accurately solve forward and inverse problems in remote sensing (Krasnopolsky, 2003).

CONCLUSION

In this chapter, LMs and ANNs applications to estimate Q^*, a significant term of the energy balance equation, over vineyard crops has been presented. Micrometeorological/soil data, averaged over a ten-minutes period, from the *FESEBAV-2007* experiment (June 18 –September 19, 2007), was used to develop and train the models.

With respect to the SOM, the maps allow to visualize the relationships between meteorological/soil parameters in an easy way, as well as to interpret physically the relationships between them. The SOM was also utilized in order to select

the parameters used as input layer in the *Multi-layer Perceptron* models. The SOM associated with *Multilayer Perceptron* allows increasing the knowledge of physical processes, as well as the interaction of the driving mechanisms concerning the surface energy balance. Taking into account that $K\downarrow$ was not used as input layer in the ANN model training, and by looking at the statistical results presented in Table 2, the ANN demonstrated to be a helpful tool to estimate Q^* at the surface from operational meteorological parameters, mainly for sites where radiation fluxes related parameters are not currently measured, showing that the modeling process using ANN is effective to estimate Q^*, when only a limited number of meteorological variables is available.

REFERENCES

Alpaydin, E. (2004). Introduction to Machine Learning (Adaptive Computation and Machine Learning). Cambridge, MA: MIT Press.

Amarakoon, D., & Chen, A. (1999). Estimating daytime net radiation using routine meteorological data in Jamaica. *Caribbean Journal of Science*, *35*(1-2), 132–141.

Åženkal, O., & Kuleli, T. (2009). Estimation of solar radiation over Turkey using artificial neural network and satellite data. *Applied Energy*, *86*(7-8), 1222–1228. doi:10.1016/j.apenergy.2008.06.003

Bennie, J., Huntley, B., Wiltshire, A., Hill, M. O., & Baxter, R. (2008). Slope, aspect and climate: Spatially explicit and implicit models of topographic microclimate in chalk grassland. *Ecological Modelling*, *216*(1), 47–59. doi:10.1016/j.ecolmodel.2008.04.010

Bishop, C. (2007). Pattern Recognition and Machine Learning (Information Science and Statistics). New York: Springer-Verlag.

Bishop, C. M. (1996). Neural Networks for Pattern Recognition. New York: Oxford University Press.

de Jong, R., Shaykewich, C. F., & Reimer, A. (1980). The calculation of the net radiation flux. *Archiv Für Meteorologie Geophysik Und Biokli-matologie. Serie B, 28,* 353–363.

Diego, G., & Loyola, R. (2006). Applications of neural network methods to the processing of earth observation satellite data. *Neural Networks, 19*(2), 168–177. doi:10.1016/j.neunet.2006.01.010

Elizondo, D., Hoogenboom, G., & McClendon, R. W. (1994). Development of neural network model to predict daily solar radiation. *Agricultural and Forest Meteorology, 7,* 115–132. doi:10.1016/0168-1923(94)90103-1

Federer, C. A. (1968). Spatial variation of net radiation, albedo and surface temperature of forests. *Journal of Applied Meteorology, 7,* 789–795. doi:10.1175/1520-0450(1968)007<0789:SVON RA>2.0.CO;2

Gardner, M. W., & Dorling, S. R. (1998). Artificial neural networks (the multilayer perceptron) - a review of applications in the atmospheric sciences. *Atmospheric Environment, 32*(14), 2627–2636. doi:10.1016/S1352-2310(97)00447-0

Gentle, J. E., Härdle, W., & Mori, Y. (2004). Handbook of Computational Statistics. Concepts and Methods. Berlin: Springer-Verlag.

Glover, J. (1972). Net radiation over tall and short grass. *Agricultural Meteorology, 10,* 455–459. doi:10.1016/0002-1571(72)90046-5

Haykin, S. (1999). Neural Networks: A Comprehensive Foundation. Englewood Cliffs, NJ: Prentice Hall International.

Haykin, S. (2008). Neural Networks and Learning Machines (3rd Ed.). Englewood Cliffs, NJ: Prentice Hall International.

Hillel, D. (2004). Introduction to Environmental Soil Physics. San Diego, CA: Elsevier Academic Press.

Irmak, S., Asce, M., Irmak, A., Jones, J. W., Howell, T. A., & Jacobs, J. M. (2003). Predicting daily net radiation using minimum climatological data. *Journal of Irrigation and Drainage Engineering, 129*(4), 256–269. doi:10.1061/(ASCE)0733-9437(2003)129:4(256)

Iziomon, M. G., Mayer, H., & Matzarakis, A. (2000). Empirical models for estimating net radiative flux: a case study for three mid-latitude sites with orographic variability. *Astrophysics and Space Science, 273,* 313–330. doi:10.1023/A:1002787922933

Jegede, O. O. (1997). Estimating net radiation from air temperature for diffusion modelling applications in a tropical area. *Boundary-Layer Meteorology, 85,* 161–173. doi:10.1023/A:1000462626302

Ji, X. B., Kang, E. S., Zhao, W. Z., Zhang, Z. H., & Jin, B. W. (2009). Simulation of heat and water transfer in a surface irrigated, cropped sandy soil. *Agricultural Water Management, 96*(6), 1010–1020. doi:10.1016/j.agwat.2009.02.008

Jiang, Y. (2008). Prediction of monthly mean daily diffuse solar radiation using artificial neural networks and comparison with other empirical models. *Energy Policy, 36,* 3833–3837. doi:10.1016/j.enpol.2008.06.030

Kalteh, A. M., Hjorth, P., & Berndtsson, R. (2008). Review of the self-organizing map (SOM) approach in water resources: analysis, modelling and application. *Environmental Modelling & Software, 23,* 835–845.

Kessler, A. (1985). World Survey Climatology, General Climatology, 1A, Heat Balance Climatology. Amsterdam: Elsevier Science Publishers.

Kjaersgaard, J. H., Cuenca, R. H., & Plauborg, F. L. (2007). Long-term comparisons of net radiation calculation schemes. *Boundary-Layer Meteorology, 123*, 417–431. doi:10.1007/s10546-006-9151-8

Kohonen, T. (2001). Self-Organizing Maps. New York: Springer.

Krasnopolsky, V. M., & Schiller, H. (2003). Some neural applications in environmental sciences. Part I: forward and inverse problems in geophysical remote measurements. *Neural Networks, 16*, 321–334. doi:10.1016/S0893-6080(03)00027-3

Landeras, G., Ortiz-Barredo, A., & López, J. J. (2008). Comparison of artificial neural network models and empirical and semi-empirical equations for daily reference evapotranspiration estimation in the Basque Country (Northern Spain). *Agricultural Water Management, 95*(5), 553–565. doi:10.1016/j.agwat.2007.12.011

Li, S., Tong, L., Li, F., Zhang, L., Zhang, B., & Kang, S. (2009). Variability in energy partitioning and resistance parameters for a vineyard in northwest China. *Agricultural Water Management, 96*(6), 955–962. doi:10.1016/j.agwat.2009.01.006

MacCann, D. W. (1992). A neural network short-term forecast of significant thunderstorm. *Forecasting Techniques, 7*, 525–534. doi:10.1175/1520-0434(1992)007<0525:ANNSTF>2.0.CO;2

Manzato, A. (2007). Sounding-derived indices for neural network based short-term thunderstorm and rainfall forecasts. *Atmospheric Research, 83*(2-4), 349–365. doi:10.1016/j.atmosres.2005.10.021

Mohandes, M. A., Rehman, S., & Halawani, T. O. (1998a). Estimation of global solar radiation using artificial neural networks. *Renewable Energy, 14*, 179–184. doi:10.1016/S0960-1481(98)00065-2

Oke, T. R. (1987). Boundary Layer Climates. Cambridge, UK: University Press.

Ortega-Farias, S., Antonioletti, R., & Olioso, A. (2000). Net radiation model evaluation at an hourly time step for Mediterranean conditions. *Agronomie, 20*, 157–164. doi:10.1051/agro:2000116

Prybutok, V. R., Yi, J., & Mitchell, D. (2000). Comparison of neural network models with ARIMA and regression models for prediction of Houston's daily maximum ozone concentrations. *European Journal of Operational Research, 122*(1), 31–40. doi:10.1016/S0377-2217(99)00069-7

Reddy, K. S., & Ranjan, M. (2003). Solar resource estimation using artificial neural networks and comparison with other correlation models. *Energy Conversion and Management, 199*, 272–294.

Rehman, S., & Mohandes, M. (2008). Artificial neural network estimation of global solar radiation using air temperature and relative humidity. *Energy Policy, 36*, 571–576. doi:10.1016/j.enpol.2007.09.033

Sentelhas, P. C., & Gillespie, T. J. (2008). Estimating hourly net radiation for leaf wetness duration using the Penman-Monteith equation. *Theoretical and Applied Climatology, 91*, 205–215. doi:10.1007/s00704-006-0290-0

Trezza, R. (2006). Evapotranspiration from a remote sensing model for water management in a irrigation system in Venezuela. *Interciencia, 31*(6), 417–423.

Venäläinen, A., Solantie, R., & Laine, V. (1998). Mean long-term surface energy balance components in Finland during the summertime. *Boreal Environment Research, 3*, 171–180.

Yi, J., & Prybutok, R. (1996). A neural network model forecasting for prediction of daily maximum ozone concentration in an industrial urban area. *Environmental Pollution, 92*(3), 349–357. doi:10.1016/0269-7491(95)00078-X

ADDITIONAL READING

Abdel-Aal, R. E., Elhadidy, M. A., & Shaahid, S. M. (2009). Modeling and forecasting the mean hourly wind speed time series using GMDH-based abductive networks. *Renewable Energy, 34,* 1686–1699. doi:10.1016/j.renene.2009.01.001

Céréghino, R., & Park, Y.-S. (2009). Review of the Self-Organizing Map (SOM) approach in water resources: Comentary. *Environmental Modelling & Software, 24,* 945–947. doi:10.1016/j.envsoft.2009.01.008

Chéruy, F., Chevallier, F., Scott, N. A., & Chédin, A. (1996). A Fast method using neural networks for computing the vertical distribution of the thermal component of the Earth radiative budget. Comptes Rendus de l'Académie des Sciences de Paris 322(S. IIb), 665-672.

Diaz-Robles, L. A., Ortega, J. C., Fu, J. S., Reed, G. D., Chow, J. C., Watson, J. G., & Moncada-Herrera, J. A. (2008). A hybrid ARIMA and artificial neural networks model to forecast particulate matter in urban areas: The case of Temuco. *Atmospheric Environment, 42*(35), 8331–8340. doi:10.1016/j.atmosenv.2008.07.020

Diaz-Robles, L. A., Ortega, J. C., Fu, J. S., Reed, G. D., Chow, J. C., Watson, J. G., & Moncada-Herrera, J. A. (2008). A new scheme to predict chaotic time series of air pollutant concentrations using artificial neural network and nearest neighbor searching. *Atmospheric Environment, 42*(18), 4409–4417. doi:10.1016/j.atmosenv.2008.01.005

Eslamloueyan, R., & Khademi, M. H. (2009). Estimation of thermal conductivity of pure gases by using artificial neural networks. *International Journal of Thermal Sciences, 48*(6), 1094–1101. doi:10.1016/j.ijthermalsci.2008.08.013

Fadare, D. A. (2009). Modelling of solar energy potential in Nigeria using an artificial neural network model. *Applied Energy, 86,* 1410–1422. doi:10.1016/j.apenergy.2008.12.005

Gurney, K. (1997). An Introduction to Neural Networks. New York: CRC Press.

Hsieh, W. W., & Tang, B. (1998). Applying neural network models to prediction and data analysis in meteorology and oceanography. *Bulletin of the American Meteorological Society, 79,* 1855–1870. doi:10.1175/1520-0477(1998)079<1855:ANNMTP>2.0.CO;2

Jain, A. K., Mao, J., & Mohiuddin, K. M. (1996). Artificial Neural Networks: A Tutorial. *Computer, 29*(3), 31–44. doi:10.1109/2.485891

Kalogirou, S. A. (2001). Artificial neural networks in renewable energy systems applications: a review. *Renewable & Sustainable Energy Reviews, 5,* 373–401. doi:10.1016/S1364-0321(01)00006-5

Kavzoglu, T. (2009). Increasing the accuracy of neural network classification using refined training data. *Environmental Modelling & Software, 24,* 850–858. doi:10.1016/j.envsoft.2008.11.012

Kim, S., & Kim, H. S. (2008). Neural networks and genetic algorithm approach for nonlinear evaporation and evapotranspiration modeling. *Journal of Hydrology (Amsterdam), 351*(3-4), 299–317. doi:10.1016/j.jhydrol.2007.12.014

Krasnopolsky, V. M., & Schiller, H. (2003). Some neural applications in environmental sciences. Part II: advancing computational efficiency of environmental numerical models. *Neural Networks, 16,* 335–348. doi:10.1016/S0893-6080(03)00026-1

Kung, S. Y., & Hwang, J. N. (1998). Neural networks for intelligent multimedia processing. *Proceedings of the IEEE, 86*(6), 1244–1272. doi:10.1109/5.687838

McNelis, P. D. (2005). Neural Networks in Finance: Gaining Predictive Edge in the Market. Orlando, FL: Elsevier Academic Press.

Principe, J. C. (1997). Neural networks for dynamics modeling. *Signal Processing Magazine, 14*(6), 33–35. doi:10.1109/MSP.1997.637300

Prokhorov, D. V. (2007). Training Recurrent Neurocontrollers for Real-Time Applications. *Neural Networks. IEEE Transactions*, *18*(4), 1003–1015.

Qi, M., & Zhang, G. P. (2008). Trend Time Series Modeling and Forecasting With Neural Networks. *Neural Networks. IEEE Transactions*, *19*(5), 808–816.

Ripley, B. (2008). Pattern Recognition and Neural Networks. Cambridge, UK: Cambridge University Press.

Samarasinghe, S. (2006). Neural Networks for Applied Sciences and Engineering: From Fundamentals to Complex Pattern Recognition. Boston, MA: Auerbach Publications.

Senkal, O., & Kuleli, T. (2009). Estimation of solar radiation over Turkey using artificial neural network and satellite data. *Applied Energy*, *86*, 1222–1228. doi:10.1016/j.apenergy.2008.06.003

Tripathy, P. P., & Kumar, S. (2009). Neural network approach for food temperature prediction during solar drying. *International Journal of Thermal Sciences*, *48*(7), 1452–1459. doi:10.1016/j.ijthermalsci.2008.11.014

Weigend, A. S., & Gershenfeld, N. A. (1993). Time Series Prediction: Forecasting the Future and Understanding the Past. Reading, MA: Addison-Wesley Publishing Co.

Widrow, B., & Lehr, M. A. (1990). 30 years of adaptive neural networks: Perceptron, Madaline, and Backpropagation. *Proceedings of the IEEE*, *78*(9), 1415–1442. doi:10.1109/5.58323

Yuhong, Z., & Wenxin, H. (2009). Application of artificial neural network to predict the friction factor of open channel flow Communications. *Nonlinear Science and Numerical Simulation*, *14*(5), 2373–2378. doi:10.1016/j.cnsns.2008.06.020

Chapter 17

Application of Machine Learning Techniques in the Study of the Relevance of Environmental Factors in Prediction of Tropospheric Ozone

Juan Gómez-Sanchis
University of Valencia, Spain

Emilio Soria-Olivas
University of Valencia, Spain

Marcelino Martinez-Sober
University of Valencia, Spain

Jose Blasco
Centro de AgroIngeniería, IVIA, Spain

Juan Guerrero
University of Valencia, Spain

Secundino del Valle-Tascón
University of Valencia, Spain

ABSTRACT

This work presents a new approach for one of the main problems in the analysis of atmospheric phenomena, the prediction of atmospheric concentrations of different elements. The proposed methodology is more efficient than other classical approaches and is used in this work to predict tropospheric ozone concentration. The relevance of this problem stems from the fact that excessive ozone concentrations may cause several problems related to public health. Previous research by the authors of this work has shown that the classical approach to this problem (linear models) does not achieve satisfactory results in tropospheric ozone concentration prediction. The authors' approach is based on Machine Learning

DOI: 10.4018/978-1-61520-893-7.ch017

(ML) techniques, which include algorithms related to neural networks, fuzzy systems and advanced statistical techniques for data processing. In this work, the authors focus on one of the main ML techniques, namely, neural networks. These models demonstrate their suitability for this problem both in terms of prediction accuracy and information extraction.

INTRODUCTION

The atmosphere provides protection and support for humans and other species without which we could not survive. It protects because its composition prevents the passage of harmful radiation to humans such as ionizing and ultraviolet radiation, and it is a medium because it contains chemical elements without which there would be no life on Earth. Therefore, models are needed to help predict the evolution of these chemical elements over time so that if trends are not desirable, control elements can be implemented to avoid problems (Corani, 2005; Hooyberghs et al., 2005). Tropospheric ozone is one component of the atmosphere that can cause severe problems. There are many research studies that demonstrate the effects of this pollutant on human health (Kinney et al., 1996; Larsen et al., 1991; Spekton et al., 1991). Moreover, humans are not the only species affected by high concentrations; adverse effects on agriculture have also been well documented (Krupa et al., 1994; Legge et al., 1995). In the European Community, these effects have been estimated to cost over one billion euros per year (Krupa et al., 1994). For example, in Europe, there has been an annual increase of tropospheric ozone concentration of between 1% and 2% over the past twenty years, with indications that this trend will continue (Stockwell et al., 1997). Harmful effects on public health, crop yields and agricultural ecology have led the governments of the EU and the USA to pass laws to reduce the concentration of this pollutant. The development and update of this legislation requires legislators to have a scientific understanding of the following:

- A rigorous and detailed knowledge of the tropospheric ozone concentration. This requires the establishment of a network to monitor the environmental air quality and subsequent numerical analysis of the data (advanced statistics).
- Predictions for the short, medium, and long term. Reliable predictions would help authorities to comply with legal regulations corresponding to advance notice to the public when tropospheric ozone concentrations reach levels that are harmful to the health of vulnerable groups (children, seniors, etc.). Long-term forecasts would also allow the species of agricultural crops that are best suited to the presence of tropospheric ozone to be selected.
- The importance of atmospheric variables and atmospheric pollutants on tropospheric ozone concentration. With this knowledge, the best decisions can be made with regard to the control of various environmental contaminants that play an important role in the formation of tropospheric ozone.

Tropospheric ozone is considered to be a secondary pollutant and is made up of complex and non-linear photochemical reactions. Its precursors (NO_x and Hydrocarbons) interact photochemically with the atmosphere to create tropospheric ozone, while tropospheric ozone is destroyed by oxidation. In a laboratory, tropospheric ozone concentrations would be easily predictable since all the conditions and concentrations of all the gases involved in their composition would be known and controlled. However, the prediction of tropospheric ozone is a complex and difficult problem when the tropospheric ozone level depends on many uncontrollable factors such as long range transport (wind), which act directly on the concentration of this pollutant in a particular place (Spellman et al., 1998).

In order to reduce the effects of tropospheric ozone on public health and on the economy, the United States and the European Union have both set limits which must not be exceeded (EU-02). In this context, predictive models for the concentration of tropospheric ozone from its precursors (Aldrin et al., 2005; Gomez-Sanchis et al., 2006) would be useful in establishing mechanisms for control of this air pollutant.

LINEAR MODELS EMPLOYED IN ENVIRONMENTAL SCIENCE

The use of mathematical models to draw conclusions about a particular problem is common in all branches of human knowledge. However, despite its usefulness, the development and adjustment of a mathematical model has a number of issues that must be taken into account: a) the model should be reasonable (i.e., the structure of the model must contain the intrinsic characteristics of the problem); b) the model must be precise (in many cases, simple models are used, but they do not provide the accuracy that is necessary for this kind of application).

For the prediction of tropospheric ozone concentration, linear models have provided poor predictions due to the inherent complexity of the problem (Balaguer et al., 2002). The following two expressions have been used in linear models:

$$y = w_0 + w_1 \cdot x_1 + \ldots\ldots + w_N \cdot x_N$$
$$y = w_0 + w_1 \cdot \varphi_1(x_1) + \ldots\ldots + w_N \cdot \varphi_N(x_N) \quad (1)$$

where w_i, x_k, φ_s are, respectively, the model parameters, the inputs to the model, and the functions that are applied to inputs to transform them (logarithms, exponentials, square roots, etc.). These two expressions (linear models) have several problems that appear when the mathematical structure is analyzed. The first expression in (1) does not reflect phenomena of saturation, hysteresis, etc. It is clear that, for the challenge of tropospheric ozone concentration modelling, the use of this expression is absurd (even though it is easy to analyze) and it should not be used.

The second expression in (1) (using an appropriate choice of nonlinear function, φ) makes it possible to implement the mathematical model in the above phenomena (saturation, hysteresis, etc.). However, another fundamental question is left unanswered: Which non-linear function φ should be chosen? In problems of this type, the high number of input variables makes it impossible to visualize the relationship between input and output using a graphic method.

One strategy for improving the performance of tropospheric ozone prediction and other similar problems is to use other techniques that have been widely applied in other fields of knowledge, such as machine learning (Abdul-Wahab et al., 2007; Giustolisi et al., 2007).

Machine learning techniques are all those techniques whose ultimate goal is the extraction of knowledge from specific data. This information can come in the form of numerical data, text, images, etc. Moreover, the extraction of knowledge can be reflected in the resolution of a specific problem (classification, system modelling, etc.) or in the extraction of certain rules. This term derives from the direct application of these methods in the field of artificial intelligence and agent theory (Mitchel et al., 1997), (Bishop et al., 2006). These techniques range from classical statistical analysis techniques to advanced techniques such as Neural

Figure 1. a) Representation of a general neural network model. b) Neuron model and its elements

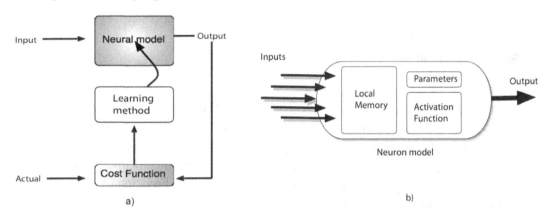

Networks, Fuzzy Logic, Support Vector Machines, Decision Trees, etc. (Alpaydin et al., 2004).

ARTIFICIAL NEURAL NETWORKS

This section presents the description of the models used in this work: neural networks. Chemical elements that make up the atmosphere and their interactions with the environment are one of the most complex systems that exist. In principle, it is logical to think that these relationships are non-linear (Balaguer, et al., 2002). There are also many variables that define the evolution of a pollutant. Thus, it is a non-linear problem with high dimensionality in which the collected data may be incomplete or have errors in measurement. This means that the models must be robust to noise.

Environmental problems are ideal for the application of neural networks (Kukkonen et al., 2003 ; Pastor-Barcenas et al., 2005; Gómez-Sanchis et al., 2006). The multilayer perceptron can be used as a universal approximator of functions (Cybenko, 1989), and, therefore, neural networks are very powerful. They have been successfully used by engineers and mathematicians in other fields, but they are not normally used in environmental science.

The approach to Artificial Neural Networks (ANN) varies according to author (Haykin, 1999), (Bishop, 1995; Ripley, 1996). For instance, some authors consider ANNs from a biological perspective; they can be used to solve problems in engineering. Other authors, however, view these systems from a mathematical perspective, establishing a correspondence between linear and non-linear models. These two approaches have coexisted throughout the development of the theory of artificial neural models creating two trends. Biological models have provided the start-up and development of many neural models, while the mathematical approach has provided an application framework and uses for these models. In this section, we analyze artificial neural models from a mathematical and operational perspective as represented in Figure 1a).

Figure 1a shows a general ANN model which has three elements. The first element is the *neural model*, which is the structure that is defined to solve the problem. This model can be either linear or non-linear and can have one or more outputs. It may also be a combination (linear, non-linear, hierarchical, etc.) from simpler neural models. The operation of this model depends on a number of parameters that establish the complexity of the neural network model.

The second element is the *cost function*, which measures the quality of the solution obtained by the neural system for the problem to be solved. The third element is the *learning algorithm*, whose mission is to determine the parameters of the neural network model to provide the solution to the problem. If this solution does not exist, it finds an optimal solution according to the criterion set by the cost function.

Thus, there are three basic elements in any ANN, and each can vary independently of the others. Therefore, the number of models / cost functions / learning algorithms is enormous. This ANN model is capable of representing complex situations. In the following paragraph, we will focus on the neural model that is the most widely used, the Multilayer Perceptron (MLP). Most applications of neural networks are based on the MLP.

The MLP is a neural network made up of processing elements which are known as neurons. Each neuron transforms a set of inputs into a single output. A general outline of a model of a neuron can be found in Figure 1b) (Hecht-Nielsen, 1990). The neuron model shown in this figure has three elements that are described below:

- *Parameters*. These are known in machine learning theory as the neural synaptic weights ($w = [w_0, w_1, ..., w_k]$). These coefficients are combined with the inputs ($x = [1, x_1, ..., x_k]$) through a function. The function most widely used to combine w and x is the dot product of the two vectors ($w_0 + w_1 \cdot x_1 + ... + w_k x_k$).

- *Activation Function*. This function provides the capability to solve complex problems. Generally, this function is non-linear and continuous and uses the dot product between synaptic weights and inputs as an argument. The most widely used activation functions are the sign function and the sigmoid function. The sign function was the first activation function used in an artificial neural network model (Arbib, 2002). This function produces a "hard separation" in the data. The expression of this function is shown in Equation (2).

$$f(x) = \begin{cases} -1 \ \text{si x} < 0 \\ 1 \ \text{si x} \geq 0 \end{cases} \tag{2}$$

The sigmoid function is the most widely used. Many learning algorithms require a differentiable function, which is the major advantage of this activation function over the sign function. The sign function is not differentiable at the origin, but the sigmoid function is. The sigmoid function is defined in Equation (3),

$$f(x) = \frac{a}{1 + e^{-b \cdot x}} \tag{3}$$

where a is the amplitude of the sigmoid and factor b defines the slope at the origin. If factor b increases, the sigmoid function approaches the sign function (but its outputs are encoded between 0 and a).

- *Local memory*. This memory is employed when neural networks are used to model time series. Since it can store previous inputs or previous outputs, the neuron remembers previous behaviour. There are many ways to implement this local memory on a large number of artificial neural models (Weigend et al., 1993).

In the MLP, the neurons are located in a series of layers. The first of these layers is called the input layer and the last layer is called the output layer. All intervening layers are known as hidden layers (Arbib, 2003). This is because the outputs of neurons are used as inputs to subsequent layers. Feedback from one layer to another is also possible (recurrent networks). The number of neurons in the input and output layers is defined by the problem to be solved. There are many examples in the literature of the fact that the multilayer perceptron with one hidden layer is a universal way of modelling continuous functions (Cybenko, 1989). If the functions have a non-continuous behaviour, two hidden layers are needed (Reed, 1999). It is important to highlight that there are guidelines for the number of hidden neurons in each layer. However, there are no works that establish the exact number of neurons. In most applications, there is a trial-and-error process to determine the number of neurons in the hidden layers.

The learning algorithm is the procedure by which the neural network model varies its parameters and architecture to solve the problem. The algorithms that are used to vary the architecture of the multilayer perceptron are known as pruning or growth methods (Haykin, 1999). Note also that there exist many learning algorithms. However, when choosing a particular algorithm, it is necessary for the learning process to be efficient, robust and independent of initial conditions. The aim of the learning algorithm is to obtain an error (the error is the difference between the actual signal value and the neural network output value) with a value that is equal to zero. In many applications, a direct solution is computationally intractable; and in many situations, a aproximated and iterative solution at a specific time is even desirable. The properties of the input to the neural network model vary over time, and the neural network model should be able to adapt to such changes. An iterative solution is needed as shown in Equation (4).

$$w_{n+1} = w_n + \Delta w_n \qquad (4)$$

where w are the parameters of the neural network model and the subscript refers to the moment in time. Using Eq. (4), there are two possibilities for learning: *On-line learning* and *Batch learning* (Haykin, 1999). In *On-line learning*, the error is measured throughout the training in terms of adjusting its synaptic weights using the learning algorithm chosen with each input pattern and the actual output value. In *Batch learning,* the error is calculated by the neural network model using all the patterns. Subsequently, the coefficients of the model are adjusted using the averaged error value.

The key in Equation (4) is to determine the optimal variation of parameters (Δw) in order to find the minimum of the cost function. The gradient of J indicates the direction of maximum growth of the cost function. The procedure that is most commonly used for this task is shown in Equation (5) (Bishop, 1995)

$$w_{n+1} = w_n - \mu \cdot \nabla_{w_n} J \qquad (5)$$

where μ is a parameter known as constant learning or constant adaptation and J is the cost function. The Backpropagation (BP) learning algorithm, which is based on Equation (5), is the most widely used learning algorithm. This process constitutes a gradient descent algorithm that propagates the error signals from the output layer to the input layer, optimizing the values of synaptic weights through an iterative process (Duda et al., 2000). Therefore, the algorithm can be divided into two phases: Forward propagation and Backpropagation. In the Forward propagation phase, first, the output of the neural network is determined. Then, the actual output is subtracted in order to calculate the error. In the Backpropagation phase, the error calculated in the previous phase is backpropagated from the output layer to the input layer through the hidden layers. It is not the aim of this section to provide a mathematical explanation of the BP algorithm; this can be found in any book on neural networks (Haykin, 1999; Ripley, 1996).

TROPOSPHERIC OZONE PREDICTION (1 YEAR) AND THE STUDY OF THE RELEVANCE OF INPUT VARIABLES

The data used in this study were obtained from the Department of Agriculture, Fisheries and Food of the Generalitat Valenciana (Spain). The center of data acquisition is located in Carcaixent, near the Mediterranean Sea about 40 km from Valencia.

Table 1. Best neural networks and results (1 ppb is a traditional measure of tropospheric ozone concentration and is equivalent to 1963 mg/m³ at 25 °C)

Learning	Layers	Neurons	R^2	MAE (ppb)	RMSE (ppb)
Batch	1	5	0.78	7.36	9.32
Batch	1	5	0.77	7.19	9.22
On-Line	1	11	0.75	7.71	10.06
On-Line	2	5-5	0.73	8.33	11.01
On-line	1	5	0.73	8.20	10.40
Batch	1	6	0.79	7.03	8.86
Batch	1	5	0.80	6.93	8.92
Batch	1	12	0.80	7.03	8.85
Batch	1	5	0.79	7.08	9.05
Batch	2	14-14	0.59	12.48	14.64

The first task was to analyze the prediction of tropospheric ozone concentration. The data set corresponds to the period of April 2002 (April 1- April 30). The reason for using April is that, during this period, there are high tropospheric ozone values in the area of data acquisition (There are also high levels of tropospheric ozone concentration in the summer, but this data was not available). In the period studied, there are usually high tropospheric ozone concentration peaks at midday and minimum levels at midnight. This is logical since tropospheric ozone formation depends on both temperature and sunlight. Data from the different variables considered were averaged at intervals of one hour, so the first 480 patterns (20 days) were used as the training set. The remaining 240 patterns (10 days) were used as the validation set.

The inputs to the neural network were chosen according to previous works of some of the authors of this paper (Balaguer et al., 2002). These variables were the following: the precursors of tropospheric ozone, NO and NO_2; and environmental factors such as temperature (T), wind speed (WS), atmospheric pressure (P), solar irradiance (SI), and relative humidity (RH). The output provided by the neural network was the tropospheric ozone concentration prediction for

the next hour. Since the variables of the neural network were standardized (all of them with zero mean value and variance unity), there was no bias in the neural network model obtained due to different ranges in the input variables to the network (Haykin, 1999).

The usual procedure when working with neural networks is to explore all the possibilities in order to arrive at a model that provides better generalization. These possibilities include the number of hidden layers (1 or 2 hidden layers), the number of neurons in each layer (from 2 to 20 neurons per layer), 50 random weight initializations, and the learning rate (0.1 to 0.9, in intervals of 0.05). *Batch* and *On-line* learning techniques were tested. In order to avoid overfitting cross validation techniques have been used. Moreover this procedure improve the generalization capability. of the models.

Table 1 shows some of the best models obtained along with their architectures, learning methods, and the adjustment parameters in the overall validation.

The indices of adjustment RMSE and MAE are defined as shown in Equation (6):

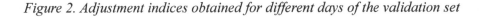

Figure 2. Adjustment indices obtained for different days of the validation set

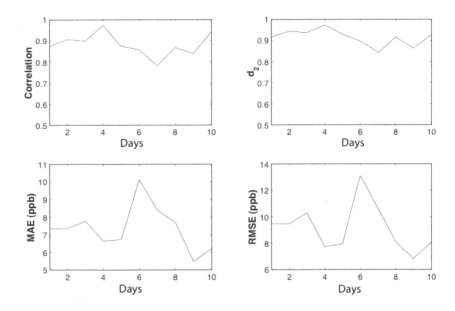

$$MAE = \frac{1}{N} \sum_{k=1}^{N} \left| cr_k - cn_k \right|$$

$$RMSE = \sqrt{\frac{1}{N} \sum_{k=1}^{N} \left| cr_k - cn_k \right|^2} \qquad (6)$$

where cr_{ki} and cn_k are, respectively, the concentrations of tropospheric ozone actually measured and the concentrations predicted by the neural network. Thus, these MAE an RMSE give an idea of the error committed by the neural network model. To establish a benchmark for comparison of the accuracy of the model, it must be taken into account that the tropospheric ozone data was acquired in a range between 50 and 70 ppb.

R^2 is the index that shows the quality of the linear fit between the signal predicted by the ANN and the actual tropospheric ozone measurement. It varies between 0 (bad fit) and 1 (perfect fit). The rates listed in Table 1 show that neural networks are an excellent tool for use in the prediction of tropospheric ozone. Note that the results of this table are obtained using data from the validation set. The use of neural networks improves the RMSE performance index obtained with linear models (Balaguer et al., 2002). Figure 2 shows the adjustment rates for each day of the validation set.

R^2 and d_2 shown in Figure 2 have the same interpretation (a value close to zero indicates a bad fit and a value close to one indicates a perfect fit). Note that the neural network model is adjusted correctly for the different days in the validation set. In a large number of situations, the indices (averaged indices for the entire validation set) defined in Table 1 mask the bad operation of the model in specific situations. However, Figure 2 shows that there are good adjustments for each day in the validation set.

Once the best prediction model is determined, tropospheric ozone profiles for different days can be simulated by varying the value of different inputs of the neural network. For example, it might be interesting to determine the profile of tropo-

Table 2. Relevance of the input variables in the 10 best models

1	2	3	4	5	6	7
T	SI	WS	RH	P	NO_2	NO
T	SI	WS	RH	P	NO_2	NO
T	SI	WS	RH	P	NO_2	NO
T	SI	RH	NO_2	WS	NO	P
T	SI	RH	WS	P	NO_2	NO
T	SI	WS	RH	P	NO_2	NO
T	SI	RH	NO_2	WS	NO	P
T	SI	RH	WS	P	NO_2	NO
T	SI	WS	RH	P	NO_2	NO
T	SI	RH	WS	NO	P	NO_2

spheric ozone on a sunny day with high values of the precursors in order to establish alert systems.

There is another way of extracting knowledge from the neural network that is seldom done. Our model can extract information about the relative importance of the inputs using the sensitivity of each variable (De et al., 1997; Pal, 1999). The procedure is simple. First, the output o_k of the neural network using all the input variables is determined. Then one of these variables is cancelled, and the new output oo_k is recalculated. The difference between o_k and oo_k is the sensitivity, which is shown in Eq. 7.

$$sensitivity = \frac{1}{N} \sum_{k=1}^{N} \left| o_k - oo_k \right| \qquad (7)$$

This measure is easy to interpret. If the sensitivity is small, it means that the output is not dependent on this input variable. Thus, it can be concluded that this variable is not important. Therefore, sensitivity is a measure of the influence of a given input on the output of the neural network.

Since the neural network is a non-linear model, conclusions cannot be drawn using only the best neural network model. Therefore, the top 10 neural

models were selected to determine the relative importance of different inputs. Table 2 shows the relative importance of the input variables (1=most important, 7=least important).

Table 2 also reflects another aspect of the quality of neural models. They corroborate knowledge that is already known by experts (i.e., the important role of the temperature and solar irradiance in tropospheric ozone formation). One aspect that initially surprised the researchers of this study is that the chemical precursors, NO and NO_2, are the least important variables. These can be attributed to long range transport such as wind speed which contain effects of chemical precursors.

Another important conclusion that can be obtained from the results shown in Table 2 is a simplification of the neural models. Given the importance of different inputs, a neural network model that uses a smaller number of input variables than the original model can be developed. These simplified models do not consider NO and NO_2. The best neural networks with a low number of relevant input variables (with 1 hidden layer and 6 neurons per layer) provided performance indices (R^2=0.78, MAE=7.73 ppb and RMSE=9.54 ppb) that were similar to those indices obtained using all the variables.

Table 3. Performance indices for the best neural networks for each year

Year	Hidden Layes	Neurons	Learning mode	MAE (ppb)	RMSE (ppb)
1997	2	5-5	On-line	8.48 9.05	6.29 7.00
1999	1	14	Batch	8.00 9.02	6.36 7.05
2000	2	5-5	On-line	6.78 7.85	5.52 6.26

TROPOSPHERIC OZONE PREDICTION (3 YEARS) AND THE RELEVANCE OF INPUT VARIABLES ON AN HOURLY BASIS

Once the ability of the neural network model for the prediction of tropospheric ozone was demonstrated for 1 year, the authors decided to replicate the study for 3 years. The data set had the same features as the initial study for the years 1997, 1999 and 2000 (the year 1998 was not included because there was no available data). The same parameters were used: sampling period of data (1 hour); the first 20 days of the month in the training set; the last 10 days in the validation set.

The main objective in this second study was to determine the importance of different input variables in the formation of tropospheric ozone, according to different temporal windows. Hourly windows were studied in order to analyze the importance of the input variables for the daily tropospheric ozone concentration. This provided important knowledge about the use of neural models for learning the mechanism for the creation of tropospheric ozone in more detail. As in the initial study, the variables were transformed to have zero mean value and variance unity. The architecture, the initialization range of coefficients, and the type of learning were varied as in the first study. Table 3 shows the rates of adjustment for training (top), and validation set (bottom). The variation range of the data over 3 years was between 62 and 71 ppb.

Figure 3 shows the predicted tropospheric ozone concentration versus the actual value for different years and for training and validation sets each year. Figure 3 a,b,c,d,e,f show that the adjustment determined by the neural model is very good (the ideal situation would be to have points on the line y = x).

Figure 4 shows the concentration of tropospheric ozone (actual and predicted) from training and validation sets for April 1999. The results shown in Figure 3 and Figure 4 demonstrate the goodness of the developed models.

As in the initial study of April 2002, a sensitivity analysis was performed of the inputs to the neural network model in order to extract as much information as possible about the phenomenon of creation/destruction of tropospheric ozone. Table 4 shows the importance of input variables in monthly intervals (as in the initial study) in determining the relevance of each variable using the sensitivity parameter.

Table 4 also illustrates important facts in the study of tropospheric ozone concentration: environmental conditions can change; and the importance of different variables in a given year may vary. Thus, as Table 4 indicates, in 1997, long range transport were mainly due to the low incidence of precursors NO and NO_2. It was later verified by experts that this transport was due to high values of the variable WS. This situation changed in 2000. There was a major influence of the elements involved in tropospheric ozone formation (temperature and precursors). Note that the temperature is reflected through several input variables (temperature (T), solar irradiance (SI) and, relative humidity (RH)).

Figure 3. Predicted and actual concentration of tropospheric ozone: a), c), and e) are all training for the years 1997, 1999, and 2000, respectively. Graphs b), d) and f) correspond to the validation sets for those years. Predicted and actual concentration of tropospheric ozone for the first five days for training set (g) and validation set (h) for the year 1999

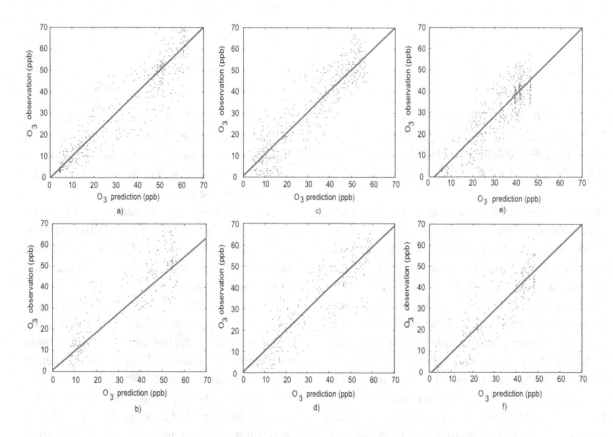

Figure 4. Predicted and actual concentration of tropospheric ozone for the first five days for training set (a) and validation sets (b) for the year 1999

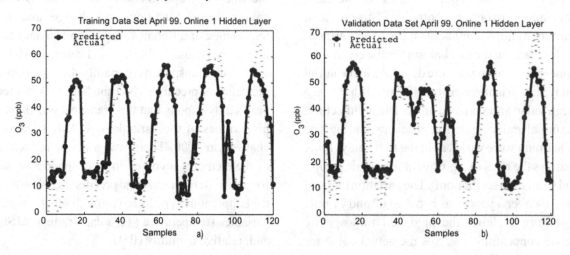

Table 4. Relevance of the input variables in the 3 best models of each year

Year	1	2	3	4	5	6	7
1997	WS	SI	T	NO2	RH	P	NO
1997	WS	SI	RH	NO	NO2	T	P
1997	T	SI	WS	P	RH	NO_2	NO
1999	T	NO_2	RH	WS	SI	P	NO
1999	T	NO_2	WS	SI	RH	P	NO
1999	T	NO_2	RH	SI	WS	P	NO
2000	NO_2	RH	WS	T	NO	P	SI
2000	RH	NO_2	T	SI	P	WS	NO
2000	RH	NO_2	T	SI	WS	P	NO

Finally, we determined the importance of environmental variables on an hourly basis to identify which variables and mechanisms were the most relevant during the day. Figure 5 shows the relevance of the most important variables for each hour. Figure 5 shows that in the central hours of the day, the temperature, solar irradiance and relative humidity are the most important variables. In the rest of the day, other variables (NO, NO2 concentrations and wind speed) increase its relevance, at the same time the relevance of the variables mentioned above decrease. This technique allows to evaluate which mechanisms are important in the tropospheric ozone formation/destruction problem in each hour of the day.

Figure 5. Importance of variables by hour: a) solar irradiance (1997); b) wind speed (1997); c) temperature (1999); d) NO (2000); e) relative humidity (2000); f) NO_2 (2000). The three lines that appear in each chart represent the best models

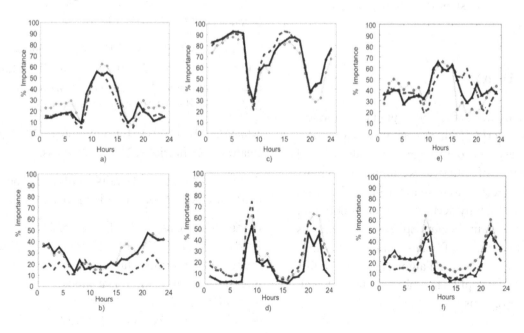

Moreover, this methodology constitute a new way to extract knowledge from neural network models.

FUTURE TRENDS

Similar models must be developed in order to study the evolution of other pollutants such as CO and CO2 from other gases responsible for climate change. The authors are currently working to replicate the study in other climatic zones.

In future research we are planning to use another type of non-linear machine learning techniques such as support vector machines (SVM). Nowadays, we are working in the use of SVM with gaussian kernels. The analysis of the support vectors, will allow the knowledge extraction in this particular problem. In order to improve the robustness of the models we want to use agent theory, mixing families of algorithms.

In order to validate the sensitivity analysis performed by using neural Networks, we are working on filter models for feature selection, such as such as minimum redundancy maximum relevance (mRMR). The filter model relies on general characteristics of the data to evaluate and select feature subsets without involving any mining algorithm

CONCLUSION

The development of effective predictive models for tropospheric ozone is very important today. In a society like ours, where the number and concentration of pollutants is continually increasing, it is important to have mathematical models that are sufficiently accurate to predict pollutant concentrations in the atmosphere. This study is specific to a region of Spain and a given pollutant, but the methods and algorithms used in this work could be applied to other pollutants as well as to other regions.

Many factors come into play in the generation / destruction of tropospheric ozone which make the prediction of pollutants an arduous task. Among these factors, particular emphasis has been given to the continuing non-linear relationship with temperature, which has been reflected in many works. In addition, there are long range transport (e.g. due to wind) that make it even more difficult to make predictions. The neural models used in this study have proven their ability to model tropospheric ozone concentration as well as to extract knowledge from this modelling.

This work represents an improvement in the prediction of pollutants in a given area without assuming any a priori assumptions. These techniques provide a set of tools to assist in determining which factors are the most important in the formation of the pollutants. They also provide a way to establish alert mechanisms to prevent damage to human health.

REFERENCES

Abdul-Wahab, S. A., & Abdo, J. (2007). Prediction of tropospheric ozone concentrations by using the design system approach. *Journal of Environmental Science and Health, 42*, 19–26.

Aldrin, M., & Horback, H. H. (2005). Generalised additive modeling of air pollution, traffic volume and meteorology. *Atmospheric Environment, 39*, 2145–2155. doi:10.1016/j.atmosenv.2004.12.020

Alpaydin, E. (2004). Introduction to Machine Learning. Cambridge, MA: MIT Press.

Arbib, M. (2002). The Handbook of Brain Theory and Neural Networks. Cambridge, MA: MIT Press.

Balaguer, E., Camps, G., Carrasco, J. L., Soria, E., & del Valle, S. (2002). Effective 1-day ahead prediction of hourly surface ozone concentrations in eastern Spain using linear models and neural networks. *Ecological Modelling, 156*, 27–41. doi:10.1016/S0304-3800(02)00127-8

Bishop, C. M. (1995). Neural Networks for Pattern Recognition. Oxford, UK: Clarendon Press.

Corani, G. (2005). Air quality prediction in Milan: feed forward neural networks, pruned neural networks an lazy learning. *Ecological Modelling, 185*, 513–529. doi:10.1016/j.ecolmodel.2005.01.008

Cybenko, G. V. (1989). Approximation by Superpositions of a Sigmoidal function. *Mathematics of Control, Signals, and Systems, 2*(4), 303–314. doi:10.1007/BF02551274

De, R., Pal, N. R., & Pal, S. K. (1997). Feature analysis: neural network and fuzzy set theoretic approaches. *Pattern Recognition, 30*(10), 1579–1590. doi:10.1016/S0031-3203(96)00190-2

Duda, R. O., Hart, P. E., & Stork, D. G. (2000). Pattern Classification (2nd ed.). New York: Wiley-Interscience.

EU. (2002). European Parliament and the European Council. 2002/3/CE O.D. C 67 E. 9-3-2002, p. 14–20.

Giustolisi, O., Doglioni, A., Savic, D. A., & Webb, B. W. (2007). A multi-model approach to analysis of environmental phenomena. *Environmental Modelling & Software, 22*, 674–682. doi:10.1016/j.envsoft.2005.12.026

Gómez-Sanchis, J., Martín-Guerrero, J. D., Soria-Olivas, E., Vila-Frances, J., Carrasco, J. L., & del Valle-Tascón, S. (2006). Neural networks for analysing the relevance of input variables in the prediction of tropospheric ozone concentration. *Atmospheric Environment, 40*, 6173–6180. doi:10.1016/j.atmosenv.2006.04.067

Haykin, S. (1999). Neural Networks: A Comprehensive Foundation. Upper Saddle River, NJ: Prentice-Hall.

Hecht-Nielsen, R. (1990). Neurocomputing. Reading, MA: Addison-Wesley.

Hooyberghs, J., Mensink, C., & Dumont, G. (2005). A neural network forecast for daily average PM10 concentrations in Belgium. *Atmospheric Environment, 39*, 3279–3289. doi:10.1016/j.atmosenv.2005.01.050

Kinney, P. L., Thurston, G. D., & Raizenne, M. (1996). The effects of ambient ozone on lung function in children: a reanalysis of six summer camp studies. *Environmental Health Perspectives, 104*, 170–174. doi:10.2307/3432785

Krupa, S. V., Nosal, M., & Legge, A. H. (1994). Ambient ozone and crop loss: establishing a cause-effect relationship. *Environmental Pollution, 83*, 269–276. doi:10.1016/0269-7491(94)90147-3

Kukkonen, J., Partanen, L., & Karpinen, A. (2003). Extensive evaluation of neural network models for the prediction of NO2 and PM10 concentrations. *Atmospheric Environment, 37*, 4539–4550. doi:10.1016/S1352-2310(03)00583-1

Larsen, R. I., McDonell, W. F., & Hortsman, D. H. (1991). An air quality data analysis system for interrelating effects, standards, and needed source reductions. Part II: A log-normal model relating human lung function decrease to ozone exposure. *J. Waste Manag. Assoc., 41*(4), 455–459.

Legge, A. H., Gräunhage, L., Nosal, M., Jagger, H. J., & Krupa, S. V. (1995). Ambient ozone and adverse crop response: an evaluation of North American and European data as they relate to exposure indices and critical levels. *J. Appl. Bot., 69*, 192–205.

Mitchel, T. (1997). Machine Learning. New York: McGraw-Hill.

Pal, N. R. (1999). Soft computing for feature analysis. *Fuzzy Sets and Systems, 103*, 201–221. doi:10.1016/S0165-0114(98)00222-X

Pastor-Bárcenas, O., Soria-Olivas, E., Martín-Guerrero, J. D., Camps-Valls, G., Carrasco-Rodríguez, J. L., & del Valle-Tascón, S. (2005). Unbiased sensitivity analysis and pruning techniques in neural networks for surface ozone modelling. *Ecological Modelling, 182*(2), 149–158. doi:10.1016/j.ecolmodel.2004.07.015

Ripley, B. P. (1996). Pattern Recognition and Neural Networks. Cambridge, UK: Cambridge University Press.

Spekton, D. M., Thurston, G. D., Mao, J., He, D., Hayes, C., & Lippman, M. (1991). Effects of single and multiday ozone exposures on respiratory function in active normal children. *Environmental Research, 55*, 107–122. doi:10.1016/S0013-9351(05)80167-7

Spellman, G. (1998). Analysing air pollution meteorology. *Weather, 53*, 34–42.

Stockwell, W. R., Kramm, G., Scheel, H. E., Mohnen, V. A., & Seiler, W. (1997). Ozone formation, destruction and exposure in Europe and the United States. In H. Sandermann, A. R. Wellburn & R. L. Heath (Eds.), Forest Decline and Ozone (pp. 1–38).

Chapter 18
Evolutionary Lagrangian Inverse Modeling for PM$_{10}$ Pollutant Dispersion

Alejandro Peña
Escuela de Ingeniería de Antioquia, Colombia

Jesús A. Hernández
Universidad Nacional de Colombia, Colombia

María Victoria Toro
Universidad Pontificia Bolivariana, Colombia

ABSTRACT

One of the main concerns when it comes to mitigating the effects of the concentration of the particulate matter PM$_x$ in an area of study is the fact to determine its behavior over time, overcoming both physical and mathematical limitations in terms of a phenomenon of dispersion. Therefore, this chapter develops and analyzes a model based on the principles of evolutionary computation (EC) in order to determine the space-time behavior of the concentration of the particulate matter PM$_x$ in a study area. The proposed model has three submodels within an integrated solution, which constitute the individual to evolve. The transformation of the possible solutions or generational population is made by using an asynchronous evolutionary model, due to genetic dependency between substructures. The proposed model was validated for configurations of n sources of emissions and m monitoring stations that measure the quality of the air in a study area.

INTRODUCTION

One of the main concerns when it comes to reducing the concentration values for particulate matter PM$_x$ in a study area, is the fact to determine their spatial behavior over time. In order to describe this behavior, it is necessary to overcome a series of physical and mathematical constraints. From the physical point of view, the restrictions are determined by the number of monitoring stations for air quality that are located in an area of study, or by the inability to carry out campaigns that enable the identification of the behavior of a pollutant over time, especially in areas where access is difficult. From a mathemati-

DOI: 10.4018/978-1-61520-893-7.ch018

cal point of view, these constraints range from the spatial representation of the concentration over time, through the estimation of emissions at the source, the type of contaminant, and the discharge of pollutants from one of the *n sources* that can affect a particular point of a study area (Aceña et al., 2007), (Martin et al., 2007). So if we try to estimate emissions from sources there is only information available with respect to the concentration values measured in selected monitoring stations, but they do not deliver any information about the dispersion of pollutants within a study area. To solve this problem, geostatistics and computational intelligence have developed different methods of representation and interpolation, which in many cases do not fit the model of a specific phenomenon, mainly due to the size and the quality of the initial sample points representing the phenomenon in a study area (Cruzado, 2004). In the case of atmospheric phenomena, the set of points of the concentration for PM_x may suffer dynamic changes over time that depend on the sources of emission, the monitoring stations and their location, or on how they are linked up due to the dispersion phenomena. So in many cases methods are required to conduct search and adaptation, or that have memory so that a number of surfaces can be generated that, in terms of the phenomenon, adapt over time, and that enable decision making regarding the mitigation of the impact of this pollutant (Peña et al., 2009(a); Peña et al., 2009(b)).

That is why this chapter analyzes and develops a model based on the principles of evolutionary computation (EC), which includes two submodels in one solution or an individual to evolve, which is based on a *Kohonen Map Features Model* (KFM) (Galvan & Isazi,2004). The first substructure is used for estimating emissions in *n sources* from a series of measurements of the concentration for PM_x taken from *m* monitoring *stations* that they measurement the air quality. This substructure is associated with the *pattern of emissions* or input to the *KFM* model. The dynamics of the

dispersion model, which is used for estimation, is governed by a *lagrangian gaussian puff tracking model* LGPT (Martín et al.,2002), which is based on the principles of a *backward gaussian puff tracking* (BGPT) (Israelsson et al.,2006). The second substructure permits to determine the spatial distribution of the concentration for PM_x, starting from identifying the concentration of *puffs* in the study area, thus *macropuffs* are generating a special type of functions, called *Non Uniform Puffs Functions* (NUPFS) (Peña & Hernandez,2007(a); Peña & Hernández,2007(b)). The model for the interpolation representation that determines the second structure is defined by the principles of a *Takagi– Sugeno Model* (TKS) (Sanchez et al., 2005) with *NUPFS* base functions. For the transformation of the possible solutions, or population of the present generation, the model uses an *asynchronous evolutionary model* (AEM), due to the genetic dependency between substructures. Finally, the proposed evolutionary model was validated in a real part of the study area, in which *n selected sources* of an industrial type and *m-monitoring stations* are located spatially. In order to validate this model, a study area, comprising an area of about 25*25 km², was selected in the Aburrá Valley, located in Antioquia, Colombia, South America.

BACKGROUND

The pollutant dispersion models have been used over time to determine the concentrations and flow and trace of elements according to the spatial distribution of sources and drains, the effect of the transport by flows mean and turbulent in the atmosphere, which are obtained from meteorological models or by detailed observation of the environment (Gallardo,1997). According to this dynamics, currently there are a number of questions that are directly related to how and in which form emissions of pollutants from different sources occur, or what is the contribution or effect generated by a source with reference to a monitoring station which measures the air quality or with respect to whichever population (Aceña et al.,2007).

In order to solve this problem various models that explain the dispersion of pollutants from a direct perspective have been developed, in which the emissions for each source are known and the concentration value for a set of monitoring stations is estimated, this is known as a *source-receptor* model (Martin et al., 2006). However, many of the models that have been developed so far, yet fail to address the problem of estimating levels of contamination in areas where it is impossible to develop measurement campaigns or where access is difficult (Aceña et al.,2007), or how and in which way an emission of particulate matter from different sources happens, which in general is called *inverse modeling* or *receptor-source* modeling (Martin et al.,2006), (Israelsson et al,2006).

For the specific case of *inverse modeling* or *receptor-source modeling*, many of the models that are used are based on models that apply *plume gaussian principles*, which show limitations when it comes to representing the phenomenon of dispersion, mainly because the dispersion of pollutants from a source is assumed to be uniform and that the winds come constantly from a prevailing direction over time, as shown in the work developed by Bein (Bein & Zao,2007). Allen (Allen et al.,2007(a)) proposes a model using Evolutionary Algorithms in order to determine the spatial location where a discharge of pollutants from a known source occurred over time, taking into account like Bein did, a dispersion model based on *plume gaussian* and a prevailing wind direction calculated by the proposed algorithm.

In that sense, different models for solving the problem of estimating emissions at the source have been developed, among them the models proposed by (Lundquist et al., 2005) stand out, who carried out a reconstruction of the emission starting from the design of monitoring networks and using the UDM model (Urban Dispersion Model), and two models proposed by Allen (Allen et al. 2007(a)), one for the optimization of variables using genetic algorithms, based on the SCIPUFF model (Second-Order Closure Integrated Puff), and a second model (Allen et al.,2007(b)) based on genetic algorithms and a *gaussian plume model* to estimate the position, the emissions, the size of the source and the wind field from a set of concentration values obtained from a set of theoretical monitoring stations that are uniformly distributed in a study area. The work of (Kyats et al.,2007) stands out as well, who used a *bayesian inference model* for the reconstruction of emissions from a set of monitoring stations. Similarly (Monache et al.,2008) proposed a model of *bayesian inference*, but this time to rebuild emissions on a continental scale.

According to the reviewed literature, we can observe a lack of models that describe the spatial-temporal behavior of the concentration for PM_x in a study area. Similarily there is a lack of models that integrate intelligent computational techniques in order to identify the dynamics of activities in a qualitative and quantitative way in sources that are considered to be fuzzy, or of models that allow an improvement of the estimation of emissions through the adjustment for eccentricity and deformation of the puffs caused by the wind fields in the area.

ISSUES, CONTROVERSIES, PROBLEMS

Six well-defined lines of research that study the concentration of the particulate matter PM_x in a study area can be highlighted:

- Characterization of the concentration of the particulate matter PM_x.

These types of research have focused on studying the behavior of the concentration metrics for PM_x over time, analyzing different variables such as road traffic, emission patterns, the characterization of sources, etc. This characterization also focuses on determining the composition of *the puffs* of the pollutant or of the *puffs* emitted from a particular source (Artiñano et al.,2006), (Martin et al.,2007).

- Development and analysis of source receptor models.

These types of research have focused on calculating concentration values for PM_x starting from emissions generated from different types of emission sources and according to meteorological variables in a study area (Martin et al.,2002), (Martin et al.,2006). Furthermore these models also allow the documentation of the behavior of parameters and variables that are related to the parameters of turbulent diffusion, height of the mixed layer, roughness of the terrain, dispersion models, etc.

- Development and analysis of receptor source models (mathematical type).

These types of research seek to determine the position and quantity of a pollutant emitted by a particular source, starting from a series of observations of the concentration for PM_x, that were made in a study area. These types of research aim to determine how and in which way a discharge of pollutants from a particular source happens, including the representation of *puffs* in the case of fuzzy sources (Aceña et al.,2007), (Israelsson et al.,2006).

- Development and analysis of receptor source models (statistical type).

These types of research seek to determine the position and quantity of a pollutant emitted by a particular source, citing the model of statistical

inference, which included MCMC models (Monte Carlo Markov Chain) and *bayesian inference* models. Many of these models focus on modeling accidental releases of pollutants at a local level and on a continental scale (Kyats et al.,2007), (Neuman et al.,2005), (Monache et al.,2008).

- Models that integrate intelligent computational techniques.

Up to date these techniques have been incorporated into the study of the dispersion of pollutants in order to describe the behavior of the concentration of the pollutants over time, favoring the prediction of the concentration for PMx in a monitoring station starting from the behavior of different meteorological variables over time. Likewise, many of these studies have focused on the prediction of the concentration for PMx over time starting from a series of variables associated with road traffic, industrial emissions and behavioral patterns of emissions over time (Perez & Reyes, 2006), (Allen et al. 2007(a)).

- Lagrangian stochastic particles models

These models have mainly focused on solving the equation of *advection diffusion* for different weather conditions, using different mathematical and computational techniques. These models are based on the use of simple particles (Moreira et al.,2005), (Israelsson et al.,2006).

These studies made clear that many of the phenomena of the dispersion of pollutants in the atmosphere implicitly have associated stochastic behaviors, that generate, with respect to the modeling of such phenomena, problems associated with uncertainty and changing dynamics of the phenomenon over time related to the weather conditions in the study area. That is why several trends have emerged that use intelligent computational techniques to solve some of the problems

Figure 1. Evolutionary Kohonen features map model

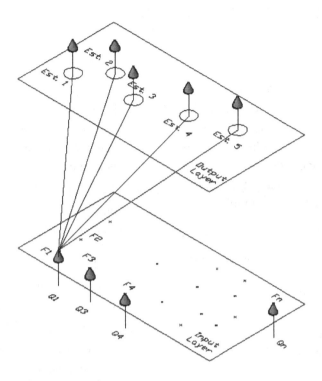

associated with uncertainty, the identification of behavioral patterns of emissions and concentrations, the identification of patterns concerning the behavior of wind fields in a study area, and the adaptation of models to the dynamics of the phenomenon.

DEVELOPMENT OF THE MODEL.

In order to determine the spatial concentration over time for PM_x in an study area it is necessary to take into account the following elements for the development of the model:

1. Submodel to estimate emissions.
2. Submodel for a Spatial Interpolation Representation.
3. Genetic manipulation of the pattern of emissions.

Estimated Emissions Submodel

In order to estimate emissions in *n specific sources* a model will be developed that is based on the principles of *evolutionary computation* (EC) and which is inspired by a model which is based on a neuronal model of the type *Kohonen Feature Map* (KFM, *Self Organization Map*-SOM) or map with the characteristics of *Kohonen* (Isazi & Galvan, 2004; Kohonen, 1982). This model consists of two layers, a first layer of inputs or layer of emissions which consists of a pattern of *n inputs* that depend on the number of emission sources that are considered for the estimation, and a second layer or output layer, which has *m cells* corresponding to the monitoring stations. Both, the input layer and the output layer, will be determined with regard to its size and shape by the study area, as shown in Figure 1.

Figure 2. Solution structure within the substructure of estimate

Q₁	Q₂	Q₃	....	Qₙ	K₁₁	K₁₂	K₁₃	....	K₁ₙ	K₂ₙ	K₃ₙ	BDL

In accordance with the principles of the EC, we can observe that the emissions will be determined for each source by a pattern of inputs, which contains the amount of pollutant (Qi) in [gr] contained in each *puff* emitted from a source (Fi). Consistent with this, the input pattern can be denoted and defined according to Figure 2.

Where:

BDL: Height of the mixed layer for the study area [m].

$K_{1,i}$: Factor depending on the size of the mouth of the chimney [m²].

$K_{2,i}$: Output flow of gases [m³ / s].

$K_{3,i}$: Quantity of pollutant emitted [gr/m³].

According to Figure 1, the connections between the input and the output layer are determined by a LGPM model (Martin et al., 2002), based on the principles of a BGPT model (Israelsson et al, 2006) and expressed by equation (1):

$$\Phi_j\left(x_j, y_j, z_j, k\right) = \sum_{j=1}^{ne} \sum_{i=1}^{nf} \sum_{k=1}^{np} \phi\left(x_{o,i,k}, y_{o,i,k}, x_j, y_j\right) . G\left(z_{o,i,k}, z_j\right)$$

(1)

Where:

$\Phi\left(x_j, y_j, z_j, k\right)$: Contribution of the puffs for a *j cell*, starting from the accumulation of puffs emitted by a group of *n sources* in the instant *k* [1/m³].

x_j, y_j, z_j: Indicate the spatial location of each *i:cell* or monitoring station within the output layer, using the coordinates UTM_x [km], UTM_y [km] and MSL (meter above sea level).

G(z,k): Effect of *n reflections* from each contaminant cloud or *puff* on the terrestrial surface and on the layer of thermal inversion located at a height of *H(k)*. (The mixed layer is located between these two surfaces).

$x_{o,i,k}, y_{o,i,k}$: Indicate the position of each of the puffs emitted from the i_source in the instant *k* with the coordinates UTM_x, UTM_y.

np: Number of *puffs* emitted [np/min].

nf: Number of Sources.

ne: Number of Monitoring Stations.

$\phi\left(x_{o,i,k}, y_{o,i,k}, x_j, y_j\right)$: Indicate the shape and size of the *puffs* emitted from one of the *i source* considered by the model. The size and shape is mathematically defined by equation (2):

$$\varphi\left(x_{o,i,k}, y_{o,i,k}, x_j, y_j\right) = \frac{1}{(2\pi)^{3/2} \sigma_x \sigma_y} Exp\left[-\frac{1}{2}\left[\left(\frac{x_j - x_{o,i,k}}{\sigma_x}\right)^2 + \left(\frac{y_j - y_{o,i,k}}{\sigma_y}\right)^2\right]\right]$$

(2)

nf: Indicates the number of sources with *i = 1,2,3,........., nf*.

ne: Indicates the number of monitoring stations or output cells with *j = 1,2,3,........, ne*

np: indicates the number of *puffs* emitted by a *i source, k = 1,2,3,.....,np*.

σ_x, σ_y: Coefficients of turbulent diffusion that determine the size and the shape of each of the *puffs* [m].

Mathematically, the concept of reflections and virtual sources is expressed in equation (3) (Martin et al., 2002):

$$G(z,k) = \sum_{n=-\infty}^{\infty} \left[\exp\left(-\frac{(2nH(k) - h_e(k) - z)}{2\sigma_z^2(t)} \right) + \exp\left(-\frac{(2nH(k) + h_e(k) - z)}{2\sigma_z^2(t)} \right) \right]$$

(3)

Where:

$h_e(k)$: Indicates the height of each of the *clouds* o contaminant *puffs* [m].

z: Indicates the height where the concept of *n reflections* is calculated [m].

For the movement of *puffs,* emitted by each of the *n soruces,* the proposed model uses the CALMET model (http://www.src.com/calpuff/calpuff1.htm) in order to determine a series of wind patterns for each of the hours included in a measurement campaign. These winds, that generate the dynamics of the model, were measured at a height of 10 m above the ground of the study area, departing from a set of meteorological data taken from NOAA (http://www.noaa.gov).

Fitness Function – *Genetic* Estimation Substructure

The values of the pattern of emissions are re-calculated by the model according to the known information about the source and according to equation (4).

$$Q_i = Q_i / IFC_i$$

(4)

Where:

IFC_i: Factor of known information about the source. This factor is denoted and defined by equation (5):

$$IFC_i = K_{1,i} * K_{2,i} * K_{3,i}$$

(5)

According to equation (4), we can observe that in order to obtain a given concentration value, a higher value for the emission is required with respect to the known information about the source. The *fitness function* (FA) that classifies the quality of a subindividual or of a pattern of estimate is given by equation (6):

$$FA = \frac{K_e}{\frac{1}{2} \sum_{j=1}^{ne} \left[\left(\sum_{i=1}^{nf} \sum_{k=1}^{np} C_{cj}\left(x_{o,i,k}, y_{o,i,k}, z_{o,i,k}\right) \right) - C_{bj}\left(x_j, y_j, z_j\right) \right]^2}$$

(6)

Where:

$C_{bj}\left(x_j, y_j, z_j\right)$: Concentration base or value of activation for the *j cell* [ug/m3].

$C_{cj}\left(x_{o,i,k}, y_{o,i,k}, z_{o,i,k}\right)$: Accumulation of the *puffs* in the *j cells* caused by the action of the connections coming from each of the *i source* due to the input pattern or subindividual of estimation [ug/m³].

Ke: Indicates the constant of proportionality for scaling the fitness function.

Validation of the submodel of estimation

In order to carry out this campaign, *5 monitoring stations* that control the quality of the air and *403 local sources* of emission within the study area were used. Also 3432 measurements of the concentration of PM$_{10}$ were captured on an hourly basis during the year 2008 and for each of the monitoring stations. According to the number of hourly measurements of the concentration that were required for the estimation of the emissions (403), 7 measurement campaigns were generated to cover periods of 20 days, or hourly 480 measurements of the concentration as stated in Table 1.

The results obtained for the estimation of emissions showed a correlation close to 90% with respect to the information known about the source and as shown in Figure 3.

Table 1. Measurement campaigns conducted in the study area

N° Campaing	Initial Hour	Initial Day	Julian Day	Final Hour	Final Day	Julian Day	IOA
1	00:00	11/04/2008	102	23:00	30/04/2008	121	0.902554
2	00:00	01/05/2008	122	23:00	20/05/2008	141	0.916340
3	00:00	21/05/2008	142	23:00	09/06/2008	161	0.899467
4	00:00	10/06/2008	162	23:00	29/06/2008	181	0.901226
5	00:00	30/06/2008	182	23:00	19/07/2008	201	0.900259
6	00:00	20/07/2008	202	23:00	08/08/2008	221	0.861771
7	00:00	09/08/2008	222	23:00	31/08/2008	243	0.925873

For the analysis of the calculation of concentrations eight metric statistics were used like the Fractional Bias (FB), Normalized Mean Square Error (NMSE), Geometric Mean (GM), Geometric Variant (VG), Index of Agreement (IOA), Accuracy of unpaired Peak (UAPC2), Within a Factor of Two (FAC2), Mean Relative Error (MRE) that are integrated in a model, and where each of them takes a qualitative value of Good (G), Fair (F) OverFair (OF), UnderFair (UF) and Poor (P). The model assigns a series of quantitative values in accordance with the quality obtained by each metric as follows G (8.5), F (5.5), OF (6.0), UF (5.0) and P (2.5), establishing a series of categories in terms of a score or performance index as follows (Park & Seok, 2007):

$$Score = NG*8.5 + NF*5.5 + NOF*6.0 + NUF*5.0 + NP*2.5 \qquad (7)$$

Where:

NG, NF, NOF, NUF, NP: Indicate the total number of attributes obtained by the model in accordance with each of the metrics used to evaluate their performance.

The results that were obtained by the proposed evolutionary model compared to the calculation

Figure 3. Index of agreement chart, information factor vs. estimate emissions

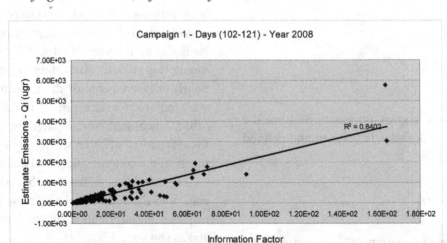

Table 2. Results obtained by the model for the calculation of the concentrations at each of the considered 5 monitoring stations

		FB	NMSE	MG	VG	FAC2	IOA	UAPC2	MRE	Score
	Ditaires	0.319337	0.125007	1.283189	1.054687	0.798434	0.752405	0.112363	0.18087	
		G	G	G	G	G	G	G	G	68
	Itagüí	-0.151128	0.09299	1.361931	1.011979	0.831349	0.756396	-0.163481	0.186400	
		G	G	G	G	G	G	G	G	68
102-121	**Politecnico**	0.190955	0.073589	1.23577	1.000028	0.845224	0.847884	0.058789	0.151028	
		G	G	G	G	G	G	G	G	68
	Univ. Nacional	1.718754	0.238193	1.983157	1.026302	0.695502	0.755810	0.196945	0.348838	
		P	G	G	G	G	G	G	G	62
	San Antonio	0.299758	0.057687	1.14901	1.087255	0.880551	0.776628	-0.252809	0.108601	
		G	G	G	G	G	G	G	G	68
									Mean	66.8
									Grade	A

of concentrations for the Campaign # 1 are shown in Table 2.

According to Table 1, we observe that the proposed evolutionary model achieves an Index of Agreement of 90% for estimating emissions with reference to the known information about the source. Looking at the graph of Figure 3, we can see that the estimated emissions show some fluctuations around the indexes that reflect the known information about the source, with indices of determination close to 85%. These results demonstrate the stability of the proposed evolutionary model in estimating emissions with regard to the information available about the source. In order to improve the process of estimating emissions, a series of additional considerations must be taken into account regarding the type of fuel used by a source, how and in which way a deter-

Figure 4. Ditaires Station – proposed evolutionary model – days (102-121) – year 2008 (a) time series for PM10 concentration (b) index of agreement chart

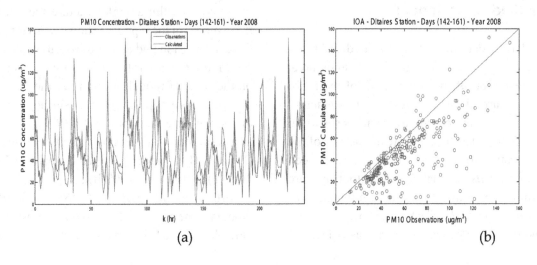

(a)   (b)

Figure 5. Activation map of the output layer by interpolation Takagi Sugeno NUPFS model

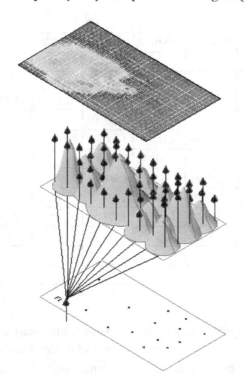

mined discharge of the pollutants occurred, the intervals of time with precipitation, the chemical transformation of pollutants, as well as a greater or lesser amount of fuel burned at a given time (See Figure 4).

Submodel of Integrated Interpolation Representation, densified EKFN model

In order to determine the spatial distribution of the concentration for PM_x in the study area, a segmentation of the connections of the KFM model is carried out, in terms of *the* segmentation of *cells* in the output layer and as shown in Figure 5. In order to determine the surface of the concentration for PM_x, the relationship between each of the *cells that* make up the output layer are determined in terms of a set of base functions or *macropuffs or NUPFS*, which identify the areas of the output layer where an increased level of

activity, or a higher concentration of *puffs* can be stated in the output layer.

Due to the limited information that a group of *m* monitoring *stacions* that control the quality of the air deliver with respect to the behavior of the concentration for PM_x within the study area, an integrated interpolation representation model of the type *Takagi Sugeno NUPFS* is proposed which incorporates within a single structure, the potential that a model of the type *TKS* shows with respect to the compression and decompression of surfaces, see Figure 6, similar to *NUPFS* functions based on the *NURBS* model, which have the ability to interpolate any type of complex surface in terms of a set of base functions or *NUPFS* that appear as a result of the dispersion model, see Figure 7 (Peña & Hernandez, 2005; & Hernandez Peña, 2007(b), Pena et al., 2009(b)).

In this way, the *TKSN (Takagi Sugeno NUPFS)* model will be composed of two fuzzy subsystems. One that shows the spatial influence of each

Figure 6. TKS model of interpolation, fuzzy spatial subsystem

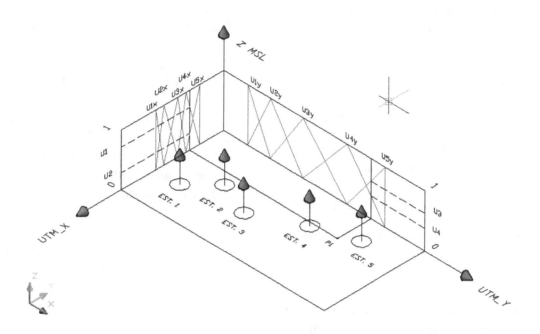

cell which belongs to the densified output layer (compression-decompression) with reference to the spatial location of each monitoring station. Accordingly, the influence of the spatial location of each *cell* is given by equation (7).

$$u_{UTM\_x} = \left[u_{1,x}, u_{2,x}, u_{3,x}, \ldots\ldots\ldots, u_{nx} \right]$$

$$u_{UTM\_y} = \left[u_{1,y}, u_{2,y}, u_{3,y}, \ldots\ldots\ldots, u_{ny} \right] \qquad (8)$$

Figure 7. TKS model of interpolation – fuzzy spatial subsystem for NUPFS

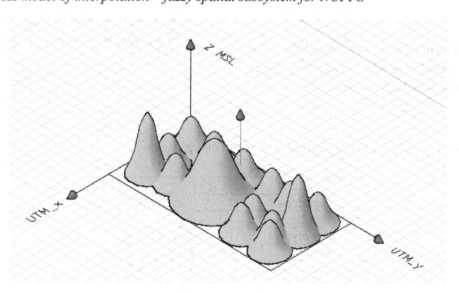

The vector of equation (8) indicates the influence that each *cell* has with respect to a point of evaluation within the study area.

Where,

n: Indicates the number of *cells* considered for the TKSN model.

u_x: Indicates the membership value of the location of the densified $\overrightarrow{cell\ x}$ with reference to each set of spatial influence on the axis UTM_x [km].

u_y: Indicates the membership value of the location of the densified $\overrightarrow{cell\ y}$ with reference to each set of spatial influence on the axis UTM_y [km].

The other fuzzy submodel permits to determine the influence that the spatial location of each *cell* in the output layer has with regard to the spatial location of each of the *macropuffs or NUPFS* functions that are considered by the model. This influence is presented in Figure 7 and is defined as shown in equation (9).

$$\varphi_y = \left[\varphi_{1,y}, \varphi_{2,y}, \ldots\ldots, \varphi_{m,y} \right]$$

$$\varphi_x = \left[\varphi_{1,x}, \varphi_{2,x}, \ldots\ldots, \varphi_{m,x} \right] \qquad (9)$$

The vectors of equation (9) indicate the influence that *macropuffs* have on a measurement point which is located in the study area.

Where,

n: Number of *macropuffs* that are considered by the proposed evolutionary model.

φ_x: Membership value associated with *macropuffs* on the axis in *UTM x* [km].

φ_y: Membership value associated with *macropuffs* on the axis in *UTM y* [km].

In an analytical way the spatial behavior over time is determined for the PM_x concentration by the *TKSN* model in terms of the phenomenon following equations (10) and (11) (Peña & Hernandez, 2005; & Hernández Peña, 2007(b), Pena et al., 2009b):

$$PM_{x,1} = \sum_{i=1}^{np} \varphi_{i,x} \left(u_{i,x} PM_x(i,j) + u_{i+1,x} PM_x(i+1,j) \right) \Big/ \sum_{i=1}^{np} \varphi_{i,x} \qquad (10)$$

$$PM_{x,2} = \sum_{i=1}^{np} \varphi_{i,x} \left(u_{i,x} PM_x(i,j+1) + u_{i+1,x} PM_x(i+1,j+1) \right) \Big/ \sum_{i=1}^{np} \varphi_{i,x} \qquad (11)$$

Based on equation (10) and (11) the output of the TKSN model is determined by equation (12) as follows:

$$PM_{x,s} = \sum_{i=1}^{np} \phi_{i,y} \left(u_{i,y} PM_{x,1} + u_{i+1,y} PM_{x,2} \right) \Big/ \sum_{i=1}^{np} \phi_{i,y} \qquad (12)$$

Where:

$PM_{x,s}$: Indicates the output of the TKSN system for a particular point within the study area.

Figure 8. Genetic substructure of representation and interpolation

C_{1x}	C_{2x}	....	C_{nx}	C_{1y}	C_{2y}	....	C_{ny}
Genotype 1				Genotype 2			
σ_{1x}	σ_{2x}	....	σ_{nx}	σ_{1y}	σ_{2y}	....	σ_{ny}
Genotype 3				Genotype 4			
K_{1x}	K_{2x}	....	K_{nx}	K_{1y}	K_{2y}	....	K_{ny}
Genotype 5				Genotype 6			

Genetic Substructure Interpolation Representation

According to equation (12), the substructure of estimation and representation is given as shown by Figure 8. Where:

Cix, Ciy: Spatial location (UTM_x [km],UTM_y [km]) of each *macropuff*.

Ωix, Ωjy: Size of each *macropuff* [m].

Kix, Kiy: Parameters for deformation due to excentricity of each *macropuff* [m].

i=1,2,…,nx: Spatial resolution of the concentration on the *UTM x* axis dependent on *cell* density in the output layer.

j=i, 2,…,ny: Saptial resolution of the concentration on the *UTM y* axis dependent on cell density in the output layer.

Fitness Function – Genetic Substructure of Estimation

According to the hourly MED of the concentration of PM_{10} which has been obtained after the estimation of the pattern of emissions and after the densification of the cells in the output layer, the fitness function for the substructure of the interplotation representation will be defined by equation (13):

$$FA = 2 \Bigg/ \sqrt{\sum_{i=1}^{(n+1)(m+1)} \left(PM10_d\left(i,j\right) - PM10\left(i,j\right)\right)^2} \quad (13)$$

Where:

FA: Represents the fitness function in terms of the inverse mean square error (MSE) for each location of each cell density

$PM_{10,d}$: MED of the concentration for PM_{10} or MED of reference obtained after terminating the process of estimation of the emissions (ug/m^3)

PM_{10}: MED of the concentration for PM_{10} obtained after terminating the process of interpolation representation by using the adaptive *TKSN* model *(ug/m^3)*.

Analysis of the Spatial Behavior of the Concentration of PM$_{10}$ within the Study Area (Case of Cell Densification in the Output Layer)

In order to carry out this analysis, a densification of the cells in the output layer was completed within the study area in terms of a segmentation of the connections or contribution of the *puffs* within the area by each source. This densification produced a set of DEM's, that show the activity in the output layer, or the temporal performance for the PM$_{10}$ concentration within the study area. In order to find an analytical spatial behavior for this activation, the genetic substructure of interpolation representation proceeded with the construction of a series of base functions or *macropuffs or NUPFS* with respect to the concentration of *puffs* in different locations in the study area until a three-dimensional analytical representation in terms of the proposed TKSN model (Peña et al., 2009(b), Pena et al. 2009(c)) was found. Accordingly, different behaviors on an hourly basis were selected at random for each of the considered measurement campaigns, and an analysis was carried out with respect to the analytical surfaces obtained as a result of the interpolation with regard to the DEM's of the local concentration for PM$_{10}$ for each campaign. In order to analyze the performance of the submodel representation interpolation, the fuzzy model proposed by Ok-Hyum (Park & Seok, 2007) was also used.

According to Table 3, we can observe that the index FB indicates that the surface, which was obtained after the interpolation process by using the TKSN model, in general contains the same amount of pollutant as the DEM of the concentration for PM$_{10}$, which was produced by the model after densifying the *cells* within the

Table 3. Behavioral analysis of the genetic substructure of interpolation representation

Day/Hour	FB	NMSE	MG	VG	FAC2	IOA	UAPC2	MRE	Score
C1	-0.01963884	0.23931241	1.41979436	1.02781217	0.6649061	0.96497154	0.26449067	0.27625628	
112/00	G	G	G	G	G	G	G	G	68
C2	0.01316245	1.80783711	1.23759688	1.00346097	0.57213954	0.82821433	0.71859054	0.11546677	
140/12	G	G	G	G	F	G	UF	G	61.5
C3	-0.0523006	0.42649075	1.44053945	1.00625259	0.6810848	0.82437959	0.61409136	0.2915801	
150/00	G	G	G	G	G	G	UF	G	64.5
C4	0.00349684	0.60217515	1.50901449	1.034545	0.58969826	0.86896319	0.49761425	0.30433925	
170/12	G	G	G	G	F	G	UF	G	61.5
C5	0.03070862	2.21084665	1.1718551	1.00005405	0.72270075	0.77242496	0.76823071	0.08608283	
185/12	G	G	G	G	G	G	UF	G	64.5
C6	0.02586803	1.31481534	1.51563521	1.00360215	0.55777861	0.77109308	0.79821841	0.16695902	
205/12	G	G	G	G	F	G	P	G	59
C7	0.02570035	1.65693406	1.2066439	1.00461615	0.6626297	0.78684456	0.64148835	-0.10368358	
2251/12	G	G	G	G	G	G	UF	G	64.5
								Mean	63.357
								Grado	A

study area. Similarly, the FAC2 index indicates that the interpolation model in general failed to achieve the maximum concentration values, which is reflected by the UAPC2 index due to an excessive rounding which the interpolation model presents with respect to some maximum values of the concentration, or when there are sudden changes with regard to the concentration

between different points in the area. Figure 9(a) provides evidence of this fact, in the figure the surface has, in general terms, the same shape, but if you look at Figure 9(b), we can observe that the peak concentration value is underestimated. With respect to the values obtained by the FAC2 index, we can observe that the points are well below the range set by this index for the estimate,

Figure 9. Surface that represents the spatial distribution of PM$_{10}$ concentration in the study area (a) DEM for PM$_{10}$ concentration (b) interpolated surface for PM$_{10}$

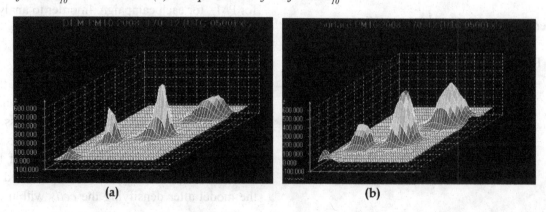

(a) (b)

Figure 10 Integrated structure of the evolutionary model - spatial temporal behavior concentration of the particulate matter PM$_x$

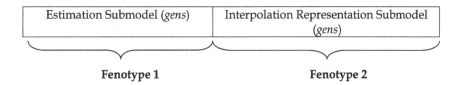

but if we look at the IOA, this index indicates that although the points are not located in the interval set by FAC2 for the measurement, the surfaces, in general, have the same shape, that generates a steady error within the study area, which easily can be eliminated by scaling the surfaces. Similarly, the rates of performance that were achieved by the evolutionary model proposed for some measurement campaigns were slightly lower, mainly due to the UAPC2 Index, which is a temporal indicator which does not reflect in general a bad behavior of a spatial model. According to the model of Ok-Hyum (Park & Seok, 2007), we can observe that the genetic substructure of the interpolation representation achieved performance rates close to 65 points, which ranks the model in the best category A.

Asynchronous Mechanism of Evolution

The proposed evolutionary model has two submodels or genetic substructures that are integrated in a single chromosome as in Figure 10.

Accordingly, the structure of the proposed evolutionary model will have three mechanisms of evolution, a mechanism of evolution which estimates emissions or a submodel of estimation, a mechanism which is in charge of the interpolation process, and a third mechanism that operates on the pattern of emissions with respect to the mutation operator in the estimation process.

Due to the dependencies of the *genetic* substructures, the proposed model provides an

algorithm for *asynchronous evolution*, according to the mechanisms of evolution that are described in the following for each substructure.

Mechanism of Evolution - Submodel for Estimating Emissions

According to Figure 11(a), the proposed evolutionary model starts with generating an initial population of individuals and with the storage of the data for concentration values collected for PM$_{10}$ using a set of *m* monitoring *stations*, which will act as a reference for the estimate. Furthermore, we can observe that this mechanism has two variables, a variable k$_2$, which allows estimation of the hourly emissions, and a variable k$_1$ that allows a relearning of the data that makes up a measurement campaign. At this point, a process of estimating hourly emissions starts, which is repeated until a minimum value for *E* (*inverse of the FA - Estimate substructure*) will be reached.

At the end of the estimation of emissions a process to densify *cells* in the output layer will start as a result of a segmentation of the connections of the KFM model. This densification delivers a MED of concentrations for PM$_x$ every hour, which shows the local behavior of the concentration in the study area. The starting point (A) indicates the completion of the hourly estimation of the emissions for each instant of time k$_2$. This point will activate the mechanism of interpolation representation for each instant of time considered for each campaign.

Furthermore, in Figure 11 (a) there are two entry points to the mechanism, where the point (C) marks the start of the process of relearning, while point (B) indicates the beginning of the hourly estimate of emissions for an instant in time. It should be noted that in order to start a new time estimate, the points (A) and (C) must be active, this marks an *asynchronous evolution* between the estimate and interpolation representation.

According to the mechanism of evolution shown in Figure 11 (a):

E: Represents the objective function that must be minimized, which, for the purpose of the model, is given as an inverse fitness function, as shown in equation (6).

MEDPM$_{10}$: Indicates the concentration MED of PM$_{10}$, which was obtained after the densification of the *cells* or by the segmentation of the connections of the KFM model (*ug/m^3*).

Cd(j,x,y,k): Indicates the concentration of the particulate matter PM$_{10}$ with reference to the *j-station*, located in the area (x, y) in an instant of time *k (ug/m^3)*.

Mechanism of Evolution – Submodel of Interpolation Representation

Figure 11 (b) shows the evolutionary mechanism which is responsible for the analytical representation of the spatial concentration for PM$_x$ in the study area. According to the population of individuals, each individual identifies the concentration of *puffs* in different areas of the study area, generating a series of *NUPFS* functions or *macropuffs*. Each of these *macropuffs* establishes an analytical relationship between each of the *cells* that are product of the densification of the *cells* in the output layer by using the interpolation model of *TKS* with *NUPFS* base functions. Each individual will be evaluated in terms of the fitness function that describes the genetic substructure interpolation representation.

Subsequently, the evolution mechanism continues with the cross operator, which provides a simple cross or a recombination of genes of the interpolation representation substructure. Likewise, the mutation operator provides a sudden adjustment or a smooth adjustment of the genes that make up this substructure. The interpolation representation process continues until the minimum for the RMS (Root Mean Square) indicator or inverse of the fitness function that describes of this substructure, is reached.

According to Figure 11 (b), the proposed evolutionary model provides two exit points and an end point, where the point (C) indicates the end of the interpolation process for each hour of a measurement campaign and a point (B) which represents the completion of the re-estimation of emissions. As a result of this mechanism, the model produces every hour a surface that represents the analytical and spatial behavior of the concentration over time within the study area. Here NH is the number of hourly measurements of the concentration for a campaign, whereas NIT indicates the number of iterations for the process of relearning for each campaign.

In tandem with this mechanism of representation interpolation, the proposed evolutionary model starts a new estimate for the next hour. In order to start with this new estimate, the point (A) and (C) must be active, this indicates that there exists a new hourly densification of the cells, symbolized by (A), and a termination of the interpolation mechanism of representation represented by (B).

Space Sensibility Mechanism

The model incorporates a description of the genes of the pattern of estimation as a stochastic process in terms of a *geometric brownian motion* (MBG). This description will enable the operator of mutation to execute a mutation which is limited by a confidence interval which is defined by the process. In this way, the mutation operator will

Figure 11. Asynchronous evolutionary model (a) submodel for estimating emissions (b) interpolation representation submodel

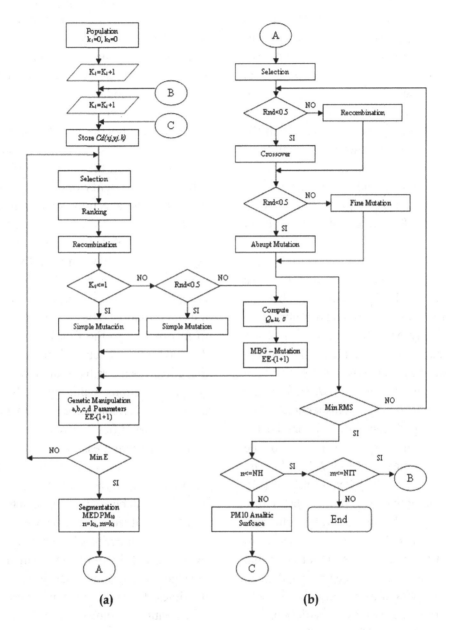

(a)   (b)

become a strategy by evolution of the type EE (1 +1), for each individual that undergoes a mutation.

CONCLUSION

The proposed evolutionary model accomplished to overcome the limitations imposed by the limited spatial information that a set of *m monitoring stations,* that control the quality of the air, deliver with respect to the spatial behavior of a phenomenon of scattering for the particulate matter PM_X in a study area. However, these *stations* imposed a series of patterns of change with respect to the shape and evolution of the surfaces of the concentration that were obtained as a result of the interpolation representation.

One of the models that delivered better results with respect to the spatial interpolation representation of the concentration of PM_X was the model of interpolation by NURBS (Non Uniform Rational Basis Splines). That was due to the capability of this model representing and interpolating any type of surface, and when it was integrated with the *Takagi Sugeno Model*, it inherited the ability of the latter to reconstruct complex surfaces starting from scattered sets, which generated a new model of interpolation called *Takagi Sugeno NURBS* (Peña et al. 2005, Peña et al., 2007(b), Pena et al., 2009(a)).

In order to further improve the spatial representation of the analytical concentration for PM_X in a study area, the NURBS functions were obtained starting from the identification and grouping of *puffs* in the study area, thus generating some larger *puffs* or *macropuffs*, that led to the concept of *NUPFS* (*Non Uniform puffs Functions*), which in turn take the properties of *NURBS* from the behavior of the phenomenon of dispersion, which converts the Takagi Sugeno interpolator NURBS in an semi-physical interpolator in terms of the phenomenon, that means into s a *Takagi Sugeno NUPFS* (Peña et al., 2009 (b), Pena et al. 2009 (c)).

The mapping of the genes of the substructure of estimation within the study area allows to carry out a series of localized mutations which leads to a reduction of the areas of the output layer that present a mayor activity o concentration of *puffs*. In this way the operator of mutation, which was modeled in terms of a strategy of evolution, will generate a series of maps of forecasts that describe the spatial-temporal behavior of the concentration of PM_X.

FUTURE RESEARCH DIRECTIONS

In order to improve the representation and interpolation of the spatial-temporal behavior of the concentration for PM_X, it is necessary to add to the NUPFS functions qualitative elements that describe the activities that were carried out at a source (EPA-42, 1995) In order to do so the use of a neuro-fuzzy system will be necessary due to its capability to integrate easily with the proposed evolutionary model.

The segmentation by genotypes and by zones within the study area, and the mapping of genes within the genetic substructure of estimation, will enable to evaluate the sensibility of a surface with reference to the behavior of a set of sources. This will make the execution of localized mutations easier as well with the aim to receive a series of activities that help to reduce the areas of the output layer, where we have more activity or a mayor concentration of *puffs* within the study area. In order to improve the uniformity of the model of the interpolation representation, it is necessary to incorporate to the fitness function, which is defined for this genetic substructure, an indicator that enhances the redistribution of macropuffs or NUPFS functions within the study area that are used by the TKS model, especially in study areas where the wind fields have a predominance with regard to certain areas of that zone.

The optimization of the behavior of the operator of mutation with respect to the estimation of the emissions can be reached through the integration of the maps of reduction that are obtained after the genetic manipulation of the pattern of emissions by areas, and that will show which locations of the study area are more sensitive with respect to the fitness function which determines the quality of the pattern of emissions.

REFERENCES

Aceña, M., Martín, F., & De Pascual, A. (2007). *Estimación de Emisiones de Partículas PM10 desde Fuentes Difusas*. Paper presented at I Congreso Colombiano de Calidad del Aire y Salud Pública, Manízales, Colombia.

Allen, C., Haupt, E., & Young, G. (2007b). Source characterization with a genetic algorithm-coupled dispersion/backward model incorporate SCIPUFF. *Journal of Applied Meteorology and Climatology, 46*(3), 273–287. doi:10.1175/JAM2459.1

Allen, C., Young, G., & Haupt, S. E. (2007a). Improving pollutant source characterization by better estimating wind direction with a genetic algorithm. *Atmospheric Environment, 41*, 2283–2289. Retrieved from doi:10.1016/j.atmosenv.2006.11.007

Artiñano, B., Gómez Moreno, F. J., Pujadas, M., et al. (2006). Measurement particulate concentrations produced during bulk material handling at Tarragona Harbour. *Atmospheric Environment, 41*, 6344-6355. Retrieved from doi:www.elsevier.com/j.atmosenv.2006.12.020

Bein, K. J., & Zao, Y. (2007). Identification of sources of atmospheric PM at the Pittsburg Supersite – Part III: Source characterization. *Atmospheric Environment, 41*, 3974–3992. Retrieved from doi:10.1016/j.atmosenv.2007.01.039

Cruzado, J. J. (2004) *Algoritmos de Estimación e Interpolación de Parámetros Geofísicos.* Unpublished Magíster Thesis, Universidad de Puerto Rico, San Juan. Retrieved from http://grad.uprm.edu/tesis/cruzadojapan.pdf

EPA-42 1995 AP 42. (1995). *Compilation of Air Pollutant Emission Factors, Volume 1: Stationary Point and Area Sources* (5th Ed.). Washington, DC: Environmental Protection Agency. Retrieved from http://www.epa.gov/ttn/chief/ap42/index.html

Gallardo, K. L. (1997). *Modelos de dispersión de contaminantes atmosféricos.* Comisión Nacional del Medio Ambiente (CONAMA), Santiago de Chile, 1997.

Isazi, V. P., & Galván, L. I. (2004). Redes de Neuronas Artificiales Un Enfoque Práctico. Upper Saddle River, NJ: Pearson, Prentice Hall.

Israelsson, P. H., Do Kim, Y., & Adams, E. E. (2006). A comparison of three Lagrangian approaches for extending near field mixing calculations. *Environmental Modeling & Software, 21*, 1631-1649. Retrieved from doi: 10.1016/j.ensoft.2005.07.008

Kohonen, T. (1982). Self-organized formation of Topologically correct feature maps. *Biological Cybernetics, 43*, 59–69. doi:10.1007/BF00337288

Kyats, A., Yee, E., Lien, F. S. (2007a). Bayesian Inference for source determination with applications to a complex urban environment. *Atmospheric Environment, 41*, 465-479. Retrieved from doi:10.1016/j.atmosenv.2006.08.044

Lundquist, J., Kosovic, B., & Belles, R. (2005). *Synthetic event reconstruction experiments for defining sensors network characteristics.* Lawrence Livermore National Laboratory Tech. Rep. UCRL-TR-217762. Retrieved from http://www.llnl.gov/tid/lof/documents/pdf/328798.pdf

Martin, L. F. (2006). *Inventario de modelos utilizados para calidad de aire.* Paper presented at V Seminario de Calidad de Aire en España, Santander, 2006.

Martín, L. F., González, C., Palomino, I., et al. (2002) Sistema Informático para el Control y Prevención de la Contaminación Atmosférica en Huelva. Centro de Investigaciones Energéticas, Medioambientales y Tecnológicas, CIEMAT.

Martín, L. F., Pujadas, M., & Artiñano, B., et al. (2007). Estimates of Atmospheric particle emissions from bulk handling of dusty materials in Spain. *Atmospheric Environment, 41*(30), 6344-6355. Retrieved from doi: 10.1016/j.atmosenv.2006.12.003

Monache, L. D., Lundquist, J. K., & Kosovic, B. (2008) Bayesian inference and Markov Chain Montecarlo sampling to reconstruct a contaminant source at continental scale. *Journal of applied meteorology and climatology, 47*(10), 2600-2613. Retrieved from doi: 10.1175/2008JAMC1766.1

Moreira, D. M., Rizza, U., Villena, M. T., & Goulart, A. (2005). Semi-analytical model for pollution dispersion in the planetary boundary layer. *Atmospheric Environment, 39*(14), 2673-2681. Retrieved from doi:10.1016/j.atmosenv.2005.03.004

Neuman, S., Glascoe, L., Kosovik, B., et al. (2005). Event reconstruction for atmospheric releases employing urban puff model UDM with stochastic inversion methodology. In *Proceedings for the American Meteorological Society Annual Meeting*, Atlanta, January 29–February 2, 2006.

Park, O. H., & Seok, M. G. (2007). Selection of an appropriate model to predict plume dispersion in coastal areas. *Atmospheric Environment, 41*, 6095–6101. doi:10.1016/j.atmosenv.2007.04.010

Peña, P., & Hernández, R. J. (2007b). *Compression of Free Surface Base don the Evolutionary Optimisation of A NURBS-Takagi Sugeno System*. Paper presented at International Conference on CAD/CAM, ROBOTICS & Factories of the Future, Bogota.

Peña, P. A. Hernández, R. J., & Toro, G. M. (2009a). Asynchronous Evolutionary Modeling for PM10 Spatial Characterization. Paper Presented at 18th World IMACS Joint Congress and MODSIM09, Cairns, Australia.

Peña, P. A., & Hernández, R. (2005). *Interpolation and Exploration of Response Surfaces using Evolutionary NURBS, LaGrange Constraint and Cylindrical Operators*. Paper presented at Genetic Evolutionary Computational Conference GECCO, Washington (ACM-1-59593-010-8/05).

Peña, P. A., Hernández, R., & Toro, M. V. (2009b). *Modelo Evolutivo Integrado para la Caracterización Espacial de Dispersión de Contaminantes*. Paper presented at 4ta. Conferencia Ibérica de Sistemas e Tecnologias de Información, Povoa de Varzim.

Peña, P. A., Hernández, R., & Toro, M. V. (2009c). *Modelo Evolutivo para Determinar el Comportamiento Espacio Temporal de la concentración de Material Particulado PMx en una Zona de Estudio* Paper presented at 4ta. Conferencia Ibérica de Sistemas e Tecnologías de Información (Simposio Doctoral), Povoa de Varzim.

Peña, P. A., Hernández, R. J., & Parra, C. (2007a). *Modelo Evolutivo Integrado para la Interpolación/ Descomposición de Modelos Digitales de Elevación*. Paper presented at 2da. Conferencia Ibérica de Sistemas y Tecnologías de Información – CISTI 2007.

Perez, P., & Reyes, J. (2006). An integrated neural network model for PM_{10} Forecasting. *Atmospheric Environment, 40*, 2845-2851. Retrieved from doi:10.1016/j.atmosenv.2006.01.010

Sánchez, A., Fernández, F., & Duarte, A. (2005). *Compresión de imágenes basada en la optimización metaheurística de un sistema Takagi Sugeno Kang*. Paper presented at: V Congreso Español sobre Metaheurísticas, Algoritmos Evolutivos y Bioinspirados (MAEB 2007), Tenerife (Spain).

Chapter 19
Artificial Intelligence Applied to Natural Resources Management

Diana F. Adamatti
Universidade Federal do Rio Grande (FURG), Brasil

Marilton S. de Aguiar
Universidade Federal de Pelotas (UFPel), Brasil

ABSTRACT

There are three computational challenges in natural resources management: data management and communication; data analysis; and optimization and control. The authors believe these three challenges can be dealt with Artificial Intelligence (AI) techniques, because they can manage dynamic activities in natural resources. There are several AI techniques such as Genetic Algorithms, Neural Networks, Multi-Agent Systems or Cellular Automata. In this chapter, the authors introduce some applications of Cellular Automata (CA) and Multi-Agent-Based Simulation (MABS) in natural resources management, because these are areas that the authors approach in their research and these areas can contribute to solve the three computational challenges. Specifically, the CA technique can face the challenge of data analysis because it can be extrapolated and new knowledge will be acquired from an area not known or experienced. Regarding the MABS technique, it can solve the challenge of optimization and control, because it works in an empiric way during the decision-making process, based on experiments and observations.

INTRODUCTION

According to Millington (2006), "the Artificial Intelligence (AI) is about making computers able to perform the thinking tasks that humans and animals are capable of". In this way, computers can already solve many problems, as arithmetic, sorting, searching, etc. Therefore, a philosophical aspect started

the AI motivation in academia: understanding the nature of thought and the nature of intelligence and building software to model how thinking might work. On the other hand, some researches works are motivated by psychology, and they try to understand the mechanics of the human brain and mental processes. In an applied field, engineers try to build algorithms to perform human-like tasks.

Natural resource management is a discipline in the management of natural resources such as land,

DOI: 10.4018/978-1-61520-893-7.ch019

water, soil, plants and animals, with a particular focus on how management affects the quality of life for both present and future generations. The discipline has given rise to the notion of sustainable development, a principle that forms the basis for land management and environmental governance throughout the world. Natural resource management specifically focuses on a scientific and technical understanding of resources and ecology and the life-supporting capacity of those resources (Holzman, 2009).

According to Fuller and colleagues (2007), there are three computational challenges in natural resources management: data management and communication; data analysis; and optimization and control. Computational tools to solve the three challenges of natural resources management could be implemented with AI techniques, because they have flexibility to treat the intrinsic dynamic of natural resources. Many techniques are available in literature, as Genetic Algorithms, Neural Networks, Multi-Agent Systems, Cellular Automata, Planning, Swam Intelligence, etc. In this chapter, our focus is on Cellular Automata and Multi-Agent Systems, because we work with such techniques in our research works.

Modern resource management increasingly depends on information systems (GIS) for interactive computational steering, high-performance computing for integrated system modeling, and geographically distributed grid computing technologies. For example, computer scientists actively engage in improving techniques for managing the large amounts of data produced by the high throughput sequencing technologies used in genomics. Often the applied computer science involvement with applied biology is mostly limited to solving molecular biologists' data management and analysis problems. Each of these areas contains a diversity of problems, many of which have great economic, social, and political importance. However, a problem might involve all three areas—for example, solutions to the control of exotic species depend on gathering information about organisms' occurrence and spread (data management/communication), understanding spatial and temporal invasion patterns (data analysis), and developing strategies to manage populations of exotic species (optimization and control).

Multi-Agent Systems (MAS) study the behavior of an independent set of agents with different characteristics, evolving in a common environment. Those agents interact with each other, and they try to perform their tasks in cooperative way, sharing information, preventing conflicts and coordinating the execution of activities (Gilbert & Troitzsch, 1999). Additionally, the use of simulation as an auxiliary tool to human-being decision-making is very efficient, because it is possible to verify specific details with great precision. Multi-Agent-Based Simulation (MABS) is the union of Multi-Agent Systems and Simulation and it is especially valuable to match different interdisciplinary perspectives. Typically, it involves researchers from various scientific areas, such as social psychology, computer science, social biology, sociology and economics.

Originally John von Neumann proposed Cellular Automata (CA) (Burks, 1970) as formal models of self-reproducing organisms. The structure studied was mostly on one- or two-dimensional infinite grids, though higher dimensions were also considered. Later, physicists and biologists began to study cellular automata for the purpose of modeling in their respective domains. The approach taken by Wolfram work (Wolfram, 1994) considered CA as models of complex systems, in the sense that simple CA rules can give rise to extremely complicated patterns. The mathematical simplicity in CA description is thought to be a significant advantage for modeling, rather than using systems of differential equations.

The proposal of this chapter is to present some of AI techniques applied to natural resources management. The chapter is structured in five sections. In Section 2 we present some research works using AI techniques such as Fuzzy Sets,

Neural Networks and Genetic Algorithms. Sections 3 and 4 are show extended applications of cellular automata and multi-agent-based simulation, respectively. Finally, Section 5 presents some conclusions and our opinion about future directions for this research area.

RELATED WORKS

The focus of our studies is on the CA and MABS techniques. However, many other applications can be done using AI techniques, as neural networks, genetic algorithms or fuzzy sets.

The idea of Neural Networks was inspired from biological nervous systems. In fact, neural networks are an attempt to create systems that work in a similar way to the human brain. The brain consists of tens of billions of neurons densely interconnected. The function of an Artificial Neural Network (ANN) is to produce an output pattern when presented with an input one. Output signals may be sent to other units along connections known as weights, which excite or inhibit the signal that is being communicated. Learning is the process of adapting or modifying the connection weights in response to stimuli being presented at the input buffer and optionally to the output buffer. A stimulus presented at the output buffer corresponds to a desired response to a given input. This desired response is provided by a knowledge "teacher". In such case learning is called "supervised learning". Though an ANN consists of units that have a very limited computing capability, when many of these units are connected together, the complete network is capable of performing a very complicated task (Picton, 2000).

The ANN has been used in several works related to natural resources management. A good example is the work of Iliadis & Maris (2006). In this work, an ANN performs an effective estimate of the Average Annual Water-Supply on an annual basis, for each mountainous watershed of Cyprus,

where there is a lack of drinking water during summer periods. Another example is the work of Ahmad & Simonovic (2005), which presents a framework to show viable alternatives when the hydrologic application requires that an accurate forecast of the stream flow behavior be provided using only the available time series data, and with relatively moderate conceptual understanding of the hydrologic dynamics of the particular watershed under investigation.

Between the 50's and 60's, scientists studied computational systems with the idea that evolution could be used as an optimization tool for problems in engineering. These systems, called Genetic Algorithms (GAs), were developed generating a population of candidates for the solution of a given problem. According to Goldberg (1989) these algorithms inspired by the natural evolution were initially applied to optimization problems and learning machine. However, their work did not give any kind of attention to the strategies of development and evolutionary programming as known currently.

The GA works with a population (a set) of some chains of bits (0's and 1's) called individuals (by convention an individual consists of a chromosome). Similar to what takes place in nature, the system evolves to the best chromosome to answer a specific problem, even without knowing what type of problem had to be resolved. The solution is found in an automatic and non-supervised way and the only information given to the system was the fitness of each chromosome. The ability of a population of chromosomes to explore the space search and combine the best result found by any mechanism reproduction is intrinsic to the natural evolution.

The AGs premise is to find approximate solutions to problems of high computational complexity through the process of *simulated evolution* that has a blind way of handling of chromosomes, i.e., the processing has no information about the problem to solve, except the value of the objective function. In the original concept of AGs, the objective function (also known as the evaluation function) is the only information about the chromosome.

Due to natural selection, each population acquires a certain amount of knowledge, which is codified and incorporated into the new formation of their chromosomes. This new population is modified by mechanisms of reproduction. The most widely used mechanisms of reproduction are mutations (inversion of chromosome parts) and crossovers (crossing of chromosome parts).

Genetic Algorithms have been used in natural resources management and several works can be cited. In (Manoliadis & Karantounias, 2003), genetic algorithms are presented as a tool for effective decision support in natural resources management specifically applied to water resources planning and management where techniques based on analytical equations often require significant simplification on the network. In this work, genetic algorithms are used for the representation of the network and a nonlinear optimization model based on AGs has been developed for the calibration of water distribution network models. The decision variables are codified and the search procedure is done in several directions simultaneously different from the traditional gradient-based models that employ unidirectional searches.

In (Wang *et al.*, 2005), genetic algorithms are employed to find optimal solutions for green building design. This work presents a multi-objective optimization model to assist designers to find better assign alternatives satisfying several conflict criteria like economical and environmental performance. A successful design requires special attention to the conceptual stage, when many potential design alternatives are generated and roughly evaluated in order to obtain the most promising solution in terms of strategies that preserve resources, reduce waste, minimize the life cycle costs, and create an healthy environment to live and work.

According to Zadeh (1965), a fuzzy set is a class of objects with a continuum of grades of membership. Such a set is characterized by a membership (characteristic) function assigning to each object a grade of membership ranging between zero and one. In natural resources, the uncertainty could be an excellent tool to develop a system more similar to reality. An example of fuzzy sets application in this area is the work of Prato (2009), where he compares three decision rules to manage natural systems: a crisp decision rule; a probability based decision rule; and a fuzzy decision rule. He concludes that a fuzzy decision rule is appropriate when the decision-maker is uncertain about the relationship between the observed and true states of ecosystem services, because under uncertainty, the decision-maker cannot assign probabilities to the true states of ecosystem services given the observed state of ecosystem services.

In (Salki, 2007), the analysis of ecological data is done using fuzzy sets. Heterogeneity is a characteristic property of the data stored in ecological databases and ecological information systems. The heterogeneity of these data results from the fact that ecologists collect and use information from various data and knowledge sources, including sources of objective (mostly quantitative) information, e.g. measurement and calculation, and sources of subjective (often only qualitative) information, e.g. expert knowledge and subjective evaluations instead of measurement data. Another problem with handling ecological data can be the high degree of uncertainty of such data. That can result from the presence of random variables, incomplete or inaccurate data, approximations instead of measurements (due to technical or financial problems) or incomparability of data (resulting from varying measurement or observation conditions).

Many other AI techniques can be applied to natural resources management, such as planning, swarm intelligence, simulated annealing, etc (Russell & Norwig, 2003). In subsequent sections we will present an extended explanation of two techniques, cellular automata and multi-agent-based simulation, applied to this domain.

CELLULAR AUTOMATA

The original concept of cellular automaton is strongly associated to John von Neumann. According to the book edited by Burks (1970), Von Neumann was interested in the connections between biology and Automata Theory. In their studies, the predominant idea was the biological phenomenon of self-reproduction.

Other authors have simplified the construction of Von Neumann, as Arbib (1969) and Myhill (1964). Stephen Wolfram presented a variation of the Von Neumann automata in Wolfram (1994). The cellular automata of Wolfram are simple mathematical models of natural systems, consisting of a mesh or reticulate of identical and discrete cells, where each one has its value on a finite set, for example, integer values. The values evolve in discrete time steps according to deterministic rules that specify the values of each cell in terms of values of neighboring cells.

According to Wolfram, the cellular automata can be considered as discrete idealizations of partial differential equations often used to describe natural systems. This discrete nature also allows to make an analogy with digital computers, because the cellular automata can be viewed as computers of parallel processing with simplified construction. Since then, physicists and biologists began to study cellular automata for the purpose of modeling in their respective domains. CA is being studied from many widely different angles, and the relationships of these structures to existing problems are being constantly sought and discovered.

In (Chopard & Lagrava, 2006), they propose a model for an ecosystem in which several species are competing and evolving and the most of evolution parameters are embedded in the model components of a cellular automaton. To compute if each individual suits the function of its genome

is a complex task because the environment is affected by the presence of other individuals and other species. A cell identifies each individual that contains its genome defined by a CA rule. Each individual has a state representing its current response to the environment and neighboring individuals. This model is a simple abstraction of an ecosystem in which several species compete and interact with an environment dynamically shaped by the spatial distribution of the species.

According to (Coulthard & De Wiel, 2006), river meandering has been often modeled using vector based methods, but these cannot simulate multiple or braided channels. In their work, a method was presented to simulate river meandering within a cellular model and a technique for determining bend radius of curvature that importantly allows regional information on bend curvature to be transferred to local points. This local curvature is then used to drive meandering and lateral erosion and can be applied to understand fluvial systems.

(Chen & Ye, 2008) proposed an unstructured cellular automata (UCA) by implementing an irregular triangular grid and used it to develop a vegetation dynamics model. This model has coupled a two-dimensional hydrodynamic model and was applied to simulate the riparian vegetation dynamics due to flow modifications by the reservoirs operations. The riparian zones are highly dynamic systems governed by interrelating physical and biological processes. It is challenging to model the riparian successions when flow patterns are largely modified by river regulations by reservoir operations.

In geophysics, an appropriate subdivision of a geographic area into segments is extremely important, because it enables us to extrapolate the results obtained in some parts of the segments (where an extensive research was made) to other parts inside the same segment and to have a good understanding of parts that had not been analyzed (Coblentz *et al.*, 2000).

Figure 1. The ICTM input data

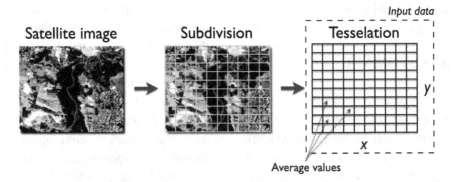

The ICTM (*Interval Categorizer Tessellation Model*) is a multi-layered and multi-dimensional tessellation model for the simultaneous categorization of geographic regions considering several different characteristics (relief, vegetation, climate, land use etc) of such regions, which uses interval techniques (Kearfort & Kreinovich, 1996; Moore, 1979) for the modeling of uncertain data and the control of discretization errors.

The analysis of the function monotonicity, which is embedded in the rules of the model, categorizes each tessellation cell, with respect to the whole considered region, according to the (positive, negative, null) signal of the cell declivity.

To perform a *simultaneous categorization*, the ICTM proceeds (in parallel) to individual categorizations considering one characteristic per layer, thus generating different subdivisions of the analyzed region. Each layer represents a tessellation for one determined property of the same analyzed region. An appropriate projection procedure of the categorizations performed in each layer into a basis layer provides the final categorization that allows for the combined analysis of all characteristics that are taken into consideration by the specialists in the considered application, allowing interesting analyzes about their mutual dependency.

The HPC-ICTM (*Multi-layered Interval Categorizer Tessellation-based Model for High Performance Computing*) was presented in (Aguiar *et al.*, 2004a) and the cluster, grid and NUMA implementations were presented in (Silva *et al.*, 2006b), (Silva *et al.*, 2006a) and (Castro *et al.*, *in press*) respectively. Whereas the formalization of the ICTM, the single-layered model for the relief categorization of geographic regions, called Topo-ICTM (*Interval Categorizer Tessellation Model for Reliable Topographic Segmentation*), was first presented in (Aguiar *et al.*, 2004b).

The ICTM Model uses a structured mesh to constitute its tessellation. Except for the boundaries all vertices of the mesh have an isomorphic local neighborhood. In three dimensions, a structured mesh is usually a deformed cubical grid. Structured meshes are simpler than the non-structured ones, and require less computer memory, as their coordinates can be calculated, rather than explicitly stored.

Data is extracted from satellite images, where the heights are given certain points referenced by their latitude and longitude coordinates. The geographic region is represented by a regular tessellation that is determined by subdividing the total area into sufficiently small rectangular subareas, each represented by one cell of the tessellation (Figure 1). This subdivision is done according to a cell size established by the geophysics or ecology analyst and it is directly associated to the refinement degree of the tessellation.

In order to categorize the regions of each layer, the ICTM Model performs sequential phases,

Figure 2. The ICTM categorization process

where each phase uses the results obtained from the previous one. The tessellation is represented as a matrix with n_r rows and n_c columns. And the phases of the ICTM Model are schematically presented in Figure 2.

In topographic analysis, usually there are too many data, most of which is geophysical irrelevant. We then take, for each subdivision, the average value of the heights at the points supplied by radar or satellite images. The first phase of the categorization process involves the input data reading (average values) and these data are stored on a matrix called *Absolute Matrix*.

We are interested in comparing the values corresponding to different cells, so we are not interested in absolute values, only in relative ones. The categorization proceeds to the next phase, to simplify the data of the matrix, we normalize them by dividing each element by the largest of these values of the Absolute Matrix.

Considering that the data extracted from the satellite images are very accurate, the errors contained in the *Relative Matrix* come from the discretization of the region into tessellation cells. Due to this fact, Interval Mathematics techniques (Moore, 1979) are used to control the errors associated to the cell values (examples of the advantages of using intervals to solve similar problems can be seen in (Coblentz *et al.*, 2000) and (Kearfort & Kreinovich, 1996). In the next phase, two *Interval Matrices* are created, in which the interval values for *x* and *y* coordinates are stored.

The creation of the *Status Matrix* is the most important phase of the entire process. In this phase, all cells are compared to its neighbors in four directions. For each cell, four directed de-

clivity registers - *reg.e*(east), *reg.w* (west), *reg.s* (south) and *reg.n* (north) - are defined, indicating the admissible declivity sign of the function that approximates the function in any of these directions, taking into account the values of the neighbor cells.

For non-border cells: i) *reg.e=0*, if there is a non-increasing relief approximation function between the cell and its neighbor in the east (and in the same way towards the west, south and north directions); ii) *reg.e, reg.w, reg.s* and *reg.n=1*, otherwise. For the east, west, south and north border cells *reg.e=0, reg.w=0, reg.s=0* and *reg.n=0*, respectively.

Let $w_{reg.e}=1$, $w_{reg.s}=2$, $w_{reg.w}=4$ and $w_{reg.n}=8$ be weights to be associated to the directed declivity registers. The status matrix is defined as an $n_r \times n_c$ matrix where each entry is the value of the corresponding cell state, calculated as the value of the binary encoding of the corresponding directed declivity registers, given as $status_{cell}=(1 \times reg.e)+(2 \times reg.s)+(4 \times reg.w)+(8 \times reg.n)$.

Thus, for a given cell, the correspondent cell can assume one and only one state represented by the value $status_{cell} = 0...15$. A limit cell is defined as the one where the relief function changes its declivity, presenting critical points (maximum, minimum or inflection points). To identify such limit cells, we use a limit register associated to each cell.

The border cells are assumed to be limit cells. The conditions of non limiting cells are: the registers *reg.e* of the cell and of its neighbor in the west are equal *1*; the registers *reg.w* of the cell and of its neighbor in the east are equal *1*; the registers *reg.s* of the cell and of its neighbor in the north

Figure 3. Land use map of the region surrounded Lagoa Pequena (light blue: wetland, dark blue: water, yellow: crops and pasture, purple: transitional, light green: riparia forest, dark green: restinga forest, red: lagoon beaches, white: without classification)

are equal *1*; the registers *reg.n* of the cell and of its neighbor in the south are equal *1*; the registers *reg.e* of the cell and of its neighbor in the west and the registers *reg.w* of the cell and of its neighbor in the east are equal *0*; the registers *reg.s* of the cell and of its neighbor in the north and the registers *reg.n* of the cell and of its neighbor in the south are equal *0*. Otherwise, the cell is assumed to be a limiting cell.

Some Examples of Categorizations

This section presents some results on the *relief* and *land use* categorizations obtained for the region surrounded the lagoon *Lagoa Pequena* (Rio Grande do Sul, Brazil). Such analyzes are to be used for the environment characterization of that region, aiming to provide subsidies for its integrated preservation/management.

Figure 3 shows the location of the lagoon and a *land use* categorization of the region that surrounds it, which shall be combined with relief categorizations. For the LANDSAT image, shown in Fig. 4, the ICTM produced the relief categorization presented in Fig. 5, for the Digital Elevation Model (DEM), and in Fig. 6(a), for a 3D visualization of this categorization. Figure 6(b) shows the ICTM relief characterization given in terms of the state and limiting matrices, where a Pleistocene marine barrier can be distinguished.

In the categorization produced by the ICTM, the state of a cell in relation to its neighbors, concerning the declivity, is shown directly by arrows (see detail in Fig. 6(b)), which have been considered a very intuitive representation by ecologists, since most geographic information systems present this kind of result by the usual

Figure 4. LANDSAT image of the region surrounding Lagoa Pequena

color encoding of declivity, with no indication of direction.

Two aspects regulate the ICTM, namely, the spatial resolution of the DEM and the neighborhood radius of the cell. Thus, regions with an agglomeration of limiting cells can be studied in more detail by just increasing the resolution of altimetry data, or reducing the neighborhood radius.

MULTI-AGENT-BASED SIMULATION

The field of Multi-Agent Systems (MAS) is a well-established research domain in Artificial Intelligence (AI). It focuses on the resolution of problems by a society of agents. The distribution of the problem solving by several agents is necessary because these problems can be too complex or too large to be solved by a single process, or still, they may need knowledge from several different domains. One of the goals of these systems is to release the researchers from low-level technical-operational issues, allowing the researcher to concentrate his/her efforts on the relevant domain application level (Wooldridge, 1999).

The computer simulation of social phenomena is a promising field of research in the intersection between the social, mathematical and computer sciences. The first developments of computer simulations in the social sciences coincided with the first use of computers in academic research, in the early 1960s. By this time, computer simulation was essentially used as a powerful implementation of mathematical modeling (Gilbert & Troitzsch, 1999).

Multi-Agent-Based Simulation (MABS) is the union of MAS and Simulation and it is especially valuable to conciliate different interdisciplinary perspectives. Typically, it involves researchers from different scientific areas, such as social psychology, computer science, social biology, sociology and economics. The interdisciplinary character of MABS is an important challenge faced by all researchers, while demanding a difficult in-

Figure 5. ICTM DEM categorization

Figure 6. Relief categorizations: (a) ICTM 3D categorization; (b) ICTM status-limits categorization

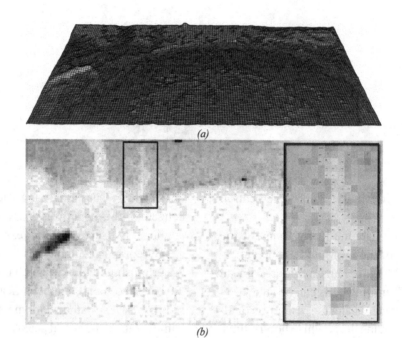

(a)

(b)

terconnection of different theories, methodologies, terminologies and points of view. The MABS field is increasingly characterized by the study, design and implementation of computational platforms to simulate societies of artificial agents.

MABS area has provided architectures and platforms for the implementation and simulation of relatively autonomous agents and it has contributed to the establishment of the agent-based computer simulation paradigm. The agent-based approach enhanced the potentialities of computer simulation as a tool for theorizing about social scientific issues. In particular, the notion of an extended computational agent, implementing cognitive capabilities, encourages the construction and exploration of artificial societies, since it facilitates the modeling of artificial societies of autonomous intelligent agents (Conte *et al.*, 1998).

The Negowat Project (Facilitating Negotiations Over Land and Water Conflicts in Latin American Peri-Urban Upstream Catchments: Combining Multi-Agent Modeling with Role-

Playing Games) was a project funded by the European Union (ICA4-CT-2002-10061) and it is a good example of MABS application in natural resource management. It studied the water problems in the São Paulo Metropolitan area (Brazil). This region is very complicated, because it is a region that includes nearly 8.000 Km² of physical area and 18 million inhabitants. Some works were developed in this project (Ducrot *et al.*, 2004).

CIRAD group (CIRAD, 2009) develops many other works using MABS technique. Barreteau *et al.* (2004) present an experiment made at the Senegal River Valley for issues of co-ordination among farmers. They also present a new approach, named Companion Modeling Approach that uses RPG (Role-Playing Games) and MABS. This approach can support collective decision processes in these systems. Etienne (2003) presents a framework where it simulates vegetation dynamics, fire propagation and agents' behavior in a game called Sylvopast. Guyot & Honiden (2006) present an alternative method, called Agent-Based

Figure 7. GMABS methodology

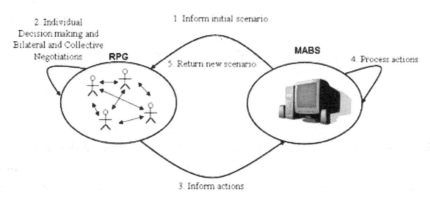

Participatory Simulations, where human beings control some software agents in a MABS. Briot *et al.* (2007) present SimParc Project, a research project aimed at methodological and computer-based support for participatory management of protected areas. The first case study is Tijuca National Park, in Rio de Janeiro, Brazil. The idea is to apply Agent-Based Participatory Simulations to help in the collective management of natural renewable resources, in order to promote biodiversity conservation and social inclusion.

GMABS Methodology

Role-Playing Games (RPGs) are a type of game where the players perform characters. These characters are created within a particular scenario (an environment), which organizes the players actions by determining the limits of what can or cannot be done (Bandini *et al.*, 2002). This way, RPGs are games where each player plays a role and takes decisions to reach its objectives. In fact, players use RPG as a "social laboratory", because they can try several possibilities, without real consequences (Barreteau *et al.*, 2003).

The use of MABS and RPG (isolated or in an integrated way) has been used in several works (Guyot & Honiden, 2006) and it shows interesting results, such as to join the dynamic capacity of MABS with the discussion and learning capacity of RPG techniques. We call the integration of

RPG and MABS as GMABS (Games and Multi-Agent-Based Simulation) methodology (Adamatti *et al.*, 2005).

Methodology steps, shown in Figure 7, are the following:

1. Players receive all the information about the game: the roles they can play, the actions and rules available to these roles, the common environment, the topological constraints. When the game starts, each player defines the role he is going to play. Each player knows then what actions he can perform, and the benefits and/or damages his action can cause to the common environment. The initial scenario defines also where the players are physically located in the common environment and what are their initial possessions (money, land, etc);

2. There are three different activities in this step:

    a. Players may reason and decide about individual actions that depend exclusively on themselves. As an example in the natural resources domain, land owners change their land use;

    b. Players have all the information necessary to initiate bilateral negotiations with other players. In order to do this, they may change information and make their decisions, according to the rules initially determined for their chosen roles. As an example in the natural resources domain, landowners can sell their lands. Normally, the duration of these two previous activities, which occur simultaneously, is defined in the beginning of the game;

c. After deciding about their individual actions and concluding the bilateral negotiations, the players can then negotiate about collective strategies for the next rounds. These collective strategies should benefit all players or just a subgroup of them. As an example in the natural resources domain, players can demand improvements on infrastructures, more jobs, tax values, etc. This negotiation process of collective strategies is just a "predisposition" to define future actions: players are not really obliged to keep their word and really use these strategies in the further rounds. This process is hence very important for each player to better understand the objectives and strategies of the other players;

3. Players inform to the MABS tool which individual actions were chosen and which bilateral negotiations were concluded;

4. Data are computed by the MABS tool: the latter actions modify the initial scenario. The properties of the environment are then modified, which implies in the modification of each player data;

5. The MABS tool returns the new scenario. If the time deadline of the game is not reached or the maximum number of rounds has not been achieved, return to step 2.

ViP-JogoMan: A Case Study in Natural Resources Management

We have chosen to implement a prototype of GMABS methodology in the natural resources management, specifically concerning water resources management. The most important aspect in the natural resources management is the negotiation process between the actors, because their objectives and strategies are different and many conflicts are generated. For example, a farmer and an industrial have different objectives and they do not necessarily reach a consensus very easily.

In fact, we have developed two prototypes for this domain: the first one, called JogoMan (Adamatti *et al.*, 2005), was based on GMABS methodology but did not use virtual players. The second one, called ViP-JogoMan (Adamatti *et al.*, 2007), used the GMABS methodology to insert virtual players.

Game Description

The roles of the players and the rules of the game are the same in both prototypes. They involve water, land use and urbanization pressure management of 3 different cities. In these games, there are four roles, each one having different goals:

*   Land Owner: a landowner has some land portions, each one with a land use type, such as forest or agriculture. For each different land use type, there are different values related to their maintenance and financial return. Owners can sell or buy their portions or they can change their land use. Landowners should ask mayors to build infrastructure in their cities.

*   Mayors: The game has different cities, each one having its mayor. The mayor goals are closely related to the city main activity (urban, agricultural, etc.). For example, if city "C" is a preservation area, then the player in the role of "Mayor C" should preserve this city. Mayors can invest on public infrastructure, such as portable water or sanitation networks, or they decide to build schools, hospitals or police headquarters.

Table 1.

Player	Profile	Objectives
Landowner	Economic	must save and earn money
	Ecologic	must improve the ecological situation of the region, has a big concern about reservoir pollution
Mayor	Social	must improve the quality of life of the population
	Economic	must improve the quality of life of people if the city has enough money for it
	Ecologic	must improve the ecological situation in the city
AguaPura Administrator	Rational	must improve water and sanitation networks with a rational use of money
	Ecologic	must improve water and sanitation networks
Migrant Representative	Economic	must allocate families without worrying about the social conditions of these families
	Social	must allocate families in good places, with facilities and near urban areas

- AguaPura Company Administrator: This role can invest on public infrastructure to improve water quality, as portable water and sanitation net.
- Migrant Representative: This role has a special role in the game, since he/she must allocate a number of new homeless families. These families arrive to the cities (urbanization pressure), and they can be allocated in settlements or in slums. The quality and/or quantity of water of the region is modified depending on where these families are placed.

Each player chooses his/her actions individually, but he/she should know that these actions have consequences to other players, because the quality and quantity of water depends on the overall land use and infrastructure. For example, if a mayor decides to decrease the land taxes for landowners that preserve the forests, various landowners can consequently decide to maintain their areas with forest or even decide to plant forest (reforestation). This action influences every player, because the water quality probably will improve. In another example, if a landowner decides to build an industry, the industry profit may be larger, but the water pollution will grow too.

Virtual Players

In the ViP-JogoMan prototype, the development of virtual players is one of the most important aspects. We have chosen the BDI architecture to model and implement the virtual players. The knowledge database of this architecture is defined in terms of players' beliefs, desires and intentions. In order to fill this knowledge base, we have mapped all the real players actions during the JogoMan prototype session tests. Our goal was to discover their objectives and strategies, aiming to build the virtual players knowledge database. Having this information in hand, we have analyzed and discovered a sequence of actions that each real player executed. This experiment was very interesting, because we could see that real players defined autonomous strategies during the game, even if we did not explain them a priori, before starting the JogoMan prototype tests, how they should choose their actions.

For each role, different objectives were discovered, and we have defined different behavioral profiles for the virtual players in Table 1.

These profiles were analyzed and evaluated by specialists in natural resources to verify if the possible strategies and actions were similar to real player activities. In order to do that, some specific variables of the game were analyzed, to measure if the proposed objective of each profile was reached. For example, when evaluating the behavioral profile Economic Land Owners, we have analyzed the amount of money in the cash box variable.

Tests and Preliminary Results

We have performed three test sessions with ViP-JogoMan prototype, involving both people and virtual players. We have defined three forms to evaluate our prototype: (i) pre and post questionnaires to be filled by real players; (ii) analysis of the behavioral profiles variables; and (iii) analysis of the message exchange flow between all players (virtual and/or real) during the negotiation process.

With the answers provided by the real players in the pre and post questionnaires, we have concluded that the ViP-JogoMan prototype gave the players interaction, entertainment and learning feelings. Moreover, real players did not discovery the virtual players easily in the game. In fact, real players just discovery some virtual players because virtual players chose their actions very quickly and real players needed more time to think and to choose theirs actions, during negotiations.

By the analysis of the behavioral profiles variables, we have concluded that the defined strategies for each type of profile reached the proposed objectives. For example, all virtual players with Economic behavioral profiles finished the game with high cash box values, as compared to other players.

Finally, by the analysis of the message exchange flow between players during the negotiation process, we have concluded that all players interacted a lot with each other, because the number of exchanged messages was significant. According to Peppet (2002), people feel more comfortable to express their opinions via Internet, because they do not have problems with shyness or prejudice. Another aspect important in ViP-JogoMan prototype is the storage of all negotiations between

players (concluded or not). McKersie & Fonstad (1997) have stated that in Internet negotiations every data and action is stored, and thus it is possible to analyze data with more attention and to better understand the negotiation process.

FUTURE DIRECTIONS AND CONCLUSIONS

The AI techniques are widely used for solving problems related to natural resources management. However, these strategies just solve problems or subset of problems in an isolated way, without realizing the whole problem, i.e., abstractions or simplifications are done from real model to computational models. If they were not connected, such approaches could leave out essential aspects of the environmental model that are relevant to the analysis.

Thus, the combination of several AI techniques could be an interesting solution, which could handle more complex environmental problems, because they could take advantage of each technique to develop a wide system. This area is known as Hybrid Intelligent Systems (HIS), which is a promising research field of modern artificial/computational intelligence concerned with the development of the next generation of intelligent systems (IJHIS, 2009).

A fundamental stimulus to the investigations of HIS is the awareness in the academic communities that combined approaches will be necessary if the remaining tough problems in artificial and computational intelligence are to be solved. Recently, HIS are getting popular due to their capabilities in handling several real world complexities involving imprecision, uncertainty and vagueness.

Despite the increase in HIS studies, with conferences and journals devoted to the topic, applications in natural resources management are rare. We believe that HIS must be applied also to ecological problems and they can provide valuable solutions.

Another possibility could be the integration of interval mathematics techniques to bring more robustness to the models based on the HIS in terms of imprecision, uncertainty and vagueness, because we can use the whole theoretical basis of interval mathematics as arithmetic operations, numerical methods, theorems, etc (Moore, 1979; Kearfort & Kreinovich, 1996).

In this work, we have presented how AI techniques could solve the three computational challenges related to natural resources management showed previously (Fuller *et al.*, 2007).

The cellular automata technique, as shown in the application presented in Section 3, can be understood as an admissible solution to the challenge of *data analysis*. Based on a simplified data representation it is possible to extrapolate the properties analyzed, for those areas with a lack of information, and global understanding emerges from local behavior.

The MABS technique, as shown in the application presented in Section 4, is a solution to the challenge of *optimization and control*, mainly to decision-making in conflicts resolution. The conflict resolution problem has a high complexity in the natural resources management, because it involves the definition of policies for different social groups.

The challenge of *data management* and *communication* was not the scope of this work. However, geographic information systems (GIS) are widely used in data management for large areas, typically used as input data models, and they use AI techniques such as Case-Based Reasoning (CBR) (Holt, 1999).

The AI techniques support the challenges resolution of natural resources management. Therefore, our main conclusion in this work is that the solution of such problems as a whole way will be possible just when these techniques could be integrated, using the HIS approach and mathematical and logic tools.

REFERENCES

Adamatti, D. F., Sichman, J., Bommel, P., Ducrot, R., Rabak, C., & Camargo, M. (2005). JogoMan: A prototype using multi-agent-based simulation and role-playing games in water management. In N. Ferrand (Ed.), *Joint Conference on Multi-Agent Modeling for Environmental Management, (CABM-HEMA-SMAGET)*, Bourg-Saint-Maurice, Les Arcs, France.

Adamatti, D. F., Sichman, J. S., & Coelho, H. (2007). Virtual players: From manual to semiautonomous RPG. In C. Frydman (Ed.), AI, Simulation and Planning in High Autonomy Systems (AIS) and Conceptual Modeling and Simulation (CMS). Joint to International Modeling and Simulation Multiconference 2007 (IMSM07), Buenos Aires – Argentina.

Aguiar, M. S., Dimuro, G. P., & Costa, A. C. R. (2004b). ICTM: An Interval Tessellation-Based Model for Reliable Topographic Segmentation. *Numerical Algorithms*, *37*(1-4), 3–11. doi:10.1023/B:NUMA.0000049453.95969.41

Aguiar, M. S., Dimuro, G. P., Costa, A. C. R., Silva, R. K. S., Costa, F. A., & Kreinovich, V. (2004a). *The multi-layered interval categorizer tesselation-based model*. In C. Iochpe & G. Câmara (Eds.), *VI Brazilian Symposium on Geoinformatics*, 22- 24 November, Campos do Jordão, São Paulo, Brazil (pp. 437–454).

Ahmad, S., & Simonovic, S. P. (2005). An artificial neural network model for generating hydrograph from hydro-meteorological parameters. *Journal of Hydrology (Amsterdam)*, *315*(1), 236–251. doi:10.1016/j.jhydrol.2005.03.032

Arbib, M. A. (1969). Theories of Abstract Automata. Upper Saddle River, NJ: Prentice-Hall.

Bandini, S., Manzoni, S., & Vizzari, G. (2002). *RPG-Profiler: a MAS for role playing games based tests in employee assessment.*

Barreteau, O., Bousquet, F., Millier, C., & Weber, J. (2004). Suitability of multi-agent simulations to study irrigated system viability: Application to case studies in the segal river valley. *Agricultural Systems, 80*(3), 255–275. doi:10.1016/j.agsy.2003.07.005

Barreteau, O., Le Page, C., & D'Aquino, P. (2003). Role-playing games, models and negotiation. *JASSS, 6*(2). Retrieved from http://jasss.soc.surrey.ac.uk/6/2/10.html

Briot, J. P., Guyot, P., & Irving, M. (2007). Participatory simulation for collective management of protected areas for biodiversity conservation and social inclusion. In C. Frydman (Ed.), International Modeling and Simulation Multiconference (IMSM07), Buenos Aires - Argentina.

Burks, A. W. (1970). Essays on Cellular Automata. University of Illinois Press, Urbana and Chicago.

Castro, M. B., Fernandes, L. G. L., Pousa, C., Méhaut, J. F., & Aguiar, M. S. (in press). NUMA-ICTM: A Parallel Version of ICTM Exploiting Memory Placement. In *PDSEC-09: The 10th IEEE International Workshop on Parallel and Distributed Scientific and Engineering Computing*, Roma.

Chen, Q., & Ye, F. (2008). *Unstructured cellular automata and the application to model river riparian vegetation dynamics.* In H. Umeo, S. Morishita, K. Nishinari, T. Komatsuzaki, & S. Bandini (Eds.), *Cellular Automata, 8th International Conference on Cellular Automata for Reseach and Industry (ACRI 2008)*, Yokohama, Japan, September 23-26, 2008 (LNCS 5191, pp. 337–344).

Chopard, B., & Lagrava, D. (2006). A cellular automata model for species competition and evolution. In S. E. Yacoubi, B. Chopard, & S. Bandini (Eds.), *Cellular Automata, 7th International Conference on Cellular Automata, for Research and Industry (ACRI 2006)*, Perpignan, France, September 20-23, 2006 (LNCS 4173, pp. 277–286).

CIRAD. (2008). *La recherche agronomique au service des pays du Sud.* Retrieved December 2008, from http://www.cirad.fr/

Coblentz, D. D., Kreinovich, V., Penn, B. S., & Starks, S. A. (2000). Towards reliable sub-division of geological areas: interval approach. In *Proc. of 19th International Conference of the North American. Fuzzy Information Processing Society (NAFIPS)* (pp. 368-372).

Conte, R., Gilbert, N., & Sichman, J. S. (1998). MAS and Social Simulation: A Suitable Commitment. In *Proceedings of the 1st International Workshop on Multi-Agent Systems and Agent-Based Simulation (MABS-98)* (LNAI 1534, pp. 1-9).

Coulthard, T. J., & De Wiel, M. J. V. (2006). A cellular model of river meandering. *Earth Surface Processes and Landforms, 31*(1), 123–132. doi:10.1002/esp.1315

Ducrot, R., Le Page, C., Bommel, P., & Kuper, M. (2004). Articulating land and water dynamics with urbanization: an attempt to model natural resources management at the urban edge. *Computers, Environment and Urban Systems, 28*(1-2), 85–106. doi:10.1016/S0198-9715(02)00066-2

Etienne, M. (2003). SYLVOPAST: a multiple target role-playing game to assess negotiation processes in sylvopastoral management planning. *JASSS, 6*(2). Retrieved from http://jasss.soc.surrey.ac.uk/6/2/5.html

Fuller, M. M., Wang, D., Gross, L. J., & Berry, M. W. (2007). Computational science for natural resource management. *Computing in Science & Engineering, 9*(4), 40–48. doi:10.1109/MCSE.2007.71

Gilbert, N., & Troitzsch, K. G. (1999). Simulation for the Social Scientist. London: Open University Press.

Goldberg, D. E. (1989). Genetic Algorithms in Search, Optimization and Machine Learning. Boston: Addison-Wesley.

Guyot, P., & Honiden, S. (2006). Agent-based participatory simulations: Merging multi-agent systems and role-playing games. *JASSS*, 9(4). Retrieved from http://jasss.soc.surrey.ac.uk/9/4/8.html

Holt, A. (1999). Applying case-based reasoning techniques in GIS. *International Journal of Geographical Information Science*, 13(1), 9–25. doi:10.1080/136588199241436

Holzman, B. A. (2009). Natural Resource Management. Retrieved May 2009, from http://bss.sfsu.edu/holzman/courses/GEOG%20657/env%20history%20lecture.pdf

IJHIS. (2009), *The International Journal of Hybrid Intelligent Systems*. Retrieved May, 2009, from http://ijhis.hybridsystem.com/

Iliadis, L. S., & Maris, F. (2007). An artificial neural network model for mountainous waterresources management: The case of cyprus mountainous watersheds. *Environmental Modelling & Software*, 22(7), 1066–1072. doi:10.1016/j.envsoft.2006.05.026

Kearfort, R. B., & Kreinovich, V. (1996). Applications of Interval Computations, Kluwer: Dordrecht.

Manoliadis, O. G., & Karantounias, G. (2003). Applications of genetic algorithms in water resources management - the koufos irrigation project in Greece. *Journal of Environmental Protection and Ecology*, (4),982–986.

McKersie, R. B., & Fonstad, N. (1997). Teaching negotiation theory and skills over the internet. *Negotiation Journal*, 13(4), 363–368.

Millington, I. (2006). Artificial Intelligence for Games. San Francisco: Morgan Kaufman.

Moore, R. E. (1979). Methods and Applications of Interval Analysis. Philadelphia, PA: Society for Industrial and Applied Mathematics.

Myhill, J. (1964). The Abstract Theory of Self-Reproduction. In M. D. Mesarovic (Ed.), Views on General Systems Theory (pp. 106-118). New York: John Wiley & Sons Inc.

Peppet, S. R. (2002). Teaching negotiation using web-based straming video. *Negotiation Journal*, 18(3), 271–283.

Picton, P. (2000). Neural Networks (2nd Ed.). New York: Palgrave.

Prato, T. (2009). Adaptive management of natural systems using fuzzy logic. *Environmental Modelling & Software*, 24(1), 940–944. doi:10.1016/j.envsoft.2009.01.007

Russel, S., & Norwig, P. (2003). Artificial Intelligence - A Modern Approach. Upper Saddle River, NJ: Prentice Hall.

Salski, A. (2007). Fuzzy clustering of fuzzy ecological data. *Ecological Informatics*, 2(1), 262–269. doi:10.1016/j.ecoinf.2007.07.002

Silva, R. K. S., Aguiar, M. S., Rose, C. A. F. D., & Dimuro, G. P. (2006a). Extending the HPC-ICTM geographical categorization model for grid computing. In B. Kagstrom, E. Elmroth, J. Dongarra, & J. Wasniewski (Eds.), PARA (LNCS 4699, pp. 850–859).

Silva, R. K. S., Aguiar, M. S., Rose, C. A. F. D., Dimuro, G. P., & Costa, A. C. R. (2006b). HPC-ICTM: a Parallel Model for Geographic Categorization. In *Proc. of The John Vincent Atanasoff Symposium*, Sofia, Bulgaria (pp. 143-148).

Wang, W., Zmeureanu, R., & Rivard, H. (2005). Applying multi-objective genetic algorithms in green building design optimization. *Building and Environment*, 11(40), 1512–1525.

Wolfram, S. (1994). Cellular Automata and Complexity. Reading, MA: Addison-Wesley.

Wooldridge, M. (1999). Intelligent agents. In G. Weiss (Ed.), Multiagent Systems - A Modern Approach to Distributed Artificial Intelligence (pp. 27-78). Cambridge, MA: The MIT Press.

Zadeh, L. A. (1965). Fuzzy Sets. *Information and Control, 8*(1), 338–353. doi:10.1016/S0019-9958(65)90241-X

Chapter 20
Applications of Self-Organizing Maps to Address Environmental Studies

M.P. Gómez-Carracedo
University of A Coruña, Spain

D. Ballabio
University of Milano-Bicocca, Italy

J.M. Andrade
University of A Coruña, Spain

R. Fernández-Varela
University of A Coruña, Spain

V. Consonni
University of Milano-Bicocca, Italy

ABSTRACT

An overview on the basic principles of Kohonen Self-Organizing Maps (SOMs), Counter-Propagation Artificial Neural Networks (i.e., a SOM with a supervised layer, called the Grossberg layer) and the so-called MOLecular Map of Atom-level Properties (MOLMAP) and their usefulness in analytical chemistry, particularly in the environmental field, was presented. Two case studies dealing with environmental studies of soil pollution by road traffic and sea pollution by spilled hydrocarbons were discussed in detail to exemplify different benefits derived from the use of these techniques.

INTRODUCTION

Artificial Neural Networks (ANNs) are increasing in uses related to several working areas within analytical chemistry and can be considered already as one of the most important tools in multivariate analysis. For this reason, several different ANN architectures and learning strategies have been proposed in literature so far (Zupan, 1994; Zupan and Gasteiger, 1993).

Kohonen Maps (or Self-Organizing Maps, SOMs, Kohonen, 1988) are one of the most

DOI: 10.4018/978-1-61520-893-7.ch020

popular Artificial Neural Networks nowadays. They mimic the action of a biological network of neurons, where each neuron accepts different signals from neighbouring neurons and processes them. Kohonen Maps are self-organising systems which are capable of solving unsupervised problems, such as clustering, exploratory analysis of data structure, and selection of relevant samples. Counter-Propagation Artificial Neural Networks (CP-ANNs) are essentially based on the Kohonen method, but combine characteristics from both supervised and unsupervised learning (Hecht-Nielsen, 1987; Zupan et al., 1995; Zupan et al., 1997). CP-ANNs are a development of Kohonen Maps, which can handle both qualitative and quantitative responses and, consequently, they allow to derive both classification and regression models. Both Kohonen Maps and CP-ANNs have been successfully applied in different research fields (Arakawa et al., 2006; Ballabio et al., 2007a; Cosio et al., 2006; Fermo et al., 2004; Marengo et al., 2006; Marini et al., 2004). Application of SOMs in the field of analytical chemistry is exploding and several examples can be cited just as a matter of example (a complete review is out of the scope of this chapter).

Lee and Scholz (2006) used SOMs to elucidate heavy metal removal mechanisms and predict heavy metal concentrations in experimental constructed wetlands treating urban runoff. Marini et al. (2007a) employed SOMs to authenticate extra virgin olive oil varieties. Samecka-Cymerman et al. (2009) applied SOMs to unravel distinct groups of soils and *Robinia pseudoacacia* leaves and bark, depending on traffic intensity. A map was developed and, then, used to recognize types of pollution in the same geographical area. Torrecilla et al. (2009) used SOMs and learning vector quantification network (LVQ) models to explore the identification of edible and vegetable oils and detect adulteration of extra virgin olive oil using the most common chemical substances in these oils, *viz.* saturated fatty (mainly palmitic and stearic) acids, oleic and linoleic acids. Fonseca

et al., (2006) showed that Kohonen SOMs classified samples of crude oils on the basis of gas chromatography-mass spectrometry (GC-MS) descriptors, in terms of geography origin, with a high degree of accuracy.

A reason that can explain the success of SOMs in analytical chemistry is their ability to solve both supervised and unsupervised problems. Besides, and very important from a pragmatic point of view, they are based on relatively easy-to-understand algorithms. Moreover, when dealing with supervised classification issues (a task that must be performed often by analytical chemists) CP-ANNs demonstrated that they can account for non-linear dependence between input and output vectors and, generally, can model classes with non-linear boundaries. On the other hand, since neural networks are non-parametric statistical methods based on adaptable parameters, most of the learning schemes require the use of a test set to optimise the structure of the model. Indeed, one of the major disadvantages of SOMs, as well as other ANN methods, is probably related to model optimisation, because this procedure suffers from some arbitrariness and can be sometimes computationally time-demanding.

Some refinements, modifications and specific implementations of the original SOM algorithm have been proposed in the literature in order to deal with specific issues (Marini et al., 2006 and 2007b; Melssen2007b et al., 2006 and 2007; Schmuker2007 et al., 2007). One of these is the so-called MOLMAP (MOLecular Map of Atom-level Properties) approach used for molecule description in the molecular modelling field (Zhang and Aires-de-Sousa, 2005 and 20072007). In this approach, the objects used for training the neural network were chemical bonds and the input variables were selected properties of bonds. By using a trained SOM, bonds in a molecule were mapped into the SOM and the pattern of activated neurons was interpreted as a fingerprint of the bonds of the molecule.

So far, the MOLMAP approach has been used for chemoinformatics studies (Gupta et al., 2006; Latino and Aires-de-Sousa, 2006) and, recently, adapted to handle multiway chemical data (Ballabio et al., 2007b). Multiway analysis is concerned with high order data, that is, data that can be arranged in multi-dimensional arrays. By means of multiway modelling, information related to each data dimension can be extracted and all the interrelations in-between dimensions can be considered at the same time. Applications of multiway analysis are getting common in several fields, such as multivariate statistical process control, metabonomics, kinetics, sensory analysis and analytical chemistry (Bro, 2006).

SOMs were also used to derive Topological Feature Maps, which are another approach for describing chemical information of molecules. Feature Maps are two-dimensional self-organizing maps of the molecular surface (Gasteiger et al., 1994), where any property of the surface can be projected into the map and visualized after scaling the property values into selected colours. Moreover, Comparative Molecular Surface Analysis (CoMSA) is a related approach that makes use of the Topological Feature Maps combined with multivariate regression methods to quantitatively predict molecular properties (Polanski and Walczak, 2000). SOMs were also used in a sort of nature-inspired approach that emulates neuro-computational principles of the olfactory system to encode, transform and classify chemical data (Schmuker and Schneider, 2007). First, molecules were encoded into a numerical representation by a number of selected molecular descriptors, and then the whole chemical space was represented by a limited number of 'virtual receptors', whose positions were determined by the positions of the SOM neurons.

In this chapter we aimed at presenting briefly the fundamentals of two applications of SOMs, that is, CP-ANN and MOLMAP, and showed two case studies where their potential to solve complex problems is demonstrated. We dealt with two environmental problems, intended to address different situations and slightly different objectives. Both case studies hold common objectives as unraveling the main patterns of the samples and justifying them, although there are also some differences, like the need to stress the behaviour of some samples on time or investigating whether the pollution patterns evolved along different sampling campaigns.

Theory of Self-Organizing Maps, Counter-Propagation ANN and MOLMAP

Notation

Scalars are indicated with italic lower-case characters (e.g. x_{ijk}) and vectors with bold lower-case characters (e.g. $\mathbf{x}$). Ordinary two-way arrays (matrices) are denoted by $\mathbf{X}$ ($I \times J$), where I is the number of objects and J the number of variables. The ijth element of the data matrix $\mathbf{X}$ is denoted as x_{ij} and represents the value of the jth variable for the ith object. Higher order arrays are denoted by $\underline{\mathbf{X}}$ ($I \times J \times K$), where I is the number of objects, J the number of variables on the second dimension (mode), and K the number of variables on the third mode. The ijkth element of $\underline{\mathbf{X}}$ is denoted by x_{ijk} where the indices run as follows: $i = 1,..., I; j = 1,..., J; k = 1,..., K$.

Self-Organizing Maps

A Self-Organizing Map or Kohonen Map is usually defined as a square toroidal space, which consists of a grid of N^2 neurons, where N is the number of neurons for each side of the square space. Toroidal basically means that each edge of the Kohonen Map has to be seen as connected with the opposite one. Each neuron contains J elements (i.e., weights), where J is the total number of input variables. The weights are initialised with random values (between 0 and 1) and updated on the basis of the I input vectors (i.e., objects).

Because objects are compared to neurons, the original data are usually range scaled between 0 and 1, in order to make them comparable to the network weights. Weights are updated for a certain number of times (called *training epochs*). Both the number of neurons and epochs to be used to train the map must be optimised by the user.

In each training epoch, one object at a time is selected randomly and introduced to the network. For each object (x_i), the most similar neuron (called *winning neuron*) is selected on the basis of the Euclidean distance. Then, the weights of the rth neuron (w_r) are changed as a function of the difference between their values and the values of the input object. This update (Δw_r) is scaled according to the topological distance from the winning neuron (d_r):

$$\Delta w_r = \eta \left(1 - \frac{d_r}{d_{max}+1} \right) \left(x_i - w_r^{old} \right) \qquad (1)$$

where η is the learning rate and d_{max} the size of the considered neighbourhood, that decreases during the training phase. The topological distance d_r is defined as the number of neurons between the considered neuron r and the winning neuron. The learning rate η changes during the training phase, as follows:

$$\eta = \left(\eta^{start} - \eta^{final} \right) \cdot \left(1 - \frac{t}{t_{tot}} \right) + \eta^{final} \qquad (2)$$

where t is the number of the current training epoch, t_{tot} is the total number of training epochs, η^{start} and η^{final} are the learning rate at the beginning and at the end of the training, respectively.

At the end of the training, objects are placed in the most similar neurons of the Kohonen Map. Consequently, data structure can be visualised and the importance of the variables in defining the data structure can be evaluated by looking at the Kohonen weights.

Counter-Propagation Artificial Neural Networks

Counter-Propagation Artificial Neural Networks (CP-ANNs) can be considered as an evolution of Kohonen Maps. CP-ANNs consist of two layers, a Kohonen layer and an output layer, where the information related to the experimental response to be modelled is collected (Figure 1). When dealing with supervised classification, the class vector containing the class labels of each sample (object) is unfolded into a matrix C, with I rows and G columns (the unfolded class information), where G is the number of classes; each entry c_{ig} of C represents the membership of the ith sample to the gth class expressed by a binary code (0 or 1). An example of class unfolding is shown in Table 1.

The weights of the rth neuron in the output layer (y_r) are updated in a supervised manner on the basis of the winning neuron selected in the Kohonen layer. Considering the class of each object i, the update is calculated as follows:

$$\Delta y_r = \eta \left(1 - \frac{d_r}{d_{max}+1} \right) \cdot \left(c_i - y_r^{old} \right) \qquad (3)$$

where d_r is the topological distance between the considered neuron r and the winning neuron selected in the Kohonen layer; c_i is the ith row of the unfolded class matrix C, that is, a G-dimensional binary vector representing the class membership of the ith object.

At the end of the network training, each neuron of the Kohonen layer can be assigned to a class on the basis of the output weights and all the objects placed in that neuron are automatically assigned to the corresponding class. CP-ANNs can recognize objects belonging to none of the class spaces. This will occur when objects become located in neurons whose output weights corresponding to the different classes do not much differ from each other, that is, the neuron cannot be assigned to a

Figure 1.

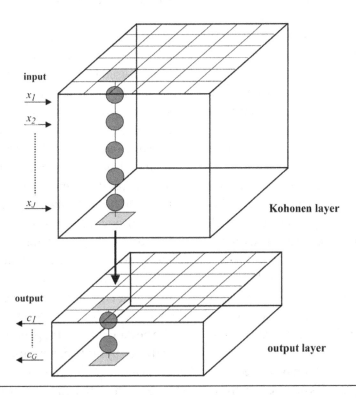

specific class, because it has the same probability to be assigned to every class.

There are several criteria to assign classes of samples to neurons. Here, two of them were employed. In the first case study, each neuron was assigned to a class on the basis of the maximum output weight in the Grossberg layer. By using this criterion, all the neurons were assigned classes.

In the second case study another approach was used which consisted in assigning classes only if the difference between the two maximum output weights of a neuron was larger than a threshold (set in advance). In this case, the neuron was assigned to the class associated to the maximum output weight. Otherwise, it was not assigned to any class.

Table 1.

Sample	Class vector	class unfolding				
		Class 1	Class 2	Class 3	....	Class G
1	1	1	0	0	....	0
2	2	0	1	0	....	0
3	3	0	0	1	....	0
4	3	0	0	1	....	0
....	....	....	....	....	....	....
I	G	0	0	0	....	1

To assess the performance of a counter-propagation network, several statistical indexes can be calculated. Most usually, they are (Frank and Todeschini, 1994):

- **Error rate (ER)**: measures categorical classification expressed as the percentage of incorrectly classified objects.
- **Non-error rate (NER)** is the percentage of the correctly classified objects.
- **Class Sensitivity:** describes the model ability to correctly recognize objects belonging to a class. Sensitivity equals 1 if all objects of the considered class are assigned to the class.
- **Class Specificity:** characterizes the ability of a class to reject objects of all the other classes. Specificity equals 1 if only objects of the considered class are assigned to the class.
- **Class Precision:** is the ratio between the number of samples classified correctly in the considered class and the total number of samples included in that class.

Cross validation is a good tool to evaluate the classification capabilities of a model when there are few samples in total (as the best option would be to prepare a validation set with a sufficiently large number of new samples). Cross validation consists of extracting a small subset of samples from the training set and developing a model with the remaining ones, then the left-out samples are projected into the model and the final responses evaluated. Next, the initially left-out samples enter the training set and another subset if extracted to be predicted once a new model is developed. This is repeated a number of times and a measure of the overall error in prediction can be obtained. In leave-one-out cross validation, each sample is left out in turn (the subset is constituted only by a sample). Cross validation was employed here in the second case study to validate the CPANN model.

MOLMAP Approach

In the original MOLMAP approach (Gupta et al., 2006; Latino and Aires-de-Sousa, 2006), the objects used for training the neural network were chemical bonds and the input variables were selected physical-chemical properties of bonds. All the bonds in all the molecules in the data set were used for network training and once the training has been completed, the SOM provides similarities among chemical bonds. Indeed, similar bonds became mapped into the same or closely adjacent neurons. By using a trained SOM, bonds in a molecule were mapped into the SOM and the pattern of activated neurons interpreted as a fingerprint of the bonds of the molecule. The map, that is, a matrix, was then transformed into a vector by concatenation of columns. This vector can be thought of as the pattern of neurons that are activated by the bonds existing in the molecule and considered as a fingerprint of molecule features.

Recently, the same approach has been applied to study multiway analytical chemical data (Ballabio et al., 2007b). In a three-way dataset, each object is represented by a two-way data matrix ($J \times K$; e.g., measured analytical variables $\times$ sampling campaigns) and, thus, I objects can be arranged in a three-way array $\mathbf{X}$ ($I \times J \times K$). In order to apply the MOLMAP procedure, data are first rearranged into a bi-dimensional matrix $\mathbf{X}_{arr}$ with $I*J$ rows ('*input vectors*') and K columns, so that the first $1,...,J$ rows of $\mathbf{X}_{arr}$ collect the information related to the first multiway sample, rows $J+1,...,J*2$ collect information on the second multiway sample, rows $J*2+1,...,J*3$ on the third one, and so forth.

The MOLMAP approach requires the Kohonen Map to be trained with the bi-dimensional matrix $\mathbf{X}_{arr}$. $I*J$ input vectors, each composed of K values, are presented to the map so that the so-called '*MOLMAP scores*' are calculated (one per sample) on the basis of the trained map. A trained Kohonen Map will show similarities between input vectors

Figure 2.

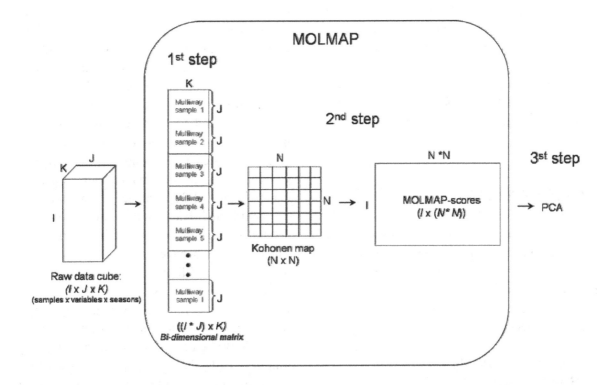

in the sense that similar input vectors are mapped into adjacent neurons. Therefore, a representation of the objects of the original multiway dataset can be obtained by projecting them onto the trained map, one at a time, and by mapping the J input vectors of each multiway sample. The pattern of activated neurons can be seen as a '*fingerprint*' of the object and constitutes its MOLMAP score.

From a technical point of view, the MOLMAP score is calculated as proposed in literature (Zhang and Aires-de-Sousa, 2005 and 20072007): each neuron of the SOM receives a value of 1 each time it is activated by the projected input vectors corresponding to a multiway sample and, in addition, a value of 0.3 is summed up to each neuron each time an inmediate neighbour is activated. This map is transformed into a vector (MOLMAP score) by concatenating the columns of the Kohonen Map: if the Kohonen Map is square and constituted by N neurons on each side, the MOLMAP score of

each object has dimension $N*N$ and the complete MOLMAP score matrix **M** has dimension $I \times N*N$, where I is the number of objects in the original three-way array **X**. Basically, **M** is a two-way matrix where the information of the original multiway dataset is compressed by codifying the input vector positions in the Kohonen Map.

Figure 2 depicts the process to perform a MOLMAP study. In this plot a principal components analysis (PCA) was applied to unravel the sample patterns hidden by the MOLMAP scores, which should be related to the original data cube. Other options exist to discover sample patterns but this was the approach presented in the case study due to its simple interpretation and fast optimization.

Software

Due to the increasing applications of both Kohonen Maps and CPANNs, several toolboxes for calculating supervised and unsupervised SOMs were proposed in literature and are at public disposal (Aires-de-Sousa, 2002; Ballabio et al., 2009; Kuzmanovski and Novič, 2008; Vesanto et al., 2000). In this work, calculations were performed by JATOON (http://www.dq.fct.unl.pt/staff/ jas/ jatoon), a MOLMAP toolbox (http://michem.di-sat.unimib.it/chm/ download/softwares.htm) and in-house programs to perform CP-ANN studies.

CASES OF STUDY

Two cases of study were chosen to show different environmental issues that can be faced nowadays using different implementations of Kohonen neural networks. To simplify exposition they will be presented sequentially despite they hold some common objectives.

Case Study 1: Analysis of Soil Pollution

Road traffic contributes significantly to air pollution in urban areas, generating particulate matter, aerosols and heavy metals around roads (Baycu et al., 2006; Campo et al., 1996;). Deposition of these heavy metals on vegetation and soil may influence the elemental composition and physiology of leaves (Baycu et al., 2006; Samecka-Cymerman et al., 2009) and, ultimately, the health of animals and human beings. Therefore, soil contamination and its monitoring is an important topic in today's environmental protection and remediation.

In this study four sampling campaigns (one per annual season) were carried out at a medium-size city (A Coruña, NW Spain, aprox 500,000 inhabitants in the metropolitan area), to assess the levels of nine heavy metals (Cd, Co, Cu, Cr, Fe, Mn, Ni, Pb and Zn) on public gardens, surroundings of a main road accessing the city (aprox. 100,000 vehicles per day –vpd-) and a highway (aprox. 50,000 vpd). In addition, three typical physicochemical parameters (humidity,

pH and loss on ignition - LOI) were determined (Carlosena et al., 1995 and 19981998). Each sampling was performed on 92 sampling points. In the AP9 highway, both roadside soils and perpendicular transects (5 to 100 m distance from the roadside) were considered: samples 1-2, 6-11, and 15-18 were collected at the border of the highway; samples 3-5 and 12-14 were from uncultivated transects, and samples 19-26 were from transects within cultivated fields. Samples 27-36 were from the roadside border of a main avenue of the city (samples 30 and 31 pertained to two transects on uncultivated fields), and samples 37-92 were taken at urban gardens (slots, gardens, parks, etc.). Three samples behaved always as outliers and they were deleted from the chemometric studies presented hereinafter. So, a total of 89 samples were considered. In the following, samples will be identified by a letter and a sequential number. Letters A, B, C and D will denote roadsoil highway samples, roadsoils from the main avenue of the city, city gardens and transects of the highway, respectively. It was expected initially that each type of samples would give rise to a different group, or class, of samples because of the different pollution levels their sampling locations suffered. Nevertheless, in environmental studies this can not be taken for granted and so patterns were extracted using SOMs.

Pattern Recognition by Kohonen SOMs

SOMs were developed autoscaled data. Note that an additional 0 to +1 scaling was performed internally by the SOM to approximate the magnitude of the (pre-processed) experimental values to the initial random weights of the neurons. Despite the results presented in the discussion of this case study corresponded to the most satisfactory models, many more assays were done varying the number of epochs, number of neighbours, and the size of the upper map.

Only a sampling campaign (the first, autumn) will be discussed in detail to illustrate the usefulness of the SOMs to unravel hidden patterns from complex environmental datasets.

After different preliminary studies, the best results (according to the original location of the samples) were obtained for a 10×10 topology, trained during 100 iterations (epochs). In effect, a good separation among four groups of samples was observed (Figure 3a). The 'pure' highway roadside samples (coded 'A') and transects (coded 'D') became well differentiated. Further, 'urban' samples (i.e., samples from the main avenue, coded 'B', and city gardens, coded 'C'), were rather well differentiated from the highway-related ones. Despite the four groups were separated, several samples occupied an intermediate position, sometimes not very well defined, and they required some further chemical/environmental justification/study.

It is worth reflecting briefly at this point on the use scientists should make of pattern recognition tools like SOMs. This is of special concern in problems where experimental data might be affected by many different uncontrolled phenomena, which is the common case in environmental studies. In effect, although the scientist knows the place where the sample was taken (e.g. a garden at a city) and he/she might expect a particular pollution profile, there are many uncontrolled physical and chemical effects (related to, e.g., the specific location of the slot, rain and/or irrigation, gardening works, accumulation of dust and heavy metals, etc.) which might change totally such an 'expected' profile. Hence, one has to accept that the geographical location of a sample would not necessarily be the main factor to classify it. Thus, samples may be classified 'correctly' even when they are in groups which do not correspond to their original location. The reason being, of course, the concentrations of pollutants they exhibit. As a conclusion, the evaluation of the results of the SOMs should consider not only the 'raw clustering' yielded by the SOM, but also a detailed study of each, apparently, 'wrong' sample.

Going back to the case study, samples C72 and C73 (two city gardens) became almost mixed with samples from the highway transects. The reason is that those gardens had been constructed very recently and they exhibited, essentially, the natural characteristics of their parent soil, with almost no influence of traffic (they had very low traffic-related metal concentrations) and high values for Co and Fe (*ca.* 15 mg/kg and 42 mg/g, respectively), compared to most gardens which exhibited contents of Co and Fe *ca.* 5 mg/kg and 20 mg/g, respectively. Besides, it was found that their lithological composition was very similar to that of the highway soils. Another city garden, sample C69, was classified as from the main avenue of the city due to its high metallic contents (particularly, Cu, *ca.* 70 mg/kg, and Pb, *ca.* 400 mg/kg), which could be caused by its proximity to a petrol station. Samples B30 and B31 corresponded to transects of the main avenue of the city, which were less affected by traffic pollution than their counterparts because of their distance to the border (20 m). In effect, the concentrations of metals typically related to road traffic for these two samples were low-medium (e.g., 25 and 90 mg/kg of Cu and Pb, respectively) and, so, they got included in the region that the SOM assigned to city gardens. Therefore, all those samples (B30, B31, C69, C72 and C73) seemed to be classified correctly from an environmental viewpoint, according to the amount of metals they contained.

Samples A16 and D12 became assigned to a neuron in an intermediate position between the two regions the SOM attributed to the highway and the transects. As they became adjacent to their correct groups, this seemed not a critical failure of the SOM. Sample A15 (from the highway) was considered as a transect, without a sound reason justifying it.

Although these explanations are fine for a general report, environmentalists would like some insights on the experimental variables responsible for the sample patterns visualized above. A straightforward way to achieve them is studying

Figure 3.

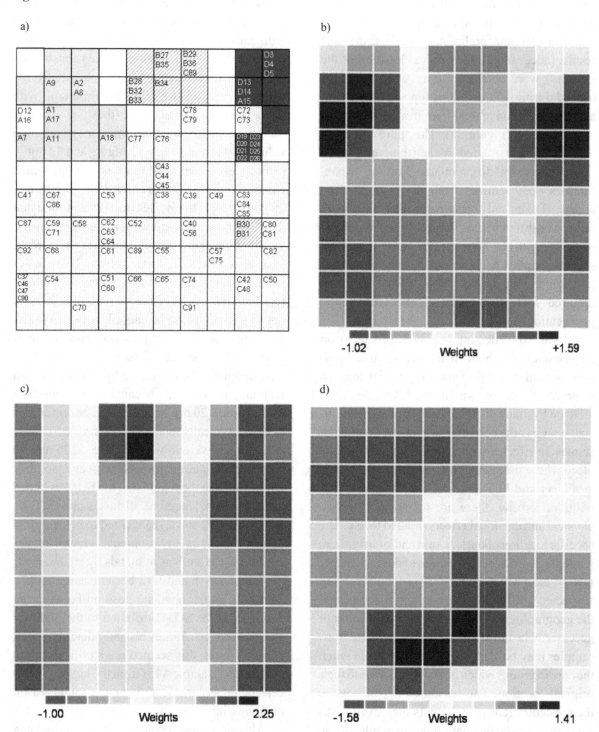

a)

b)

c)

d)

graphically the layers of weights of the neurons. A layer of weights may display a pattern that may

be related to the final distribution of the groups of samples on the map. Figure 3b shows the weights of the 5th level of the SOM detailed above. There it was observed that neurons with high weights corresponded to neurons where highways and transects got clustered. Hence, it was concluded that the 5th analytical variable (Fe) had in general high values for the highway-related samples (*ca.* 30-40 mg/g). The 2nd level of the SOM (Co) yielded a very similar pattern, though slightly less defined. Level 8 (Pb) seemed closely related to the samples of the main avenue of the city (Figure 3c) whereas level 10 (humidity) characterized the city gardens (Figure 3d), along with level 7 (low values for Ni). Besides, high weights at the 7th level (Ni) became associated to the highway.

The results presented in this section illustrate that SOMs provided a satisfactory visualization of the samples and of the relationships between the experimental variables and the classes of samples. In order to 'validate' the results, they were compared to previous studies where well-known and established multivariate methods had been used (Andrade et al., 2007; Carlosena et al, 1995 and 19981998) and an excellent agreement was observed. This demonstrated that SOMs constituted a reliable alternative to perform pattern recognition and that inspection of their layers of weights can yield insightful conclusions to characterize groups of samples by specific experimental values of the original variables.

Classification by CP-ANNs

After several preliminary studies, the most satisfactory results (according to the original location of the samples) were obtained by a 10x10 map, trained during 150 iterations (epochs) and autoscaling the raw data. The nets were optimized using cross validation and studying the error rate, non-error rate, class sensitivity, class specificity and class precision statistics defined above. In effect, a good separation among the four groups of samples was observed (Figure 4a). The highway roadsoil samples (A) and transects (D) became well differentiated. Further, urban samples (i.e.,

codes B and C), were rather well differentiated from the highway-related ones. A major difference with respect to what happened in the SOM (section above) was that group D got divided in two parts. The upper one (upper, left corner) considered the samples from uncultivated transects, whereas the other one in the middle considered those from the cultivated ones (plus sample D12 which was from an uncultivated transect).

Samples C72 and C73, two city gardens, became adjacent to the cultivated highway transects, which was correct from a chemical point of view (the reason was already explained in the section above). Samples B30 and B31 corresponded to transects of the main avenue of the city, which were less affected by traffic pollution (as mentioned above) and, therefore, became located correctly with the samples from the gardens. Sample A7 was classified in a neuron which occupy a borderline position with the 'pure' highway samples. The neuron was assigned to the transects because of its proximity to two samples from this group (see Figure 4b), accordingly this misclassification seemed not critical.

Figure 4b shows the weights of the 2nd level of the CP-ANN, which corresponded to cobalt, together with the codes of the classes assigned at the Grossberg layer. It was seen that high weights were associated to neurons where highway roadsoils and transects got clustered. Hence, it was concluded that Co had in general characteristic high values for the highway-related samples (*ca.* 10-25 mg/kg; along with samples C72 and C73 mentioned above). A similar pattern was observed for the 4th and 5th levels of weights (Chromium and Iron, respectively).

The statistical indexes explained above were calculated to assess the behaviour of the model in a more objective way. For a training considering the overall set of samples and considering the four geographical locations, NER and ER were 98.88% and 1.12%, respectively. The following table shows the class precision, sensitivity and specificity parameters for the calibration set

Figure 4.

a)

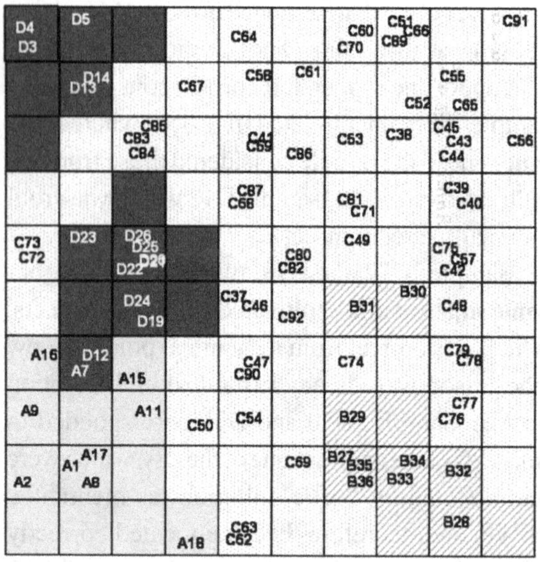

b)

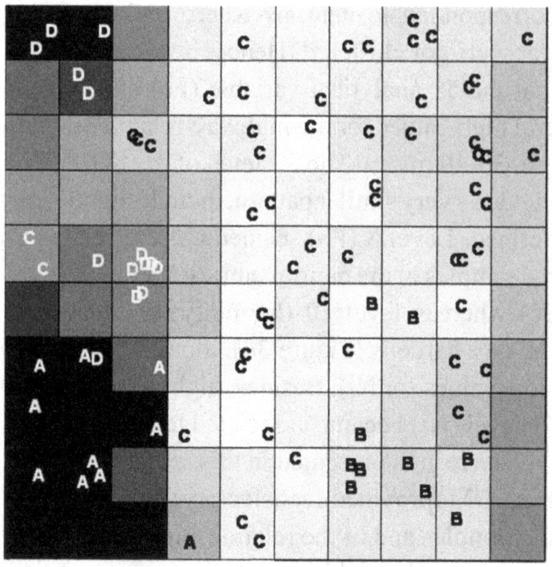

and it demonstrates that the four classes were modelled quite well and that only the highway roadsoils and transects either received undue samples (specificity) or lack of some of their own samples (sensitivity). Note that the percentage of incorrectly classified samples was only 1.12%.

As CP-ANN is a classification technique, we were interested not only on getting a model using all the samples but to evaluate how well such a model would predict the class of new samples. This was studied by cross-validation. When only 4 groups of samples were considered (a proportional number of samples of each class was included in each group), results were also good: NER=91.01%, ER=8.99%. When leave-one-out cross validation (CV-LOO) was used, similar results were obtained (see table 2).

This demonstrated that CP-ANN can be used as a reliable technique to classify new samples taken on the geographical region under study in one of the four main classes of roadsoils, which in turn showed different pollution patterns due to –mainly- the different road traffic characteristics.

CASE Study 2: Identification and Monitoring of Oil Spillages

World economy is dependent on the exploration, production, transportation, and refining of petroleum. The demand for petroleum continues to increase as developing countries move from agricultural- to industrial-based economies (Douglas et al., 2007). To cope with the demand for oil over the next two decades, the world oil supply of crude oil increased by over 45 million barrels/day and most of it will be transported by large ship tankers (NRC, 2003). Thus, the risk of accidental discharges of petroleum to the environment – either as crude oil from production operations or as marine fuels from the discharge of maritime cargo vessels- augmented.

Worldwide oil spillages harm deeply the ocean environment. Hundreds of different species of plants and animals are constantly threatened and in great danger because of the harmful effects of some hydrocarbons. Furthermore, in coastal and intertidal areas, oil pollution is a critical issue for

Table 2.

	Parameters/Classes	Class 1 (highway roadsoils)	Class 2 (main avenue)	Class 3 (city gardens)	Class 4 (highway transects)
Calibration (ER=1.12%)	**Class Precision**	1	1	1	0.9333
	Class Sensitivity	0.9000	1	1	1
	Class Specificity	1	1	1	0.9867
CV (4 groups) (ER=8.99%)	**Class Precision**	0.7000	0.9000	0.9643	0.8462
	Class Sensitivity	0.7000	0.9000	0.9818	0.7857
	Class Specificity	0.9620	0.9873	0.9412	0.9733
CV-LOO (ER=8.99%)	**Class Precision**	0.6667	0.9091	0.9818	0.7857
	Class Sensitivity	0.6000	1	0.9818	0.7857
	Class Specificity	0.9620	0.9873	0.9706	0.9600

fisheries, seafood and sea farms. Nowadays, oil spills from tankers either accidental or intentionally man made (i.e., illegal cleaning of bilges, release of ballast, etc.) continue to be a hot topic and of great concern in many countries. Particularly, Europe has 89,000 kilometres of coastline whose protection against accidental wrecks or deliberate pollution is a keystone of European Union (EU).

The strategic location of the Galician coast (NW Spain) caused repeated threats of hydrocarbon pollution, including accidental oil spills from tankers, undue ballast releases and residues of ship bilges cleanups. The wreckage of the ship *Prestige-Nassau* was the fifth large oil tanker spillage occurred at the Galician coast since 1970 and, as it happened with other recent disasters (e.g. *Cosco Busan*, at San Francisco Bay, releasing 220 oil tons, and *Hebei Spirit*, South Corea, pouring ca. 10,000 oil tons) caused important environmental damages. The oil tanker *Prestige* became damaged in a heavy storm on the 13th of November of 2002, suffering a breach on her hull. On Tuesday, 19th November, the vessel split in two halves and sank off the Galician coast. She carried out ca. 77,000 tons of a heavy fuel oil, of which circa 63,000 tons were released to the marine ecosystem. This was a very viscous product, almost insoluble, with an oil-characteristic smell,

difficult to disperse and with a pronounced trend to form stable emulsions. The dramatic short-term environmental impact affected more than 2,500 km of coastal areas from N Portugal to SW France, and it boostered the international scientific community to study the spillage.

The fingerprinting of crude oil spills is a very complex analytical problem as many of their components are present in very low quantities. When oils enter the environment a plethora of processes occur. The particular evolution an oil undergoes while it is floating and drifting on the sea is affected by many physicochemical processes which, in turn, are strongly dependent on the particular composition of the spilled product and the physical, marine and solar conditions. These phenomena are collectively known as weathering and include evaporation, dissolution, dispersion, photooxidation and biodegradation (Douglas et al., 2002). Moreover fuel persistence, toxicity and bioavailability are strongly determined by its particular composition as well.

Four typical crude oils (Ashtart, Brent, Maya and Sahara Blend) and two heavy fuel oils (a IFO fuel and the *Prestige*'s fuel oil) were selected for this study. All products were released (ca. 500 mL) on a special metallic container equipped with a closed-circuit water pump to agitate continuously

Figure 5.

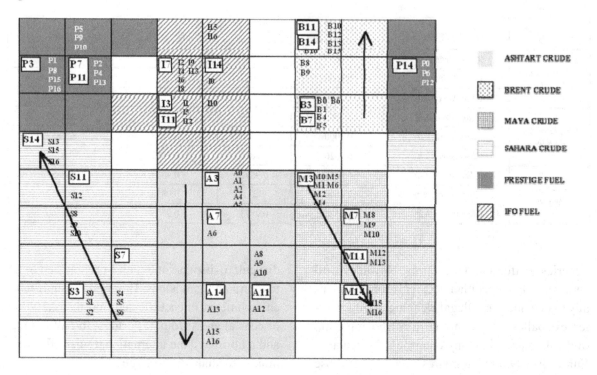

the system by pouring water over the oil–water surface so that washing, emulsion, wave agitation and sea movement were simulated as close as possible. The container was filled with sea water (60–70 L) and the oils weathered for three and a half months. Samples identified as 0 in the figures correspond to original unweathered fuels. The other samples were numbered sequentially. The letter before the number indicates the type of product (e.g., A=Ashtart, B=Brent, etc.).

Hence, this case study considered 102 samples, corresponding to the unweathered and weathered samples of all products, on which 50 polycyclic aromatic hydrocarbons (PAHs, many of which are carcinogenic) were measured using the analytical technique known as CG-MS (Gas Chromatography-Mass Spectrometry) (Fenández-Varela et al., 2005, Fresco-Rivera, 2007).

Pattern Recognition by Kohonen SOM

Different assays were made varying the topology of the SOMs from 8x8 to 10x10 neurons, and from 50 to 200 epochs.

The best clustering results were obtained for a 9x9 topology, trained during 100 epochs, and autoscaled data. In effect, Figure 5 showed a good separation between the six products (recall the toroidal topology of the SOMs). They became differentiated clearly in separate regions, likely according to the total concentration of PAHs; which were 16,450; 16,150; 15,650; 14,350; 13,580 and 8,060 µg/g for Sahara, Prestige, Brent, Ashtart, IFO and Maya, respectively.

In addition, samples ordered within each group according to the extent of their weathering, from the first almost unweathered to the oldest more weathered ones (e.g., from A0 to A16; S0 to S16, etc.). It is worth noting that each product presented a slightly different behaviour. The weathering pattern for each was resumed by arrows in Figure 5, where the tips point towards the most weathered samples. The IFO and *Prestige* fuel oils did not show a definite trend, as expected due to their heavy and recalcitrant nature (they were heavy distillates, almost without volatile components, constituted by complex molecules, not easy to degrade). The other products became ordered, although in different directions. Thus, lightest products (Brent and Sahara) had the most weathered samples on the upper part of the map, whereas the heaviest ones (Ashtart and Maya) became ordered in the opposite direction.

In order to evaluate the adequacy of the results, a small set of four samples ('*test set*') of each product had been initially left out of the training set and they were projected into the model. These samples were selected systematically so that each one represented a part of the weathering process. All of them corresponded to weathering stages in the middle of the overall weathering period, neither at the very beginning of the ageing, nor at its end. Figure 5 showed that such testing samples (identified by labels surrounded by squares) were projected correctly within the particular group they belonged to. Further, they were projected in locations which corresponded to their expected (already known) age, which can be visualized by the sequential numbers in the labels.

This constituted a very interesting result because it demonstrated that the SOM was capable not only of differentiating between the six products (even when they were weathered) but of modelling what occurred within each. Further, the model seemed trustworthy after testing it with a small set of samples.

Pattern Recognition by MOLMAP Approach

Despite the typical arrangement of the 3-way experimental data would be a cube of dimension $17 \times 50 \times 6$ (i.e., samples × analytical variables × products studied), we found out the best results using a data cube of dimension $17 \times 6 \times 50$, that

is, samples × products × analytical variables. As in the previous section, four samples (or weathering stages) per oil product were left out to be finally projected into the estimated model and, thus, evaluate the usefulness of the models. Hence, the learning set was of dimension ($13 \times 6 \times 50$), whereas the test set was composed of four samples ($4 \times 6 \times 50$). The latter was not used at all to develop models. They were coded 's' and 'v' on the figures, respectively.

The unfolding yielded a ($(13*6) \times 50$) or 78 × 50 bi-dimensional matrix. Then, calculation of the Molmap-scores was carried out. To get them, raw data were first range-scaled (from 0 to 1) in the variables-dimension. The scaled unfolded data were input to an inner MOLMAP-SOM (7 x 7 topology, 100 epochs).

Figure 6 presents the Kohonen top map where all the 78 calibration samples and 24 test samples (the original 3-way test set ($4 \times 6 \times 50$) was unfolded to a (24×50) matrix) were projected. There, the 78 and 24 input vectors were labelled on the basis of the class membership of the related samples. The input vectors were coded in the following way:

1. a initial number to indicate the product to which the input vector is related: 1=Ashtart, 2=Brent, 3=Maya, 4=Sahara, 5=IFO and 6=Prestige;
2. a letter: 's' or 'v' to indicate training or test samples, respectively;
3. a sequential number to indicate the stage of the weathering process, from 0=unweathered sample to 16=the most weathered one.

It was observed that all products became well separated, except for the two most weathered samples of the Asthart crude oils (i.e., codes 1-s15 and 1-s16), which got mixed with the most weathered samples of the Maya crude oil (i.e., codes 3-s13, 3-s15 and 3-s16, placed in the left corner of Figure 6). Despite the input vectors related to the six products gave rather compact

Figure 6.

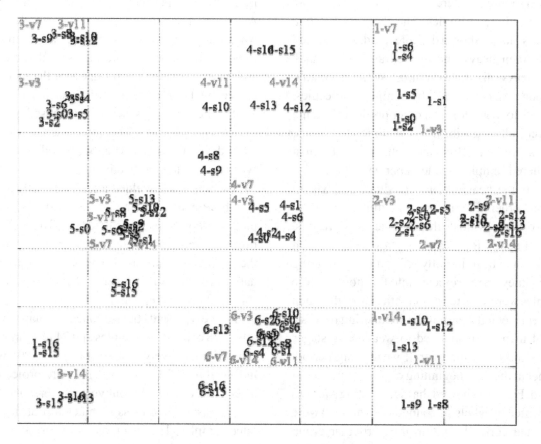

groups, a good ordering of the samples with their weathering stage can be visualized and characterized by several neurons (recall the cyclic nature of the SOMs).

In the next paragraphs the ordering of each class and the chemical interpretation of the associated weights is given. To simplify the explanations and the visualization, the neurons characterizing each class will be identified by two numbers defining their position in the top map presented in Figure 6. Thus neuron (2,5) corresponds to the neuron located at the second row and fifth column.

Group 1 (Ashtart) was characterized by neurons (1,6), (2,6), (6,6), (7,6) along with (6,1). The last one is associated to the two most weathered samples that got mixed with product 3 (Maya). The profiles of the weights of the first four neurons showed a clear predominance of the original C_2-

benzothiophene and C_4-dibenzothiophene PAHs, respectively (i.e., variables 13 and 28; Figure 7a), whereas the last neuron was more related to the 15th variable (i.e., C_4-benzothiophene) than to the 13th one, although this can be attributed to the influence of the Maya samples. Neuron (2,6) clustered all samples with a slight weathering (codes from 0 to 5), whereas neuron (6,6) contained weathered samples (codes from 10 to 14) but for the most weathered ones that are located with the Maya samples, as early noted.

Group 2 (Brent) got associated to neurons (4,6)–the least weathered samples–and (4,7)–the weathered samples–. These neurons had characteristic small weights for almost all variables (Figure 7b), of which only variable 20 (fluorene) had a weight larger than 0.2 (recall that all weights

346

Figure 7.

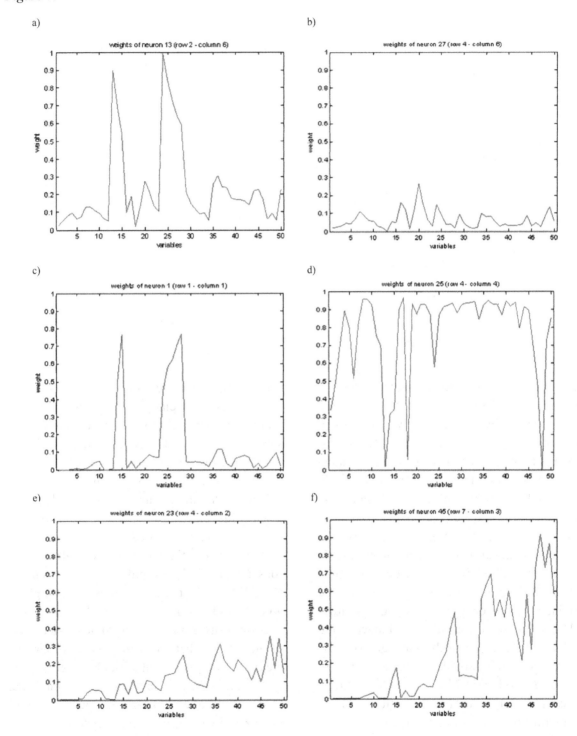

range from 0 to 1). The weights were even lower for the neuron with the most weathered samples.

Group 3 (Maya) was related to neurons (1,1), (2,1) and (7,1). The most important weights char-

Figure 8.

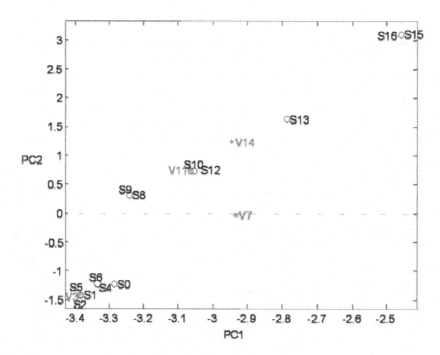

acterizing these neurons were essentially those of variables 15 and 28 (i.e., C_4-benzothiophene and C_4-dibenzothiophene, respectively), as it can be seen from Figure 7c, although with a different relative importance for neuron (7,1), where variable 28 was much more important. This is probably due to the fact that such molecule was much less prone to be degraded and, thus, pointed out those samples that suffered from strong weathering.

Group 4 (Sahara) spread from neuron (4,4) –least weathered samples– to neuron (1,4) –most weathered aliquots–. Those neurons showed large weights for many original PAHs (e.g., variables 8, 16 and 36; i.e., C_2-naphthalene, biphenyl and C_2-fluoranthene, respectively) although, noteworthy, very small for variables 13 (studied above), 18 and 48 (see Figure 7d). This might be due to the large depletion most PAHs suffered during weathering of this very light crude oil. Hence not only a variable can be used to characterize its ageing, but a suite of them.

Group 5 (IFO) restricted to neurons (4,2) and (5,2) –the last two samples of the ageing process–.

Their distinctive pattern consists on low values of the weights associated to variables 1 to 25 and more relevant weights for the heaviest molecules, see Figure 7e (e.g., PAHs numbered 36, 47 and 49; C_2-fluoranthene, benzo(g,h,i)perylene and dibenzo(a,h)anthracene, respectively). This was coherent with the fact that the IFO product was a heavy fuel oil, with small quantities of volatile species and hard to degrade.

Group 6 (Prestige) located essentially in neurons (6,4) and (7,3) –the oldest samples–. Similar to the IFO product, these neurons were weighted almost only by the heaviest original PAHs (Figure 7f), although the weights were almost twice those of the IFO (so that both products got differentiated). The most relevant variables were 34, 35, 36, 47 and 49 (i.e., fluoranthene, C_1-fluoranthene, C_2-fluoranthene, benzo(g,h,i)perylene and dibenzo(a,h)anthracene, respectively).

It is worth noting that all test samples were projected correctly into the top map (considering their weathering stage), being located near the products they belong to.

Then, a PCA was applied to the MOLMAP-scores; no further scaling was performed at this stage. Two principal components accounted for 87.7% of the total variance. Figure 8 revealed a nice ordering of the 13 weathering stages of the training set (from the first weathering stages –from 0 to 6– to the last ones –15 and 16) in the PC1-PC2 subspace. Unfortunately, the first stages could not be differentiated well, although this seemed reasonable because of the small timeframe where the first 6 samples were obtained (i.e., three days), which is not enough to get a definite pattern (evaporation of the lightest chains of hydrocarbons is the most significant fact within this period). Note that each point in the plot represents the average behaviour on time of the sequential samples for all six products and, so, this plot suggests that, on average, the different stages of the weathering process can be differentiated (despite for Prestige and IFO this might be not absolutely true, as seen in the previous studies). Projection of the test samples in this model yielded good results as they became located in a region that can be logically associated to their age (see Figure 8, samples coded with 'v'). The weathering stage v7 (used only for testing) became slightly displaced from the apparent linear behaviour, although this can be justified by the complex chemical processes that may occur with the varying atmospheric conditions.

As a conclusion, the MOLMAP strategy was capable of unravelling insightful phenomena present on the 3-way data set. Trends were observed among the samples, which were related to specific behaviours of some analytical variables.

REFERENCES

Aires de Sousa, J. (2002). JATOON: Java tools for neural networks. *Chemometrics and Intelligent Laboratory Systems*, *61*(1-2), 167–173. doi:10.1016/S0169-7439(01)00171-X

Andrade, J. M., Kubista, M., Carlosena, A., & Prada, D. (2007). 3-Way characterization of soils by Procrustes rotation, matrix-augmented principal components analysis and parallel factor analysis. *Analytica Chimica Acta*, *603*(1), 20–29. doi:10.1016/j.aca.2007.09.043

Arakawa, M., Hasegawa, K., & Funatsu, K. (2006). QSAR study of anti-HIV HEPT analogues based on multi-objective genetic programming and counter-propagation neural network. *Chemometrics and Intelligent Laboratory Systems*, *83*(2), 91–98. doi:10.1016/j.chemolab.2006.01.009

Ballabio, D., Consonni, V., & Todeschini, R. (2007b). Classification of multiway analytical data based on MOLMAP approach. *Analytica Chimica Acta*, *605*(2), 134–146. doi:10.1016/j.aca.2007.10.029

Ballabio, D., Consonni, V., & Todeschini, R. (2009). The Kohonen and CP-ANN toolbox: a collection of MATLAB modules for Self Organizing Maps and Counterpropagation Artificial Neural Networks. *Chemometrics and Intelligent Laboratory Systems*, *98*, 115–122. doi:10.1016/j.chemolab.2009.05.007

Ballabio, D., Kokkinofta, R., Todeschini, R., & Theocharis, C. R. (2007a). Characterization of the traditional Cypriot spirit Zivania by means of Counterpropagation Artificial Neural Networks. *Chemometrics and Intelligent Laboratory Systems*, *87*(1), 52–58. doi:10.1016/j.chemolab.2006.09.002

Baycu, G., Tolunay, D., Özden, H., & Günebakan, S. (2006). Ecophysiological and seasonal variations in Cd, Pb, Zn, and Ni concentrations in the leaves of urban deciduous trees in Istanbul. *Environmental Pollution*, *143*(3), 545–554. doi:10.1016/j.envpol.2005.10.050

Bro, R. (2006). Review on Multiway Analysis in Chemistry – 2000-2005. *Critical Reviews in Analytical Chemistry, 36*(3-4), 279–293. doi:10.1080/10408340600969965

Campo, G., Orsi, M., Badino, G., Giacomelli, R., & Spezzano, P. (1996). Evaluation of motorway pollution in a mountain ecosystem. Pilot project: Susa Valley (Northwest Italy) years 1990-1994. *The Science of the Total Environment, 189/190,* 161–166. doi:10.1016/0048-9697(96)05205-9

Carlosena, A., Andrade, J. M., Kubista, M., & Prada, D. (1995). Procrustes Rotation as a Way to Compare Different Sampling Seasons in Soils. *Analytical Chemistry, 67*(14), 2373–2378. doi:10.1021/ac00110a008

Carlosena, A., Andrade, J. M., & Prada, D. (1998). Searching for heavy metals grouping roadside soils as a function of motorized traffic influence. *Talanta, 47*(3), 753–767. doi:10.1016/S0039-9140(98)00117-9

Cosio, M. S., Ballabio, D., Benedetti, S., & Gigliotti, C. (2006). Geographical origin and authentication of extra virgin olive oils by an electronic nose in combination with artificial neural networks. *Analytica Chimica Acta, 567*(2), 202–210. doi:10.1016/j.aca.2006.03.035

Douglas, G. S., Owens, E. H., Hardenstine, J., & Prince, R. (2002). The OSSA II pipeline oil spill: the character and weathering of the spilled oil. *Spill Science & Technology Bulletin, 7*(3-4), 135–148. doi:10.1016/S1353-2561(02)00046-4

Douglas, G. S., Stout, S. A., Uhler, A. D., McCarthy, K. J., & Emsbo-Mattingly, S. D. (2007). Advantages of quantitative chemical fingerprinting in oil spill source identification. In Wang, Z. and Stout, S.A. Oil spill Environmental Forensics. Fingerprinting and source identification. Academic Press, United States of America.

Fermo, P., Cariati, F., Ballabio, D., Consonni, V., & Bagnasco, G. (2004). Classification of ancient Etruscan ceramics using statistical multivariate analysis of data. *Applied Physics. A, Materials Science & Processing, 79*(2), 299–307. doi:10.1007/s00339-004-2520-6

Fernández-Varela, R., Suárez-Rodríguez, D., Gómez-Carracedo, M. P., Andrade, J. M., Fernández, E., Muniategui, S., & Prada, D. (2005). Screening the origin and weathering of oil slicks by attenuated total reflectance mid-IR spectrometry. *Talanta, 68*(1), 116–125. doi:10.1016/j.talanta.2005.04.061

Fonseca, A. M., Biscaya, J. L., Aires-de-Sousa, J., & Lobo, A. M. (2006). Geographical classification of crude oils by Kohonen self-organizing maps. *Analytica Chimica Acta, 556*(2), 374–382. doi:10.1016/j.aca.2005.09.062

Frank, I. E., & Todeschini, R. (1994). The data analysis handbook. Amsterdam: Elsevier.

Fresco-Rivera, P., Fernández-Varela, R., Gómez-Carracedo, M. P., Ramírez-Villalobos, F., Prada, D., Muniategui, S., & Andrade, J. M. (2007). Development of a fast analytical tool to identify oil spillages employing infrared spectral indexes and pattern recognition techniques. *Talanta, 74*(2), 163–175. doi:10.1016/j.talanta.2007.05.047

Gasteiger, J., Li, X., Rudolph, C., Sadowski, J., & Zupan, J. (1994). Representation of Molecular Electrostatic Potentials by Topological Feature Maps. *Journal of the American Chemical Society, 116*(11), 4608–4620. doi:10.1021/ja00090a009

Gupta, S., Matthew, S., Abreu, P. M., & Aires-de-Sousa, J. (2006). QSAR analysis of phenolic antioxidants using MOLMAP descriptors of local properties. *Bioorganic & Medicinal Chemistry, 14*(4), 1199–1206. doi:10.1016/j.bmc.2005.09.047

Hecht-Nielsen, R. (1987). Counter-propagation Networks. *Applied Optics*, *26*(23), 4979–4984. doi:10.1364/AO.26.004979

Kohonen, T. (1988). Self-Organization and Associative Memory. Berlin: Springer Verlag.

Kuzmanovski, I., & Novič, M. (2008). Counter-propagation neural networks in Matlab. *Chemometrics and Intelligent Laboratory Systems*, *90*(1), 84–91. doi:10.1016/j.chemolab.2007.07.003

Latino, D. A. R. S., & Aires-de-Sousa, J. (2006). Genome-Scale Classification of Metabolic Reactions: A Chemoinformatics Approach. *Angewandte Chemie International Edition*, *45*, 2066–2069. doi:10.1002/anie.200503833

Lee, B.-H., & Scholz, M. (2006). Application of the self-organizing map (SOM) to asses the heavy metal removal performance in experimental constructed wetlands. *Water Research*, *40*(18), 3367–3374. doi:10.1016/j.watres.2006.07.027

Marengo, E., Bobba, M., Robotti, E., & Liparota, M. C. (2006). Modeling of the Polluting Emissions from a Cement Production Plant by Partial Least-Squares, Principal Component Regression, and Artificial Neural Networks. *Environmental Science & Technology*, *40*(1), 272–280. doi:10.1021/es0517466

Marini, F., Magrì, A. L., & Bucci, R. (2007b). Multilayer feed-forward artificial neural networks for class modeling. *Chemometrics and Intelligent Laboratory Systems*, *88*(1), 118–124. doi:10.1016/j.chemolab.2006.07.004

Marini, F., Magrì, A. L., Bucci, R., & Magrì, A. D. (2007a). Use of different artificial neural networks to resolve binary blends of monocultivar Italian olive oils. *Analytica Chimica Acta*, *599*(2), 232–240. doi:10.1016/j.aca.2007.08.006

Marini, F., Zupan, J., & Magrì, A. L. (2004). On the use of counterpropagation artificial neural networks to characterize Italian rice varieties. *Analytica Chimica Acta*, *510*(2), 231–240. doi:10.1016/j.aca.2004.01.009

Marini, F., Zupan, J., & Magrì, A. L. (2006). Class-modeling using Kohonen artificial neural networks. *Analytica Chimica Acta*, *544*(1-2), 306–314. doi:10.1016/j.aca.2004.12.026

Melssen, W., Ustun, B., & Buydens, L. (2007). SOMPLS: A supervised self-organising map-partial least squares algorithm for multivariate regression problems. *Chemometrics and Intelligent Laboratory Systems*, *86*(1), 102–120. doi:10.1016/j.chemolab.2006.08.013

Melssen, W., Wehrens, R., & Buydens, L. (2006). Supervised Kohonen networks for classification problems. *Chemometrics and Intelligent Laboratory Systems*, *83*(2), 99–113. doi:10.1016/j.chemolab.2006.02.003

NRC (National Research Council). (2003). Oil in the Sea III. Washington, DC: National Academic Press.

Polanski, J., & Walczak, B. (2000). The Comparative Molecular Surface Analysis (COMSA): A Novel Tool for Molecular Design. *Computers & Chemistry*, *24*(5), 615–625. doi:10.1016/S0097-8485(00)00064-4

Samecka-Cymerman, A., Stankiewicz, A., Kolon, K., & Kempers, A. J. (2009). Self-organizing feature map (neural networks) as a tool to select the best indicator of road traffic pollution (soil, leaves or bark of Robinia pseudoacacia L). *Environmental Pollution*, *157*(7), 2061–2065. doi:10.1016/j.envpol.2009.02.021

Schmuker, M., & Schneider, G. (2007). Processing and classification of chemical data inspired by insect olfaction. *Proceedings of the National Academy of Sciences of the United States of America, 204*(51), 20285–20289. doi:10.1073/pnas.0705683104

Schmuker, M., Schwarte, F., Brück, A., Proschak, E., Tanrikulu, E., & Givehchi, A. (2007). SOMMER: self-organising maps for education and research. *Journal of Molecular Modeling, 13*(1), 225–228. doi:10.1007/s00894-006-0140-0

Torrecilla, J. S., Rojo, E., Oliet, M., Dominguez, J. C., & Rodriguez, F. (2009). Self-Organizing Maps and Learning Vector Quantization Networks As Tools to Identify Vegetable Oils. *Journal of Agricultural and Food Chemistry, 57*(7), 2763–2769. doi:10.1021/jf803520u

Vesanto, J., Himberg, J., Alhoniemi, E., & Parhankangas, J. (2000). *SOM Toolbox for Matlab 5*. Technical Report A57, Helsinki University of Technology.

Zhang, Q. Y., & Aires-de-Sousa, J. (2005). Structure-Based Classification of Chemical Reactions without Assignment of Reaction Centers. *Journal of Chemical Information and Modeling, 45*(6), 1775–1783. doi:10.1021/ci0502707

Zhang, Q. Y., & Aires-de-Sousa, J. (2007). Random Forest Prediction of Mutagenicity from Empirical Physicochemical Descriptors. *Journal of Chemical Information and Modeling, 47*(1), 1–8. doi:10.1021/ci050520j

Zupan, J. (1994). Introduction to Artificial Neural Network (ANN) Methods: What They Are and How to Use Them. *Acta Chimica Slovenica, 41*, 327–352.

Zupan, J., & Gasteiger, J. (1993). Neural Networks for Chemists: An Introduction. Weinheim, Germany: VCH-Verlag.

Zupan, J., Novič, M., & Ruisánchez, I. (1997). Kohonen and counterpropagation artificial neural networks in analytical chemistry. *Chemometrics and Intelligent Laboratory Systems, 38*(1), 1–23. doi:10.1016/S0169-7439(97)00030-0

Chapter 21
Neural Models for Rainfall Forecasting

A. Moreno
Universidad de Valencia, Spain

E. Soria
Universidad de Valencia, Spain

J. García
Universidad de Valencia, Spain

J. D. Martín
Universidad de Valencia, Spain

R. Magdalena
Universidad de Valencia, Spain

ABSTRACT

This chapter is focused on obtaining an optimal forecast of one month lagged rainfall in Spain. It is assessed by analyzing 22 years of both satellite observations of vegetation activity (e.g. NDVI) and climatic data (precipitation, temperature). The specific influence of non-spatial climatic indices such as NAO and SOI is also addressed. The approaches considered for rainfall forecasting include classical Auto-Regressive Moving-Average with Exogenous Inputs (ARMAX) models and Artificial Neural Networks (ANN), the so-called Multilayer Perceptron (MLP), in particular. The use of neural models is proven to be an adequate mathematical prediction tool in this problem due the non-linearity of the problem. These models enable us to predict, with one month foresight, the general rainfall dynamics, with average errors of 44 mm (RMSE) in a test series of 4 years with a rainfall standard deviation equal to 73 mm. Also, the sensitivity analysis in the neural network models reveals that observations in the status of the vegetation cover in previous months have a predictive power greater than other considered variables. Linear models yield average results of 55 mm (RMSE) although they need a large number of error terms (12) to obtain acceptable models. Nevertheless, they provide means for assessing the seasonal influence of the precipitation regime with the aid of linear dummy regression parameters, thereby offering an immediate interpretation (e.g. coherent maps) of the causality between vegetation cover and rainfall.

DOI: 10.4018/978-1-61520-893-7.ch021

INTRODUCTION

Rainfall is a climatic phenomenon characterized by extremely irregular space-time distribution. Rainfall forecasting is a challenging task especially in the modern world where we are facing major environmental problems such as global warming. One of the most crucial issues of global climatic variability is its effect on water resources (Aida, 1996). Scenarios for rainfall forecasting are relevant for a wide range of Land Biosphere Applications, such as, agriculture and forestry, environmental management and land use, hydrology, natural hazards monitoring and management (e.g., river training works and flood warning systems), vegetation-soil dynamics monitoring, drought conditions and fire scar extent.

There are numerous factors that affect rainfall, such as terrain orography (in the particular case of Iberian Peninsula it is very complex and compartmentalized), land and sea surface temperature, soil moisture, vegetation, wind and pressure (Goosse, 2008; McGuffie & Henderson, 2005).

A brief of studies indicate that rainfall over the Iberian Peninsula is influenced by different modes of long term variability like the North Atlantic Oscillation (NAO) and El Niño South Oscillation (ENSO) (Rodó, 1997). The NAO index refers to a southern oscillation in atmospheric mass with centers of action near Iceland and over the subtropical Atlantic from the Azores across the Iberian Peninsula. The NAO controls the strength and direction of westerly winds and storm tracks across the North Atlantic (Parker & Folland, 1988). The SOI (Southern Oscillation Index) is an index used to quantify the strength of the coupled ocean-atmosphere phenomenon El Niño-Southern Oscillation (ENSO), by reflecting the fluctuations in the air pressure difference between Tahiti and Darwin, Australia.

Another important element affecting climate is vegetation cover. Far from being a passive component of the climate system, it acts on climate regulating exchanges of energy, mass, and momentum between the surface and atmosphere. In a general way, there are two competing effects on local climate. First, vegetation modifies albedo, and it tends to cool down the surface because solar energy is reflected. Second, more leaves mean more surface area to evaporate water from, so decreasing them also decreases evaporation and, consequently, raise the local temperature. The balance between these two effects varies between different vegetation types (Adams, 2007; Bounoua, 2000; Schwartz & Karl, 1990). A wealth of studies indicates that land surface vegetation can considerably feedback on climate. Results obtained over the North American grasslands indicate that positive vegetation anomalies earlier in the growing season significantly "Granger cause" lower rainfall (and higher temperatures) later in summer (Wang, 2006). Recent observational works have also shown that there is a significant local impact of the vegetation state on monthly mean rainfall anomalies. At the same time, these studies have suggested that vegetation could have much higher impacts on rainfall at seasonal and longer time scales (Liu, 2006).

The global nature of precipitation regime is very complicated and requires sophisticated computer modeling and simulation to predict accurately. A variety of methods have been proposed for this purpose at different time scales. The classical approaches include conceptual (physical) and empirical (statistical) models. They attempt to model the fluid and thermal dynamic systems for gridpoint time series forecasting based on boundary meteorological data. These techniques often require intensive computations involving complex differential equations and computational algorithms (Beniston, 1998). In general, due to the complex nature of rainfall processes, the physical approaches are still unsatisfactory. Besides, the accuracy depends on certain constraints such as the adoption of incomplete boundary conditions, model assumptions and numerical instabilities.

The number of publications related to the application of Machine Learning to time series prediction has increased exponentially last years (Min & Zhang, 2008; Dong, 2009). These techniques have several advantages over other classical (linear) models (Bishop, 1996; Haykin, 2008; Alpaydin, 2004):

- There is no need of a priori knowledge of the problem. This is especially relevant in non-linear modeling problems in which the relationship between input variables and the output variable might take any shape. The use of a non-parametric universal function approximator, like a neural network (Haykin, 2008) or a neuro-fuzzy system (Jang, 1997) is a great advantage in the presence of non-linear and complex problems.
- They are able to find relationships in high-dimensional problems.
- They show a certain noise immunity, which is shown up in the data errors. These errors might be due to different causes: data acquisition mistakes, data transcription mistakes, errors exporting from one format to another one, …
- Due to their non-linear nature, these techniques can model phenomena which are very difficult to be modeled by linear problems, like the hysteresis.

All these advantages make these techniques an alternative to rainfall forecasting at different time scales, which range from short term (hours-days) (Valverde, 2005) to long term (from seasons to years) (Karamouz, 2008). This approach is essentially data driven. The two primary objectives pursued in this work are:

- The implementation of procedures based on linear and non linear models (neural networks) for rainfall modeling within one month foresight. The developed models bring the value of rainfall in a given period from the time evolution of five variables -vegetation, temperature, rainfall, NAO index and SOI index - during former months.
- The evaluation of the forecasting potential of considered variables through sensitivity analyses. After obtaining the nonlinear models, a sensitivity analysis is done to identify sensitive parameters or processes associated with model output.

The work is organized as follows: in next section the observational datasets used are described and the developed forecasting techniques are introduced. The section entitled "results" is devoted to show the achieved outcomes and, the last two sections contain a discussion of future research directions and the conclusions of this study, respectively.

MATERIALS AND METHODS

This work is focused on developing appropriate models for rainfall forecasting in Spain. The complexity and nonlinearity inherent in rainfall patterns make it attractive to apply non-linear methods such as Artificial Neural Networks (ANN). Linear models were also considered to compare the efficiency of both approaches to solve the problem. To show the spatial distribution of causality between anomalies of vegetation cover and drought, and assess the specific influence of the seasonal effects on precipitation regime, an additional Dummy-Variable regression model was developed.

Data Sets

Depending on the way of acquisition, two kinds of variables can be taken into account. First, remotely sensed data to characterize the vegetation cover (Normalized Difference Vegetation Index, NDVI) and second, data from in situ measures, such as the considered climatic variables (rainfall, temperature, NAO index and SOI index).

Vegetation has been traditionally monitored using time series of satellite based vegetation indices such as the NDVI (Tucker, 1979). The Global Inventory Modeling and Mapping Studies (GIMMS) NDVI data sets were generated to provide one of the longest time series currently available (covering the 1981-2003 period) with a temporal resolution of 15 days. Key features of this dataset include reduced NDVI variations arising from calibration, view geometry, volcanic aerosols, and other effects not related to actual vegetation change. In particular, NOAA-9 descending node data from September 1994 to January 1995, volcanic stratospheric aerosol correction for 1982-1984 and 1991-1994, and improved NDVI using empirical mode decomposition/reconstruction (EMD) to minimize effects of orbital drift (Pinzon, 2005). Spatial and temporally consistent estimates of the biophysical variables such as Fractional Vegetation Cover (FVC) and Leaf Area Index (LAI) were obtained in the context of DULCINEA Project. These variables offered a mean for obtaining direct indicators of vegetation biomass, structure and condition from a regional to global scale. Adapted variants of a probabilistic spectral mixture analysis algorithm (García, 2005), which is currently used operationally in the context of the EUMETSAT/LSA SAF mission, were used. The considered data set covered a 9-year period (February'2000-January'2009), presenting a 1km spatial resolution over 16-day periods. Vegetation indices (NDVI and FVC) were time-sampled at a monthly resolution in order to have a homogenous sampling time for all the input variables.

Climatic data such as precipitation and temperature control differences in the Earth's vegetation cover, affecting growth rate, plant reproduction, and frost damage. In this study, monthly climatic maps of precipitation and temperature in Spain were derived during the 1950-2007 period at a 2-km spatial resolution. The acute estimation of the spatial distribution of precipitation requires a very dense network of measuring gaugement. The climatic data used in the study were obtained from

AEMET (*Agencia Estatal de Meteorología*, State Agency of Meteorology) in Spain and were derived during the 1950-2008 period at a 2-km spatial resolution. They correspond to between 2500 and 4800 records (depending on the period) recording termo-pluviometric stations and major observatories distributed over Spain (García, 2008). From the monthly maps, annual and monthly averages for the analyzed period were computed. It was also used a commonly used drought index derived from precipitation, Standard Precipitation Index (SPI). It is derived by fitting historical precipitation data to a Gamma probability distribution function for a specific time period and location, and transforming the Gamma distribution to a normal distribution (McKee, 1993). Several global and regional land cover datasets were used to identify the major biomes (vegetation cover type) in the Iberian Peninsula. In particular, the CORINE Land Cover classification (CLC2000 at 100m resolution) was used to discard urban and irrigated areas (anthropogenic landscapes).

Temporal variations of the different variables were quite different: while vegetation and temperature showed a smooth evolution along the year (Figure 1a and Figure 1b), with a typical unimodal annual cycle, monthly rainfall showed an irregular seasonal pattern (Figure 1c). Different temporal filters were found to be ineffective since they removed extreme rainfall events that could be adequately described by the model for some of the cases.

Modeling Techniques

Linear Models

Amongst the several linear models for time series analysis the ARMAX (*Autoregressive Moving Average with Exogenous Inputs*) approach was chosen because of its extended noise model and simplicity (Nelles 2001). The ARMAX model is probably the second most popular linear after ARX model. This technique includes the historic of the

Figure 1. An example of temporal evolution of temperature, vegetation cover (NDVI) and rainfall

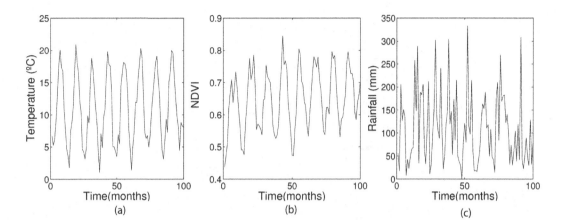

Box 1.

$$y(t) + a_1 y(t-1) + \ldots + a_{n_a} y(t-n_a) = b_1 u(t-n_k) + \ldots + b_{n_b} u(t-n_k-n_b+1) + c_1 e(t-1) + \ldots + c_{n_c} e(t-n_c) + e(t) \qquad (1)$$

variable to model, other explicative variables and a noise modeling which purpose is the description of the variance that considered variables are unable to model. Compared with ARX models (the most commonly used), ARMAX models have an additional flexibility because of an extended noise model is included in its parameters. The mathematical expression of this model is given by equation 1 (see Box 1).

where $y(t)$ is the desired output of the model in the instant t, n_a is the number of delays of the variable y, n_b is the number of delays of every input variable u (in our case there are four variables, NDVI, T, index NAO and index SOI), n_c is the number of delays used in noise modelling and n_k is the delay that represents the number of observations that take place before the input variables have effect in the output variable to be predicted.

The model represented by Equation (1) is aimed at finding both the number of delays that are optimal for each variable and also the model

parameters. The optimal number of parameters is based on a trade-off between the modeling capability and the number of delays, because if the number of delays is high, then the model will not be able to validate for new data (Nelles, 2001). There are different criteria to obtain the optimal number of delay. In this work, we used the Akaike's criterion, which is widely used in this kind of applications. The parameters were obtained using least-square modeling (Weigend & Gershenfeld, 1992).

Artificial Neural Networks

Artificial Neural Networks (ANN) provide a non-linear forecasting method over the time series considered. In this work, the classical Multilayer Perceptron (MLP) was used, which is currently the most widely used network due to its great range of application (Haykin, 2008). The MLP has proven to be very powerful in dealing with a

Figure 2. Multilayer perceptron structure

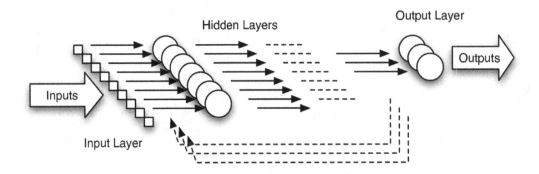

broad range of complicated forecasting problems (prediction of tropospheric ozone concentration, rainfall-runoff process, economic forecasting) (Gómez, 2006; De & Meneghetti, 2000; Franses, 1999) and are particularly well suited to address the rainfall forecast. There is a number of reasons that justify its wide use, firstly, they enable to infer the complex relations between the existing variables; secondly, they are built upon data, not considering any a priori relation amongst variables; and thirdly, they can be applied to relatively big data sets, because the computational load is constant when the net is fully trained.

An MLP is formed by a set of elementary units (neurons); each of these units carries out a non-linear transformation of its inputs defined by the following expression:

$$y = \phi\left(\sum\nolimits_{i=1}^{m} w_i \cdot x_i + b\right) \qquad (2)$$

where m is the number of inputs to the neuron, w_i are the synaptic weights (parameters of the system), b is the bias coefficient (other parameter to be set) and ϕ is a non linear function (in this work the most widely used function was chosen, the hyperbolic tangent). The non-linear function provides MLP with its non-linear characteristics. In general, an MLP consists of a lowermost input layer, any number of hidden layers, and an output layer at the top (see Figure 2).

Neurons are arranged in layers; the first layer is known as input layer, the last one as output layer and the layers in between are the so-called hidden layers (Figure 2). It is mathematically proven that a MLP with two hidden-layers is able to model any relationship between two sets of variables (Haykin, 2008). The MLP have been trained with the Levenberg-Marquardt (LM) algorithm. This algorithm is an iterative technique that locates the minimum of a function. When the current solution is far from the minimum, the algorithm behaves like a steepest descent method (that is, minimization along the direction of the gradient), but guaranteed to converge. When the current solution is close to the minimum, it becomes a Gauss-Newton method (it uses a quadratic model to speed up the process of finding the minimum). This algorithm shows a better performance than other more widely used and classical algorithms (e.g., backpropagation).

Due to the method of minimum local search, it is necessary to test different initializations in order to avoid the problem of falling into a local minimum. Another approach, not followed in this work, is based on a minimum global search, such as genetic algorithms (Alpaydin, 2004).

In order to simplify the obtained models and assess the importance of the involved variables, a sensitivity analysis over the MLP's was carried out. This technique assumes that after a MLP has successfully trained to model a data set, the weights between the neurons are so adjusted that removing irrelevant features does not influence the output of the neural network in a great extent (Pal, 1999; De, 1997).

A representative sample (100) of the networks that best model the training data set was taken. Then the difference between the outputs of these models when excluding a given variable was calculated. Values of this difference close to zero would imply that the excluded variable was not required by the model and was thus discarded. This methodology sorts the importance of variables in order to reject those that do not significantly contribute to the predictive model.

Experimental Design

Most statistical forecasting methods are based on the assumption that the time series can be rendered approximately stationary through the use of mathematical transformations. In order to work with linear models a data pre-processing was necessary because the input data was not stationary. Autocorrelation and differencing methods were used to achieve stationary. Seasonal differences were taken and the remaining non-stationarity in the mean was removed with a further first difference.

It was developed around 4000 linear models with different number of parameters and delays for every pixel in order to minimize the prediction error and the number of parameters. This selection was performed in two stages. First the best 200 models were selected in base of the Akaike information criteria (AIC); this method enables to maximize the determination coefficient (R^2) penalizing the model according to the number of considered variables. Finally the model with lower Root Mean Squared Error (RMSE) was selected.

Variables were standardized in order to ensure that all variables had the same a priori relevance for the models (Maier & Dandy, 2000). A critical issue in developing prediction models in general, and ANNs in particular, is related to generalization. ANNs can suffer from either over-fitting or under-

fitting the training set. To achieve generalization, the early stopping method was used. According to this method, the data was split into three datasets, namely training set, validation (or generalization) set and a test set. The validation set was used to test the performance of the network during training process. When the error of validation set reached a minimum, then the training process was stopped. Finally, the performances of the ANN were evaluated on test data set which had not been used in the training process. In this work, 22 years (1981-2003) of climatic and remotely sensed standardized data were used. The first 18 years were used for training the prediction models and the remaining four years for testing purposes.

The approach based on the MLP is a four-step approach:

1. *An exhaustive initialization of the model parameters.* Around 6000 ANN were trained for every pixel, trying different architectures with a fixed number of inputs (7 delays of rainfall, temperature, NDVI, NAO index and SOI index), and initializing the parameters randomly (Jain & Fanelli, 2000). This method allowed to determine the optimal complexity of the MLP appropriate to rainfall forecasting (determine the number of hidden layers and the number of neurons in each hidden layer).

Since the algorithm is based on a local minimum search, different synaptic weights initializations were employed (Jain, 2000).

2. *Selection of the models that present the best performance.* As a result of a heuristic adjustment, only the 100 ANNs presenting the lowest RMSE values were chosen.
3. *Sensitivity analysis.* Based on the preselected models, a sensitivity analysis was undertaken to select the most meaningful variables.

Table 1. Characteristics of a subset sites representing the major biomes(vegetation cover types)

Zone	Latitude	Longitude	Vegetation Cover
1	43°52'30"N	8°57'51"W	Broad-leaved forest
2	42°41'28"N	0°0'36"E	Bare rocks/Sparsely veg.
3	43°14'59"N	9°35'21"W	Broad-leaved forest
4	36°52'22"N	2°23'24"W	Sparsely vegetated areas

4. *Selection of best model with reduced inputs.* Using the reduced input features' data set, other 6000 MLPs were trained testing different architectures. The best ANN model was selected based upon the model performance (minimum RMSE) over a four year (1999-2003) test set.

Results

In order to analyze the response to rainfall of different vegetation types and climatic regions, a stratified analysis was performed considering the major regional climates and vegetation communities in Spain. The analysis is focused on a representative subset of selected sites (see table 1). Table 2 summarizes the outcomes obtained by the two modeling techniques over the selected sites. It shows that the number of variables is relatively large (34-38) for linear models although the Akaike's Information Criterion (AIC) was used.

AIC penalizes the model according to the number of considered variables.

About neural models, the sensitivity analysis step over the MLP caused a considerable reduction, from 35 to 8-14 inputs. The comparative performance in terms of RMSE suggests that using the ANN (table 2), significantly improves the overall forecast accuracy for 1 month ahead rainfall. This evidences that the non-linear models offer a superior generalization capability, which can only be partly accounted by the use of noise terms in the considered linear model. RMSE values are lower than standard deviation of rainfall time series in both cases (linear and non linear models). A similar result was obtained over a larger number of sites. The **standard** deviation gives the RMSE when the mean value of the time series is used as predictor. While classical linear models give a better and easier interpretation of the described relationships, ANNs are more versatile and can reflect accurately non linear relationships among the input variables taken into consideration.

Table 2. Characteristics of the prediction -with one month foresight- achieved by the linear models. (ARMAX) and the non-linear ones (ANN) in the test and training data sets. RMSE and MAE (Mean Absolute Error) models correspond to the test data set covering a four-year period. Note that in the ARMAX model, the number of variables includes the noise parameters

Zone	Input variables		RMSE (rainfall, mm)			MAE (rainfall, mm)			std. rainfall (mm)
	ARMAX	ANN	ARMAX	ANN train	ANN test	ARMAX	ANN train	ANN test	
1	34	8	55.3	42.7	43.9	44.5	40.8	42.6	73.0
2	36	14	91.7	71.3	91.0	75.3	65.1	73.9	114.3
3	37	11	99.0	63.5	92.2	83.5	56.3	69.1	121.6
4	38	10	18.9	17.2	16.4	14.7	13.7	12.8	22.5

Figure 3. One-month ahead prediction of rainfall for 4 years (test set) using ARMAX model for site 1

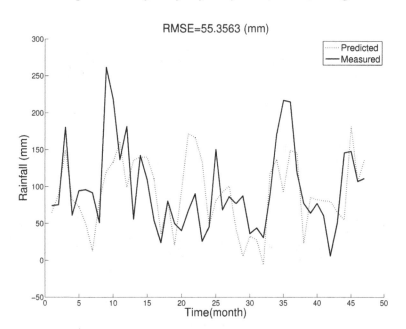

Figures 3 and 4 show some examples of the predicted rainfall series for site 1, for a further analysis of the prediction performance. These figures show that both modeling techniques are able to follow reasonably well the overall dynamics of the rainfall pattern in this evergreen forest site. Note however, that the non-linear model requires a considerably lower number of input parameters (8) compared to the linear one (34) and a noticeably higher fit to the test set. The non-linear model is able to follow the dynamics of the rainfall series from the vegetation evolution, while the linear ones offer a poorer modeling.

Figure 5 shows the results of a sensitivity analysis. Variables related with NVDI (with its seven delays) were the most relevant variables for the prediction in case *a*. This area of study corresponds with a broad-leaved forest biome (according with Corine Land cover classification), and clearly the most relevant input feature for the MLP was NDVI(t-6). In case *b*, vegetation also had the most relevant input feature. In particular, NDVI (t-5) was the most influencing input. This

zone of study corresponded with a semi-arid region of the South-Eastern Spain (Almeria), where the predominant vegetation cover in this area was sparsely vegetated areas. The temperature shows a great influence on rainfall according with results of sensitivity analysis. Outcomes of the models obtained suggest that the relationship between vegetation and rainfall lasts at least seven months, except for zone 2, which is a rocky surface with very scarce high-mountain vegetation. The sensitivity analysis also suggests that the significance of NAO and SOI indices as predictors of rainfall was weaker than the other variables considered. However, it should be taken into account the short time period of influence for our analysis (7 months) which made difficult to find connections between the factors showing dependent cycles of several years.

The spatial and temporal dynamics of fractional vegetation cover (FVC) and SPI enabled spatially explicit comparisons of precipitation condition in response to vegetation. A regression model with seasonal dummy variables was used

Figure 4. One-month ahead prediction of rainfall for 4 years (test set) using ANN model corresponding for site 1

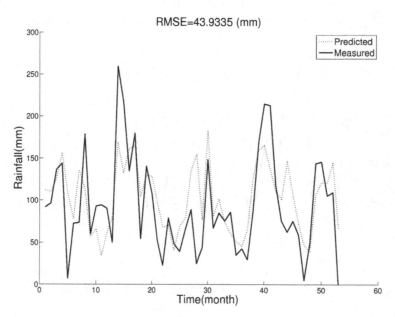

to build a relationship between the FVC and SPI at different time scales and considering different lags. Dummy variables were appropriate to handle seasonal variations of FVC. In order to evaluate the effect of seasonal timing, different temporal windows covering a 3 month period were considered (1-3,4-6,7-9,10-12). The regression model contained 6 coefficients assigned to the 3 intercepts and 3 slopes of the linear relationship and used to account for the effect of the "month" on SPI. The coefficients obtained with these categorical variables reflected the average difference in the forecast variable between months. Some of the estimated parameters might be insignificant (p-values larger than 0.05), in particular, the 3 intercepts. If this occurs, the dummy model was

Figure 5. Normalized relevance of the different features for zone 1(a) and zone 4(b). Variables 1-7 are Temperature delays, 8-14 are NVDI delays, 15-21 are rainfall delays, 22-28 are NAO delays and 29-35 stand for the SOI delays

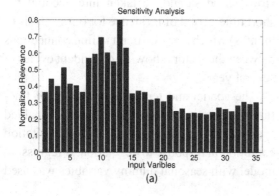
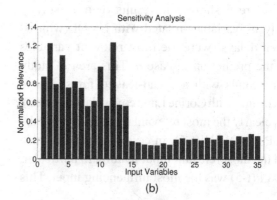

Figure 6. Determination coefficient (R^2) of the linear regression model with seasonal dummy variables between SPI-1 one month lagged and anomaly of fractional vegetation cover (FVC). It is represented the period from April to June over a nine-year (2000-2008) period. FVC was first retrieved from MODIS data, and then reprojected to geographical coordinates system at a 2km spatial resolution

revised and the insignificant terms were omitted. Dummy variables significantly increased model fit, but at a cost of fewer degrees of freedom.

Figure 6 shows the spatial distribution of the determination coefficient (R^2) between SPI-1 and anomaly of FVC for the April-June period, which covers the growing season in most of the area. Despite the simplicity of the employed model, statistically significant correlations were found between satellite-derived anomalies of vegetation activity and the water drought index in certain areas, which reveals a geographically coherent pattern. Since vegetation was coupled with the rainfall rate in different time scales, one key issue was to assess the predictive potential of variables that comprised relevant information regarding the evolution of the vegetation cover (as assessed from remotely sensed observations) on rainfall. This variable could reflect upon its time signature previous climate events, bringing an interesting and scarcely reported explaining

potential (Alessandri & Navarra, 2008). The relationships were highly dependent on the regional climate and vegetation community (Woodard, 1987). In general, they were more significant in semi-arid regions and are also dependent of the vegetation type and seasonal period.

FUTURE RESEARCH

Although the results in the use of MLPs have been satisfactory, some improvements can be proposed for the future research:

The addition of new climatic variables to evaluate their influence on rainfall. In future work, the ANN methodology will be applied at the satellite image level (thousand of pixels), rather than over a reduced number of sites. Also, the advent of modern satellites (e.g. MODIS, MERIS, SEVIRI, VEGETATION) has improved the possibilities to retrieve new vegetation properties because of a better radiometric, spectral and angular performance of imaging instruments. Biophysical variables derived from such instruments such as Fractional Vegetation Cover (FVC) will be used to improve the characterization of vegetation activity.

Extension of the analysis to bigger regions. This extension can be carried out using a global model for the entire region or developing local models for sub-areas within the studied regions, so that the different sub-area models can be combined later. This extension could indicate the goodness of the global solution as well as the need (or not) of using local models.

Another important issue would be to account for the seasonal timing of the precipitation, which has been ignored by both the classical linear and nonlinear models. This fact would involve another input to the models (to characterize this factor) or new models could be proposed which should be analyzed altogether in order to draw conclusions about the relevance of the new factor.

The use of other universal function approximators, such as regression trees and neuro-fuzzy systems (Alpaydin, 2004), which can provide predictions in terms of rules could be useful in order to provide a qualitative knowledge of the problem. Likewise, other neural model, the Self-Organizing Map, can also help in providing this kind of knowledge.

CONCLUSION

The focus of this work has been to develop appropriate models for rainfall forecasting in Spain. The global nature of this phenomenon is very complicated and the relationship between the different physical variables involved in the process is extremely complex and not well understood. Sophisticated computer modeling such as the ARMAX model and the ANN techniques have emerged as an alternative to rainfall forecasting. These approaches are essentially data driven, and

the appropriate model obtained has to extract the internal physical processes involved.

In this study, it has been shown that, the MLP was capable of approximating the rainfall regime by one month ahead time step with typical RMSE values around 44-90 mm/month. The ANN forecasting models has potential utility for conditioning water resources outlook, particularly where there is a strong relationship between the variables taken into consideration. Also, the sensitivity analysis of the calculated models has revealed that temporal evolution of vegetation activity plays a key role on climate and, more precisely, on rainfall. The non-linear approach improvement of forecast accuracy relative to the ARMAX model has been significant, although accuracy offered by the linear models has also been acceptable. It should also be pointed out that error modeling has a too high weight in the linear models, thus showing up the non-linearity of the models to be taken into account. This could partly explain the better prediction accuracies offered by the ANN approach.

To show the spatial distribution of causality between anomalies of vegetation cover and drought, and assess the specific influence of seasonal effects on precipitation regime, a Dummy-Variable linear regression model has also been developed. The results of applying this modeling technique has allowed us to obtain image-scale (thousands of pixels) results of causality between vegetation biophysical variables (FVC) and drought indices (SPI).

The work has also evidenced the potential of remotely sensed observations of vegetation activity to improve rainfall prediction over land in Spain. Vegetation has appeared to provide a biophysical memory of climatic events and is supposed to act through delayed feedbacks on rainfall. More specifically, changes in the precipitation can be related to changes in the vegetation activity as a result of changes in the soil moisture and temperature. The vegetation activity has the ability to capture in its temporal signature past climatic events, giving an interesting and poorly understood explanatory power.

ACKNOWLEDGMENT

This work was supported by the DULCINEA (CGL2005-04202) and ÁRTEMIS (CGL2008-00381) projects.

REFERENCES

Adams, J. (Ed.). (2007). Vegetation-Climate Interaction. Chichester, UK: Springer-Praxis.

Aida, M. J., Francisco, R. V., & Cruz, N. A. (1996). A study on impact of climate variability/change on water resources in the Philippines. Chemosphere, 33(9), 1687–1704. doi:10.1016/0045-6535(96)00185-3

Alessandri, A., & Navarra, A. (2008). On the coupling between vegetation and rainfall inter-annual anomalies: Possible contributions to seasonal rainfall predictability over land areas. Geophysical Research Letters, 35, L02718. doi:10.1029/2007GL032415

Alpaydin, E. (Ed.). (2004). Introduction to Machine Learning. Adaptive Computation and Machine Learning. Cambridge, MA: MIT Press.

Beniston, M. (Ed.). (1998). From turbulence to climate: numerical investigations of the atmosphere with a hierarchy of models. Berlin: Springer.

Bishop, C. M. (1996). Neural Networks for Pattern Recognition. Oxford, UK: Clarendon Press.

Bounoua, L., Collatz, G. J., Los, S. O., Sellers, P. J., Dazlich, D. A., Tucker, C. J., & Randall, D. A. (2000). Sensitivity of climate to changes in NDVI. Journal of Climate, 13, 2277–2292. doi:10.1175/1520-0442(2000)013<2277:SOCTCI>2.0.CO;2

De, R., Pal, N. R., & Pal, S. K. (1997). Feature analysis: neural network and fuzzy set theoretic approaches. Pattern Recognition, 30(10), 1579–1590. doi:10.1016/S0031-3203(96)00190-2

De, T., & Meneghetti, A. (2000). The production planning process for a network of firms in the textile-apparel industry. International Journal of Production Economics, 65, 17–32. doi:10.1016/S0925-5273(99)00087-0

Dong, M., Yang, D., Kuang, Y., Hec, D., Erdald, S., & Kenskie, D. (2009). PM concentration prediction using hidden semi-Markov model-based times series next term data mining. Expert Systems with Applications, 36(5), 9046–9055. doi:10.1016/j.eswa.2008.12.017

Franses, P. H. (1999). Time Series Models for Business and Economic Forecasting. Cambridge, UK: Cambridge University Press.

García-Haro, F. J., Belda, F., & Poquet, D. (2008). *Estimation of climatological variables in Spain during the 1950-2008 period using geostatistical techniques*. Paper presented at the 8th Annual Meeting of the EMS / 7th ECAC EMS8/ECAC7 Abstracts, Vol. 5, EMS2008-A-00319, 2008.

García-Haro, F. J., Sommer, S., & Kemper, T. (2005). Variable multiple endmember spectral mixture analysis (VMESMA). International Journal of Remote Sensing, 26, 2135–2162. doi:10.1080/01431160512331337817

Gómez, J., Martín, J. D., Soria, E., Vila, J., Carrasco, J. L., & Valle, S. (2006, October). Neural networks for analysing the relevance of input variables in the prediction of tropospheric ozone concentration. Atmospheric Environment, 40(32), 6173–6180. doi:10.1016/j.atmosenv.2006.04.067

Goosse, H., Barriat, P. Y., Lefebvre, W., Loutre, M. F., & Zunz, V. (2008). *Introduction to climate dynamics and climate modeling*. Online textbook. Retrieved from http://www.climate.be/textbook

Haykin, S. (Ed.). (2008). Neural Networks and Learning Machines. Upper Saddle River, NJ: Prentice Hall.

Jain, L., & Fanelli, A. M. (Eds.). (2000). Recent Advances in Artificial Neural Networks: Design and Applications. Boca Raton, FL: CRC Press, Inc.

Jang, J. S., Sun, C. T., & Mizutani, E. (Eds.). (1997). Neuro-Fuzzy and Soft Computing: A Computational Approach to Learning and Machine Intelligence. Upper Saddle River, NJ: Prentice Hall.

Karamouz, M., Razavi, S., & Araghinejad, S. (2008). Long-lead seasonal rainfall forecasting using time-delay recurrent neural networks: a case study. Hydrological Processes, 22(2), 229–241. doi:10.1002/hyp.6571

Liu, Z., Notaro, M., & Kutzbach, J. (2006). Assessing global vegetation climate feedbacks from observations. Journal of Climate, 19, 787–814. doi:10.1175/JCLI3658.1

Maier, H. R., & Dandy, G. C. (2000). Neural Networks for the prediction and forecasting of water resources variables: a review of modeling issues and applications. Environmental Modelling & Software, 15, 101–123. doi:10.1016/S1364-8152(99)00007-9

McGuffie, K., & Henderson-Sellers, A. (2005). A Climate Modelling Primer (3rd Ed.). Hoboken, NJ: John Wiley & Sons, Ltd.

McKee, T. B., Doesken, N. J., & Kliest, J. (1993). The relationship of drought frequency and duration to time scales. In *Proceedings of the 8th Conference of Applied Climatology,* 17-22 January, Anaheim, CA (pp. 179-184). Boston, MA: American Meterological Society.

Min, Q., & Zhang, G. P. (2008). Trend Time–Series Modeling and Forecasting With Neural Networks. IEEE Transactions on Neural Networks, 19(5), 808–816. PubMeddoi:10.1109/TNN.2007.912308

Nelles, O. (Ed.). (2001). Nonlinear System Identification. Berlin: Springer-Verlag.

Pal, N. R. (1999). Soft computing for feature analysis. Fuzzy Sets and Systems, 103(2), 201–221. doi:10.1016/S0165-0114(98)00222-X

Parker, D. E., & Folland, C. K. (1988). The nature of climatic variability. Meteorological Magazine, 117, 201–210.

Pinzon, J., Brown, M. E., & Tucker, C. J. (2005). Satellite time series correction of orbital drift artifacts using empirical mode decomposition. In N. Huang (Ed.), Hilbert-Huang Transform: Introduction and Applications (pp. 167-186).

Rodó, X., Baert, E., & Comin, A. (1997). Variations in seasonal rainfall in Southern Europe during the present century: relationships with the North Atlantic Oscillation and El Niño-Southern Oscillation. Climate Dynamics, 13, 275–284. doi:10.1007/s003820050165

Schwartz, M. D., & Karl, T. R. (1990). Spring phenology: Nature's experiment to detect the effect of 'green up' on surface maximum temperatures. Monthly Weather Review, 118, 883–890. doi:10.1175/1520-0493(1990)118<0883:SPNETD>2.0.CO;2

Tucker, C. J. (1979). Red and photographic infrared linear combinations for monitoring vegetation. Remote Sensing of Environment, 8, 127–150. doi:10.1016/0034-4257(79)90013-0

Valverde, M. C., de Campos, H. F., & Ferreira, N. J. (2005). Artificial neural network technique for rainfall forecasting applied to the Sao Paulo region. Journal of Hydrology (Amsterdam), 301, 1–4. doi:10.1016/j.jhydrol.2004.06.018

Wang, W. (2006). *Detecting and modeling large-scale interactions between vegetation, precipitation, and temperature over temperate-semiarid and boreal climate regimes.* Ph.D. dissertation, Boston University, MA, USA.

Weigend, A. S., & Gershenfeld, N. A. (1992). Time Series Prediction: Forecasting The Future And Understanding The Past. Santa Fe Institute Studies in the Sciences of Complexity. Boulder, CO: Westview Press.

Woodard, F. I. (Ed.). (1987). Climate and plant distribution. Cambridge, UK: Cambridge University Press.

ADDITIONAL READING

Abuelgasim, A. A., Ross, W. D., Gopal, S., & Woodcock, C. E. (1999). Change detection using adaptive fuzzy neural networks: environmental damage assessment after the Gulf War. Remote Sensing of Environment, 70, 208–223. doi:10.1016/S0034-4257(99)00039-5

Balestrassi, P. P., Popova, E., Paiva, A. P., & Marangon Lima, J. W. (2009). Design of experiments on neural network's training for nonlinear time series forecasting. Neurocomputing, 72(4-6), 1160–1178. doi:10.1016/j.neucom.2008.02.002

Bishop, M. (Ed.). (2007). Pattern Recognition and Machine Learning (Information Science and Statistics). Berlin: Springer.

Canty, M. J., & Nielsen, A. A. (2004). Unsupervised classification of changes in multispectral satellite imagery. In L. Bruzzone (Ed.), *Proc. SPIE on Image and Signal Processing for Remote Sensing X* (Vol. 5573, pp. 356-363).

Canty, M. J. (Ed.). (2007). Image Analysis, Classification and Change Detection in Remote Sensing, with Algorithms for ENVI/IDL. Boca Raton, FL: CRC.

Chan, S. H., Ngan, H. W., Rad, A. B., David, A. K., & Kasabov, N. (2006). Short-term ANN load forecasting from limited data using generalization learning strategies. Neurocomputing, 70(1-3), 409–419. doi:10.1016/j.neucom.2005.12.131

Coppin, P., Nackaerts, K., Queen, L., & Brewer, K. (2001). Operational monitoring of green biomass change for forest management. Photogrammetric Engineering and Remote Sensing, 67, 603–611.

Coppin, P. R., & Bauer, M. E. (1996). Digital change detection in forest ecosystems with remote sensing imagery. Remote Sensing Reviews, 13, 207–234.

Díaz, L. A., Ortega, J. C., Fu, J. S., Reed, G. D., Chow, J. C., Watson, J. G., & Moncada, J. A. (2008). A hybrid ARIMA and artificial neural networks model to forecast particulate matter in urban areas: The case of Temuco. Chile Atmospheric Environment, 42(35), 8331–8340.

Elizondo, D., Hoogenboom, G., & McClendon, R. W. (1994). Development of a neural network model to predict daily solar radiation. Agricultural and Forest Meteorology, 71(1-2), 115–132. doi:10.1016/0168-1923(94)90103-1

Engelbrecht, P. (Ed.). (2007). Computational Intelligence: An Introduction. New York: Wiley.

García-Haro, F. J., Belda, F., Gilabert Navarro, M. A., Meliá, J., Moreno, A., Poquet, D., et al. (2008). Monitoring drought conditions in the Iberian Peninsula using moderate and coarse resolution satellite data. In Proc. of the '2nd MERIS / (A) ATSR User Workshop', Frascati, Italy, 22-26 September 2008.

García-Haro, F. J., Gilabert, M. A., & Melia, J. (1996). Linear spectral mixture modelling to estimate vegetation amount from optical spectral data. International Journal of Remote Sensing, 17(17), 3373–3400. doi:10.1080/01431169608949157

García-Haro, F. J., Gilabert, M. A., & Meliá, J. (2001). Monitoring fire-affected areas using TM data. International Journal of Remote Sensing, 22, 533–549. doi:10.1080/01431160050505847

Gautam, A. K., Chelani, A. B., Jain, V. K., & Devotta, S. (2008). A new scheme to predict chaotic time series of air pollutant concentrations using artificial neural network and nearest neighbour searching. Atmospheric Environment, 42(18), 4409–4417. doi:10.1016/j.atmosenv.2008.01.005

Gilabert, M. A., González-Piqueras, J., & Martínez, B. (2009). Theory and applications of vegetation indices. In F. Maselli, M. Menenti, P. A. Brivio (Eds.), Remote Sensing optical observations of vegetation properties and processes.

Gómez, J., Martín, J. D., Soria, E., Vila, J., Carrasco, J. L., & Valle, S. (2006). Neural networks for analysing the relevance of input variables in the prediction of tropospheric ozone concentration. Atmospheric Environment, 40(32), 6173–6180. doi:10.1016/j.atmosenv.2006.04.067

Gonzalez-Alonso, F., Cuevas, J. M., Calle, A., Casanova, J. L., & Romo, A. (2004). Spanish vegetation monitoring during the period 1987–2001 using NOAA-AVHRR images. International Journal of Remote Sensing, 25, 3–6. doi:10.1080/0143116031000115229

Grivas, G., & Chaloulakou, A. (2006). Artificial neural network models for prediction of PM10 hourly concentrations in the Greater Area of Athens, Greece. Atmospheric Environment, 40(7), 1216–1229. doi:10.1016/j.atmosenv.2005.10.036

Guarize, R., Matos, N. A. F., Sagrilo, L. V. S., & Lima, E. C. P. (2007). Neural networks in the dynamic response analysis of slender marine structures. Applied Ocean Research, 29(4), 191–198. doi:10.1016/j.apor.2008.01.002

Ito, E., Ono, K., Ito, Y. M., & Araki, M. (2008). A neural network approach to simple prediction of soil nitrification potential: A case study in Japanese temperate forests. Ecological Modelling, 219(1–2), 200–211. doi:10.1016/j.ecolmodel.2008.08.011

Jeong, K. S., Kim, D. K., Jung, J. M., Kim, M. C., & Joo, G. J. (2008). Non-linear autoregressive modelling by Temporal Recurrent Neural Networks for the prediction of freshwater phytoplankton dynamics. Ecological Modelling, 211(3-4), 292–300. doi:10.1016/j.ecolmodel.2007.09.029

Kukkonen, J., Partanen, L., Karppinen, A., Ruuskanen, J., Junninen, H., Kolehmainen, M., et al. (2003). Extensive evaluation of neural network models for the prediction of NO2 and PM10 concentrations, compared with a deterministic modelling system and measurements in central Helsinki. Atmospheric Environment, 37(32), 4539–4550. doi:10.1016/S1352-2310(03)00583-1

Lee, C., Chiang, Y., Shih, C., & Tsai, C. (2009). Noisy time series prediction using M-estimator based robust radial basis function neural networks with growing and pruning techniques. Expert Systems with Applications, 36(3). PubMed

López, G., Rubio, M. A., Martínez, M., & Batlles, F. J. (2001). Estimation of hourly global photosynthetically active radiation using artificial neural network models. Agricultural and Forest Meteorology, 107(4), 279–291. doi:10.1016/S0168-1923(01)00217-9

Lu, H., Hsieh, J., & Chang, T. (2006). Prediction of daily maximum ozone concentrations from meteorological conditions using a two-stage neural network. Atmospheric Research, 81(2), 124–139. doi:10.1016/j.atmosres.2005.11.007

Martínez, B., García-Haro, F. J., & Camacho-de Coca, F. (2009). Derivation of high-resolution leaf area index maps over Barrax test site for validation activities. Agricultural and Forest Meteorology, 149, 130–145. doi:10.1016/j.agrformet.2008.07.014

Nourani, V., Mohammad, T., & Mohammad, H. A. (2009). A combined neural-wavelet model for prediction of Ligvanchai watershed precipitation. Engineering Applications of Artificial Intelligence, 22(3), 466–472. doi:10.1016/j.engappai.2008.09.003

Pastor, O., Soria, E., Martín, J. D., Camps, G., Carrasco, J. L., & Valle, S. (2005). Unbiased sensitivity analysis and pruning techniques in neural networks for surface ozone modelling. Ecological Modelling, 182(2), 149–158. doi:10.1016/j.ecolmodel.2004.07.015

Roger, J. S., Sun, C. T., & Mizutani, E. (Eds.). (1997). Neuro-Fuzzy and Soft Computing: A Computational Approach to Learning and Machine Intelligence (Matlab Curriculum Series). Upper Saddle River, NJ: Prentice Hall.

Rojas, I., Valenzuela, O., Rojas, F., Guillen, A., Herrera, L. J., Pomares, H., et al. (2008). Soft-computing techniques and ARMA model for time series prediction. Neurocomputing, 71(4-6), 519–537. doi:10.1016/j.neucom.2007.07.018

Sedki, A., Ouazar, D., & El Mazoudi, E. (2009). Evolving neural network using real coded genetic algorithm for daily rainfall-runoff forecasting. Expert Systems with Applications, 36(3), 4523–4527. doi:10.1016/j.eswa.2008.05.024

Weigend, A. S., & Mangeas, M. (1995). Avoiding Overfitting by Locally Matching the Noise Level of the Data. In Artificial Intelligence Applications on Wall Street (pp. 298-307). New York: Software Engineering Press.

Compilation of References

Abdul-Wahab, S. A., & Abdo, J. (2007). Prediction of tropospheric ozone concentrations by using the design system approach. Journal of Environmental Science and Health, 42, 19–26.

Abo-Sinna, M. A., & Amer, A. H. (2005). Extensions of TOPSIS for multiobjective large-scale nonlinear programming problems. Applied Mathematics and Computation, 162, 243–256. doi:10.1016/j.amc.2003.12.087

ABS. (2009). Smart Look. Retrieved June 30, 2009, from http://www.smart-mirror.com

Aceña, M., Martín, F., & De Pascual, A. (2007). Estimación de Emisiones de Partículas PM10 desde Fuentes Difusas. Paper presented at I Congreso Colombiano de Calidad del Aire y Salud Pública, Manízales, Colombia.

ACI Committee. 209. (1982). Prediction of Creep, Shrinkage and Temperature Effects in Concrete Structures. ACI 209-82. American Concrete Institute, Detroit.

Activisu. (2009). Activisu Expert. Retrieved June 29, 2009, from http://www.activisu.com

Adamatti, D. F., Sichman, J. S., & Coelho, H. (2007). Virtual players: From manual to semiautonomous RPG. In C. Frydman (Ed.), AI, Simulation and Planning in High Autonomy Systems (AIS) and Conceptual Modeling and Simulation (CMS). Joint to International Modeling and Simulation Multiconference 2007 (IMSM07), Buenos Aires – Argentina.

Adamatti, D. F., Sichman, J., Bommel, P., Ducrot, R., Rabak, C., & Camargo, M. (2005). JogoMan: A prototype using multi-agent-based simulation and role-playing games in water management. In N. Ferrand (Ed.), Joint Conference on Multi-Agent Modeling for Environmental Management, (CABM-HEMA-SMAGET), Bourg-Saint-Maurice, Les Arcs, France.

Adams, J. (Ed.). (2007). Vegetation-Climate Interaction. Chichester, UK: Springer-Praxis.

Afonso, V. X., Tompkins, W. J., Nguyen, T. Q., & Luo, S. (1999). ECG beat detection using filter banks. IEEE Transactions on Bio-Medical Engineering, 46, 192–201. doi:10.1109/10.740882

Aguiar, M. S., Dimuro, G. P., & Costa, A. C. R. (2004b). ICTM: An Interval Tessellation-Based Model for Reliable Topographic Segmentation. Numerical Algorithms, 37(1-4), 3–11. doi:10.1023/B:NUMA.0000049453.95969.41

Aguiar, M. S., Dimuro, G. P., Costa, A. C. R., Silva, R. K. S., Costa, F. A., & Kreinovich, V. (2004a). The multi-layered interval categorizer tesselation-based model. In C. Iochpe & G. Câmara (Eds.), VI Brazilian Symposium on Geoinformatics, 22-24 November, Campos do Jordão, São Paulo, Brazil (pp. 437–454).

Ahmad, S., & Simonovic, S. P. (2005). An artificial neural network model for generating hydrograph from hydro-meteorological parameters. Journal of Hydrology (Amsterdam), 315(1), 236–251. doi:10.1016/j.jhydrol.2005.03.032

Aida, M. J., Francisco, R. V., & Cruz, N. A. (1996). A study on impact of climate variability/change on water resources in the Philippines. Chemosphere, 33(9), 1687–1704. doi:10.1016/0045-6535(96)00185-3

Aires de Sousa, J. (2002). JATOON: Java tools for neural networks. Chemometrics and Intelligent Laboratory Systems, 61(1-2), 167–173. doi:10.1016/S0169-7439(01)00171-X

Akaike, H. (1969). Fitting autoregressive models for prediction. Annals of the Institute of Statistical Mathematics, 20, 425–439. doi:10.1007/BF02911655

Aldec Active, H. D. L. (2009). Retrieved from http://www.aldec.com/ActiveHDL/

Aldrin, M., & Horback, H. H. (2005). Generalised additive modeling of air pollution, traffic volume and meteorology. Atmospheric Environment, 39, 2145–2155. doi:10.1016/j.atmosenv.2004.12.020

Alessandri, A., & Navarra, A. (2008). On the coupling between vegetation and rainfall inter-annual anomalies: Possible contributions to seasonal rainfall predictability over land areas. Geophysical Research Letters, 35, L02718. doi:10.1029/2007GL032415

Ali, B., Almaini, A., & Kalganova, T. (2004). Evolutionary Algorithms and Their Use in the Design of Sequential Logic Circuits. []. Amsterdam: Kluwer Academic Publisher.]. Genetic Programming and Evolvable Machines, 5, 11–29. doi:10.1023/B:GENP.0000017009.11392.e2

Allen, C., Haupt, E., & Young, G. (2007b). Source characterization with a genetic algorithm-coupled dispersion/backward model incorporate SCIPUFF. Journal of Applied Meteorology and Climatology, 46(3), 273–287. doi:10.1175/JAM2459.1

Allen, C., Young, G., & Haupt, S. E. (2007a). Improving pollutant source characterization by better estimating wind direction with a genetic algorithm. Atmospheric Environment, 41, 2283–2289. Retrieved from doi:10.1016/j.atmosenv.2006.11.007

Allende, C., Rebolo, R., Garcia, R., & Serra-Ricart, M. (2000). The INT Search for Metall-Poor Stars. Spectroscopic Observations and Classification via Artificial Neural Networks. The Astronomical Journal, 120, 1516–1531. doi:10.1086/301533

Alpaydin, E. (2004). Introduction to Machine Learning (Adaptive Computation and Machine Learning). Cambridge, MA: MIT Press.

Altera. (2009). Retrieved from http://www.altera.com/products/software/quartus-ii/subscription-edition/qts-se-index.html

Amarakoon, D., & Chen, A. (1999). Estimating daytime net radiation using routine meteorological data in Jamaica. Caribbean Journal of Science, 35(1-2), 132–141.

Amiguet-Vercher, J., Szarowicz, A., & Forte, P. (2001). Synchronized Multi-agent Simulations for Automated Crowd Scene Simulation. In AGENT-1 Workshop Proceedings, IJCAI 2001, August 2001.

Anderson, J. (1995). Learning and Memory: An Integrated Approach. New York: John Wiley and Sons.

Andrade, J. M., Kubista, M., Carlosena, A., & Prada, D. (2007). 3-Way characterization of soils by Procrustes rotation, matrix-augmented principal components analysis and parallel factor analysis. Analytica Chimica Acta, 603(1), 20–29. doi:10.1016/j.aca.2007.09.043

Angelov, P., & Zhou, X. (2008). Evolving Fuzzy-Rule-Based Classifiers From Data Streams, Fuzzy Systems. IEEE transactions on Fuzzy Systems, 16(6), 1462–1475. doi:10.1109/TFUZZ.2008.925904

Angelov, P., Zhou, X., & Klawonn, F. (2007). Evolving fuzzy rule-based classifiers. In Computational Intelligence in Image and Signal Processing (pp. 220-225).

Arakawa, M., Hasegawa, K., & Funatsu, K. (2006). QSAR study of anti-HIV HEPT analogues based on multi-objective genetic programming and counter-propagation neural network. Chemometrics and Intelligent Laboratory Systems, 83(2), 91–98. doi:10.1016/j.chemolab.2006.01.009

Arbib, M. (2002). The Handbook of Brain Theory and Neural Networks. Cambridge, MA: MIT Press.

Arbib, M. A. (1969). Theories of Abstract Automata. Upper Saddle River, NJ: Prentice-Hall.

Arciszewski, T., & De Jong, K. A. (2001). Evolutionary computation in civil engineering: research frontiers. In B. H. V. Topping (Ed.), Proceedings of the Eight International Conference on Civil and Structural Engineering Computing, Eisenstadt, Vienna, Austria.

Arias, G., Ciurana, J., Planta, X., & Crehuet, A. (2007). Analyzing Process Parameters that influence laser machining of hardened steel using Taguchi method. In Proceedings of 52nd International Technical Conference SAMPE 2007, Baltimore.

Armitage, P. (1995). Test for linear trends in proportions and frequencies. Biometrics, 11, 375–386. doi:10.2307/3001775

Arrhythmia Database, M. I. T.-B. I. H. (n.d.). Retrieved April 14, 2009, from http://www.physionet.org/physiobank/mitdb

Artiñano, B., Gómez Moreno, F. J., Pujadas, M., et al. (2006). Measurement particulate concentrations produced during bulk material handling at Tarragona Harbour. Atmospheric Environment, 41, 6344-6355. Retrieved from doi:www.elsevier.com/j.atmosenv.2006.12.020

Ashburner, M., Ball, C. A., Blake, J. A., Botstein, D., Butler, H., & Cherry, J. M. (2000). Gene Ontology: tool for the unification of biology. Nature Genetics, 25(1), 25–29. doi:10.1038/75556

Ashour, A. F., Alvarez, L. F., & Toropov, V. V. (2003). Empirical modelling of shear strength of RC deep beams by genetic programming. Computers & Structures, 81, 331–338. doi:10.1016/S0045-7949(02)00437-6

Asuncion, A., & Newman, D. J. (2007). UCI Machine Learning Repository. Irvine, CA: University of California, School of Information and Computer Science. Retrieved from http://www.ics.uci.edu/~mlearn/ML-Repository.html

Åženkal, O., & Kuleli, T. (2009). Estimation of solar radiation over Turkey using artificial neural network and satellite data. Applied Energy, 86(7-8), 1222–1228. doi:10.1016/j.apenergy.2008.06.003

Azuma, R. T. (1997). A survey of augmented reality. Presence (Cambridge, Mass.), 6, 355–385.

Bahoura, M., Hassani, M., & Hubin, M. (1997). DSP implementation of wavelet transform for real time ECG wave forms detection and heart rate analysis. Computer Methods and Programs in Biomedicine, 52, 35–44. doi:10.1016/S0169-2607(97)01780-X

Bailer-Jones, C. A. L. (2000). Stellar parameters from very low resolution spectra and medium band filters. Astronomy & Astrophysics, 357, 197–205.

Bailer-Jones, C. A. L. (2008). A method for exploiting domain information in astrophysical parameter estimation. In Astronomical Data Analysis Software and Systems XVII. ASP Conference Series (Vol. 30).

Bakker, P., & Kuniyoshi, Y. (1996). Robot see, Robot do: an overview of robot imitation. In the AISB Workshop on Learning in Robots and Animals, Brighton, UK.

Balaguer, E., Camps, G., Carrasco, J. L., Soria, E., & del Valle, S. (2002). Effective 1-day ahead prediction of hourly surface ozone concentrations in eastern Spain using linear models and neural networks. Ecological Modelling, 156, 27–41. doi:10.1016/S0304-3800(02)00127-8

Balding, D. (2006). A tutorial on statistical methods for population association Studies. Nature Reviews. Genetics, 7, 781–791. doi:10.1038/nrg1916

Ballabio, D., Consonni, V., & Todeschini, R. (2007b). Classification of multiway analytical data based on MOLMAP approach. Analytica Chimica Acta, 605(2), 134–146. doi:10.1016/j.aca.2007.10.029

Ballabio, D., Consonni, V., & Todeschini, R. (2009). The Kohonen and CP-ANN toolbox: a collection of MATLAB modules for Self Organizing Maps and Counterpropagation Artificial Neural Networks. Chemometrics and Intelligent Laboratory Systems, 98, 115–122. doi:10.1016/j.chemolab.2009.05.007

Ballabio, D., Kokkinofta, R., Todeschini, R., & Theocharis, C. R. (2007a). Characterization of the traditional Cypriot spirit Zivania by means of Counterpropagation Artificial Neural Networks. Chemometrics and Intelligent Laboratory Systems, 87(1), 52–58. doi:10.1016/j.chemolab.2006.09.002

Bandini, S., Manzoni, S., & Vizzari, G. (2002). RPG-Profiler: a MAS for role playing games based tests in employee assessment.

Bandivadekar, A., Cheah, L., Evans, C., Groode, T., Heywood, J., & Kasseris, E. (2008). Reducing the fuel use and greenhouse gas emissions of the US vehicle fleet. Energy Policy, 36(7), 2754–2760. doi:10.1016/j.enpol.2008.03.029

Banzhaf, W., Beslon, G., Christensen, S., Foster, J. A., Kepes, F., & Lefort, V. (2006). Guidelines: from artificial evolution to computacional evolution: a research agenda. Nature Reviews. Genetics, 7(9), 729–735. doi:10.1038/nrg1921

Barreteau, O., Bousquet, F., Millier, C., & Weber, J. (2004). Suitability of multi-agent simulations to study irrigated system viability: Application to case studies in the segal river valley. Agricultural Systems, 80(3), 255–275. doi:10.1016/j.agsy.2003.07.005

Barreteau, O., Le Page, C., & D'Aquino, P. (2003). Role-playing games, models and negotiation. JASSS, 6(2). Retrieved from http://jasss.soc.surrey.ac.uk/6/2/10.html

Barron, F. H., & Barrett, B. E. (1996). Decision Quality Using Ranked Attribute Weights. Management Science, 42(11), 1515–1523. doi:10.1287/mnsc.42.11.1515

Bas, J. L. (2007). Real Time Suggestion of Related Ideas in the Financial Industry. W3C Semantic Web use cases and case Studies. Retrieved May 5, 2009, from http://www.w3.org/2001/sw/sweo/public/UseCases/Bankinter/

Basso, M., Bencivenni, F., & Giarre, L. Groppi, S., & Zappa., G. (2002, December). Experience with NARX Model Identification of an Industrial Power Plant Gas Turbine. In 41st IEEE Conference on Decision and Control, Las Vegas, Nevada, USA (pp. 3710–3711).

Battocchi, A., & Pianesi, F. (2004). Dafex: Un database di espressioni facciali dinamiche. In SLI-GSCP Workshop Comunicazione Parlata e Manifestazione delle Emozioni.

Baycu, G., Tolunay, D., Özden, H., & Günebakan, S. (2006). Ecophysiological and seasonal variations in Cd, Pb, Zn, and Ni concentrations in the leaves of urban deciduous trees in Istanbul. Environmental Pollution, 143(3), 545–554. doi:10.1016/j.envpol.2005.10.050

Bazant, Z. P., & Baweja, S. (1995). Creep and Shrinkage Prediction Model for Analysis and Design of Concrete Structures - Model B3. Materials and Structures, 28, 357–365. doi:10.1007/BF02473152

Beasley, D., Bull, D. R., & Martin, R. R. (1993). A sequential niche technique for multimodal function optimization. Evolutionary Computation, 1(2), 101–125. doi:10.1162/evco.1993.1.2.101

Beccali, M., Cellura, M., & Ardente, D. (1998). Decision Making in Energy Planning: The ELECTRE Multicriteria Analysis Approach Compare to a Fuzzy-Sets methodology. Energy Conversion and Management, 39(16-18), 1869–1881. doi:10.1016/S0196-8904(98)00053-3

Beg, M. M. S., & Ahmad, N. (2003). Soft Computing Techniques for Rank Aggregation on the World Wide Web. World Wide Web: Internet and Web Information Systems, 6, 5–22.

Bein, K. J., & Zao, Y. (2007). Identification of sources of atmospheric PM at the Pittsburg Supersite – Part III: Source characterization. Atmospheric Environment, 41, 3974–3992. Retrieved from doi:10.1016/j.atmosenv.2007.01.039

Beniston, M. (Ed.). (1998). From turbulence to climate: numerical investigations of the atmosphere with a hierarchy of models. Berlin: Springer.

Bennett, K. P., & Mangasarian, O. L. (1992). Robust linear programming discrimination of two linearly inseparable sets. Optimization Methods and Software, 1, 23–34. doi:10.1080/10556789208805504

Bennie, J., Huntley, B., Wiltshire, A., Hill, M. O., & Baxter, R. (2008). Slope, aspect and climate: Spatially explicit and implicit models of topographic microclimate in chalk grassland. Ecological Modelling, 216(1), 47–59. doi:10.1016/j.ecolmodel.2008.04.010

Bentley, P. J. (2002). Digital Biology. New York: Simon and Schuster.

Berners-Lee, T., Hendler, J., & Lassila, O. (2001). The semantic web. Scientific American, 284(5), 34–43. doi:10.1038/scientificamerican0501-34

Bidel, S., Lemoine, L., & Piat, F. (2003). Statistical machine learning for tracking hypermedia user behavior. In Proceedings of the 2nd workshop on machine learning, information retrieval and user modeling (pp. 56-65).

Bishop, C. (2007). Pattern Recognition and Machine Learning (Information Science and Statistics). New York: Springer-Verlag.

Bishop, C. M. (1996). Neural Networks for Pattern Recognition. Oxford, UK: Clarendon Press.

Blake, C., & Merz, C. (1998). UCI repository of ML databases. Retrieved April 14, 2009, from http://archive.ics.uci.edu/ml/

Bland, I. M., & Megson, G. M. (1996). Systolic random number generation for genetic algorithms. Electronic Letters.Bland, I. M., & Megson, G. M. (1997, June). Efficient operator pipelining in a bit serial genetic algorithm engine. Electronic Letters.

Bodenhofer, U., Hüllermeier, E., Klawonn, F., & Kruse, R. (2007). Special issue on soft computing for information mining. Soft Computing, 11, 397–399. doi:10.1007/s00500-006-0105-3

Boneva, B., Quinn, A., Kraut, R., Kiesler, S., Cummings, J., & Shklovski, I. (2006). Instant messaging in teen life. In R. Kraut, M. Brynin & S. Kiesler (Eds.), Computers, Phones, and the Internet: The Social Impact of Information Technology. Oxford, UK: Oxford University Press.

Bouckaert, R. R. (2004). Bayesian networks in Weka. Computer Science Department. University of Waikato, 14.

Bouguet, J. (1999). Pyramidal implementation of the Lucas Kanade feature tracker. Technical report, Intel Corporation, Microprocessor Research Labs, OpenCV documents.

Bounoua, L., Collatz, G. J., Los, S. O., Sellers, P. J., Dazlich, D. A., Tucker, C. J., & Randall, D. A. (2000). Sensitivity of climate to changes in NDVI. Journal of Climate, 13, 2277–2292. doi:10.1175/1520-0442(2000)013<2277:SOCTCI>2.0.CO;2

Bradski, G. R. (1998). Computer vision face tracking as a component of a perceptual user interface. In Workshop on Applications of Computer Vision (pp. 214-219).

Brans, J. P., Mareschal, B., & Vincke, P. H. (1984). PROMETHEE: A New Family of Outranking Methods in MCDM. In International Federation of Operational Research Studies (IFORS 84), North Holland (pp. 470-490).

Brans, J. P., Vincke, P. H., & Mareschal, B. (1986). How to select and how to rank projects: the PROMETHEE method. European Journal of Operational Research, 24, 228–238. doi:10.1016/0377-2217(86)90044-5

Briot, J. P., Guyot, P., & Irving, M. (2007). Participatory simulation for collective management of protected areas for biodiversity conservation and social inclusion. In C. Frydman (Ed.), International Modeling and Simulation Multiconference (IMSM07), Buenos Aires - Argentina.

Bro, R. (2006). Review on Multiway Analysis in Chemistry – 2000-2005. Critical Reviews in Analytical Chemistry, 36(3-4), 279–293. doi:10.1080/10408340600969965

Brun, A., Bonnin, G., & Boyer, A. (2009). History dependent Recommender Systems based on Partial Matching. In G-J. Houben, G. McCalla, F. Pianesi & M. Zancanari (Eds.), User Modeling, Adaptation and Personalization 2009 (pp. 343-348). Berlin: Springer-Verlag.

Bruno, F., Caruso, F., & Pisacane, O. (2008). A web3D application for the bin-packaging problem. In 20th European Modeling and Simulation Symposium (Simulation in Industry), EMSS08, Calabria, Italy.

Buechner, A. G., Baumgarten, M., Anand, S. S., Mulvenna, M. D., & Hughes, J. G. (1999). Navigation Pattern Discovery from Internet Data. Workshop on Web Usage Analysis and User Profiling (pp.92-111), Springer.

Bull, S., Gardner, P., Ahmad, N., Ting, J., & Clarke, B. (2009). Use and Trust of Simple Independent Open Learner Models to Support Learning Within and Across Courses, in G-J. Houben, G, McCalla, F. Pianesi and M. Zancanari (eds), User Modeling, Adaptation and Personalization 2009 (pp. 42-53). Springer-Verlag, Berlin Heidelberg.

Burges, C. (1998). A Tutorial on Support Vector Machines for Pattern Recognition. Data Mining and Knowledge Discovery, 2(2), 121–167. doi:10.1023/A:1009715923555

Burks, A. W. (1970). Essays on Cellular Automata. University of Illinois Press, Urbana and Chicago.

Campo, G., Orsi, M., Badino, G., Giacomelli, R., & Spezzano, P. (1996). Evaluation of motorway pollution in a mountain ecosystem. Pilot project: Susa Valley (Northwest Italy) years 1990-1994. The Science of the Total Environment, 189/190, 161–166. doi:10.1016/0048-9697(96)05205-9

Campos, A., Fernández, M. J., Berrueta, D., Polo, L., & Mínguez, I. (2008). CRUZAR: An application of semantic matchmaking for eTourism in the city of Zaragoza. W3C Semantic Web case studies and use cases. Retrieved April 16, 2009, from http://www.w3.org/2001/sw/sweo/public/UseCases/Zaragoza-2/

Cantu-Paz, E. (1995). A summary of research on parallel genetic algorithms. University of Illinois.

Carl Zeiss Vision. (2009). Lens Frame Assistant. Retrieved June 30, 2009, from http://www.zeiss.com

Carlosena, A., Andrade, J. M., & Prada, D. (1998). Searching for heavy metals grouping roadside soils as a function of motorized traffic influence. Talanta, 47(3), 753–767. doi:10.1016/S0039-9140(98)00117-9

Carlosena, A., Andrade, J. M., Kubista, M., & Prada, D. (1995). Procrustes Rotation as a Way to Compare Different Sampling Seasons in Soils. Analytical Chemistry, 67(14), 2373–2378. doi:10.1021/ac00110a008

Carnevale, C., Finzi, G., Pisoni, E., Singh, V., & Volta, M. (2007). Neuro-fuzzy and neural network systems for air quality control. In Urban Air Quality 2007, UAQ 2007, March 27-29, Cyprus.

Castrillón, M., Déniz, O., Hernández, M., & Guerra, C. (2007). ENCARA2: Real-time detection of multiple faces at different resolutions in video streams. Journal of Visual Communication and Image Representation, 18(2), 130–140. doi:10.1016/j.jvcir.2006.11.004

Castro, M. B., Fernandes, L. G. L., Pousa, C., Méhaut, J. F., & Aguiar, M. S. (in press). NUMA-ICTM: A Parallel Version of ICTM Exploiting Memory Placement. In PDSEC-09: The 10th IEEE International Workshop on Parallel and Distributed Scientific and Engineering Computing, Roma.

Chaitin, G. J. (1997). Algorithmic information theory. Cambridge, UK: Cambridge University Press.

Chan, H., & Mazumder, P. (1995). A systolic architecture for high speed hypergraph partitioning using genetic algorithms. Berlin: Springer-Verlag.

Chen, Q., & Ye, F. (2008). Unstructured cellular automata and the application to model river riparian vegetation dynamics. In H. Umeo, S. Morishita, K. Nishinari, T. Komatsuzaki, & S. Bandini (Eds.), Cellular Automata, 8th International Conference on Cellular Automata for Reseach and Industry (ACRI 2008), Yokohama, Japan, September 23-26, 2008 (LNCS 5191, pp. 337–344).

Chen, S., & Billings, S. A. (1989). Representations of Non-linear Systems: The Narmax model. International Journal of Control, 49(3), 1013–1032.

Chen, T. Q., & Lu, Y. (2002). Color image segmentation: an innovative approach. Pattern Recognition, 35(2), 395–405. doi:10.1016/S0031-3203(01)00050-4

Cheng, H. D., Jiang, X. H., Sun, Y., & Wang, J. L. (2001). Color image segmentation: advances and prospects. Pattern Recognition, 34(12), 2259–2281. doi:10.1016/S0031-3203(00)00149-7

Cheng, H., Jiang, X., & Wang, J. (2002). Color image segmentation based on histogram thresholding and region merging. Pattern Recognition, 35(2), 373–393. doi:10.1016/S0031-3203(01)00054-1

Chirn, G., Wang, G. T., & Wang, Z. (1997). Scientific Data Classification: A Case Study. In Tools with Artificial Intelligence (pp. 216-222).

Chiu, B. C., & Webb, G. I. (1999). Dual-model: An Architecture for Utilizing Temporal Information in Student Modeling, International conference on Computers in Education, Amsterdam, vol. 1., (pp. 111-118). IOS Press.

Chiunhsiun, L. (2007). Face detection in complicated backgrounds and different illumination conditions by using YCbCr color space and neural network. Pattern Recognition Letters, 28, 2190–2200. doi:10.1016/j.patrec.2007.07.003

Chopard, B., & Lagrava, D. (2006). A cellular automata model for species competition and evolution. In S. E. Yacoubi, B. Chopard, & S. Bandini (Eds.), Cellular Automata, 7th International Conference on Cellular Automata, for Research and Industry (ACRI 2006), Perpignan, France, September 20-23, 2006 (LNCS 4173, pp. 277–286).

Christlieb, N., Wisotzki, L., & Graßhoff, G. (2002). Statistical Methods of automatic spectral classification and their application to the Hamburg/ESO sourvey. Astronomy & Astrophysics, 391, 397–406. doi:10.1051/0004-6361:20020830

CIRAD. (2008). La recherche agronomique au service des pays du Sud. Retrieved December 2008, from http://www.cirad.fr/

Ciurana, J., Arias, G., & Ozel, T. (2009). Neural network modeling and particle swarm optimization of process parameters in pulsed laser micro-machining of hardened AISI H13 steel. Materials and Manufacturing Processes, 24, 358–368. doi:10.1080/10426910802679568

Cladera, A., & Marí, A. R. (2004). Shear design procedure for reinforced normal and high-strength concrete beams using artificial neural networks. Part I: beams without stirrups. Engineering Structures, 26, 917–926. doi:10.1016/j.engstruct.2004.02.010

Clark, T. G., De Iorio, M., Griffiths, R. C., & Farrall, M. (2005). Finding associations in dense genetic maps: a genetic algorithm approach. Human Heredity, 60, 97–108. doi:10.1159/000088845

Co, C. B. C. (2009). Camirror. Retrieved June 30, 2009, from http://www.camirror.com

Coblentz, D. D., Kreinovich, V., Penn, B. S., & Starks, S. A. (2000). Towards reliable sub-division of geological areas: interval approach. In Proc. of 19th International Conference of the North American. Fuzzy Information Processing Society (NAFIPS) (pp. 368-372).

Coello Coello, C. A., Van Veldhuizen, D. A., & Lamont, G. B. (2002). Evolutionary Algorithms for Solving Multi-Objective Problems. New York: Kluwer Academic Publishers.

Cohen, P. R., Perrault, C. R., & Allen, J. F. (1982). Beyond Question Answering, In W. G. Lehnert and M. H. Ringle(Ed.), Strategies for Natural Language Processing, 245-274. Hillsdale, NJ.

Cohoon, J. P., Martin, W. N., & Richards, D. S. (1991). Genetic algorithms and punctuated equilibria in VLSI. In Proceedings of 1st Workshop, October 1991. Berlin: Springer-Verlag

Collin, R. E. (1966). Foundations for Microwave Engineering. New York: McGraw-Hill Book Co.

Comaniciu, D., & Meer, P. (1997). Robust analysis of feature spaces: color image segmentation. In IEEE Conference on Computer Vision and Pattern Recognition (pp. 750-55).

Company, P. (1997). Integrating Creative Steps in CAD Process. In International Seminar on Principles and Methods of Engineering Design. Proceedings, 1, 295–322.

Conte, R., Gilbert, N., & Sichman, J. S. (1998). MAS and Social Simulation: A Suitable Commitment. In Proceedings of the 1st International Workshop on Multi-Agent Systems and Agent-Based Simulation (MABS-98) (LNAI 1534, pp. 1-9).

Cook, N. R., Zee, R. Y. L., & Ridker, P. M. (2004). Tree and spline based association analysis of gene-gene interaction models for ischemic stroke. Statistics in Medicine, 23, 1439–1453. doi:10.1002/sim.1749

Cooley, J. W., & Tukey, J. W. (1965). An algorithm for the machine calculation of complex Fourier series. Mathematics of Computation, 19, 297–301. doi:10.2307/2003354

Corani, G. (2005). Air quality prediction in Milan: feed forward neural networks, pruned neural networks an lazy learning. Ecological Modelling, 185, 513–529. doi:10.1016/j.ecolmodel.2005.01.008

Corchado, E., & Fyfe, C. (2003). Connectionist Techniques for the Identification and Suppression of Interfering Underlying Factors. International Journal of Pattern Recognition and Artificial Intelligence, 17(8), 1447–1466. doi:10.1142/S0218001403002915

Corchado, E., Han, Y., & Fyfe, C. (2003). Structuring Global Responses of Local Filters Using Lateral Connections. Journal of Experimental & Theoretical Artificial Intelligence, 15(4), 473–487. doi:10.1080/09528130310001611603

Corchado, E., MacDonald, D., & Fyfe, C. (2004). Maximum and Minimum Likelihood Hebbian Learning for Exploratory Projection Pursuit. Data Mining and Knowledge Discovery, 8(3), 203–225. doi:10.1023/B:DAMI.0000023673.23078.a3

Cordell, H. J., & Clayton, D. G. (2002). A unified stepwise regression approach for evaluating the relative effects of polymorphisms within a gene using case/control or family data: application to HLA in type 1 diabetes. American Journal of Human Genetics, 70, 124–141. doi:10.1086/338007

Cosio, M. S., Ballabio, D., Benedetti, S., & Gigliotti, C. (2006). Geographical origin and authentication of extra virgin olive oils by an electronic nose in combination with artificial neural networks. Analytica Chimica Acta, 567(2), 202–210. doi:10.1016/j.aca.2006.03.035

Coull, S. E., Branch, J. W., Szymanski, B. K., & Breimer, E. (2003). Intrusion Detection: A Bioinformatics Approach. In Computer Security Applications Conference (pp.24-33).

Coulthard, T. J., & De Wiel, M. J. V. (2006). A cellular model of river meandering. Earth Surface Processes and Landforms, 31(1), 123–132. doi:10.1002/esp.1315

Cristianini, N., & Shawe-Taylor, J. (2000). An introduction to support vector machines. Cambridge, UK: Cambridge University Press.

Cruzado, J. J. (2004) Algoritmos de Estimación e Interpolación de Parámetros Geofísicos. Unpublished Magíster Thesis, Universidad de Puerto Rico, San Juan. Retrieved from http://grad.uprm.edu/tesis/cruzadojapan.pdf

Cybenko, G. V. (1989). Approximation by Superpositions of a Sigmoidal function. Mathematics of Control, Signals, and Systems, 2(4), 303–314. doi:10.1007/BF02551274

CyberImaging. (2009). CyberEyes. Retrieved from http://www.cyber-imaging.com

Darwin, C. (1859). On the origin of species by means of natural selection or the preservation of favoured races in the struggle for life. Cambridge, UK: Cambridge University Press.

Darwin, C. (1859). On the Origin of the Species by Means of Natural Selection.

Daubechies, I. (1988). Orthonormal bases of compactly supported wavelets. Communications on Pure and Applied Mathematics, 41, 909–996. doi:10.1002/cpa.3160410705

Davis, L. (1991). Handbook of Genetic Algorithms. New York: Van Nostrand Reinhold.

De Jong, K. A. (1988). Learning with genetic algorithms: an overview. Machine Learning, 3(2/3), 121–138. doi:10.1023/A:1022606120092

De Jong, K. A., Spears, W. M., & Gordon, D. F. (1993). Using genetic algorithms for concept learning. Machine Learning, 13(2/3), 161–188. doi:10.1023/A:1022617912649

de Jong, R., Shaykewich, C. F., & Reimer, A. (1980). The calculation of the net radiation flux. Archiv Für Meteorologie Geophysik Und Bioklimatologie . Serie B, 28, 353–363.

De, R., Pal, N. R., & Pal, S. K. (1997). Feature analysis: neural network and fuzzy set theoretic approaches. Pattern Recognition, 30(10), 1579–1590. doi:10.1016/S0031-3203(96)00190-2

De, T., & Meneghetti, A. (2000). The production planning process for a network of firms in the textile-apparel industry. International Journal of Production Economics, 65, 17–32. doi:10.1016/S0925-5273(99)00087-0

Delabie, C., Villegas, M., & Picon, O. (1997). Creation of new shapes for resonant microstrip structures by means of a genetic algorithm. Electronics Letters, 33, 1509–1510. doi:10.1049/el:19971017

Dellaert, F., & Beer, R. D. (1996). A Developmental Model for the Evolution of Complete Autonomous Agent. In From animals to animats: Proceedings of the Forth International Conference on Simulation of Adaptive Behaviour, Massachusetts, 9-13 September 1996 (pp. 394-401). Cambridge, MA: MIT Press.

Den Dunnen, J. T., & Antonarakis, S. E. (2000). Mutation Nomenclature Extensions and Suggestions to Describe Complex Mutations: A Discussion. Human Mutation, 15, 7–12. doi:10.1002/(SICI)1098-1004(200001)15:1<7::AID-HUMU4>3.0.CO;2-N

Déniz, O., Hernández, M., Lorenzo, J., & Castrillón, M. (2007). An Engineering Approach to Sociable Robots. Journal of Experimental & Theoretical Artificial Intelligence, 19(4), 285–306. doi:10.1080/09528130701208174

deRidder, D., & Handels, H. (2002). Image processing with neural networks – a review. Pattern Recognition, 35, 2279–2301. doi:10.1016/S0031-3203(01)00178-9

Deschamps, G. A. (1953). Microstrip Microwave Antennas. In The Third Symposium on The USAF Antenna Research and Development Program (pp. 18-22), University of Illinois, Monticello, Illinois.

Diaconis, P., & Freedman, D. (1984). Asymptotics of Graphical Projections. Annals of Statistics, 12(3), 793–815. doi:10.1214/aos/1176346703

Diego, G., & Loyola, R. (2006). Applications of neural network methods to the processing of earth observation satellite data. Neural Networks, 19(2), 168–177. doi:10.1016/j.neunet.2006.01.010

Ding, Y., & Foo, S. (2002). Ontology research and development. Part 2-a review of ontology mapping and evolving. Journal of Information Science, 28(5), 375.

Dong, G., & Xie, M. (2005). Color clustering and learning for image segmentation based on neural networks. IEEE Transactions on Neural Networks, 16(4). doi:10.1109/TNN.2005.849822

Dong, M., Yang, D., Kuang, Y., Hec, D., Erdald, S., & Kenskie, D. (2009). PM concentration prediction using hidden semi-Markov model-based times series next term data mining. Expert Systems with Applications, 36(5), 9046–9055. doi:10.1016/j.eswa.2008.12.017

Dote, Y., & Ovaska, S. J. (2001). Industrial Applications of Soft Computing: A Review. Proceedings of the IEEE, 89(9), 1243–1265. doi:10.1109/5.949483

Douglas, G. S., Owens, E. H., Hardenstine, J., & Prince, R. (2002). The OSSA II pipeline oil spill: the character and weathering of the spilled oil. Spill Science & Technology Bulletin, 7(3-4), 135–148. doi:10.1016/S1353-2561(02)00046-4

Douglas, G. S., Stout, S. A., Uhler, A. D., McCarthy, K. J., & Emsbo-Mattingly, S. D. (2007). Advantages of quantitative chemical fingerprinting in oil spill source identification. In Wang, Z. and Stout, S.A. Oil spill Environmental Forensics. Fingerprinting and source identification. Academic Press, United States of America.

Ducrot, R., Le Page, C., Bommel, P., & Kuper, M. (2004). Articulating land and water dynamics with urbanization: an attempt to model natural resources management at the urban edge. Computers, Environment and Urban Systems, 28(1-2), 85–106. doi:10.1016/S0198-9715(02)00066-2

Duda, R. O., Hart, P. E., & Stork, D. G. (2000). Pattern Classification (2nd ed.). New York: Wiley-Interscience.

Edwards, W., & Barron, F. H. (1994). SMARTS and SMARTER: Improved simple methods for multiattribute utility measurement. Organizational Behavior and Human Decision Processes, 60, 306–325. doi:10.1006/obhd.1994.1087

Eggenberger, P. (1996). Cell Interactions as a Control Tool of Developmental Processes for Evolutionary Robotics. In From animals to animats: Proceedings of the Forth International Conference on Simulation of Adaptive Behaviour, Massachusetts, 9-13 September 1996 (pp. 440-448). Cambridge, MA: MIT Press.

Ehrig, M. (2007). Ontology alignment: bridging the semantic gap. New York: Springer-Verlag Inc.

Elizondo, D., Hoogenboom, G., & McClendon, R. W. (1994). Development of neural network model to predict daily solar radiation. Agricultural and Forest Meteorology, 7, 115–132. doi:10.1016/0168-1923(94)90103-1

EPA-42 1995 AP 42. (1995). Compilation of Air Pollutant Emission Factors, Volume 1: Stationary Point and Area Sources (5th Ed.). Washington, DC: Environmental Protection Agency. Retrieved from http://www.epa.gov/ttn/chief/ap42/index.html

Esen, H., & Inalli, M. (2009). Modelling of a vertical ground heat pump system by using Artificial Neural Networks. Expert Systems with Applications, 36(7), 10229–10238. doi:10.1016/j.eswa.2009.01.055

Esen, H., Ozgen, F., Esen, M., & Sengur, A. (2009). Modelling of a new solar air heater through least-squares support vector machines. Expert Systems with Applications, 36(7), 10673–10682. doi:10.1016/j.eswa.2009.02.045

Etienne, M. (2003). SYLVOPAST: a multiple target role-playing game to assess negotiation processes in sylvo-pastoral management planning. JASSS, 6(2). Retrieved from http://jasss.soc.surrey.ac.uk/6/2/5.html

EU. (2002). European Parliament and the European Council. 2002/3/CE O.D. C 67 E. 9-3-2002, p. 14–20.

Eurocode 2. (2004). Design of Concrete Structures (EN 1992-1-1:2004). European Committee for Standardization.

Europa. (2007). Commission proposal to limit the CO2 emissions from cars to help fight climate change, reduce fuel costs, and increase European competitiveness. Retrieved June 19, 2008, from http://europa.eu/rapid/pressReleasesAction.do?reference=IP/07/1965

Euzenat, J., & Shvaiko, P. (2007). Ontology matching. Berlin: Springer-Verlag.

Euzenat, J., & Valtchev, P. (2004). Similarity-based ontology alignment in OWL-Lite. In Proceedings of 16th European Conference on Artificial Intelligence (ECAI), Amsterdam (pp. 333-337).

Euzenat, J., Le Bach, T., Barrasa, J., Bouquet, P., De Bo, J., Dieng, R., et al. (2004). State of the art on ontology alignment. Deliverable D2.2.3 v1.2. Knowledge Web. Retrieved December 21, 2008, from http://knowledgeweb.semanticweb.org/

Fan, H.-Y., & Lampinen, J. (2003). A Trigonometric Mutation Operation to Differential Evolution. Journal of Global Optimization, 27, 105–129. doi:10.1023/A:1024653025686

Farzan, R., & Brusilovsky, P. (2009). Social Navigation Support for Information Seeking: If You Build It, Will The Come? In G-J. Houben, G, McCalla, F. Pianesi and M. Zancanari (Ed.), User Modeling, Adaptation and Personalization 2009 (pp. 66-77). Springer-Verlag, Berlin Heidelberg.

Fasel, B., & Luettin, J. (2003). Automatic facial expression analysis: a survey. Pattern Recognition, 36, 259–275. doi:10.1016/S0031-3203(02)00052-3

Federer, C. A. (1968). Spatial variation of net radiation, albedo and surface temperature of forests. *Journal of Applied Meteorology*, 7, 789–795. doi:10.1175/1520-0450(1968)007<0789:SVONRA>2.0.CO;2

Federici, D. (2004). Using embryonic stages to increase the evolvability of development. In *Proceedings of WORLDS Workshop on Regeneration and Learning in Developmental Systems hosted by GECCO 2004*. New York: ACM Press.

Fermo, P., Cariati, F., Ballabio, D., Consonni, V., & Bagnasco, G. (2004). Classification of ancient Etruscan ceramics using statistical multivariate analysis of data. *Applied Physics. A, Materials Science & Processing*, 79(2), 299–307. doi:10.1007/s00339-004-2520-6

Fernandez-Blanco, E., Dorado, J., Rabuñal, J. R., Gestal, M., & Pedreira, N. (2007). A New Evolutionary Computation Technique for 2D Morphogenesis and Information Processing. In *WSEAS Transactions on Information Science & Applications*, April 2007 (Vol. 4, pp. 600-607).

Fernández-Castro, A. S., & Jiménez, M. (2005). PROMETHEE: an extension through fuzzy mathematical programming. *The Journal of the Operational Research Society*, 56, 119–122. doi:10.1057/palgrave.jors.2601828

Fernández-Varela, R., Suárez-Rodríguez, D., Gómez-Carracedo, M. P., Andrade, J. M., Fernández, E., Muniategui, S., & Prada, D. (2005). Screening the origin and weathering of oil slicks by attenuated total reflectance mid-IR spectrometry. *Talanta*, 68(1), 116–125. doi:10.1016/j.talanta.2005.04.061

Fiala, M. (2004). Artag, an improved marker system based on artoolkit. Technical Report ERB-1111, NRC Canada.

Fichera, A., & Pagano, A. (2002). Neural Network based Prediction of the oscillating behaviour of a closed loop Thermosyphon. *International Journal of Heat and Mass Transfer*, 45, 3875–3884. doi:10.1016/S0017-9310(02)00095-9

Fiorentin, P. R., Bailer-Jones, C. A. L., Lee, Y. S., Beers, T. C., Sivarani, T., & Wilhelm, R. (2007). Estimation of stellar atmospheric parameters from SDSS/SEGUE spectra. *Astronomy & Astrophysics*, 467, 1373–1387. doi:10.1051/0004-6361:20077334

Fogarty, T., Miller, J., & Thompson, P. (1998). Evolving digital logic circuits on Xilinx 6000 family FPGAs. In P. Chawdhry, R. Roy, & R. Pant (Eds.), *Soft Computing in Engineering Design and Manufacturing* (pp. 299–305). Springer: Berlin.

Fogel, L. J., Owens, A. J., & Walsh, M. A. (1966). *Artificial Intelligence through Simulated Evolution*. New York: Wiley.

Fonseca, A. M., Biscaya, J. L., Aires-de-Sousa, J., & Lobo, A. M. (2006). Geographical classification of crude oils by Kohonen self-organizing maps. *Analytica Chimica Acta*, 556(2), 374–382. doi:10.1016/j.aca.2005.09.062

Force, A., Lynch, M., Pickett, F. B., Amores, A., Lin Yan, Y., & Poshlethwait, J. (1999). Preservation of duplicate genes by complementary, degenerative mutations. *Genetics*, 151, 1531–1545.

Frank, I. E., & Todeschini, R. (1994). *The data analysis handbook*. Amsterdam: Elsevier.

Franses, P. H. (1999). *Time Series Models for Business and Economic Forecasting*. Cambridge, UK: Cambridge University Press.

Freeman, S., & Herron, J. (2002). *Análisis Evolutivo*. Madrid: Prentice Hall.

Fresco-Rivera, P., Fernández-Varela, R., Gómez-Carracedo, M. P., Ramírez-Villalobos, F., Prada, D., Muniategui, S., & Andrade, J. M. (2007). Development of a fast analytical tool to identify oil spillages employing infrared spectral indexes and pattern recognition techniques. *Talanta*, 74(2), 163–175. doi:10.1016/j.talanta.2007.05.047

Friedman, J. H., & Tukey, J. W. (1974). Projection Pursuit Algorithm for Exploratory Data-Analysis. *IEEE Transactions on Computers*, 23(9), 881–890. doi:10.1109/T-C.1974.224051

Fuchs, M. (1998). Crossover Versus Mutation: An Empirical and Theoretical Case Study. In J. R. Koza, W. Banzhaf, K. Chellapilla et al. (Eds.), 3rd Annual Conference on Genetic Programming (pp. 78-85) Madison, WI: Morgan-Kauffman.

Fuller, M. M., Wang, D., Gross, L. J., & Berry, M. W. (2007). Computational science for natural resource management. Computing in Science & Engineering, 9(4), 40–48. doi:10.1109/MCSE.2007.71

Fung, E., Wong, Y., Ho, H. F., & Mignolet, P. (2003). Modelling and Prediction of Machining Errors using ARMAX and NARMAX Structures. Applied Mathematical Modelling, 27, 611–627. doi:10.1016/S0307-904X(03)00071-4

Fyfe, C., & Corchado, E. (2002). Maximum Likelihood Hebbian Rules. In Proc. of the 10th European Symposium on Artificial Neural Networks (ESANN 2002) (pp. 143-148).

Gaia. (2009). The galactic census problem. Retrieved from http://www.rssd.esa.int/gaia/

Gaines, B. R., & Compton, P. (1995). Induction of Ripple-Down Rules Applied to Modeling Large Databases. Journal of Intelligent Information Systems, 5(3), 211–228. doi:10.1007/BF00962234

Gal, A., & Shvaiko, P. (2009). Advances in Ontology Matching. In Advances in Web Semantics, I: Ontologies, Web Services and Applied Semantic Web (pp. 176).

Gallardo, K. L. (1997). Modelos de dispersión de contaminantes atmosféricos. Comisión Nacional del Medio Ambiente (CONAMA), Santiago de Chile, 1997.

García-Haro, F. J., Belda, F., & Poquet, D. (2008). Estimation of climatological variables in Spain during the 1950-2008 period using geostatistical techniques. Paper presented at the 8th Annual Meeting of the EMS / 7th ECAC EMS8/ECAC7 Abstracts, Vol. 5, EMS2008-A-00319, 2008.

García-Haro, F. J., Sommer, S., & Kemper, T. (2005). Variable multiple endmember spectral mixture analysis (VMESMA). International Journal of Remote Sensing, 26, 2135–2162. doi:10.1080/01431160512331337817

Gardner, M. W., & Dorling, S. R. (1998). Artificial neural networks (the multilayer perceptron) - a review of applications in the atmospheric sciences. Atmospheric Environment, 32(14), 2627–2636. doi:10.1016/S1352-2310(97)00447-0

Garner, S. (1995). WEKA: The waikato environment for knowledge analysis. In Proc. of New Zealand Computer Science Research Students Conference (pp. 57-64).

Gasteiger, J., Li, X., Rudolph, C., Sadowski, J., & Zupan, J. (1994). Representation of Molecular Electrostatic Potentials by Topological Feature Maps. Journal of the American Chemical Society, 116(11), 4608–4620. doi:10.1021/ja00090a009

Geib, C. W., & Goldman, R. P. (2001). Plan Recognition in Intrusion Detection Systems, In DARPA Information Survivability Conference and Exposition (DISCEX).

Gentle, J. E., Härdle, W., & Mori, Y. (2004). Handbook of Computational Statistics. Concepts and Methods. Berlin: Springer-Verlag.

Georgopoulou, E., Sarafidis, Y., & Diakoulaki, D. (1998). Design and implementation of a group DSS for sustaining renewable energies exploitation. European Journal of Operational Research, 109, 483–500. doi:10.1016/S0377-2217(98)00072-1

Gilbert, N., & Troitzsch, K. G. (1999). Simulation for the Social Scientist. London: Open University Press.

Giles, C. L., & Gori, M. (1998). Adaptive Processing of Sequences and Data Structures. Summer School on Neural Networks, 1387, Springer.

Giordana, A., & Neri, F. (1995). Search intensive concept induction. Evolutionary Computation, 3(4), 375–416. doi:10.1162/evco.1995.3.4.375

Giustolisi, O., Doglioni, A., Savic, D. A., & Webb, B. W. (2007). A multi-model approach to analysis of environmental phenomena. Environmental Modelling & Software, 22, 674–682. doi:10.1016/j.envsoft.2005.12.026

Glover, J. (1972). Net radiation over tall and short grass. Agricultural Meteorology, 10, 455–459. doi:10.1016/0002-1571(72)90046-5

Godoy, D., & Amandi, A. (2005). User Profiling for Web Page Filtering. IEEE Internet Computing, 9(4). doi:10.1109/MIC.2005.90

Goldberg, D. E. (1989). Genetic Algorithms in Search, Optimization and Machine Learning. Boston, MA: Addison-Wesley Longman Publishing Co. Inc.

Goldberg, D. E., & Deb, K. (1991). A comparative analysis of selection schemes used in genetic algorithms. San Francisco: Morgan Kaufmann.

Goldberg, D., Nichols, D., Oki, B. M., & Terry, D. (1992). Using collaborative filtering to weave an information tapestry. Communications of the ACM, 35, 61–70. doi:10.1145/138859.138867

Gómez, J., Martín, J. D., Soria, E., Vila, J., Carrasco, J. L., & Valle, S. (2006, October). Neural networks for analysing the relevance of input variables in the prediction of tropospheric ozone concentration. Atmospheric Environment, 40(32), 6173–6180. doi:10.1016/j.atmosenv.2006.04.067

Gómez-Pérez, A., & Villazon-Terrazas, B. (2006). Legal Ontologies for the Spanish e-Government. In Lecture Notes in Computer Science, 11th Conference of the Spanish Association for Artificial Intelligence.

Gómez-Pérez, A., Fernández-López, M., & Corcho, O. (2004). Ontological Engineering: with examples from the areas of Knowledge Management, e-Commerce and the Semantic Web. Berlin: Springer.

Gómez-Sanchis, J., Martín-Guerrero, J. D., Soria-Olivas, E., Vila-Frances, J., Carrasco, J. L., & del Valle-Tascón, S. (2006). Neural networks for analysing the relevance of input variables in the prediction of tropospheric ozone concentration. Atmospheric Environment, 40, 6173–6180. doi:10.1016/j.atmosenv.2006.04.067

González, A., & Herrera, F. (1997). Multi-stage genetic fuzzy systems based on the iterative rule learning approach. Mathware & Soft Computing, 4(3), 233–249.

Gonzalez, R. C., & Woods, R. E. (2000). Digital Image Processing. São Paulo, Brasil: Edgard Blücher.

Goosse, H., Barriat, P. Y., Lefebvre, W., Loutre, M. F., & Zunz, V. (2008). Introduction to climate dynamics and climate modeling. Online textbook. Retrieved from http://www.climate.be/textbook

Gordon, V. S., & Whitley, D. (1994, June). A machine-independent analysis of parallel genetic algorithms. Complex Systems, Complex Systems Publication.

Goumas, M., & Lygerou, V. (2000). An extension of the PROMETHEE method for decision making in fuzzy environment: Ranking of alternative energy exploitation projects. European Journal of Operational Research, 123, 606–613. doi:10.1016/S0377-2217(99)00093-4

Graham, P., & Nelson, B. (1995). A hardware genetic algorithm for the travelling salesman problem on SPLASH, Lecture Notes in Computer Science, Springer – Verlag.

Greene, D. P., & Smith, S. F. (1993). Competition based induction of decision models from examples. Machine Learning, 13(2), 229–257. doi:10.1023/A:1022622013558

Grieg, D. D., & Englemann, H. F. (1952). Microstrip –A New Transmission Technique for the Kilomegacycle Range. Proceedings of The IRE, 40(12), 1644–1650. doi:10.1109/JRPROC.1952.274144

Gruau, F. (1994). Neural networks synthesis using cellular encoding and the genetic algorithm. Doctoral dissertation, Ecole Normale Superiere de Lyon, France.

Gruber, T. R. (1995). Toward principles for the design of ontologies used for knowledge sharing. International Journal of Human-Computer Studies, 43(5-6), 907–928. doi:10.1006/ijhc.1995.1081

Guarino, N. (1998). Formal ontology in information systems. Amsterdam: IOS press.

Gupta, S., Matthew, S., Abreu, P. M., & Aires-de-Sousa, J. (2006). QSAR analysis of phenolic antioxidants using MOLMAP descriptors of local properties. Bioorganic & Medicinal Chemistry, 14(4), 1199–1206. doi:10.1016/j.bmc.2005.09.047

Gustafsson, M., & Falkman, G. (2005). Representing clinical knowledge in oral medicine using ontologies. Studies in Health Technology and Informatics, 116, 743.

Guyot, P., & Honiden, S. (2006). Agent-based participatory simulations: Merging multi-agent systems and role-playing games. JASSS, 9(4). Retrieved from http://jasss.soc.surrey.ac.uk/9/4/8.html

Haber, R., & Keviczky, L. (1999). Nonlinear System Identification, Input-Output Modeling Approach, Part 1: Nonlinear System Parameter Estimation. London: Kluwer Academic Publishers.

Haber, R., & Keviczky, L. (1999). Nonlinear System Identification, Input-Output Modeling Approach, Part. 2: Nonlinear System structure Identification. London: Kluwer Academic Publishers.

Hackos, J. T., & Redish, J. C. (1998). User and Task Analysis for Interface Design. Hoboken, NJ: Wiley.

Han, K., & Veloso, M. (2000). Automated Robot Behavior Recognition Applied to Robotic Soccer. In Robotics Research: the Ninth International Symposium, (pp. 199-204). London: Springer-Verlag.

Harinder, P., Gulati, R. K., & Gupta, R. (1998). Stellar Spectral Classification using Principal Component Analysis and Artificial Neural Networks. Monthly Notices of the Royal Astronomical Society, 295, 312–318. doi:10.1046/j.1365-8711.1998.01255.x

Hartley, R. I., & Zisserman, A. (2000). Multiple View Geometry in Computer Vision. Cambridge, UK: Cambridge Univ. Press.

Haupt, R. L., & Haupt, S. E. (1998). Practical genetic Algorithm. New York: John Wiley & Sons.

Haykin, S. (1999). Neural Networks: A Comprehensive Foundation. Englewood Cliffs, NJ: Prentice Hall International.

Haykin, S. (2008). Neural Networks and Learning Machines (3rd Ed.). Englewood Cliffs, NJ: Prentice Hall International.

He, X., & Asada, H. (1993). A new method for identifying orders of input-output models for nonlinear dynamic systems. In Proc. Of the American Control Conf., California (pp. 2520–2523).

Hecht-Nielsen, R. (1987). Counter-propagation Networks. Applied Optics, 26(23), 4979–4984. doi:10.1364/AO.26.004979

Hecht-Nielsen, R. (1990). Neurocomputing. Reading, MA: Addison-Wesley.

Heckerman, D., Geiger, D., & Chickering, D. M. (1995). Learning Bayesian Networks: The Combination of Knowledge and Statistical Data. Machine Learning, 20(3), 197–243.

Heywood, M. I., & Zincir-Heywood, A. N. (2000). Register based genetic programming on FPGA computing platforms. In R. Poli, W. Banzhaf, W. B. Langdon, J. F. Miller, P. Nordin, & T. C. Fogarty (Eds.), Genetic Programming, Proc. EuroGP'2000, Edinburgh, 15–16 April 2000 (LNCS 1802, pp. 44–59). Berlin: Springer.

Hillel, D. (2004). Introduction to Environmental Soil Physics. San Diego, CA: Elsevier Academic Press.

Hipp, J., Guntzer, U., & Nakaeizadeh, G. (2000) Algorithms for Association Rule Mining - a General Survey and Comparison. In U. Fayyad (Ed.), Sixth ACM SIGKDD International Conference on Knowledge Discovery and Data Mining (Vol. 2, pp. 58 - 64). Boston: ACM.

Holland, J. H. (1975). Adaptation in natural and artificial systems. Ann Arbor, MI: University of Michigan Press.

Holland, J. H., & Reitman, J. S. (1978). Cognitive Systems Based on Adaptive Algorithms. In D. A. Waterman & F. Hayes-Roth (Eds.), Pattern-Directed Inference Systems (pp. 313-329). New York: Academic Press.

Holt, A. (1999). Applying case-based reasoning techniques in GIS. International Journal of Geographical Information Science, 13(1), 9–25. doi:10.1080/136588199241436

Holte, R. C., Acker, L., & Porter, B. W. (1989). Concept Learning and the Problem of Small Disjuncts (Tech. Rep. AI89-106). Austin, TX: University of Texas at Austin, Computer Sciences Department.

Holzman, B. A. (2009). Natural Resource Management. Retrieved May 2009, from http://bss.sfsu.edu/holzman/courses/GEOG%20657/env%20history%20lecture.pdf

Hooyberghs, J., Mensink, C., & Dumont, G. (2005). A neural network forecast for daily average PM10 concentrations in Belgium. Atmospheric Environment, 39, 3279–3289. doi:10.1016/j.atmosenv.2005.01.050

Horman, Y., & Kaminka, G. (2007). Removing biases in unsupervised learning of sequential patterns. Intelligent Data Analysis, 11(5), 457–480.

Hornby, G. S., & Pollack, J. B. (2001). The advantages of generative grammatical encodings for physical design. In Proceedings of the 2002 Congress on Evolutionary Computation. Piscataway, NJ: IEEE Press.

Hosseini, H., & Reynolds, K. J. (2001). A Multi-stage Neural Network Classifier for ECG Events. In Proceedings of the 23rd International Conference of the IEEE Engineering in Medicine and Biology Society (Vol. 2, pp. 1672-1675).

Hsieh, N. (2004). An integrated data mining and behavioural scoring model for analyzing bank customers. Expert Systems with Applications, 27, 623–633. doi:10.1016/j.eswa.2004.06.007

Huang, J., Blanz, V., Heisele, B., Lee, S. W., & Verri, A. (2002). Face Recognition Using Component-Based SVM Classification and Morphable Models. Lecture Notes in Computer Science, 2388, 334–341. doi:10.1007/3-540-45665-1_26

Huang, Z., Yang, Y., & Chen, X. (2003). An approach to plan recognition and retrieval for multi-agent systems. In Workshop on Adaptability in Multi-Agent Systems (AORC 2003).

Hubley, R. M., Zitzler, E., & Roach, J. C. (2003). Evolutionary algorithms for the selection of single nucleotide polymorphisms. BMC Bioinformatics, 4(30), 30–39. doi:10.1186/1471-2105-4-30

Hugues, L., & Bredeche, N. (2006). Simbad: an Autonomous Robot Simulation Package for Education and Research. In Proceedings of The International Conference on the Simulation of Adaptive Behavior 2006.

Hummel, R., Krasenbrink, A., & De Santi, G. (2000). Characterisation of Vehicle Emissions. Journal of Aerosol Science, 31(Supplement 1), S246–S247. doi:10.1016/S0021-8502(00)90255-6

Hyde, K. M., & Maier, H. R. (2006). Distance-based and stochastic uncertainty analysis for multi-criteria decision analysis in Excel using Visual Basic for Applications. Environmental Modelling & Software, 21(12), 1695–1710. doi:10.1016/j.envsoft.2005.08.004

Hyde, K. M., Maier, H. R., & Colby, C. B. (2003). Incorporating Uncertainty in the PROMETHEE MCDA Method. Journal of Multi-Criteria Decisions Analysis, 12, 245–259. doi:10.1002/mcda.361

ICCT. (2007). Passenger vehicle greenhouse gas and fuel economy standards: a global update. Sacramento, CA: International Council on Clean Transportation.

Iglesias, J. A., Ledezma, A., & Sanchis, A. (2007). Sequence classification using statistical pattern recognition. Intelligent Data Analysis, 2007, 207–218. doi:10.1007/978-3-540-74825-0_19

Iglesias, J. A., Ledezma, A., & Sanchis, A. (2009). Modelling Evolving User Behaviours. In ESDIS 2009 IEEE Workshop on Evolving and Self-Developing and Self-Developing Intelligent Systems (pp. 16-23).

Iglesias, J. A., Ledezma, A., & Sanchis, A. (2009). CAOS Coach 2006 Simulation Team: An opponent modelling approach. Computing and Informatics Journal, 28(1), 57–80.

IJHIS. (2009), The International Journal of Hybrid Intelligent Systems. Retrieved May, 2009, from http://ijhis.hybridsystem.com/

Iliadis, L. S., & Maris, F. (2007). An artificial neural network model for mountainous waterresources management: The case of cyprus mountainous watersheds. Environmental Modelling & Software, 22(7), 1066–1072. doi:10.1016/j.envsoft.2006.05.026

Ionescu, L., Mazare, A., Serban, G., & Sofron, E. (2008). Evolved synthesis of digital circuits. In J. R. Rabunal Dopico, J. Dorado de la Calle, & A. Pazos Sierra (Eds.), Encyclopedia of Artificial Intelligence (pp. 609-617). Hershey, PA: IGI Global.

Irmak, S., Asce, M., Irmak, A., Jones, J. W., Howell, T. A., & Jacobs, J. M. (2003). Predicting daily net radiation using minimum climatological data. Journal of Irrigation and Drainage Engineering, 129(4), 256–269. doi:10.1061/(ASCE)0733-9437(2003)129:4(256)

Isaacs, E., Walendowski, A., Whittaker, S., Schiano, D., & Kamm, C. (2002). The character, functions, and styles of instant messaging in the workplace. In Proceedings of the 2002 ACM conference on Computer supported cooperative work (pp. 11-20).

Isard, M., & MacCormick, J. (2001). BraMBLe: A Bayesian Multiple-Blob tracker. In International Conference on Computer Vision, 34-31.

Isazi, V. P., & Galván, L. I. (2004). Redes de Neuronas Artificiales Un Enfoque Práctico. Upper Saddle River, NJ: Pearson, Prentice Hall.

Israelsson, P. H., Do Kim, Y., & Adams, E. E. (2006). A comparison of three Lagrangian approaches for extending near field mixing calculations. Environmental Modeling & Software, 21, 1631-1649. Retrieved from doi: 10.1016/j.ensoft.2005.07.008

Ito, A., Wang, X., Suzuki, M., & Makino, S. (2005). Smile and laughter recognition using speech processing and face recognition from conversation video. In Procs. of the 2005 IEEE Int. Conf. on Cyberworlds (CW'05).

Iziomon, M. G., Mayer, H., & Matzarakis, A. (2000). Empirical models for estimating net radiative flux: a case study for three mid-latitude sites with orographic variability. Astrophysics and Space Science, 273, 313–330. doi:10.1023/A:1002787922933

Jain, L., & Fanelli, A. M. (Eds.). (2000). Recent Advances in Artificial Neural Networks: Design and Applications. Boca Raton, FL: CRC Press, Inc.

Jang, G. J., & Kweon, I. O. (2001). Robust Real-time Face Tracking Using Adaptive Color Model. In International Conference on Robotics and Automation (pp. 138-149).

Jang, J. S., Sun, C. T., & Mizutani, E. (Eds.). (1997). Neuro-Fuzzy and Soft Computing: A Computational Approach to Learning and Machine Intelligence. Upper Saddle River, NJ: Prentice Hall.

Janikow, C. Z. (1993). A knowledge-intensive genetic algorithm for supervised learning. Machine Learning, 13(2/3), 189–228. doi:10.1023/A:1022669929488

Jankowski, S., & Oreziak, A. (2003). Learning System for Computer-Aided ECG Analysis Based on Support Vector Machines. International Journal of Bioelectromagnetism, 5(1), 175–176.

Jegede, O. O. (1997). Estimating net radiation from air temperature for diffusion modelling applications in a tropical area. Boundary-Layer Meteorology, 85, 161–173. doi:10.1023/A:1000462626302

Jepson, A., Fleet, D., & El-Maraghi, T. (2001). Robust Online Appearance Models for Visual Tracking. Computer Vision and Pattern Recognition, 25(10), 415–422.

Ji, X. B., Kang, E. S., Zhao, W. Z., Zhang, Z. H., & Jin, B. W. (2009). Simulation of heat and water transfer in a surface irrigated, cropped sandy soil. Agricultural Water Management, 96(6), 1010–1020. doi:10.1016/j.agwat.2009.02.008

Jiang, Y. (2008). Prediction of monthly mean daily diffuse solar radiation using artificial neural networks and comparison with other empirical models. Energy Policy, 36, 3833–3837. doi:10.1016/j.enpol.2008.06.030

Jimenez, P., Thomas, F., & Torras, C. (2001). A neural networks based collision detection engine for multi-armrobotic systems. Computers & Graphics, 25(2), 269–285. doi:10.1016/S0097-8493(00)00130-8

Johnson, J. M., & Samii, Y. R. (1997). Genetic Algorithms In Engineering Electromagnetics. IEEE Magazine on Antennas and Propagation, 39, 7–25. doi:10.1109/74.632992

Jourdan, L., Dhaenens, C., Talbi, E.-G., & Gallina, S. (2002). A Data Mining Approach to Discover Genetic and Environmental Factors involved in Multifactorial Diseases. Knowledge-Based Systems, 15(4), 235–242. doi:10.1016/S0950-7051(01)00145-9

Jurado, F. (2004). Modelling SOFC plants on the distribution system using identification algorithms. Journal of Power Sources.

Kaempf, T. A., Willemsen, P. G., Bailer-Jones, C. A. L., & de Boer, K. S. (2005). Parameterisation of RVS spectra with Artificial Neural Networks First Steps. In 10th RVS workshop, Cambridge.

Kahl, F., & Henrion, D. (2005) Globally Optimal Estimates for Geometric Reconstruction Problems. In 10th IEEE International Conference on Computer Vision (ICCV 2005) (pp. 978-985).

Kalfoglou, Y., & Schorlemmer, M. (2003). Ontology mapping: the state of the art. The Knowledge Engineering Review, 18(1), 1–31. doi:10.1017/S0269888903000651

Kalteh, A. M., Hjorth, P., & Berndtsson, R. (2008). Review of the self-organizing map (SOM) approach in water resources: analysis, modelling and application. Environmental Modelling & Software, 23, 835–845.

Kaminka, G., Fidanboylu, M., Chang, A., & Veloso, M. (2002). Learning the sequential coordinated behavior of teams from observations. In RoboCup 2002 (pp. 111-125). Berlin: Springer.

Kaneko, K. (2006). Life: An Introduction to Complex Systems Biology. Berlin: Springer Press.

Kanungo, T. (1999). UMDHMM: Hidden Markov Model Toolkit. Extended Finite State Models of Language, Cambridge University Press.

Karaboga, D., Güney, K., Sagiroglu, S., & Erler, M. (1999). Neural Computation Of Resonant Frequency Of Electrically Thin And Thick Rectangular Microstrip Antennas. Microwaves, Antennas and Propagation . IEEE Proceedings, 146(2), 155–159.

Karamouz, M., Razavi, S., & Araghinejad, S. (2008). Long-lead seasonal rainfall forecasting using time-delay recurrent neural networks: a case study. Hydrological Processes, 22(2), 229–241. doi:10.1002/hyp.6571

Karlsson, H. L. (2004). Ammonia, nitrous oxide and hydrogen cyanide emissions from five passenger vehicles. The Science of the Total Environment, 335, 125–132. doi:10.1016/j.scitotenv.2004.04.061

Kauffman, S. A. (1969). Metabolic stability and epigenesis in randomly constructed genetic nets. Journal of Theoretical Biology, 22, 437–467. doi:10.1016/0022-5193(69)90015-0

Kearfort, R. B., & Kreinovich, V. (1996). Applications of Interval Computations, Kluwer: Dordrecht.

Kelemen, A., Vasilakos, A. V., & Liang, Y. (2009). Computational Intelligence for genetic association study in complex diseases: review of theory and applications. International Journal of Computational Intelligence in Bioinformatics and System Biology, 1(1), 15–31. doi:10.1504/IJCIBSB.2009.024041

Kephart, J. O., & Chess, D. M. (2003). The vision of Autonomic Computing. IEEE Computer Magazine, (January), 41-50.

Kerr, J. L. (1977). Other Microstrip Antenna Applications. In Proc. 1977 Antenna Applications Symp., Univ. Illinois.

Kessler, A. (1985). World Survey Climatology, General Climatology, 1A, Heat Balance Climatology. Amsterdam: Elsevier Science Publishers.

Kinney, P. L., Thurston, G. D., & Raizenne, M. (1996). The effects of ambient ozone on lung function in children: a reanalysis of six summer camp studies. Environmental Health Perspectives, 104, 170–174. doi:10.2307/3432785

Kitano, H. (2005). Using process diagrams for the graphical representation of biological networks . Nature Biotechnology, 23(8), 961–966. doi:10.1038/nbt1111

Kjaersgaard, J. H., Cuenca, R. H., & Plauborg, F. L. (2007). Long-term comparisons of net radiation calculation schemes. Boundary-Layer Meteorology, 123, 417–431. doi:10.1007/s10546-006-9151-8

Kohonen, T. (1982). Self-organized formation of Topologically correct feature maps. Biological Cybernetics, 43, 59–69. doi:10.1007/BF00337288

Kohonen, T. (1988). Self-Organization and Associative Memory. Berlin: Springer Verlag.

Kohonen, T. (1997). Self-Organizing Maps (2nd Ed.). Berlin: Springer-Verlag.

Kohonen, T. (2001). Self-Organizing Maps. New York: Springer.

Kowalik, U., Aoki, T., & Yasuda, H. (2005). Broaference - a next generation multimedia terminal providing direct feedback on audience's satisfaction level. In INTERACT (pp. 974-977).

Kowalik, U., Aoki, T., & Yasuda, H. (2006). Using automatic facial expression classification for contents indexing based on the emotional component. In EUC (pp. 519-528).

Koza, J. (1990). Genetic Programming: A paradigm for genetically breeding populations of computer programs to solve problems (Tech. Rep.). Stanford, CA: Stanford University, Computer Science Department.

Koza, J. (1992). Genetic Programming. On the Programming of Computers by means of Natural Selection. Cambridge, MA: The MIT Press.

Koza, J. R., Bennett, F. H., III, Andre, D., & Keane, M. A. (1999). Genetic Programming III: Darwinian Invention and Problem Solving. San Francisco, CA: Morgan Kaufmann Publishers.

Koza, J. R., Bennett, F. H., III, Hutchings, J. L., Bade, S. L., Keane, M. A., & Andre, D. (1997). Evolving sotring networks using genetic programming and the rapidly reconfigurable xilinx 6216 Field Programmable Gate Array. In Proc. 31st Asilomar Conf. Signals, Systems, and Comp. New York: IEEE Press.

Krasnopolsky, V. M., & Schiller, H. (2003). Some neural applications in environmental sciences. Part I: forward and inverse problems in geophysical remote measurements. Neural Networks, 16, 321–334. doi:10.1016/S0893-6080(03)00027-3

Krupa, S. V., Nosal, M., & Legge, A. H. (1994). Ambient ozone and crop loss: establishing a cause-effect relationship. Environmental Pollution, 83, 269–276. doi:10.1016/0269-7491(94)90147-3

Kukkonen, J., Partanen, L., & Karpinen, A. (2003). Extensive evaluation of neural network models for the prediction of NO2 and PM10 concentrations. Atmospheric Environment, 37, 4539–4550. doi:10.1016/S1352-2310(03)00583-1

Kumar, S. (2004). Investigating Computational Models of Development for the Construction of Shape and Form. PhD Thesis, Department of Computer Science, University Collage London.

Kumar, S., & Bentley, P. J. (Eds.). (2003) On Growth, Form and Computers. London: Elsevier Academic Press.

Kuniyoshi, Y., Rougeaux, S., Ishii, M., Kita, N., Sakane, S., & Kakikura, M. (1994). Cooperation by observation - the framework and the basic task patterns. In IEEE International Conference on Robotics and Automation (pp. 767–773).

Kunzmann, U., Von Wagner, G., Schöchlin, J., & Bolz, A. (2002). Parameter extraction of the ECG-signal in real-time. Biomedizinische Technik, 47, 875–878. doi:10.1515/bmte.2002.47.s1b.875

Kuzmanovski, I., & Novič, M. (2008). Counter-propagation neural networks in Matlab. Chemometrics and Intelligent Laboratory Systems, 90(1), 84–91. doi:10.1016/j.chemolab.2007.07.003

Kyats, A., Yee, E., Lien, F. S. (2007a). Bayesian Inference for source determination with applications to a complex urban environment. Atmospheric Environment, 41, 465-479. Retrieved from doi:10.1016/j.atmosenv.2006.08.044

Lagerholm, M. (1998). Mean Field Neural Network Techniques. (Tech. Rep.). Lund, Sweden: Lund University, Department of Theoretical Physics.

Lai, Y. J., Liu, T. Y., & Hwang, C. L. (1994). TOPSIS for MODM. European Journal of Operational Research, 76, 486–500. doi:10.1016/0377-2217(94)90282-8

Lambrix, P., & Tan, H. (2007). Ontology alignment and merging. Anatomy Ontologies for Bioinformatics: Principles and Practice, 133.

Landeras, G., Ortiz-Barredo, A., & López, J. J. (2008). Comparison of artificial neural network models and empirical and semi-empirical equations for daily reference evapotranspiration estimation in the Basque Country (Northern Spain). Agricultural Water Management, 95(5), 553–565. doi:10.1016/j.agwat.2007.12.011

Lane, T., & Brodley, C. E. (1999). Temporal sequence learning and data reduction for anomaly detection. International Journal ACM Transactions on Information and System Security, 2(3), 150–158.

Langdon, W. (2001). Long random linear programs do not generalize. []. Amsterdam: Kluwer Academic Publishers.]. Genetic Programming and Evolvable Machines, 2, 95–100. doi:10.1023/A:1011590227934

Larsen, R. I., McDonell, W. F., & Hortsman, D. H. (1991). An air quality data analysis system for interrelating effects, standards, and needed source reductions. Part II: A log-normal model relating human lung function decrease to ozone exposure. J. Waste Manag. Assoc., 41(4), 455–459.

Latino, D. A. R. S., & Aires-de-Sousa, J. (2006). Genome-Scale Classification of Metabolic Reactions: A Chemoinformatics Approach. Angewandte Chemie International Edition, 45, 2066–2069. doi:10.1002/anie.200503833

Lee, B.-H., & Scholz, M. (2006). Application of the self-organizing map (SOM) to asses the heavy metal removal performance in experimental constructed wetlands. Water Research, 40(18), 3367–3374. doi:10.1016/j.watres.2006.07.027

Lee, J.-S., Jung, Y.-Y., Kim, B.-S., & Sung-Jea, K. (2001). An advanced video camera system with robust AF, AE and AWB control. IEEE Transactions on Consumer Electronics, 47(3), 694–699. doi:10.1109/30.964165

Legge, A. H., Gräunhage, L., Nosal, M., Jagger, H. J., & Krupa, S. V. (1995). Ambient ozone and adverse crop response: an evaluation of North American and European data as they relate to exposure indices and critical levels. J. Appl. Bot., 69, 192–205.

Lepetit, V., Vacchetti, L., Thalmann, D., & Fua, P. (2003). Fully automated and stable registration for augmented reality applications. In Proceedings of International Symposium on Mixed and Augmented Reality, Tokyo, Japan.

Leshno, M., & Schocken, S. (1993). Multilayer Feedforward Networks with non-Polynomial Activation Functions can Approximate any Function. Center for Digital Economy Research, Stern School of business. Working Paper IS-91-26.

Levi, D., & Guccione, S. (1999, July). Genetic FPGA: evolving stable circuits on mainstream FPGA devices. In A. Stoica, D. Keymeulen, & J. Lohn (Eds.), Proc. First NASA/DoD Workshop on Evolvable Hardware (pp. 12–17). Silver Spring, MD: IEEE Computer Society.

Li, C., Zheng, C., & Tai, C. (1995). Detection of ECG characteristic points using wavelet transforms. IEEE Transactions on Bio-Medical Engineering, 42, 21–28. doi:10.1109/10.362922

Li, S., Tong, L., Li, F., Zhang, L., Zhang, B., & Kang, S. (2009). Variability in energy partitioning and resistance parameters for a vineyard in northwest China. Agricultural Water Management, 96(6), 955–962. doi:10.1016/j.agwat.2009.01.006

Lindenmayer, A. (1968). Mathematical models for cellular interaction in development: Part I and II. Journal of Theoretical Biology, 18, 280–315. doi:10.1016/0022-5193(68)90079-9

Little, R. J. A., & Rubin, D. B. (2002). Statistical Analysis with Missing Data. New York: John Wiley.

Liu, F., Wu, X., & Cheng, W. (2007). Visual Intelligent Simulation For Railway Container Yard Based on Agent. International Conference on Intelligent Systems and Knowledge Engineering (ISKE2007).

Liu, J. J., Cheng, S., Kung, I., Chang, H., & Billings, S. A. (2001). Non-linear System Identification and fault diagnosis using a new gui interpretation tool. Mathematics and Computers in Simulation, 54, 425–499. doi:10.1016/S0378-4754(00)00274-3

Liu, W., Shen, P., Yingge, Q., & Xia, D. (2001). Fast Algorithm of Support Vector Machines in Lung Cancer Diagnosis. In International Workshop on Medical Imaging and Augmented Reality (pp. 188).

Liu, Z., Notaro, M., & Kutzbach, J. (2006). Assessing global vegetation climate feedbacks from observations. Journal of Climate, 19, 787–814. doi:10.1175/JCLI3658.1

Ljung, L. (1999). System Identification, Theory for the User. Upper Saddle River, NJ: Prentice-Hall.

Lockman, M. J. (2000). Compliance, relaxation and creep recovery of normal strength concrete (Thesis). Ottawa, Canada: University of Ottawa, Department of Civil Engineering.

Lorenzo, J., Castrillón, M., Hernández, M., & Déniz, O. (2004). Introduction of Homeostatic Regulation in Face Detection. In A. Fred (Ed.), Proceedings of the 4th International Workshop on Pattern Recognition in Information Systems, PRIS 2004, Porto (Portugal), April 13-14, 2004 (pp. 5-14).

Lorenzo, J., Déniz, O., Guerra, C., & Hernández, D. (2003). A Proposal of a Homeostatic Regulation Mechanism for a Vision System. In X Conferencia de la Asociación Española para la Inteligencia Artificial, CAEPIA, San Sebastián.

Lucrédio, D., Almeida, E. S., & Prado, A. F. (2004). A Survey on Software Components Search and Retrieval. In R. Steinmetz & A. Mauthe (Eds.), 30th IEEE EURO-MICRO Conference. Component-Based Software Engineering Track (pp. 152-159). Rennes, France: IEEE Press.

Lundquist, J., Kosovic, B., & Belles, R. (2005). Synthetic event reconstruction experiments for defining sensors network characteristics. Lawrence Livermore National Laboratory Tech. Rep. UCRL-TR-217762. Retrieved from http://www.llnl.gov/tid/lof/documents/pdf/328798.pdf

Lyons, M., Akamatsu, S., Kamachi, M., & Gyoba, J. (1998). Coding facial expressions with gabor wavelets. In Procs. of the Third IEEE International Conference on Automatic Face and Gesture Recognition.

Lyu, M. R., King, I., Wong, T. T., Yau, E., & Chan, P. W. (2005). Arcade: Augmented reality computing arena for digital entertainment. In Proceedings 2005 IEEE Aerospace Conference, Big Sky (pp. 5-12).

Ma, Q., Wang, J. T., Shasha, D., & Wu, C. H. (2001). DNA sequence classification via an expectation maximization algorithm and neural networks: a case study. International Journal IEEE Transactions on Systems, Man, and Cybernetics . Part C, 31(4), 468–475.

Macaire, L., Ultre, V., & Postaire, J.-G. (1996). Determination of compatibility coefficients for color edge detection by relaxation. In International Conference on Image Processing (pp. 1045-1048).

MacCann, D. W. (1992). A neural network short-term forecast of significant thunderstorm. Forecasting Techniques, 7, 525–534. doi:10.1175/1520-0434(1992)007<0525:ANNSTF>2.0.CO;2

Macedo, A. A., Truong, K. N., Camacho-Guerrero, J. A., & Pimentel, M. G. (2003). Automatically sharing web experiences through a hyperdocument recommender system. In ACM conference on Hypertext and hypermedia (pp. 48-56). New York: ACM.

Maher, M. L., & Gero, J. S. (2003). Agent models of 3D virtual worlds. In Proceedings of ACADIA 2002, Panoma, California.

Maier, H. R., & Dandy, G. C. (2000). Neural Networks for the prediction and forecasting of water resources variables: a review of modeling issues and applications. Environmental Modelling & Software, 15, 101–123. doi:10.1016/S1364-8152(99)00007-9

Mallat, S. (1989). A theory for Multiresolution Signal Decomposition: The Wavelet representation. Proc. IEEE Trans on Pattern Anal., & Math. Intel., 7(11).

Mallat, S. (1998). Wavelet Tour of signal Processing. Boston: American Press.

Manoliadis, O. G., & Karantounias, G. (2003). Applications of genetic algorithms in water resources management - the koufos irrigation project in Greece. Journal of Environmental Protection and Ecology, (4),982–986.

Manzato, A. (2007). Sounding-derived indices for neural network based short-term thunderstorm and rainfall forecasts. Atmospheric Research, 83(2-4), 349–365. doi:10.1016/j.atmosres.2005.10.021

Marengo, E., Bobba, M., Robotti, E., & Liparota, M. C. (2006). Modeling of the Polluting Emissions from a Cement Production Plant by Partial Least-Squares, Principal Component Regression, and Artificial Neural Networks. Environmental Science & Technology, 40(1), 272–280. doi:10.1021/es0517466

Marini, F., Magrì, A. L., & Bucci, R. (2007b). Multilayer feed-forward artificial neural networks for class modeling. Chemometrics and Intelligent Laboratory Systems, 88(1), 118–124. doi:10.1016/j.chemolab.2006.07.004

Marini, F., Magrì, A. L., Bucci, R., & Magrì, A. D. (2007a). Use of different artificial neural networks to resolve binary blends of monocultivar Italian olive oils. Analytica Chimica Acta, 599(2), 232–240. doi:10.1016/j.aca.2007.08.006

Marini, F., Zupan, J., & Magrì, A. L. (2004). On the use of counterpropagation artificial neural networks to characterize Italian rice varieties. Analytica Chimica Acta, 510(2), 231–240. doi:10.1016/j.aca.2004.01.009

Marini, F., Zupan, J., & Magrì, A. L. (2006). Class-modeling using Kohonen artificial neural networks. Analytica Chimica Acta, 544(1-2), 306–314. doi:10.1016/j.aca.2004.12.026

Martin, L. F. (2006). Inventario de modelos utilizados para calidad de aire. Paper presented at V Seminario de Calidad de Aire en España, Santander, 2006.

Martín, L. F., González, C., Palomino, I., et al. (2002) Sistema Informático para el Control y Prevención de la Contaminación Atmosférica en Huelva. Centro de Investigaciones Energéticas, Medioambientales y Tecnológicas, CIEMAT.

Martín, L. F., Pujadas, M., & Artiñano, B., et al. (2007). Estimates of Atmospheric particle emissions from bulk handling of dusty materials in Spain. Atmospheric Environment, 41(30), 6344-6355. Retrieved from doi: 10.1016/j.atmosenv.2006.12.003

Martin, N. J., St. Onge, B., & Waaub, P.-W. (1999). An integrated decision aid system for the development of Saint Charles river alluvial plain, Quebec, Canada. International Journal of Environment and Pollution, 12(2/3), 264–279.

Martinez Lastra, J. L., López-Torres, E., & Colombo, A. W. (2005). A 3D Visualization and Simulation Framework for Intelligent Physical Agents. HoloMAS, 2005, 23–38.

Martinez, A. M., & Benavente, R. (1998). The AR Face Database. CVC Technical Report #24.

Martinez, J. P. (2004). A Wavelet-Based ECG Delineator. Evaluation on Standard Databases. IEEE Transactions on Bio-Medical Engineering, 51(4), 570–581. doi:10.1109/TBME.2003.821031

McCulloch, W. S., & Pitts, W. (1990). A logical calculus of the ideas immanent in nervous activity. The Bulletin of Mathematical Biophysics, 5, 115–133. doi:10.1007/BF02478259

McGuffie, K., & Henderson-Sellers, A. (2005). A Climate Modelling Primer (3rd Ed.). Hoboken, NJ: John Wiley & Sons, Ltd.

McKee, T. B., Doesken, N. J., & Kliest, J. (1993). The relationship of drought frequency and duration to time scales. In Proceedings of the 8th Conference of Applied Climatology, 17-22 January, Anaheim, CA (pp. 179-184). Boston, MA: American Meterological Society.

McKenna, S., Raja, Y., & Gong, S. (1999). Tracking Colour Objects using Adaptive Mixture Models. Image and Vision Computing, 17(3-4), 225–231. doi:10.1016/S0262-8856(98)00104-8

McKersie, R. B., & Fonstad, N. (1997). Teaching negotiation theory and skills over the internet. Negotiation Journal, 13(4), 363–368.

Megson, G. M. (1992). An Introduction to Systolic Algorithm Design. Oxford, UK: Clarendon Press.

Megson, G. M. (1994). Transformational approaches to systolic design, Chapman-Hall Parallel and Distributed Computing, Megson, G. M., & Bland, I. M. (1997, March). Generic systolic array for genetic algorithms. IEEE Proc. Computers and Digital Techniques.

Melssen, W., Ustun, B., & Buydens, L. (2007). SOMPLS: A supervised self-organising map-partial least squares algorithm for multivariate regression problems. Chemometrics and Intelligent Laboratory Systems, 86(1), 102–120. doi:10.1016/j.chemolab.2006.08.013

Melssen, W., Wehrens, R., & Buydens, L. (2006). Supervised Kohonen networks for classification problems. Chemometrics and Intelligent Laboratory Systems, 83(2), 99–113. doi:10.1016/j.chemolab.2006.02.003

Meng, H., Wang, Z., & Llu, G. (2000). Performance of the Daubeschies wavelet filters compared with other orthogonal transforms in random signal processing. In Proceedings ICSP.

Mentor Graphics. (2009). Retrieved from http://www.mentor.com/products/fpga/do-254/

Michalewicz, Z. (1998). Genetic Algorithms + Data Structures = Evolution Programs, 3rd revised & extended Ed. Berlin: Springer.

Mierlo, J. V., Timmermans, J.-M., Maggetto, G., Bossche, P. V., Meyer, S., & Hecq, W. (2004). Environmental rating of vehicles with different alternative fuels and drive trains: a comparison of two approaches. Transportation Research Part D, Transport and Environment, 9, 387–399. doi:10.1016/j.trd.2004.08.005

Mierlo, J. V., Vereeken, L., Maggetto, G., Favrel, V., Meyer, S., & Hecq, W. (2003). How to define clean vehicles? Environmental impact rating of vehicles. International Journal of Automotive Technology, 4(2), 77–86.

Mihir, K., & Kishor, N. (2009). Adaptive Fuzzy Model Identification to Predict the Heat Transfer coefficient in pool boiling of distilled water. Expert Systems with Applications, 36(2-1), 1142 – 1154.

Miller, J., Job, D., & Vassiliev, V. (2000). Principles in the evolutionary design of digital circuits – Part 1. []. Amsterdam: Kluwer Academic Publishers.]. Genetic Programming and Evolvable Machines, 1, 7–35. doi:10.1023/A:1010016313373

Miller, J., Job, D., & Vassiliev, V. (2000). Principles in the evolutionary design of digital circuits – Part 2. []. Amsterdam: Kluwer Academic Publishers.]. Genetic Programming and Evolvable Machines, 1, 259–288. doi:10.1023/A:1010066330916

Millington, I. (2006). Artificial Intelligence for Games. San Francisco: Morgan Kaufman.

Min, Q., & Zhang, G. P. (2008). Trend Time–Series Modeling and Forecasting With Neural Networks. IEEE Transactions on Neural Networks, 19(5), 808–816. PubMeddoi:10.1109/TNN.2007.912308

Mitchel, T. (1997). Machine Learning. New York: McGraw-Hill.

Mitchell, M. (1996). An introduction to Genetic Algorithms. Cambridge, MA: Bradford Books.

Mjolsness, E., Sharp, D. H., & Reinitz, J. (1995). A Connectionist Model of Development. Journal of Theoretical Biology, 176, 291–300. doi:10.1006/jtbi.1995.0199

Mohandes, M. A., Rehman, S., & Halawani, T. O. (1998a). Estimation of global solar radiation using artificial neural networks. Renewable Energy, 14, 179–184. doi:10.1016/S0960-1481(98)00065-2

Molitor, J., Marjoram, P., & Thomas, D. (2003). Fine-scale mapping of disease genes with multiple mutations via spatial clustering techniques. American Journal of Human Genetics, 73, 1368–1384. doi:10.1086/380415

Monache, L. D., Lundquist, J. K., & Kosovic, B. (2008) Bayesian inference and Markov Chain Montecarlo sampling to reconstruct a contaminant source at continental scale. Journal of applied meteorology and climatology, 47(10), 2600-2613. Retrieved from doi: 10.1175/2008JAMC1766.1

Montana, D. J. (1993). Strongly Typed Genetic Programming. Evolutionary Computation, 3, 199–230. doi:10.1162/evco.1995.3.2.199

Moore, J. H. (2004). Computational analysis of gene–gene interactions using multifactor dimensionality reduction. Expert Review of Molecular Diagnostics, 4, 795–803. doi:10.1586/14737159.4.6.795

Moore, J. H., & White, B. C. (2006). Exploiting expert knowledge for genome-wide genetic analysis using genetic programming. In T. P. Runarsson, H-G. Beyer, E. Burke, J. J. Merelo-Guervos, L. D. Whitley & X. Yao (Eds.), Parallel Problem Solving from Nature – PPSN IX (Vol. 4193, pp.969-977). Reykjavik, Iceland: Springer.

Moore, R. E. (1979). Methods and Applications of Interval Analysis. Philadelphia, PA: Society for Industrial and Applied Mathematics.

Moraes, J., Freitas, M., Vilani, F., & Costa, E. (2002). A QRS complex detection algorithm using electrocardiogram leads. Computers in Cardiology, 29, 205–208.

Moreira, D. M., Rizza, U., Villena, M. T., & Goulart, A. (2005). Semi-analytical model for pollution dispersion in the planetary boundary layer. Atmospheric Environment, 39(14), 2673-2681. Retrieved from doi:10.1016/j.atmosenv.2005.03.004

Morgan, E. (2004). Dispensing's new wave. Eyecare Business. Retrieved from http://www.eyecarebiz.com

Motsinger, A. A., Lee, S. L., Mellick, G., & Ritchie, M. D. (2006). GPNN: power studies and applications of a neural network method for detecting gene-gene interactions in studies of human disease. BMC Bioinformatics, 7(39).

Mulcahy, N. J., & Call, J. (2006). Apes save tools for future use. Science, 312(5776), 1038–1040. doi:10.1126/science.1125456

Müller, H. S., & Hilsdorf, H. K. (1990). Evaluation of the Time Dependent Behavior of Concrete. (Bulletin d'Information No. 199). France: CEB Comite Euro-International du Beton.

Myhill, J. (1964). The Abstract Theory of Self-Reproduction. In M. D. Mesarovic (Ed.), Views on General Systems Theory (pp. 106-118). New York: John Wiley & Sons Inc.

Nagendra, I. V., & Gujar, U. (1988). 3-d objects from 2-D Orthographic Views – A survey. Computer Graphics, 12(1), 111–114. doi:10.1016/0097-8493(88)90015-5

Nagl, S. B., Parish, J. H., Paton, R. C., & Warner, G. J. (1998). Macromolecules, Genomes and Ourselves. In R. Paton, H. Bolouri, M. Holcombe, J. H. Parish & R. Tateson (Eds.), Computation in cells and tissues. Perspective and tools of thought. Berlin: Springer Press.

Namkung, J., Hines, E. L., Green, R. J., & Leeson, M. S. (2007). Probe-fed microstrip antenna feed point optimisation using genetic algorithms and the method of moments. Microwave and Optical Technology Letters, 49(2), 325-329. Pattnaik, S. S., Panda, D. C., & Devi, S. (2002). Input Impedance Of Rectangular Microstrip Patch Antenna Using Artificial Neural Networks. Microwave and Optical Technology Letters, 32(5), 381–383.

Nammuni, K., Levine, J., & Kingston, J. (2002). Skill-based Resource Allocation using Genetic Algorithms and an Ontology. In Proceedings of the International Workshop on Intelligent Knowledge Management Techniques (I-KOMAT 2002).

Nanda, H., & Cutler, R. (2001). Practical calibrations for a real-time digital onmidirectional camera. In Proceedings of the Computer Vision and Pattern Recognition Conference (CVPR 2001).

National Instruments Corporation. (2004). LABVIEW System Identification Toolkit User Manual.

Neches, R., Fikes, R., Finin, T. W., Gruber, T. R., Patil, R., & Senator, T. E. (1991). Enabling technology for knowledge sharing. AI Magazine, 12(3), 36–56.

Nelles, O. (2001). Nonlinear System Identification, From Classical Approaches to Neural Networks and Fuzzy Models. Berlin: Springer.

Nelles, O. (Ed.). (2001). Nonlinear System Identification. Berlin: Springer-Verlag.

Neophytos, C., Evans, C., & Rees, D. (2002, June). Non-linear Gas Turbine Modelling using Feedforward Neural Networks. In Proceedings of ASME TURBO EXPO 2002, GT-2002-30035, Amsterdam, The Netherlands. Nögaard, M., Ravn, O., Poulsen, N. K., & Hansen, L. K. (2000). Neural Networks for Modelling and Control of Dynamic Systems. London, U.K: Springer-Verlag.

Neuman, S., Glascoe, L., Kosovik, B., et al. (2005). Event reconstruction for atmospheric releases employing urban puff model UDM with stochastic inversion methodology. In Proceedings for the American Meteorological Society Annual Meeting, Atlanta, January 29–February 2, 2006.

Nikolaev, D., & Nikolayev, P. (2004). Linear color segmentation and its implementation. Computer Vision and Image Understanding, 94(3), 115–139. doi:10.1016/j.cviu.2003.10.012

Nikravesh, M. (2008). Soft Computing for Intelligent Reservoir Characterization and Decision Analysis. In M. Nikravesh et al. (Eds.), Forging the New Frontiers: Fuzzy Pioneers II. Berlin: Springer-Verlag.

Noblet, C. L., Tiesl, M. F., & Rubin, J. (2006). Factors affecting consumer assessment of eco-labelled vehicles. Transportation Research Part D, Transport and Environment, 11, 422–431. doi:10.1016/j.trd.2006.08.002

NRC (National Research Council). (2003). Oil in the Sea III. Washington, DC: National Academic Press.

Nummiaro, K., Koller-Meier, E., & Van-Gool, L. (2002). A color-based Particle Filter. In Proceedings of the 1st International Workshop on Generative-Model-Based Vision (pp. 353-358).

OfficeMate Software Systems. (2009). iPointVTO. Retrieved June 30, 2009, from http://www.opticalinnovations.com

Ohlander, R., Price, K., & Reddy, D. R. (1980). Picture segmentation using a recursive region splitting method. Computer Graphics Image Processing, 8, 313–333. doi:10.1016/0146-664X(78)90060-6

Oke, T. R. (1987). Boundary Layer Climates. Cambridge, UK: University Press.

OMB. (2004). Analytical statement in support of 2004 budget: transportation. Retrieved December 30, 2004, from http://www.whitehouse.gov/omb/budget/fy2004/text/energy.html.

Omron Corp. (2008). Omron OKAO vision system. Retrieved from http://www.omron.com/r_d/technavi / vision/okao/authentication.html

Ong, S. H., Yeo, N. C., Lee, K. H., Venkatesh, Y. V., & Cao, D. M. (2002). Segmentation of color images using a two-stage self-organizing network. Image and Vision Computing, 20, 279–289. doi:10.1016/S0262-8856(02)00021-5

Online, A. B. C. (2004). Website rates environmental performance of cars. Retrieved July 12, 2004, from http://www.abc.net.au/newsitems/200408/s1169582.htm

Ordóñez, D., Dafonte, C., Arcay, B., & Manteiga, M. (2007). A canonical integrator environment for the development of connectionist systems. Dynamics of continuous . Discrete and Impulsive Systems, 14, 580–585.

Ortega-Farias, S., Antonioletti, R., & Olioso, A. (2000). Net radiation model evaluation at an hourly time step for Mediterranean conditions. Agronomie, 20, 157–164. doi:10.1051/agro:2000116

Pacheco, R., & Steffen, V. (2004). On the identification of non-linear mechanical systems using orthogonal functions. International Journal of Non-linear Mechanics, 39, 1147–1159. doi:10.1016/S0020-7462(03)00112-4

Page, I. (1996). Closing the gap between hardware and software: Hardware-software cosynthesis at Oxford. IEEE Colloquium Digest.

Pal, N. R. (1999). Soft computing for feature analysis. Fuzzy Sets and Systems, 103, 201–221. doi:10.1016/S0165-0114(98)00222-X

Pal, S. K., & Mitra, S. (1999). Neuro-Fuzzy Pattern Recognition: Methods in Soft Computing. New York: Wiley.

Pantic, M. S., & Rothkrantz, L. J. M. (2000). Automatic analysis of facial expressions: The state of the art. IEEE Transactions on Pattern Analysis and Machine Intelligence, 22, 1424–1445. doi:10.1109/34.895976

Paperless Practice. (2009). FrameCam. Retrieved June 30, 2009, from http://www.paperlesspractice.com

Park, O. H., & Seok, M. G. (2007). Selection of an appropriate model to predict plume dispersion in coastal areas. Atmospheric Environment, 41, 6095–6101. doi:10.1016/j.atmosenv.2007.04.010

Park, S. H., Yun, I. D., & Lee, S. U. (2001). Color image segmentation based on 3D clustering: morphological approach. Pattern Recognition, 31(8), 1061–1076. doi:10.1016/S0031-3203(97)00116-7

Parker, D. E., & Folland, C. K. (1988). The nature of climatic variability. Meteorological Magazine, 117, 201–210.

Pastor-Bárcenas, O., Soria-Olivas, E., Martín-Guerrero, J. D., Camps-Valls, G., Carrasco-Rodríguez, J. L., & del Valle-Tascón, S. (2005). Unbiased sensitivity analysis and pruning techniques in neural networks for surface ozone modelling. Ecological Modelling, 182(2), 149–158. doi:10.1016/j.ecolmodel.2004.07.015

Pazzani, M., & Billsus, D. (1997). Learning and revising user profiles: The identification of interesting web sites. Machine Learning, 27, 313–331. doi:10.1023/A:1007369909943

Peña, P. A. Hernández, R. J., & Toro,G. M. (2009a). Asynchronous Evolutionary Modeling for PM10 Spatial Characterization. Paper Presented at 18th World IMACS Joint Congress and MODSIM09, Cairns, Australia.

Peña, P. A., & Hernández, R. (2005). Interpolation and Exploration of Response Surfaces using Evolutionary NURBS, LaGrange Constraint and Cylindrical Operators. Paper presented at Genetic Evolutionary Computational Conference GECCO, Washington (ACM-1-59593-010-8/05).

Peña, P. A., Hernández, R. J., & Parra, C. (2007a). Modelo Evolutivo Integrado para la Interpolación/Descomposición de Modelos Digitales de Elevación. Paper presented at 2da. Conferencia Ibérica de Sistemas y Tecnologías de Información – CISTI 2007.

Peña, P. A., Hernández, R., & Toro, M. V. (2009b). Modelo Evolutivo Integrado para la Caracterización Espacial de Dispersión de Contaminantes. Paper presented at 4ta. Conferencia Ibérica de Sistemas e Tecnologias de Información, Povoa de Varzim.

Peña, P. A., Hernández, R., & Toro, M. V. (2009c). Modelo Evolutivo para Determinar el Comportamiento Espacio Temporal de la concentración de Material Particulado PMx en una Zona de Estudio Paper presented at 4ta. Conferencia Ibérica de Sistemas e Tecnologías de Información (Simposio Doctoral), Povoa de Varzim.

Peña, P., & Hernández, R. J. (2007b). Compression of Free Surface Base don the Evolutionary Optimisation of A NURBS-Takagi Sugeno System. Paper presented at International Conference on CAD/CAM, ROBOTICS & Factories of the Future, Bogota.

Peppet, S. R. (2002). Teaching negotiation using web-based straming video. Negotiation Journal, 18(3), 271–283.

Pepyne, D. L., Hu, J., & Gong, W. (2004). User Profiling for Computer Security. In Proceedings of the American Control Conference (pp. 982-987).

Perez, P., & Reyes, J. (2006). An integrated neural network model for PM10 Forecasting. Atmospheric Environment, 40, 2845-2851. Retrieved from doi:10.1016/j.atmosenv.2006.01.010

Perez, P., Hue, C., Vermaak, J., & Gangnet, M. (2002). Color-Based Probabilistic Tracking. In European Conference on Computer Vision (pp. 661-675).

Perkins, S., Porter, R., & Harvey, N. (2000). Everything on the chip: A hardware-based self-contained spatially-structured genetic algorithm for signal processing. In J. Miller, A. Thompson, P. Thompson, and T. Fogarty (Eds.), Proc. 3rd Int. Conf. Evolvable Systems: From Biology to Hardware (ICES 2000), Edinburg, UK (LNCS 1801, pp. 165–174). Springer: Berlin.

Picton, P. (2000). Neural Networks (2nd Ed.). New York: Palgrave.

Pietikainen, M. (2008). Accurate color discrimination with classification based on feature distributions. In International Conference on Pattern Recognition (pp. pp. 833-838).

Pinzon, J., Brown, M. E., & Tucker, C. J. (2005). Satellite time series correction of orbital drift artifacts using empirical mode decomposition. In N. Huang (Ed.), Hilbert-Huang Transform: Introduction and Applications (pp. 167-186).

Plumbaum, T., Stelter, T., & Korth, A. (2009). Semantic Web Usage Mining: Using Semantics to Understand User Intentions. In G-J. Houben, G. McCalla, F. Pianesi & M. Zancanari (Eds.), User Modeling, Adaptation and Personalization 2009 (pp. 391-396). Berlin: Springer-Verlag.

Pohekar, S. D., & Ramachandran, M. (2004). Application of multi-criteria decision making to sustainable energy planning – A review. Renewable & Sustainable Energy Reviews, 8, 365–381. doi:10.1016/j.rser.2003.12.007

Polanski, J., & Walczak, B. (2000). The Comparative Molecular Surface Analysis (COMSA): A Novel Tool for Molecular Design. Computers & Chemistry, 24(5), 615–625. doi:10.1016/S0097-8485(00)00064-4

Popovic, B. D., Dragovic, M. B., & Djordjevic, A. R. (1982). Analysis and synthesis of wire antennas. New York: Research studies Press.

Pozar, D. M., & Schaubert, D. H. (Eds.). (1995). Microstrip Antennas. New York: IEEE Press.

Prada, R., & Paiva, A. (2005). Intelligent virtual agents in collaborative scenarios. In Proceedings of the 5th International Working Conference on Intelligent Virtual Agents (IVA 2005), Kos, Greece.

Prato, T. (2009). Adaptive management of natural systems using fuzzy logic. Environmental Modelling & Software, 24(1), 940–944. doi:10.1016/j.envsoft.2009.01.007

Prothero, A. (1994). Green marketing in the car industry. In P. Nieuwenhuis & P. Wells (Eds.), Motor Vehicles in the Environment: Principles and Practice. Chichester, UK: John Wiley.

Prybutok, V. R., Yi, J., & Mitchell, D. (2000). Comparison of neural network models with ARIMA and regression models for prediction of Houston's daily maximum ozone concentrations. European Journal of Operational Research, 122(1), 31–40. doi:10.1016/S0377-2217(99)00069-7

Qazvinian, V., Abolhassani, H., Haeri, S. H., & Hariri, B. B. (2008). Evolutionary coincidence-based ontology mapping extraction. Expert Systems: International Journal of Knowledge Engineering and Neural Networks, 25(3), 221–236. doi:10.1111/j.1468-0394.2008.00462.x

Rahm, E., & Bernstein, P. A. (2001). A survey of approaches to automatic schema matching. The International Journal on Very Large Data Bases, 10(4), 334–350. doi:10.1007/s007780100057

Raja, Y., McKenna, S., & Gong, S. (1998). Tracking and Segmenting People in Varying Lighting Condition using Color. In International Conference on Face and Gesture Recognition (pp. 228-233).

Rana, A. S., & Zalzala, A. M. (1997). Fifth International Conference on Artificial Neural Networks (Conf. Publ. No. 440).

Raychowdhury, A., Gupta, B., & Bhattacharjee, R. (2000). Bandwidth improvement of microstrip antennas through a genetic-algorithm based design of feed network. Microwave and Optical Technology Letters, 27, 273–275. doi:10.1002/1098-2760(20001120)27:4<273::AID-MOP17>3.0.CO;2-8

Recio-Blanco, A., Bijaoui, A., & de Laverny, P. (2002). Automated derivation of stellar atmospheric parameters and chemical abundances: the MATISSE algorithm. R. Astron. Soc.

Recio-Blanco, A., de Laverny, P., & Plez, B. (2005). RVS-ARB-001. European Space Agency technical note.

Reddy, K. S., & Ranjan, M. (2003). Solar resource estimation using artificial neural networks and comparison with other correlation models. Energy Conversion and Management, 199, 272–294.

Reed, M., Gigliotti, A., McDonald, J., Seagrave, J., Seilkop, J., & Manderly, J. (2004). Health effects of subchronic exposure to environmental levels of diesel exhaust. Inhalation Toxicology, 16(4), 177–193. doi:10.1080/08958370490277146

Rehman, S., & Mohandes, M. (2008). Artificial neural network estimation of global solar radiation using air temperature and relative humidity. Energy Policy, 36, 571–576. doi:10.1016/j.enpol.2007.09.033

Reif, D. M., White, B. C., & Moore, J. H. (2004). Integrated analysis of genetic, genomic and proteomic data. Expert Review of Proteomics, 1, 67–75. doi:10.1586/14789450.1.1.67

Reimondo, A. (2007). OpenCV Swiki. Retrieved from http://alereimondo.no-ip.org/OpenCV/

Rickel, J., & Johnson, W. L. (1999). Animated Agents for Procedural Training in Virtual Reality: Perception, Cognition, and Motor Control. Applied Artificial Intelligence, 13(4-5), 343–382. doi:10.1080/088395199117315

RILEM. (2009). Réunion Internationale des Laboratoires et Experts des Matériaux, systèmes de constructionet ouvrages. Retrieved from http://www.rilem.net

Ripley, B. P. (1996). Pattern Recognition and Neural Networks. Cambridge, UK: Cambridge University Press.

Risch, N. (2000). Searching for genetic determinants in the new millennium. Nature, 405, 847–856. doi:10.1038/35015718

Ritchie, M. D., Hahn, L. W., & Roodi, N. (2001). Multifactor dimensionality reduction reveals high-order interactions among estrogen metabolism genes in sporadic breast cancer. American Journal of Human Genetics, 69, 138–147. doi:10.1086/321276

Ritchie, M. D., White, B. C., Parker, J. S., Hahn, L. W., & Moore, J. H. (2003). Optimization of neural network architecture using genetic programming improves detection and modelling of gene-gene interactions in studies of human diseases. BMC Bioinformatics, 4(28).

Rocchio, J. (1971). Relevance feedback in information retrieval. In The SMART retrieval system: Experiments in Automatic Document Processing (pp. 313-323).

Rocha, F. E. L., Costa, J. V., & Favero, E. L. (2004). A new approach to meaningful learning assessment using concept maps: Ontologies and genetic algorithms. In Proceedings of the First International Conference on Concept Mapping.

Rodenstock. (2009). ImpressionIST. Retrieved June 30, 2009, from http://www.rodenstock.com

Rodó, X., Baert, E., & Comin, A. (1997). Variations in seasonal rainfall in Southern Europe during the present century: relationships with the North Atlantic Oscillation and El Niño-Southern Oscillation. Climate Dynamics, 13, 275–284. doi:10.1007/s003820050165

Romero-Legarreta, I., Addison, P. S., Reed, M. J., Grubb, N. R., Clegg, G. R., Robertson, C. E., & Watson, J. N. (2005). Continuous wavelet transform modulus maxima analysis of the electrocardiogram: Beat-to-beat characterization and beat-to-beat measurement. International Journal of Wavelets, Multresolution, and Information Processing, 3, 19–42. doi:10.1142/S0219691305000774

Rova, M., Haataja, R., & Marttila, R. (2004). Data mining and multiparameter analysis of lung surfactant protein genes in bronchopulmonarydysplasia. Human Molecular Genetics, 13, 1095–1104. doi:10.1093/hmg/ddh132

Rumelhart, D. E., Hilton, G. E., & Williams, R. J. (1986). Learning internal representations by error propagation. In Parallel distributed processing: Explorations in the microstructure of cognition (Vol. 1, pp. 318-362). Cambridge, MA: MIT Press.

Rumelhart, D. E., Hinton, G. E., & Williams, R. J. (1986). Learning representations by back-propagating errors. Nature, 323, 533–536. doi:10.1038/323533a0

Russel, S., & Norvig, P. (1995). Artificial Intelligence, A modern approach. Upper Saddle River, NJ: Prentice-Hall, Inc.

Sahambi, J., Tandon, S., & Bhatt, R. (1997). Using wavelet transforms for ECG characterization an on-line digital signal processing system. IEEE Engineering in Medicine and Biology Magazine, 16, 77–83. doi:10.1109/51.566158

Salmond, D. (1990). Mixture Reduction Algorithms for Target Tracking in Clutter. SPIE Signal and Data Processing of Small Targets, 1305, 434–445.

Salski, A. (2007). Fuzzy clustering of fuzzy ecological data. Ecological Informatics, 2(1), 262–269. doi:10.1016/j.ecoinf.2007.07.002

Salton, G. (1989). Automatic Text Processing: The Transformation, Analysis, and Retrieval of Information by Computer. Reading, MA: Addison-Wesley Longman Publishing Co., Inc.

Samecka-Cymerman, A., Stankiewicz, A., Kolon, K., & Kempers, A. J. (2009). Self-organizing feature map (neural networks) as a tool to select the best indicator of road traffic pollution (soil, leaves or bark of Robinia pseudoacacia L). Environmental Pollution, 157(7), 2061–2065. doi:10.1016/j.envpol.2009.02.021

Samii, R., & Michielson, E. (1999). Electromagnetic Optimization by Genetic algorithm. Hoboken, NJ: John Wiley & Sons Inc.

Sánchez, A., Fernández, F., & Duarte, A. (2005). Compresión de imágenes basada en la optimización metaheurística de un sistema Takagi Sugeno Kang. Paper presented at: V Congreso Español sobre Metaheurísticas, Algoritmos Evolutivos y Bioinspirados (MAEB 2007), Tenerife (Spain).

Sánchez-Nielsen, E., Antón-Canalís, L., & Guerra-Artal, C. (2005). An autonomous and user-independent hand posture recognition system for vision-based interface tasks. In Procs. of the 11th Conference of the Spanish Association for Artificial Intelligence (CAEPIA 2005) (pp. 113-122).

Saxena, A., Sun, M., & Ng, A. (2007). Make3D: Learning 3-D Scene Structure from a Single Still Image. ICCV workshop on 3D Representation for Recognition (3dRR-07).

Schmuker, M., & Schneider, G. (2007). Processing and classification of chemical data inspired by insect olfaction. Proceedings of the National Academy of Sciences of the United States of America, 204(51), 20285–20289. doi:10.1073/pnas.0705683104

Schmuker, M., Schwarte, F., Brück, A., Proschak, E., Tanrikulu, E., & Givehchi, A. (2007). SOMMER: self-organising maps for education and research. Journal of Molecular Modeling, 13(1), 225–228. doi:10.1007/s00894-006-0140-0

Schöfkopf, B., Burges, C., & Smola, A. (1999) Pairwise Classification and Support Vector Machines. Cambridge, MA: The MIT Press.

Schonlau, M., Dumouchel, W., Ju, W. H., Karr, A. F., Theus, M., & Vardi, Y. (2001). Computer Intrusion: Detecting Masquerades. Statistical Science, 16(1), 58–74. doi:10.1214/ss/998929476

Schwartz, M. D., & Karl, T. R. (1990). Spring phenology: Nature's experiment to detect the effect of 'green up' on surface maximum temperatures. Monthly Weather Review, 118, 883–890. doi:10.1175/1520-0493(1990)118<0883:SPNETD>2.0.CO;2

Scott, D., Seth, S., & Samal, A. (1997, July 4). A hardware engine for genetic algorithms. Technical Report UNL-CSE-97-001, Dept. Computer Science and Engineering, University of Nebraska-Lincoln.

Scott, S. D., Samal, A., & Seth, S. (1995). HGA: A hardware-based Genetic Algorithm. In Proc of the ACM-SIGDA Third Int. Symposium on Field-Programmable Gate Arrays (pp. 53-59).

Seitz, S. M., Curless, B., Diebel, J., Scharstein, D., & Szeliski, R. (2006). A comparison and evaluation of multiple stereo reconstruction algorithms. CVPR, 519–528.

Senhadji, L., Carrault, G., Bellanger, J. J., & Passariello, G. (1995). Comparing wavelet transforms for recognizing cardiac patterns. IEEE Engineering in Medicine and Biology Magazine, 14, 167–173. doi:10.1109/51.376755

Sentelhas, P. C., & Gillespie, T. J. (2008). Estimating hourly net radiation for leaf wetness duration using the Penman-Monteith equation. Theoretical and Applied Climatology, 91, 205–215. doi:10.1007/s00704-006-0290-0

Seung, H. S., Socci, N. D., & Lee, D. (1998). The Rectified Gaussian Distribution. Advances in Neural Information Processing Systems, 10, 350–356.

Shackleford, B., Okushi, E., Yasuda, M., Koizumi, H., Seo, K., & Iwamoto, T. (1997, July). Hardware framework for accelerating the execution speed of a genetic algorithm. IEICE Transactions on Electronics.

Shackleford, B., Snider, G., Carter, R., Okushi, E., Yasuda, M., Seo, K., & Yasuura, H. (2001). A high performance, pipelined, FPGA-based genetic algorithm machine. Genetic Programming and Evolvable Machines, 2(1), 33–60. doi:10.1023/A:1010018632078

Shaefer, C. G. (1987, July). The ARGOT strategy: adaptive representation genetic optimizer technique. In Proceedings of the 2nd International, Conference on Genetic Algorithmsi and their Applications. New York: Lawrence Erlbaum Associates.

Sharma, V., & Gupta, G. K. (2007). Using Artificial Neural Network to Model Microstrip Inset Fed Rectangular Patch Antenna. In Microwave and Millimeter Wave Technology, ICMMT International Conference (pp. 1-2).

Shinohara, Y., & Otsu, N. (2004). Facial expression recognition using Fisher weight maps. In Procs. of the IEEE Int. Conf. on AFGR.

Shvaiko, P., & Euzenat, J. (2005). A Survey of Schema-based Matching Approaches. [JoDS]. Journal on Data Semantics, 4, 146–171.

Shyu, L.Y., & al. (2004). Using Wavelet Transform and Fuzzy Neural Network for VPC Detection From the Holter ECG. IEEE Transactions on Bio-Medical Engineering, 51(7), 1269–1273. doi:10.1109/TBME.2004.824131

SIBTRA. (2009). Sistema Inteligente de Bajo Coste Para el Transporte y la Vigilancia en Entornos Ecológicos No Estructurados. Ministerio de Educación y Ciencia. Plan Nacional de I+D (DPI2007-64137).

Silippo, R., Zong, W., & Berthold, M. (1999). ECG Feature Relevance in a Fuzzy Arrhythmia Classifier. Computers in Cardiology, 679–682.

Silva, R. K. S., Aguiar, M. S., Rose, C. A. F. D., & Dimuro, G. P. (2006a). Extending the HPC-ICTM geographical categorization model for grid computing. In B. Kagstrom, E. Elmroth, J. Dongarra, & J. Wasniewski (Eds.), PARA (LNCS 4699, pp. 850–859).

Silva, R. K. S., Aguiar, M. S., Rose, C. A. F. D., Dimuro, G. P., & Costa, A. C. R. (2006b). HPC-ICTM: a Parallel Model for Geographic Categorization. In Proc. of The John Vincent Atanasoff Symposium, Sofia, Bulgaria (pp. 143-148).

Simo, A., Kitamura, K., & Nishida, Y. (2005). Behavior based Children Accidents' Simulation and Visualization: Planning the Emergent Situations. Computational Intelligence, 164–169.

Simon, U., Brüggemann, R., & Pudenz, S. (2004). Aspects of Decision Support in Water Management - Example Berlin and Potsdam (Germany) I - Spatially Differentiated Evaluation. Water Research, 38, 1809–1816. doi:10.1016/j.watres.2003.12.037

Sison, R., & Shimura, M. (1998). Student Modeling and Machine Learning. International Journal of Artificial Intelligence in Education, 9, 128–158.

Sivannarayana, N., & Reddy, D. C. (1999). Biorthogonal wavelet transforms for ECG. Medical Engineering & Physics, 21, 167–174. doi:10.1016/S1350-4533(99)00040-5

Smith, B., & Brochhausen, M. (2008). Establishing and Harmonizing Ontologies in an Interdisciplinary Health Care and Clinical Research Environment. Studies in Health Technology and Informatics, 134, 219.

Smith, S. F. (1980). A learning system based on genetic adaptive Algorithms. Doctoral dissertation, University of Pittsburgh.

SMMT. (2004). The 4th Annual Sustainability Report. London: Society of Motor Manufacturers and Traders.

Snae, C., & Brueckner, M. (2007). Ontology-driven e-learning system based on roles and activities for Thai learning environment. Interdisciplinary Journal of Knowledge and Learning Objects, 3, 1–17.

Söderström, T., & Stoica, P. (1989). System identification. Englewood Cliffs, NJ: Prentice Hall.

Solymosi, T., & Dombi, J. (1986). A method for determining weights of criteria: The centralized weights. European Journal of Operational Research, 26, 35–41. doi:10.1016/0377-2217(86)90157-8

Song, M. H., Lee, J., Cho, S. P., Lee, K. J., & Yoo, S. K. (2005). Support Vector Machine Based Arrhythmia Classification Using Reduced Features. International Journal of Control, Automation, and Systems, 3(4), 571–579.

Soto, M., & Allongue, S. (2002). Modeling Methods for Reusable and Interoperable Virtual Entities in Multimedia Virtual Worlds. Multimedia Tools and Applications, 16(1/2), 161–177. doi:10.1023/A:1013249920338

Soule, T. (1998). Code Growth in Genetic Programming (Thesis). Moscow, ID: University of Idaho.

Soule, T., & Foster, J. A. (1997). Code Size and Depth Flows in Genetic Programming. Genetic Programming. In Proceedings of the Second Annual Conference. San Francisco, CA (pp. 313-320).

Spasic, I., Ananiadou, S., McNaught, J., & Kumar, A. (2005). Text mining and ontologies in biomedicine: making sense of raw text. Briefings in Bioinformatics, 6(3), 239–251. doi:10.1093/bib/6.3.239

Spekton, D. M., Thurston, G. D., Mao, J., He, D., Hayes, C., & Lippman, M. (1991). Effects of single and multi-day ozone exposures on respiratory function in active normal children. Environmental Research, 55, 107–122. doi:10.1016/S0013-9351(05)80167-7

Spellman, G. (1998). Analysing air pollution meteorology. Weather, 53, 34–42.

Spiliopoulou, M., & Faulstich, L. C. (1998). WUM: A Web Utilization Miner. In EDBT Workshop WebDB98 (pp. 109-115). Berlin: Springer Verlag.

Srikant, R., & Agrawal, R. (1995). Mining generalized association rules. In U. Dayal, P. Gray & S. Nishio (Eds.), 21st International Conference on Very Large Data Bases (pp. 407-419). Zurich, Germany: Morgan Kaufmann.

Stanley, K., & Miikkulainen, R. (2003). A Taxonomy for Artificial Embryogeny. In Proceedings []. Cambridge, MA: MIT Press.]. Artificial Life, 9, 93–130. doi:10.1162/106454603322221487

Stefan, G. (2000). Circuits and digital systems (Circuite si sisteme digitale). Bucharest: Tehnical Publishing House.

Stikoff, N., Wazlowski, M., Smith, A., & Silverman, H. (1995). Implementing a genetic algorithm on a parallel custom computing machine. IEEE Workshop on FPGAs for Custom Computing Machines.

Stockwell, W. R., Kramm, G., Scheel, H. E., Mohnen, V. A., & Seiler, W. (1997). Ozone formation, destruction and exposure in Europe and the United States. In H. Sandermann, A. R. Wellburn & R. L. Heath (Eds.), Forest Decline and Ozone (pp. 1–38).

Stoica, P., & Söderström, T. (1982). A useful parametrization for optimal experimental design. In IEEE Trans. Automatic. Control, AC-27. The Math Works, Inc. (n.d.). The Matlab and Simulink products. Retrieved from http://www.mathworks.com/

Storn, R., & Price, K. (1997). Differential Evolution - A Simple and Efficient Heuristic for Global Optimisation over Continuous Spaces. Journal of Global Optimization, 11, 341–359. doi:10.1023/A:1008202821328

Sugihara, K. (1986). Machine interpretation of line Drawings. Cambridge, MA: The MIT Press.

Sun, L., Hines, E. L., Mias, C., Green, R., & Udrea, D. (2005). Quarter-wave phase-compensating multidielectric lens design using genetic algorithms. Microwave and Optical Technology Letters, 44(2), 165–169. doi:10.1002/mop.20577

Sun, R., Merrill, E., & Peterson, T. (2001). From implicit skills to explicit knowledge: a bottom-up model of skill learning. Cognitive Science, 25(2), 203–244.

Swain, M. J., & Ballard, D. H. (1991). Color indexing. International Journal of Computer Vision, 7(1), 11–32. doi:10.1007/BF00130487

Sydbom, A., Blomberg, A., Parnia, S., Stenfors, N., Sandstrom, T., & Dahlen, S.-E. (2001). Health effects of diesel exhaust emissions. The European Respiratory Journal, 17(4), 733–746. doi:10.1183/09031936.01.17407330

Syldatke, T., Chen, W., Angele, J., Nierlich, A., & Ullrich, M. (2007). How Ontologies and Rules Help to Advance Automobile Development. Lecture Notes in Computer Science, 4824, 1. doi:10.1007/978-3-540-75975-1_1

Syswerda, G. (1989). Uniform crossover in genetic algorithms. In Proceedings of the Third International Conference on Genetic Algorithms and their Applications. San Francisco: Morgan Kaufmann.

Tahri-Daizadeh, N., Tregouet, D. A., & Nicaud, V. (2003). Automated detection of informative combined effects in genetics association Studies of complex traits. *Genome Research*, 13, 1952–1960.

The r project. (n.d.). The R Project for Statistical Computing. Retrieved from http://www.r-project.org/

Thomas, D. C. (2004). *Statistical Methods in Genetic Epidemiology*. Oxford, UK: Oxford University Press.

Thompson, A. (1996). Silicon evolution. In J. R. Koza, D. E. Goldberg, D. B. Fogel, & R. L. Riolo (Eds.), Genetic Programming 1996: Proc. First Ann. Conf., Stanford University, CA, 28–31 July 1996 (pp. 444–452). Cambridge, MA: MIT Press.

Thompson, A., & Layzell, P. (1999). Analysis of unconventional evolved electronics. *Communications of the ACM*, 42(4), 71–79. doi:10.1145/299157.299174

Toivonen, H., Onkamo, P., Hintsanen, P., et al. (2005). Data mining for gene mapping. In M. M. Kantardzic & J. Zurada (Eds.), New Generation of Data Mining Applications (pp. 263-293). Hoboken, NJ: IEEE Press.

Tomita, D. (2001). Whole-cell simulation: A grand challenge of the 21st century. *Trends in Biotechnology*, 19(6), 205–210. doi:10.1016/S0167-7799(01)01636-5

Torrecilla, J. S., Rojo, E., Oliet, M., Dominguez, J. C., & Rodriguez, F. (2009). Self-Organizing Maps and Learning Vector Quantization Networks As Tools to Identify Vegetable Oils. *Journal of Agricultural and Food Chemistry*, 57(7), 2763–2769. doi:10.1021/jf803520u

Tran, V. T., Yang, B. S., & Chiow Tan, A. C. (2009). Multi-step Ahead Direct Prediction for a Machine Conditions Prognosis using regression trees and Neuro-fuzzy Systems. *Expert Systems with Applications*, 36(5), 9378–9387. doi:10.1016/j.eswa.2009.01.007

Tremeau, A., & Borel, N. (1997). A region growing and merging algorithm to color segmentation. *Pattern Recognition*, 30(7), 1191–1203. doi:10.1016/S0031-3203(96)00147-1

Trezza, R. (2006). Evapotranspiration from a remote sensing model for water management in a irrigation system in Venezuela. *Interciencia*, 31(6), 417–423.

Troxell, G. E., Raphael, J. M., & Davis, H. E. (1958). Long term creep and shrinkage test of plain and reinforced concrete. In Proceedings of the American Society for Testing and Materials (ASTM), Philadelphia, PA (Vol. 58, pp. 1101-1120).

Tucker, C. J. (1979). Red and photographic infrared linear combinations for monitoring vegetation. *Remote Sensing of Environment*, 8, 127–150. doi:10.1016/0034-4257(79)90013-0

Tufte, G., & Haddow, P. (1999). Prototyping a GA pipeline for complete hardware evolution. In A. Stoica, D. Keymeulen, & J. Lohn (Eds.), Proc. First NASA/DoD Workshop on Evolvable Hardware (pp. 18–25). New York: IEEE Computer Society.

Tufte, G., & Haddow, P. C. (2005). Towards Development on a Silicon-based Cellular Computing Machine. *Natural Computing*, 4(4), 387–416. doi:10.1007/s11047-005-3665-8

Tulving, E. (2004). The Missing Link in Cognition: Evolution of Self-Knowing Consciousness. (H. Terrace & J. Metcalfe, Eds.). New York: Oxford Univ. Press.

Turing, A. (1952). The chemical basis of morphogenesis. *Philosofical Transactions of the Royal Society B*, 237, 37–72. doi:10.1098/rstb.1952.0012

Turon, B. C. H., & Arslan, T. (1995). A parallel genetic VLSI architecture for combinatorial real-time application. IEEE Int. Conf. Genetic Algorithms in Engineering Systems: Innovations and Applications.

Tzeng, J. Y., Devlin, B., & Wasserman, L. (2003). On the identification of disease mutations by the analysis of haplotype similarity and goodness of fit. *American Journal of Human Genetics*, 72, 891–902. doi:10.1086/373881

Valverde, M. C., de Campos, H. F., & Ferreira, N. J. (2005). Artificial neural network technique for rainfall forecasting applied to the Sao Paulo region. Journal of Hydrology (Amsterdam), 301, 1–4. doi:10.1016/j.jhydrol.2004.06.018

Van Dam, K. H., & Lukszo, Z. (2006). Modelling Energy and Transport Infrastructures as a Multi-Agent System using a Generic Ontology. In Systems, Man and Cybernetics IEEE International Conference 2006 (SMC06).

Van Rijsbergen, C. J. (1975). Information Retrieval. London: Butterworth.

Vapnik, V. (1995). The Nature of Statistical Learning Theory. Berlin: Springer.

Vazquez Feijoo, J. A., Worden, K., & Stanway, R. (2004). System identification using associated linear equations. Mechanical Systems and Signal Processing, 18, 431–455. doi:10.1016/S0888-3270(03)00078-5

VCA. (2004). Vehicle Certification Agency Car Fuel / CO2 data. Retrieved from http://www.vca.gov.uk/carfueldata/index.shtm

Venäläinen, A., Solantie, R., & Laine, V. (1998). Mean long-term surface energy balance components in Finland during the summertime. Boreal Environment Research, 3, 171–180.

Venkatesh, S. (2004). Necessary and sufficient conditions for robust identification of uncertain LTI systems. Systems & Control Letters, 53, 117–125. doi:10.1016/j.sysconle.2003.10.007

Venturini, G. (1993). SIA: A supervised inductive algorithm with genetic search for learning attributes based concepts. In P. Brazdil (Ed.), Machine Learning: ECML-93: Vol. 667. European Conference on Machine Learning (pp. 280-296). Vienna: Springer.

Vermeulen-Jourdan, L., Dhaenens, C., & Talbi, E.-G. (2005). Linkage disequilibrium study with a parallel adaptive GA. International Journal of Foundations of Computer Science, 16(2), 241–260. doi:10.1142/S0129054105002978

Vesanto, J., Himberg, J., Alhoniemi, E., & Parhankangas, J. (2000). SOM Toolbox for Matlab 5. Technical Report A57, Helsinki University of Technology.

Viola, P., & Jones, M. J. (2004). Robust real-time face detection. International Journal of Computer Vision, 57(2), 151–173. doi:10.1023/B:VISI.0000013087.49260.fb

Visionix. (2009). 3DiView 3D virtual try-on. Retrieved June 30, 2009, from http://www.visionix.com

Von Hippel, T., Allende, C., & Sneden, C. (2002). Automated Stellar Spectral Classification and Parameterization for the Masses. The Garrison Festschrift conference proceedings.

Vosinakis, S., & Panayiotopoulos, T. (2005, February). A tool for constructing 3D Environments with Virtual Agents. Multimedia Tools and Applications, 25(2), 253–279. doi:10.1007/s11042-005-5607-y

Voss, G., Behr, J., Reiners, D., & Roth, M. (2002). A Multi-Thread Safe Foundation for Scenegraphs and its Extension to Clusters. Eurographics Workshop on Parallel Graphics and Visualisation.

Waddell, M., Page, D., Zhan, F., et al. (2005). Predicting cancer susceptibility from single-nucleotide polymorphism data: A case study in multiple myeloma. In S. Parthasarathy, W. Wang & M.J. Zaki (Eds.), Fifth ACM SIGKDD Workshop on Data Mining in Bioinformatics (BIOKDD) (pp. 21-28). Chicago: ACM.

Walton, D., Thomas, J. A., & Dravitzki, V. (2004). Commuters' concern for the environment and knowledge of the effects of vehicle emissions. Transportation Research Part D, Transport and Environment, 9, 335–340. doi:10.1016/j.trd.2004.04.001

Wang, B. F., & Lo, Y. T. (1984). Microstrip Antennas For Dual Frequency Operation. IEEE Transactions on Antennas and Propagation, 32, 938–943. doi:10.1109/TAP.1984.1143459

Wang, H. (2005). Bayesian shrinkage estimation of quantitative trait loci parameters. Genetics, 170, 465–480. doi:10.1534/genetics.104.039354

Wang, J., Ding, Z., & Jiang, C. (2006). GAOM: Genetic Algorithm Based Ontology Matching. In Proceedings of IEEE Asia-Pacific Conference on Services Computing 2006 (APSCC2006).

Wang, W. (2006). Detecting and modeling large-scale interactions between vegetation, precipitation, and temperature over temperate-semiarid and boreal climate regimes. Ph.D. dissertation, Boston University, MA, USA.

Wang, W., & Grinstein, G. (1993). A Survey of 3D Solid Reconstruction from 2D Projection Line Drawings. Computer Graphics Forum, 12(2), 137–158. doi:10.1111/1467-8659.1220137

Wang, W., Zmeureanu, R., & Rivard, H. (2005). Applying multi-objective genetic algorithms in green building design optimization. Building and Environment, 11(40), 1512–1525.

Wang, X., & Triantaphyllou, E. (2008). Ranking irregularities when evaluating alternatives by using some ELECTRE methods. Omega, 36, 45–63. doi:10.1016/j.omega.2005.12.003

Wasserman, P. (1989). Neural Computing. New York: Van Nostrand Reinhold.

Watson, J. D., & Crick, F. H. (1953). Molecular structure of Nucleic Acids. Nature, 171, 737–738. doi:10.1038/171737a0

Weigend, A. S., & Gershenfeld, N. A. (1992). Time Series Prediction: Forecasting The Future And Understanding The Past. Santa Fe Institute Studies in the Sciences of Complexity. Boulder, CO: Westview Press.

Wendland, J., Harrison, P. M., Henry, M., & Brownell, M. (2005). Deep Engraving of Metals for the Automotive Sector Using High Average Power Diode Pumped Solid State Lasers. In Proceedings of the 23nd International Conference on Applications of Lasers and Electro-Optics (ICALEO 2005) Laser Institute of America, Miami, USA.

Wexelblat, A. (1996). An environment for aiding information-browsing tasks. AAAI Spring Symposium on Acquisition, Learning and Demonstration: Automating Tasks for Users. Birmingham, UK, AAAI Press.

Wikipedia. (2009). Article on 3D modelling. Retrieved from http://en.wikipedia.org/wiki/3D_modelling

Wilcox, M. A., Wyszynski, D. F., & Panhuysen, C. I. (2003). Empirically derived phenotypic subgroups - qualitative and quantitative trait analyses. BMC Genetics, 4(1), S15. doi:10.1186/1471-2156-4-S1-S15

Wilkinson, M. I., Vallenary, A., & Turon, C. (2005). Spectroscopic survey of the Galaxy with Gaia- II. The expected science yield from the Radial Velocity Spectrometer. Monthly Notices of the Royal Astronomical Society, 359, 1306. doi:10.1111/j.1365-2966.2005.09012.x

Witten, I. H., & Frank, E. (2005). Data Mining: Practical machine learning tools and techniques (2nd Ed.). San Francisco, CA: Morgan Kaufmann.

Wittke-Thompson, J. K., Pluzhinikov, A., & Cox, N. J. (2005). Rational Inferences about departures from Hardy-Weinberg equilibrium. American Journal of Human Genetics, 76, 967–986. doi:10.1086/430507

Wolberg, W. H., & Mangasarian, O. L. (1990). Multisurface method of pattern separation for medical diagnosis applied to breast cytology. Proceedings of the National Academy of Sciences of the United States of America, 87(23), 9193–9196. doi:10.1073/pnas.87.23.9193

Wolfram, S. (1994). Cellular Automata and Complexity. Reading, MA: Addison-Wesley.

Woodard, F. I. (Ed.). (1987). Climate and plant distribution. Cambridge, UK: Cambridge University Press.

Wooldridge, M. (1999). Intelligent agents. In G. Weiss (Ed.), Multiagent Systems - A Modern Approach to Distributed Artificial Intelligence (pp. 27-78). Cambridge, MA: The MIT Press.

Woolson, I. H. (1905). Some remarkable tests indicating flow of concrete under pressure. Engineering News, 54, 454.

Wu, J. Z., Xiong, P., & Sheng, H. (2007). Mining Personalization Interest and Navigation Patterns on Portal. In PAKDD (pp. 948-955). Berlin: Springer.

Xia, P. (2003). An inverse model of MR damper using optimal neural network and system identification. Journal of Sound and Vibration, 266, 1009–1023. doi:10.1016/S0022-460X(02)01408-6

Xilinx. (2009). Retrieved from http://www.xilinx.com/ise/logic_design_prod/foundation.htm

Yam, L. H., Yan, Y. J., & Jiang, J. S. (2003). Vibration-based damage detection for composite Structures using wavelet transform and Neural Network identification. Composite Structures, 60, 403–412. doi:10.1016/S0263-8223(03)00023-0

Yasunaga, M., Kim, J., & Yoshihara, I. (2001). Evolvable reasoning hardware: its prototyping and performance evaluation. []. Amsterdam: Kluwer Academic Publishers.]. Genetic Programming and Evolvable Machines, 2, 211–230. doi:10.1023/A:1011939025340

Yeo, N. C., Lee, K. H., Venkatesh, Y. V., & Ong, S. H. (2005). Colour image segmentation using the self-organizing map and adaptive resonance theory. Image and Vision Computing, 23, 1060–1079. doi:10.1016/j.imavis.2005.07.008

Yi, J., & Prybutok, R. (1996). A neural network model forecasting for prediction of daily maximum ozone concentration in an industrial urban area. Environmental Pollution, 92(3), 349–357. doi:10.1016/0269-7491(95)00078-X

Young, S. S., & Ge, N. (2005). Recursive partitioning analysis of complex disease pharmacogenetic studies I. Motivation and overview. Pharmacogenetics, 6, 65–75.

Zachariadis, T., Ntziachristos, L., & Samaras, Z. (2001). The effect of age and technological change on motor vehicle emissions. Transportation Research Part D, Transport and Environment, 6, 221–227. doi:10.1016/S1361-9209(00)00025-0

Zadeh, L. A. (1965). Fuzzy Sets. Information and Control, 8(3), 338–353. doi:10.1016/S0019-9958(65)90241-X

Zadeh, L. A. (1994). Fuzzy logic, neural networks, and soft computing. Communications of the ACM, 37, 77–84. doi:10.1145/175247.175255

Zenso, S. (1986). A note on the gradient pf multi-image. Computer Vision Graphics and Image Processing, 33(1), 116–125. doi:10.1016/0734-189X(86)90223-9

Zhang, Q. Y., & Aires-de-Sousa, J. (2005). Structure-Based Classification of Chemical Reactions without Assignment of Reaction Centers. Journal of Chemical Information and Modeling, 45(6), 1775–1783. doi:10.1021/ci0502707

Zhang, Q. Y., & Aires-de-Sousa, J. (2007). Random Forest Prediction of Mutagenicity from Empirical Physicochemical Descriptors. Journal of Chemical Information and Modeling, 47(1), 1–8. doi:10.1021/ci050520j

Zhu, T., Greiner, R., & Häubl, G. (2003). Predicting Web Information Content, Intelligent Techniques for Web Personalization. In B. Mobasher & S. S. Anand (Eds.), ITWP 2003 (pp. 1-36). Berlin: Springer-Verlag.

Zimmerman, M. W., & Povinelli, R. J. (2004). On Improving the Classification of Myocardial Ischemia Using Holter ECG Data. Computers in Cardiology, 377–380. doi:10.1109/CIC.2004.1442951

Zupan, J. (1994). Introduction to Artificial Neural Network (ANN) Methods: What They Are and How to Use Them. Acta Chimica Slovenica, 41, 327–352.

Zupan, J., & Gasteiger, J. (1993). Neural Networks for Chemists: An Introduction. Weinheim, Germany: VCH-Verlag.

Zupan, J., Novič, M., & Ruisánchez, I. (1997). Kohonen and counterpropagation artificial neural networks in analytical chemistry. Chemometrics and Intelligent Laboratory Systems, 38(1), 1–23. doi:10.1016/S0169-7439(97)00030-0

About the Contributors

Daniel Rivero was born in A Coruña on the January, 30th 1978. He has obtained his MS degree in Computer Science by the University of A Coruña, A Coruña, Spain in 2001 and the PhD degree in Computer Science in 2007 by the same university. He is currently an assistant professor at the Faculty of Computer Science of the University of A Coruña. Before he gets that academic role, he has received different research grants from different administrations for more than four years. His main research interests are Artificial Neural Networks, Genetic Algorithms, Genetic Programming and Adaptative Systems.

Marcos Gestal is an assistant professor in the Computer Science Faculty (University of A Coruña) and member of the research laboratory Artificial Neural Networks and Adaptative Systems. He has obtained his PhD degree in Computer Science in 2007, with a thesis about multimodal problem resolution using several approaches based on Genetic Algorithms. His actual research interests are focused on evolutionary computation (mainly genetic algorithms), artificial neural networks and their interaction to perform variable selection. Also he is interested in security task, so he is actually teaching in the information systems security subject. He has participated in several research projects and published papers in many international journals and books.

***

Leopoldo Acosta received his MS degree in applied physics in 1987 and his PhD degree in Computer Science in 1991 from the University of La Laguna, Tenerife, Spain. From 1988 to 1998, he was an assistant professor and associate professor in the Department of Applied Physics, Electronics and Systems at the same university. Currently, he works as Professor at the University de La Laguna. His areas of interest include robotics and Control. He has issued several papers in conferences and journals in these fields. Furthermore, he has participated in different research projects related with his research areas of interest.

Luis Antón Canalís received his Graduate in Computer Science from the Universidad de La Laguna, and he is currently finishing his PhD on Computer Vision in the Universidad de Las Palmas de Gran Canaria. His current research interests include Artificial Intelligence, Swarm Intelligence, Object Tracking and Object Detection.

Diana Francisca Adamatti received her PhD from Escola Politécnica da Universidade de São Paulo, Brazil, in Electrical Engineering (2007). She has a MSc from Universidade Federal do Rio Grande do Sul (2003) and BSc from Universidade de Caxias do Sul (2000), both in Brazil, in Computer Science. Currently, she is a lecturer at Universidade Federal do Rio Grande, Brazil. Her main research is Artificial Intelligence and Computer Games, mainly Multi-Agent Systems and Role-Playing Games.

Vanessa Aguiar was born in Paris (France), in 1985. She received the MS degree in Computer Science at the University of A Coruña, Spain in 2008. She is currently a Ph.D. student in Information and Communication Technologies at the Faculty of Informatics of the University of A Coruña. She has received different research grants from different administrations for two years. She is member of the Galician Bioinformatics Network. Her main research interests are data mining, evolutionary computation and bioinformatics.

Jesus B. Alonso (S'01-M'06) received the Telecommunication Engineer degree (honors) in 2001 and the Ph.D. degree (honors) in 2006 from University of Las Palmas de Gran Canaria (ULPGC-Spain) where he is an Associate Professor in the Department of Signal and Communications from 2002. He has researched in more than 20 International and Spanish Research Projects. He has more than 140 papers published in international journals and conferences. He has been reviewer in different international journals and conferences since 2001. His research interests include signal processing in biocomputing, biometrics, nonlinear signal processing, recognition systems, audio characterization and data mining. He is head of excellent network in biomedical engineering in ULPGC. He is Vice-Dean from 2009 in Higher Technical School of Telecommunication Engineers in ULPGC.

Jose Manuel Andrade, M.Sc. in Chemistry in 1990 (Univ. Santiago de Compostela), Ph.D. in Analytical Chemistry in 1995 (Univ. A Coruña). He is an Associated Professor at the Department of Analytical Chemistry, Univ. A Coruña, Spain. His main research interests deal with applying pattern recognition, multivariate regression and variable selection techniques to environmental and industrial Quality Control applications. He works with infrared molecular spectrometry and collaborates with groups focused on atomic spectroscopy to develop multivariate regression models. He published a book on Quality Management, edited 'Basic Chemometric Techniques in Atomic Spectroscopy' (RSC) and coauthored five chapters of books and more than seventy papers on international journals. He delivered training courses to governmental and private laboratories (most of them on basic Quality Control, Basic Chemometric Techniques and/or Environmental Management), as well as more specialized lectures in international conferences and Pittcon. He collaborates with MuldiD Analyses AB, a Swedish software company.

Bernardino Arcay Varela graduated from the electronics program at the Faculty of Physics, University of Santiago, Spain. Since 1986, he has been a member of the Laboratory of Applied Biophysics in Artificial Intelligence in the same faculty. He received the Ph.D. in Applied Physics from the University of Santiago in 1990. He currently is Full Professor in the Department of Computer Science, University of A Coruña, Spain. His current research area is intelligent monitoring research, real-time systems, tele-control systems and signal processing.

Davide Ballabio received the MSc degree in environmental science in 2002 from the Università di Milano – Bicocca and since January 2003 he has an on-going collaboration with the Milano QSAR and Chemometrics Group, at the same University. In 2007 he received the PhD degree in food technology from the Università Statale di Milano and, during his Thesis, he spent nine months in the Chemometrics Group of The Royal Veterinary and Agricultural University, Copenhagen, Denmark. He is author of twenty-six peer reviewed papers published on international scientific journals and five chapters, published on international books. His main research interests are mathematical modelling and multivariate analysis applied on chemical data., QSAR/QSPR modelling, artificial neural networks, pattern recognition and variable selection algorithms. He is referee for several international scientific journals and, in particular, top referee for Analytica Chimica Acta (2008) and Journal of Pharmaceutical and Biomedical Analysis (2006).

Malcolm J. Beynon is Professor of Uncertain Reasoning in Business/Management in Cardiff Business Cardiff at Cardiff University (UK). He gained his BSc and PhD in pure mathematics and computational mathematics, respectively, at Cardiff University. His research areas include the theoretical and application of uncertain reasoning methodologies, including Dempster-Shafer theory, fuzzy set theory and rough set theory. Also the introduction and development of multi-criteria based decision making and classification techniques, including the Classification and Ranking Belief Simplex. He has published over 140 research articles. He is a member of the International Rough Set Society, International Operations Research Society and the International Multi-Criteria Decision Making Society.

José Blasco received a B.Sc. (1994) and Ph.D. degree in Computer Science from Polytechnic University of Valencia, UPV, (2001). He also received a M.Sc. in Computer Aided Design and Manufacturing (CAD/CAM) from UPV in 1995. He worked during two years at Industrial Business Machine (IBM) Spain as system analyst before he joined at the Public Research Institute, IVIA in 1996. Since then, he is the manager of the Computer Vision Lab at the Agricultural Engineering Centre of IVIA. His field of interest is mainly focused on Computer Vision, Image Processing, Real time inspection and Machine vision.

Marco Block-Berlitz received the PhD degree from Freie Universität Berlin, Germany in 2009. He is chief of the game-programming group of Freie Universität Berlin and since 2008 member of the autonomous car project "Spirit of Berlin".

Ionel Bostan was born in Arefu, Romania, on January 2, 1968. He receives the Ph.D. degree from University of Pitesti in 2002 with thesis "Robotics and artificial intelligence" in the field of design of artificial intelligence, robotics and reconfigurable circuits. Current is professor to University of Pitesti, Department of Electronics, Communication and Computers. It activates in the fields of digital and analog circuits design, automatic systems, programmable machine and reconfigurable circuits. He has published more than 90 papers in the field of digital and analog circuits design and applications and reconfigurable circuits. He is author for 2 books in the area of the digital and analog circuits design, and reconfigurable circuits.

Gloria Bueno received her MsC from Universidad Complutense de Madrid in 1993, and her PhD from Coventry University in 1998. From 1998 to 2000 Gloria worked as a postdoctoral researcher at Université Louis Pasteur, Strasbourg. In 2000-2001 she worked at CNRS-Institut de Physique Biologique-Hôpital Civil and from 2001 to 2003 she was a senior researcher at CEIT (Centro de Estudios e Investigaciones Técnicas de Gipuzkoa), San Sebastián, Spain. She is currently an Associate Professor at Universidad de Castilla-La Mancha, Spain. Her main research interests include image processing –particularly for biomedical engineering applications- computer vision, artificial intelligence, modeling and simulation.

Andres Bustillo is a Lecturer at the University of Burgos (Spain). He received his Ph.D. in Physics from University of Valladolid (Spain). His Ph.D. topic was laser development for Plasma Diagnostic with an experimental set-up developed at the Physikalish-Technische Bundesanstalt (PTB) Berlin. After his Ph.D. degree he worked for 7 years as R&D Project Manager at Nicolas Correa S.A., a Spanish world leader in the design of huge milling machines. During this time he accumulated a wide experience in the simulation and optimization of high speed milling, laser cladding and other industrial technologies related with the Manufacturing Industry. Nowadays, his research interests are focused on the application to industry of different soft-computing techniques like neural networks, fuzzy logic, multiple classifier systems and Hybrid Systems.

Modesto Castrillón is an Assistant Professor at the Department of Computer Science and a research member of the Institute of Intelligent Systems and Numerical Applications in Engineering at the ULPGC (University of Las Palmas de Gran Canaria), Spain. His research interests include facial detection and recognition, and computer vision for human-computer interaction. He holds since 2003 a PhD from the ULPGC, and is member of AEPIA, AERFAI and the IEEE.

Viviana Consonni received her PhD in Chemical Sciences at the University of Milano in 2000 and is now full researcher in chemometrics and chemoinformatics at the Department of Environmental Sciences of the University of Milano-Bicocca (Milano, Italy). She is a member of the Milano Chemometrics and QSAR Research Group and has 10 years experience in multivariate analysis, QSAR, molecular descriptors, multicriteria decision making and software development. She is author of more than 40 publications in peer reviewed journals and of the book "Handbook of Molecular Descriptors", by R. Todeschini and V. Consonni; Wiley-VCH, 2000. In 2006 she obtained the International Academy of Mathematical Chemistry Award for distinguished young researchers.

Emilio Corchado is an Associated Professor at the University of Burgos (Spain). He received his Ph.D. in Computer Science and his degree in Physics from University of Salamanca (Spain). His research interests include neural networks, with a particular focus on exploratory projection pursuit, maximum likelihood hebbian learning, self-organising maps, multiple classifier systems and Hybrid Systems. He has published over 80 peer-reviewed articles in a range of topics from knowledge management and risk analysis, intrusion detection systems, food industry, artificial vision, and recently modelling of industrial processes. He is the director of the GICAP Research Group at the University of Burgos, Spain. He is Coeditor-in-Chief of International Journal of Computational Intelligence Research (IJCIR) and member of the Editorial Boards of the International Journal of Computational Intelligence and Applications (IJCIA) and also of the International Journal of Reasoning-based Intelligent Systems (IJRIS).

He is the Director of HAIS international Series of Conferences and Co-Director of CISIS international Series of Conferences.

Jorge Corsino-Espino was born in Spain in 1985. He received the Sc. degree in 2007 in Telecommunication Engineering at University of Las Palmas de Gran Canaria (ULPGC), Spain. Actually he is studying the M.Sc degree in Telecommunication at the same institution. He has been introduced into different researches about medical signal processing and classification systems. He has 1 international paper published an explained in the International Conference on Bio-inspired System and Signal Processing (Portugal 2008).

Leticia Curiel is an assistant Lecturer at the University if Burgos. She obtained the Computer Sciencies Degree at the University of León (Spain). Nowadays she is working in her PhD and her supervisors are PhD. Emilio Corchado and PhD. Javier Sedano. She has been member of the program Comittee of some conference like International Conference on Intelligent Data Engineering and Automated Learning (IDEAL), International Conference on Hybrid Artificial Intelligence Systems (HAIS), International Workshop on Computational Intelligence in Security for Information Systems (CISIS), International Workshop on Soft Computing Models in Industrial Applications (SOCO) and International Workshop on Practical Applications of Agents and Multiagent Systems. (IWPAAMS).

José Carlos Dafonte Vázquez graduated with a degree in Computer Science from the University of A Coruña, Spain, in 1994 and received his first postgraduate degree for research in Computer Science in 1995. He received the Ph.D. in Computer Science from the University of A Coruña in 2002. He currently is Associate Professor in the Department of Information and Communications Technologies, University of A Coruña. His research interest includes information systems, intelligent systems for real-time control and signal processing.

Óscar Deniz received his MsC and PhD from Universidad de Las Palmas de Gran Canaria, Spain, in 1999 and 2006, respectively. He has been associate professor at Universidad de Las Palmas de Gran Canaria from 2003 to 2007 and currently at Universidad de Castilla-La Mancha, Spain. His main research interests are human-robot interaction and computer vision. He is a research fellow of the Institute of Intelligent Systems and Numerical Applications in Engineering and member of IEEE, AEPIA and AERFAI.

Julián Dorado was born in A Coruña, Spain in 1970. He is associate professor in the Department of Information and Communications Technologies of the University of A Coruña. He finished his studies on Computer Engineering in 1993, and on 1999 he became Doctor in Computer Science with his thesis "Methodology for the Development of Knowledge Extraction Systems in ANNs". He has worked on several Spanish and European projects, and he has published many books and papers on several international journals. He is currently working on Evolutionary Computation, Artificial Neural Networks and Knowledge Extraction systems.

Enrique Fernández-Blanco was born in Frankfurt, Germany in 1981. He received his M.S. degree in Computer Science from the University of A Coruña in 2005. Since that date he has been working with the research group RNASA/IMEDIR of the University of A Coruña. Actually, he is developing his

PhD thesis in Computer Science under the direction of Julian Dorado in the Department of Information Technologies and Communications. His current research interests include artificial neural networks, Artificial Embryogeny, Swarm Intelligence, image processing and Evolutionary Computation.

Raquel Fernández-Varela received her MSc in Chemistry in 2003 from the University of A Coruña, Spain, and since September 2002 she collaborates with the Department of Analytical Chemistry at the same University. On 2010 she will defend her Thesis on Seaborne Hydrocarbon Spills Monitoring to get her Ph.D. in Analytical Chemistry. She coauthored several peer reviewed papers published on international scientific journals. Her main interests concern the measurement of hydrocarbon mixtures using different analytical techniques (MIR, NIR, GC-FID, GC-MS) and the analyses of the associated datasets employing different pattern recognition methods (PCA, LDA, Hierarchical Clustering, Potential Curves, SOMs, CP-ANN, MOLMAP, PARAFAC, MA-PCA) and variable selection methods (Genetic Algorithms and Procrustes rotation). Current applications include environmental and industrial problems (monitoring of oil spills, hydrocarbon distillates, crude oils, etc.). On 2006 she was awarded the Ignacio Rivas Marques Prize to young Galician researchers.

Miguel A. Ferrer was born in Spain in 1965. He received his M.Sc. degree in Telecommunications in 1988 and Ph.D. in 1994, both from the Universidad Politécnica de Madrid, Spain. He is an Associate Professor at Universidad de Las Palmas de Gran Canaria, where he has taught since 1990 and heads the Digital Signal Processing Group there. His research interests lie in the fields of biometrics and audio quality evaluation. He is a member of the IEEE Carnahan Conference on Security Technology advisory Committee.

Ana Freire was born in Rábade (Galicia, Spain), in 1983. She received the MS degree in Computer Science at the University of A Coruña, Spain in 2008. She is currently a Ph.D. student in Information and Communication Technologies at the Faculty of Informatics of the University of A Coruña. She has received a research grant for one year. She is member of the Galician Bioinformatics Network and the IBERO-NBIC Network. Her main research interests are data mining, evolutionary computation, bioinformatics, proteomics and information retrieval.

F. Javier García-Haro received the M.S. and Ph.D. degrees in physics from the University of Valencia, Spain, in 1994 and 1997, respectively. He has been also a Post-Doctoral Fellow at the Joint Research Centre, Ispra, Italy, from 1998 to 2000. He has held a research position since 2001 and is currently a Lecturer in Environmental Physics with the University of Valencia, position held since 2008. His main research interests span spectral mixture and BRDF modeling, image analysis algorithms for retrieval of vegetation parameters and product validation.

Antonio Geraldo Ferreira received a B.Sc. and License degree in Physics in 1990 from the University Estadual Júlio de Mesquita Filho – UNESP, Rio Claro, Brazil, and a M.Sc. degree in Tropical Marine Sciences (concentration area: Remote Sensing Techniques for Environmental Monitoring) in 2005 from the University Federal do Ceará - Laboratório de Ciências do Mar, Fortaleza, Brazil. From August 1996 to September 2005 he was Head of the FUNCEME´s Department of Meteorology and Oceanography from FUNCEME-Meteorology and Water Resources Ceara's Foundation, Fortaleza. Currently he is finishing his Ph.D. in the Department of Physics of the Earth and Thermodynamics at the University of Valencia, Spain with the Climatology from Satellites Group, where he is applying remote sensing techniques and neural network to land-surface process studies.

María Paz Gómez-Carracedo, MSc in Chemistry in 1998 (University of Santiago de Compostela). PhD in Analytical Chemistry in 2005 (University of A Coruña), Special Award. During her thesis, she spent two months in the Department of Analytical Chemistry (University of Valencia). She coauthored seventeen peer reviewed papers published on international scientific journals and four chapters published on international books. Her main interest is in combining molecular analytical techniques (MIR, NIR, TGA) with pattern recognition and regression chemometric methods (PLS, PCA, PLS-DA, PCA-LDA, LDA/QDA, kNN, Potential Curves, SOMs, CP-ANN, MOLMAP, backpropagation neural networks) to address environmental and industrial problems (oil spills, urban soils, apple juice, hydrocarbon distillation, etc.). She is also interested in variable selection methods by genetic algorithms and Procrustes rotation. At present she is performing research stays in different European Chemometrics groups (Universidade Nova de Lisboa, Portugal and Milano Chemometrics and QSAR Research Group, Italy).

Juan Gómez-Sanchis received a B.Sc. degree in Physics (2000) and a B.Sc. degree in Electronics Engineering from the University of Valencia (2003). He joined at the Public Research Institute IVIA in 2004, developing is Ph.D. in hyperspectral computer vision systems applied to the agriculture. He joined to the Department of Electronics Engineering at University of Valencia in 2008, where he currently works as assistant lecturer in pattern recognition using neural networks

Evelio Gonzalez received the MS degree in Applied Physics in 1998 and his PhD degree in Computer Science in 2004 from the University of La Laguna, Tenerife, Spain. From 1998 to 2001, he was a Research Student in the Department of Applied Physics, Electronics and Systems at the same university. Currently, he works as Assistant Professor in the University de La Laguna. His areas of interest include Simulation, Digital Control, Computer Architecture, Artificial Intelligence and Intelligent Agents.

Juan F. Guerrero received the B.Sc. degree in physics and the Ph.D. degree in electronic engineering in 1985 and 1988, respectively, from the Universitat de Valencia, Spain. Since 1985, he has been with the Digital Signal Processing Group (GPDS), Department of Electronic Engineering, University of Valencia, where he is an Associate Professor. His research interests include biomedical digital signal processing and biosignal instrumentation.

Ling Guo obtained her B.S degree at the Department of Electrical Engineering of Yangzhou University (China). She received her Master degree in Electrical Engineering from Delft University of Technology (The Netherlands). She joined University of A Coruña (Spain) as a Ph.D. student in Information and Communication Technologies. Her research interests involve the biomedical signal processing, wavelet theory, evolutionary computation and artificial intelligence technology.

Angela Hernández received the MS degree in Applied Physics in 2008 from the University of La Laguna, Tenerife, Spain. Currently, She is a research student at University de La Laguna. Her areas of interest include Simulation, Control, Neuro-Fuzzy Systems.

Mario Hernández received his Graduate in Electrical Engineering and PhD in Computer Science from the Universidad de Las Palmas de Gran Canaria. He is currently a Full Professor of Computer Science and Engineering at the Computer Science and Systems Department of the Las Palmas de Gran Canaria University. His current research interests span Autonomous Systems, Knowledge-Based Systems, Active Vision, Visual Learning, Scene Analysis, Mobile Robotics and Interactive Robotic Systems. He has been the author or coauthor of more than 60 research papers and chapters. He is member of the International Association of Pattern Recognition (IAPR), the Asociación Española de Reconocimiento de Formas y Análisis de Imágenes (AERFAI) and the Asociación Española para la Inteligencia Artificial (AEPIA).

Jesús Antonio Hernández, E. E. and MIS DEA, has been working, for over fifteen years managing and developing large scale software systems for engineering and business. In 1991-1992 he was hired by The National University of Colombia as a Special Professor for the Graduate School of Computer Sciences and Systems Engineering. He is still an active member of the staff of this university. At the present time, he is working on his Ph.D. with the software engineering researching group of the Polytechnic University of Valencia-Spain (UPV). He won the RDV Fellowship grant. Mr. Hernández is a recognized consultant engineer in Colombia. Some Interest Areas: Software and Business Systems Renovation, Software Quality, Software Projects Management, Automated Environments.

Evor Hines joined Warwick University in 1984 and he is a Reader in the School of Engineering. He became a Fellow of the Higher Education Academy (FHEA) in 2000 and was awarded his DSc(Warwick) in 2007. He is a chartered Engineer and a Fellow of IET. His main research interest is concerned with Intelligent Systems (also known by other names such as Computational Intelligence and Soft Computing) and their applications. Most of his work has focused on Artificial Neural Networks, Genetic Algorithms, Fuzzy Logic, Neuro-Fuzzy Systems and Genetic Programming. Typical application areas include intelligent sensors (e.g. electronic nose); medicine; non-destructive testing of, for example, composite materials; computer vision; telecommunications; amongst others. He has for example co-authored some 215 articles and supervised more 30 successful research students. He currently leads the School's Intelligent Systems Engineering Laboratory which he established in 1990 and the School's Information and Communication Technologies Research Group. His work has been funded by numerous organisations including several EPRSC and EU and he acts as a referee for a range of journals.

Gabriel Iana was born in Stefanesti, Romania, on May 1, 1975. He receives the Ph.D. degree from University of Pitesti in 2004 with thesis "Digital filter using sigma delta modulators" in the field of digital signal processing using reconfigurable structures. Current is assistant professor to University of Pitesti, Department of Electronics, Communication and Computers. It activates in the fields of digital signal processing, microprocessors and microcontrollers and hardware description languages. He has published more than 50 papers in the field of digital filters, digital signal processing, sigma delta modulators, hardware implementation of digital filter and embedded system design for signal processing applications. He is coauthor for 2 books in the field of digital signal processing and reconfigurable structures.

José Antonio Iglesias is a Teaching Assistant of computer science and member of the CAOS research group at Carlos III University of Madrid (UC3M), Spain. He received his M. Sc. in computer science at UC3M in 2006 and he is pursuing his Ph.D. since then. He has a B. Sc. in computer science (2002) from Valladolid University. He takes part in several national research projects. He has published over

10 conference and journal papers and he is committee member of several international conferences. His research interests include user modeling, plan recognition, sequence learning, machine learning and evolving fuzzy systems. His web page is: http://www.caos.inf.uc3m.es/~jiglesia/

Laurentiu Ionescu was born in Arges, Romania, on February 20, 1978. He receives the Ph.D. degree from University of Pitesti in 2007 with thesis "Modeling, design, simulation, implementation of the evolvable hardware structures" in bio-inspired solution for logic circuits design . Current is assistant professor to University of Pitesti, Department of Electronics, Communication and Computers. It activates in the fields of reconfigurable structures, real time systems, microprocessors and computers. He has published more than 40 papers in the field of hardware implementation of bio – inspired structures like evolutionary algorithms and artificial neural networks, computing optimization using parallel hardware structures, dynamic reconfiguration and real time processing.

Agapito Ledezma is an Associate Professor of computer science and member of the CAOS research group at Carlos III University of Madrid (UC3M). He obtained his Ph.D. in computer science from UC3M in 2004. He has a B. S. in computer science (1997) from Universidad Latinoamericana de Ciencia y Tecnologia (ULACIT) of Panamá. He has contributed to several national research projects on data mining and image processing. His research interests span data mining, user modeling, ensemble of classifiers and cognitive robotics. He has written more than 30 technical papers for computer science journals and conferences and he is a committee member of several international conferences. His web page is: http://www.caos.inf.uc3m.es/~ledezma/

Ernesto López-Baeza, Associate Professor of Applied Physics at the University of Valencia, Spain, is currently coordinating the activities of the Climatology from Satellites Group applying remote sensing techniques to climate process studies. Their main scientific activity is the development of validation methologies for low spatial resolution Earth Observation missions related to radiative balance, net radiation, and soil moisture. They count on the Valencia and the Alacant Anchor Stations (www.uv.es/elopez/) which are two robustly equipped meteorological stations, respectively located and representative of large reasonably homogeneous areas in the natural regions of Utiel-Requena Plateau (Valencia) and Vinalopo River Valley (Alicante), Spain. In that framework significant scientific activities are progressively being developed. Dr Lopez-Baeza is currently involved in five scientific groups related to satellite missions at different development stages, namely GERB, SMOS, EarthCARE, CERES and EPS/MetOp. He is currently Vice-Chair of the COSPAR Scientific Sub-Commission A3 on Land Processes and Morphology.

Javier Lorenzo is an Associate Professor at the Department of Computer Science and a research member of the Institute of Intelligent Systems and Numerical Applications in Engineering of the University of Las Palmas de Gran Canaria (ULPGC), Spain. He is currently teaching graduate courses in Computer Vision, Pattern Recognition and Artificial Intelligence at Facultad de Informática and Escuela Técnica Superior de Ingenieros Industriales. He received his PhD in Computer Science in 2001 on feature selection in Machine Learning. Since 2001, his research interests have been in Computer Vision applied to Human-Computer Interaction, Bioinspired Computer Vision Systems, Machine Learning and Web Usage Mining. Dr. Lorenzo has been co-author of chapters in the books Pattern Recognition and Image Analysis (AERFAI, 1998) and Artificial Intelligence (Inteligencia Artificial, McGraw-Hill, 2008). He has also participated as research member and project coordinator in several research projects.

Rafael Magdalena received the M.S. and the Ph.D. degrees in Physics from the University of Valencia, Spain in 1991 and 2000 respectively. He has also been a lecturer with the Polytechnic University of Valencia, a funded researcher with the Research Association in Optics and has held industrial positions with several electromedicine and IT companies. Currently he is a Labour Lecturer in Electronic Engineering with the University of Valencia, position held since 1998. He has conducted research in telemedicine, biomedical engineering and signal processing.

Minia Manteiga graduated in Physics at the Faculty of La Laguna in 1986. Since that date, she entered the postgraduated program at the Spanish Instituto de Astrofísica de Canarias (IAC, Tenerife, Spain) and received the Ph.D in Astrophysics in 1990. She spent two years as a postdoctoral researcher at the Italian Istituto di Astrofísica Spaziale (IAS, at Frascati-Rome) and 3 years at the INTA (Spanish National Institute for Aerospacial Studies, Madrid, Spain). In 1997 she got a position as Associate Professor at the Applied Physics Department of the University of Vigo. She currently is Associate Professor in the Navigation and Earth Sciences Department of the University of A Coruña. She is a member of the IAU (International Asstrophysics Union) and President of the GEA (Group of Astrophysics) of the Spanish Royal Society of Physics. Her current research area is stellar evolution and the study of stellar populations.

G. Nicolás Marichal received the MS degree in Applied Physics in 1993 and his PhD degree in Computer Science in 1999 from the University of La Laguna, Tenerife, Spain. From 1994 to 2001, he was an assistant professor in the Department of Applied Physics, Electronics and Systems at the same university. Currently, he works as Associate Professor at the University de La Laguna. His areas of interest include Simulation, intelligent Control, Artificial Intelligence and Robotics. He has issued several papers in conferences and journals in these fields. Furthermore, he has participated in different research projects related with his research areas of interest.

Jose D. Martin received the B.Sc. degree in Theoretical Physics from the University of Valencia in 1997. Afterwards, he received B.Sc. degree and M.Sc. degrees in Electronic Engineering from the University of Valencia, Valencia, Spain, in 1999, and 2001, respectively. He got a PhD from the University of Valencia in 2004. He is currently an Assistant Professor in the Electronic Engineering Department, University of Valencia. His research interests are focused on neural networks and reinforcement learning. Dr. Martín-Guerrero is a Member of the European Neural Network Society.

Fernando Martínez-Abella is a Full Professor in Construction Engineering for the Civil Engineering School of the Universidade da Coruña (Spain), and is also presently the Chair for the Construction Technology Department. He obtained his MSc and PE in Civil and Structural Engineering in 1989 and his PhD in 1993, all of them in the Universidad Politécnica de Cataluña. Dr Martínez-Abella's research interests are steel –concrete bond in reinforced and prestressed concrete structures, recycled aggregate concrete, alkali-aggregate expansions in concrete, structural testing of full size civil and industrial structural elements and Artificial Intelligence techniques applications for Civil Engineering. He has headed over 15 public and 30 privately funded R+D projects along these lines, producing over 40 research papers and presentations and authoring or co-authoring 15 books and chapters in manuals.

Marcelino Martinez received his B.S. and Ph.D. degrees in Physics in 1992 and 2000 respectively from the Universitat de Valencia(Spain). Since 1994 he has been with the Digital Signal Processing Group at the Department of Electronics Engineering. He is currently an Asistant Professor. He has worked on several industrial projects with private companies (in the areas such as industrial control, real-time signal processing and digital control) and with public funds (in the areas of foetal electrocardiography and ventricular fibrillation). His research interests include real time signal processing, digital control using DSP and biomedical signal processing.

Marcos Martínez Romero received the M.S. in Computer Science from the University of A Coruña (Spain) in 2007. Since 2006, he has been a member of the Medical Informatics and Radiological Diagnosis Center (IMEDIR Center) from that University. He is currently a Computer Science PhD candidate at the Department of Information and Communications Technologies from the University of A Coruña. His main research interests include health information systems, ontologies, semantic web, ontology based data integration, ontology alignment, semantic annotation and security in medical information systems. He is a member of several outstanding research projects, including the Galician Network for Colorectal Cancer Research (REGICC), the Galician Bioinformatics Network (RGB) and the IBERO-NBIC research network.

Alin Mazare was born in Bucharest, Romania, on December 22, 1967. He receives the Ph.D. degree from University of Pitesti in 2008 with thesis "Modeling, simulation and implementation of AI based structures for embedded equipments" in artificial intelligence solutions: full integration and optimization for embedded systems. Current is assistant professor to University of Pitesti, Department of Electronics, Communication and Computers. It activates in the fields of embedded system design, PCB design and reconfigurable structures. He has published 35 papers in the field of embedded systems and sensors, embedded computing, embedded system design, electromagnetic compatibility and artificial intelligence.

Álvaro Moreno received the B.Sc. degree in Physics from the University of Valencia in 2005. Afterwards, he has held a research position as research technician for three years. Currently, he has started his Ph.D. degree in physics. His main research interests are machine learning and remote sensing.

Pinaki Mukherjee is a Professor and H.O.D in the Department of Electronics & Telecommunication Engineering, Institute of Engineering & management, Salt Lake Kolkata,INDIA, where he has been teaching from 1999. He was born in Kolkata in 1972 and obtained his B.Tech and M.Tech degree from Institute of Radiophysics and Electronics, University of Kolkata (INDIA) in the years 1996 and 1999. He obtained his Ph.D. (Engg.) degree from Jadavpur University (INDIA) in the year 2005. He is a Member of IEEE. He has published many research articles in refereed journals and conferences. He has guided a large number of postgraduate theses and served as referee in different internationally acclaimed journals. His present area of interest is Planar Antennas, Application of Artificial Intelligence Paradigms in Microwave Engineering and Antennas and Radio frequency properties of Carbon Nanotube.

Cristian R. Munteanu received the Ph.D. degree in theoretical and computational chemistry from the University of Santiago de Compostela (Spain) in 2005. From 2005 to 2009, he worked in structural protein bioinformatics, complex network applications and quantum chemistry studies of van der Waals complexes. He is currently a biomedical researcher of the Artificial Neural Networks and Adaptative Systems group in the department of Information and Communication Technologies at the University of A Coruña, Spain. His research interests include signal analysis, data mining for complex diseases, graph software design and applications. He is a member of IBERO-NBIC research network.

Diego Ordóñez Blanco graduated with a degree in Computer Science from the University of A Coruña, Spain, in 2006. He received his first postgraduate degree for research in Computer Science in 2008. He is currently a Phd Student with a contract of the Ministry of Education from the Spanish Government to collaborate in a project of the ESA (European Space Agency) called Gaia. His research area includes the study of the spectral information of sky objects from the Milky Way and the development of new connectionist algorithms and tools to deal with artificial neural networks.

Alejandro Pazos Sierra received the M.S. degree in Medicine from the University of Santiago de Compostela (Spain) in 1987 and the Ph.D. in Computer Science from the Polytechnic University of Madrid in 1989. In 1996, he received the Ph.D. in Medicine from the Complutense University of Madrid. Since 1989, he has worked with several research groups such as the "Graphics,Visualization and Usability Laboratory ", at Georgia Institute of Technology, the "Decision Systems Group", at Harvard Medical School, or the "Section on Medical Informatics", at Stanford University. In 1995, he founded the "Artificial Neural Networks and Adaptive Systems Laboratory" at the University of A Coruña, which he currently manages. At the moment, he is a professor at the Department of Information and Communications Technologies at the same University. His current research interests include artificial neural networks, medical image, evolutionary computation, adaptive systems, medical information systems, telemedicine and ontologies.

Nieves Pedreira is an assistant professor in the Department of Information and Communicaton Technologies, Univesity of A Coruña (Spain). She earned a degree in Computer Science from the Univerity of A Coruña (1993). This was followed by a master's degree in communications and real time systems. After having worked in private enterprises, she returned to the university in 1997 as PhD student, and in 2003, she became a doctor of Computer Science with the thesis entitled "A Model for Virtual Learning to Learn". She is also a tutor at the UNED (Spanish Distance Education National University) since 1998. Her research interests are focused on distance learning and new technologies.

Alejandro Peña is professor of the School of Engineering of Antioquia in the area of Mechatronics Engineering. Mr. Peña has developed studies of Mechanical Engineering, and the pursuit of their degrees in Systems Engineering Master's and Doctorate in Engineering, with focus on the identification of dynamic systems using evolving system. Professor Pena has developed various research and publications on the development of models for assessing air quality in a study area, using the principles of natural systems that provide the basis for computational intelligence. Some Interest Areas: Computational Intelligence, Evolutionary Computation, Lagrangian Dispersion Models, Particulate Matter, .NET Technologies.

Javier Pereira Loureiro received the M.S. in Computer Science from the University of A Coruña (Spain) in 1995, and the Ph.D. degree in Computer Science from the same University in 2004. He is an Associated Professor in the area of Radiology and Physical Medicine at the Department of Medicine in the Faculty of Health Sciences, at the University of A Coruña. His current research interests include medical information systems, DICOM, PACS, medical informatics, accessibility in Information and Communication Technologies, disability and informatics, and technical aids development. He is a member of the Medical Informatics and Radiological Diagnosis Center (IMEDIR Center) from the University of A Coruña, and of the Artificial Neural Network and Adaptative Systems Group from the Faculty of Computer Sciences in the same university. He has participated, and is participating in multiple research projects, funded by either public autonomous, national and international organisations or private companies.

Juan L. Pérez has received the BSc degree in Computer Science in 2001, the MS degree in Computer Science in 2004 and the CPh in Computer Science in 2006, all of them from the University of A Coruña, Spain. He is presently a PhD student at the Department of Information and Communications Technologies at University of A Coruña. Additionally, he is enjoying a FPI research fellowship from the Spanish Ministry of Science and Innovation at the School of Civil Engineering (Department of Construction Technology) at the University of A Coruña. He also is a teaching assistant in both departments. He is author of about 25 publications (book chapters, journal papers and conference papers). He also has worked in more than 15 research projects. His research interests include artificial neural networks, genetic programming, genetic algorithms, and artificial intelligence applied to civil engineering.

Marco Antonio Perez-Cisneros received the B.S. degree with distinction in Electronics and Communications Enginering from the University of Guadalajara, Mexico in 1995 and the M.Sc. degree in Industrial Electronics from ITESO University, Mexico in 2000, and the PhD degree from the University of Manchester Institute of Science and Technology, UMIST, Manchester, UK in 2004. He was a research consultant on robotic manipulators for TQ Ltd, UK in 2003 and since 2005 he has been with University of Guadalajara, where he is currently a Professor and Head of Department of Computer Science. He is a member of the Mexican National Research System (SNI) from 2007. His current research interest includes robotics and computational vision, especially visual servoing and humanoid walking control.

Juan R. Rabuñal has obtained his BSc degree in Computer Science in 1996, the MS degree in Computer Science in 1999 and the PhD degree in Computer Science in 2002, all of them by the University of A Coruña, Spain. He has also obtained a PhD degree in Civil Engineering in 2008. Nowadays, he shares his time between his lecturer position at the Faculty of Computer Science of the University of A Coruña and the direction of the Centre of Technological Innovations in Construction and Civil Engineering. He has also headed several research projects for the regional government and also the national government. He is the co-editor of the Encyclopedia of Artificial Intelligence, Information Science Reference, 2008. His principal research interests are artificial neural networks, genetic programming, genetic algorithms and artificial intelligence and computer vision in civil engineering.

Araceli Sanchis has been a University Associate Professor of computer science at Carlos III University of Madrid (UC3M) since 1999. She received her Ph.D. in physical chemistry from Complutense University of Madrid in 1994 and in computer science from Polytechnic University of Madrid in 1998. She has a B. Sc. in chemistry (1991) from the Complutense University of Madrid. She had been Vice-Dean of the Computer Science degree at UC3M and, currently, she is head of the CAOS group (Grupo de Control, Aprendizaje y Optimización de Sistemas) based on machine learning and optimization. She has led several research projects founded by the Spanish Ministry of Education and Science and also by the European Union. She has published over 50 journal and conference papers mainly in the field of machine learning. Her topics of interests are multi-agent systems, user modeling, data mining and cognitive robotics.

Marilton Sanchotene de Aguiar received a degree in Computer Science from the Universidade Católica de Pelotas (UCPel), in 1996. He also received the M.Sc. and Ph.D. degrees in Computer Science from the Universidade Federal do Rio Grande do Sul (UFRGS), in 1998 and 2004, respectively. He is an Associate Professor at Universidade Federal de Pelotas (UFPel), where he has been since 2009. He was an Associate Professor at Universidade Católica de Pelotas (UCPel) from 2001 to 2009. His current research interests include Artificial Intelligence, Soft Computing, Interval Mathematics and Fuzzy Logic, Geographical Information Systems and Image Processing.

José Luis Saorín is an Assistant Professor of Engineering Graphics and CAD at La Laguna University (ULL). He earned an MS degree in Energy Engineering in 1999, and a Ph.D. in Industrial Engineering in 2006 from UPV. He worked for private companies from 1992, as a project engineer in water supply systems. He joined La Laguna University in 2001 and his research interests include development of spatial abilities using multimedia technologies and sketch-based modeling.

Javier Sedano obtained his Ph.D. at the University of León, degree in Industrial Engineering. He has participated in the development and management of more than twenty-five technological development projects and pre-funded in regional and national programs, and prototypes most cases, training of professionals in all disciplines of production technologies and project management. He has published articles in international prestige, as well as over twenty-five contributions, including book chapters and conference communications. He is the author of intellectual property records, which are in operation.

José A. Seoane was born in Ferrol (Spain), in 1980. He received the MS in Computer Science from the University of A Coruña (A Coruña, Spain) in 2008. In 2009 he finished his MS in Statistical Learning and Data Mining from the Spanish National University of Distance Learning. He is scientific/technical personnel of the same university since his 2004. He has participated in several research projects related with biomedicine and artificial intelligence. He is member of the Galician Bioinformatics Network since 2007. His work lines are focused in artificial neural networks, evolutionary computation, data mining and bioinformatics.

José Andrés Serantes was born in Cedeira, Spain, in 1983. He received his BS degree in Computer Science from the university of A Coruña in 2006. He has been working with the RNASA/IMEDIR group of the University of A Coruña since 2007. Actually, he is doing his last year of M.S. degree in Computer Science in the University of A Coruña. His current research interests include Artificial Embryogeny, Artificial Neural Networks and Evolutionary Computation.

Gheorghe Serban was born in Pitesti, Romania, on January 25, 1958. He receives the Ph.D. degree from University of Brasov in 1996 with thesis "Increase of processing speed by using parallelism in digital circuits design" in the field of design of digital circuits, hardware description languages and reconfigurable circuits. Current is professor to University of Pitesti, Department of Electronics, Communication and Computers. It activates in the fields of computers, microprocessors and microcontrollers, embedded systems, hardware description languages and reconfigurable circuits. He has published more than 150 papers in the field of embedded systems, microprocessors and microcontrollers and reconfigurable circuits. He is author for 4 books in the area of the simulation of the analog and digital circuits, microcontrollers and microprocessors and embedded system design. He is member of IEEE Computer Society and IEEE Industrial Electronics Society.

Antonio J. Serrano received a B.Sc. degree in Physics in 1996, a M.Sc. degree in Physics in 1998 and a Ph.D. degree in Electronics Engineering in 2002, from the University of Valencia, Spain. He is currently an associate professor in the Electronics Engineering Department at the same university. His research interest is machine learning methods for biomedical engineering and signal processing.

Emilio Soria-Olivas received his B.Sc. in 1982 in Physics and the Ph.D. degree in Electronic Engineering in 1997 from the Universitat of Valencia, Spain. Since 1994 he has been with the Department of Electronic Engineering at the University of Valencia, where he belongs to the GPDS (Digital Signal Processing Group). He is an Assistant Professor. His research activities include Advanced Signal Processing using neural networks and fuzzy systems.

María Victoria Toro is a Chemical engineer, master in environmental pollution at the Polytechnic University of Madrid and Ph.D. at the Polytechnic University of Catalonia Spain. During more than 10 years has worked on the study of the air quality and atmospheric dispersion modeling. Currently she is the director of the air quality network in Medellín City and director of the Metropolitan air quality Information System. Some Interest Areas: Pollutants Dispersion, Particulate Matter, .NET Technologies, Atmospheric Dispersion Modeling.

Carlos M. Travieso-González was born in Spain in 1971. He received the M.Sc. degree in 1997 in Telecommunication Engineering at Polytechnic University of Catalonia (UPC), Spain. Besides, he received Ph.D. degree in 2002 at University of Las Palmas de Gran Canaria (ULPGC-Spain). He is an Associate Professor from 2001 in ULPGC, teaching subjects on signal processing and learning theory. His research lines are biometrics, classification system, medical signal processing, environmental intelligence, and data mining. He has researched in more than 20 International and Spanish Research Projects, some of them as head researcher. He has more than 140 papers published in international journals and conferences. He has been reviewer in different international journals and conferences since 2001. He is Image Processing Technical IASTED Committee Member. He is Vice-Dean from 2004 in Higher Technical School of Telecommunication Engineers in ULPGC.

Erik Valdemar Cuevas-Jimenez received the B.S. degree with distinction in Electronics and Communications Enginering from the University of Guadalajara, Mexico in 1995 and the M.Sc. degree in Industrial Electronics from ITESO, Mexico in 2000, and the PhD degree from Freie Universität Berlin, Germany in 2005. Since 2006 he has been with University of Guadalajara, where he is currently a Professor in the Department of Computer Science. From 2008, he is a member of the Mexican National Research System (SNI). His current research interest includes biped robots design, computational vision and humanoid walking control.

Secundino del Valle Tascón received the B.Sc. degree from Barcelona University in 1969 and the Ph. D. degree (biology) from Madrid University in 1975, followed by postdoctoral experience at Leiden University and California University at Berkeley. Following teaching appointments in plant physiology at the Extremadura University, he joined the Plant Physiology at Valencia University, where he is now Professor. His recent research interests include have mainly been in numerical methods for remote sensing, biophysics and stress physiology.

José Manuel Vázquez Naya received the M.S. in Computer Science from the University of A Coruña (Spain) in 2004. Since June 2000, he has been a member of the Medical Informatics and Radiological Diagnosis Center (IMEDIR Center) from that University. Currently, he is a Computer Science PhD candidate and a lecturer at the Department of Information and Communications Technologies from the University of A Coruña. His main research interests include health information systems, ontologies, semantic web, ontology based data integration, ontology alignment, semantic annotation and security in medical information systems. José M. Vázquez has been an author of several journal papers and multiple book chapters and conference papers. He is also a member of a variety of research projects, including the Galician Network for Colorectal Cancer Research (REGICC), the Galician Bioinformatics Network (RGB) and the IBERO NBIC research network.

José R. Villar was born in October, 11th, 1967 in Santo Domingo, Dominican Republic. He obtained the Engineering Degree at the University of Oviedo and the PHD in Computer Sciences at University of León, both in Spain. He had worked with several engineering consultancies. He began his educational career at University of León. Currently he is with the Computer Science Department at University of Oviedo. He is the author of several articles published in different international and indexed journals, more than fifty international conference contributions, three patents and more than ten research projects funded by national grants or private investment.

Peter Wells is Reader in the Centre for Automotive Industry Research (CAIR) in Cardiff Business Cardiff at Cardiff University (UK). He joined the CAIR at its inception in 1990 and has since specialised on economic, strategic and environmental aspects of the world automotive industry. He is particularly interested in small scale, decentralised economic organisation as a means to achieve sustainable consumption and production. His research areas of interest include; Industrial ecology; socio-technical transformations and the distributed economy as they apply to the automotive industry; alternative business models. He is an associate member of the Centre for Business Relationships, Accountability, Sustainability & Society at Cardiff University.

Daniel Zaldivar-Navarro received the B.S. degree with distinction in Electronics and Communications Engineering from the University of Guadalajara, Mexico in 1995 and the M.Sc. degree in Industrial Electronics from ITESO, Mexico in 2000, and the PhD degree from Freie Universität Berlin, Germany in 2005. Since 2006 he has been with University of Guadalajara, where he is currently a Professor in the Department of Computer Science. From 2008, he is a member of the Mexican National Research System (SNI).

Index